The POLISH-ENGLISH Dictionary of SLANG AND COLLOQUIALISM

The POLISH-ENGLISH Dictionary of SLANG AND COLLOQUIALISM

Maciej Widawski

with Consulting Editors:
Robert Urbanski, Phillip Lee Goss,
Mary Kobrzak, and Marta Trejtowicz

HIPPOCRENE BOOKS
New York

For information, address:
HIPPOCRENE BOOKS, INC.
171 Madison Avenue
New York, NY 10016

Library of Congress Cataloging-in-Publication Data
Widawski, Maciej.
The Polish-English dictionary of slang and colloquialism / Maciej Widawski ; with consulting editors Robert Urbanski, Phillip Lee Gross, Mary Kobrzak, and Marta Trejtowicz.
p. cm.
Includes bibliographical references and index.
ISBN 0-7818-0570-8
1. Polish language--Slang--Dictionaries. 2. Polish language--Spoken Polish--Dictionaries. 3. Polish language--Dictionaries--English. I. Urbanski, Robert.
PG6815.W53 1997
491.8'5321--dc21 97-38303
CIP

Printed in the United States of America.

Contents

Introduction

This dictionary is a novelty in Polish-English lexicography. There are two reasons which account for this. Firstly, it is the first Polish-English dictionary of such a specific nature and extensive format; most Polish dictionaries, bilingual or monolingual, published on either side of the Atlantic have, until mid 1990's, generally neglected slang and colloquialisms. Secondly, it is the first dictionary of this type aimed specifically at readers whose first language is not Polish, although its design makes it possible to be used by both Americans and Poles.

The dictionary contains nearly 5,000 terms and expressions of current Polish slang along with their American English equivalents. The slang and colloquial terms described in this dictionary include so-called broad Polish, which is the modern non-standard spoken language of a highly colloquial and idiomatic nature known to most Polish adults and teenagers; it is also a salient feature of the Polish language and culture. Dialect, jargon, as well as standard idioms have generally been excluded from the dictionary. Although most of the examples have been edited or invented by the consultants, all headword data comes from the *Corpus of Colloquial Polish*, generated between 1990 and 1996. The *Corpus* is roughly 50% written Polish (of which 75% comes from newspapers and magazines, the rest is literature) and 50% spoken Polish (of which 75% consists of notes or recordings done by volunteers, the rest having been recorded from radio, television, and film). American equivalents have also been based on the corpus in similar proportions; however the greatest contribution in matching American equivalents came from bilingual consultants who gave the dictionary its final shape. In both cases, many slang and colloquialism dictionaries have been consulted. These are duly presented in the bibliography.

The purpose of this dictionary is to provide both Americans and Poles with access to vocabulary that has never been taught in the classroom, but has high usage in everyday informal speech. It is hoped that this dictionary will prove useful for various groups of readers. Americans (and Americans of Polish descent) who study Polish may find it an interesting addition the standard language they have been learning. Polish immigrants living in the United States (or elsewhere) may discover some new words and meanings of contemporary Polish. Finally, the dictionary will give Poles an instant key to the understanding of American slang and colloquial everyday speech.

Anyone familiar with the language knows how intangible and quivocal slang is. This is true for both American and Polish slangs: Each of these alone constitutes an enormous and constantly changing territory. Recording, selecting, editing, and, above all, matching these two was truly arduous work. As any pioneer endeavor, this dictionary is by no means free from oversights. It is hoped that the reader will judge the merits of this dictionary solely on the whole entity.

Grateful acknowledgment is made to numerous students of the University of Gdańsk, specifically of the Department of English, for their invaluable help in verifying the dictionary entries. My heartfelt gratitude goes to Robert Urbanski, chief consulting editor, for his dedication in searching for English equivalents and editing examples. Most of all, I must credit Marta Trejtowicz and Mary Kobrzak for their support and assistance in this project.

Maciej Widawski
New York City
Fall, 1996

Guide to the Dictionary

I have tried to make the apparatus of this book clear and self-explanatory, but a few guidelines may help the reader. These are given more or less in the order of the elements in the definition block itself.

The Main Entry

Main entries are shown in **bold typeface**. Phrases are given as they normally appear in actual usage, and not according to the key word principle. This was done to ease the process of finding a given phrase in the dictionary. Additionally, the meticulously prepared cross-refernce index is incorporated within the main text.

Polish Pronunciation

Phonetic spellings are given in brackets [] for all Polish entries and their variants. The pronunciation recorded in the dictionary conforms to standard Polish pronunciation and reflects no regional accent markers. The phonetic spelling system is designedly very simple and aimed at Americans who would want to pronounce Polish words. The pronunciations are to be interpreted using the following conventions:

(1) All syllables are divided by hyphens, for example **nafaszerować się** [nah-fah- sheh-ROH-vahch shyeh] or **luzara** [loo-ZAH-rah].
(2) Stressed syllables are shown in capital letters, for example **blondyna** [blohn-DI- nah] or **kasa** [KAH-sah]; one-syllable words (or those treated as such) are typically not stressed, for example **dziad** [jaht] or **iść** [eeshch].
(3) The following are all vowels and consonants for which Polish spelling differs considerably from English (the remaining consonants are pronounced more or less as they are in English):

Polish Spelling	English Sound	PEDSC System	Sample Word
a	as in father	[ah]	**rura** [ROO-rah]
e	as in men	[eh]	**duperele** [doo-peh-REH-leh]
i	as in see	[ee]	**siki** [SHEE-kee]
o	as in talk	[oh]	**zdrowo** [ZDROH-voh]
u	as in rude	[oo]	**lulu** [LOO-loo]
y	as in sin	[i]	**typ** [tip]
ę	almost as in hang	[eh]	**prosię** [PROH-shyeh]
		[ehn]	**gęś** [gensch]
		[ehm]	**gęba** [GEHM-bah]

ą	almost as in don't	[oh]	**gąska** [GOHN-skah]
		[ohn]	**flądra** [FLOHN-drah]
		[ohm]	**trąba** [TROHM-bah]
c	as in bits	[ts]	**cycki** [TSI-tskee]
ć	softer than in beach	[ch]	**srać** [srahch]
ch	as in German nacht	[kh]	**cholera** [khoh-LEH-rah]
cz	as in beach	[ch]	**czubek** [CHOO-behk]
dz	as in holds	[dz]	**jędza** [YEHN-dzah]
dż	as in jump	[j]	**dżampreza** [jahm-PREH-zah]
dź	softer than jump	[j]	**wiedźma** [VYEHJ-mah]
g	as in dog	[g]	**gały** [GAH-wi]
j	as in yellow	[y]	**jaja** [YAH-yah]
ł	as in window	[w]	**połówka** [poh-WOOF-kah]
ń	as in canyon	[ń]	**koń** [kohń]
r	as in rolled Scots far	[r]	**bary** [BAH-ri]
rz	as in vision	[zh]	**rzygać** [ZHI-gahch]
ś	softer than in sheep	[sh]	**ścierwo** [SHCHYEHR-voh]
sz	as in sheep	[sh]	**szmal** [shmahl]
w	as in very	[v]	**wóda** [VOO-dah]
ź	softer than in vision	[zh]	**źdźiebko** [ZHJEHP-koh]
ż	as in vision	[zh]	**żur** [zhoor]

Notes On Pronunciation

(1) Polish vowels are inherently short, although stressed vowels tend to be slightly longer than unstressed ones.

(2) Polish has two nasal vowels similar to French nasals, as in *en garde* and *bon ton.* In informal speech they are pronounced as [eh], [ehn], [ehm] as in **prosię** [PROH-shyeh], **gęś** [gensch], **gęba** [GEHM-bah] and as [oh], [ohn], [ohm] **gąska** GOHN-skah], **flądra** [FLOHN-drah], **trąba** [TROHM-bah].

(3) Hard consonants [p], [b], [k], [g], [m], [n], [l], [f], [v] have soft or palatalized counterparts. These counterparts are indicated in Polish script by the softening vowel letter "i" and by [y] in the PEDSC spelling, for example, **pierdzieć** [PYEHR-jehch], **biegać** [BYEH-gahch], **kiep** [kyehp], **gie** [gyeh], **miastowy** [myahs-TOH-vi], **gniot** [gnyoht], **italianiec** [ee-tah-LYAH-nyehts], **fiut** [fyoot], **wiedzieć** [VYEH-jehch].

(4) Voiced consonants become voiceless at the end of a word and before a voiceless consonants, for example **łeb** [wehp], **badylarz** [bah-DI-lahsh], **kubek w kubek** [KOO-behk f KOO-behk], **nie w sosie** [nyeh f SOH-shyeh], **babsztyl** [BAHP-shtil].

(5) The consonants [p], [t], [k] are pronounced without the puff of air which follows them in English before stressed vowels, for example **pała** [PAH-wah], **tango** [TAHN-goh], **kutwa** [KOOT-fah].

(6) The consonant [t] is never pronounced like the American English flap, as in *letter* or *city*, but is always voiceless, for example **bity** [BEE-ti], **napity** [nah- PEE-ti], **chata** [KHAH-tah].

(7) The consonant [r] is never silent and is pronounced like rolled Scots "r" in all positions, for example **fart** [fahrt], **rura** [ROO-rah], **kafar** [KAH-fahr].

(8) The consonant [kh] resembles the German sound of "nacht" or Scottish "loch," and must never be pronounced as [k]. Examples are **chata** [KHAH-tah], **chujowy** [khoo-YOH-vi], or **łach** [wahkh].

Variant Forms

Variants are shown in parentheses () and given in **boldface**. They are introduced by "or," colons and semicolons may be further used to separate various levels of variant forms. Variants of parts of longer phrases are introduced by the phrases "may replace," "may precede," etc. Variable pronouns are indicated by **ktoś** "someone" and **coś** "something," or (where necessary) by their declined forms, such as **komuś, kogoś, kimś, czemuś, czegoś, czymś**. For example, **dać komuś w łapę, chodzić komuś po głowie, lecieć na kogoś, puszczać do kogoś oko, żyć z kimś na kocią łapę, kręcić z kimś, skręcić czemuś kark, umyć ręce od czegoś, nie mieć głowy do czegoś, do dupy z czymś, położyć łapę na czymś**. The description of variants is intended to be a general, not absolute, guide to the possibilities.

Note on gender. Polish, like French, is a very gender-oriented language. Although effort has been made to offer both masculine and feminine forms of adjectives and nouns, very often only masuline forms are given (and treated as a canonical form). This was done to save space and in no way should be considered sexist.

Part-of-speech Labels

Parts of speech and a few other grammatical particulars are indicated by rather self-explanatory labels:

adjective	*adj*	przymiotnik, przymiotnikowy
adverb	*adv*	przysłówek, przysłówkowy
conjunction	*conj*	spójnik
exclamation	*excl*	wykrzyknienie, wykrzyknikowy
noun (feminine)	*nf*	rzeczownik rodzaju żeńskiego
noun (masculine)	*nm*	rzeczownik rodzaju męskiego
noun (neuter)	*nn*	rzeczownik rodzaju nijakiego
plural noun	*npl*	rzeczownik w liczbie mnogiej
particle	*part*	partykuła
perfective (verb)	*perf*	(czasownik) dokonany
phrase	*phr*	fraza
plural	*pl*	liczba mnoga

preposition	*prep*	przyimek
pronoun	*pron*	zaimek
verb	*v*	czasownik, czasownikowy

Asterisks and Impact labels

This dictionary contains a sizable number of words and phrases, Polish or American, that some readers may find offensive or inflammatory. For the sake of caution, words considered to have stronger social or emotional impact are indicated by asterisks following them. The asterisks are assigned on a two-level principle: Terms of strongest imapact are marked with ** (and considered extremely offensive and vulgar), those of lesser impact are marked with * (and considered less offensive). For example and pierdolić**, pizda**, skurwysyn**, and pieprzyć*, dupa*, gówniarz*. Terms devoid of asterisks are generally presumed to be used without any reservations, although it must be remembered that slang (or colloquialism) is by nature boorish, defiant, derisive, or bawdy; hence some of them may be potentially offensive in certain contexts. Moreover, the assignment of asterisks was a matter of editorial judgment, and not everyone will agree with it.

English Definitions and Equivalents

English definitions were written in what most readers will accept as standard English. In case of polysemous headwords, their individual senses (along with their definitions) are labeled with boldfaced Arabic numerals. The definitions are subsequently appended by direct slang or colloquial equivalents in American English, shown in <> brackets. Care has been taken to most adequately render the meaning of the Polish words and expressions; very often longer strings of more-or-less synonymous expressions are given to offer readers more choice and variety.

It must be noted that finding appropriate slang equivalents was not easy; in many cases there were no direct American English equivalents; sometimes there were no equivalents at all. Moreover, not everyone will agree with some of the suggested equivalents. Such is the fate of a slang lexicographer, not to mention a lexicographer of a bilingual slang dictionary. It is hoped, however, that most of the readers will *generally* agree that the body of words recorded in this dictionary does depict the spoken language(s) they know, and, as for bilingual readers, it is hoped that they will find the suggested equivalents as being accurate.

Examples

Usage examples constitute an integral part of this book and are intended to append definitions. Examples have either been invented by the consultants or edited from original citations based on the corpus. In the former case, all citation sources have been eliminated for the sake of brevity. Each headword (or, in case of polysemous headwords, each sense) is typically accompanied by one example, which is further translated into English. Both the example and its translation are given in italics.

Cross-references, Phrases and Phrase-finder Index

This dictionary locates phrases by the first word of the phrase (placing **patrzeć komuś na ręce** under **patrzeć**; or **na jednej nodze** under **na**, for example), which is believed to be the most appropriate for the purpose of this dictionary and in line with the increasingly common American practice. Additionally, an extraordinary attempt has been made to help the reader find the term in question by cross-referencing nearly every important term in every phrase (prepositions, particles, pronouns, and the like not cross-referenced). Rather than placed at the end of the dictionary, this phrase-finder index was incorporated within the main text, that is, spread under the most important (or clue) words. As another user-friendly device, all perfective verb forms have been cross-referenced to their non-perfective canonical forms, for example **zapierdolić** is cross-referenced to **pierdolić**; or **iść** is cross-referenced to **pójść**.

English Index

The English Index contains all American English slang and colloquial equivalents of the Polish headwords, listed in alphabetical order along with the page numbers where they may be found. This feature makes the dictionary virtually bi-directional and is likely to prove very useful for both Americans (who wish to find Polish equivalents of English words) and Poles (who may want to find English equivalents of Polish words).

Note about the Author

Dr. Maciej Widawski is one of the few scholars in Poland who specializes in slang. Formerly in the diplomatic service, he is now a professor for the Department of English at the University of Gdańsk, where he has been teaching linguistics and communication. As a lexicographer, he authored *Słownik Slangu i Potocznej Angielszczyzny (English-Polish Thesaurus of Slang and Colloquialisms)* and *Słownik Wyrażeń z F**k (The F**ktionary)*.

The POLISH-ENGLISH Dictionary of SLANG AND COLLOQUIALISM

A

aby zbyć [AH-bi ZBICH] (or **byle zbyć** [BI-leh ZBICH]) *adv phr* Carelessly and cursorily, esp because of haste; haphazardly <half-assedly, half-heartedly, helter-skelter, hit-or-miss, hit-and-miss, harum-scarum, higgedly-piggedly, ramble-scramble, arsy-varsy, with a lick and a promise, slapdash, slapbang, skewgeely, scratching the surface> eg *Zmiatał podłogę, aby zbyć (He was mopping the floor half-assedly)*

aby-aby See na aby-aby

adidas [ah-DEE-dahs] *nm* Acquired Immune Deficiency Syndrome; AIDS <gay plague, blood disease, big A, slim> eg *Zmarł na adidasa (He died of the gay plague)*

adolf* [AH-dohlf] *nm* A male German <kraut, krauthead, sauerkraut, Fritz, Heinie, Jerry> eg *Jakiś adolf nadjechał Beemką (Some krauthead pulled up in his Beemer)*

agent [AH-ghent] (or **agregat** [ah-GREH-ghat] or **artysta** [ahr-TIS-tah] or **aparat** [ah-PAH-raht]) *nm* A man impressive, extravagant, or disorderly in behavior <artist, joker, clown, article, ham, character, item, number> eg *Z tego twojego kuzyna to prawdziwy agent; poszedł na egzamin końcowy w szortach! (Your cousin is a real joker: He went to his final exam wearing shorts!); Nieprzeciętny z niego artysta! Załatwił wszystko w jeden dzień! (He's a real character! It took him one day to fix everything up!)*

agentka [ah-GHENT-kah] (or **artystka** [ahr-TIS-tkah]) *nf* A woman impressive, extravagant, or disorderly in behavior <artist, joker, clown, article, ham, character, item, number> eg *Z niej to była agentka! Potrafiła przegadać całą imprezę (She was a real artist! She could gab for the whole party)*

akademik [ah-kah-DEH-meek] *nm* A dormitory <dorm, frat, frat house, fratority, sorenity, birdcage> eg *Mieszkasz w akademiku? (Do you live in a dorm?)*

akumulatory See naładować akumulatory

akuratnie [ah-koo-RAHT-nyeh] *adj* Properly and precisely; just as desired; according to procedures <by the book, according to Hoyle, by the numbers, on the ball, on the right track, on the button, on the dot, on the nose, on the bean, to a tee, just what the doctor ordered> eg *Zrobimy wszystko akuratnie (We'll do everything by the book)*

akuratny [ah-koo-RAHT-ni] *adj* Proper; decent; just as desired <solid, stone, straight, square> eg *Akuratny z niego młodzieniec (He's a straight young man)*

alfons* [AHL-fohns] *nm* A man who solicits business for a prostitute <pimp, mack, flesh-peddler> eg *Ten facet z diamentowym sygnetem wygląda na alfonsa (The guy with the diamond ring looks like a pimp)*

amen See jak amen w pacierzu

Ameryka [ah-meh-RI-kah] *nf* United States of America <US of A, States, stateside, mainland> eg *Jest prosto z Ameryki. Chcesz z nim pogadać? (He's fresh from the States. You want to talk to him?)*

amerykan [ah-meh-RI-kahn] (or **amerykaniec** [ah-meh-ri-KAH-nyehts]) *nm* A citizen of (or a person born) in the United States of America <Yank, Yankee, Americano> eg *Kim jest ten Amerykan? (Who's that Yank?)*

amfa [AHM-fah] *nf* Amphetamine <speed, amp, leaper, jumper, pepper-upper, pep pill, up, upper, lid popper, lid opener, co-pilot> eg *Dzieciaki myślą, że amfa nie wpędzi i ch w kłopoty (Kids think that speed won't get them into trouble); Widać, że jest na amfie. Jest narąbany jak cholera (You can tell he's on leapers. He's wired as hell)*

amigo [AH-mee-goh] *nm* A man, esp impressive, extravagant, or disorderly in behavior <artist, joker, clown, article, ham, character, item, number> eg *Te, amigo, nie jesteś w cyrku (Hey, clown, you're not in the circus)*

amory [ah-MOH-ri] *npl* Love <amore, crush, yen, itch, mash, pash, the hots> eg *Wiesz, dlaczego zachowują się tak, jak się zachowują? Chodzi o amory (You know why they act the way they do? It's about amore)*

anal* [AH-nahl] *nm* Anal sex in general or an anal intercourse <Greek way, Hershey highway, buggering, cornholing, brownholing, bungholing, buttfucking, assfucking, backdooring, reaming> eg *Powiedział, że anal jest super (He said buttfucking is cool)*

angol [AHN-gohl] *nm* **1** An Englishman <Brit, Britisher, limey, limejuicer, beefeater, Tommy> eg *Angole są nieszczęśliwi z powodu niskiej pozycji funta (The Brits are unhappy over the weakness of the pound sterling)* **2*** The English language, esp as a subject in school <no slang equivalent> eg *Wiesz, że dostał pałę z klasówy z angola? (Do you know that he got an F on his English test?)*

ani be ani me [AH-nee BEH AH-nee MEH] (or **ani be ani me ani kukuryku** [AH-nee BEH AH-nee MEH AH-nee koo-koo-RI-koo]) *adv phr* **1** Unable to understand or express oneself clearly <not get, not get it, not catch, not get the drift, not get the picture, get the message, not get the hang of, not savvy, not dig, not click, not capeesh, not read, not be with it, not see where one is coming from, not to know where one is coming from> eg *Tłumaczył jej dwa razy, ale ona ani be ani me (He explained it to her twice but she didn't get the drift)* **2** Silent <clammed up, closed up like a clam, buttoned up, tight-lipped, tongue-tied, unflappable, like a grave> eg *Liczyła, że jej się oświadczy na imprezie, ale on ani be ani me (She hoped he would propose to her during the party, but he got tongue-tied)*

ani centa [AH-nee TSEHN-tah] *nm* (Of an amount of money) Nothing at all; zero <zilch, beans, damn, diddly-squat, doodly-squat, duck egg, goose egg, hoot, one red cent, one thin dime, rat's ass, zero, zippo, shit-all, fuck-all> eg *Nie dali mi ani centa (They gave me zilch)*

ani mi się śni [AH-nee mee shyeh SHNEE] *excl* You will never discover me doing this <catch me, catch me doing this, not on your life, eat shit, eat dirt, eat my shorts, not on your life> eg *You want me to undress? Catch me doing this! (Chcesz, żebym się rozebrała? Ani mi się śni!)*

ani pary z gęby [AH-nee PAH-ri z GEHM-bi] (or **ani mru-mru** [AH-nee mroo-MROO] or **gęba na kłódkę** [GEHM-bah nah KWOOT-keh] or **gęba w kubeł** [GEHM-bah f KOO-beh-oo] or **morda na kłódkę*** [MOHR-dah nah KWOOT-keh] or **morda w kubeł*** [MOHR-dah f KOO-beh-oo]) *excl phr* An exclamation urging someone not to spread the secret <shush, mum's the word, put a sock in it, button your lip, zip your lip, bag your head, keep your mouth shut, don't let out a peep, shut your yap, shut up, can it, cork it, button it, bottle it, clam up> eg *Nie* *mów nikomu tego, co ci powiedziałam. Pamiętaj, ani mru mru (Don't tell anyone what I told you. Remember, mum's the word)*

ani pisnąć [AH-nee PEES-nohnch] (or **nie pisnąć ani słówka** [nyeh PEES-nohnch AH-nee SWOOF-kah]) *v phr* To remain silent; not to reveal a secret <not let the cat out of the bag, not spill the beans, not make the shit hit the fan> eg *Nasz agent nie pisnął ani słówka (Our agent didn't spill out the beans)*

ani rusz [AH-nee ROOSH] *adv phr* By no means; impossible <out of the question, no way, no way Jose, no dice, not on your life, nothing doing, no can do> eg *Poprosiłem tę laskędo tańca, a ona ani rusz (I asked that chick to dance but no can do)*

ani w ząb [AH-nee v ZOHMP] (or **ni w ząb** [nee v ZOHMP]) *adv phr* Nothing at all; zero <zilch, beans, damn, diddly-squat, doodly-squat, duck egg, goose egg, hoot, not one red cent, not one thin dime, rat's ass, zero, zippo, shit-all, fuck-all> eg *Ani w ząb nie znam się na matematyce (I know zilch about mathematics)*

ani ziębić ani grzać kogoś [AH-nee ZHYEHM-beech AH-nee GZHAHCH] *v phr* To make no difference; to be indifferent to someone <make no diff, be all the same, be same old shit, be same difference, no matter how you slice it, make no never mind, be no big deal, could care less about, not care, not care a damn, not care a shit, not care a fuck, not give a damn, not give a shit, not give a fuck, be no skin off one's ass> eg *Czy ja go chcę wyrzucić? Ani on mnie ziębi ani grzeje (Do I want to fire him? I don't give a damn about him)*

antenki [ahn-TEHN-kee] *npl* The ears, esp big <flappers, flaps, sails, cauliflowers> eg *Ten facet za dużymi antenkami wydaje się mi znajomy (That guy with big flappers seems familiar to me)*

aparat See agent

aparatczyk [ah-pah-RAHT-chik] *nm* (Esp in former communist times) A high-ranking party official <aparatchik, party boss, party hack> eg *Jej ojciec był wpływowym aparatczykiem (Her father was an influential aparatchik)*

arbajt [AHR-bah-eet] *nm* Work, esp tedious <old nine-to-five, daily grind, salt mines, nine-to-five, rat race, donkeywork, bullwork, elbow grease> eg *Miałem tydzień wolnego, a teraz znów arbajt! (I had a week off, and now it's back to the salt mines!)*

armia [AHR-myah] *nf* Armed Forces <Uncle Sam, green machine, khaki tit> eg *Armia go zabrała (Uncle Sam's got him)*

artysta See agent

artystka See agentka

as [ahs] *nm* A person of extraordinary skill in specified activity; an expert <ace, whiz, whiz-kid, wiz, maven, mavin, guru> eg *Naszą szkołę reprezentował as komputerowy (Our school was represented by a computer ace); Nie jesteś asem giełdowym (You're not a stock market mavin)*

as w rękawie [ahs v rehn-KAH-vyeh] *nm phr* Something or someone held secretly in reserve; anything which can help in an emergency <ace up one's sleeve, ace in the hole> eg *Ten banknot pięćdziesięciodolarowy był moim asem w rękawie (The fifty-dollar bill was my ace in the hole)*

asfalt* [AHS-fahlt] *nm* A black person <nigger, niggra, bro, brother, jungle bunny, chocolate drop, darky, groid, inky-dink, blue-skin, boogie, jigaboo, zigaboo, shade, shadow, smoke, spade, spook, coon, Hershey bar> eg *W holu paru asfaltów krzyczało na siebie (There were a couple of niggers in the hall shouting at each other)*

astronomiczny [ah-stroh-noh-MEECH-ni] *adj* (Esp about a price or sum) exorbitant; expensive <astronomical, pricey, up to here, out of sight> eg *Przed świętami ceny były astronomiczne (The prices before Christmas were astronomical)*

audik [AH-oo-deek] *nm* An Audi <no slang equivalent> eg *Wczoraj kupił nowiutkiego audika (Yesterday he bought a brand new Audi)*

autobus See narąbany

autograf [ah-oo-TOH-grahf] *npl* One's signature <John Hancock, John Henry> eg *Postaw to swój autograf i forsa jest twoja (Put your John Hancock here and the money's yours)*

B

bałwan* [BAH-oo-vahn] (or **bęcwał*** [BEHNTS-vah-oo] or **bezmózgowiec*** [behz-mooz-GOH-vyehts]) *nm* A silly, clumsy or ineffectual person <airbrain, airhead, birdbrain, blockhead, squarehead, bonehead, bubblebrain, bubblehead, buckethead, cluckhead, cementhead, clunkhead, deadhead, dumbbell, dumbcluck, dumbhead, dumbass, dumbbrain, fatbrain, fathead, flubdub, knukclebrain, knucklehead, lamebrain, lardhead, lunkhead, meathead, musclehead, noodlehead, numbskull, pointhead, scatterbrain, jerk, jerk-off, klutz, chump, creep, nerd, dork, dweeb, gweeb, geek, jackass, lummox, twerp, nerd, bozo, clod, cluck, clunk, dimwit, dingbat, dipstick, dodo, dopey, dufus, goofus, lump, lunk, nitwit, schnook, schlep, schlemiel, schmendrick, schmo, schmuck, simp, stupe> eg *Ale bałwan ze mnie. Zapomniałem prawa jazdy, panie władzo (I'm such a birdbrain. I forgot my driver's license, officer); Rzucił się na profesora z pyskiem? Bęcwał! (He started yelling at the professor. What a dumbass!)*

baba [BAH-bah] *nf* **1** A woman <gal, dame, lady, missy, ma'am, dudette> eg *Ma facet przerąbane: w domu pięć bab i ani jednego chłopa (Man, does he have it bad: five dames in the house)* **2** Someone's wife <old lady, old woman, ball-and-chain, little woman, significant other, better half> eg *On chce jechać, ale jego baba mu nie pozwoli (He wants to go, but his old lady won't let him)* **3** A timid, weak, or effeminate male, a weakling <lady, wimp, wuss, pussy, fraidy cat, gutless wonder, milquetoast> eg *Nie bądź taka baba! Weź się w garść (Don't be such a wimp. Get hold of yourself); Nie bądź baba. Skacz! (Don't be a fraidy cat. Go ahead, jump!)*
See babiarz, chodzić na dupy, cięty na baby

babcia See jak bum cyk-cyk

babiarz [BAH-byahsh] (or **pies na baby** [pyehs nah BAH-bi]) *nm* A man who pursues and otherwise devotes himself to women to an unususal degree <ladies' man, lech, skirt-chaser, lady-killer, operator, player, playboy, hound-dog, cocksman, pistol Pete> eg *Uważa się za babiarza. Laski uważają go za starego zbereźnika. (He thinks he is a lady-killer. The chicks see him as a dirty old man)*

babiniec [bah-BEE-nyehts] *nm* A group of women <ladies' club> eg *Moje biuro to istny babiniec - dwóch facetów i dwadzieścia bab! (My office is a real ladies' club: There are just 2 guys and 20 gals)*

babka See na dwoje babka wróżyła

babka [BAHP-kah] *nf* A young and attractive woman <chick, broad, gal, pussy, cunt, ass, piece of ass, piece, dish, babe, baby, dame, beauty, beaut, beauty queen, baby doll, doll, dolly, dollface, dreamboat, dream girl, eating stuff, eyeful, flavor, looker, good-looker, head-turner, traffic-stopper, honey, killer, hot number, package, knockout, oomph girl, peach, bombshell, sex bunny, sex job, sex kitten, sex pot, table grade, ten, bunny, centerfold, cheesecake, date bait, dazzler, heifer, fluff, quail, sis, skirt, tail, job, leg, tart, tomato, pussycat, cooz, twat> eg *Twoja szefowa to podobno ładna babka (They say your boss is a nice little lady)*

babochłop* [bah-BOH-khwohp] *nm* A woman that appears or behaves like a man <butch, butch-dyke, bull-dyke, tomboy> eg *Wygląda jak jakiś babochłop, tylko wąsów jej brakuje (She looks real butch. She's only missing a mustache)*

babrać się [BAHB-rach shyeh] *v* To do something very slowly, sluggishly, or arduously; to dawdle <poke along, sit on one's ass, sit on one's butt, play around with, play with, fool around with, fool with, mess around with, mess with, diddle around with, diddle with, fart around with, fart with, fiddle around with, fiddle with, monkey around with, monkey with, screw around with, screw with, fuck around with, fuck with, schlep around, drag around, drag-ass> eg *Na twoim miejscu nie babrałbym się tym przełącznikiem (I wouldn't fool around with that switch if I were you)*

babska impreza [BAHP-skah eem-PREH-zah] *nf phr* A party for women only <hen party, ladies' night> eg *Nie lubiła chodzić na babskie imprezy (She didn't like to go to hen parties)*

babski [BAHP-skee] *adj* Characteristic of a woman <girly, chick, chick's> eg *Myślę, że Melrose Place to babski serial (I think that Melrose place is a chick show)*

babsko* [BAHP-skoh] (**babsztyl*** [BAHP-shtil] or **babon*** [BAH-bohn]) *nn* A woman, esp a heavy, ugly, or mean one <beasty, skag, skank, pig, bag, dog, cow> eg *Ale z niej babon! Mogłaby trochę schudnąć (She's such a cow! She really should lose weight); Bez makijażu to babsztyl (She looks like a skag without makeup)*

bachor* [BAH-khohr] *nm* A child, esp a young one <brat, kid, punk> eg *Jej brat to prawdziwy bachor. Nie wie, kiedy trzymać gębę na kłódkę (Her brother is a little brat. He doesn't know when to keep his mouth shut)*

badyl [BAH-dil] *nm* A stalk <stick> eg *Zabierz ode mnie te badyle (Get these sticks away from me)*

badylarz [bah-DI-lahsh] *nm* An owner of an agricultural enterprise; a rich but rustic and unsophisticated businessman <white-trash aristocrat, backwood baron, hayseed tycoon> eg *Robi się na kulturalną, ale widać, że to córka badylarza (She tries to act sophisticated, but you can say she's a daughter of a backwood baron)*

bagno [BAHG-noh] *nn* The most immoral and loathsome place or situation imaginable, esp the one from which it is almost impossible to free oneself <the pits, the armpit, the cellar, the asshole, bottom rung, rock bottom> eg *Mówi, że jej uniwersytet to bagno (She says her university is the pits)*

bajda See bajka

bajeczka See bajka

bajer [BAH-yehr] (or **bajer bongo** [BAH-yehr BOHN-goh]) *nm* **1** (or **blaga** [BLAH-gah] *nf*) (Ability to say) A lie or an exaggeration meant to impress or win the approval; manipulating someone to think or act as one wishes <bluff, mind-

fucking, head-fucking, pushing around, upstaging, showing off, grandstanding, grandstand play, circus play, showboating, hotdogging, bullshitting, blowing off, signifying> eg *Ona nie uwierzy w takie bajery (She won't believe such bullshitting)* **2** Anything attractive, stylish or unusual that makes impression <swank, knock-out, kill-out, whizbang, humdinger, killer, killer-diller, fireworks, doozie> eg *Przywiózł masę bajerów z Ameryki (He brought a lot of humdingers from America); Rety, ale bajer! (Geez, what a knockout is is!)*

See bajerować

bajerancki See bombowy

bajerancko See bombowo

bajerant [bah-YEH-rahnt] (or **blagier** [BLAH-gyehr]) *nm* A man who has the ability to manipulate someone to think or act as one wishes; someone who tries to impress or win the approval, esp by lying or exaggerating <bluffer, mind-fucker, head-fucker, bullshitter, bullshit artist, hot-air artist, showboater, grandstander, blowhard> eg *Twój kuzyn to prawdziwy bajerant. Wszystkie moje przyjaciółki mają świra na jego punkcie (Your cousin is a real head-fucker. All of my friends are crazy about him)*

bajerować [bah-yeh-ROH-vahch] (perf **zbajerować** [zbah-yeh-ROH-vahch]; or **brać kogoś na bajer** [brahch KOH-gohsh nah BAH-yehr] or **brać kogoś pod bajer** [brahch KOH-gohsh pohd BAH-yehr]; or **blagować** [blah-GOH-vahch]) *v* To manipulate someone to think or act as one wishes; (to try) to impress or win the approval, esp by lies or exaggeration <bluff, mind-fuck, head-fuck, push around, upstage, wind around one's finger, wrap around one's finger, twist around one's finger, show off, grandstand, showboat, pile it on, hotdog, bullshit, blow one's horn, blow one's trumpet, blow smoke, blow off, blow hard, signify, bigmouth, talk big> eg *W przeciągu dwóch godzin kompletnie zbajerował ją (Within two hours he managed to totally wrap her around his finger)*

bajka [BAH-ee-kah] (or **bajeczka** [bah-YEHCH-kah] or **bujda** [BOO-ee-dah] or **bajda** [BAH-ee-dah] or **banialuki** [bah-nyah-LOO-kee] *npl*; **na resorach** [nah reh-SOH-rahkh] may be added) Deceitful talk; a lie <bull, bullshit, bullshine, BS, bunk, baloney, applesauce, eyewash, hogwash, hot air, crock, crock of shit, piece of shit, pile of shit, shit, dogshit, horseshit, shit for the birds, crap, crapola, poppycock, smoke, hokum, garbage, trash, horsefeathers, smoke, all that jazz, jazz, jive, malarkey, gobbledygook, double-talk, bafflegab, blah-blah, phony-baloney, fiddle-faddle, twiddle-twaddle, mumbo-jumbo, yackety-yack> eg *Nie wciskaj mi bujdy, koleś (Don't give me that applesause, man)*

bajzel See burdel

bajzelmama See burdelmama

bakcyl See połknąć bakcyla

bakier See być na bakier

bal See po balu

bal samców [bahl SAHM-tsoof] *nm phr* A party for men only <stag party, bachelor party> eg *Jak się udał wczorajszy bal samców? (How was the stag party last night?)*

balanga [bah-LAHN-gah] *nf* A drinking party; a carousal <bash, bender, bust, twister, wingding, winger> eg *Balanga rozpoczęła się o godzinie ósmej i trwała do rana (The bender started at eight and lasted till the morning)*

balety [bah-LEH-ti] *nm pl* Sexual or amorous activity of any kind <action, dirty deed, little heavy breathing, fun and games, bouncy-bouncy, boom-boom, in-and-out, hootchie-coochie, jig-jig, roll in the hay, jelly roll, night baseball, bush patrol, hanky-panky, lovey-dovey, grab-ass, you-know-what> eg *Zwykli zaciągać dziewczyny do lasu na balety (They would drag girls into the woods for a little heavy breathing)*

balon See baniak, zrobić kogoś w konia

balować [bah-LOH-vahch] (perf **zabalować** [zah-bah-LOH-vahch]) *v* To carouse or celebrate <party, ball, have a ball, jam, paint the town red, raise hell, bar-hop, bar-crawl, go on a bender> eg *Postanowili gdzieś zabalować (They decided to go and party someplace)*

bamber [BAHM-behr] *nm* A farmer, esp rich <hick, hayseed, apple-knocker, hillbilly, shitkicker, big-time bumpkin, hayseed tycoon, hillbilly baron> eg *Bambrom ciężko jest przyzwyczaić się do życia w mieście (It's hard for these hayseeds to adjust to city life)*

bambetle [bahm-BEHT-leh] *npl* Personal belongings, esp small and numerous articles of various kinds <stuff, crap, shit, junks, props, odds and ends, bits and pieces, thingies, gadgets, widgets, dingbats, gimmicks> eg *Zabieraj swoje bambetle z mojej szafki (Get your stuff out of my locker)*

bambo See bambus

bambuko See zrobić kogoś w konia

bambus* [BAHM-boos] (or **bambo*** [BAHM-boh] *nn*) *nm* A black person <nigger, niggra, bro, brother, jungle bunny, chocolate drop, darky, groid, inky-dink, blue-skin, boogie, jigaboo, zigaboo, shade, shadow, smoke, spade, spook, coon, Hershey bar> eg *Ich rząd składa się z samych bambusów (Their government is composed of niggers only)*

See pierdolić, zrobić kogoś w konia

banda [BAHN-dah] *nf* A group of people <folks, pack, bunch, crew, gang, clan, crowd, boys> eg *Instytut Anglistyki to banda wariatów (The English Department is a pack of nuts)*

bandzioch See bebech

bandzior [BAHN-johr] *nm* A bandit or thug; a violent and reckless criminal <cowboy, gangster, hood, hoodlum, hooligan, goon> eg *Pobiły go jakieś bandziory (Some hoods beat him)*

bania See do dupy, na gazie

baniak [BAH-nyah] (or **bańka** [BAHÑ-kah] *nf*) *nm* **1** (or **bania** [BAH-nyahk] *nf*) The head <bean, noggin, conk, dome, gourd, skull> eg *(Załóż czapkę na baniak i walimy (Put your cap on your conk, and let's cruise)* **2** (or **balon** [BAH-lohn] *nm*) A million zloty <M, mil> eg *To cię będzie kosztowało bańkę (It'll set you back a mil)*

banialuki See- bajka

banie* [BAH-nyeh] (or **baniaki*** [bah-NYAH-kee]) *npl* A woman's large breasts <tits, melons, knockers, bazooms, boobs, headlights, hooters, hemispheres> eg *Z takimi baniami, powinna grać w filmach (With boobs like that, she ought to be in the movies)*

bankowo [bahn-KOH-voh] (or **jak w banku** [yahk v BAHN-koo] or **na bank** [nah BAHNK]) *adv phr* Certainly; secure; very sure <sure, fer sure, sure as hell, sure as shit, sure as can be, for real, indeedy, really truly, absitively, posilutely, real, cert,

def, no buts about it, wired up, cinched, taped, racked, sewed up, iced, in the bag, tied up, nailed down> eg *Wybiorą naszego kandydata. Mamy to jak w banku (They will chose our candidate. We got it cinched)*

bankowy [bahn-KOH-vi] *adj* Sure; secured <sure, fer sure, sure as hell, sure as shit, sure as can be, for real, real, cert, def, wired up, cinched, taped, racked, sewed up, iced, in the bag, tied up, nailed down> eg *To bankowy zwycięzca (He's a sure winner)*

barłóg [BAHR-wook] *nm* A bed <hay, pad, sack, flop, rack, snooze bin, fleabag, fart sack, whank-pit, workbench> eg *Nie zmieniał pościeli w swoim barłogu przez miesiąc (He hasn't changed the sheets in his sack for a month)*

bara-bara [BAH-rah BAH-rah] *nn phr* Amorous or sexual activity of any kind, esp playful <action, dirty deed, little heavy breathing, fun and games, bouncy-bouncy, boom-boom, in-and-out, hootchie-coochie, jig-jig, roll in the hay, jelly roll, night baseball, bush patrol, hanky-panky, lovey-dovey, grab-ass, you-know-what> eg *Oznajmił, że bara-bara go nie bawi (He said he's not interested in doing the dirty deed)*

barachło [bah-rah-KHWOH] *nn* Anything worthless, useless, or of shoddy quality; trash <schlock, dreck, garbage, junk, lemon, crap, piece of crap, shit, piece of shit, dogshit, sleaze> eg *Gdzie kupiłeś to barachło? (Where did you buy this lemon?)*

baran* [BAH-rahn] (or **barani łeb*** [bah-RAH-nee WEHP] or **ośli łeb*** [OSH-lee WEHP] or **zakuty łeb*** [zah-KOO-ti WEHP]) *nm* A stupid, clumsy or ineffectual person; an idiot <airbrain, airhead, birdbrain, blockhead, squarehead, bonehead, bubblebrain, bubblehead, buckethead, cluckhead, cementhead, clunkhead, deadhead, dumbbell, dumbcluck, dumbhead, dumbass, dumbbrain, fatbrain, fathead, flubdub, knukclebrain, knucklehead, lamebrain, lardhead, lunkhead, meathead, musclehead, noodlehead, numbskull, pointhead, scatterbrain, jerk, jerk-off, klutz, chump, creep, nerd, dork, dweeb, gweeb, geek, jackass, lummox, twerp, nerd, bozo, clod, cluck, clunk, dimwit, dingbat, dipstick, dodo, dopey, dufus, goofus, lump, lunk, nitwit, schnook, schlep, schlemiel, schmendrick, schmo, schmuck, simp, stupe> eg *Ale baran ze mnie. Zapomniałem prawa jazdy, panie władzo (I'm such a birdbrain. I forgot my driver's license, officer); Rzucił się na profesora z pyskiem? Zakuty łeb! (He started yelling at the professor. What a dumbass!)*
See na barana

barani wzrok [bah-RAH-nee VZROHK] (or **barania mina** [bah-RAH-nyah MEE-nah] *nf phr*) *nm phr* A surprised confused, or stupid look <glassy eyes, bug eyes> eg *Tylko nie rób baraniej miny (Don't give me these glassy eyes)*

barszcz See tani jak barszcz

bary [BAH-ri] *npl* The shoulders, the arms <wings, fins, delts, soupbones, brace of broads> eg *Bary mnie bolą jak cholera (My wings hurt like hell)*

bas [bahs] *nm* A bass guitar <bass> eg *Posłuchaj mnie, tu grasz na bębnach, a kto na basie? (Listen to me, You play the drums, and who plays bass?)*
See pół litra

baty See dać po dupie, dostać po dupie

bawełna See nie owijać w bawełnę

bawić się [BAH-veech shyeh] (or **zabawiać się** [zah-BAH-vyahch shyeh]; perf **pobawić się** [poh-BAH-veech shyeh] or **zabawić się** [zah-BAH-veech shyeh]) *v* **1** To handle or tamper with something, esp slowly or sluggishly <play around with, play with, fool around with, fool with, mess around with, mess with, diddle

around with, diddle with, fart around with, fart with, fiddle around with, fiddle with, monkey around with, monkey with, screw around with, screw with, fuck around with, fuck with, schlep around, drag around, drag-ass> eg *Na twoim miejscu nie zabawiałbym się tym przełącznikiem (I wouldn't fool around with that switch if I were you)* **2** To do something casually <play around with, fool around with, mess around with, diddle around with, fart around with, fiddle around with, monkey around with, screw around with, fuck around with> eg *Ostatnio bawi się sprzedawaniem choinek (Recently he's been messing around selling Christmas trees)* **3** To tease; to banter; to treat someone unseriously and frivolously; to have fun at someone's expense <poke fun at, kid, kid around, pull someone's leg, pull someone's string, fool around, jive, josh, shuck, lark, spoof, send up, cut down> eg *Powiedziała mu, żeby przestał się z nią bawić (She told him to stop fooling around with her)*

bawić się w chowanego [BAH-veech shyeh f khoh-vah-NEH-goh] (or **bawić się w ciuciubabkę** [BAH-veech shyeh chyoo-chyoo-BAHP-keh] or **bawić się w kotka i myszkę** [BAH-veech shyeh KOHT-kah ee MISH-keh]) *v phr* To delude; to deceive; to avoid answering <play cat and mouse with, play a cat and mouse game with, beat around the bush, play games, jerk someone around, dick someone around, pussyfoot around, snow, blow smoke, pull the wool over someone's eyes> eg *Przestań się bawić w chowanego i powiedz mi prawdę (Stop pussyfooting around and tell me the truth)*

baza See kumać

bazgrać [BAHZ-grahch] (perf **nabazgrać** [nah-BAHZ-grahch]; or **bazgrolić** [bah-ZGROH-leech] perf **nabazgrolić** [nah-bah-ZGROH-leech]; **jak kura pazurem** [yahk KOO-rah pah-ZOO-rehm] may be added) *v* To handwrite illegibly or write anything which is meaningless <scribble, scratch> eg *Zawsze bazgrał jak kura pazurem (He always used to scribble)*

bazgranina [bahz-grah-NEE-nah] (or **bazgroły** [bahz-GROH-wi] *npl*) *nf* Illegible handwriting or any meaningless piece of writing <scribble, scribbling, scratching, hen tracks, chicken tracks, hen scratches, chicken scratches, hen writing, chicken writing> eg *Nie mogę rozczytać tych bazgrołów (I can't read these hen tracks)*

bąbelki [bohm-BEHL-kee] *npl* **1** Any carbonated non-alcoholic drink <soda, pop, coke, fizzle-water, sizz-water> eg *Dolać ci trochę bąbelków? (You want me to pour you some more soda?)* **2** Champagne or sparkling wine <bubbly, bubbles, bubble water, giggle water, sparkle water> eg *Więcej bąbelków, czy może chciałabyś coś mocniejszego? (More bubbly, or do you want something stronger?)*

bąk [bohnk] *nf* A release of intestinal gas, perhaps with a noise <fart, cheese, ass noise> eg *Czy słyszałem bąka? (Did I hear a fart?)*
See puszczać bąka, zbijać bąki

be [beh] *adj* Bad; loathsome; disgusting <no-good, gross, barfy, scuzzy, sleazy, grody, icky, yucky, gooky, grungy, ech, yech, kaka, caca, no-no> eg *Nadwaga jest be (Overweight is no-no)*

bełkot [BEH-oo-koht] *nm* Trivial or platitudinous talk; nonsense <small talk, bull, bullshit, BS, bullshine, bunk, baloney, applesauce, eyewash, hogwash, hot air, crock, crock of shit, piece of shit, pile of shit, shit, dogshit, horseshit, shit for the birds, crap, crapola, poppycock, smoke, hokum, garbage, trash, horsefeathers, smoke, all that jazz, jazz, jive, malarkey, gobbledygook, double-talk, bafflegab,

blah-blah, phony-baloney, fiddle-faddle, twiddle-twaddle, mumbo-jumbo, yackety-yack> eg *Mam już dość twojego intelektualnego bełkotu (I'm sick and tired of your intellectual mumbo-jumbo)*

bełt [BEH-oot] *nm* Cheap and inferior wine <plonk, red ink, veeno, Mad Dog 20/20, Nighttrain, Wild Irish Rose> eg *Co powiesz na butelkę bełta? (How about a bottle of plonk?)*

bebech [BEH-behkh] (or **bęben** [BEHN-behn] or **bandzioch** [BAHN-johkh]) *nm* The stomach, esp large <belly, breadbasket, gut, gutbucket, labonza> eg *Walnęła go prosto w bebech (She poked him right in the gut); Ten twój bandzioch robi się coraz większy, co? (Your gutbucket is getting sort of big, isn't it?)*

bebechy [beh-BEH-khi] *npl* The intestines <guts, kishkes, innards> eg *Postrzelili go w bebechy (He was shot in the guts)*

bęcwał See bałwan

beczeć [BEH-chehch] (perf **pobeczeć się** [poh-BEH-chehch shyeh] or **rozbeczeć się** [rohz-BEH-chehch shyeh]) **1** *v* To cry or weep noisily <blubber, bawl, break down, break down and cry, turn on the waterworks, cry one's eyes out, cry me a river, shed bitter tears, weep bitter tears, sing the blues, put on the weeps, let go, let it out> eg *Rozbeczała się, gdy to usłyszała (She turned on the waterworks when she heard that)*

beczka See z innej parafii, zjeść z kimś beczkę soli

beemwica [beh-ehm-VEE-tsah] *nf* (or **beemka** [beh-EHM-kah]) A BMW <Beemer, Beamer, Bimmer> eg *Ile kosztowała ta beemka? (How much did that Beemer cost?)*

beka [BEH-kah] *nf* An obese person <fatty, fatso, blimp, fat-ass, lard-ass, tub of lard, crisco> eg *Ta beka ledwo mieści się w drzwiach (That tub of lard can hardly get through the door)*

bekać [BEH-kahch] (perf **beknąć** [BEHK-nohnch]) *v* To bring up stomach gas <burp, berp, belch> eg *Staraj się nie bekać przy stole (Try not to burp at the table); Beknąłem i wszyscy zaczęli się śmiać (I belched and everybody started to laugh)*

beknąć za coś [BEHK-nohnch zah tsohsh] *v* To become responsible for the consequences of someone else's wrongdoings <carry the can, hold the bag, hold the sack, take the rap, take the heat, take the fall, bite the bullet, face the music, take it, put one's ass on the line> eg *Jeśli ją złapią, to ja za nią beknę (If she gets caught, I'll take the rap for her)*

beksa [BEHK-sah] (or **beksalala** [behk-sah-LAH-lah]) *nf* A person given to weeping or lamenting at the least adversity <crybaby, whiner> eg *Przestań się drzeć i nie bądź taka beksa! (Stop lamenting. Don't be such a cry baby!)*

bela See pijany jak świnia, upić się jak świnia

belfer [BEHL-fehr] *nm* A teacher <prof, teach, guru, baby-sitter> eg *Ile zarabia taki belfer? (How much does a prof like him earn?)*

bengal [BEHN-gahl] *nm* A soundless but horrendous smelling release of intestinal gas <S.B.D., silent but deadly, cheese, silent killer> eg *Kto puścił tego bengala? (Who let the S.B.D.?)*

berbeć See brzdąc

beret See jaja, rzut beretem

betka [BEHT-kah] *nf* Anything unimportant, trivial, or easy; a trifle; a bagatelle <big deal, no big deal, no biggie, Mickey Mouse, small potatoes, small beer, fly speck,

piece of cake, cake, cakewalk, cherry pie, duck soup, kid stuff, picnic, pushover, snap, tea party, walkaway, walkover, breeze, stroll, cinch, pipe, plain sailing> eg *Otrzymanie paszportu to betka (Getting a passport is no big deal); Ten egzamin to prawdziwa betka (This exam is a real cakewalk)*

beton [BEH-tohn] *nm* **1** A person or people adversive to change; dogmatics; conservatives; stalwarts <hard-liner, hard-core, hard-shell, die-hard, fogy, fud, stonewall, brickwall> eg *Większość z nich to partyjny beton (Most of them are hard-liners)* **2** A slow-witted or foolish person <slow on the draw, slow on the uptake, slow on the trigger, slow-mo> eg *Ale z niego beton. Nic nie zrozumiał (He's really slow on the draw. He didn't get a single thing)* **3** A very drunk person <alkied, bagged, blitzed, blotto, blown away, bent, boiled, bombed, blasted, boozed, bottled, boxed, buzzed, canned, clobbered, cooked, corked, crashed, drunk as a skunk, edged, embalmed, fractured, fried, gassed, ginned, grogged, have one too many, half under, high, hooched up, in bad shape, impaired, illuminated, juiced, knocked out, liquored, lit, loaded, looped, lubricated, lushed, smashed, oiled, pickled, plastered, plonked, polluted, sauced, shitfaced, slugged, sloshed, soaked, stewed, stiff, stinking drunk, swizzled, tanked, three sheets to the wind, wiped, zonked, lit up like a Christmas tree> eg *Facet był kompletny beton (The guy was lit up like a Christmas tree)*

See mur beton

bety [BEH-ti] *npl* **1** Personal belongings, esp small and numerous articles of various kinds <stuff, crap, shit, junks, props, odds and ends, bits and pieces, thingies, gadgets, widgets, dingbats, gimmicks> eg *Zabieraj swoje bety z mojej szafki (Get your gadgets out of my locker)* **2** Bedsheets; bedding <dreamers, white lilies, lily whites> eg *Wciąż leżała w betach (She was still lying in the dreamers)*

bez ładu i składu [behz WAH-doo ee SKWAH-doo] *adv phr* In a state or disorder; chaotically and carelessly, esp because of haste; haphazardly <hit-or-miss, hit-and-miss, half-assedly, half-heartedly, slapdash, slapbang, helter-skelter, harum-scarum, higgedly-piggedly, ramble-scramble, arsy-varsy, ass backwards, assed-up, balled-up, fucked-up, screwed-up, messed-up, fubar, snafu, every which way, all anyhow, skewgeely> eg *Napisała ten esej bez ładu i składu (She wrote this essay helter-skelter)*

bez echa [behz EH-khah] (or **bez huku** [behs KHOO-koo]) *adv phr* Without any response or repercussions, esp scandalous; unnoticed <without a splash, without a bang, without a fallout, without a follow-up, without a follow-through, without a spin-off, without a feedback, without a kickback, without making waves> eg *Przyjazd prezydenta odebrano w mediach bez echa (The President's arrival was met without a bang in the media)*

bez grosza [behz GROH-shah] (or **bez grosza przy duszy** [behz GROH-shah pshi DOO-shi]) *adj phr* Penniless; destitute <broke, dead broke, flat broke, stone broke, busted, cleaned out, cold in hand, down and out, piss-poor, poor as a church mouse, strapped, tapped out, drained, without a red cent> eg *Nie mogę iść z wami. Jestem bez grosza (I can't go with you. I'm dead broke)*

bez jaj [behz YAH-ee] **1*** *adj phr* (Esp about a man) Cowardly, fearful, or effeminate; timorous <gutless, chicken-hearted, chicken-livered, paper-assed, soft-assed, pucker-assed, candy-assed, pansified, sissified, wimpish, wimpy, sissy, pansy, wussy, pussy, weak-kneed, cold-feeted, scared shitless, yellow> eg *Ten facet* *jest kompletnie bez jaj. Wszystkiego się boi (This guy is totally gutless. He's afraid of everything)* **2** *phr* (or **bez kitu** [behs KEE-too]) A phrase of disbelief urging someone to stop treating one unseriously or making fun of one <are you kidding me, no kidding, you gotta be kidding, are you pulling my leg, are you fooling me, no way, no way Jose, no dice, not on your life, nothing doing, no can do, will eat one's hat, in a pig's eye, in a pig's ass, in a pig's ear, like hell, like fun, like shit, my ass, someone will be damned if, someone will be fucked if, says you> eg *Widziałaś już wyniki? Bez jaj! (Did you see the results yet? No kidding); Oddał jej całą forsę? Bez kitu! (He gave her the money back. No kidding!)*

bez krępacji [behs krehm-PAHTS-yee] *adv phr* Freely or unrestrainedly; without feeling embarrassed or uncomfortable <feel free> eg *Bez krępacji. Podejdź do baru i weź co chcesz (Feel free to help yourself to the bar and take anything you want)*

bez mydła See włazić komuś do dupy, zrobić kogoś na szaro

bez ogródek [behs oh-GROO-dehk] *adv phr* Directly; bluntly; frankly; holding nothing back <straight from the shoulder, from the shoulder, straight out> eg She always speaks straight from the shoulder. You never have to guess what she really means

bez przegięcia [behs psheh-GYEHN-chyah] (or **bez przesadyzmu** [behs psheh-sah-DIZ-moo]) *adv phr* A phrase urging someone not to exaggerate <don't go too far, don't push it, don't stretch it, don't hype it, don't ham it> eg *Tylko bez przegięcia z tym! (Just don't hype the thing to death!)*

bez pudła [behs POOD-wah] *adv phr* Certainly; surely <sure, fer sure, sure as hell, sure as shit, sure as can be, for real, indeedy, really truly, absitively, posilutely, real, cert, def, no buts about it, wired up, cinched, taped, racked, sewed up, iced, in the bag, tied up, nailed down> eg

bez różnicy [BEHS roo-ZHNEE-tsi] *adv phr* (Something makes) No difference; (Something is) insignificant <no diff, all the same, same old shit, same difference, no matter how you slice it, makes no never mind, makes no difference, anything goes> eg *Czy go wyrzucą, czy sam odejdzie, to bez różnicy (They fire him or he quits, it's the same difference)*

bez wazeliny See włazić komuś do dupy

bezbłędnie See obłędnie

bezbłędny See obłędny

bezcen See za bezcen

bezmózgowiec See bałwan

bezpłciowy [beh-spoow-CHYOH-vi] *adj* Sexually frigid, sexless <cold as a fish, tight-assed, iceberg> eg *Ta jego nowa dziewczyna jest bardzo bezpłciowa (His new girlfriend is cold as a fish)*

bezpieka [behs-PYEH-kah] *nf* (Esp in former communist times) Secret Police <the eye, undercovers, plainclothes, spooks, peepers, dicks, ops> eg *Bezpieka go dorwała (The plainclothes caught him)*

beztalencie [behs-tah-LEHN-chyeh] *nn* Someone devoid of any talent; a mediocre, insignificant, or ineffectual person; a mediocrity or failure <underachiever, loser, born loser, second-rater, schlemiel, schmendrick, schmo, schnook, screwup, fuckup, hacker, muffer, scrub, dub, dool tool, turkey, lump, buterfingers, fumble-fist, goof, goof-off, goofball, eightball, foulball, klutz, also-ran, never-was, nonstarter, zero, lightweight, nobody, non, nonentity, noname, small potatoes,

small timer, bush-leaguer> eg *Nowy dyrektor Instytutu to beztalencie. Zrobił doktorat po czterdziestce (The new director of the Institute is a real loser. He did his PhD when he turned forty)*

bi [bee] (or **biseks** [BEE-sehks]) *nm* A bisexual person <bi, AC-DC, AM-FM, ambidextrous, double-gaited, he/she, switch-hitter, swinging both ways> eg *Mówi, że on jest bi, ale ja w to nie wierzę (She said he is AC-DC, but I don't believe it)*

bić kogoś na głowę [beech KOH-gohsh nah GWOH-veh] *v phr* To be or do better than someone else; to outdo or outsmart; to surpass <top, outgun, outfox, beat, beat one's time, burn, clobber, lick, put in the shade, skin, sweep, take the cake, come out on top, be cut above, be way far cry better> eg *Europejczycy na pewno biją ich na głowę, jeśli chodzi o piwo (Europeans sure top them, when it comes to beer)*

bić konia See walić konia

bić po kieszeni [beech poh kyeh-SHEH-nee] (or **uderzać po kieszeni** [oo-DEH-zhahch poh kyeh-SHEH-nee] or **dostać po kieszeni** [DOH-stahch poh kyeh-SHEH-nee]) *v phr* To consume a lot of money; to cost a very high price <cost an arm and a leg, cost a bundle> eg *Obawiam się, że to nas uderzy po kieszeni (I'm afraid this is going to cost us an arm and a leg)*

biały See czarno na białym, dostać cholery, rozbój w biały dzień, w biały dzień, widzieć białe myszki

biadolić [byah-DOH-leech] (perf **pobiadolić** [poh-byah-DOH-leech]; or **brzęczeć** [BZHEHN-chehch] or **brzęczeć nad uchem** [BZHEHN-chehch nahd OO-khehm] may be added, perf **zabrzęczeć** [zah-BZHEHN-chehch]) *v* To complain or lament, esp over trivialities; esp groundlessly <fuss, stink, scene, make a ceremony, beef, bleed, hassle, kvetch, bitch, beef, gripe, piss, bellyache, grouse, growl, squawk, cut a beef, make a stink, piss up a storm, raise a stink, blow up a storm, kick up a storm, eat someone's heart out, fuck around, screw around, mess around, trip> eg *Biadoliła, bo nie mieli tego, co chciała (She was pissing up a storm, because they didn't have what she wanted)*

biba [BEE-bah] (or **bibka** [BEEP-kah]) *nf* A drinking party; a carousal <bash, bender, bust, twister, wingding, winger> eg *Lubię iść na dobrą bibkę co jakiś czas (I like a good bender every now and then)*

bida [BEE-dah] (or **bida z nędzą** [BEE-dah z NEHN-dzoh] or **bida aż piszczy** [BEE-dah ahsh PEESH-chi] or **stara bida** [STAH-rah BEE-dah]) *nf* Poverty, destitution, or very troublesome and difficult situation <the rims, same old shit, SOS, gas, fuss, stink, hot potato, bad scene, bad news, can of worms, bag of worms, takedown, putdown, shit, serious shit, deep shit, deep water, drag, bind, bitch, bummer, downer, headache, double trouble, snafu, pain in the ass, pain in the neck, spot, mess, holy mess, pickle, squeeze, hard time, glitch, stinker, skeleton, skeleton in the closet, sizzler, scorcher, dynamite, Watergate, fine kettle of fish, fine how do you do, fine cup of coffee, big stink, curtains, lights out, game's over> eg *No to co nowego u Ciebie? Stara bida. Nie chcą mi dać awansu (So what's new with you? Same old shit. They don't want to give me a promotion)*

bidować [bee-DOH-vahch] (or **biedować** [byeh-DOH-vahch] or **klepać bidę** [KLEH-pahch BEE-deh]) *v* To be poor or destitute <be down and out, be on the edge, be on one's ass, be on the hog, be on the rims, be down to one's last cent, be without a red cent, be without a dime to rub against another, feel the pinch, be

cold in hand, be dead broke, be flat broke, be stone broke> eg *W zaszłym miesiącu klepałem bidę (Last month I was down and out)*

bieda See od biedy, pół biedy

bieg See w biegu

biegać o coś [BYEH-gahch OH tsohsh] *v* To mean; to have in mind; to attempt or want to say <be up, be up to, drive at, get at, go on, go down, come off, come down> eg *Nie rozumiem, o co biega (I don't understand what's coming off)*

biegać za kimś See latać za kimś

biegiem [BYEH-gyehm] *adv* Immediately; very quickly <pretty damn quick, PDQ, ASAP, on the spot, on the double, double time, double clutching, like a shot, in half a mo, like now, before you know it, before you can say Jack Robinson, in a jiffy, in a flash, in half a shake, right off the bat, like a bat out of hell, like a shot out of hell, hubba-hubba, horseback, like greased lightning> eg *Biegnij tam szybko, biegiem! (Run over there quick, on the double!)*

bigos See burdel

bimbać [BEEM-bahch] (or **bimbać sobie** [BEEM-bahch SOH-byeh]; perf **przebimbać** [psheh-BEEM-bahch] or **pobimbać** [poh-BEEM-bahch]) *v phr* **1** To loaf or idle; to pass time lazily <bum around, hang around, hang out, goof around, fuck around, screw around, fiddle around, fiddle fart around, fart around, jack around, mess around, hack around, monkey around, knock around, kick around, fool around, horse around, piddle around, play around, rat around, schloomp around, ass around, beat around, dick around, fuck around, fuck off, screw off, goof off, jerk off, fuck the dog, rat fuck, flub the dub, sit on one's ass, sit on one's butt, lollygag, veg out> eg *Bimbał sobie przez całę wakacje (He gooffed off for the whole vacation)* **2** To be indifferent; not to care at all; to ignore; to show disrespect <not give a damn, not give a fuck, not give a shit, not give a diddly-shit, not give a diddly-damn, not give a flying fuck, not give a hoot, not give a rat's ass, not give a squat, pass up, diss, skip, ig, ice, chill, freeze, cut, brush off, give the brush, give the cold shoulder, turn the cold shoulder, cold-shoulder, give the go-by, high-hat, kiss off> eg *Bimbam na to, co myślisz (I don't give a shit what you think)*

bimber [BEEM-behr] *nm* Cheap, inferior, or illicit liquor, esp home-made <moonshine, moonlight, mountain dew, rotgut, swipe, tiger sweat, panther piss, coffin varnish> eg *Ten bimber cię zabije (This moonshine's going to kill you)*

bimbrownia [beem-BROH-vnyah] *nf* A place where illegal or inferior alcohol is produced or sold, usually a nightclub <bootleg joint, speakeasy> eg *Mój dziadek pamięta bimbrownie. Były to bardzo prymitywne miejsca (My grandfather remembers speakeasies. They were very crude places)*

biola [BYOH-lah] *nf* A biology, esp as a subject in school <bio, bugs, frog slicing> eg *Dostał pionę z bioli (He got an A in bio)*

bity [BEE-ti] *adj* Entire <whole damn> eg *Po tym jak pożyczyłem mu te pieniądze, bity miesiąc czekałem, aż odda (After I loaned him the money I had to wait a whole damn month to get it back)*

biurwa* [BYOOR-vah] *nf* **1** An arrogant and impolite female clerical worker <office bitch> eg *Co ta biurwa sobie myśli do jasnej cholery, że kim jest? (Who the hell does that office bitch think she is?)* **2** A female secretary who readily copulates with her superiors <office fuker, office ass> eg *Ta biurwa lubi szybkie numerki (That office ass likes quickies)*

blać* [blahch] *excl* An exclamation of anger, irritation, disappointment, shock <shit, fuck, hell, heck, damn, damn it, goddamn it, gosh, golly, gee, jeez, holy fuck, holy cow, holy moly, holy hell, holy mackarel, holy shit, jumping Jesus, fucking shit, fucking hell> eg *Blać! Nie ma bynzyny! (Fucking hell! We're out of gas!)*

blachy [BLAH-khi] *npl* Automotive license plates <pads, plates, tags, numbers> eg *The Mazda was wearing German plates (Mazda miała niemieckie blachy)*

blade pojęcie See nie mieć zielonego pojęcia

blaga See bajer

blagier See bajerant

bliźniak [BLEE-zhnyahk] *nm* A house that is one of a pair of joined houses; a duplex <double home> eg *Mieszkamy w bliźniaku (We live in a double home)*

blondas [BLOHN-dahs] *nm* A blond man <blond guy, whitey> eg *Czego chciał ten blondas? (What did the blond guy want?)*

blondyn See świński blondyn

blondyna [blohn-DI-nah] *nf* A blond woman <blondie, whitey, goldilocks> eg *Ta blondyna naprawdę go jara (That blondie really drives him crazy)*

blus See czuć blusa, kumać

bluzg [bloosk] *nm* An obscene word or phrase; a swearword or curse <French word, four-letter word, cuss word, dirty word, dirty talk, dirt> eg *Możebyś tak przestał używać bluzgów w mojej obecności (I wish you'd stop using cuss words in my presence)*

bluzgać [BLOOZ-gahch] (perf **bluzgnąć** [BLOOZ-gnohnch] or **bluznąć** [BLOOZ-nohnch] or **zbluzgać** [ZBLOOZ-gahch]) *v* To curse (someone), swear (at someone), or otherwise use foul language <cuss, talk dirty> eg *Przestań bluzgać w obecności dzieci! (Stop cussing in the presence of children)*

błoto [BWOH-toh] *nn* Defamation; slander or libel; false degrading matters <dirt, dirty linen, dirty wash, dirty laundry, mud, slime, rap, slam, smear> eg *Nie mam nic wspólnego z tym błotem (I have nothing to do with this smear)*
See wyrzucić w błoto

błyskotka [bwis-KOHT-kah] *nf* A piece of jewelry, esp cheap and fake; a trinket <sparkler, brass, stone, rock, ice, glass, junk jewelry, gewgaw> eg *Kupił jej jakieś błyskotki (He bought her some junk jewelry)*

bobas See brzdąc

Bóg See chwycić Boga za nogi, czuć się jak młody bóg, jak u Pana Boga za piecem, za cholerę

bohomaz [boh-KHOH-mahs] *nm* A worthless or mediocre painting <doodle, kitsch, schlock> eg *Jak mogłaś powiesić taki bohomaz na ścianie? (How could you hang such a kitsch on the wall?)*

bok See mieć kogoś na boku, robić coś na boku, robić komuś boki, skok w bok, zrywać boki

boki [BOH-kee] *npl* A part-time job or any job of an assignment nature <gig> eg *Miałem boki w zwszłym tygodniu. Miałem napisać kolejny artykuł dla naszej miejscowej gazety (I had a gig last week. I had to write another article for our local paper)*

bokser See damski bokser

ból See do bólu, znać ten ból

bomba [BOHM-bah] *nf* Anything sensational or exciting, esp news; a sensation <bomb, bombshell, barnburner, flash, blast, eye-popper, breath-taker, heart-stopper, grabber, stand-out, stunner, gasser, sensaysh, hit, smash-hit, blockbuster, sockeroo> eg *Ta informacja okazała się być prawdziwą bombą (This piece of news turned out to be a real bombshell)*

bombowo [bohm-BOH-voh] (or **bajerancko** [bah-yeh-RAHN-tskoh] or **byczo** [BI-choh]) *adv* Extremely well; superbly <great, cool, swell, fab, rad, def, far-out, awesome, frantic, terrific, funky, gorgeous, groovy, hellacious, neat, peachy, dandy, baddest, mean, solid, super-dooper, wailing, wicked, gnarly, top-notch, ten, ace-high, A-OK, A-1, some> eg *Czuję się po prostu bombowo (I just feel great)*

bombowy [bohm-BOH-vi] (or **bajerancki** [bah-yeh-RAHN-tskee] or **byczy** [BI-chi]) *adj* Excellent; wonderful; impressive <great, cool, swell, fab, rad, def, far-out, awesome, frantic, terrific, funky, gorgeous, groovy, hellacious, neat, peachy, dandy, baddest, mean, solid, super-dooper, wailing, wicked, gnarly, top-notch, ten, ace-high, A-OK, A-1, some> eg *Ale masz byczy samochód! (What a gorgeous car you got!)*

bonanza [boh-NAHN-zah] *nf* A very profitable venture; a lucrative business <bonanza, gold mine, pay dirt, gravy train, cash cow> eg *Wydaje się, że to przedsięwzięcie to jest bonanza (This enterprise seems to be a cash cow)*

Bozia [BOH-zhah] *nf* God <Almighty, Man Upstairs, Lordy, Dad, Head Knock> eg *Ona modli się do Bozi codziennie (She prays to the Man Upstairs everyday)*
See iść do piachu

brać [brahch] (perf **wziąć** [vzhyohnch]) *v* **1** To excite someone, esp to arouse someone sexually <turn on, bring on, heat up, fire up, steam up, send> eg *Nie bierze mnie ten typ kobiet (That kind of women doesn't turn me on)* **2*** (Of a man) To copulate with a woman in a particular way <fuck, screw, lay, ball, bang, boink, boff, boogie, bop, frig, hump, poke, shag> eg *Na początku zawsze lubił brać ją od tyłu (At the beginnig he always liked to bang her from the rear)* **3** To take drugs <do drugs, fix, take a fix, take a hit, take> eg *Słyszałem, że bierze od dawna (I hear he's been doing drugs for a long time)*

brać coś na siebie [brahch tsohsh nah SHYEH-byeh] *v phr* To accept responsibility for something <be someone's job, be someone's problem, take care of, leave it up to someone> eg *Wygramy. Biorę to na siebie (We'll win. Leave it up to me)*

brać coś z sufitu [brahch tsosh s soo-FEE-too] (or **brać coś z głowy** [brahch tsosh z GWOH-vi]) *v phr* To devise or invent, esp impromptu, something not based on facts; to hastily fabricate <think up, fake up, cook up, dream up, cobble up, take it off the top of one's head, take it off the cuff, take it spur-of-the-moment> eg *Całą tę historię wziął z sufitu (He cooked up the all story)*

brać do buzi* [brahch doh BOO-zhee] (or **dawać do buzi*** [DAH-vahch doh BOO-zhee]) *v phr* To perform fellatio <suck off, blow, eat, give head, dick-lick, go down on, play the skin flute> eg *Prostytutka chciała mu wziąć do buzi za darmo (The prostitute wanted to blow him free of charge); Bierze do buzi? (Does she give head?)*

brać do ust See nie brać do ust

brać dupę w troki* [brahch DOO-peh f TROH-kee] *v* To leave or depart, esp hastily <split, beat it, ankle, bag ass, blow, breeze off, burn rubber, butt out, buzz off, check out, cruise, cut and run, cut ass, cut out, drag ass, dust, ease out, fade,

fade away, fade out, fuck off, get the fuck out, get the hell out , get going, get moving, get lost, get off the dime, get on one's horse, go south, haul ass, hightail, hit the bricks, hit the road, hop it, make tracks, pull out, scram, set sail, shove off, shuffle along, skate, skip out, split the scene, take off> eg *Bierz dupę w troki. Natychmiast! (Beat it. Right now!)*

brać kogoś [brahch KOH-gohsh] *v* **1** (perf **wziąć** [vzhyohnch]) To arouse or excite, esp sexually; to delight extremely <turn on, steam up, stir up, send, knock out, knock someone dead, knock someone' socks off, knock someone for a loop, throw someone for a loop, kill, murder, slay, slaughter, put someone away, tickle pink, tickle to death, tickle the piss out of someone> eg *Popatrz, jak rusza biodrami. Dziewczyny strasznie to bierze (Look the way he moves his hips. It turns the girls on)* **2** (perf **wziąć** [vzhyohnch] or perf **zabierać** [zah-BYEH-rahch]) (Of disease) To start affecting someone <catch, come down with> eg *Czuję, że zabiera mnie grypa (I feel like I'm coming down with the flu)*

brać kogoś do galopu [brahch KOH-gohsh doh gah-LOH-poo] (or **brać kogoś w obroty** [brahch KOH-gohsh oh-BROH-ti]) *v phr* To make someone actively engaged in something; to make someone accelerate or concentrate one's efforts <put the smack down on, come down on, get someone's ass in gear, get someone's ass, get the finger out of someone's asshole, get off someone's ass> eg *Wzięła mnie do galopu (She put the smack down on me)*

brać kogoś na bajer See bajerować

brać kogoś na chatę [brahch KOH-gohsh nah KHAH-teh] *v phr* To take someone to one's home, where sexual activity may be started <drag someone to one's place, go for a night cap> eg *Po imprezie wziął ją na chatę i robili to przez dalszą część nocy (After the party he dragged his to his place and they were doing it for the rest of the night); Zabrał ją na chatę (He went for a night cap with her)*

brać kogoś na dywanik See wezwać kogoś na dywanik

brać kogoś na języki [brahch KOH-gohsh nah yehn-ZI-kee] (or **brać kogoś na spytki** [brahch KOH-gohsh nah SPIT-kee]) *v phr* (To start) To gossip about someone; to spread rumors about someone; to denigrate or criticize <wag some tongues, have one's name bandied about, badmouth someone, blackball someone, spitball someone, dish the dirt about someone, chew the fat about someone, cut someone up and down, cut someone into little pieces, schmooze about someone, run someone down, bring someone down, dump all over someone, dump on someone, put the shit on someone> eg *Po tym wypadku ludzie wzięli ją na języki (After that accident people started to badmouth her)*

brać kogoś na muszkę See brać kogoś pod lupę

brać kogoś pod bajer See bajerować

brać kogoś pod lupę [brahch KOH-gohsh pohd LOO-peh] (or **brać kogoś na muszkę** [brahch KOH-gohsh nah MOOSH-keh] or **mieć kogoś pod lupą** [myehch KOH-gohsh pohd LOO-poh] or **mieć kogoś na muszce** [myehch KOH-gohsh nah MOOSH-tseh]) *v phr* (To start) To carefully observe and examine someone or something; to be or become interested in someone or something <put under the microscope, check out, scope out, figure out, case, dig, kick around, let the sunlight in, let the daylight in, get a load of, size up and down> eg *Wezmę ich pod lupę i dam ci znać, jak coś znajdę (I'll case them out and I'll let* *you know when I find something); Na chwilkę weźmy jego pomysł pod lupę (Let's kick his idea around for a while)*

brać kogoś pod pic See picować

brać kogoś pod włos [brahch KOH-gohsh pohd WVOHS] *v phr* To tease; to banter; to treat someone unseriously and frivolously; to have fun at someone's expense <poke fun at, kid, kid around, pull someone's leg, pull someone's string, fool around, jive, josh, shuck, lark, spoof, send up, cut down> eg *Powiedziała mu, żeby przestał brać ją pod włos (She told him to stop fooling around with her)*

brać kogoś w obroty See brać kogoś do galopu

brać na warsztat [brahch nah VAHR-shtaht] (or **brać na tapetę** [brahch nah tah-PEH-teh]) *v phr* To start dealing with something, esp analyzing or discussing something; to become actively interested in something; to concentrate on <set about, go about, get down to, get down to business, get down to cases, zero in, home in, narrow down, pin down, spot, spotlight, pinpoint> eg *Ostatnio wziąłem na warsztat coś zupełnie innego (Recently I've got down to something entirely new)*

brać się [brahch shyeh] (or **brać się do roboty** [brahch shyeh doh roh-BOH-ti] or **brać się do galopu** [brahch KOH-gohsh doh gah-LOH-poo]; perf **wziąć się** [vzhyohnch shyeh]) *v* To become actively engaged in something; to apply oneself to something; to energetically get into action; to accelerate or concentrate one's efforts <set about, go about, get down to, get down to business, get one's ass in gear, snap it up, snap to it, make it snappy, step on it, get the lead out, get a hump on, get a hustle on, get a move on, get one's ass, get cracking, get going, get one's finger out of one's asshole, get off one's ass, get it on, get off the dime, hop to it, hump, hustle, pour it on, pour on the coal, shake a leg, shake the lead out, gas up, goose up, hop up, jump up, pump up, rev up, buckle down> eg *Lepiej bierz się do roboty (You'd better get down to business)*

brać się za łby [brahch shyeh zah WBI] (or **brać się za czuby** [brahch shyeh zah CHOO-bi]) *v phr* To quarrel; to actively disagree; to fight <bump heads, hassle, take on, lock horns, set to, scrap, cross swords, pick a bone, tangle with, tangle ass with, go up against, put up a fight, bicker, go round and round, go toe to toe, go to it, go to the mat, have a pissing contest, have a pissing match, have a run-in, kick up a row, make the fur fly, put on the gloves, lead a cat-and-dog life, have a cat-and-dog life, fight like cat and dog, jump down someone's throat, be at loggerheads with> eg *Bez przerwy brali się za łby (They were constantly at loggerheads with one another)*

brać w łapę [brahch v WAH-peh]) *v phr* To accept bribe money < be on the take, be on the pad, take it under the table> eg *Czy pułkownik też bierze w łapę? (Is the colonel on the pad as well?)*

brać w łeb [brahch v WEHP] *v phr* To come to nothing; to fail to be completed <fall through, fall down, fall flat, drop through, tumble down, fuck up, get fucked up, screw up, get screwed up, get crimped, get cramped, get stymied> eg *Nasze plan wziął w łeb i w ogóle nie jedziemy do Europy (Our plan fell through and we won't be going to Europe at all)*

brakować komuś piątej klepki See nie mieć piątej klepki

bramka See stać na bramce

bramkarz [BRAHM-kahsh] *nm* A person employed to eject unwanted customers from a saloon or restaurant <bouncer> eg *Jej brat miał czarny pas w karate i został* *bramkarzem w jakimś nocnym klubie (Her brother had a black belt in karate and became a bouncer in a night club)*

brandzlerka** [brahn-DZLEHR-kah] (or **branzlerka**** [brahn-ZLEHR-kah] *nf*, **brandzlowanie**** [brahn-dzloh-VAH-nyeh] *nn*, **branzlowanie**** [brahn-zloh-VAH-nyeh] *nn*) *nf* (Of women) Masturbation, esp by inserting a finger into the vulva <finger-job, finger-fuck, hand job, frigging, fingering, finger-fucking> eg *Myślę, że wolałaby brandzlerkę od prawdziwego bara-bara (I think she'd rather have a finger-fuck than the real thing)*

brandzlować się** [brahn-DZLOH-vahch] (or **branzlować się**** [brahn-ZLOH-vahch]) *v* (Of women) To masturbate, esp by inserting a finger into the vulva <finger, finger-fuck, frig, play stinky-finger, play stinky-pinky> eg *Dwie studentki brandzlowały się na podłodze (The two students were finger-fucking on the floor)*

brat See jak z młodszego brata, jak ze starszego brata

brednie [BREH-dnyeh] (or **bzdety** [BZDEH-ti]) *npl* Nonsense; absurdities <bull, bullshit, bullshine, BS, bunk, baloney, applesauce, eyewash, hogwash, hot air, crock, crock of shit, piece of shit, pile of shit, shit, dogshit, horseshit, shit for the birds, crap, crapola, poppycock, smoke, hokum, garbage, trash, horsefeathers, smoke, all that jazz, jazz, jive, malarkey, gobbledygook, double-talk, bafflegab, blah-blah, phony-baloney, fiddle-faddle, twiddle-twaddle, mumbo-jumbo, yackety-yack> eg *Za dużo już się nasłuchałem jego bredni (I've heard enough of his bullshit)*

bredzić [BREH-jeech] *v* To talk nonsense <bullshit, talk bull, talk bullshit, talk bullshine, talk BS, talk bunk, talk baloney, talk applesauce, jazz, jive, shovel the shit, blow off, blow off one's mouth> eg *Ten facet bredzi. Nie słuchajcie go (This guy is talking bullshit. Don't listen to him)*

breja [BREH-yah] (or **bryja** [BRI-yah]) *nf* **1** Any viscous and unappetizing, semi-liquid food <glop, goo, gook, goop, gunk, slop, pigswill> eg *Mam zjeść tę breję? (Am I supposed to eat this slop?)* **2** Silt or mud <goo, gooey, glop, gloppy, gunk, gumbo, gook, slime> eg *W basenie była breja (There was goo in the swimming pool)*

broda See kawał z brodą, pluć sobie w brodę

broszka See nie czyjaś broszka

browar [BROH-vahr] *nm* Beer <brew, brewski, suds, swill, froth, chill, cold one, wet one> eg *Mogę dostać jeszcze trochę browaru? (Could I get some more brew?)*

brud See tyle co kot napłakał

brudas [BROO-dahs] *nm* A sloppy, shabby, and loathsome man <dirt-bag, scum-bag, douche-bag, scum> eg *Nikt nie powie o nim, że jest brudasem (No one will say that he's a dirt-bag)*

brudna robota See mokra robota

brudny [BROOD-ni] *adj* Illegal, unethical, or dishonest <dirty, sleazy, crooked, crummy, foul, shady, shabby, salty, raw, heavy, hung-up, below the belt, under the counter, under the table, underhand> eg *Wiem jedynie, że robili jakieś brudne interesy (For all I know, they had some underhand dealings)*

brudzio [BROO-joh] *nm* A drink which symbolizes an agreement to stop using "sir" form and to start using a mere "you" (and being on first-name terms) <no slang equivalent> eg *Wypili brudzia (They dranked to their friendship and were on first name terms)*

bruk See iść na zieloną trawkę, posłać na zieloną trawkę

brukowiec [broo-KOH-vyehts] *nm* A tabloid, esp disreputable <rag, dirt rag, blat, bladder, scandal sheet, fish wrapper, toilet paper> eg *Gdzie to wyczytałeś? W jakimś brukowcu (Where did you read this? In some rag)*

brukowy [broo-KOH-vi] *adj* Of a tabloid <sleazy, dirty, dirt-rag> eg *Ta informacja pochodzi z jakiejś brukowej gazety (his information comes from some sleazy paper)*

Brunner See nie ze mną te numery

brutal [BROO-tahl] *nm* A rough, aggressive or intimidating man; a brute <toughie, tough customer, rough customer, roughneck, hardboiled egg, hard case, goon, ape, bruiser, cowboy, gorilla, John Wayne> eg *Nie mam nic wspólnego z tym brutalem (I have nothing to do with this roughneck)*

bryja See breja

bryka [BRI-kah] (or **bryczka** [BRICH-kah]) *nf* An automobile <wheels, set of wheels, crate, ride, cage, trans, transportation, four wheeler, boat, buggy> eg *Jak Ci się podoba moja bryka? (How do you like my wheels?)*

brykać [BRI-kahch] (perf **bryknąć** [BRIK-nohnch]) *v* **1** To leave or depart, esp hastily <split, beat it, ankle, bag ass, blow, breeze off, burn rubber, butt out, buzz off, check out, cruise, cut and run, cut ass, cut out, drag ass, dust, ease out, fade, fade away, fade out, fuck off, get the fuck out, get the hell out , get going, get moving, get lost, get off the dime, get on one's horse, go south, haul ass, hightail, hit the bricks, hit the road, hop it, make tracks, pull out, scram, set sail, shove off, shuffle along, skate, skip out, split the scene, take off> eg *Gliny już tu są. Brykamy! (The cops are already here. Let's split!)* **2** To insolently defy, challenge, or oppose <defi, face off, face down, fly in the face, fly in the teeth, meet eyeball to eyeball, make my day, hang tough, hang in there, take one on, stick fast, stick it out, kick over traces, lip, brace, cross, put one's life on the line, stand up to, knock the chip off one's shoulder, step over the line, tangle, bump heads with, cross, square off, put down, have a bone to pick, hold no brief for, put up a fight, mess with, mess around with, fool with, fool around with, fuck with, fuck around with, screw with, screw around with, dick with, dick around with, diddle with, diddle around with, fiddle with, fiddle around with, fart with, fart around with, monkey with, monkey around with> eg *Jest niebezpieczny. Lepiej z nim nie brykaj (He's dangerous. You'd better not fuck around with him)*

bryle [BRI-leh] *npl* Spectacles <specs, goggles, windows, cheaters> eg *Stłukłem bryle (I broke my specs)*

brylować [bri-LOH-vahch] (perf **zabrylować** [zah-bri-LOH-vahch]) *v* To behave in an ostentatiously skilled, assured, or intellectual way in order to impress others <show off, grandstand, showboat, pile it on, hotdog, bullshit, blow one's horn, blow one's trumpet, blow smoke, blow off, blow hard, signify, bigmouth, talk big> eg *Brylował na balu dobroczynnym (He was grandstanding at the charity ball)*

brytol* [BRI-tohl] *nm* An Englishman <Brit, Britisher, limey, limejuicer, beefeater, Tommy> eg *Brytole są nieszczęśliwi z powodu niskiej pozycji funta (The Brits are unhappy over the weakness of the pound sterling)*

brzdąc [bzhdohnts] (or **berbeć** [BEHR-behch] or **bobas** [BOH-bahs]) *nm* A baby or a young child <knee biter, carpet rat, rug rat, little fella> eg *W poczekalni siedziała kobieta z brzdącem na kolanach (A woman with a knee biter on her lap was sitting in the waiting room); Jak tam się ma twój berbeć? (How is that knee biter of yours?)*

brzdąkać [BZHDOHN-kahch] *v* To play a musical instrument <wail, smoke, rip, strum, thrum, thump> eg *Brzdąkał na swojej gitarze (He was wailing on his guitar)*

brzęczeć See biadolić

brzeg See cicha woda

brzuch See leżeć bykiem, mieć brzucha, z brzuchem, zrobić komuś dzieciaka

brzydal [BZHI-dahl] *nm* **1** An ugly man <beast, dog> eg *Kim jest ten brzydal w olbrzymim kapeluszu? (Who is that beast with the big hat?)* **2** A sweetheart or other cherished man <big lunk> eg *Chodź tu. Daj mi buzi, ty brzydalu (Come here. Give me a kiss, you big lunk)*

brzydki See dwa razy brzydszy od gówna

brzydki jak noc [BZHIT-kee yahk NOHTS] *adj phr* Very ugly, repulsive <fugly, piss-ugly, plug-ugly, ugly as cat-shit, ugly as sin, homely as a mud fence> eg *Jest brzydka jak noc, ale dobrze gotuje (She's ugly as sin but she's a good cook)*

brzydula [bzhi-DOO-lah] *nf* An ugly woman <beasty, skag, skank, pig, bag, dog, cow> eg *Spytaj tę brzydulę, czy ma lustro (Aks that skank if she has a mirror)*

bubek [BOO-behk] *nm* A pretensionally elegant man, often fawning on women <dandy, fancypants, poser> eg *Jakiś bubek zajechał właśnie swoją beemką (Some poser just pulled up in his beemer)*

bubel [BOO-behl] *nm* Anything defective, unsatisfactory, or of shoddy quality; trash <lemon, schlock, dreck, garbage, junk, crap, piece of crap, shit, piece of shit, dogshit, sleaze> eg *Twój samochód to prawdziwy bubel (Your car is a real lemon)*

buc* [boots] *nm* A slow-witted or uncultured man, esp from the country <bumpkin, hick, hillbilly, clodhopper> eg *Nie zachowuj się jak buc (Don't act like you were a country bumpkin)*

buchnąć [BOOKH-nohnch] *v* To steal; to rob <heist, boost, burgle, nurn, bag, buzz, highjack, hoist, hold up, hook, hustle, jump, kick over, knock off, knock over, lift, move, mug, nab, nick, nip, pinch, pluck, roll, rustle, snatch, snitch, stick up, swipe, take off, put the grab on, go south with> eg *Buchnęli prawie sto tysięcy w gotówce (They heisted nearly a hundred thousand in cash)*

bucior [BOO-chyohr] *nm* A shoe or boot, esp heavy or sturdy <stomper, wafflestomper, boondocker, clodhopper, shitkicker> eg *Zabieraj buciory z mojego biurka (Get your clodhoppers out of my desk)*

buda [BOO-dah] *nf* **1** A school, esp a public high school <hi, high, jail, knowledge box, blackboard jungle, brainery> eg *Nasza buda jest spoko (Our high is okay)* **2** An old or dilapidated house <ruin, hole, den, joint, shack, dump, cave, flophouse> eg *Nie masz zamiaru kupować tej budy, prawda? (You're not going to buy that ruin, are you?)* **3** A police van, esp one used to transport prisoners <paddy wagon, Black Maria> eg *Policjanci zaciągnęli go do budy (The policemen dragged him to the paddy wagon)*

See psu na budę

budować się [boo-DOH-vahch shyeh] (perf **wybudować się** [vi-boo-DOH-vahch shyeh]) *v* To have a house built or to build a house on one's own <knock together a house, throw together a house, fudge together a house> eg *Słyszałem, że się budują (I heard they are knocking together a house)*

budowlaniec [boo-doh-VLAH-nyehts] *nm* A construction worker <hard hat> eg *Budowlańcy siedzieli sobie gwiżdżąc za przechodzącymi dziewczynami (The hard hats sat around whistling at the passing girls)*

bufory* [boo-FOH-ri] *npl* A woman's large breasts <tits, melons, knockers, bazooms, boobs, headlights, hooters, hemispheres> eg *Widziałeś bufory tej laski? (Did you see the knockers on that chick?)*

bujać [BOO-yahch] (perf **nabujać** [nah-BOO-yahch]) *v* To tell lies in order to deceive someone <bull, bullshit, shit, shovel the shit, string along, snow, fake it, talk through one's hat, speak with forked tongue, put someone on, pull someone's leg, pull someone's string, give someone a leg, have someone on, jack someone around, jerk someone around, kid someone around, fool someone around, jack someone's chain, spoof, cut down, mind-fuck, head-fuck, push around, upstage> eg *Mnie się zdaje, że pan buja (I think you're shitting me)*

bujać się [BOO-yahch shyeh] *v* **1** (perf **zabujać się** [zah-BOO-yahch shyeh]) To love someone or to fall in love with <fall for, have a crush on, be sweet on, be stuck on, be wild about, be mad about, be crazy about, take a shine to, have a thing for, be head over heels> eg *Zakochał się w jakiejś striptizerce (He fell for some stripper)* **2** (Esp in the imperative as a brusque command) To leave or depart, esp hastily <split, beat it, ankle, bag ass, blow, breeze off, burn rubber, butt out, buzz off, check out, cruise, cut and run, cut ass, cut out, drag ass, dust, ease out, fade, fade away, fade out, fuck off, get the fuck out, get the hell out , get going, get moving, get lost, get off the dime, get on one's horse, go south, haul ass, hightail, hit the bricks, hit the road, hop it, make tracks, pull out, scram, set sail, shove off, shuffle along, skate, skip out, split the scene, take off> eg *Bujaj się, ty gnojku (Beat it, you little punk)*

bujda See bajka

bulić [BOO-leech] (perf **wybulić** [vi-BOO-leech] or **zabulić** [zah-BOO-leech]) *v* To pay <cough up, ante up, dig up, dish up, fork out, fork over, kick in, lay down, plunk down, shell out> eg *Strach pomyslec, ile jeszcze będziemy musieli wybulić (It's scary to think how much more we'll have to shell out)*

bumelanctwo [boo-meh-LAHNT-stfoh] *nn* An act of shirking work or duty <goldbricking, goofing around, jerking off, screwing off, ass-dragging, lollygagging, sitting on one's ass, clock-watching, fucking the dog> eg *Nieznoszę wielu rzeczy, ale najbardziej nieznoszę bumelanctwa (I can't stand many things, but most of all, goldbricking)*

bumelant [boo-MEH-lahnt] *nm* A person who regulary and chronically avoids work; a shirker <goldbricker, bunk lizard, coffee cooler, feather merchant, lazybones, lazy-ass, lazy bum, bum, clock watcher, dog-fucker> eg *Powiedz temu bumelantowi, żeby brał się do roboty (Tell that lazybones to get to work)*

bumelować [boo-meh-LOH-vahch] *v* To avoid work; to shirk duty <goldbrick, goof off, goof around, fuck around, screw around, jerk off, screw off, drag-ass, drag one's ass, drag it, dragtail, fake off, flub the dub, fuck off, fuck the dog, dog it, lollygag, sit on one's ass, soldier, skate, watch the clock> eg *On zawsze bumelował (He's always been goldbricking)*

bura suka See suka

burak* [BOO-rahk] *nm* A slow-witted or uncultured man from the country <bumpkin, hick, hillbilly, clodhopper> eg *Mówiłem dyplomatycznie, żeby nie rozsierdzić tych buraków (I tried being diplomatic not to antagonize the clodhoppers)*

burdel [BOOR-dehl] (or **bajzel** [BAH-ee-zehl]) *nm* **1** A brothel <whore-house, call-house, cat-house> eg *Pracowała w burdelu jako recepcjonistka, tak przynajmniej* *mówiła (She worked in a whore-house as a receptionist, at least that's what she said)* **2** (or **bigos** [BEE-gohs]; **na kółkach** [nah KOOW-kahkh] may be added) *nm* A confusing situation; confusion <mess, mess-up, mix-up, fuck-up, screw-up, mess and a half, holy mess, unholy mess, all hell broke loose, ruckus, discombobulation, foofaraw, srew, sweat, swivet, tizzy, hassle, rat's nest, SNAFU> eg *Kto jest odpowiedzialny za cał ten burdel? (Who is responsible for this whole mix-up?)*

burdelmama [boor-dehl-MAH-mah] (or **bajzelmama** [bah-ee-zehl-MAH-mah]) *nf* The madame of a brothel <aunt, mama-san, house-mother> eg *Wszyscy byli spłukani, ale spytali burdelmamę, czy by ich nie wpuściła (They were all broke but they asked the aunt if she would let them in)*

burek [BOO-rehk] *nm* A dog, esp a mongrel <doggie, mutt, pooch, pup, Fido, Heinz, flea bag, tail wagger, bone eater, pot hound> eg *Gdzie jest burek? (Where's Fido?)*

but See głupszy niż ustawa przewiduje

butelczyna [boo-tehl-CHI-nah] *nf* A liquor bottle, esp empty <soldier, dead soldier, marine, dead marine, dead man, dead one> eg *Wyrzuć butelczynę do śmietnika, co? (Toss your soldier into the garbage, will you?)*

butelka See nabić kogoś w butelkę, pijany jak świnia, upić się jak świnia

buzia See brać do buzi

buziak [BOO-zhayhk] (or **buzi** [BOO-zhee] or **buźka** [BOOSH-kah]) *nm* A kiss <smacker, smackeroo, kissy-kissy, kissy-poo, kissy-face> eg *Dała mu buziaka prosto w usta (She planted a smacker square on his lips)*

była [BI-wah] *nm* A former girlfriend, lover, or wife <ex, old flame, back number> eg *Przedstawił swoją byłą raczej dość zwyczajnie zważywszy, że byli razem przez 15 lat (He introduced his ex rather casually considering they were together 15 years)*

były [BI-wi] *nm* A former boyfriend, lover, or husband <ex, old flame, back number> eg *Pozwól, że przedstawię ci mojego byłego (Let me introduce you to my ex)*

być albo nie być [OHCH-koh v GWOH-vyeh] *nn phr* Something very important <matter of life or death> eg *Jest to dla niego być albo nie być (It's a matter of life or death to him)*

być do przodu [bich doh PSHOH-doo] *v phr* To make a net profit; to earn <be in the black, pull down, pull in, rack in, pick up, clean up, rack up, pile up, stack up, cash in, make a bundle> eg *Jeśli to zareklamujemy, to będziemy do przodu (If we advertize it, we will clean up); Mieliśmy przez jakiś czas kłopoty, ale teraz jesteśmy do przodu (We had some problems for a while, but now we're in the black)*

być do tyłu [bich doh TI-woo] *v phr* To lose money <be in the red, lose out, blow, drop a bundle, go to the cleaners, take a bath, tap out, wash out> eg *Korporacja była do tyłu przez pięć lat (The corporation has been in the red for five years)*

być gorzej komuś [GOH-zheh-ee KOH-moosh] *adv phr* To be or to behave as if one were insane or stupid; to lose one's senses <be off one's rocker, be off one's nut, be off one's base, be off the track, be off the trolley, be out one's skull, be out of one's mind, be crazy, be crazy as a loon, blow one's cork, blow one's top, blow a fuse, crack up, freak out, flip out, be ape, be bananas, be bent, be bonkers, be cracked, be dopey, be ga-ga, be half-baked, be loony, be loopy, be mental, be nerts, be nuts, be nutty, be psycho, be schizo, be screwy, be wacky, be weird, be wild, schiz out, psych out, come unglued, come unstuck, come unwrapped, come

unzipped> eg *Co ona mówi? Jest jej gorzej, czy jak? (What is she talking about? Is she out of her rocker, or what?)*

być jedną nogą w grobie [bich YEHD-noh NOH-goh v GROH-byeh] (or **być jedną nogą na tamtym świecie** [bich YEHD-noh NOH-goh nah TAHM-tim SHFYEH-chyeh]) *v phr* To be nearly dead <be one foot in the grave, have one foot in the grave, be a goner> eg *Nie zostanie prezydentem. Jest jedną nogą w grobie (He won't become president. He's one foot in the grave)*

być komuś łyso See czuć się łyso

być na bakier [bich nah BAH-kyehr] *v phr* **1** To be ignorant, unfamiliar, or disoriented; not to be knowledgeable <not know from nothing, not know one's ass from first base, not know one's ass from a hole in the ground, not know one's ass from one's elbow, not know a rock from a hard place, not know diddly-shit, not know shit, not know shit from Shinola, not know zilch, not have a clue, not know the score, not know the time of day, not have the foggiest idea, search me, beats me> eg *Jest na bakier z nowymi przepisami (He doesn't know diddly-shit about the new regulations)* **2** To be unable to perform well because of lack of recent practice <be rusty, be out of shape, slip, lose one's touch> eg *Zgodziłem się zagrać mecz, chociaż jestem z piłką trochę na bakier (I agreed to play in the soccer game, although I'm very rusty)*

być na bramce See stać na bramce

być na czyimś garnuszku [bich nah CHI-eemsh gahr-NOOSH-koo] (or **być u kogoś na garnuszku** [bich oo KOH-gohsh nah gahr-NOOSH-koo]; **żyć** [ZHICH] may replace **być**) *adj phr* To get one's food and income from someone; to take financial advantage of someone <live off, sponge, mooch, scrounge, milk> eg *Od wielu lat jest na ciotki garnuszku (He's been living off his aunt for many years)*

być na minusie [bich nah mee-NOO-shyeh] (or **wyjść na minus** [VI-eeshch nah MEE-noos]) *v phr* To lose money <be in the red, lose out, blow, drop a bundle, go to the cleaners, take a bath, tap out, wash out> eg *Jestem na minusie od miesiąca (I've been in the red for a month)*

być na plusie [bich nah PLOO-shyeh] (or **wyjść na plus** [VI-eeshch nah PLOOS] or **wyjść na swoje** [VI-eeshch nah SFOH-yeh]) *v phr* To make a net profit; to earn <be in the black, pull down, pull in, rack in, pick up, clean up, rack up, pile up, stack up, cash in, make a bundle> eg *Mieliśmy przez jakiś czas kłopoty, ale teraz jesteśmy na plusie (We had some problems for a while, but now we're in the black)*

być na tej samej fali [bich nah teh-ee SAH-meh-ee FAH-lee] (or **nadawać na tej samej fali** [nah-DAH-vahch nah teh-ee SAH-meh-ee FAH-lee]) *v* To be perfectly understood of felt by someone; to have identical perception as someone else <be on the same wavelength, be on someone's wavelength, have the same vibes, be tuned in, find a common ground> eg *Wyglądało na to, że nie nadawaliśmy na tej samej fali, więc zerwaliśmy ze sobą (It looked like we were not on the same wavelength, so we broke up)*

być nie tak [bich nyeh TAHK] *v phr* To be suspicious or dubious <be phony, ring phony, be fishy, be funny, not be kosher> eg *Skoro mówimy o tej propozycji, to coś jest nie tak (Talking about this proposal, it is somewhat fishy)*

być pępkiem świata [bich PEHMP-kyehm SHFYAH-tah] *v phr v phr* To be very conceited and to think one is the most important or in the center of everyone's attention <think one's shit doesn't stink, be too big for someone's shoes, ego-trip,

get stuck-up, get puffed-up, get high-hat, get swelled-up, get swell-headed, get big-headed, get high-nosed, get blown-up, get stuck on oneself, get chesty, get stuffy, get gassy, get windy, get hatty, get hinkty, get uppity, get biggety> eg *Zawsze był szpanerem, ale gdy w 1996 został dyrektorem Instytutu, to myśli, że jest pępkiem świata (He had always been a blowhard, but since he became the director of the Institute in 1996, he's thought that his shit doeasn't stink)*

być w trasie [bich f TRAH-shyeh] *v phr* To be traveling or be on one's way, esp as a truck driver <be on the road, be on the move, be on the trail, hit the road, trek, city-hop> eg *Gdzie jest twój kolega? Jest w trasie (Where's your colleague? He's on the road)*

byczek See bysio

byczo See bombowo

byczy See bombowy

byczyć się [BI-chich shyeh] (perf **wybyczyć** [vi-BI-chich shyeh] or **pobyczyć** [poh-BI-chich shyeh]) *v phr* To loaf or idle; to pass time lazily <bum around, hang around, hang out, goof around, fuck around, screw around, fiddle around, fiddle fart around, fart around, jack around, mess around, hack around, monkey around, knock around, kick around, fool around, horse around, piddle around, play around, rat around, schloomp around, ass around, beat around, dick around, fuck around, fuck off, screw off, goof off, jerk off, fuck the dog, rat fuck, flub the dub, sit on one's ass, sit on one's butt, lollygag, veg out> eg *W te wakacje mam zamiar po prostu się pobyczyć się (I'm just going to goof off during this vacation)*

bydło* [BI-dwoh] *nn* Worthless, badly-behaved, and often poor people <riff-raff, rabble, mob, gang, scum, scum of the earth, hoods> eg *Nie lubię tej dzielnicy. Same tu bydło (I don't like this neighborhood. The people here are the scum of the earth)*

bydlak* [BID-lahk] (or **bydlę*** [BI-dleh] *nn*) *nm* **1** A man one dislikes or disapproves of <asshole, fuck, fucker, fuckhead, fuckface, motherfucker, shit, shitface, shithead, shitheel, bastard, jerk, SOB, son of a bitch, son of a whore, cocksucker, prick, dick, dickhead, cuntface, schmuck, scum, scumbag, sleazebag, slimebag, dipshit, pisshead, piece of shit, pain in the ass> eg *Na twoim miejscu zignorowałabym tego bydlaka (If I was you, I would ignore that bastard); Bydlak nie wiedział nawet gdzie, kurde, jest (The asshole didn't even know where the hell he was)* **2** Any large animal <beast, critter, monster> eg *O rety! Co za bydę! Czy to twój pies? (Geez! What a beast! Is that your dog?)*

byk [bik] *nm* **1** A failing grade <flunk, flush, F, zip, zippo> eg *Dostał byka z tego testu (He got an F on that test)* **2** A careless but blatant mistake <slip, slip-up, flub, fluff, foozle, goof-up, screw-up, fuck-up, ball-up, mess-up, louse-up, blooper> eg *Ale byk! (What a slip-up)*

See bysio, jak byk, leżeć bykiem, patrzeć na kogoś krzywo, po byku, z byka spaść, zdrowy jak ryba

byle zbyć See aby zbyć

bysio [BI-shyoh] (or **byczek** [BI-chehk] or **byk** [bik] or **kawał byka** [KAH-vah-oo BI-kah] *nm phr*) *nm* A tall, big, and usually attractive man <hunk, stud, stud-muffin, beefcake, he-man, macho, muscleman, v-man> eg *Twój kuzyn to prawdziwy kawał byka (Your cousin is a real hunk)*

bystrzak [BIST-shahk] (or **bystrzacha** [bist-SHAH-khah] *nf*) *nm* A very bright and intelligent person <brain, smart apple, whiz, whiz kid, wiz, wizard> eg *Ja* *wiedziałem, że on jeden to potrafi. To prawdziwy bystrzak! (I knew he was the only one who could do that. He's a real smart apple!)*

bzdety See brednie

bzik [bzheek] *nm* Obsession, eccentricity, or lack of mental stability <thing, kick, bag, bug, craze, freak, frenzy, weakness, bug up one's ass, bug in one's ear, bee in one's bonnet, bee, flea in one's nose, maggot, maggot in one's brain, hang-up, jones, monkey, ax to grind> eg *Ma bzika na punkcie tego, że joga jest lekarstwem na wszystkie złe rzeczy tego świata (He's got a bee in his bonnet about yoga curing all the world's ills); Judo to jego ostatni bzik (Judo is his latest craze)*
See dostać świra, mieć świra

bzikować [bzhee-KOH-vahch] (perf **zbzikować** [zbzhee-KOH-vahch]) *v* To become obsessed, insane or eccentric; to lose mental stability <go crazy, go crazy as a loon, blow one's cork, blow one's top, blow a fuse, crack up, freak out, flip out, go ape, go bananas, go bent, go bonkers, go cracked, go dopey, go ga-ga, go half-baked, go loony, go loopy, go mental, go nerts, go nuts, go nutty, go off one's nut, go off one's rocker, go off one's base, go off the track, go off the trolley, go out one's skull, go psycho, go schizo, go screwy, go wacky, go weird, go wild, schiz out, psych out, come unglued, come unstuck, come unwrapped, come unzipped, go to pieces> eg *Od wojny każdy może zbizkować (War is enough to make anyone go crazy); Jego siostra zbzikowała gdy zdechł jej kot (His sister came unglued after the cat got killed)*

bzyk* [bzik] *nm* A sexual intercourse, esp a quick one <screw, fuck, lay, bang, boink, boff, hump, poke, quickie> eg *Zatrzymał się przed domem swojej dziewczyny na bzyka (He stopped off at his girlfriend's house for a hump)*

bzykać się* [BZI-kahch shyeh] *v* To copulate <get screwed, get fucked, get laid, screw, fuck, fork, frig, ball, bang, boink, bonk, boff, hump, poke, shag> eg *Dyrektor znalazł ich, jak bzykali się w szatni (The headmaster found them screwing in the locker room)*

bzykać* [BZI-kahch] (perf **bzyknąć*** [BZIK-nohnch] or **wybzykać*** [vi-BZI-kahch]) *v* To copulate with someone, esp quickly <fuck, screw, lay, ball, bang, boink, boff, hump, poke, shag, bunny-fuck> eg *Naprawdę chciałbym ją bzyknąć! (I really would like to screw her!)*

bździć* [BZHJEECH] (perf **nabździć*** [NAH-bzhjeech] or **zabździć*** [ZAH-bzhjeech]) *v* To release intestinal gas, perhaps with a noise <fart, cut a fart, lay a fart, blow a fart, let a fart, cut the cheese, backfire, break wind, pollute the air> eg *Najedli się fasoli i bździli jak cholera (They ate beans and farted like hell)*

bździna* [BZHJEE-nah] *nf* A release of intestinal gas, perhaps with a noise <fart, cheese, ass noise> eg *Czy słyszałem bździnę? (Did I hear a fart?)*

C

całą gębą [TSAH-woh GEHM-boh] (or **pełną gębą** [PEH-oo-noh GEHM-boh]) *adv phr* Truly; fully; to an extreme degree <sure, fer sure, sure as hell, sure as shit, sure as can be, for real, indeedy, really truly, absitively, posilutely, real, cert,

def, no buts about it, flat-out, all-out, all the way, like hell, like all get-out, like sin, to beat the band, like all creation, to the max, as blazes, as can be, as hell, like hell, in full swing> eg *Twój brat jest profesjonalistą pełną gębą (Your brother is a sure pro); Zima jest całą gębą (The winter has come for real)*

całkiem See inna para kaloszy

całkiem-całkiem [TSAH-oo-kyehm TSAH-oo-kyehm] *adj phr* **1** Handsome, sexually attractive <ten, drop-dead gorgeous, knock-out gorgeous, dishy, hunky, laid out> eg *Myślę, że ta twoja kumpela jest całkiem-całkiem (I think your friend is a ten)* **2** Quite good, attractive or wonderful <great, cool, swell, fab, rad, def, far-out, awesome, frantic, terrific, funky, gorgeous, groovy, hellacious, neat, peachy, dandy, baddest, mean, solid, super-dooper, wailing, wicked, gnarly, top-notch, ten, ace-high, A-OK, A-1, some, pretty good, dishy, hunky> eg *Ten samochód jest na prawdę całkiem-całkiem (This car is real cool)*

całość See iść na całość

całować kogoś w dupę See lizać komuś dupę

całus See cmok

cały w nerwach See w nerwach

cackać się [TSAHTS-kahch shyeh] *v* To handle someone or something too gently or slowly; to tamper with something or someone <treat with kid gloves, handle with kid gloves, play around with, play with, fool around with, fool with, mess around with, mess with, diddle around with, diddle with, fart around with, fart with, fiddle around with, fiddle with, monkey around with, monkey with, screw around with, screw with, fuck around with, fuck with, schlep around, drag around, drag-ass> eg *Cackał się z nią, jakby była prawiczką (He handled her with kid gloves, as if she was a cherry)*

cacko [TSAH-tskoh] *nn* Anything or anyone attractive, admirable, wonderful, esp precious but small and meant for play <baby, gem, humdinger, hummer, beaut, corker, crackerjack, cat's pajamas, cat's meow, hot shit, hot spit, hot stuff, killer, killer-diller, knockout, lollapalooza, pisser, piss-cutter, ripsnorter, whizbang, tsatske, tchochke, doozie> eg *Daj mi ze dwa takie cacka (Give me two of these babies)*

cacy [TSAH-tsi] (or **cacuś** [TSAH-tsoosh]) *adj* Excellent; wonderful; extremely good <great, cool, swell, fab, rad, def, far-out, awesome, frantic, terrific, funky, gorgeous, groovy, hellacious, neat, peachy, dandy, baddest, mean, solid, super-dooper, wailing, wicked, gnarly, top-notch, ten, ace-high, A-OK, A-1, some, pretty good> eg *Ten samochód jest na prawdę cacy (This car is real cool)*

cap* [tsahp] (or **cep*** [tsehp]) *nm* A man, esp sloppy, loathsome, slow-witted, or old <dirt-bag> eg *Nienawidziłam tego starego capa (I hated this dirt-bag)*

capnąć [TSAHP-nohnch] *v* **1** To catch a criminal; to arrest <bust, bag, claw, clip, collar, cop, flag, grab, haul in, jab, knock, pinch, nab, nail, nick, pick up, pull in, run in, sidetrack, put the collar on, put the sleeve on> eg *Wiedziałem, że policja prędzej czy później go capnie (I knew the police would nab him sooner or later)* **2** To steal; to rob <heist, boost, burgle, nurn, bag, buzz, highjack, hoist, hold up, hook, hustle, jump, kick over, knock off, knock over, lift, move, mug, nab, nick, nip, pinch, pluck, roll, rustle, snatch, snitch, stick up, swipe, take off, put the grab on, go south with> eg *Capnęli prawie sto tysięcy w gotówce (They heisted nearly a hundred thousand in cash)*

cegła [TSEH-gwah] *nf* A thick and usually boring or worthless book <potboiler, spyboiler, pulp> eg *Napisał tę cegłę w dwa miesiące (It took him two months to write this potboiler)*

cent See ani centa

centralnie [tsehn-TRAHL-nyeh] (or **czadownie** [chah-DOH-vnyeh]) *adv* Extremely; exceedingly; very <awful, god-awful, real, mighty, plenty, damn, damned, goddamn, goddamned, darn, darned, effing, flipping, forking, freaking, frigging, fucking, one's ass off, one's brains out, one's head off, to the max, like all get-out, like sin, to beat the band, like all creation, as blazes, as can be, as hell, like hell> eg *Ona jest centralnie zgrabna (She's damn shapely)*

ceregiele [tseh-reh-GYEH-leh] *npl* Complaining, hesitant and objectionable behavior, esp with regard to trifles, formalities, and details <fuss, scene, ceremony, stink> eg *Przestań robić ceregiele i zostaw nas w spokoju (Stop making a fuss and leave us alone); Poszła z nim do łóżka bez ceregieli (She went to bed with him without much fuss)*

ceregielić się [tseh-reh-GYEH-leh] (or **certolić się** [tsehr-TOH-leech shyeh]) *v* To handle someone or something too gently or slowly; to tamper with something or someone <treat with kid gloves, handle with kid gloves, play around with, play with, fool around with, fool with, mess around with, mess with, diddle around with, diddle with, fart around with, fart with, fiddle around with, fiddle with, monkey around with, monkey with, screw around with, screw with, fuck around with, fuck with, schlep around, drag around, drag-ass> eg *Ceregielił się z nią, jakby była prawiczką (He handled her with kid gloves, as if she was a cherry)*

cesarka [tseh-SAHR-kah] *nf* Cesarean section <cesarean, C-section> eg *Their first baby was born by cesarean (Ich pierwsze dziecko przyszło na świat przez cesarkę)*

chłam [khwahm] *nm* Anything worthless, useless, or of shoddy quality; trash <schlock, dreck, garbage, junk, lemon, crap, piece of crap, shit, piece of shit, dogshit, sleaze> eg *Skądżeś wziął ten chłam? (Where did you get this garbage from?)*

chłop [khwohp] *nm* **1** A man <fella, dude, guy, dude> eg *Wszyscy wiedzą, że to swój chłop (Everybody knows he's a good fella)* **2** A husband, fiance, or boyfriend <old man> eg *Mój chłop jest tego wart (My old man is worth it)*
See swój chłop

chłopaczek See chłoptaś

chłopisko [khwoh-PEE-skoh] (or **kawał chłopa** [KAH-wah-oo KHWOH-pah] *nm phr*) *nm* A tall, big, and usually attractive man teddy bear, hunk, stud, stud-muffin, beefcake, he-man, macho, muscleman, v-man> eg *Ten twój kuzyn to prawdziwe chłopisko (Your cousin is such a teddy bear)*

chłopski filozof [KHWOHP-skee fee-LOH-zohf] *nm phr* A person who speaks authoritatively or impudently but not convincingly on matters where that person lacks knowledge or experience; someone who pretends to virtual omiscience <smart aleck, smart ass, smart mouth, smartypants, wise ass, know-it-all, armchair general, armchair strategist> eg *Kto chciałby słuchać tego chłopskiego filozofa? (Who would like to listen to that know-it-all?)*

chłoptaś [KHWOHP-tahsh] (or **chłopaczek** [khwoh-PAH-chehk]) *nm* A boy or young man <punk, guy, dude, brat> eg *Naprawdę spodobał mi się chłopaczek (I really liked that guy); Więc ten chłoptaś podszedł do mnie i chciał papierosa (So this punk came up to me and wanted a cigarette)*

chałtura [khah-oo-TOO-rah] *nf* **1** (or **chała** [KHAH-wah]) Shoddy workmanship <hack-work, hacking> eg *Kto jest odpowiedzialny za tę chałturę? (Who's responsible for this hack-work)* **2** A part-time job or any job of an assignment nature <gig> eg *Miałem jedną chałturę w zwszłym tygodniu. Miałem napisać kolejny artykuł dla naszej miejscowej gazety (I had a gig last week. I had to write another article for our local paper)*

chałturnik [khah-oo-TOOR-neek] *nm* Someone who works slovenly or carelessly, esp without motivation <hacker, slacker> eg *Co tu robi ten chałturnik? (What is this hacker doing here?)*

chałturzyć [khah-oo-TOO-zhich] *v* **1** To work slovenly or carelessly, esp without motivation <hack, slack> eg *Co tu robisz? A chałturzę (What are you doing here? Just hacking)* **2** To have a part-time job, esp of an assignment nature <gig, moonlight, have a job on the side> eg *Jestem najszczęśliwszy, gdy chałturzę (I'm the happiest when I'm gigging); Musiał chałturzyć, żeby mieć na wykarmienie rodziny (He had to moonlight to earn enough to feed his family)*

chałupa See chata

chachmęcić [khah-KHMEHN-cheech] (or **nachachmęcić** [nah-khah-KHMEHN-cheech]) *v* **1** To make something unclear, esp deliberately; to confuse, complicate, or lie <stir, stir up, adjy, bull, bullshit, shit, shovel the shit, string along, snow, fake it, talk through one's hat, speak with forked tongue> eg *Myślę, że facet chachmęci (I think the guy is bullshitting)* **2** (perf **zachachmęcić** [zah-khah-KHMEHN-cheech]) To steal; to rob <heist, boost, burgle, nurn, bag, buzz, highjack, hoist, hold up, hook, hustle, jump, kick over, knock off, knock over, lift, move, mug, nab, nick, nip, pinch, pluck, roll, rustle, snatch, snitch, stick up, swipe, take off, put the grab on, go south with> eg *Zachachmęcił prawie sto tysięcy w gotówce (He heisted nearly a hundred thousand in cash)*

chajtać się See hajtać się

cham* [khahm] (or **chamidło*** [khah-MEED-woh] *nn*) *nm* A rude, insensitive man, esp from the country; a boor <badass, son of a bitch, jerk, toughie, roughneck, country bumpkin, hick, hayseed, apple-knocker, hillbilly, shitkicker> eg *Na imprezę zaprosił pełno chamów (He invited many badasses to the party)*

chamka* [KHAHM-kah] (or **chamidło*** [khah-MEED-woh] *nn*) *nf* A rude, coarse, insensitive woman, esp from the country; a boor <badass, bitch, jerk, toughie, roughneck, country bumpkin, hick, hayseed, apple-knocker, hillbilly, shitkicker> eg *Jego nowa dziewczyna to prawdziwa chamka (His new girlfriend is a real hick)*

chamowaty* [khah-moh-VAH-ti] *adj* Rude; boorish; impudent; impertinent <cheeky, sassy, cocky, brassy, raw, filthy, bitchy, lippy, fresh> eg *Nie bądź taki chamski do twojej dziewczyny (Don't be so cheeky to your girlfriend)*

chandra [KHAHND-rah] *nf* A state of melancholy; depression; low spirits <blues, blue devils, blue funk, funk, bummer, downer, down trip, dismals, dumps, grumps, mokers, blahs> eg *Ma chandrę po tym, jak rzuciła go dziewczyna (After his girlfriend dumped him, he's come down with the blues)*

chandryczyć się [khahnd-RI-chich shyeh] *v* To quarrel; to actively disagree; to fight <bump heads, hassle, take on, lock horns, set to, scrap, cross swords, pick a bone, tangle with, tangle ass with, go up against, put up a fight, bicker, go round and round, go toe to toe, go to it, go to the mat, have a pissing contest, have a pissing match, have a run-in, kick up a row, make the fur fly, put on the gloves, lead a cat-and-dog life, have a cat-and-dog life, fight like cat and dog, jump down

someone's throat, be at loggerheads with> eg *Bez przerwy się chandryczyli (They were constantly at loggerheads with one another)*

chapać [KHAH-pahch] (perf **nachapać się** [nah-KHAH-pahch shyeh] or **chapnąć** [KHAHP-nohnch]) *v* **1** To acquire or gather something, esp by taking advantage of an opportunity <get, catch, grab, bag, collar, cop, dig up, drag, hook, land, nab, nail, snag, pull down, pull in, rack in, knock down, get hold of, get one's hands on, lay one's hands on, glom on to> eg *Zachapał wszystko, co się dało i ożenił się po raz drugi (He grabbed everything he could and he married for the second time)* **2** To steal; to rob <heist, boost, burgle, nurn, bag, buzz, highjack, hoist, hold up, hook, hustle, jump, kick over, knock off, knock over, lift, move, mug, nab, nick, nip, pinch, pluck, roll, rustle, snatch, snitch, stick up, swipe, take off, put the grab on, go south with> eg *Złodziej chapnął prawie sto tysięcy w gotówce (The thief heisted nearly a hundred thousand in cash)*

charakterek [khah-rahk-TEH-rehk] *nm* A trouble-making or dishonest person; a person of nasty and unbearable character <scalawag, gremlin, eel, snake, weasel, rat, jerk> eg *Your little sister is a real scalawag. She is responsible for that awful rumor (Twoja siostrzyczka to prawdziwy charakterek. To ona jest odpowiedzialna za tę okropną plotkę)*

chark* [khahrk] *nm* A large and nasty mass of phlegm coughed up from the lungs and spat out <hawker, lunger, loogie> eg *Odkrył chark w swoim bucie (He discovered a lunger in his shoe)*

charkać* [KHAHR-kahch] (perf **charknąć*** [KHAHRK-nohnch]) *v* To spit or to cough something up <hawk, let one fly, let a hawker fly, let a lunger fly, let a loogie fly> eg *Charknęła i uśmiechnęła się (She let one fly and smiled)*

chata [khah-WOO-pah] (or **chałupa** [KHAH-tah]) *nf* An apartment or a house <place, crib, pad, crash pad, cave, den, joint, box, dump, heave, camp, setup, layout, castle, palace, flop, flophouse, shack, rack, homeplate> eg *Ma bardzo wygodną i elegancką chatę (He has a very comfy and elegant setup); Chodź do mnie do chaty (Come over to my place)*

See brać kogoś na chatę

chcica [KHCHEE-tsah] (or **chętka** [KHEHNT-kah] or **chrapka** [KHRAHP-kah]) *nf* Strong desire, esp sexual; lust <hots, hot pants, hard-on, horniness, lech, heat, nasties, stonies, itch, pash, beaver fever, fever> eg *Myślę, że ta blondyna ma na ciebie chętkę (I think that blonde's got the hots for you); Uwierz mi, on ma na ciebie chcicę (Believe me, he has a hard-on for you)*

chcieć się rzygać* [khchyehch shyeh ZHI-gahch] *v phr* To be repelled, disgusted, irritated, or bored with something <be grossed out, be scuzzed out, be turned off, be barfed out, be grody, have a bellyful, have a skinful, be fed up with, be up to here with, have it up to here with, be sick and tired of> eg *Za każdym razem jak go widzę, rzygać mi się chce (I'm barfed out everytime I see him)*

cherlak [KHEHR-lahk] (or **chuchro** [KHOO-khroh]) *nm* A sickly or frail man <walking corpse> eg *Jej mąż to wygląda jak cherlak (Her husband looks like a walking corpse)*

chichrać [KHEEKH-rahch] (perf **pochichrać** [poh-KHEEKH-rahch]; **się** [shyeh] may be added) *v* To burst with laughter <crack up, break up, split, split one's sides, die laughing, roll in the aisles, tear one apart, be in stiches, laugh fit to burst, bust a gut laughing, pee in one's pants laughing, fall out laughing, howl,

scream, horselaugh, stitch, be blue in the face, laugh till one is blue in the face> eg *Pochichrała się, gdy usłyszała tę wiadomość (She was just rolling in the aisles when she heard the news)*

chinol* [kee-TAH-yehts] *nm* A Chinese male <Chink, Chinaman, chino, slant eyes> eg *Chinole mówią, że ich język jest łatwy (Chinks say their language is easy)*

chińszczyzna [kheeñ-SHCHIZ-nah] *nf* Something beyond one's understanding; something inconmprehensible <all double Dutch, all Greek, gobbledygook, bafflegab, fiddle-faddle, twiddle-twaddle, mumbo-jumbo, yackety-yack> eg *Ich rozmowa o komputerach to była dla mnie chińszczyzna (Their conversation about computers was all double Dutch to me); Usiłował mi tłumaczyć, ale to dla mnie chińszczyzna (He tried to explain it, but it's all Greek to me)*

chlać [khlahch] (perf **schlać się** [skhlahch shyeh] or **nachlać się** [NAH-khlahch shyeh] or **pochlać** [POH-khlahch] or **ochlać się** [OH-khlahch shyeh] or **uchlać się** [OO-khlahch shyeh] or **wychlać** [VI-khlahch]; **jak świnia** [yahk SHFEE-nyah] may be added) *v* To drink alcohol, esp in large quantities <booze up, guzzle, gargle, bend the elbow, hit the bottle, hit the sauce, knock back, lap, tank up, wet one's whistle, hang a few on, slug down, swig> eg *Chlali przez godzinę lub dwie (They tanked up for an hour or two)*

chlapa [KHLAH-pah] *nf* Drizzly or wet weather <slush, spit> eg *Spojrzał przez okno. Na zewnątrz była chlapa (He looked through the window. There was slush outside)*

chlapać [KHLAH-pahch] (perf **chlapnąć** [KHLAHP-nohnch] or **wychlapać** [vi-KHLAH-pahch]) *v* To reveal a secret or a surprise by accident <let the cat out of the bag, spill the beans, make the shit hit the fan> eg *To sekret. Staraj się tego nie wychlapać (It's a secret. Try not to spill the beans)*
See mleć jęzorem

chleb See ciężki kawałek chleba, mieć na chleb, przeciętniak, zarabiać na chleb

chlew [khlehf] *nm* Any dirty, shabby, dilapidated, or repulsive place, esp an apartment <dump, hole, hellhole, rathole, shithole, shithouse, joint, firetrap, pigsty> eg *Mieszka w okropnym chlewie (He lives in a terrible rathole)*

chlor [khlohr] *nm* A heavy drinker; an alcoholic <lush, bar-fly, alky, boozehound, boozer, bottle baby, dipso, elbow bender, ginhead, juicehead, loadie, sponge, soak, wino> eg *Ten chlor chciał trochę pieniędzy na piwo (That boozer wanted some money for beer)*

chlupnąć [KHLOOP-nohnch] (or **chlusnąć** [KHLOOS-nohnch] or **chlapnąć** [KHLAHP-nohnch]) *v* To have a quick drink of liquor <knock back, down, slug down, swig, tank, tank up, sling back> eg *Chlapnął całą butelkę i zaczął bekać (He knocked back the whole bottle and started to burp)*

chmara [KHMAH-rah] *nf* Much; many; plenty <helluva lot, lotsa, lotta, oodles, scads, heaps, bags, barrels, loads, piles, tons, wads, jillions, zillions, enough to choke a horse, shitload, fuckload, truckload> eg *Ona ma chmarę forsy. Zastanawiam się skąd go wzięła (She has lotsa money. I wonder where did she get it from?)*

chmurka See pod chmurką

chodliwy [KHOHD-leevi] *adj* (Of a merchandise) Popular and easily sold <hot, selling like hotcakes, going like hotcakes, sellling like it's going out of style, sellling like it's the best thing since sliced bread, hip, trendy> eg *Ten gadżet jest bardzo chodliwy (This new gadget is selling like hot cakes)*

chodu See dawać chodu

chody [KHOH-di] *npl* Powerful contacts; influenial connections; influence <clout, drag, pull, juice, network, channels, ropes, strings, wires, suction> eg *Ma chody i może wszystko załatwić (He's got the pull and he can get everything)*

chodzić [KHOH-jeech] *v* **1** (Of mechanical appliances) To function; to operate <go, work, run on, run off, perk, tick, click, hum, cook> eg *To chodzi na baterie (It runs on batteries)* **2** To have a particular price at a given moment <go for> eg *Pamiętam stare dobre czasy, gdy kilo złota chodził po stówie (I remember the good old days when a kilo of gold would cost a hundred)* **3** (or **chodzić ze sobą** [KHOH-jeech zeh SOH-boh]) *v* To have a steady relationship with a member of the opposite sex, esp in the teenage context <date, go steady, go together, go out, step out, have a thing going, be an item> eg *Chodzą ze sobą od września (They've been going together since September)*

chodzić koło czegoś See chodzić za czymś, kręcić się koło kogoś

chodzić koło kogoś na palcach [KHOH-jeech KOH-woh KOH-gohsh nah PAHL-tsahkh] *v phr* To treat someone with excessive care and tenderness <treat with kid gloves, handle with kid gloves> eg *On jest tutaj guru i wszyscy chodzą wokół niego na palcach (He's a guru around here and everybody treats him with kid gloves)*

chodzić komuś po głowie [KHOH-jeech KOH-moosh poh GWOH-vyeh] (or **chodzić za kimś** [KHOH-jeech zah KEEMSH]) *v phr* (Of anything or anyone) To keep nagging someone; to be an object of someone's intense thinking <be on someone's mind, prey on someone's mind, noodle around, percolate, perk, head trip, skull drag, be up to, eat, bug> eg *You were always on my mind (Zawsze chodziłaś mi po głowie); Ta piosenka chodzi za mną przez cały dzień (That song has been preying on my mind all day)*

chodzić na dupy* [KHOH-jeech nah DOO-pi] (or **chodzić na baby** [KHOH-jeech nah BAH-bi] or **chodzić na ksiuty** [KHOH-jeech nah KSHYOO-ti]) *v phr* (Of men) To go about seeking sexual encounters; be sexually promiscuous <chase, cruise, tail, troll, run around, dog someone's footsteps, hunt for cunt> eg *Powiedział swojej dziewczynie, że grał w pokera, ale na prawdę to poszedł na dupy (He told his girlfriend he was playing poker, but he was really cruising for chicks)*

chodzić na rzęsach See stawać na głowie

chodzić o coś [KHOH-jeech OH tsohsh] (or **rozchodzić się o coś** [rohs-KHOH-jeech shyeh OH tsohsh]) *v* To mean; to have in mind; to attempt or want to say <be up, be up to, drive at, get at, go on, go down, come off, come down> eg *Nie rozumiem, o co mu się rozchodzi (I don't understand what he's driving at)*

chodzić za czymś [KHOH-jeech zah chimsh] (or **chodzić koło czegoś** [KHOH-jeech KOH-woh CHEH-gohsh]) *v phr* To intensively look for something, esp a desired merchandise in a store <hunt, shop around for> eg *Chodziłam za tą bluzką cały dzień (I've been shopping for this blouse the whole day)*

chodzić za kimś See latać za kimś

chojrak [KHOH-ee-rahk] *nm* A brave, self-confident man who shows off his fearlessness; a daredevil <fire-eater, harum-scarum, John Wayne> eg *Nie bądź taki chojrak (Don't be such a John Wayne)*

cholera [khoh-LEH-rah] *nf* **1** A fit of extreme anger; fury; rage <fit, storm, blow-up, blow-off, flare-up, swivet, conniption fit, catfit, stew, snit, pucker, tantrum, hemorrhage, shit hemorrhage> eg *Dostał cholery, gdy zdał sobie sprawę z tego, że przegrali (He had a swivet when he realized they'd lost)* **2** (or **cholernica** [khoh-lehr-

NEE-tsah]) *nf* A woman one dislikes or disapproves of <bitch, slut, cunt, broad, wench, hag, old hag, old biddy, old bag, old tart, piece of shit> eg *Ty cholero, ja się z tobą porachuję! (You piece of shit, I'll get even with you!)* **3** (or **cholerstwo** [khoh-LEH-rah] *nn*) Anything arduous, despicable, or disagreeable <shit, bitch, fucker, motherfucker, sucker, bastard> eg *Palę tylko paczkę papierosów dziennie, bo drogie cholery (I only smoke a pack of cigarettes a day, because motherfuckers are expensive)* **4** (or **jasna cholera** [YAHS-nah khoh-LEH-rah] or **choroba** [khoh-ROH-bah] or **do cholery** [doh khoh-LEH-ri] or **do jasnej cholery** [doh YAHS-neh-ee khoh-LEH-ri] or **do ciężkiej cholery** [doh CHYEHN-skyeh-ee khoh-LEH-ri]; **choroby** [khoh-ROH-bi] may replace **cholery**) An exclamation of anger, irritation, disappointment, shock <shit, fuck, hell, heck, damn, damn it, goddamn it, gosh, golly, gee, jeez, holy fuck, holy cow, holy moly, holy hell, holy mackarel, holy shit, jumping Jesus, fucking shit, fucking hell> eg *Przegraliśmy ten mecz! Do jasnej cholery! (We lost that game! Fuck!)*

See dostać cholery, iść w cholerę, jak chuj, na cholerę, od cholery, pierdolnąć

cholera kogoś bierze [khoh-LEH-rah KOH-gohsh BYEH-zheh] (or **kurwica kogoś bierze**** [koor-VEE-tsah KOH-gohsh BYEH-zheh]) *phr* To become furious or irritated <get pissed off, get peed off, get p'd off, get bent out of a shape, get pushed out of a shape, get browned off, get cranky, get edgy, get sore, get mad as a hornet, get steamed up, get ticked off, get tee'd off, get burned up, go ballistic> eg *Cholera mnie bierze za każdym razem, jak widzę takiego idiotęza kierownicą mojego samochodu (I get pissed off every time I see such an idiot behind the steering wheel of my car)*

cholera wie [khoh-LEH-rah VYEH] (or **chuj wie**** [KHOO-ee VYEH] or **czort wie** [chohrt VYEH] or **diabli wiedzą** [DYAHB-lee VYEH-dzoh] or **licho wie** [LEE-khoh VYEH]) *adv phr* Unknown; unpredictable <hell knows, who the hell knows, fuck knows, who the fuck knows, fucked if I know> eg *Myślisz, że wygrają? Cholera wie (Do you think they will win? Hell knows)*

cholernie [khoh-LEHR-nyeh] *adv* Extremely; exceedingly; very <awful, god-awful, real, mighty, plenty, damn, damned, goddamn, goddamned, darn, darned, effing, flipping, forking, freaking, frigging, fucking, one's ass off, one's brains out, one's head off, to the max, like all get-out, like sin, to beat the band, like all creation, as blazes, as can be, as hell, like hell, in full swing> eg *Poczułem się cholernie głupio (I felt real stupid); Ten siniak cholernie mnie boli (This bruise hurts like hell)*

cholernik [khoh-LEHR-neek] *nm* A man one dislikes or disapproves of <asshole, fuck, fucker, fuckhead, fuckface, motherfucker, shit, shitface, shithead, shitheel, bastard, jerk, SOB, son of a bitch, son of a whore, cocksucker, prick, dick, dickhead, cuntface, schmuck, scum, scumbag, sleazebag, slimebag, dipshit, pisshead, piece of shit, pain in the ass> eg *Na twoim miejscu zignorowałabym tego cholernika (If I was you, I would ignore that bastard)* .

cholerny [khoh-LEHR-ni] (or **chujowy**** [khoo-YOH-vi] or **chrzaniony** [khshah-NYHOH-ni]) *adj* Cursed; damnable; bad <fucking, damn, damned, goddamn, goddamned, god-awful, blasted, darn, darned, effing, flipping, forking, freaking, frigging, pesky> eg *W tym chujowym upale nie można było pracować (You couldn't work in that fucking heat); Zabieraj ode mnie twe cholerne łapy (Get your damn hands off me)*

chomikować [khoh-mee-KOH-vahch] (perf **zachomikować** [zah-khoh-mee-KOH-vahch]) *v* To hide and save for the future <squirrel away, sock away, stash, stache, rathole, put aside for a rainy day, save for a rainy day> eg *Myślę, że zachomikował trochę pieniędzy (I think he stashed some money)*

chorągiewka [kho-rohn-GYEHF-kah] *nf* Someone who changes his beliefs or decisions; an opportunist <weasel, coat-turner, coat-changer, snake in the grass, sneaky dicky, two-faced liar, rat> eg *Ta chorągiewka doniosła o mnie szefowi (That snake in the grass reported me to the boss)*

choroba See cholera

chorobowe See na chorobowym

chory [KHOH-ri] *adj* Insane, stupid or thoughtless <crazy, creazy as a loon, loony, nerts, nuts, nutso, nutsy, nutty, sick, sick in the head, sicko, wacko, wacky, psycho, shizo, screwy, off one's rocker, out of one's skull, fruity, airbrained, airheaded, birdbrained, blockheaded, squareheaded, boneheaded, bubblebrained, bubbleheaded, bucketheaded, cluckheaded, cementheaded, clunkheaded, deadheaded, dumbclucked, dumbheaded, dumbassed, dumbbrained, fatbrained, fatheaded, flubdubbed, knukclebrained, knuckleheaded, lamebrained, lardheaded, lunkheaded, meatheaded, muscleheaded, noodleheaded, numbskulled, pointheaded, scatterbrained, nerdy, dorky, jackassed, lummoxed, dopey, goofy> eg *On musi być chory! Rzucić się na profesora z pyskiem? (He must be nuts! To start yelling at the professor)*

chować [KHOH-vahch] (perf **odchować** [oht-KHOH-vahch]) *v* To bring up children; to raise <no slang equivalent> eg *Odchowali dwóch chłopaków (They brought up two boys)*

chować się przy kimś/czymś [KHOH-vahch shyeh pshi keemsh/chimsh] *v phr* To be far worse when compared with someone or something else; not to be fit to be compared with <pale compared with, pale by comparison with, pale in comparison with, not hold a candle to, not hold a stick to> eg *Mój samochód chowa się przy jego (My car pales compared to his)*

chrapka See chcica

chrapnąć sobie komara [KHRAHP-nohnch SOH-byeh koh-MAH-rah] *v phr* To get some sleep; take a nap <catch some Z's, cop some Z's, cut some Z's, bag some Z's, grab some Z's, catch a nod, cop a nod, bag a nod, grab a nod, konck a nod, collar a nod, take forty winks, bag it, snooze, conk off, caulk off, dope off, drop off, sack out, zonk out, conk out, caulk out, fall out, saw wood, rack, crash, doss, sack up, sack in, zizz, get some blanket drill, get some bunk fatigue, get some sack time, get some shuteye, hit the hay, hit the pad, hit the sack> eg *Muszę chrapnąć sobie komara, bo inaczej padnę (I've got to catch some Z's before I drop)*

chromolić See chrzanić

chryja [KHRI-yah] *nf* A scandalous fact or situation; a scandal or disturbance <gas, fuss, stink, hot potato, bad scene, bad news, can of worms, bag of worms, takedown, putdown, shit, serious shit, deep shit, deep water, drag, bind, bitch, bummer, downer, headache, double trouble, snafu, pain in the ass, pain in the neck, spot, mess, holy mess, pickle, squeeze, hard time, glitch, stinker, skeleton, skeleton in the closet, sizzler, scorcher, dynamite, Watergate, fine kettle of fish, fine how do you do, fine cup of coffee, big stink, curtains, lights out, game's over> eg *Jak mnie złapią, to będzie chryja (Bad scene for me if they find me)*

chrzan See do dupy

chrzanić [KHSHAH-neech] (or **chromolić** [khroh-MOH-leech]) *v* To be indifferent to or contemptuous of; not to care at all; to ignore; to show disrespect <not give a damn, not give a fuck, not give a shit, not give a diddly-shit, not give a diddly-damn, not give a flying fuck, not give a hoot, not give a rat's ass, not give a squat, pass up, diss, skip, ig, ice, chill, freeze, cut, brush off, give the brush, give the cold shoulder, turn the cold shoulder, cold-shoulder, give the go-by, high-hat, kiss off> eg *Chrzanię to, co myślisz (I don't give a shit what you think)*

chrzaniony See cholerny

chuch [khookh] *nm* Bad breath, esp as a result of drinking alcohol <beer breath, dry mouth> eg *Czemu mnie nie pocałowała? Z powodu twojego chuchu, stary (Why didn't she kiss me? Bad breath, man)*

chuchać [KHOO-khahch] *v* To handle someone or something with excessive care or tenderness; to pamper <treat with kid gloves, handle with kid gloves, treat someone as an apple of someone's eye, give someone the red carpet treatment, pet> eg *Jego matka chuchała na niego, ale ją zostawił (His mother treated him with kid gloves, but he left her)*

chuchro See cherlak

chudzielec [khoo-JEH-lehts] (or **chudzina** [khoo-JEE-nah] *nf*) *nm* A skinny, usually tall person <beanpole, long drink of water, stringbean, skin and bones, skeleton, bag of bones> eg *Kiedyś byłem chudzielcem (I used to be a beanpole); Była wysoka, ale nie chudzina (She was tall, but no beanpole)*

chuj ci w dupę** [KHOO-ee chee v DOO-peh] (or **kij ci w dupę*** [keey chee v DOO-peh] or **chuj ci w oko**** [KHOO-ee chee v OH-koh] or **kij ci w oko** [keey chee v OH-koh]) *excl* (Esp as an exclamation of defiance and contempt) To invite someone to perform or submit to a humiliating act <fuck you, screw you, chuck you Farley, fuck you Charley, drop dead, eat shit, eat my shorts, get lost, get fucked, get screwed, get stuffed, go fly a kite, go fuck yourself, fuck yourself, go screw yourself, screw yourself, go shit in your hat, go to hell, take a flying fuck, kiss my ass, bite my ass, piss on you, shit on you, cram it, stuff it, shove it, stick it, stick it in your ear, stick it in your ass, up your ass, up yours> eg *Chuj ci w dupę, jeśli tak myślisz! (Fuck you, if that's what you think)*

chuj wie See cholera wie

chuj** [KHOO-ee] **1** *nm* The penis <cock, prick, dick, stick, joystick, dipstick, bone, meat, beef, wang, yang, dong, dummy, hammer, horn, hose, jock, joint, knob, pork, putz, rod, root, tool, flute, skin flute, love-muscle, sausage, schmuck, schlong, schvantz, cream-stick, third leg, middle leg, business, apparatus, John, Johnny, Johnson, John Thomas, Jones, pecker, peter, peepee, pisser, weenie, peenie, dingus, dingbat, thingy> eg *Ugryzła go w chuja, uwierzyłbyś? (She bit him on his penis, would you believe that?)* **2** *nm* (or **kawał chuja**** [KAH-vah-oo KHOO-yah] *nm phr*) *nm* A man one dislikes or disapproves of <asshole, fuck, fucker, fuckhead, fuckface, motherfucker, shit, shitface, shithead, shitheel, bastard, jerk, SOB, son of a bitch, son of a whore, cocksucker, prick, dick, dickhead, cuntface, schmuck, scum, scumbag, sleazebag, slimebag, dipshit, pisshead, piece of shit, pain in the ass> eg *Czy ty wiesz, co ten chuj mi powiedział? Że spał z moją dziewczyną (You know what that prick told me? He slept with my girlfriend)* **3** *excl* (or **do chuja**** [doh KHOO-yah] or **u chuja**** [oo KHOO-yah] or **takiego chuja**** [tah-

KYEH-goh KHOO-yah] or **taki chuj**** [TAH-kee KHOO-ee]) An exclamation of irritation, anger, or defiance <shit, fuck, hell, heck, damn, damn it, goddamn it, gosh, golly, gee, jeez, holy fuck, holy cow, holy moly, holy hell, holy mackarel, holy shit, jumping Jesus, fucking shit, fucking hell> eg *Przegraliśmy ten mecz! Chuj! (We lost that game! Fuck!)* **4** *nm* Nothing at all; zero <shit, shit-all, fuck-all, zilch, beans, damn, diddly-squat, doodly-squat, duck egg, goose egg, hoot, one red cent, one thin dime, rat's ass, zero, zippo> eg *Byłam piękna, bogata, wykształcona - wszystko chuj (I was beautiful, rich, educated -- it was all shit); Myślał, że dostanie duży spadek, a tu chuj (He thought he'd inherit a lot of money, but he got fuck-all)*
See kłaść na czymś/kimś lachę, lecieć sobie w chuja, móc komuś skoczyć, na chuj, od cholery, po byku, rzucać mięsem, tak że hej, taki że hej, za cholerę, zrobić kogoś w konia

chuja wart** [KHOO-yah vahrt] *adj* Bad, poor, worthless, or of inferior quality <worth shit, lousy, awful, bush-league, cheap, crappy, shitty, cruddy, crummy, doggy, low-rent, low-ride, no-good, raggedy-ass, schlocky, stinking, tacky, trashy, two-bit, dime-a-dozen, fair to middling, garden variety, of a sort, of sorts, piddling, pissy-ass, piss-poor, run-of-the-mill, small-time> eg *Cała jego ciężka praca była chuja warte (His entire work was worth shit)*

chujowo** [khoo-YOH-voh]) *adv* Extremely bad; terribly; awfully <lousy, shitty, awful> eg *Chujowo się dzisiaj czuję (I feel really lousy today)*

chujowy See cholerny

chujoza** [khoo-YOH-zah] *nf* Any object or situation that is wretched, unpleasant, or bothersome <shit, crap, bitch, bummer, drag, motherfucker, fucker> eg *Musiałem dziś wstać o 7.30. Co za chujoza! (I had to get up at 7.30 today. What a drag!)*

chwila [KHFEE-lah] (or **chwila moment** [KHFEE-lah MOH-mehnt]) *excl* An exclamation telling someone to wait a little, esp for one's decision or agreement <just a mo, just a sec, wait a mo, wait a sec, hold on, hold your water, hold your horses> eg *Te, chwila moment, co to ma wszystko znaczyć? (Hey, hold on. What's that supposed to mean?)*

chwycić Boga za nogi [KHFI-cheech BOH-gah zah NOH-gee] *v phr* To think one is very important or successful, and is free to do anything; to become conceited or self-impressed <think one's shit doesn't stink, be too big for someone's shoes, ego-trip, get stuck-up, get puffed-up, get high-hat, get swelled-up, get swell-headed, get big-headed, get high-nosed, get blown-up, get stuck on oneself, get chesty, get stuffy, get gassy, get windy, get hatty, get hinkty, get uppity, get biggety, dog it, put on the dog, give oneself airs, put on airs, put on, put on the ritz> eg *Jest dyrektorem i myśli, że chwycił Boga za nogi (He's the director and thinks his shit doesn't stink)*

chwyt poniżej pasa See cios poniżej pasa

chwytać [KHFI-tahch] *v* (perf **chwycić** [KHFI-cheech]) **1** (or **chwytać w lot** [KHFI-tahch v LOHT]) To understand; to comprehend <get, get it, catch, get the drift, get the picture, get the message, get the hang of, savvy, dig, click, capeesh, read, be with it, see where one is coming from, know where one is coming from> eg *Usiłowałem mu wytłumaczyć, ale nie chwycił (I tried to explain it to him but he didn't get the drift); Skoro dyrektor nie chwycił, to myślisz, że oni to chwycą? (If the director didn't get it, do you think they will?)* **2** To win approval or recognition; to prove successful, appealing or valid <do, wash, work, go down, cut it, make the

grade, make the cut, make it, cut the mustard, pass in the dark, fill the bill, fit in, fit the bill> eg *Ten pomysł jest zbyt dziwaczny. Nie chwyci (This idea is too bizarre. It won't wash)* **3** To get sunburned <catch some rays, bag some rays, get nuked, get fried, get barbecued> eg *Chwyciło ją już po pół godziny w słońcu (She caught some rays after one hour in the sun)*

ciągnąć See obciągać

ciągnąć [CHYOHNG-nohnch] *v* **1** (perf **wyciągnąć** [vi-CHYOHNG-nohnch] or **pociągnąć** [poh-CHYOHNG-nohnch]) To drink alcohol, esp quickly or in large quantities <booze up, guzzle, gargle, bend the elbow, hit the bottle, hit the sauce, knock back, lap, tank up, wet one's whistle, hang a few on, slug down, swig> eg *Facet ciągnie regularnie (The guy hits the sauce regularly)* **2** (perf **wyciągnąć** [vi-CHYOHNG-nohnch]) *v phr* To take financial advantage of someone; to wheedle money out of someone <sponge, mooch, scrounge, milk> eg *Od wielu lat ciągnie kasę od ciotki (He's been sponging on his aunt for many years)* **3** (Of cold air from the outside) To flow through a room <no slang equivalent> eg *Ciągnie od okna (There's a draft coming from the window)* **4** To use up gasoline <guzzle> eg *Ten model ciągnie dużo benzyny (This model guzzles a lot of gas)* **5** (or **ciągać** [CHYOHN-gahch]) (To try) To take someone with one somewhere, esp against someone's will; to accompany <get, drag along, drag around, schlep along, schlep around, tag along, tag around, push> eg *Ciągał mnie po sklepach przez cały dzień (He was dragging me around shops all day); On zawsze ciągnie mnie na wódkę (He's always pushing me to go and drink with him)* **6** To be attracted to someone or something; to cling <hang onto, be really into, be heavily into, get sold into, get hooked, get caught, eat sleep and breathe something> eg *Ciągnie mnie do takich świrów (I am really into such freaks)*

ciągnąć kogoś za język [CHYOHNG-nohnch zah YEHN-zik] *v phr* To induce someone to reveal some information, esp to cross-examine <make someone spill the beans, male someone let the cat out of the bag, put the third degree, drag info out of> eg *Przestań ciągnąć mnie za język (Stop dragging info out of me)*

ciągnąć nosa [CHYOHNG-nohnch NOH-sah] (or **dać sobie w nosa** [dahch SOH-byeh v NOH-sah]; **nocha** [NOH-khah] may replace **nosa**) *v phr* To insufflate a powdered drug, espacially cocaine <sniff, snort, blow, scoop, toot> eg *Patrz na tę, co ciągnie nosa (Look at the one who's snorting); Musiała wyjść z biura, żeby pociągnąć nocha (She had to leave the office to toot); Wolę sobie pociągnąć nosa niż walnąć w żyłę (I'd rather snort it than shoot it)*

ciągnąć się [CHYOHNG-nohnch shyeh] (or **ciągnąć się jak smród w gaciach** [CHYOHNG-nohnch shyeh yahk SMROOT v GAH-chyakh] or **przeciągać się** [psheh-CHYOHN-gahch shyeh]) *v* (Esp about time or an activity) To linger; to move very slowly and, esp be delayed <lag behind, drag on, drag out, drag one's feet, drag one's ass, schlep along, stretch out, crawl, move at a snail's pace, toddle, tool, tail, jelly, hang around, hang up, hold up, slow up, tie up, bind, stall, put on hold, put off, have lead in one's pants, put on the shelf> eg *Jego proces ciągnął się przez rok (His trial dragged on for a year)*

ciągnąć sobie łacha z kogoś See drzeć sobie łacha z kogoś

ciągoty [chyohn-GOH-ti] *npl* Strong inclination or penchant, esp sexual <hots, hot pants, hard-on, horniness, lech, heat, nasties, stonies, itch, pash, beaver fever,

fever> eg *Mój młodszy brat ma ciągoty do starszych kobiet (My younger brother has a hard-on for older women)*

ciało See dać dupy

ciamajda [chyah-MAH-ee-dah] (or **ciemięga** [cheh-MYEHN-gah] or **ciapa** [CHYAH-pah]) *nf* An awkward, sluggish, inept, or ineffectual person; a bungler; a fumbler <screw-up, loser, dool tool, turkey, schmendrick, duffer, flubdub, lummox, lump, foozler, buterfingers, fumble-fist, goof, goof-off, goofball, eightball, foulball, klutz, also-ran, never-was, nonstarter, drag-ass, foot-dragger, schlepper, slowpoke> eg *Nie chcę żadnych ciamajd w moim zespole (I don't want any klutzes on my unit)*

ciapek [CHYAH-pehk] *nm* A dog, esp a mongrel <doggie, mutt, pooch, pup, Fido, Pluto, Goofy, Heinz, flea bag, tail wagger, bone eater, pot hound> eg *Gdzie jest ciapek? (Where's Fido?)*

cicha woda [CHEE-khah VOH-dah] (or **cicha woda brzegi rwie** [CHEE-khah VOH-dah BZHEH-gee RVYEH]) *nf phr* A person who is quiet but may have very strong feelings, deep knowledge, etc <still waters, still waters run deep, iron fist in the velvet glove> eg *Mój brat zawsze był cicha woda. Nigdy nie wiadomo, o co mu chodzi (My brother has always been still waters. You never know what he's up to)*

cichacz [CHEE-khahch] *nm* A soundless but horrendous smelling release of intestinal gas <S.B.D., silent but deadly, cheeser, silent killer> eg *Kto puścił tego cichacza? (Who let the S.B.D.?)*

cichaczem [chee-KHAH-chehm] (or **cichcem** [CHEEKH-tsehm]) *adv phr* Secretly; quietly; inconspicuously <on the quiet, on the QT, on the sly, in a hole-and-corner way, in holes and corners, under one's hat, under wraps, soft-pedaled, hush-hush> eg *Burmistrz cichcem wziął łapówkę (The mayor accepted a bribe on the QT)*

cichodajka* [chee-khoh-DAH-ee-kah] *nf* A woman who enjoys frequent yet discreet sexual encounters, likely with more than one partner; a sexually promiscuous woman <floozy, bimbo, chippy, quiff, easy lay, easy make, alley cat, dirty-leg, roundheels, nympho> eg *Zawsze ci mówiłam, że to cichodajka. A ty się z nią ożeniłeś! (I always told you she was an alley cat. You're the one who married her!); Ma reputację cichodajki (She's got a reputation as an easy make)*

ciężki See cholera, przystojniak

ciężki kawałek chleba [CHYEHN-shkee kah-VAH-wehk KHLEH-bah] *nm phr* Not very remunerative but very hard work <ball-buster, bone-breaker, back-breaker, bitch, killer, grind, donkeywork, bullwork, dirty work> eg *Pisanie słowników to ciężka robota, ale pisanie słowników slangu to ciężki kawałek chleba! (Writing dictionaries is a hard job but writing slang dictionaries is a bitch!)*

ciężki przystojniak See przystojniak

ciężkie pieniądze [CHEHNSH-kyeh pyeh-NYOHN-dzeh] (or **duże pieniądze** [DOO-zheh pyeh-NYOHN-dzeh] or **grube pieniądze** [GROO-beh pyeh-NYOHN-dzeh] or **ładne pieniądze** [WAHD-neh pyeh-NYOHN-dzeh]) *npl phr* A large amount of money <bundle, bankroll, big bucks, megabucks, heavy bread, mint, package, hard coin> eg *Ten samochód musiał kosztować ciężkie pieniądze (That car must have cost a bundle); Jego brat zarabia teraz grube pieniądze (His brother is earning megabucks these days)*

cieć [chehch] *nm* **1** A man one dislikes or disapproves of <asshole, fuck, fucker, fuckhead, fuckface, motherfucker, shit, shitface, shithead, shitheel, bastard, jerk,

SOB, son of a bitch, son of a whore, cocksucker, prick, dick, dickhead, cuntface, schmuck, scum, scumbag, sleazebag, slimebag, dipshit, pisshead, piece of shit, pain in the ass> eg *Weź spytaj ciecia, o której zamykają (Go ask this asshole when they close)* **2** A janitor, gate-keeper or night watchman <stick, night-stick, house sitter> eg *Cieć nie chciał ich wpuścić (The night-stick didn't want to let them in)*

cięcie [CHYEHN-chyeh] **1** *nn* A planned reduction in size or amount <cut, slash> eg *Rząd sprzeciwia się cięciom w budżecie (The administration is opposed to cuts in budget)* **2** (Usually) Sudden stop of filming by a camera <cut, rap> eg *Dobra! Uwaga wszyscy, cięcie! (Okay! Attention everybody, that's a rap!)*

ciekawski [chyeh-KAHF-skee] *adj* Rudely prying; overly inquisitive <nosey, snoopy> eg *Powiedz twojemu ciekawskiemu bratu, żeby pilnował swego nosa (Tell your nosey brother to mind his own business)*

cielak [CHYEH-lahk] *nn* **1** (or **cielę** [CHYEH-leh]) A slow, awkward, sluggish, or ineffectual person; a bungler; a fumbler <screw-up, loser, dool tool, turkey, schmendrick, duffer, flubdub, lummox, lump, foozler, buterfingers, fumble-fist, goof, goof-off, goofball, eightball, foulball, klutz, also-ran, never-was, nonstarter, drag-ass, foot-dragger, schlepper, slowpoke> eg *Kiedy to cielę wreszcie skończy? (When will this goofball ever finish?)* **2** A calf <no slang equivalent> eg *Sprzedał dzisiaj dwa cielaki (He sold two calves today)*

ciemięga See ciamajda

ciemniak [CHYEHM-nyahk] (or **ciemna masa** [CHEHM-nah MAH-sah] *nf phr*) *nm* A slow-witted, stupid or thoughtless person <airbrain, airhead, birdbrain, blockhead, squarehead, bonehead, bubblebrain, bubblehead, buckethead, cluckhead, cementhead, clunkhead, deadhead, dumbbell, dumbcluck, dumbhead, dumbass, dumbbrain, fatbrain, fathead, flubdub, knukclebrain, knucklehead, lamebrain, lardhead, lunkhead, meathead, musclehead, noodlehead, numbskull, pointhead, scatterbrain, jerk, jerk-off, klutz, chump, creep, nerd, dork, dweeb, gweeb, geek, jackass, lummox, twerp, nerd, bozo, clod, cluck, clunk, dimwit, dingbat, dipstick, dodo, dopey, dufus, goofus, lump, lunk, nitwit, schnook, schlep, schlemiel, schmendrick, schmo, schmuck, simp, stupe> eg *Powiedz tej ciemnej masie, że może tu więcej nie przychodzić (Tell that lamebrain not to show up here anymore); Tłumaczyłam mu trzy razy, ale on nic nie zrozumiał. Ale ciemniak! (I explained it to him three times but he didn't understand anything. What a birdbrain!)*

ciemno że w mordę daj* [CHYEHM-noh zheh v MOHR-deh DAH-ee] (**ciemno jak w dupie u murzyna*** [CHYEHM-noh yahk v DOO-pyeh oo moo-ZHI-nah]) *adv phr* Very dark <pitch dark, pitch black> eg *Było ciemno, że w mordę daj (It was pitch dark)*

Ciemnogród [chehm-NOH-groot] (or **ciemnota** [chyehm-NOH-tah] *nf*) *nm* Stupidity or a group of people who are stupid and thoughtless <stupid thing, silly-ass thing, stupidom, klutzdom> eg *Co za ciemnogród! (What a stupid thing to do!)*

ciemny [CHYEHM-ni] (or **czarny** [CHAHR-ni]) *adj* Illegal, unethical, or dishonest <dirty, sleazy, crooked, crummy, foul, shady, shabby, salty, raw, heavy, hung-up, below the belt, under the counter, under the table, underhand> eg *Wiem jedynie, że robili jakieś ciemne interesy (For all I know, they had some underhand dealings)*

ciemny [CHYEHM-ni] *adj* Slow-witted, stupid or thoughtless <airbrained, airheaded, birdbrained, blockheaded, squareheaded, boneheaded, bubblebrained,

bubbleheaded, bucketheaded, cluckheaded, cementheaded, clunkheaded, deadheaded, dumbclucked, dumbheaded, dumbassed, dumbbrained, fatbrained, fatheaded, flubdubbed, knukclebrained, knuckleheaded, lamebrained, lardheaded, lunkheaded, meatheaded, muscleheaded, noodleheaded, numbskulled, pointheaded, scatterbrained, nerdy, dorky, jackassed, lummoxed, dopey, goofy> eg *Może i jest ciemna, ale ma świetne ciało (Maybe she is dumbheaded, but she's got great body)*

cienias [CHYEH-nyahs] (or **cienki bolek** [CHYEHN-kee BOH-lehk]) *nm* A mediocre, insignificant, or ineffectual person; a mediocrity or failure <underachiever, loser, born loser, second-rater, schlemiel, schmendrick, schmo, schnook, screwup, fuckup, hacker, muffer, scrub, dub, dool tool, turkey, lump, buterfingers, fumble-fist, goof, goof-off, goofball, eightball, foulball, klutz, also-ran, never-was, nonstarter, zero, lightweight, nobody, non, nonentity, noname, small potatoes, small timer, bush-leaguer> eg *Nowy dyrektor Instytutu to cienias. Zrobił doktorat po czterdziestce (The new director of the Institute is a real loser. He did his PhD when he turned forty)*

cienki [CHYEHN-kee] *adj* Of inferior quality; shoddy; poor <lousy, awful, bush-league, cheap, crappy, shitty, cruddy, crummy, doggy, low-rent, low-ride, no-good, raggedy-ass, schlocky, stinking, tacky, trashy, two-bit, dime-a-dozen, fair to middling, garden variety, of a sort, of sorts, piddling, pissy-ass, piss-poor, run-of-the-mill, small-time> eg *Co myślisz o ich najnowszej płycie? Myślę, że jest bardzo cienka (What do you think about their latest album? I think it's very crappy)*

cienko [CHYEHN-koh] *adv* Extremely bad; terribly; awfully <lousy, shitty, awful> eg *Cienko mi poszło na egzaminie (I did lousy in the exam)*

cienko śpiewać [CHYEHN-koh SHPYEH-vahch] (or **inaczej śpiewać** [ee-NAH-cheh-ee SHPYEH-vahch]; **prząść** [pshohnshch] may replace **śpiewać**) *v phr* To stop behaving in a superior, haughty, or self-assured manner; to moderate one's behavior <sing another tune, whistle a different tune, change one's tune, come down a peg, take down a notch, climb down, come off one's perch, get off one's high horse, eat dirt, eat humble pie, pull in one's horns, take off one's high hat> eg *Na początku zaczął się popisywać, ale teraz inaczej śpiewa (At the beginning he started to show off but now he sings another tune)*

ciepłe kluchy [CHYEH-pweh KLOO-khi] *npl phr* A soft, apathetic, sluggish or ineffectual person; a weakling <wimp, wuss, pussy, big baby, candy ass, milktoast, milquetoast, featherweight, gutless wonder, limp-dick, pantywaist, hard-off> eg *Czy na prawdę myślisz, że mogłabym pójść na randkę z twoim bratem? On to są ciepłe kluchy (Do you really think I could go out on a date with your brother? He's a wimp)*

ciepło [CHYEHP-woh] *adv* Very nearly correct; not quite the thing <close but no cigar> eg *Jeśli odpowiedzieliście „pięć", to było ciepło (If you answered "five," you were close but no cigar)*

cięty [CHYEHN-ti] (or **cięty jak osa** [CHYEHN-ti yahk OH-sah] may be added) *adj* Spiteful, rancorous, malicious or vindictive <bitchy, mean, cussed, bad-assed, nasty-assed, rough, tough, hard on> eg *Dlaczego ona jest taka cięta na mnie? (Why is she so hard on me?)*

cięty na baby [CHYEHN-ti nah BAH-bi] *adj phr* (Of a man) pursuing and otherwise devoting himself to women to an unususal degree <pussy-simple,

pussy-happy, cunt-simple, cunt-happy, letching> eg *Twój profesor jest naprawdę cięty na baby (Your professor is really letching)*

cinkciarz [CHEENK-chahsh] *nm* A money changer, esp illegal <no slang equivalent> eg *Jego brat jest cinkciarzem (His brother is a money changer)*

cios poniżej pasa [chyohs poh-NEE-zheh-ee PAHsah] (or **chwyt poniżej pasa** [KHFIT poh-NEE-zheh-ee PAHsah]) *nm phr* A remark or action that takes advantage of someone else's vulnerability <hit below the belt, blow below the belt, below the belt tactic, cheap shot> eg *Twoje pytanie było ciosem poniżej pasa (Your question was a hit below the belt); Politycy często używają ciosów poniżej pasa (Politicians often use below the belt tactics)*

cios w plecy [chyohs f PLEH-tsi] (or **nóż w plecy** [noosh f PLEH-tsi]) *nm phr* An act of betrayal <stab in the back, double-crossing, Judas kiss, let-down, sell-out> eg *Ta decyzja była dla niego prawdziwym nożm w plecy (This decision was a real stab in the back for him)*

ciota** [CHYOH-tah] (or **ciotka**** [CHYOHT-kah]) *nf* **1** A male homosexual; gay <fag, faggot, fairy, queer, fruitcake, homo, pansy, sissy, swish, daisy, limp-wrist, queen> eg *Nie zachowuj się jak ciota! (Don't act like a faggot!)* **2** A menstrual period <the curse, the rag, ragtime, the monthlies, red flag, that time of the month, little visitor> eg *Od rana mam ciotę (The curse struck this morning)*

cipa* [CHEE-pah] (or **cipka*** [CHEEP-kah] or **cipencja*** [chee-PEHN-tsyah]) *nf* **1** A woman treated as a sexual object, esp young and attractive <chick, broad, gal, pussy, cunt, ass, piece of ass, piece, dish, babe, baby, dame, beauty, beaut, beauty queen, baby doll, doll, dolly, dollface, dreamboat, dream girl, eating stuff, eyeful, flavor, looker, good-looker, head-turner, traffic-stopper, honey, killer, hot number, package, knockout, oomph girl, peach, bombshell, sex bunny, sex job, sex kitten, sex pot, table grade, ten, bunny, centerfold, cheesecake, date bait, dazzler, heifer, fluff, quail, sis, skirt, tail, job, leg, tart, tomato, pussycat, cooz, twat> eg *Jak się nazywa ta cipa z twojego biura? (What's the name of this broad that works in your office?)* **2** A woman, esp whom one dislikes or disapproves of <bitch, slut, cunt, broad, wench, hag, old hag, old biddy, old bag, old tart, piece of shit> eg *Jak się nazywa ta cipa z twojego biura? (What's the name of this broad that works in your office?)* **3** The vulva, vagina <pussy, slit, slot, snatch, twat> eg *Ma ogoloną cipkę (She has a shaved pussy)*
See lizać

ciszej See dawać ciszej

ciułać [CHYOO-wahch] (perf **uciułać** [oo-CHYOO-wahch]) *v* To save money for the future, esp with difficulty <put aside for a rainy day, save for a rainy day, squirrel away, sock away, stash, stache> eg *Ciułał przez całe życie (He's been socking away his entire life)*

ciułacz [CHYOO-wahch] *nm* A petty saver, esp a senior citizen and parsimonious person; a miser <tightwad, piker, cheapskate, scrooge, pinchfist, penny-pincher, pinchpenny, nickel-nurser, nickel-squeezer> eg *Jej mąż to ciułacz. Nie pozwoli jej kupić tego futra (Her husband is a tightwad. He won't let her buy that fur coat)*

ciuch See wyskoczyć z ciuchów

ciuchcia [CHOOKH-chah] *nf* A steam-driven locomotive or train <choo-choo, puffer, boiler, smoker, kettle> eg *Ta ciuchcia jest bardzo stara (This choo-choo is very old)*

ciuchy [CHYOO-khi] (or **ciuszki** [CHYOOSH-kee]) *npl* Clothes or clothing; dress <threads, drapes, duds, rags, togs, weeds, outfit> eg *Podobają mi się twoje ciuchy. Gdzie je kupiłaś? (I like your threads. Where did you buy them?)*

ciuciubabka See **bawić się w chowanego**

ciul* [chyool] *nm* **1** A man one strongly dislikes or disapproves of <dickhead, cocksucker, pisshead> eg *Gówno ode mnie dostaniesz, ty ciulu jeden! (You'll get nothing from me, you dickhead!)* **2** The penis <cock, prick, dick, stick, joystick, dipstick, bone, meat, beef, wang, yang, dong, dummy, hammer, horn, hose, jock, joint, knob, pork, putz, rod, root, tool, flute, skin flute, love-muscle, sausage, schmuck, schlong, schvantz, cream-stick, third leg, middle leg, business, apparatus, John, Johnny, Johnson, John Thomas, Jones, pecker, peter, peepee, pisser, weenie, peenie, dingus, dingbat, thingy> eg *Siedział w parku na ławce i babom ciula pokazywał (He was sitting on a park bench, flasking his dick to women walking by)*

ciupa [CHYOO-pah] *nf* A prison; a jail <slam, slammer, jug, can, bucket, cage, big cage, big house, caboose, calaboose, cannery, cooler, hole, hoosegow, icebox, lockup, mill, stir, pen, tank, college, crossbar hotel, booby hatch, pink clink, quad> eg *Siedzi w ciupie już od dwóch lat (He's been in the slammer for two years now)*

ciupciać się* [CHYOOP-chahch shyeh] *v* To copulate <get screwed, get fucked, get laid, screw, fuck, fork, frig, ball, bang, boink, bonk, boff, hump, poke, shag> eg *Dyrektor znalazł ich, jak ciupciali się w szatni (The headmaster found them screwing in the locker room)*

ciupciać* [CHYOOP-chahch] (or **ciupciać sobie*** [CHYOOP-chahch SOH-byeh]; perf **pociupciać*** [poh-CHYOOP-chahch] or **wyciupciać*** [vi-CHYOOP-chahch]) *v* To copulate with someone <fuck, screw, lay, ball, bang, boink, boff, boogie, bop, frig, hump, poke, shag> eg *Naprawdę chciałbym ją wyciupciać! (I really would like to screw her!)*

ciupcianie* [chyoop-CHAH-nyeh] *nn* Sex or a sexual intercourse in general <screw, screwing, fuck, fucking, lay, bang, banging, boink, boinking, boff, boffing, hump, humping, poke, poking> eg *Zatrzymał się przed domem swojej dziewczyny na ciupcianie (He stopped off at his girlfriend's house for a hump)*

ciurkiem [CHYOOR-kyehm] *adv* Non stop; continuously; all the time <<around the clock, day and night, forever and a day, over and over, again and again> eg *Nowe zlecenia przychodziły ciurkiem (New orders would come day and night)*

ciut [chyoot] (or **ciut-ciut** [chyoot-CHYOOT] or **ciutkę** [CHYOOT-keh]) **1** *nn* A little bit <smidgen, tad, wee bit, itty bit> eg *I don't want the whole thing. Give me jus a smidgen (Nie chcę wszystkiego. Daj mi tylko ciutkę)* **2** *adv* A little; not much <bit wee, tad, wee bit, itty bit> eg *Myślę, że ciasto jest ciut za słodkie (I think the cake is we too sweet)*

ciut-ciut See od cholery

cizia [CHEE-zhyah] *nf* A young, attractive, and usually fashionably dressed woma <chick, broad, gal, pussy, cunt, ass, piece of ass, piece, dish, babe, baby, dame beauty, beaut, beauty queen, baby doll, doll, dolly, dollface, dreamboat, drear girl, eating stuff, eyeful, flavor, looker, good-looker, head-turner, traffic-stoppe honey, killer, hot number, package, knockout, oomph girl, peach, bombshell, se bunny, sex job, sex kitten, sex pot, table grade, ten, bunny, centerfol cheesecake, date bait, dazzler, heifer, fluff, quail, sis, skirt, tail, job, leg, ta

tomato, pussycat, cooz, twat> eg *Była to dwudziestoparoletnia cizia z małym mózgiem, ale dużą ambicją (She was a babe in her 20s with more ambition than brains)*

cmok [tsmohk] (or **całus** [TSAH-woos]) *nm* A kiss <smacker, smackeroo, kissy-kissy, kissy-poo, kissy-face> eg *Dała mu całusa prosto w usta (She planted a smacker square on his lips)*

cmokać [TSMOH-kahch] (perf **cmoknąć** [TSMOHK-nohnch]) *v* To give someone a kiss; to kiss <suck face, swap spit, play kissy-kissy, play kissy-poo, play kissy-face, smooch, mash, neck, pet, smack, give someone a buzz, give someone a peck, give someone a smack, give someone a smooch, give someone a kissy-face, give someone a kissy-poo, give someone one on the cheek> eg *Bardzo się cieszę, że Cię widzę. Cmoknij mnie! (I'm so glad to see you. Give me a smooch!)*

cmoknąć w mankiet [TSMOHK-nohnch v MAHN-kyeht] *v phr* To kiss a woman on her hand <peck on the hand, smack on the hand, smooch on the hand, suck the hand, lay one on the hand> eg *Cmoknął ją w mankiet i wyszedł (He laid one on her hand and left)*

cnotka* [TSNOHT-kah] (or **cnota*** [TSNOH-tah]; **niewydymka**** [nyeh-vi-DIM-kah] may be added) *nf* **1** A prim and ostentatiously virtuous person, esp a woman; a prude <tight-ass, goody-goody, goody two-shoes, old maid, bluenose> eg *Nie bądź taka cnotka. Daj sobie na luz! (Don't be such a tight-ass. Loosen up!)* **2** A virgin, of either sex <cherry, canned goods> eg *Myślę, że ona wciąż jest cnotką (I think she's still a cherry)*

co dusza pragnie [tsoh DOO-shah PRAHG-nyeh] *phr* You cannot designate anything not included here; whatever you want <you name it> eg *Ma ciało, talent, inteligencję, czego dusza zapragnie (She got looks, talent, intelligence, you name it)*

co jest [TSOH yehst] (or **co jest grane** [TSOH yehst GRAH-neh] may be added) *phr* What's happening? What's the matter? What do you mean? <what's up, what are you up to, what are you driving at, what's going on, what's going down, what's coming off, what's coming down, what's the deal, what's the story> eg *Hej, co jest grane? (Hey, what's the deal?)*

co ma piernik do wiatraka [TSOH mah PYEHR-neek doh vyaht-RAH-kah] *excl phr* (An exclamation of irritation) These things or persons are completely unrelated <what's that got to do with anything, what's that got to do with it> eg *Nie było cię wczoraj w szkole. Wiem, ale co ma piernik do wiatraka? (You didn't come to school yesterday. I know, but what's that got to do with it)*

co popadnie [coh poh-PAHD-nyeh] *phr* Anything; whatever <any old thing, any which way, all, whatever is at hand> eg *Weź co popadnie (Take any old thing you want)*

co rusz [tsoh ROOSH] (or **co krok** [tsoh KROHK]) *adv phr* From time to time <every now and then, every now and again, every so often, on and off> eg *Co rusz wymyślał nowe powody, żeby nie dać mi awansu (He would make up new excuses every now and then to block my advance)*

co siła [tsoh SHEE-wah] *adv phr* Immediately or quickly; as soon as possible <pretty damn quick, PDQ, ASAP, on the spot, on the double, double time, double clutching, like a shot, in half a mo, like now, before you know it, before you can say Jack Robinson, in a jiffy, in a flash, in half a shake, right off the bat, like a bat out of hell, like a shot out of hell, hubba-hubba, horseback, like greased lightning> eg *Biegnij tam szybko, co siła! (Run over there quick, on the double!)*

coś koło tego [TSOSH KOH-woh TEH-goh] *adv phr* About; approximately <around, in the ballpark of, pretty near, something like, close shave to, in the neighborhood of, damn near, pretty near> eg *Zapłaciłem dwa tysiące, lub cośkoło tego (I paid two thousand or something like that)*

coś mocniejszego [tsohsh mohts-nyeh-ee-SHEH-goh] *nn phr* Potent liquor such as vodka or whiskey <hard liquor, hard stuff, hooch, booze, stiff drink, poison> eg *Po czymś mocniejszym robi mi się niedobrze (Hard liquor makes me sick)*

coś na ząb [TSOSH nah ZOHMB] *nn phr* A light snack or any light meal <bite, snack, nosh, finger food, munchies, something to chew on, something to munch on> eg *Daj coś na ząb (Give me something to munch on)*

coś niecoś [tsohsh NYEH-tsohsh] *adv phr* A little; not much <bit, wee, tad, wee bit, itty bit> eg *Myślę, że on ma coś niecoś na koncie (I think she does have a bit on her account)*

coś w tym rodzaju [TSOSH f TIM roh-DZAH-yoo] *phr* Something similar or approximate; something to that effect <something like that, something pretty near, something like, close shave, something in the neighborhood of, damn near, pretty near> eg *Zapłaciłem dwa tysiące, lub coś w tym rodzaju koło tego (I paid two thousand or something like that)*

córa [TSOO-rah] *nf* A daughter <sprout, little beaver, little missy, little pumpkin, pride and joy> eg *Ile twoja córa ma lat? (How old is your little beaver?)*

cuchnąć [TSOOKH-nohnch] To have an illegal, immoral, or scandalous quality <smell, stink, stink on ice> eg *Cała ta sprawa naprawdę cuchnie (This whole affairs really stinks)*

cudo [TSOO-doh] (or **cudeńko** [tsoo-DEHÑ-koh] *nn*, **cud-miód** [TSOOT-MYOOT] *nm phr*) Anything beautiful, attractive, extraordinary, admirable <humdinger, hummer, beaut, corker, crackerjack, cat's pajamas, cat's meow, hot shit, hot spit, hot stuff, killer, killer-diller, knockout, lollapalooza, pisser, piss-cutter, ripsnorter, whizbang, tsatske, tchochke, doozie> eg *Jak ci się podoba mój samochód? Cudo, nie? (How do you like my car? A humdinger, isn't it?)*

cudzes See na sępa

cug See iść w cug

cuks [tsooks] *nm* A piece of candy, esp hard candy <jawbreaker> eg *Dasz mi trochę cuksów? (Will you give me some jawbreakers?)*

cwaja [TSFAH-yah] *nf* A failing grade <flunk, flush, F, zip, zippo> eg *Masz trzy cwaje. Nie sądzisz, że powinieneś coś z tym zrobić? (You have three F's. Don't you think you should do something about it?)*

cwaniactwo [tsfah-NYAHTS-tfoh] *npl* Smart, shrewd, or cunning people <smartasses, wiseasses, sharpies, sharks, smoothies> eg *Cwaniactwo chciało dostać podwyżkę (Smartasses wanted to get a pay rise)*

cwaniak [TSFAH-nyahk] (or **cwaniaczek** [tsfah-NYAH-chehk]; **z miodem w uszach** [z MYOH-dehm v OO-shahkh] may be added) *nm* A smart, shrewd, or cunning man <smartass, wiseass, sharpie, shark, smoothie> eg *Ten cwaniaczek zażądał dwóch tysięcy gotówką (That smartass wanted two thousand in cash)*

cwaniara [tsfah-NYAH-rah] *nf* A smart, shrewd, or cunning woman <smartass, wiseass, sharpie, shark, smoothie> eg *Czego chciała ta cwaniara? (What did this wiseass want?)*

cwany [TSFAH-ni] *adj* Smart, shrewd, or cunning <smart-ass, street-smart, street-wise, sly, cagey, foxy, sharp, smooth, in the know, on the inside> eg *Uważaj, to cwany facet (Be careful, he's a foxy guy)*

cwel** [TSFEHL] *nm* **1** A man forced to perform homosexual acts, esp in prison; a passive homosexual <sugar boy, bitch, fag, faggot, fairy, queer, fruitcake, homo, pansy, sissy, swish, daisy, limp-wrist, queen> eg *Wypierdolmy tego cwela (Let's fuck this sugar boy)* **2** A man one dislikes or disapproves of <asshole, fuck, fucker, fuckhead, fuckface, motherfucker, shit, shitface, shithead, shitheel, bastard, jerk, SOB, son of a bitch, son of a whore, cocksucker, prick, dick, dickhead, cuntface, schmuck, scum, scumbag, sleazebag, slimebag, dipshit, pisshead, piece of shit, pain in the ass> eg *Ten cwel nie zapłacił mi ani grosza (That son of a bitch didn't pay me a red cent)*

cyc* [tsits] (or **cycek*** [TSI-tsehk]) *nm* A woman's breast <tit, titty> eg *Myślisz tylko o cycach (All you think about is knockers); Ta lola ma świetne cyce (This doll has real bazooms)*

cycata* [tsi-TSAH-tah] (or **cycasta*** [tsi-TSAHS-tah]) *adj* A large-breasted woman <constructed, stacked, built like a brick shithouse> eg *Panienka z agencji musi być cycate (A call-girl has to be built like a brick shithouse)*

cyce jak donice* [TSI-tseh yahk doh-NEE-tseh] *nm pl* A woman's large breasts <tits, melons, knockers, bazooms, boobs, headlights, hooters, hemispheres> eg *Jego siostra to ma dopiero ma cyce jak donice! (His sister really has some melons!)*

cyk See na gazie

cykać się [TSI-kahch shyeh] *v* To be afraid; to be frightened; to be intimidated <chicken out, turn chicken, turn yellow, run scared, have cold feet, be scared stiff, be scared shitless, shit one's pants, piss one's pants, shit bullets, shit a brick, shit green, be spooked, push the panic button, wimp out> eg *Nie chciał wyjeżdżać. Myślę, że cykał się (He didn't want to leave. I guess he was scared stiff)*

cykor [TSI-kohr] *nm* **1** Fear; nervousness <creeps, shivers, cold feet, jitters, needles, pins and needles, zingers, all-overs, butterflies, dithers, fidgets, heebie-jeebies, jimjams, jumps, quivers, screaming meemies, shakes, shpilkes, willies, goose bumps, stew> eg *On tego nie zrobi, bo ma cykora (He's not going to do it, because he's got the jitters)* **2** A fearful person; a coward <chicken, chicken heart, candy-ass, fraidy cat, scaredy cat, gutless wonder> eg *Jej chłopak, to prawdziwy cykor. Boi się myszy (Her boyfriend is a real candy-ass. He's scared at the sight of mice)*
See dostać cykora, mieć cykora

cymbał See czubek

cynk [tsink] *nm* A piece of important information, given or obtained in advance <tip, hot tip, tipoff, pointer, steer> eg *Gliny dostały cynk o tym napadzie (The cops got a tip about that robbery)*
See dać cynk, dostać cynk

cyrk [tsirk] *nm* A very funny, amusing, or foolish situation <laugh, laugh and a half, laugher, laughing stock, horselaugh, merry ha-ha, hoot, howl, riot, laff riot, laffer, scream, stitch, boffo, panic, knee-slapper, rib-tickler, side-splitter> eg *Powiedział, że zna się na leksykograii. Ale cyrk! (He said he knows lexicography. That's a laugh!)*

cywil See iść do cywila

czacha [CHAH-khah] (or **czaszka** [CHAHSH-kah] *nf* or **czerep** [CHEH-rehp] *nm* or **czajnik** [CHAH-ee-neek] *nm*) *nf* The head <bean, noggin, conk, dome,

gourd, skull> eg *Podrapał się po czaszce (He scratched his noggin; Chcesz dostać w czajnik? (You want me to punch you on the bean?); Skąd masz takiego okropnego siniaka na czerepie? (Where did you get that nasty bump on your conk?)*

See mieć pod czachą

czad [chaht] *nm* A delightful and euphoric sensation; thrill <good time, barrel of laughs, ball, blast, gas, groove, boot, charge, bang, kick, belt, buzz, charge, drive, flash, flip, jolt, lift, rush, upper, wallop, whoopee, fun and games> eg *Ale będzie czad! (Are we going to have a ball!)*

czadownie See centralnie

czadowy [chah-DOH-vi] (or **czadowny** [chah-DOH-vni]) *adj* Excellent; wonderful; extremely good <great, cool, swell, fab, rad, def, far-out, awesome, frantic, terrific, funky, gorgeous, groovy, hellacious, neat, peachy, dandy, baddest, mean, solid, super-dooper, wailing, wicked, gnarly, top-notch, ten, ace-high, A-OK, A-1> eg *Ostry wygląd, czadowa muzyka, piwo w dłoni, nieskrępowany seks - Nowy Wamp*

czaić się [CHAH-eech shyeh] *v* To be frightened or bashful (and esp to delay doing something as a result of this) <chicken out, turn chicken, turn yellow, run scared, have cold feet, be scared stiff, be scared shitless, shit one's pants, piss one's pants, shit bullets, shit a brick, shit green, be spooked, push the panic button, wimp out> eg *Myślę, że ona chce to zrobić, ale się czai (I think she wants to do it but she is chickening out)*

czarna owca [CHAHR-nah OHF-tsah] *nf* Someone who is thought by his family to have brought shame to the family; the worst member in the family <black sheep, black sheep of the family, rotten apple> eg *Moja siostra jest czarną owcą w naszej rodzinie. Zawsze ma problemy z policją (My sister is the black sheep in our family. She's always in trouble with the police)*

czarna robota [CHAHR-nah roh-BOH-tah] *nf phr* Very hard work; a Herculean labor <ball-buster, bone-breaker, back-breaker, bitch, killer, grind, donkeywork, bullwork, dirty work> eg *Potrzebujemy ich do czarnej roboty (We need them for doing donkeywork)*

czarno na białym [CHAHR-noh nah BYAH-wim] *adv phr* Simply; straightforwardly; evidently <in black and white, down in black and white, carved in stone, etched in stone, up front, open and shut, like it is, laid on the line, what you see is what you get, wysiwyg> eg *Tu jest napisane czarno na białym, że to moja własność (It says right here in black and white that it's my property)*

czarnuch* [CHAHR-nookh] (or **czarny** [CHAHR-ni]) *nm* **1** A black person <nigger, niggra, bro, brother, jungle bunny, chocolate drop, darky, groid, inky-dink, blue-skin, boogie, jigaboo, zigaboo, shade, shadow, smoke, spade, spook, coon, Hershey bar> eg *Same czarnuchy i żółtki w tej dzielnicy! (There are only niggers and chinks in this neighborhood)* **2** A Roman Catholic priest <black coat, padre, sky pilot, sky merchant, sky scout, gospel pusher, bible thumper, bible banger, sin hound, rev, abbey, Holy Joe, preacher man> eg *Co ten czarny od ciebie chciał? (What did the padre want from you?)*

See ciemny, mała czarna, na czarną godzinę, pracować na czarno

czarnula [chahr-NOO-lah] (or **mała czarna** [MAH-wah CHAHR-nah] *nf phr*) *nf* A brunette <no slang equivalent> eg *Widzisz tę mała czarną? (Can you see that brunette?)*

czarować się [chah-ROH-vahch shyeh] *v* To be under the illusion; to deceive oneself <kid oneself, play cat and mouse with oneself, beat around the bush, play games, jerk oneself around, dick oneself around, pussyfoot oneself around, snow, blow smoke, pull the wool over one's eyes> eg *Nie czarujmy się. Popsuliśmy całą imprezę (Let's not kid oneselves: We spoiled the whole party)*

czas See kawał czasu, zabijać czas

czaszka See czacha

czekoladowy* [cheh-koh-lah-DOH-vi] *nm* A black person <nigger, niggra, bro, brother, jungle bunny, chocolate drop, darky, groid, inky-dink, blue-skin, boogie, jigaboo, zigaboo, shade, shadow, smoke, spade, spook, coon, Hershey bar> eg *Moja sąsiadka wyszła za czekoladowego (My neighbor married a chocolate drop)*

czepek See w czepku urodzony

czerep See czacha

czerwony* [chehr-VOH-ni] *nm* A communist <commie, comrade, red, pink, lefty, left-winger> eg *Czerwoni wygrali w ostatnich wyborach (The commies won the last elections)*

czeski [CHEHS-kee] (or **czeski niebieski** [CHEHS-kee nyeh-BYEHS-kee]) *adj phr* Not knowlegeable; not acquainted with something; poor at something <not knowing from nothing, not know one's ass from first base, not know one's ass from a hole in the ground, not know one's ass from one's elbow, not know a rock from a hard place, not know diddly-shit, not know shit, not know shit from Shinola, not know zilch, not have a clue, not know the score, not know the time of day, not have the foggiest idea, search me> eg *Jest na bakier z nowymi przepisami (He doesn't know diddly-shit about the new regulations)*

często gęsto [CHEHN-stoh GEHN-stoh] *adv phr* Very frequently <much, all the time, over and over, again and again> eg *Jak był kawalerem, to często gęsto do niej przychodził (When he was a bachelor, he used to visit her much)*

czkawka See odbijać się czkawką

człon* [chwohn] *nm* The penis, esp large <cock, prick, dick, stick, joystick, dipstick, bone, meat, beef, wang, yang, dong, dummy, hammer, horn, hose, jock, joint, knob, pork, putz, rod, root, tool, flute, skin flute, love-muscle, sausage, schmuck, schlong, schvantz, cream-stick, third leg, middle leg, business, apparatus, John, Johnny, Johnson, John Thomas, Jones> eg *Jakiś robak ugryzł go w człona (Some bug bit him on his dick)*

człowiek See swój chłop, zrobić z kogoś człowieka

czołg See jedzie mi tu czołg

czoło See puknąć się w czoło

czort wie See cholera wie

czterdziestka See rycząca czterdziestka

cztery kółka [CHTEH-ri KOOW-kah] *npl phr* An automobile <wheels, set of wheels, four wheeler, crate, ride, cage, trans, transportation, boat, buggy> eg *Ciężko podrywać laski, jak się nie ma własnych czterech kółek (It's hard to pick up chicks without a set of wheels)*

cztery litery [CHTEH-ri lee-TEH-ri] *nn phr* The buttocks, the posterior <ass, butt, bum, behind, back, back seat, seat, bottom, heinie, rear, tush, fanny, derriere, tail, bucket, tokus, keister, kazoo> eg *Siadłabyś na czterech literach i dała mi skończyć (Why don't you sit on your heinie and let me finish)*

czuć blusa [CHOOCH BLOO-sah] (or **kumać blusa** [KOO-mahch BLOO-sah]) *v phr* To understand; to comprehend <get, get it, catch, get the drift, get the picture, get the message, get the hang of, savvy, dig, click, capeesh, read, be with it, see where one is coming from, know where one is coming from> eg *On w ogóle nie poczuł blusa (He didn't get the picture at all)*

czuć do kogoś miętę [CHOOCH doh KOH-gohsh MYEHN-teh] *v phr* To incur a liking, love or affection to someone; to like <take a shine to, have a thing about, take to> eg *Poczuła do niego miętę prawie natychmiast (She took a shine to him almost instantly)*

czuć pismo nosem See mieć nosa

czuć przez skórę See mieć nosa

czuć się łyso [CHOOCH shyeh WI-soh] (or **być komuś łyso** [bich KOH-moosh WI-soh]) *v phr* To be embarrassed, ashamed, or uneasy <feel stupid, be redfaced, have egg on one's face, be uptight, be jittery, be caught short> eg *Nie wiedział co powiedziać. Czuł się bardzo łyso (He didn't know what to say. He felt stupid)*

czuć się jak młody bóg [chooch shyeh yahk MWOH-di book] *v phr* To feel well and healthy, both physically and mentally <feel like a million dollars, feel like a million bucks, feel like a million, be in the pink> eg *Kiedy jestem na wakacjach i jest piękny ranek, czuję sięjak młody bóg (When I'm on vacation and it's a beautiful morning, I feel like a million dollars)*

czuć się jak ryba w wodzie [chooch shyeh yahk RI-bah v VOH-jeh] *v phr* To be comfortable and proficient in a given field or circumstance <feel at home, feel right at home, be at home, be right at home> eg *Wydawało mi się, że ona tam się czuje jak ryba w wodzie (It seemed that she feels right at home)*

czub See brać się za łby, mieć w czubie

czubek* [CHOO-behk] (or **cymbał** [TSIM-bah-oo]) *nm* A stupid, clumsy or ineffectual person; an idiot <airbrain, airhead, birdbrain, blockhead, squarehead, bonehead, bubblebrain, bubblehead, buckethead, cluckhead, cementhead, clunkhead, deadhead, dumbbell, dumbcluck, dumbhead, dumbass, dumbbrain, fatbrain, fathead, flubdub, knukclebrain, knucklehead, lamebrain, lardhead, lunkhead, meathead, musclehead, noodlehead, numbskull, pointhead, scatterbrain, jerk, jerk-off, klutz, chump, creep, nerd, dork, dweeb, gweeb, geek, jackass, lummox, twerp, nerd, bozo, clod, cluck, clunk, dimwit, dingbat, dipstick, dodo, dopey, dufus, goofus, lump, lunk, nitwit, schnook, schlep, schlemiel, schmendrick, schmo, schmuck, simp, stupe> eg *Ten czubek rozbił mój samochód! (That schlemiel crashed my car!); Ale cymbał ze mnie. Zapomniałem prawa jazdy, panie władzo (I'm such a birdbrain. I forgot my driver's license, officer)*

czupiradło [choo-pee-RAHD-woh] *nn* A person with unkempt hair <hippie, hairball, furball, mop> eg *Lepiej byś się uczesała. Wyglądasz jak czupiradło (You'd better comb your hair. You look like a hairball)*

czyjaś w tym głowa [CHI-yahch f tim GWOH-vah] *phr* (It is) Someone's responsibility or ingenuity <it is someone's job, it is someone's problem, someone will take care of this, leave it up to someone> eg *Wygramy. Moja w tym głowa (We'll win. Leave it up to me)*

czysta [CHIS-tah]' (or **czyściocha** [chish-CHYOH-khah]) *nf* Pure, non-flavored vodka <no slang equivalent> eg *Przez cały wieczór piliśmy czystą (We were drinking pure vodka for the whole evening)*

czystka [CHIS-tkah] *nf* An act of getting rid of one's unwanted associates, esp by killing them; a purge <clean house, cleaning, reshuffling, offing, bumping-off, bump-off, knocking-off, knock-off, wiping-off, wipe-off, wiping-out, wipe-out, cleaning-out, clean-out, shaking-out, shake-out, rubbing-out, rub-out, kissing-off, kiss-off, wasting, scragging, liquidation, neutralization> eg *Kto jest odpowiedzialny za tę czystkę? (Who's responsible for the wipe-out?)*

czysto See na rękę, wyjść na czysto

czysty [CHIS-ti] *adj* **1** Legal or lawful <clean, legit, kosher, on the legit> eg *Prowadzą tylko czyste interesy (They conduct only legit businesses)* **2** Sheer; utter; complete <total, pure plain, clean, awful, god-awful, real, mighty, plenty, damn, damned, goddamn, goddamned, blasted, darn, darned, effing, flipping, forking, freaking, frigging, pesky> eg *To czyste wariactwo jechać tam w środku zimy! (It's total madness to go there in the middle of winter)*
See mieć czyste ręce

Ć

ćmok [chmohk] (or **ćwok** [chfohk]) *nm* A silly, clumsy or ineffectual person <airbrain, airhead, birdbrain, blockhead, squarehead, bonehead, bubblebrain, bubblehead, buckethead, cluckhead, cementhead, clunkhead, deadhead, dumbbell, dumbcluck, dumbhead, dumbass, dumbbrain, fatbrain, fathead, flubdub, knukclebrain, knucklehead, lamebrain, lardhead, lunkhead, meathead, musclehead, noodlehead, numbskull, pointhead, scatterbrain, jerk, jerk-off, klutz, chump, creep, nerd, dork, dweeb, gweeb, geek, jackass, lummox, twerp, nerd, bozo, clod, cluck, clunk, dimwit, dingbat, dipstick, dodo, dopey, dufus, goofus, lump, lunk, nitwit, schnook, schlep, schlemiel, schmendrick, schmo, schmuck, simp, stupe> eg *Ale ćwok ze mnie. Zapomniałem prawa jazdy, panie władzo (I'm such a birdbrain. I forgot my driver's license, officer)*

ćpać [chpahch] (perf **naćpać się** [NAH-chpahch shyeh]) *v* To take drugs <do drugs, fix, take a fix, take a hit, take> eg *Jego siostra ćpała w pokoju obok (His sister was in the other room fixing)*

ćpun [chpoon] (or **ćpacz** [chpahch]) *nm* A narcotics user or addict <junkie, druggie, drughead, dopehead, freak> eg *Mamy tu paru załamanych ćpunów, którzy chcieli popełnić samobójstwo (We've got here a few depressed junkies who have tried suicide)*

ćwiartka [CHFYAHRT-kah] *nf* A quarter-liter bottle of vodka <micky, miky> eg *Kupił tylko dwie ćwiartki (He only bought two mickies)*

D

dać [dahch] *v* To assess or estimate someone's age <give, size up, size, check, peg, read, nick, figure, figure out, take one's measure> eg *Ja bym jej dał 20 lat (I'd give her 20)*

dać baty See dać po dupie

dać bobu See dać wycisk

dać ciała See dać dupy

dać cynk [dahch TSINK] *v phr* To give someone a piece of important information, esp in advance <tip, tip off, steer, give a pointer> eg *Jak się dowiem, to dam ci cynk (As soon as I know, I'll tip you off)*

dać do wiwatu See dać wycisk

dać drapaka See dać nogę

dać drapaka See drapnąć

dać dupy* [dahch DOO-pi] (or **dać ciała*** [dahch CHYAH-wah] or **dać plamę*** [dahch PLAH-meh]) *v phr* To fail spectacularly, esp by blundering; to perform very poorly and disgrace oneself <fuck up, screw up, blow, bomb, crash, flop, fold, drop the ball, lose out, strike out, fall flat on one's ass, do an el foldo, lay an egg, lose face, be shot down in flames, go down the tube, step on one's dick> eg *Aleśmy wczoraj dali dupy na meczu! (Did we really blew the game yesterday!)*

dać dyla See dać nogę

dać głowę [dahch GWOH-veh] (or **dać sobie głowę uciąć** [dahch SOH-byeh GWOH-veh OO-chyohnch] or **dać sobie rękę uciąć** [dahch SOH-byeh REHN-keh OO-chyohnch]) *v phr* (To be sure enough) To give something of great value <give one's right arm, bet one's bottom dollar, bet one's life, bet one's boots> eg *Nigdy nie zrobic tego po raz drugi. Dam sobie głowę uciąć (He will never do it a second time. You can bet your bottom dollar on that)*

dać grabę [dahch GRAH-beh] (or **uścisnąć grabę** [oosh-CHEES-nohnch GRAH-beh]) *v phr* To shake hands, as a sign of agreement or reconciliation <slip five, slap five, give someone five, give someone high-five, give someone some skin> eg *No to jak? Dasz grabę? (So what do you say? Will you give me five?)*

dać komuś święty spokój [dahch KOH-moosh SHFYEHN-ti SPOH-koo-ee] *nm phr* To leave someone alone; to stop bothering someone <leave someone alone, lay off, back off, butt out, give someone a break, get off someone's back> eg *Daj mi święty spokój. Pracuję (Lay off me. I'm working)*

dać komuś w łapę [dahch KOH-moosh v WAH-peh] *v phr* (or **posmarować komuś łapę** [poh-smah-ROH-vahch KOH-moosh WAH-peh]) To bribe someone <grease someone's palm, cross someone's palm, oil someone's palm, smear, shmear, pay off> eg *Adwokat dał w łapę sędziemu, żeby orzekł na jego korzyść (The lawyer paid off the judge for deciding the case in the lawyer's favor)*

dać kopa [dahch KOH-pah] (or **dać z kopa** [dahch s KOH-pah] or **dać z lacza** [dahch z LAH-chah] or **dać z fleka** [dahch z fleh-KAH] or **skopać** [SKOH-pahch] or **dokopać** [doh-SKOH-pahch] or **nakopać** [nah-KOH-pahch]) *v phr* To kick someone <kick someone's ass, boot, kick the bejesus out of, kick the shit

out of, kick the living shit out of, kick the bejejus out of, kick the daylights out of, kick someone into the middle of next week, kick the daylights out of, kick someone where he lives> eg *Dał jej z kopa i odszedł (He kicked the shit out of her and left)*

dać kosza [dahch KOH-shah] *v phr* To reject a person who makes a romantic or sexual advance to one <turn down, turn down cold, thumb down, turn thumbs down, give someone his walking papers, give someone his walking ticket, give someone his running shoes, bag, ditch, dump, deep-six, shitcan, chuck, bounce, give the bounce, give the heave-ho, give the kiss-off, kiss goodbye, put the skids> eg *Był zawsze nieogolony, więc dała mu kosza (He was constantly unshaved, so she turned him down)*

dać manto See dać po dupie

dać nogę [dahch NOH-geh] (or **dać dyla** [dahch DI-lah] or **dać drapaka** [dahch drah-PAH-kah]) *v* To leave, depart, or desert, esp hastily <split, beat it, ankle, bag ass, blow, breeze off, burn rubber, butt out, buzz off, check out, cruise, cut and run, cut ass, cut out, drag ass, dust, ease out, fade, fade away, fade out, fuck off, get the fuck out, get the hell out , get going, get moving, get lost, get off the dime, get on one's horse, go south, haul ass, hightail, hit the bricks, hit the road, hop it, make tracks, pull out, scram, set sail, shove off, shuffle along, skate, skip out, split the scene, take off> eg *Jak tylko dotarli do miasta, facet dał nogę (When they reached the town, the guy split)*

dać plamę See dać dupy

dać po dupie* [dahch poh DOO-pyeh] (**w dupę*** [v DOO-peh] or **w skórę** [f SKOO-reh] or **po łapach** [poh WAH-pahkh] or **po uszach** [poh OO-shahkh] or **po głowie** [poh GWOH-vyeh] or **po nosie** [poh NOH-shyeh] or **łupnia** [WOOP-nyah] or **baty** [BAH-ti] or **manto** [MAHN-toh] may replace **po dupie**) *v phr* To beat someone up, esp as a punishment; (figuratively) to punish someone <kick someone's ass, sock, bash, trash, clobber, bang, belt, clock, duke, dust, hammer, land one, lay one on, spank, wham, whack, bam, whip, bust, smack, poke, blast, beat the shit out of, beat the living shit out of, beat the bejejus out of, beat the daylights out of, beat someone into the middle of next week, knock the bejejus out of, knock the daylights out of, knock someone into the middle of next week, hit someone where he lives> eg *Jak zaraz nieprzestaniesz, to dam ci w skórę (If you don't stop right now, I'll beat the shit out of you)*

dać popalić See dać wycisk

dać pyska [dahch PIS-kah] To kiss someone cordially and, usually hug <give someone a buzz, give someone a peck, give someone a smack, give someone a smooch, give someone a kissy-face, give someone a kissy-poo, give someone one on the cheek> eg *Bardzo się cieszę, że Cię widzę. Daj pyska! (I'm so glad to see you. Give me a smooch!)*

dać się nabrać See nabrać się

dać się zwariować See nie dać się zwariować

dać sobie głowę uciąć See dać głowę

dać sobie na luz [dahch SOH-byeh nah LOOS] (or **wziąć sobie na luz** [vzhyohnch SOH-byeh nah LOOS]; **spoko** [SPOH-koh] may replace **luz**) *v phr* (Esp in the imperative as a command) To moderate one's behavior; to calm oneself; to relax <take it easy, hang it easy, go easy, hang loose, lay back, cool out,

cool it, keep it cool, play it cool, give it a rest, don't sweat it, mellow out, lighten up, hold one's horses, keep one's shirt on> eg *Hej, wyluzakuj się. Test jest dopiero jutro (Hey, take it easy. The test's only tomorrow)*

dać sobie na wstrzymanie [dahch SOH-byeh nah fstshi-MAH-nyeh] (or **wziąć sobie na wstrzymanie** [vzhyohnch SOH-byeh nah fstshi-MAH-nyeh]) *v phr* To stop or give up doing something; to resign, surrender, or abandon <knock it off, call it quits, drop it, bag it, can it, stow it, caulk off, come off, cut out, hang it up, lay off, take a break, drop, pull out, bail out, bow out, walk out, check out, drop out, cop out, butt out, push out, snake out, fase out, pass up, pass on, throw in the towel, throw in the sponge, toss in the sponge, toss in the towel, cry uncle, say uncle, toss it in, pack it in, cave in, buckle under, back down, fold, duck, slide, walk, leg, ditch, dump, kick off, knock off, take a walk, quit cold turkey, sideline, call it a day> eg *Te, weź na wstrzymanie i daj spokój, co? Zrobiło się dosyć późno (Why don't you call it quits? It's gotten kind of late)*

dać sobie rękę uciąć See dać głowę

dać sobie w żyłę See ładować sobie w żyłę

dać sobie w gaz [dahch SOH-byeh f GAHS) (or **dać sobie w palnik** [dahch SOH-byeh f PAHL-neek] or **dać sobie w rurę** [dahch SOH-byeh v ROO-reh]; **uderzyć** [oo-DEH-zhich] may replace **dać**) *v phr* To drink alcohol to excess; to get drunk <hit the booze, hit the bottle, hit the sauce, bend the elbow, tank up, guzzle, get alkied, get bagged, get blitzed, get blotto, get blown away, get bent, get boiled, get bombed, get boozed up, get blasted, get bottled, get boxed, get canned, get clobbered, get cooked, get corked, get drunk as a skunk, get edged, get embalmed, get fractured, get fried, get gassed, get ginned, get grogged, get high, get hooched up, get impaired, get illuminated, get juiced, get liquored up, get lit, get loaded, get looped, get lubricated, get smashed, get oiled, get pickled, get plastered, get plonked, get polluted, get sauced, get shitfaced, get sloshed, get soaked, get stewed, get stiff, get stinking drunk, get swizzled, get tanked up, get wiped, get zonked> eg *Zawsze pierwszego lubi dać sobie w palnik (He always gets sauced on payday)*

dać sobie w kaszę dmuchać See **nie dać sobie w kaszę dmuchać**

dać sobie w nosa See ciągnąć nosa

dać szkołę See dać wycisk

dać w długą See iść w długą

dać w dupę See dać po dupie

dać w głowę See dać po dupie

dać w kość See dać wycisk

dać w lewo [DAH-vahch v LEH-voh] *v phr* To turn left <hang a left, hang a louie> eg *Miń trzy przecznice i daj w lewo (Go three blocks and hang a left)*

dać w prawo [DAH-vahch f PRAH-voh] *v phr* To turn right <hang a right, hang a ralph> eg *Czemu nie dałeś w lewo? (Why didn't you hang a right?)*

dać w skórę See dać po dupie

dać wciry See dać wycisk

dać wpierdol** [dahch FPYEHR-dohl] (or **spuścić wpierdol**** [SPOOSH-cheech FPYEHR-dohl]; **wpieprz*** [fpyehpsh] may replace **wpierdol**) *v phr* To beat someone up <kick someone's ass, sock, bash, trash, clobber, bang, belt, clock, duke, dust, hammer, land one, lay one on, spank, wham, whack, bam, whip,

bust, smack, poke, blast, beat the shit out of, beat the living shit out of, beat the bejejus out of, beat the daylights out of, beat someone into the middle of next week, knock the bejejus out of, knock the daylights out of, knock someone into the middle of next week, hit someone where he lives, work over> eg *Zaraz ci dam wpierdol! (I'm going to beat the shit out of you soon!)*

dać wycisk [dahch VI-cheesk] (or **w kość** [f KOHSHCH] or **wciry** [FCHEE-ri] or **do wiwatu** [doh vee-VAH-too] or **szkołę** [SHKOH-weh] or **bobu** [BOH-boo] or **popalić** [poh-PAH-leech] To make someone's life miserable; to torment <kick someone's ass, give someone a hard time, give someone a bad time, give someone hell, jump all over, put the heat on, put the squeeze on, put someone through the wringer, break someone's balls, bust someone's ass, lean on, twist someone's arm, hassle> eg *Jeśli nam dzisiaj nie zapłaci, damy mu wycisk (If he doesn't pay us today, we'll have to lean on him)*

dać z fleka See dać kopa

dać z kopa See dać kopa

dać z lacza See dać kopa

dachować [dah-KHOH-vahch] *v* (Of an automobile) To turn upside down; to capsize <turn turtle, roof, roll> eg *Na skutek kolizji, oba samochody dachowały (After colliding, both cars turned turtle)*

dachowanie [dah-khoh-VAH-nyeh] *nn* (Of an automobile) Turning upside down; capsizing <turtle, turning turtle, roofing, rolling> eg *Jazda skończyła się dachowaniem. Szczęśliwym trafem nikt nie zginął (The ride ended up in turning turtle. Luckily nobody got killed)*

dachowiec [dah-KHOH-vyehts] *nm* A cat, esp a mongrel <kitty, kitty cat, pussy, pusycat, meow meow, Garfield, Sylvester> eg *To zwykły dachowiec (It's an ordinary meow meow)*

daleko w lesie See w lesie

damski bokser [DAHM-skee BOHK-sehr] *nm phr* A man who beats his wife <wife-beater> eg *Jej mąż to damski bokser (Her husband is a wife-beater)*

damulka [dah-MOOL-kah] *nf* A young, attractive, and usually fashionably dressed woman <chick, broad, gal, pussy, cunt, ass, piece of ass, piece, dish, babe, baby, dame, beauty, beaut, beauty queen, baby doll, doll, dolly, dollface, dreamboat, dream girl, eating stuff, eyeful, flavor, looker, good-looker, head-turner, traffic-stopper, honey, killer, hot number, package, knockout, oomph girl, peach, bombshell, sex bunny, sex job, sex kitten, sex pot, table grade, ten, bunny, centerfold, cheesecake, date bait, dazzler, heifer, fluff, quail, sis, skirt, tail, job, leg, tart, tomato, pussycat, cooz, twat> eg *Czego chciała ta damulka? (What did that dame want?)*

darmocha [dahr-MOH-khah] *nf* An act of acquiring something free of charge or anything enjoyed free of charge <freebie, free-o, free gratis, free lunch> eg *Nie ma czegoś takiego jak darmocha (There ain't such a thing as a free lunch)*

dawać [DAH-vahch] (perf **dać** [dahch]) *v* **1** To broadcast over the radio or TV <air, get out, go on the air, telecast, televise> eg *Dawali same powtórki (They aired only reruns)* **2** (or **dawać gazu** [DAH-vahch GAH-zoo]) To drive at very high speed or to accelerate <barrel, barrel along, barrel ass, haul ass, tear, tool, burn rubber, burn the breeze, burn the road, dust, floorboard, fly, step on it, step up, step on the gas, hit the gas, nail it, floor it, push it to the floor, put the pedal to the metal,

put the heel to the steel, drop the hammer down, hammer on, pour on it, pour on the coal, put on the afterburners, gun, rev, rev up, open her up, go flat-out, go full blast, go hell-bent, go like a bat out of hell, go like a blue streak, go like blazes, go like the devil, let her rip, rip-ass, vroom, varoom, zoom> eg *Dawał gazu swoim Porsche na autostradzie (He flew down the highway in his Porsche)* **3** (Esp in the imperative as a command) To bring or call someone, esp instantly <get someone, give someone> eg *Daj mi tego w szarym garniturze. Chcę z nim pogadać (Get me the one in the gray suit. I want to talk with him)* **4*** (or **dawać dupy*** [DAH-vahch DOO-pi]) (Of women) To readily consent to sexual intercourse <put out, give out, spread for, come across> eg *Nie da mu dupy jeśli on nie kupi jej prezentu (She won't put out unless he buys her a present)* **5*** (or **dawać dupy*** [DAH-vahch DOO-pi] or **dawać na prawo i lewo*** [DAH-vahch nah LEH-voh ee PRAH-voh] may be added) (Of women) To be sexually promiscuous <sleep around, screw around, fuck around, screw around the block, fuck around the block, get around, chippy around, swing, shack up, bedhop> eg *Myślał, że jego dziewczyna jest wierna, ale ona dawała dupy na prawo i lewo (He thought his girlfriend was faithful, but she has been screwing around)*

dawać chodu [DAH-vahch KHOH-doo] *v phr* To leave or depart, esp hastily <split, beat it, ankle, bag ass, blow, breeze off, burn rubber, butt out, buzz off, check out, cruise, cut and run, cut ass, cut out, drag ass, dust, ease out, fade, fade away, fade out, fuck off, get the fuck out, get the hell out , get going, get moving, get lost, get off the dime, get on one's horse, go south, haul ass, hightail, hit the bricks, hit the road, hop it, make tracks, pull out, scram, set sail, shove off, shuffle along, skate, skip out, split the scene, take off> eg *Gliny już tu są. Dajemy chodu! (The cops are already here. Let's split!)*

dawać ciszej [DAH-vahch CHEE-sheh-ee] *v phr* To decrease the volume; to reduce the loudness <turn down> eg *Daj ciszej to radio! (Turn that radio down!)*

dawać do buzi See brać do buzi

dawać głośniej [DAH-vahch GWOHSH-nyeh-ee] *v phr* To increase the volume <turn up, pump it up, pump up the volume, crank it, blast it> eg *Daj głośniej radio, nic nie słyszę (Turn the radio up, I can't hear anything)*

dawać komuś po oczach [DAH-vahch KOH-moosh poh OH-chahkh] *v phr* To dazzle or blind <flash, flash in someone's eyes, be flashy, be in someone's eyes> eg *Te światła dają po oczach. Nic nie widzę (These lights are really flashing in my eyes. I can't see anything)*

dawno i nieprawda [DAHV-noh ee nyeh-PRAHV-dah] *adv phr* (Gone) A long time ago <dead and gone, ages ago, jurassic time ago, God knows when, when Hector was a pup> eg *Słyszałam, że byłeś dyplomatą. Tak, ale to było dawno i nieprawda (I heard you were a diplomat. Yes, but it is dead and gone)*

debil* [DEH-beel] *nm* A very stupid, clumsy or ineffectual person; an idiot <airbrain, airhead, birdbrain, blockhead, squarehead, bonehead, bubblebrain, bubblehead, buckethead, cluckhead, cementhead, clunkhead, deadhead, dumbbell, dumbcluck, dumbhead, dumbass, dumbbrain, fatbrain, fathead, flubdub, knukclebrain, knucklehead, lamebrain, lardhead, lunkhead, meathead, musclehead, noodlehead, numbskull, pointhead, scatterbrain, jerk, jerk-off, klutz, chump, creep, nerd, dork, dweeb, gweeb, geek, jackass, lummox, twerp, nerd, bozo, clod, cluck, clunk, dimwit, dingbat, dipstick, dodo, dopey, dufus, goofus,

lump, lunk, nitwit, schnook, schlep, schlemiel, schmendrick, schmo, schmuck, simp, stupe> eg *Ten debil rozbił mój samochód! (That schlemiel crashed my car!)*

decha [DEH-khah] (or **deska** [DEHS-kah]) *nf* A woman with small breast <flast-chested, flat as a board> eg *Z twarzy jest całkiem ładna, szkoda, że taka deska (She's pretty. Too bad she's flat-chested)*
See do gobowej deski, dziura, gaz, od deski do deski, w dechę

decyzja See męska decyzja

deczko [DEHCH-koh] (or **zdeczko** [ZDEHCH-koh] or **zdziebko** [ZHJEHP-koh] *adv* Not much; a little <bit, wee, tad, wee bit, itty bit> eg *Myślę, że ciasto jest ździebko za słodkie (I think the cake is wee to sweet)*

dekować się [deh-KOH-vahch shyeh] (perf **zadekować się** [zah-deh-KOH-vahch shyeh]) *v phr* To avoid work; to shirk duty <goldbrick, goof off, goof around, fuck around, screw around, jerk off, screw off, drag-ass, drag one's ass, drag it, dragtail, fake off, flub the dub, fuck off, fuck the dog, dog it, lollygag, sit on one's ass, soldier, skate, watch the clock> eg *On zawsze dekował (He's always been goldbricking)*

delirka [deh-LEER-kah] *nf* Delirium tremens <shakes, clanks, creeps, DTs, heebie-jeebies, horrors, jim-jams, jumps, screaming meemies, blue devils> eg *Ma fatalną delirkę (He has a bad case of DT's)*

demolka [deh-MOHL-kah] *nf* An act of demolitioning, destroying, or ruining, esp of equipment <smash, squash, trash, smash-up, wrack-up, crack-up, mess-up, screw-up, wipe-off, wipe-out, tear-down, wash-out, knock-out, rub-out, X-out> eg *Ale demolka! (What a smash-up!)*

demoludy [deh-MOH-loot] *npl* The former Eastern Bloc; countries of Eastern Europe that used to be under Soviet domination <iron curtain> eg *To znany uchodźca polityczny. Właśnie uciekł z demoludów (He's a well-known political refugee. He just escaped from behind the iron curtain)*

denat [DEH-naht] (or **dętka** [DEHNT-kah]) *nm* **1** Someone who is very tired or exhausted <dead, dead on one's feet, dead-tired, dog-tired, out of it, out of gas, out of juice, all in, all shot, pooped, bagged, beat, beat to the ground, beat to the ankles, bone-tired, burned out, bushed, chewed, crapped out, done, done in, dragged out, frazzled, played out, fucked out, knocked out, tuckered out, tapped out, had it, ready to drop, on one's last legs> eg *Jestem denat. Zaraz padnę (I'm dead-tired. I'm gonna drop in a second)* **2** Someone who is very drunk <alkied, bagged, blitzed, blotto, blown away, bent, boiled, bombed, blasted, boozed, bottled, boxed, buzzed, canned, clobbered, cooked, corked, crashed, drunk as a skunk, edged, embalmed, fractured, fried, gassed, ginned, grogged, have one too many, half under, high, hooched up, in bad shape, impaired, illuminated, juiced, knocked out, liquored, lit, loaded, looped, lubricated, lushed, smashed, oiled, pickled, plastered, plonked, polluted, sauced, shitfaced, slugged, sloshed, soaked, stewed, stiff, stinking drunk, swizzled, tanked, three sheets to the wind, wiped, zonked, lit up like a Christmas tree> eg *Facet był kompletny denat (The guy was lit up like a Christmas tree)*

dennie [DEHN-nyeh] *adv* Extremely bad; terribly; awfully <lousy, shitty, awful> eg *Dennie się dzisiaj czuję (I feel really lousy today)*

denny [DEHN-ni] *adj* Of inferior quality; shoddy; poor <lousy, awful, bush-league, cheap, crappy, shitty, cruddy, crummy, doggy, low-rent, low-ride, no-good,

raggedy-ass, schlocky, stinking, tacky, trashy, two-bit, dime-a-dozen, fair to middling, garden variety, of a sort, of sorts, piddling, pissy-ass, piss-poor, run-of-the-mill, small-time> eg *Co myślisz o ich najnowszej płycie? Myślę, że jest denna (What do you think about their latest album? I think it's crappy)*

deptać komuś po piętach [DEHP-tahch KOH-moosh poh PYEHN-tahkh] *v phr* To follow very closely behind someone, esp to chase <tread on someone's heels, step on someone's heels, dog someone's heels, dog, shadow, tail, tailgte, trail, track, run down, go after, tag after, stick to> eg *Policja depcze mu po piętach od miesiąca (The police's been tailing him for a month)*

deptak [DEHP-tahk] *nm* A promenade, walk, or a pedestrian zone, esp in downtown <strip, stroll, trail, boardwalk> eg *Klub usytuowany jest na deptaku (The club is located on the main strip)*

deska See decha, do gobowej deski, od deski do deski

deska rodzielcza [DEHS-kah rohz-JEHL-chah] *nf phr* A dashboard <dash> eg *Podoba Ci się deska rodzielcza? (Do you like the dash?)*

deszcz See z deszczu pod rynnę

dętka See denat

dewizowiec [deh-vee-ZOH-vyehts] *nm* (Esp in former communist times) A foreigner who is likely to have or pay with hard currency, esp US dollars; any foreigner <furriner, outsider, stranger, jaboney, jiboney> eg *Coraz więcej dewizowców przyjeżdża to naszego miasta (More and more furriners come to see our city)*

diabeł See iść w cholerę, na diabła, pierdolnąć, tam gdzie pieprz rośnie

diabelnie [dyah-BEHL-nyeh] (or **diabelsko** [dyah-BEHL-skoh] or **diablo** [DYAH-bloh]) *adv* Extremely; exceedingly; very <awful, god-awful, real, mighty, plenty, damn, damned, goddamn, goddamned, darn, darned, effing, flipping, forking, freaking, frigging, fucking, one's ass off, one's brains out, one's head off, to the max, like all get-out, like sin, to beat the band, like all creation, as blazes, as can be, as hell, like hell, in full swing> eg *Słyszałam, że on jest diabelnie inteligentny (I heard he's goddamn intelligent)*

diabli See jak chuj

diabli kogoś biorą [DYAH-blee KOH-gohsh BYOH-roh] *v phr* To get angry or irritated <get pissed off, get peed off, get p'd off, get bent out of a shape, get pushed out of a shape, get browned off, get cranky, get edgy, get sore, get mad as a hornet, get steamed up, get ticked off, get tee'd off, get burned up, go ballistic> eg *Diabli mnie biorą za każdym razem, jak widzę takiego idiotę za kierownicą mojego samochodu (I get pissed off every time I see such an idiot behind the steering wheel of my car)*

diabli wiedzą See cholera wie

dings [deenks] (or **dyngs** [dinks] or **dzyndzel** [DZIN-dzehl]) *nm* Any object, esp unspecified or unspecifiable <thingy, thingamajig, thingum, thingdad, gismo, giz, gadget, widget, dingbat, dingus, grabber, gimmick, whatchamacallit, whatzis, goofus, jigamaree, gigmaree, doodad, doodle, doofunny, doohickey, doojigger, jigger, stuff, bitch, fucker, baby> eg *Po co jest ten dinks? (What is this thingamajig for?)*

dizel [DEE-zehl] *nm* A diesel automobile <smudge potter, boiler, buzz-wagon, oil burner> eg *Ten tu to diesel (This one here is a smudge potter)*

dla jaj [dlah YAH-ee] (or **dla draki** [dlah DRAH-kee] or **dla kawału** [dlah kah-VAH-woo] or **dla zgrywy** [dlah ZGRI-vi] or **dla picu** [dlah PEE-tsoo]) *adv phr* For mere fun or pleasure <for kicks, for laughs, for the hell of it> eg *Dam mu na imię Lothar, dla draki (I'm going to name the baby Lothar, just for kicks); Czemuś to zrobił? Dla jaj (Why did you do it? Just for the hell of it)*

dla ludzi [dlah LOO-jee] *phr* (Developed in such a way so as to be) Easy to use or understand; not sophisticated <user-friendly, for the people, for the common man, plain as mud fence, plain enough to stop a clock, low-tech, folksy, homey, haymish, clean, open and shut, meat-and-potatoes> eg *Musiałem obniżyć trochę jej poziom, tak aby była bardziej dla ludzi (I had to lower its level, so that it could be more folksy)*

dla niepoznaki [dlah nyeh-poh-ZNAH-kee] *adv phr* Meant to disguise or deceive <as a cover-up, as a bluff, as a phony-up, bluffing, putting up a front> eg *Dla niepoznaki miał na sobie mundur policjanta (He was wearing a police uniform as a cover-up)*

dla ubogich [DLAH oo-BOH-geekh] *adj phr* Of inferior quality; shoddy; poor <lousy, awful, bush-league, cheap, crappy, shitty, cruddy, crummy, doggy, low-rent, low-ride, no-good, raggedy-ass, schlocky, stinking, tacky, trashy, two-bit, dime-a-dozen, fair to middling, garden variety, of a sort, of sorts, piddling, pissy-ass, piss-poor, run-of-the-mill, small-time> eg *Cały ten film to porno dla ubogich (The entire movie is a lousy porn)*

dla zmyłki [dlah ZMI-oo-kee] *adv phr* (Of a fact or remark) Intended to mislead, esp to draw people's attention away from the main point <as a red herring, as a put-on, as a frame-up, as a set-up, fake> eg *Oskarżenie zostało zaprojektowane dla zmyłki (The charge was designed as a red herring)*

dłużyzna [DWOO-zhiznah] *nf* A very dull, long, or unnecessary part, esp, of a film; longueur <padding, boost, stretch-out, drag-on, drag-out, spun-out, run-out, hold-off> eg *W tym filmie było dużo niepotrzebnych dłużyzn (The movie was full of unnecessary padding)*

długi See iść w długą, mieć długi język

dmuchać See nie dać sobie w kaszę dmuchać, nie w kij dmuchał

dmuchnąć See dupnąć

dnice See cyce jak donice

dno [dnoh] *nn* The worst and most loathsome place or situation imaginable <the pits, the armpit, the cellar, the asshole, bottom rung, rock bottom> eg *Ta szkoła to dno (This school is the pits)*

do łopaty See iść do łopaty

do bani See do dupy

do cholery See cholera, iść w cholerę

do chrzanu See do dupy

do chuja See chuj

do diabła See iść w cholerę

do diabła [doh DYAHB-wah] (or **u diabła** [oo DYAHB-wah]; **do wszystkich diabłów** [doh FSHIST-keekh DYAHB-woof] or **do jasnej anielki** [doh YAHS-neh-ee ah-NYEHL-kee] or **do licha** [doh LEE-khah] or **do pioruna** [doh pyoh-ROO-nah] or **do stu piorunów** [do stoo pyoh-ROO-noof] or **do jasnej ciasnej** [doh YAHS-neh-ee CHYAHS-neh-ee]) *excl* An exclamation of anger, irritation, disappointment, shock <shit, fuck, hell, heck, damn, damn it, goddamn it, gosh, golly, gee, jeez, holy fuck, holy cow, holy moly, holy hell, holy mackarel, holy shit, jumping Jesus, fucking shit, fucking hell> eg *Do diabła, przegraliśmy ten mecz! (Shit! We lost that game!)*

do dupy See wlazić komuś do dupy

do dupy z czymś/kimś* [doh DOO-pi s chimsh/keemsh] *phr* (An exclamation of irritation or anger) Something or someone is bad, poor, worthless, or of inferior quality <to hell with, to heck with, to fuck with, the hell with, the heck with, the fuck with> eg *Do dupy z takim telefonem! (To hell with that phone!)*

do dupy* [doh DOO-pi] (or **do bani** [doh BAH-nee] or **do chrzanu** [doh KHSHAH-noo] or **do kitu** [doh KEE-too] or **do luftu** [doh LOOF-too] or **do niczego** [doh nee-CHEH-goh]) *adj phr* Bad, poor, worthless, or of inferior quality <lousy, awful, bush-league, cheap, crappy, shitty, cruddy, crummy, doggy, low-rent, low-ride, no-good, raggedy-ass, schlocky, stinking, tacky, trashy, two-bit, dime-a-dozen, fair to middling, garden variety, of a sort, of sorts, piddling, pissy-ass, piss-poor, run-of-the-mill, small-time> eg *Ten magnetowid, który kupiłeś jest naprawdę do dupy (The VCR that you bought is real shitty); Silnik jest w porządku, ale zawieszenie jest do luftu (The engine's OK, but the suspension is trashy)*

do galopu See brać kogoś do galopu, brać się

do gazu [doh GAH-zoo] *phr* (An exclamation used to show opposition and dislike) We do not want someone <down with, to hell with, fuck someone, screw someone, nuke someone, give someone the chair> eg *Ludzie krzyczeli: komuniści do gazu! (The people shouted: Down with communists!)*

do gobowej deski [doh groh-BOH-veh-ee DEH-skee] (or **do gobowej dechy** [doh groh-BOH-veh-ee DEH-khi] or **do usranej śmierci*** [doh oo-SRAH-neh-ee SHMYEHR-chee] or **do upadłego** [doh oo-pahd-WEH-goh]) *adv phr* Till the very end, esp till your life's end; forever; endlessly, interminably, or permanently <for keeps, for ever so long, forever and amen, for good, around the clock, day and night, forever and a day, till hell freezes over, till the cows come home, for a dog's age, for a month of Sundays, for donkey's years, for God knows how long, for ages> eg *Mój profesor powiedział mi, że będę pisał te słowniki do usranej śmierci (My professor told me that I'm going to write dictionaries till hell freezes over)*

do góry nogami [doh GOO-ri noh-GAH-mee] *adv phr* In the wrong order, esp, in a reversed position; in a state of complete disorder <upside down, ass backwards, back asswards, topsy turvy, cart before the horse> eg *Cały system wywrócony jest do góry nogami (The entire system is topsy turvy)*

do jasnej anielki See do diabła

do jasnej ciasnej See do diabła

do kitu See do dupy

do kupy See wziąć się do kupy

do kurwy nędzy See kurwa

do licha See do diabła

do luftu See do dupy

do niczego See do dupy

do ściany See jak groch o ścianę

do oporu [doh oh-POH-roo] (or **do bólu** [doh BOO-loo]) *adv phr* To an extreme degree <to the max, flat-out, all-out, all the way, like hell, like all get-out, like sin,

to beat the band, like all creation, like it had gone out of style, like there was no tomorrow, like nobody's business, one's ass off, one's brains out, one's head off, the whole nine yards, nine to the dozen> eg *Pił z beczułki do oporu (He was drinking from the keg like nobody's business)*

do pioruna See do diabła

do ręki See na rękę

do roboty See brać się

do rzeczy [doh ZHEH-chi] **1** *adj phr* (Esp about a person) Quite good, attractive or wonderful <great, cool, swell, fab, rad, def, far-out, awesome, frantic, terrific, funky, gorgeous, groovy, hellacious, neat, peachy, dandy, baddest, mean, solid, super-dooper, wailing, wicked, gnarly, top-notch, ten, ace-high, A-OK, A-1, some, pretty good, ten, drop-dead gorgeous, knock-out gorgeous, dishy, hunky> eg *Na pierwszy rzut oka dziewczyna była całkiem do rzeczy (At first glance, the girl was real cool)* **2** *adv phr* Relevant to the subject; making sense <to the point, on target, just what the doctor ordered, on the right track, right-on> eg *Obawiam się, że muszę panu przerwać. Proszę mówić do rzeczy (I'm afraid I'll have to interrupt you. Please, get on the right track); Jego wykład był do rzeczy (His lecture was right-on)*

do słupa See jak groch o ścianę

do stu piorunów See do diabła

do szpiku kości See przemarznąć na kość

do tańca i różańca [doh TAHÑ-tsah ee roo-ZHAHÑ-tsah] *adj phr* (Of a person) Amiably balanced; agreeable; both joyous and responsible <Mr. Nice Guy, good Joe, total package, princey, pussycat, all reet, all root, all righty, all-around, righteous, fine and dandy, kopasetic, hunky-dory> eg *Ten twój kuzyn to do tańca i różańca! (That cousin of yours is a total package!)*

do upadłego See do gobowej deski

do usranej śmierci See do gobowej deski

do wszystkich diabłów See do diabła

do wyboru do koloru [doh vi-BOH-roo doh koh-LOH-roo] *phr* You cannot designate anything not included here; whatever you want <you name it, any old thing you want> eg *Ma ciało, talent, inteligencję, do wyboru do koloru (She got looks, talent, intelligence, you name it)*

dół See iść w dół

doładować See dopierdolić

dołożyć See dopierdolić

dołożyć [doh-WOH-zhich] *v* (In sports) To defeat decisively; to beat; to trounce <bash, trash, dish, whack, whomp, whip, KO, kayo, bust, total, zap, waste, bump, kick someone's ass, kick someone's butt, put down, smack down, shoot down, tear down, shoot down in flames, punch out, wipe out, beat up, beat the shit out of, beat the bejejus out of, beat the hell out of, beat the shit out of, beat the living shit out of, knock dead, knock out, knock the shit out of, knock the bejejus out of, blast, kill, squash, finish off, blow off, blow away, clobber, bushwack, butcher, ice, knock off, knock out, murder, nuke, polish off, put away, roll over, rub out, sandbag, scalp, scrag, shellac, stomp, trash, work over> eg *Dołóżmy im! (Let's knock them dead!); Dołożyliśmy im (We kicked their ass)*

dołować [doh-WOH-vahch] (perf **zdołować** [zdoh-WOH-vahch]) *v* To depress someone <bring down, down, drag, bug, damper, chill, faze, beat, beat down, bum

out, turn off, put down, run down, play down, be a downer, be a bummer, give someone the blues, give someone a bad trip, throw cold water on, throw a wet blanket on, put the needle in> eg *Ta wiadomość naprawdę mnie zdołowała (This news really brought me down)*

dobierać się [do-BYEH-rahch shyeh] (perf **dobrać się** [DOH-brahch shyeh]) *v* **1** To invite or request sexual favors; to attempt to fondle <make a pass at, put a move on, make a play for, cop a feel, feel up, grope, pet, neck, grab-ass> eg *Gdy wszyscy wyszli, zaczął się do niej dobierać (After everybody left, he started to feel her up)* **2** (or **dobierać się do skóry** [do-BYEH-rahch shyeh doh doh SKOO-ri] or **dobierać się do dupy*** [do-BYEH-rahch shyeh doh DOO-pi] To start to make someone's life miserable <get to someone, kick someone's ass, give someone a hard time, give someone a bad time, give someone hell, jump all over, put the heat on, put the squeeze on, put someone through the wringer, break someone's balls, bust someone's ass, lean on, twist someone's arm, hassle> eg *Dobiorą się do ciebie prędzej czy później (They'll kick your ass sooner or later)*

dobra w te klocki [DOHB-ri f teh KLOHTS-kee] *adj phr* (Of a woman) Able to copulate well or satisfactorily <good in bed, G.I.B., good in bed, sex machine, fuck machine, nympho> eg *Słyszałem, że twoja przyjaciółka jest naprawdę dobra w te klocki (I heard your friend is a real fuck machine)*

dobroć See dzień dobroci dla zwierząt

dobry [DOHB-ri] *adj* (Esp about a distance or period of time) Big <way, whale, helluva, whaling, spanking, whopping, mother> eg *To jeszcze dobry kawał drogi (It's still a helluva a distance to go)*

See dobry w te klocki, mieć spust

dobry w te klocki [DOHB-ri f teh KLOHTS-kee] *adj phr* (Of a man) Able to copulate well or satisfactorily <good in bed, G.I.B., good in bed, sex machine, fuck machine, nympho> eg *Pali i ma zły oddech, ale jest dobry w te klocki (He smokes, and he has bad breath, but he's G.I.B.)*

dobrze See robić komuś dobrze, robić sobie dobrze

dobrze [DOHB-zheh] *adv* Very; extremely <way, far cry, good bit, fair bit, fair sight> eg *Było już dobrze po północy (It was way after midnight)*

dochodzeniówka [doh-khoh-dzheh-NYOOF-kah] *nf* The police unit in charge of homicide; police in general <kojaks, cops, coppers, flatfeet, flatties, fuzzies, pigs, gumshoes, nabs, paddies, finest, elbows, bluecoats, big Johns, arms, yard bulls, smokies, bears, smokey bears> eg *Zabierzcie stąd tych z dochodzeniówki (Get these kojaks out of here)*

dociągnąć [doh-CHYOHNG-nohch] *v* To live to be of a certain age <gun for, push, hit, get> eg *Mam nadzieję, że dociągnę do trzydziestki (I'm hoping to push thirty)*

docierać [doh-CHEH-rahch] (perf **dotrzeć** [DOHT-shehch]) *v* To become understood or comprehended by someone <sink in, get, get it, catch, get the drift, get the picture, get the message, get the hang of, savvy, dig, click, capeesh, read, be with it, see where one is coming from, know where one is coming from> eg *Wiadomość była takim szokiem, że jeszcze do mnie nie dotarła (The news was such a shock it still hasn't sunk in yet); Nic do niego nie dotarło (He didn't get it at all)*

docierać się [doh-CHYEH-rahch shyeh] (perf **dotrzeć się** [DOHT-shehch shyeh]) *v* (Esp about a relationship) To adjust itself; to shape up well <work out,

work itself out, work out fine, fit in, fix up> eg *Wszystko się niedługo dotrze (Everything will soon work itself out)*

dogadywać się [doh-gah-DI-vahch shyeh] (perf **dogadać się** [doh-GAH-dahch shyeh]) *v* **1** To make oneself understood; to communicate <get across, get one's point across, interface, relate, touch base, be on the same wavelength, be on someone's wavelength, have the same vibes, be tuned in, find a common ground> eg *Nie dogadywali się za bardzo (They weren't getting their point across too well)* **2** To reach an agreement; to compromise <okay, OK, shake hands, shake on, sign on, clinch, cut, go along with, play ball, come across, come around, trade off, meet halfway, strike a happy medium, make a deal, fit in> eg *Nie martw się, w końcu się dogadają (Don't worry, they'll eventually shake hands)*

doić [DOH-eech] (perf **wydoić** [vi-DOH-eech]) *v* **1** To drink alcohol, esp quickly or in large quantities <knock back, guzzle, gargle, lap, tank up, slug down, swig, sling back> eg *Wydoił trzy piwa pod rząd (He knocked back three beers in a row)* **2** To take financial advantage of someone; to wheedle money out of someone <sponge, mooch, scrounge, milk> eg *Od wielu lat doi pieniądze od ciotki (He's been sponging on his aunt for many years)*

doigrać się [doh-EE-grahch shyeh] *v* (Of a person) To come to a bad end, esp to get the punishment one deserves <get one's comeuppance, get what is coming to someone, get what one's asked for, serve someone right, be in line for> eg *Zawsze obraża ludzi, no i w końcu się doigrał (He's always insulting people, but he finally got his comeuppance)*

doje* [DOH-yeh] *nf* A woman's large breasts <tits, melons, knockers, bazooms, boobs, headlights, hooters, hemispheres> eg *Widziałeś doje tej laski? (Did you see the knockers on that chick?)*

dojeść See przejeść się

dojna krowa See krowa dojna

dojścia [DOH-eesh-chyah] *nm pl* Powerful contacts; influenial connections; influence <clout, drag, pull, juice, network, channels, ropes, strings, wires, suction> eg *Znasz kogoś, kto ma dojścia u prezesa banku? Do you know anyone who has some pull with the bank president?)*

dokładka [doh-KWAHT-kah] *nf* An additional serving of food at a meal; a second helping <seconds> eg *Poprosił o dokładkę (He asked for seconds)*
See na dokładkę

dokopać See dać kopa

dokumentnie [doh-koo-MEHNT-nyeh] *adv* Extremely; exceedingly; very <awful, god-awful, real, mighty, plenty, damn, damned, goddamn, goddamned, darn, darned, effing, flipping, forking, freaking, frigging, fucking, one's ass off, one's brains out, one's head off, to the max, like all get-out, like sin, to beat the band, like all creation, as blazes, as can be, as hell, like hell, in full swing> eg *Ona jest dokumentnie zgrabna (She's damn shapely)*

dokumentny [doh-koo-MEHNT-ni] *adj* Cursed; damnable; bad <fucking, damn, damned, goddamn, goddamned, god-awful, blasted, darn, darned, effing, flipping, forking, freaking, frigging, pesky> eg *Twój brat to dokumentny idiota (Your brother is a damn idiot)*

dola [DOH-lah] *nf* One's share of a sum <bite, whack, cut, divvy, piece, slice, takeout, chunk, take> eg *Kto wziął jego dolę? (Who took his cut?)*

dolać See dopierdolić

dolec [DOH-lehts] *nm* A US dollar <buck, green, greenie, greenback, smacker, bone, clam> eg *Będzie cię to kosztowało dwieście dolców (It'll set you back two hundred bucks)*

dolewka [doh-LEHF-kah] *nf* An additional serving of soup at a meal; a second helping <seconds, refill> eg *Poprosił o dolewkę (He asked for a refill)*

doliniarz [doh-LEE-nyahsh] *nm* A professional pickpocket, esp operating in a crowd <dip, cannon, tool, wire, meachanic, cutpurse, digger, file, forks, five fingers, finger, fingersmith, greasy finger, gun, knucker, picks, friskers, hooks, spitter, jostler, clipper, stickup man, lifter> eg *Policjanci właśnie aresztowali dwóch doliniarzy (The policemen just arrested two dips)*

dom bez klamek See **dom wariatów**

dom wariatów [DOHM vah-RYAH-toof] (or **dom bez klamek** [DOHM behs KLAH-mehk] or **wariatkowo** [vahr-yaht-KOH-voh] *nn*) *nm phr* A mental hospital; an insane asylum <bughouse, loony bin, bin, booby hatch, crazy house, nut house, nut farm, nut college, nut box, nut hatch, nut factory, funny farm, cackle factory, laughing academy, warehouse, rubber room, soft walls> eg *Zaraz pójdę do domu wariatów! (I feel like I'm about ready for the loony bin!)*

domowy See **kura domowa**

dopierdalać się** [doh-pyehr-DAH-lahch shyeh] (perf **dopierdolić się**** [doh-pyehr-DOH-leech shyeh]; or **dopieprzać się*** [doh-PYEHP-shahch shyeh] perf **dopieprzyć się*** [doh-PYEHP-shich shyeh]; or **dopierniczać się*** [doh-pyehr-NEE-chahch shyeh] perf **dopierniczyć się*** [doh-pyehr-NEE-chich shyeh]; or **dopierdzielać się*** [doh-pyehr-JEH-lahch shyeh] perf **dopierdzielić się*** [doh-pyehr-JEH-leech shyeh]; or **dowalać się** [doh-VAH-lahch shyeh] perf **dowalić się** [doh-VAH-leech shyeh]) *v* To criticize someone or something, esp if not deserved; to have ungrounded complaints or remarks <pick on, trip on, nitpick, trash, bash, knock, slam, hit, clobber, blast, rake, needle, bitch, go after, stick to someone, give someone the needle, give someone the heat, give someone a hard time, give someone a bad time, give someone hell, kick someone's ass, cut in half, cut to bits, jump all over, jump on, lean on, land on, come down hard on, put down, run down, take down, throw the book at, put the heat on, put the squeeze on, put someone through the wringer, break someone's balls, bust someone's ass, twist someone's arm, hassle> eg *Czemu on się zawsze do mnie dopierdala? (Why is he always picking on me?)*

dopierdolić** [doh-pyehr-DOH-leech] (or **dopieprzyć*** [doh-PYEHP-shich] or **dopierniczyć*** [doh-pyehr-NEE-chich] or **dopierdzielić*** [doh-pyehr-JEH-leech] or **dołożyć** [doh-WOH-zhich] or **dosolić** [doh-SOH-leech] or **dosunąć** [doh-SOO-nohnch] or **doładować** [doh-wah-DOH-vahch] or **dolać** [DOH-lahch] or **dowalić** [doh-VAH-leech] *v* To beat someone up <kick someone's ass, sock, bash, trash, clobber, bang, belt, clock, duke, dust, hammer, land one, lay one on, spank, wham, whack, bam, whip, bust, smack, poke, blast, beat the shit out of, beat the living shit out of, beat the bejejus out of, beat the daylights out of, beat someone into the middle of next week, knock the bejejus out of, knock the daylights out of, knock someone into the middle of next week, hit someone where he lives, work over> eg *Zagroził, że mi dopierdoli (He threatened to beat the living shit out of me)*

doprawić się See zaprawić się

dorabiać [doh-RAH-byahch] (or **dorabiać sobie** [doh-RAH-byahch SOH-byeh] may be added, perf **dorobić** [doh-ROH-beech]) *v* To have a part-time job, esp of an assignment nature <gig, moonlight, have a job on the side> eg *Jestem najszczęśliwszy, gdy dorabiam (I'm the happiest when I'm gigging)*

dorobkiewicz [doh-rohp-KYEH-veech] *nm* A person having only recently become rich and tending to tastelessly spend a lot of money to prove one's wealth; a nouveau riche <slick, new rich, new money, Johnny-come-lately> eg *Nie ma nic bardziej obrzydliwego niż dorobkiewicze (There's nothing more disgusting than the new rich)*

dorwać się [DOHR-vahch shyeh] *v* **1** To get access to something desired; to acquire or gather something <get, catch, grab, bag, collar, cop, dig up, drag, hook, land, nab, nail, snag, pull down, pull in, rack in, knock down, get hold of, get one's hands on, lay one's hands on, glom on to, get down to> eg *W parę sekund dorwał się do tego laptopa (He got his hands on this laptop within a few seconds)* **2** To become actively engaged in something; to apply oneself to something; to energetically get into action; to accelerate or concentrate one's efforts <set about, go about, get down to, get down to business, get one's ass in gear, snap it up, snap to it, make it snappy, step on it, get the lead out, get a hump on, get a hustle on, get a move on, get one's ass, get cracking, get going, get one's finger out of one's asshole, get off one's ass, get it on, get off the dime, hop to it, hump, hustle, pour it on, pour on the coal, shake a leg, shake the lead out, gas up, goose up, hop up, jump up, pump up, rev up, buckle down> eg *Szybko dorwał się do roboty (He quickly got down to business)*

doskok See z doskoku

dosolić See dopierdolić

dostać baty See dostać po dupie

dostać bobu See dostać wycisk

dostać bzika See dostać świra

dostać cholery [DOH-stahch khoh-LEH-ri] (or **dostać kurwicy**** [DOH-stahch koor-VEE-tsi] or **dostać białej gorączki** [DOH-stahch BYAH-weh-ee goh-ROHNCH-kee]) *v phr* To become furious or irritated <get pissed off, get peed off, get p'd off, get bent out of a shape, get pushed out of a shape, get browned off, get cranky, get edgy, get sore, get mad as a hornet, get steamed up, get ticked off, get tee'd off, get burned up, go ballistic> eg *Mój ojciec dostanie cholery, jak się tego dowie (My father is going to get peed off when he learns about that); Dostaję białej gorączki za każdym razem, jak widzę takiego idiotę za kierownicą mojego samochodu (I get pissed off every time I see such an idiot behind the steering wheel of my car)*

dostać cykora [DOH-stahch tsi-KOH-rah] (or **dostać pietra** [DOH-stahch PYEHT-rah] or **dostać stracha** [DOH-stahch STRAH-khah]) *v phr* To become afraid; to become frightened; to become intimidated <chicken out, turn chicken, turn yellow, run scared, get cold feet, get scared stiff, get scared shitless, shit one's pants, piss one's pants, shit bullets, shit a brick, shit green, get spooked, push the panic button, wimp out> eg *Nie chciał wyjeżdżać. Myślę, że dostał pietra (He didn't want to leave. I guess he got spooked)*

dostać cynk [DOH-stahch TSINK] *v phr* To obtain a piece of important information, esp in advance <get a tip, get a tipoff, get a hot tip, get a tipoff, get a pointer, get a steer> eg *Gliny dostały cynk o tym napadzie (The cops got a tip about that robbery)*

dostać do wiwatu See dostać wycisk

dostać kopa [DOH-stahch KOH-pah] (or **dostać z kopa** [DOH-stahch s KOH-pah] or **dostać z lacza** [DOH-stahch z LAH-chah] or **dostać z fleka** [DOH-stahch z fleh-KAH]) *v phr* To get kicked <get kicked, get kicked on the ass, get booted> eg *Dał jej z kopa i odszedł (He kicked the shit out of her and left)*

dostać kopa w górę [DOH-stahch KOH-pah v GOO-reh] *v phr* To advance; to get promoted, esp in order to remove one from their position <get kicked upstairs, get upped, upgrade, win one's wings> eg *Dwa tygodnie temu dostał kopa w górę i jest teraz wicedyrektorem (Two weeks ago he got upped and he's now deputy president)*

dostać kosza [DOHS-tahch KOH-shah] *v phr* To get rejected by a person whom one makes a romantic or sexual advance <get turned down, get turned down cold, get thumbed down, get one's walking papers, get one's walking ticket, get one's running shoes, get bagged, get ditched, get dumped, get deep-sixed, get shitcanned, get chucked, get bounced, get the bounce, get the heave-ho, get the kiss-off> eg *Dostał kosza dwa razy w tym tygodniu (He got dumped two times this week)*

dostać kurwicy See dostać cholery

dostać manto See dostać po dupie

dostać świra [DOH-stahch SHFEE-rah] (**bzika** [BZHEE-kah] or **fioła** [FEE-yoh-wah] or **fisia** [FEE-shyah] or **hopla** [KHOHP-lah] or **kota** [KOH-tah] or **kręćka** [KREHNCH-kah] or **pierdolca**** [pyehr-DOHL-tsah] or **zajoba*** [zah-YOH-bah] or **szmergla** [SHMEHRG-lah] or **szajbę** [SHAH-ee-beh] or **kuku na muniu** [KOO-koo nah MOO-nyooh] or **kiełbie we łbie** [KYEH-oo-byeh VEH-oo-byeh] or **fiksum-dyrdum** [FEEK-soom DIR-doom] may replace **świra**) *v phr* To become obsessed, insane or eccentric <go crazy, go crazy as a loon, blow one's cork, blow one's top, blow a fuse, crack up, freak out, flip out, go ape, go bananas, go bent, go bonkers, go cracked, go dopey, go ga-ga, go half-baked, go loony, go loopy, go mental, go nerts, go nuts, go nutty, go off one's nut, go off one's rocker, go off one's base, go off the track, go off the trolley, go out one's skull, go psycho, go schizo, go screwy, go wacky, go weird, go wild, schiz out, psych out, come unglued, come unstuck, come unwrapped, come unzipped, go to pieces> eg *Od wojny każdy może dostać kota (War is enough to make anyone go crazy); Dostał hopla na punkcie zarabiania pieniędzy (He went nerts about earning money); Dostał kręćka na punkcie tej dziewczyny (He went bananas over that girl); Facet dostał kuku na muniu, gdy mu napisała, że chce się z nim kochać (The guy went bananas when she wrote him she wanted to make love to him); Jego siostra dostała pierdolca, gdy zdechł jej kot (His sister came unglued after the cat got killed)*

dostać pietra See dostać cykora

dostać po łapach See dostać po dupie

dostać po dupie* [DOH-stahch poh DOO-pyeh] (**w dupę*** [v DOO-peh] or **w skórę** [f SKOO-reh] or **po łapach** [poh WAH-pahkh] or **po uszach** [poh OO-shahkh] or **po głowie** [poh GWOH-vyeh] or **po nosie** [poh NOH-shyeh] or **łupnia** [WOOP-nyah] or **baty** [BAH-ti] or **manto** [MAHN-toh] may replace **po dupie**) *v phr* To be beaten up, esp as a punishment; (figuratively) to be punished

<get kicked on the ass, get socked, get bashed, get trashed, get clobbered, get banged, get belted, get clocked, get duked, get dusted, get hammered, get spanked, get whammed, get whacked, get bammed, get whipped, get busted, get smacked, get poked, get blasted, get worked over> eg *Jak zaraz nieprzestaniesz, to dam ci w skórę (If you don't stop right now, I'll beat the shit out of you)*

dostać po kieszeni See bić po kieszeni

dostać wpierdol** [DOH-stahch FPYEHR-dohl] (or **dostać wpieprz*** [DOH-stahch fpyehpsh]) *v phr* To be beaten someone up <get kicked on the ass, get socked, get bashed, get trashed, get clobbered, get banged, get belted, get clocked, get duked, get dusted, get hammered, get spanked, get whammed, get whacked, get bammed, get whipped, get busted, get smacked, get poked, get blasted, get worked over> eg *Zaraz ci dam wpierdol! (I'm going to beat the shit out of you soon!)*

dostać wycisk [DOH-stahch VI-cheesk] (or **w kość** [f KOHSHCH] or **wciry** [FCHEE-ri] or **do wiwatu** [doh vee-VAH-too] or **szkołę** [SHKOH-weh] or **bobu** [BOH-boo] or **popalić** [poh-PAH-leech] To be subjected to maltreatment, misery, and torment <get kicked on the ass, get a hard time, get a bad time, get hell, get the heat, get the squeeze, be put through the wringer, have one's balls broken, have one's ass busted, get leaned on, have one's arm twisted> eg *Jeśli nam dzisiaj nie zapłaci, damy mu wycisk (If he doesn't pay us today, we'll have to lean on him)*

dostać z fleka See dostać kopa

dostać z kopa See dostać kopa

dostać z lacza See dostać kopa

dostać zajoba See dostać świra

dosunąć See dopierdolić

dowalać się See dopierdalać się

dowalić See dopierdolić

dowcipas [dohf-CHEE-pahs] *nm* A witty, extravagant, disorderly or man <artist, joker, kidder, clown, article, ham, character, item, number> eg *Z tego twojego kuzyna to prawdziwy dowcipas; poszedł na egzamin końcowy w szortach! (Your cousin is a real joker: He went to his final exam wearing shorts!)*

drągal See dryblas

drab See dryblas

draka See dla jaj

draka [DRAH-kah] *nm nf* A scandalous fact or situation; a scandal <gas, hot potato, bad scene, bad news, can of worms, bag of worms, takedown, putdown, shit, serious shit, deep shit, deep water, drag, bind, bitch, bummer, downer, headache, double trouble, snafu, pain in the ass, pain in the neck, spot, mess, holy mess, pickle, squeeze, hard time, glitch, stinker, skeleton, skeleton in the closet, sizzler, scorcher, dynamite, Watergate, fine kettle of fish, fine how do you do, fine cup of coffee, big stink, curtains, lights out, game's over> eg *Jak mnie złapią, to będzie granda (Bad scene for me if they find me)*

drań [drahñ] (or **zimny drań** [ZHEEM-ni DRAHÑ]) *nm* A ruthless and unscrupled man one dislikes or disapproves of <asshole, fuck, fucker, fuckhead, fuckface, motherfucker, shit, shitface, shithead, shitheel, bastard, jerk, SOB, son of a bitch, son of a whore, cocksucker, prick, dick, dickhead, cuntface, schmuck, scum,

scumbag, sleazebag, slimebag, dipshit, pisshead, piece of shit, pain in the ass> eg *Na twoim miejscu zignorowałabym tego drania (If I was you, I would ignore that bastard)*

drapnąć [DRAHP-nohnch] *v* **1** To steal; to rob <heist, boost, burgle, nurn, bag, buzz, highjack, hoist, hold up, hook, hustle, jump, kick over, knock off, knock over, lift, move, mug, nab, nick, nip, pinch, pluck, roll, rustle, snatch, snitch, stick up, swipe, take off, put the grab on, go south with> eg *Drapnęła to z drogerii (He lifted that from a drugstore)* **2** To catch a criminal; to arrest <bust, bag, claw, clip, collar, cop, flag, grab, haul in, jab, knock, pinch, nab, nail, nick, pick up, pull in, run in, sidetrack, put the collar on, put the sleeve on> eg *Wiedziałem, że policja prędzej czy później go drapnie (I knew the police would nab him sooner or later)* **3** (or **dać drapaka** [dahch drah-PAH-kah]) To leave, depart, or desert, esp hastily <split, beat it, ankle, bag ass, blow, breeze off, burn rubber, butt out, buzz off, check out, cruise, cut and run, cut ass, cut out, drag ass, dust, ease out, fade, fade away, fade out, fuck off, get the fuck out, get the hell out , get going, get moving, get lost, get off the dime, get on one's horse, go south, haul ass, hightail, hit the bricks, hit the road, hop it, make tracks, pull out, scram, set sail, shove off, shuffle along, skate, skip out, split the scene, take off> eg *Jak tylko dotarli do miasta, facet dał nogę (When they reached the town, the guy split)*

drętwa mowa See mowa-trawa

drętwy [DREHNT-fi] *adj* Boring, monotonous, insipid, or too official and conventional <lame, flat, flat as a pancake, dull as dishwater, ho-hum, hum-drum, dullsville, deadsville, dragsville, square, beige, blah, yawny, dragass, draggy> eg *Impreza była naprawdę drętwa (The party was real lame)*

drink [dreenk] (or **drynk** [drink]) *nm* A drink of liquor, esp potent <snort, finger, jigger, pull, shot, nip, gargle, guzzle, slug, hit> eg *Co powiesz na kolejnego drinka? (How about another shot?)*

drinkować [dreen-KOH-vahch] (or **drynkować** [drin-KOH-vahch]; perf **zadrinkować** [zah-dreen-KOH-vahch] or **zadrynkować** [zah-drin-KOH-vahch]) *v* To drink alcohol, esp in large quantities <booze, guzzle, gargle, bend the elbow, hit the bottle, hit the sauce, knock back, lap, tank up, wet one's whistle, hang a few on, slug down, swig> eg *Twój brat to dopiero lubi dryknować (Your brother sure likes to wet his whistle)*

drobiazg [droh-BYAHSK] *nm* A baby or a young child <knee biter, carpet rat, rug rat, little fella> eg *Jak tam się mają twje dwa drobiazgi? (How are the two knee biters of yours?)*

drobne [DROHB-neh] (or **drobniak** [drohb-NYAH-kee]) *npl* Money at hand and to spare, usually in coins of low denominations <loose change, spare change, nickles, dimes, nickles and dimes> eg *Chciałem pomóc, ale nie miałem przy sobie drobnych (I wanted to help but I didn't have any loose change)*

droga See kpisz czy o drogę pytasz

droga wolna [DROH-gah VOHL-nah] *excl phr* There is noone or nothing to stop you, esp no enemy or danger is in sight <coast is clear> eg *Strażnik odszedł! Droga wolna! (The watchman's gone! The coast is clear!)*

drogówka [droh-GOOF-kah] *nf* Traffic police, esp a highway patrol <bear, black and white, battlewagon, paddywagon, bearmobile, pigmobile, fuzzmobile, Black Maria> eg *Pod tamtym mostem jest drogówka (There's a bear hiding under that bridge)*

drugie [DROO-gyeh] *nn* A main course <no slang equivalent> eg *Co jest na drugie? (What's for the main course?)*

drut See obciągać prosty jak drut

drutociąg* [droo-TOH-chyohng] (or **druciara*** [droo-CHYAH-rah] *nf*) *nm* A person who performs fellatio <cock-sucker, dick-sucker, peter-eater, come-freak> eg *Ten drutociąg podszedł do mnie i chciał wiedzieć, spod jakiego jestem znaku (This dick-sucker came up to me and wanted to know my sign)*

dryblas [DRIB-lahs] (or **drągal** [DROHN-gahl] or **drab** [drahp]) *nm* A tall and big man <he-man, macho, muscleman> eg *Był najwiekszym dryblasem z całej szkoły (He was the biggest muscleman in our school)*

dryg [drig] *nf* A special natural skill or ability <bent, knack, hang, feel, what it takes> eg *On nie ma drygu do sztuki (He doesn't have a knack for art)*

dryndać [DRIN-dahch] (or **dryndnąć** [DRIND-nohnch]; perf **przedryndać** [psheh-DRIN-dahch]) *v* To telephone <make a call, buzz, ring, jingle, honk, horn, give someone a buzz, give someone a ring, give someone a jingle, give someone a honk, give someone a tinkle, get one on the line, get one on the horn> eg *Myślę, że powinieneś do niej przedryndać (I think you should give her a buzz)*

drynk See drink

drynkować See drinkować

drzeć mordę* [dzhehch MOHR-deh] (**pysk** [psik] or **pyska** [PIS-kah] or **ryj*** [RI-ee] or **ryja*** [RI-yah] or **ryło*** [RI-woh] or **gębę** [GEHM-beh] may replace **mordę**; or **drzeć się** [DZHEHCH shyeh]) *v phr* To scream; to shout; to complain loudly <holler, holler out, beller, yawp, fuss, stink, scene, make a ceremony, beef, bleed, hassle, kvetch, bitch, beef, gripe, piss, bellyache, grouse, growl, squawk, cut a beef, make a stink, piss up a storm, raise a stink, blow up a storm, kick up a storm, eat someone's heart out, fuck around, screw around, mess around, trip> eg *Zrobię, co chcesz, tylko przestań drzeć mordę! (I'll do what you want, just stop bitching)*

drzeć sobie łacha z kogoś [DZHEHCH SOH-byeh WAH-khah s KOH-gohsh] (or **ciągnąć sobie łacha z kogoś** [CHYOHNG-nohnch SOH-byeh WAH-khah s KOH-gohsh]) *v phr* To deceive in fun; to have fun at someone's expense <poke fun at, kid, kid around, pull someone's leg, pull someone's string, fool around, jive, josh, shuck, lark, spoof, send up, cut down> eg *To nie może być prawda. Ciągniesz sobie ze mnie łacha (That can't be true. You're kidding me); Zawsze drą sobieze mnie łacha (They're always cutting me down)*

drzwi See pi razy oko

duże niebieskie oczy [DOO-zheh nyeh-BYEHS-kyeh OH-chi] *npl phr* A woman's breasts, esp large <big brown eyes, melons, knockers, bazooms, boobs, headlights, hooters, hemispheres> eg *Jestem całkowicie normalny. Tylko marzę o lasce z dużymi niebieskimi oczami (I am normal. I only dream about a chick with big brown eyes)*

duże pieniądze See ciężkie pieniądze

dużo wody w Wiśle upłynie [DOO-zhoh VOH-di v VEESH-leh oop-WI-nyeh] *phr* Much time will have to pass before something happens <much water will pass under the bridge> eg *Zapewne dużo jeszcze wody w Wiśle upłynie zanim to nastąpi (Much water will pass under the bridge before that happens)*

dudek See wystrychnąć kogoś na dudka

dupa* [DOO-pah] (or **dupcia*** [DOOP-chyah] or **dupka*** [DOOP-kah] or **dupeńka*** [doo-PEHÑ-kah] or **dupeczka*** [doo-PEHCH-kah] or **dupencja*** [doo-PEHN-tsyah]) *nf* **1** A young and attractive woman <chick, broad, gal, pussy, cunt, ass, piece of ass, piece, dish, babe, baby, dame, beauty, beaut, beauty queen, baby doll, doll, dolly, dollface, dreamboat, dream girl, eating stuff, eyeful, flavor, looker, good-looker, head-turner, traffic-stopper, honey, killer, hot number, package, knockout, oomph girl, peach, bombshell, sex bunny, sex job, sex kitten, sex pot, table grade, ten, bunny, centerfold, cheesecake, date bait, dazzler, heifer, fluff, quail, sis, skirt, tail, job, leg, tart, tomato, pussycat, cooz, twat> eg *Fajna z niej dupcia, chociaż trochę gadatliwa (She' s a nice babe, but a little talkative); Jest piątek wieczór. Gdzie tu zarwać jaką dupę? (It's Friday evening. Where am I going to get a piece of ass?); Myślę, że jesteś niezła dupa i chcesz mnie bardzo (I think you're a nice piece of ass and you want me); Słyszałem, że wasza matematyca to całkiem niezła dupcia (I hear you math teacher is a fine broad)* **2** The buttocks; the posterior <ass, butt, bum, behind, back, back seat, seat, bottom, heinie, rear, tush, fanny, derriere, tail, bucket, tokus, keister, kazoo> eg *Zabieraj stąd swoją dupę (Get your ass out if here); Dupęmi odmroziło (My ass got freezed off)* **3** (or **dupeusz*** [doo-PEH-oosh] *nm* or **dupa wołowa*** [DOO-pah voh-WOH-vah]) *nf* An ineffectual or sluggish person; a botcher <underachiever, loser, born loser, second-rater, schlemiel, schmendrick, schmo, schnook, screwup, fuckup, hacker, muffer, scrub, dub, dool tool, turkey, lump, buterfingers, fumble-fist, goof, goof-off, goofball, eightball, foulball, klutz, also-ran, never-was, nonstarter> eg *Ta dupa wołowa nawet nie wiedziała, jak włączyć toster (That shlemiel didn't even know how to turn on the toaster)*

See móc kogoś pocałować, brać dupę w troki, chuj ci w dupę, ciemno że w mordę daj, dać dupy, dać po dupie, dawać, dobierać się, dostać po dupie, ganiać za kobietami, leżeć bykiem, lizać komuś dupę, mieć coś/kogoś gdzieś, mieć robaki w dupie, móc sobie w dupę wsadzić, nie ma dupy, pierdolić w dupę, pijany jak świnia, robić komuś koło dupy, trząść dupą, upić się jak świnia, własna skóra, włazić komuś do dupy, wrzód na dupie, z palcem, zarabiać na dupie, zawracać komuś głowę, zawracać sobie głowę, zawracanie głowy, zimno że dupę urywa

dupczyć się* [DOOP-chich shyeh] *v* **1** (Of a woman) To be sexually promiscuous <fuck around, screw around, screw around the block, fuck around the block, sleep around, chippy around, swing, shack up, bedhop> eg *Ludzie mówią, że dupczy się od paru miesięcy (She's been known to fuck around for several months)* **2** To copulate <get screwed, get fucked, get laid, screw, fuck, fork, frig, ball, bang, boink, bonk, boff, hump, poke, shag> eg *Dupczył się z jakąś kelnerką po pracy (He used to fuck some waitress after hours)*

dupczyć* [DOOP-chich] (perf **wydupczyć*** [vi-DOOP-chich]) *v* To copulate with someone <fuck, screw, lay, ball, bang, boink, boff, boogie, bop, frig, hump, poke, shag> eg *Dupczył ją tylko dwa razy (He only fucked her two times)*

dupek* [DOO-pehk] *nm* A man one dislikes or disapproves of, esp a fool <asshole, fuck, fucker, fuckhead, fuckface, motherfucker, shit, shitface, shithead, shitheel, bastard, jerk, SOB, son of a bitch, son of a whore, cocksucker, prick, dick, dickhead, cuntface, schmuck, scum, scumbag, sleazebag, slimebag, dipshit, pisshead, piece of shit, pain in the ass> eg *Czy ten dupek wie z kim rozmawia? (Does that asshole know whom he's talking to?)*

duperele* [doo-peh-REH-lah] *npl* **1** Unimportant or unnecessary things; trifles <excess baggage, deadwood, third wheels> eg *Wywal te wszystkie duperele (Get rid of all this excess baggage)* **2** (or **dyrdymały** [dir-di-MAH-wi]) Nonsense; absurdities; pretentious or deceitful talk <bull, bullshit, BS, bullshine, bunk, baloney, applesauce, eyewash, hogwash, hot air, crock, crock of shit, piece of shit, pile of shit, shit, dogshit, horseshit, shit for the birds, crap, crapola, poppycock, smoke, hokum, garbage, trash, horsefeathers, smoke, all that jazz, jazz, jive, malarkey, gobbledygook, double-talk, bafflegab, blah-blah, phony-baloney, fiddle-faddle, twiddle-twaddle, mumbo-jumbo, yackety-yack> eg *Za dużo już się nasłuchałem twoich dupereli (I've heard enough of your bullshit)*

dupeusz See dupa

dupiata* [doo-PYAH-tah] (or **dupiasta*** [doo-PYAH-stah]) *adj* A woman with large buttocks <lard-assed, fat-assed> eg *Dajcie mi jaką dupiastą piczkę, i to szybko! (Give me some fat-assed broad, fast!)*

dupnąć* [DOOP-nohnch] *v* **1** (or **dmuchnąć** [DMOOKH-nohnch]) To steal; to rob <heist, boost, burgle, nurn, bag, buzz, highjack, hoist, hold up, hook, hustle, jump, kick over, knock off, knock over, lift, move, mug, nab, nick, nip, pinch, pluck, roll, rustle, snatch, snitch, stick up, swipe, take off, put the grab on, go south with> eg *Dupnął to z drogerii (He nicked that from a drugstore)* **2** To catch a criminal; to arrest <bust, bag, claw, clip, collar, cop, flag, grab, haul in, jab, knock, pinch, nab, nail, nick, pick up, pull in, run in, sidetrack, put the collar on, put the sleeve on> eg *Wiedziałem, że policja prędzej czy później go dupnie (I knew the police would nab him sooner or later)*

dupowaty* [doo-poh-VAH-ti] *adj* Ineffectual or sluggish <underachiever, loser, born loser, second-rater, schlemiel, schmendrick, schmo, schnook, screwup, fuckup, hacker, muffer, scrub, dub, dool tool, turkey, lump, buterfingers, fumble-fist, goof, goof-off, goofball, eightball, foulball, klutz, also-ran, never-was, nonstarter> eg *O rety, ale on jest dupowaty! (Geez, he's a real goofball of a person)*

dupsko* [DOOPS-koh] *nn* Large buttocks <fat-ass, lard-ass> eg *Luknij na dupsko tej damulki (Check out the lard-ass on that dame)*

dureń* [DOO-rehñ] *nm* A stupid, foolish, or ineffectual person; an idiot <shit for brains, airbrain, airhead, birdbrain, blockhead, squarehead, bonehead, bubblebrain, bubblehead, buckethead, cluckhead, cementhead, clunkhead, deadhead, dumbbell, dumbcluck, dumbhead, dumbass, dumbbrain, fatbrain, fathead, flubdub, knukclebrain, knucklehead, lamebrain, lardhead, lunkhead, meathead, musclehead, noodlehead, numbskull, pointhead, scatterbrain, jerk, jerk-off, klutz, chump, creep, nerd, dork, dweeb, gweeb, geek, jackass, lummox, twerp, nerd, bozo, clod, cluck, clunk, dimwit, dingbat, dipstick, dodo, dopey, dufus, goofus, lump, lunk, nitwit, schnook, schlep, schlemiel, schmendrick, schmo, schmuck, simp, stupe> eg *Ten twój chłopak to prawdziwy dureń. Oblał taki łatwy egzamin (That boyfriend of yours is a real airbraind. He flunked such an easy exam)* See wychodzić na durnia

durnieć [DOOR-nyehch] (perf **zdurnieć** [ZDOOR-nyehch]) *v* **1** To lose mental fitness; to become obsessed, insane or eccentric <go crazy, go crazy as a loon, blow one's cork, blow one's top, blow a fuse, crack up, freak out, flip out, go ape, go bananas, go bent, go bonkers, go cracked, go dopey, go ga-ga, go half-baked, go loony, go loopy, go mental, go nerts, go nuts, go nutty, go off one's nut, go off

one's rocker, go off one's base, go off the track, go off the trolley, go out one's skull, go psycho, go schizo, go screwy, go wacky, go weird, go wild, schiz out, psych out, come unglued, come unstuck, come unwrapped, come unzipped, go to pieces> eg *Całkowicie zdurniała, gdy zdechł jej kanarek (She went to pieces when her canary died)* **2** To become bewildered, disoriented, or confused <get spaced out, get mixed up, get discombobulated, get flabbergasted, get messed up, get unscrewed, get farmisht, get balled up, get shook up, get floored, get unglued, get unzipped, get fried, get screwed-up, get fucked-up, get flummoxed, get kerflooey, get caught off base> eg *Zdurniała, gdy to usłyszała (She got farmisht when she heard that)*

durnota [door-NOH-tah] *nf* Stupidity <stupid thing, silly-ass thing, stupidom, klutzdom> eg *Co za durnota! (What a stupid thing to do!)*

durnowaty See durny

durny [DOOR-ni] (or **durnowaty** [door-noh-VAH-ti]) *adj* **1** Senseless, idiotic, or clownish <loony, batty, daffy, jackass, screwloose, jerky, nerdy, kooky, sappy, crazy, crazy as a loon, dopey, ga-ga, half-baked, loopy, mental, nerts, nuts, nutty, psycho, schizo, screwy, wacky, weird, wild> eg *Nie lubię takich durnych filmów (I don't like such loony movies)* **2** Unimportant, worthless, paltry or derisory <measly, piddly, pissy> eg *Ile go to kosztowało? Durne dwa tysiące (How much did it set him back? Measly two thousand)*

dusza See bez grosza, co dusza pragnie

duszkiem See pić duszkiem

dwa razy brzydszy od gówna* [dvah rah-zi BZHIT-shi ohd GOOV-nah] (or **trzy razy brzydszy od gówna*** [tshi rah-zi BZHIT-shi ohd GOOV-nah]) *adj phr* Very ugly, repulsive <fugly, fucking ugly, piss-ugly, plug-ugly, ugly as cat-shit, ugly as sin, homely, homely as a mud fence> eg *Jego narzeczona jest dwa razy brzydsza od gówna (His fiancee is homely as a mud fence)*

dwója [DVOO-yah] *nf* A failing grade <flunk, flush, F, zip, zippo> eg *Mam dwa zaliczenia i trzy dwóje (I got two passes and three flunks)*

dwójarz [DVOO-yahsh] *nm* A failing student <flunky, dropout> eg *Nie zadawaj się z tym dwójarzem (Don't hang around with that flunky)*

dwudziestka [dvoo-JEHST-kah] (or **dwudziecha** [dvoo-JEH-khah]) *nf* Any bill or coin valued twenty; esp a twenty zloty bill <double saw, twenty-spot> eg *Masz dla mnie dwudziestkę? (You got a double saw for me?)*

dycha [DI-khah] (or **dziesiątka** [jeh-SHYOHNT-kah]) *nf* **1** Any bill or coin valued ten, esp a ten zloty bill <tenner, ten-spot, saw> eg *Mówi, że chce za to tylko pięc dych (He says he only wants five tenners for it)* **2** Ten years, esp a ten-year prison sentence <both hands, tenner, ten-spot> eg *Dostał dychę za tę kradzież (He got a tenner for that theft)*

dykta [DIK-tah] *nf* Methylated spirits or any other alcohol not intended for drinking, but consumed by an addict who is in need <no slang equivalent> eg *Wypije nawet dyktę (He will even drink metyhyl)*

dym [dim] (or **dymy** [DI-mi]*npl*) *nm* A scandalous fact or situation; a scandal or disturbance <gas, fuss, stink, hot potato, bad scene, bad news, can of worms, bag of worms, takedown, putdown, shit, serious shit, deep shit, deep water, drag, bind, bitch, bummer, downer, headache, double trouble, snafu, pain in the ass, pain in the neck, spot, mess, holy mess, pickle, squeeze, hard time, glitch, stinker,

skeleton, skeleton in the closet, sizzler, scorcher, dynamite, Watergate, fine kettle of fish, fine how do you do, fine cup of coffee, big stink, curtains, lights out, game's over> eg *Jak mnie złapią, to będzie dym (Bad scene for me if they find me)*
See puścić coś z dymem

dymać* [DI-mahch] (perf **wydymać*** [vi-DI-mahch]) *v* (Of a man) To copulate with someone <fuck, screw, lay, ball, bang, boink, boff, boogie, bop, frig, hump, poke, shag> eg *Często udaje nam się poderwać jakąś małolatę i ostro razem ją wydymać (Sometimes we manage to pick up a teenage girl and ball her)*

dyngs See dings

dynie* [DI-nyeh] *npl* A woman's large breasts <tits, melons, knockers, bazooms, boobs, headlights, hooters, hemispheres> eg *Widziałeś dynie tej laski? (Did you see the knockers on that chick?)*

dyr [DIR] (or **dyro** [DI-roh]) *nm* A director, leader or executive <boss, chief, big boy, big cheese, big enchilada, top brass, honcho, big man, man upstairs, top dog, key player, exec, numero uno> eg *Co powiedział dyr? (What did the big cheese say?)*

dyrdymały See duperele

dyrektorować [di-rehk-toh-ROH-vahch] (or **dyrektorzyć** [di-rehk-TOH-zhich]) *v* To work as a director, leader or executive; to control; to manage <boss, be at the helm, be in the driver's seat, call the shots, crack the whip, head up, mastermind, rule the roost> eg *On dyrektoruje tu od pięciu lat (She's been in the driver's seat here for five years)*

dyscyplinarka [dis-tsi-plee-NAHR-kah] *nf* Discharge or discharge notice <ax, air, boot, bum's rush, kiss-off, sack, pink slip, walking papers, walking ticket> eg *Wszystek 2000 pracowników dostało dziś dyscyplinarki (All 2,000 employees got pink slips today)*

dysko [DIS-koh] (or **dysk** [DISK] *nm*) *nn* A discotheque <disco> eg *Chcesz iść na dysk? (Do you want to go to a disco?)*

dywanik See wezwać kogoś na dywanik

działka [JAH-oo-kah] *nf* **1** One's share of a sum <bite, whack, cut, divvy, piece, slice, takeout, chunk, take> eg *Kto wziął jego działkę (Who took his bite?)* **2** One's profession, occupation or concern <racket, line, bag, kick, biz, game, cup of tea> eg *Leksykografia to moja działka (Lexicography is my racket)* **3** Money given to someone illegally or unethically; a bribe <graft, gravy, payoff, payola, smear, shmear, grease, palm grease, palm. oil, boodle, kickback, envelope> eg *Wszyscy policjanci byli skorumpowani, brali działki od prostytutek (All the policemen were corrupt, getting kickbacks from the prostitutes)* **3** A dose of a narcotic <fix, bang, hit> eg *Ile kosztuje tu jedna działka? (How much is a hit here?)*
See odpalać

dziabnąć [JAHB-nohnch] *v* To have a quick drink of liquor <knock back, down, slug down, swig, tank, tank up> eg *Dziabnął cztery piwa i zaczął bekać (He downed three beers and started to burp)*

dziad [jahd] (or **dziadyga*** [jah-DI-gah]) *nm* **1** A man, esp an old one <gramps, old fart, old bugger, geezer, gaffer, old-timer, fossil> eg *Dziad myślał, że mu wszystko wolno (That old fart thought that he could do anything)* **2** A slow-witted, conventional or uncultured man, esp from the country <bumpkin, hick, hillbilly, clodhopper> eg *Nie zachowuj się jak dziad (Don't act like you were a country bumpkin)*

dziadostwo [jah-DOH-stfoh] *npl* **1** The poor <have-nots, white trash, lower folk> eg *Dziadostwo szuka jakiejś szansy (The have-nots are looking for a chance)* **2** Anything worthless, useless, or of shoddy quality; trash <schlock, dreck, garbage, junk, lemon, crap, piece of crap, shit, piece of shit, dogshit, sleaze> eg *Skądżeś wziął to dziadostwo chłam? (Where did you get this garbage from?)*

dziadowski [jah-DOHF-skee] *adj* Bad, poor, worthless, or of inferior quality <lousy, awful, bush-league, cheap, crappy, shitty, cruddy, crummy, doggy, low-rent, low-ride, no-good, raggedy-ass, schlocky, stinking, tacky, trashy, two-bit, dime-a-dozen, fair to middling, garden variety, of a sort, of sorts, piddling, pissy-ass, piss-poor, run-of-the-mill, small-time> eg *To jedzenie było naprawdę dziadowskie (The food was real lousy)*

dziany See nadziany

dzieci See robić dzieci

dzieciak See dzieciuch, zrobić komuś dzieciaka

dzieciarnia [jeh-CHAHR-nyah] *nf* A group of children <brat pack, kiddies> eg *Dzieciarnia poszła na lekcje (The kiddies went to class)*

dzieciaty [jeh-CHYAH-ti] *adj* Having children <no slang equivalent> eg *Czy on jest dzieciaty? (Does he have any children?)*

dzieciorób* [jeh-CHYOH-roop] *nm* A man who has many children <children-maker> eg *Zadaje się z tym dzieciorobem (She's been hanging around this children-maker)*

dzieciuch [JEH-chyookh] (or **dzieciak** [JEH-chyahk]) *nm* **1** A boy or young man <boyo, kid, shrimp, sprout, little man> eg *Nie zabijaj go. To tylko dzieciak (Don't kill him. He's just a kid)* **2** An adult who is unreasonable and immature <childish> eg *Nie bądź taka dzieciak i przestań się mazać (Don't be so childish and stop whining)*

dziecko See wylać dziecko z kąpielą, zrobić komuś dzieciaka

dzień See mieć ciche dni, na dniach, na wejściu, rozbój w biały dzień, w biały dzień

dzień dobroci dla zwierząt [jehñ doh-BROH-chee dlah ZVYEH-zhohnt] *nm phr* A day when someone is exceptionally friendly, polite, or helpful for others, esp because of good mood <love-your-neighbor day, be-good-to-someone's-day> eg *Dlaczego jej pomógł? Nie wiadomo, może dla niego to był akurat dzień dobroci dla zwierząt? (Why did he help her? Nobody knows. Maybe it was be-good-to-her day?)*

dziesiąta woda po kisielu [jeh-SHOHN-tah VOH-dah poh kee-SHYEH-loo] (or **dziewiąta woda po kisielu** [jeh-VYOHN-tah VOH-dah poh kee-SHYEH-loo] or **siódma woda po kisielu** [SHYOOD-mah VOH-dah poh kee-SHYEH-loo]) *nf phr* A distant relative, for example third and fourth cousin <shirttail kin, kissing cousin> eg *To mój daleki krewny. Dziesiąta woda po kiesielu (He's my distant cousin. A shirttail kin)*

dziesiątka See dycha, strzał w dziesiątkę, strzelić w dziesiątkę

dziewczynka [jehf-CHIN-kah] *nf* A prostitute <hooker, hustler, pro, call girl, floozy, chippy, bimbo, quiff, slut, working girl, street walker> eg *Impreza była świetna. Była trawka, alkohol, dziewczynki (The party was great. We had grass, booze, call girls)* See ganiać za kobietami

dziewczynka na telefon [jehf-CHIN-kah nah teh-LEH-fohn] (or **panienka na telefon** [pah-NYEHN-kah nah teh-LEH-fohn]) *nf phr* A prostitute who is always on call <call girl, dial-a-pussy, rent-a-fuck> eg *Pracowała przez rok jako dziewczynka* *na telefon zanim nie wyszła za niego (She had worked as a call-girl for a year before she married him)*

dziewucha [jeh-VOO-khah] *nf* A teenage girl or a young woman <chick, chicklet, teen, teener, teeny-bopper, bubble-gummer, little lady> eg *W naszej klasie są same brzydkie dziewuchy (Our class is nothing but ugly chicks); To dziewuchy strasznie jara (This really turns on all the chicks)*

dziki [JEE-kee] *adj* Madly and crudely exuberant; untamed; uncouth <crazy-asssed, wild-assed, wild and woolly, screwloose> eg *Skądżeś wziął tego dzikiego faceta? (Where'd you get that wild-assed guy from?)*

dziób [joop] *nm* The mouth <yap, bazoo, kisser, trap> eg *Nie rozmawiaj z pełnym dziobem (Don't talk with a full bazoo); Zamknij dziób! (Shut your trap!)*

dziunia [JOON-yah] (or **dziumdzia** [JOOM-jah]) *nf* A young and unintelligent woman <chick, silly goose> eg *Nie wiem co się stało, ale dziunia wyglądała na przestraszoną (I don't know what happened, but the chick looked scared)*

dziura [JOO-rah] *nf* **1*** (or **dziurka*** [JOOR-kah]) The vulva, vagina <hole, slit, slot> eg *Wygoliłem jej dziurkę (I shaved her slit); Nie jest taka znowu młoda. Wie od czego jest dziurka (She's not so young. She knows what a hole is for)* **2** (or **dziupla** [JOOP-lah]) Any dirty, shabby, dilapidated, or repulsive place, esp an apartment <dump, hole, hellhole, rathole, shithole, shithouse, joint, firetrap> eg *Urodził się w okropnej dziurze (He was born in a terrible rathole)* **3** (or **dziura zabita dechami** [JOO-rah zah-BEE-tah deh-KHAH-mee] or **wieś zabita dechami** [VYEHSH zah-BEE-tah deh-KHAH-mee]) A small town, esp in the country; any place far from civilization <jerk town, jerkwater town, backwater, hellhole, rathole, mudhole, real hole, noplaceville, hicksville, whistle stop, dump, armpit, East Jesus, Bumfuck Egypt> eg *To miejsce to prawdziwa dziura (This place is a real hole); Dość mam życia w tej dziurze (I have enough of living in this mudhole)*

dziurawiec [joo-RAH-vyehts] *nm* A daughter <sprout, little beaver, little missy, pride and joy> eg *Ile twoje dziurawce mają lat? (How old are your little beavers?)*

dziwka* [JEEF-kah] *nf* **1** A prostitute or promiscuous woman <floozy, bimbo, slut, bitch, cunt, whore, hooker, chippy, quiff, swinger, easy lay, easy make, alley cat, dirty-leg, roundheels, nympho, piece of ass, punchboard, town bike> eg *Tylko wam wódka i dziwki w głowie (All you care is booze and quiffs)* **2** A woman, esp despicable or promiscuous one <slut, bitch> eg *Ona go tylko naciąga. Dziwka jedna (She's using him as a free ride. Bitch!); Odkrył, że jego dziewczyna spała z jego najlepszym przyjacielem. Ale z niej dziwka! He found out that his girlfriend was sleeping with his best friend. What a slut!)*

See męska dziwka

dziwkarz* [JEEF-kahsh] *nm* A sexually voracious man, esp one who often goes to prostitutes <whore-hopper, whore-hound, whore-monger> eg *Nie był żadnym dziwkarzem, ale porządnym mężem (He was no whore-hopper, but a decent husband)*

dzwony [DZVOH-ni] *npl* Pants with legs that become wider at the bottom <bell-bottoms, bells, bottoms> eg *Luknij na tego faceta w dzwonach (Check out the guy in bell-bottoms); Ta laska miała na sobie dzwony (The chick had bottoms on)*

dzyndzel See dings

dżampreza See impreza

dżoint [JOH-eent] (or **dżojnt**) *nm* A marijuana cigarette <joint, reefer, weed, killer stick, tea stick, hemp, Mary Jane, MJ> eg *Zawsze pali dżointy (He always smokes joints)*

E

echo See bez echa

ekipa [eh-KEE-pah] *nf* A group of people who are intimate and close <folks, pack, bunch, crew, gang, clan, crowd, boys> eg *Cała ekipa w końcu dortarła tu wczoraj (The whole crew finally got here yesterday); Lubiłem naszą ekipę (I really loved our gang)*

ekstra [EHK-strah] **1** *adj* Excellent; wonderful <great, cool, swell, fab, rad, def, far-out, awesome, frantic, terrific, funky, gorgeous, groovy, hellacious, neat, peachy, dandy, baddest, mean, solid, super-dooper, wailing, wicked, gnarly, top-notch, ten, ace-high, A-OK, A-1, some> eg *Ten samochód jest na prawdę ekstra (This car is real cool)* **2** *adv* Extremely; exceedingly <awful, god-awful, real, mighty, plenty, damn, damned, goddamn, goddamned, darn, darned, effing, flipping, forking, freaking, frigging, fucking, one's ass off, one's brains out, one's head off, to the max, like all get-out, like sin, to beat the band, like all creation, as blazes, as can be, as hell, like hell> eg *Byliśmy ekstra zmęczeni (We were mighty tired)* **3** *adv* (Esp about money) Additionally; extra <gravy, jelly, cake> eg *Jest z tego jakiś ekstra profit? (Is there any gravy out of it?)*

elegancik [eh-leh-GAHN-cheek] *nm* A pretensionally elegant man <dandy, fancypants, poser> eg *Jakiś bubek chaiał ze mną zatańczyć (Some fancypants wanted to dance with me)*

elegancja-francja [FRAHNTS-yah eh-leh-GAHNTS-yah] (or **francja-elegancja** [eh-leh-GAHNTS-yah FRAHNTS-yah]) *nf phr* Something elegant, stylish, or admirable; elegance; stylishness <class, high class, spiff, snazz, ritz, swank, posh, plush, shine, dash, splash, splurge, fancy-schmancy> eg *Facet wie, jak się ubierać. Prawdziwa elegancja-francja (The guy knows how to dress properly. Real class)*

em [ehm] *nn* An apartment <place, crib, pad, crash pad, cave, den, joint, box, dump, heave, camp, setup, layout, flop, flophouse, shack, rack, homeplate> eg *Ma własne em w centrum miasta (He has his own pad downtown)*

enty [EHN-ti] *adj* (Esp about repetitions) Of a large and unspecified ordinal number <umpty-umpth, umpteenth, umptieth, zillionth, jillionth> eg *Wygłosił tę samą mowę po raz enty (He made the same speech for the umpteenth time)*

erka [EHR-kah] *nf* An ambulance <meat wagon, butcher wagon, crash wagon, fruit wagon, band-aid wagon, blood box, bone box> eg *Erka pojawiła się 15 minut później (The meat wagon showed up 15 minutes later)*

esbek* [EHS-behk] (or **SB-ek*** [EHS-behk]) *nm* (In former communist times) A member of Secret Police <the eye, undercover, plainclothes, spook, peeper, dick, op> eg *Zabito wczoraj dwóch esbeków (Two spooks were killed yesterday)*

F

fałszywka [fah-oo-SHIF-kah] *nf* A counterfeit bill or document <paper, wallpaper, bad paper, phony money, hot dough, long green, gypsy bankroll, queer, boodle, bogus> eg *Dwóch z nich rozprowadzało fałszywki (Two of them passed the wallpaper)*

facet [FAH-tseht] (or **facio** [FAH-chyoh] or **facior** [FAH-chyohr] or **facecik** [fah-TSEH-cheek]) *nm* A man <fella, guy, dude, bud, budy, pal, mack> eg *Co to za facio w przyciemnianych okularach? (Who's the fella with the dark glasses?); Daj mi spokój, facet! (Give me a break, man!)*

facet od czegoś [FAH-tseht oht CHEH-gohsh] *nm phr* A teacher of a given subject in school <teach, prof, guru> eg *To jest mój facet od matmy (He's my math prof)*

facetka [fah-TSEHT-kah] *nf* A woman <gal, dame, lady, missy, ma'am, dudette> eg *Jedna facetka była mi winna kupę pieniędzy (Some gal owed me a lot of money); Te dwie facetki szukały czegoś innego (These two ladies were looking for something else)*

fach [FAHKH] *nm* One's trade, profession or occupation <racket, line, bag, kick, biz, game, cup of tea> eg *Nie wiem, jaki jest jego fach (I don't know what his number can be)*

fachman [FAHKH-mahn] (or **fachura** [fah-KHOO-rah]) *nm* (Usually with reference to repairs) A specialist or an expert; professional <pro, ace, whiz, whiz-kid, wiz, maven, mavin, guru> eg *Słyszałem, że twój brat to prawdziwy fachman w tych sprawach (I heard your brother is a real pro in these matters)*

facjata [fahts-YAH-tah] *nf* The face <kisser, puss, mug, map, phiz, mask, pan> eg *Spójrz na tego faceta! Nigdy nie w życiu widziałem tak okropnej facjaty (Look at that guy! I never saw such an ugly kiser in my life)*

fagas* [FAH-gahs] *nm* A man one dislikes or disapproves of <asshole, fuck, fucker, fuckhead, fuckface, motherfucker, shit, shitface, shithead, shitheel, bastard, jerk, SOB, son of a bitch, son of a whore, cocksucker, prick, dick, dickhead, cuntface, schmuck, scum, scumbag, sleazebag, slimebag, dipshit, pisshead, piece of shit, pain in the ass> eg *Zakochała się w jednym z tych fagasów (She fell in love in one of these dickheads)*

fajczyć się [FAH-ee-chich shyeh] (perf **sfajczyć się** [SFAH-ee-chich shyeh]) *v* To burn; to be on fire <fry, burn down, cook down, nuke, roast, sizzle> eg *Dom obok się sfajczył (The house next door got fried)*

fajka [FAH-ee-kah] (or **faja** [FAH-yah]) *nf* A cigarette <smoke, butt, cig, ciggie, fag, faggot, nail, coffin nail, stick, cancer stick, drag, bonfire, lung duster, root, cigaroot, cigareete, spark, dope, dope stick, grit, joint, pimp stick, slim, toke, weed> eg *Rety, ale mi się chce fajki! (Man, do I need a smoke!)*

fajnie [FAH-ee-nyeh] (or **fajowo** [fah-YOH-voh] or **fallicznie** [fahl-LEECH-nyeh]) *adv* Extremely well; superbly <great, cool, swell, fab, rad, def, far-out, awesome, frantic, terrific, funky, gorgeous, groovy, hellacious, neat, peachy, dandy, baddest, mean, solid, super-dooper, wailing, wicked, gnarly, top-notch, ten, ace-high, A-OK, A-1, some> eg *Jak się dzisiaj masz? Po prostu świetnie. Nie mogłoby być lepiej (How are you today? I'm just great. It couldn't be better)*

fajny [FAH-ee-ni] (or **fajowy** [fah-YOH-vi] or **falliczny** [fahl-LEECH-ni]) *adj* Excellent; wonderful; extremely good <great, cool, swell, fab, rad, def, far-out, awesome, frantic, terrific, funky, gorgeous, groovy, hellacious, neat, peachy, dandy, baddest, mean, solid, super-dooper, wailing, wicked, gnarly, top-notch, ten, ace-high, A-OK, A-1, some> eg *Ten samochód jest na prawdę fajny (This car is real cool); Na pewno poznasz fajnych ludzi (You're sure going to meet great people)*

fajrant [FAH-ee-rahnt] (or **fajerant** [fah-YEH-rahnt]) *nm* End of work or a rest period <five o'clock whistle, five o'clock bell, quitting time, breather, breathing spell, time-out, five, ten, break, time to go home, off> eg *Jak tylko mamy fajrant, to znów trzeba do roboty (As soon as we've had a breather, it's back to work); Zostało tylko 10 minut do fajrantu (It's only ten minutes to the five o'clock bell)*

fajtłapa See fujara

fala [FAH-lah] *nf* **1** Time remaining to the end of one's enlistment; keeping track of one's enlistment period <sign-on time, sign-up time, call-up time> eg *Myśli o fali bez przerwy (He's constantly thinking about his sign-on time)* **2** Soldiers of the same draft <boots, rookies, tenderfeet, cannon fodder, sad sacks> eg *Trzeba coś zrobić z falą (We have to do something with the rookies)*
See być na tej samej fali, na topie

falowiec [fah-LOH-vyehts] *nm* A massive, concrete apartment building with cheap apartments for working class, common in former communist times <no slang equivalent> eg *Mieszka w tym mrówkowcu (She lives in this massive apartment building)*

fan [fahn] *nm* A male enthusiast or devotee, esp of a musical group <fan, freak, groupie> eg *Jrgo fani o mało go nie zabili (His fans nearly killed him)*

fanka [FAHN-kah] *nf* A female enthusiast or devotee <fan, freak, groupie> eg *Dwie fanki chciały z nim pójść do łóżka (Two fans wanted to go to bed with him)*

farba [FAHR-bah] *nf* Blood <claret> eg *Wszędzie było pełno krwi (There was claret all over)*

farcić [FAHR-cheech] (perf **przyfarcić** [pshi-FAHR-cheech] or **pofarcić** [poh-FAHR-cheech]) *v* To enjoy good luck; to get something by good luck <luck out, luck up, get lucky, strike oil, strike it lucky, make a lucky strike, turn a lucky strike, hit it big, have Lady Luck on one's side> eg *W zeszłym roku pofarciło mi (Last year I lucked out); Boy, did he luck out with the new job! (Stary, ale mu przyfarciło z tą nową pracą!)*

farfocel [fahr-FOH-tsehl] *nm* A shred of anything or a cloud of dust <dustball, dust bunny, dust kitty, kitten, pussie, slut's wool, house moss, ghost turd, lint> eg *Sprzątnęłabyś te farfocle z podłogi (You could take those dustballs off the floor); Zawsze sterczy mu farfocel z pępka (He always has lint sticking out of his belly button)*

fart [fahrt] (or **fuks** [fooks]) *nm* Luck <mazel, mazeltov, fluke, mojo, streak of luck, lucky strike, lucky hit, lucky scratch, lucky break, Dame Fortune, Lady Luck> eg *Dostaliśmy się na ten lot przez fart (We got onto that flight by fluke); Wygrałem, bo miałem farta (I won because I had Lady Luck on my side)*

fartowny [fahr-TOHV-ni] *adj* Lucky <fluky> eg *To był bardzo fartowny dzień (It was a very fluky day)*

fason See stracić fason, trzymać fason, z fasonem

faszerować się [fah-sheh-ROH-vahch shyeh] (perf **nafaszerować się** [nah-fah-sheh-ROH-vahch shyeh]) *v* **1** To swallow many pills of narcotics <hit, pop, drop>

eg *Faszeruje się Prozakiem codziennie (He pops Prozac everyday)* **2** To overeat, eat greedily and more than needed <stuff oneself, pig out, scarf out, pork out> eg *Jak skończę z tą dietą, to mam zamiar nafaszerować się ciastkami i lodami (When I get off this diet, I'm going to pig out on cake and ice cream)*

fatałaszki [fah-tah-WAH-shehk] *nm* Clothes or clothing, esp fashionable or ostentatious <zoot suit, fine feathers, threads, drapes, duds, rags, togs, weeds, outfit> eg *Podobają mi się twoje fatałaszki. Gdzie je kupiłaś? (I like your weeds. Where did you buy them?)*

faza See mieć fazę

fąfel [FOHN-fehl] *nm* **1** A minor skin lesion or a pimple <zit, whitehead, blackhead, guber, goober, pip> eg *Nie wyciskuj swoich fąfli na moim lustrze! (Don't squeeze your zits on my mirror!)* **2** A blob of nasal mucus <snot, booger, boogie, nose-lunger, skeet> eg *Na twojej twarzy jest fąfel (There's snot on your face)*
See funfel

feler [FEH-lehr] *nm* A flaw, defect, or malfunction <bug, glitch, wart, catch, slip-up, wrinkle> eg *Nowy program ma jeden feler (The new program has one wart)*

felerny [feh-LEHR-ni] *adj* Flawed, defected, or malfunctioning <crappy, shitty, lousy, bugged, glitched, warted, slipped-up, wrinkled, lemon> eg *Gdzie kupiłeś ten felerny magnetofon? (Where did you buy this glitched tape recorder?)*

ferajna [feh-RAH-ee-nah] *nf* A group of people who are intimate and close; a company <folks, pack, bunch, crew, gang, clan, crowd, boys> eg *Cała ferajna w końcu dortarła tu wczoraj (The whole crew finally got here yesterday)*

fest [fehst] **1** *adj* Excellent; wonderful <great, cool, swell, fab, rad, def, far-out, awesome, frantic, terrific, funky, gorgeous, groovy, hellacious, neat, peachy, dandy, baddest, mean, solid, super-dooper, wailing, wicked, gnarly, top-notch, ten, ace-high, A-OK, A-1, some> eg *Z niej to jest fest dziewczyna (She's a swell girl)* **2** *adv* Extremely; exceedingly <awful, god-awful, real, mighty, plenty, damn, damned, goddamn, goddamned, darn, darned, effing, flipping, forking, freaking, frigging, fucking, one's ass off, one's brains out, one's head off, to the max, like all get-out, like sin, to beat the band, like all creation, as blazes, as can be, as hell, like hell> eg *Byliśmy fest zmęczeni (We were mighty tired); Jadłem na fest (I ate to the max)*

feta [FEH-tah] *nf* A party or other usually noisy celebration <ball, bash, blast, blowout, brawl, fest, rally, shindig> eg *Podobała ci się feta? (Did you like the ball?)*

fifty-fifty [FEEF-ti FEEF-ti] *adv phr* Fairly; evenly; equably <fifty-fifty, even-steven, half-way, the Dutch way> eg *Podzielmy to fifty-fifty, co?) Let's split it fifty-fifty, okay?)*

figa [FEE-gah] (or **figa z makiem** [FEE-gah z MAH-kyehm]) *nf* Nothing at all; zero <zilch, beans, damn, diddly-squat, doodly-squat, duck egg, goose egg, hoot, one red cent, one thin dime, rat's ass, zero, zippo, shit-all, fuck-all> eg *Co od niej dostałeś? Figę z makiem! (What did she get from her? Zilch!)*

figo-fago [fee-goh FAH-goh] *nm phr* **1** A male homosexual; gay <fag, faggot, fairy, queer, fruitcake, homo, pansy, sissy, swish, daisy, limp-wrist, queen> eg *Wydaje mi się, że twój szef jest figo-fago (It seems to me that your boss is a fruitcake)* **2** (or **fiki-miki** [FEE-kee MEE-kee]) or **fiku-miku** [FEE-koo MEE-koo] Playful amorous or sexual activity, esp quick <action, dirty deed, little heavy breathing, fun and games, bouncy-bouncy, boom-boom, in-and-out, hootchie-coochie, jig-jig, roll in

the hay, jelly roll, night baseball, bush patrol, hanky-panky, lovey-dovey, grab-ass, you-know-what, quickie, quick one, wham bam thank you ma'am, bunny fuck, fast fuck> eg *Oznajmiła, że figo-fago ją nie bawi (She said she's not interested in doing the dirty deed)*

figura [fee-GOO-rah] *nf* A very important, influential, or well-known person <big shot, big cheese, big enchilada, big fish, big guy, big wheel, wheel, biggie, topsider, celeb, big time operator, head honcho, BTO, VIP> eg *To figura w polityce krajowej (He's a big shot in national politics)*

fikać [FEE-kahch] (perf **pofikać** [poh-FEE-kahch]) *v* To caress sexually or to copulate <play with someone, feel up, cop a feel, grope, pet, neck, smooch, get physical, play grab-ass, play doctor> eg *Najbardziej lubimy fikać z rana (We prefer to play with ourselves in the morning)*

fikołek [fee-KOH-wehk] *nm* An alcoholic cocktail; a drink <highball, mixer> eg *Możesz mi zrobić jeszcze jednego fikołka? (Can you get me another highball?)*

fiksować [feek-SOH-vahch] (perf **sfiksować** [sfeek-SOH-vahch]) *v* To lose mental fitness; to become insane or eccentric <go crazy, go crazy as a loon, blow one's cork, blow one's top, blow a fuse, crack up, freak out, flip out, go ape, go bananas, go bent, go bonkers, go cracked, go dopey, go ga-ga, go half-baked, go loony, go loopy, go mental, go nerts, go nuts, go nutty, go off one's nut, go off one's rocker, go off one's base, go off the track, go off the trolley, go out one's skull, go psycho, go schizo, go screwy, go wacky, go weird, go wild, schiz out, psych out, come unglued, come unstuck, come unwrapped, come unzipped, go to pieces> eg *Całkowicie sfiksowała, gdy zdechł jej kanarek (She went to pieces when her canary died)* **2** To become bewildered, disoriented, or confused <get spaced out, get mixed up, get discombobulated, get flabbergasted, get messed up, get unscrewed, get farmisht, get balled up, get shook up, get floored, get unglued, get unzipped, get fried, get screwed-up, get fucked-up, get flummoxed, get kerflooey, get caught off base> eg *Sfiksowała, gdy to usłyszała (She got farmisht when she heard that)*

fiksum-dyrdum See dostać świra, mieć świra

film się komuś urwał [feelm shyeh KOH-moosh OOR-vah-oo] *v phr* To lose consciousness as a result of heavy drinking <be knocked out, crash, pass out, conk out, zonk out, black out> eg *Przez tę whiskey urwał mu się film i nic nie pamięta (He drank so much whiskey that he blacked out and does not remember anything); Koło północy urwał mi się film (Around midnight I crashed)*

filozof See chłopski filozof

fioł [FEE-yoh-oo] (or **fiś** [feesh] or **fiź** [feesh] or **fiksum-dyrdum** [FEEK-soom DIR-doom]) *nm* Obsession, insanity, or eccentricity <thing, kick, bag, bug, craze, freak, frenzy, weakness, bug up one's ass, bug in one's ear, bee in one's bonnet, bee, flea in one's nose, maggot, maggot in one's brain, hang-up, jones, monkey, ax to grind> eg *Ma fioła na punkcie tego, że joga jest lekarstwem na wszystkie złe rzeczy tego świata (He's got a bee in his bonnet about yoga curing all the world's ills); Surfing to jego fiksum-dyrdum (Surfing is his thing)*
See dostać świra, mieć świra

firmować [feer-MOH-vahch] *v* To be personally responsible for someone else's actions, esp poor workmanship or failure <take the rap, take the heat, take the fall, take the heat, take it, face the music, stand for it, stand the gaff, grin and bear

it, carry the can, carry the load, carry the mail> eg *Nie mam zamiaru firmować tej klapy (I'm not about to take the rap because of this flop)*

fisza [FEE-shah] *nf* A very important, influential, or well-known person <big shot, big cheese, big enchilada, big fish, big guy, big wheel, wheel, biggie, topsider, celeb, big time operator, head honcho, BTO, VIP> eg *Wyszła za miejscową fiszę (He married a local big shot)*

fiu-bździu [fyoo-BZHJOO] **1** *nn phr* Trivial, platitudinous or deceitful talk; nonsense <small talk, bullshit, BS, applesauce, baloney, blah-blah, crap, crock of shit, eyewash, hogwash, garbage, horseshit, hot air, jive, jazz, phony-baloney, piece of shit, pile of shit, poppycock, shit, smoke, gobbledygook, double-talk, hokum, horsefeathers, hokum, bunk> eg *Za dużo już się nasłuchałem tego fiu-bździu (I've heard enough of that baloney)* **2** *excl phr* An exclamation of incredulity or disbelief <in a pig's eye, in a pig's ass, in a pig's ear, like hell, like fun, like shit, my ass, there's no way, someone will be damned if, someone will be fucked if, says you> eg *Dostaniemy podwyżkę w przyszłym miesiącu. Fiu-bździu! (We'll get a pay hike next month. Says you!)*

fiut* [fyoot] (or **flet*** [fleht]) *nm* The penis <cock, prick, dick, stick, joystick, dipstick, bone, meat, beef, wang, yang, dong, dummy, hammer, horn, hose, jock, joint, knob, pork, putz, rod, root, tool, flute, skin flute, love-muscle, sausage, schmuck, schlong, schvantz, cream-stick, third leg, middle leg, business, apparatus, John, Johnny, Johnson, John Thomas, Jones, pecker, peter, peepee, pisser, weenie, peenie, dingus, dingbat, thingy> eg *Myślałam, że ma większego fiuta (I thought he has a bigger dick)*

fiza [FEE-zah] *nf* A physics or science, esp as a subject in school <sci> eg *Słyszałem, że znów dostałeś jedynkę z fizy (I heard you got an F in sci again)*

fizol [FEE-zohl] (or **fizyczny** [fee-ZICH-ni]) *nm* An unqualified menial worker; an unskilled laborer <grave-digger, wetback, blue collar, workhorse, hard hat, stiff, working stiff> eg *Umysłowi i fizyczni odrzucili te propozycje (Blue collars and white collars rejected these proposals)*

flądra [FLOHN-drah] *nf* A promiscuous woman <floozy, bimbo, slut, bitch, cunt, chippy, quiff, swinger, easy lay, easy make, alley cat, dirty-leg, roundheels, nympho, piece of ass, punchboard, town bike> eg *W każdy sobotni wieczór przyprowadza do domu innego faceta. Prawdziwa z niej flądra (She comes home with a different man every Saturday night. She's a real floozy)*

flacha [FLAH-khah] (or **flaszka** [FLAHSH-kah] or **flakon** [FLAH-kohn]) *nf* A liquor bottle <soldier> eg *Czemu pan nie mówił, że przyszedł pan z flaszką? (Why didn't you say you brought a soldier with you?)*

flaczeć [FLAH-chehch] (perf **sflaczeć** [SFLAH-chehch]) *v* To lose strength or energy; to become very tired or exhausted <get dead, get dead on one's feet, get dead-tired, get dog-tired, get out of it, get out of gas, get out of juice, get all in, get all shot, get pooped, get bagged, get beat, get beat to the ground, get beat to the ankles, get bone-tired, get burned out, get bushed, get chewed, get crapped out, get done, get done in, get dragged out, get frazzled, get played out, get fucked out, get knocked out, get tuckered out, get tapped out, had it, get ready to drop, get on one's last legs> eg *Sflaczał bardzo szybko, bo wyszedł z wprawy (He got dead-tired real soon, because he's out of practice)*

flak [flahk] *nm* **1** A punctured automotive tire <flat, blow-up, blown tire> eg *Spójrz na tego flaka (Check out this flat)* **2** Someone who is very tired or exhausted <dead, dead on one's feet, dead-tired, dog-tired, out of it, out of gas, out of juice, all in, all shot, pooped, bagged, beat, beat to the ground, beat to the ankles, bone-tired, burned out, bushed, chewed, crapped out, done, done in, dragged out, frazzled, played out, fucked out, knocked out, tuckered out, tapped out, had it, ready to drop, on one's last legs> eg *Ale jestem flak! Zaraz padnę (Am I dead-tired! I'm gonna drop in a second)*

flaki [FLAH-kee] *npl* The intestines <guts, kishkes, innards> eg *Jest doktorem. Widok flaków go nie przestraszy (He's a doctor. The sight of guts won't frighten him)*
See wypruwać sobie flaki, nudny jak flaki z olejem

flaki się komuś przewracają [FLAH-kee shyeh KOH-moosh psheh-vrah-TSAH-yoh] (or **kiszki się komuś przewracają** [KEESH-kee shyeh KOH-moosh psheh-vrah-TSAH-yoh]; **w kimś** [f KEEMSH] may replace **komuś**) *v phr* To be very angry, irritated, or disgusted <be pissed off, be peed off, be p'd off, be bent out of a shape, be pushed out of a shape, be browned off, be cheesed off, be uptight, be cranky, be edgy, be sore, be mad as a hornet, be steamed up, be ticked off, be tee'd off, be burned up, be ballistic, be grossed out, be scuzzed out, be turned off, be barfed out, be grody, have a bellyful, have a skinful> eg *Za każdym razem jak go widzę, mi się flaki przewracają (I'm peed off everytime I see him)*

fleja [FLEH-yah] *nf* A sloppy, shabby, or ugly woman <dirt-bag, dirt-ball, beasty, skag, skank, pig, bag, dog, cow> eg *Twoja sąsiadka to prawdziwa fleja (Your neighbor is a real dirt-bag)*

flejtuch [FLEY-tookh] *nm* A sloppy, shabby, and loathsome man <dirt-bag> eg *Twój współlokator to prawdziwy flejtuch (Your roommate is a real dirt-bag)*

flek See na gazie

flet See fiut, obciągać

flinta [FLEEN-tah] *nf* A rifle, esp old <flintlock, flint stick, blowpipe, long rod, smoke pole, slim, stick, boom stick, hardware, artillery> eg *Facet ponownie załadował flintę (The guy reloaded his flint stick)*

fochy [FOH-khi] *npl* Groundless dissatisfaction or discontent; unfounded complaints; fret <fuss, stink, scene, ceremony, beef, bleed, hassle, kvetch, bitch, beef, gripe, piss, bellyache, grouse, growl, squawk> eg *Po co te całe fochy? (What's this fuss all about?)*
See stroić fochy

forsa [FOHR-sah] *nf* Money <dough, bread, bank, cabbage, change, coin, folding, green, lettuce> eg *Przyjdź w środę po forsę (Come on Wednesday to pick up the bread)*
See ładować w coś forsę, mieć forsy jak lodu, przy forsie, robić kokosy

forsiasty [fohr-SHAHS-ti] *adj* Very rich; affluent <loaded, flush, filthy rich, stinking rich, dirt richy, lousy rich, in the bucks, in the dough, in the money, rolling in it, made of money> eg *Słyszałem, że chodzi z jakimś forsiastym facetem (I hear she's been dating some flush guy)*

fotka [FOHT-kah] (or **foto** [FOH-toh] *nn*) *nf* A photograph <photo, pic, pix, snap, shot, eight by ten glossy> eg *Jedna dobra fotka jest warta więcej (One good pix is worth much more)*

fotomontaż See pic

frajda [FRAH-ee-dah] *nf* A delightful sensation; fun; thrill <good time, barrel of laughs, ball, blast, gas, groove, boot, charge, bang, kick, belt, buzz, charge, drive, flash, flip, riot, jolt, lift, rush, upper, wallop, whoopee, fun and games> eg *Stary, ale mieliśmy frajdę! (Man, did we have a ball!); Zobaczenie jej jeszcze raz było wielką frajdą (Seeing her again was quite a kick)*

frajer [FRAH-yehr] *nm* **1** (or **frajer pompka** [FRAH-yehr POHMP-kah]) A naive and easily victimized man; a dupe <sucker, patsy, easy mark, mark, fall guy, pushover, schnook, babe in the woods, sitting duck, goat, babe in the woods> eg *Uważaj, bo on nie jest frajerem (Be careful, because he's no pushover)* **2** An easy task or job; anything easy <piece of cake, cake, cakewalk, cherry pie, duck soup, kid stuff, picnic, pushover, snap, tea party, walkaway, walkover, breeze, stroll, cinch, pipe, plain sailing> eg *Dla niego to frajer (It's a kid stuff for him)*
See za frajer

frajerka [frah-YEHR-kah] *nf* A naive and easily victimized woman; a dupe <sucker, patsy, easy mark, mark, fall guy, pushover, schnook, babe in the woods, sitting duck, goat, babe in the woods> eg *Ale z niej frajerka. Dała się nabrać przez niego (What a patsy she is! To get fooled by him)*

frajerstwo [frah-YEHR-stfoh] *npl* Naivety; gullibility <suckerdom, patsydom> eg *Nie znoszę frajerstwa (I hate suckerdom)*

franca* [FRAHN-tsah] *nf* **1** Anything or anyone despicable, annoying, repulsive <shit, bitch> eg *Zabierz od mnie tę francę i to szybko (Get this shit away from me, fast)* **2** An unpleasant, nagging disease, esp veneral <bug, crud, scrud, double scrud, creeping crud, VD, clap, dose, dose of claps, drip, blue balls, syph, siph, head cold, crabs> eg *Nie używał prezerwatyw i złapał jakąś francę (He didn't use any condoms so he caught a clap)* **3** A prostitute <hooker, hustler, pro, call girl, floozy, chippy, bimbo, quiff, slut, working girl, street walker> eg *Ile ta franca bierze za numerek? (How much does that pro charge a trick?)* **4** Any insect, esp a sizable and noisy fly <bug, crum, crumb, grayback> eg *Zaraz zabiję tę francę (I'm going to kill that bug)* **5** A woman, esp old or shrewish one <bitch, slut, cunt, broad, wench, hag, old hag, old biddy, old bag, old tart, piece of shit> eg *Chciała, żebym zapłacił z góry, franca jedna! (She wanted me to pay up front, the old tart!)*

francja-elegancja See elegancja-francja

francowaty* [frahn-tsoh-VAH-ti] *adj* Cursed; damnable; bad <damn, damned, goddamn, goddamned, god-awful, blasted, darn, darned, effing, flipping, forking, freaking, frigging, pesky> eg *Ten francowaty klucz nie pasuje (This goddamn key doesn't fit in)*

francuz [FRAHN-tsoos] *nm* **1** The French language, esp as a subject in school <Frog> eg *Muszę się uczyć do egzaminu z francuza (I have to study for the Frog exam)* **2*** Oral sex <blow job, face job, head job, French job, deep throat> eg *Lubi wszystko a najbardziej francuza (She likes everything, but blow jobs most of all)*

friko See za frajer

fryc* [frits] *nm* A male German <kraut, krauthead, sauerkraut, Fritz, Heinie, Jerry> eg *Jakiś fryc nadjechał Mercem (Some krauthead pulled over his Merc)*

fucha [FOO-khah] *nf* A part-time job or any job of an assignment nature <gig> eg *Miałem jedną fuchę w zwszłym tygodniu. Miałem napisać kolejny artykuł dla naszej miejscowej gazety (I had a gig last week. I had to write another article for our local paper)*

fujara [foo-YAH-rah] *nf* **1*** The penis <cock, prick, dick, stick, joystick, dipstick, bone, meat, beef, wang, yang, dong, dummy, hammer, horn, hose, jock, joint, knob, pork, putz, rod, root, tool, flute, skin flute, love-muscle, sausage, schmuck, schlong, schvantz, cream-stick, third leg, middle leg, business, apparatus, John, Johnny, Johnson, John Thomas, Jones, pecker, peter, peepee, pisser, weenie, peenie, dingus, dingbat, thingy> eg *O, mam pryszcza na mojej fujarze! (Oh, there's a zit on my dick!)* **2** (or **fajtłapa** [fah-eet-WAH-pah]) An ineffectual or sluggish person; a botcher <underachiever, loser, born loser, second-rater, schlemiel, schmendrick, schmo, schnook, screwup, fuckup, hacker, muffer, scrub, dub, dool tool, turkey, lump, buterfingers, fumble-fist, goof, goof-off, goofball, eightball, foulball, klutz, also-ran, never-was, nonstarter> eg *Ta dupa wołowa nawet nie wiedziała, jak włączyć toster (That shlemiel didn't even know how to turn on the toaster)*

fuks See fart

ful [fool] *adv* Plenty; many <helluva lot, lotsa, lotta, oodles, scads, heaps, bags, barrels, loads, piles, tons, wads, jillions, zillions, enough to choke a horse, shitload, fuckload, truckload> eg *W barze było ful ludzi (There was a helluva lot people in the bar)*

See na ful

fundować [foon-DOH-vahch] (perf **fundnąć** [FOOND-nohnch]) *v* (To ask someone out and) To pay the cost of something, esp of a drink; to treat someone to something <stand, buy, pop for, spring for, be on one, someone will get it, pick up the check, pick up the tab> eg *Może poszlibyśmy do jakiejś knajpy. Ja funduję (Why don't we go to some joint. I'm buying)*

funfel [FOON-fehl] (or **fumfel** [FOOM-fehl] or **fąfel** [FOHN-fehl]) *nm* A male colleague or friend <bro, brother, buddy, amigo, pal, sidekick, bosom buddy> eg *Jego funfel ma na niego zły wpływ (His sidekick has a bad influence on him)*

fura [FOO-rah] *nf* **1** An automobile <wheels, set of wheels, crate, ride, cage, trans, transportation, four wheeler, boat, buggy> eg *Ta fura kosztowała mnie 10 tysięcy (This ride set me back 10 thousand)* **2** Plenty; many many <helluva lot, lotsa, lotta, oodles, scads, heaps, bags, barrels, loads, piles, tons, wads, jillions, zillions, enough to choke a horse, shitload, fuckload, truckload> eg *Dostał furę pieniędzy (He got oddles of money)*

G

gały [GAH-wi] *npl* The eyes <peepers, blinkers, lamps, oglers, peekers> eg *Gały mi się zmęczyły (My peepers are tired); Jak tylko otworzyłem oczy, jak myślisz, kogo zobaczyłem? (As I opened my blinkers, guess who I saw?)*

See widziały gały co brały

gablota [gah-BLOH-tah] *nf* An automobile <wheels, set of wheels, crate, ride, cage, trans, transportation, four wheeler, boat, buggy> eg *Skądżeś wziął taką gablotę? (Where'd you get such a crate?)*

gach [gahkh] *nm* A male lover, esp older and one who provides money <sugar daddy, bank account, sponsor> eg *Chodzą słuchy, że ma nowego gacha (Rumor has it that she has a new sugar daddy)*

gacie [GAH-chyeh] (or **galoty** [gah-LOH-ti] or **gatki** [GAHT-kee]) *npl* **1** Underwear, esp male; briefs, shorts, or long johns <undies, underthings, unmentionables, step-ins, drawers, BVD's, woolilies, skivvies, longies, long ones, Hanes> eg *Jak Ci się podobają moje gacie? (How do you like my undies?)* **2** Pants; trousers <slacks, jeans, cords, ducks, hip huggers, kneebusters, baggies, jammies, dungarees, pegs, striders, strides, britches, knickers, drawers, longies, bags> eg *Załóż gacie. Ktoś puka do drzwi (Put your slacks on. Somebody is knocking at the door)* See ciągnąć się, mieć cykora, robić w gacie

gad See glizda

gadać [GAH-dahch] (or **ględzić** [GLEHN-jeech] or **gadać jak nakręcony** [GAH-dahch yahk nah-krehn-TSOH-ni]; perf **pogadać** [poh-GAH-dahch] or **poględzić** [poh-GLEHN-jeech]) *v* To talk, chat, or converse, esp idly <go, gab, rap, yap, yack, yam, blab, flap, drool, patter, jaw, gum, lip, chin, chew, rattle, crack, blow, breeze, buzz, noise off, sound off, chew the fat, chew the rag, bat one's gums, beat one's gums, shoot the breeze, shoot the shit, flip one's lip, flap one's jaw, run one's mouth, talk one's ear off, talk one's ass off, wag the tongue> eg *Pogadajmy sobie trochę (Let's chew the fat for a while)*

gadać od rzeczy [GAH-dahch ohd ZHEH-chi] (or **gadać jak potłuczony** [GAH-dahch yahk poh-twoo-CHOH-ni]) *v phr* To talk nonsense <bullshit, talk bull, talk bullshit, talk bullshine, talk BS, talk bunk, talk baloney, talk applesauce, jazz, jive, shovel the shit, blow off, blow off one's mouth> eg *Ten facet gada od rzeczy. Nie słuchajcie go (This guy is talking bullshit. Don't listen to him)*

gadka szmatka [GAHT-kah] (or **gadka szmadka** [GAHT-kah SHMAHT-kah]) *nf phr* **1** *nf phr* Trivial, platitudinous or deceitful talk; nonsense <small talk, applesauce, baloney, blah-blah, crap, crock of shit, eyewash, hogwash, garbage, horseshit, hot air, jive, jazz, phony-baloney, piece of shit, pile of shit, poppycock, shit, smoke, gobbledygook, double-talk, hokum, horsefeathers, hokum, bunk> eg *Za dużo już się nasłuchałem tej gadki-szmatki (I've heard enough of that baloney)* **2** *excl phr* An exclamation of incredulity or disbelief <in a pig's eye, in a pig's ass, in a pig's ear, like hell, like fun, like shit, my ass, there's no way, someone will be damned if, someone will be fucked if, says you> eg *Powiedział, że nam pomoże. Gadka-szmadka, akurat nam pomoże! (He said he'd help us. My ass! Like hell he would help us!)*

gaduła [gah-DOO-wah] *nf* A person who talks too much; a logorrheic person <blabbermouth, babbler, blabber, bag of wind, big breeze, bigmouth, chatterbox, ear-bender, flapjaw, gabbler, gum-beater, jabberer, jawsmith, loudmouth, satchelmouth, spieler, tongue-wagger, windbag, windjammer, motormouth> eg *Twoja siostra to prawdziwa gaduła. Gadała przez cała imprezę (Your sister is a real chatterbox. She talked for the whole party)*

gadzina See glizda

gafa [GAH-fah] *nf* A careless but blatant mistake; a gaffe <blooper, clinker, howler, fox paw, fox pass, slip, slip-up, flub, fluff, foozle, goof-up, screw-up, fuck-up, ball-up, mess-up, louse-up> eg *Ale gafa! (What a slip-up)*

gajer [GAH-yehr] *nm* A suit <vine, flute, gray flannel, front, getup, rig, zoot suit, flash, frock, tux, drape, set of drapes, set of threads, outfit> eg *Jak Ci się podoba mój gajer? (How do you like my zoot suit?)*

galareta [gah-lah-REH-tah] *nf* Someone who is nervous, anxious, or completely off-balance <basket case, nervous wreck, bundle of nerves, uptight, jumpy, jittery, shaky, shivery, nervy, edgy, antsy, clutchy, hitchy, fretty, itchy, wired, tightened-up, strung-out, on pins and needles, all hot and bothered, all shook up, worried stiff, hot and bothered, shitting razorblades, in the anxious seat, in a stew, in a sweat, in a swivet, in a tizzy, on edge> eg *Facet jest galareta. Nie zrobi tego, przynajmniej teraz (They guy is all shook up. He won't do it, at least not at this moment)*

galimatias [gah-lee-MAHT-yahs] *nm* A confusing situation; confusion <mess, mess-up, mix-up, fuck-up, screw-up, mess and a half, holy mess, unholy mess, all hell broke loose, ruckus, discombobulation, foofaraw, srew, sweat, swivet, tizzy, hassle, rat's nest, SNAFU> eg *Kto jest odpowiedzialny za cał ten galimatias? (Who is responsible for this whole mix-up?)*

galop See brać kogoś do galopu, brać się

galopem [gah-LOH-pehm] (or **gazem** [GAH-zehm]) *adv* Immediately; very quickly <pretty damn quick, PDQ, ASAP, on the spot, on the double, double time, double clutching, like a shot, in half a mo, like now, before you know it, before you can say Jack Robinson, in a jiffy, in a flash, in half a shake, right off the bat, like a bat out of hell, like a shot out of hell, hubba-hubba, horseback, like greased lightning> eg *Biegnij tam szybko, galopem! (Run over there quick, on the double!)*

galoty See gacie

ganc egal [gahnts eh-GAHL] (or **ganc pomada** [gahnts poh-MAH-dah]) *adv phr* (Something makes) No difference; (Something is) insignificant <no diff, all the same, same old shit, same difference, no matter how you slice it, makes no never mind, makes no difference, anything goes> eg *Czy go wyrzucą, czy sam odejdzie, to ganc egal (They fire him or he quits, it makes no difference)*

ganiać za kimś See **latać za kimś**

ganiać za kobietami [GAH-nyahch zah koh-byeh-TAH-mee] (or **uganiać się za kobietami** [oo-GAH-nyahch shyeh zah koh-byeh-TAH-mee]; **dziewczynkami** [jehf-chin-KAH-mee] or **dupami*** [doo-PAH-mee] may replace **kobietami**) *v* To go about seeking sexual encounters; be sexually promiscuous <chase, cruise, tail, troll, run around, dog someone's footsteps, hunt for cunt> eg *Przez całe życie uganiał się za dziewczynkami (He's been cruising all his life)*

gapa [GAH-pah] (or **gamoń** [GAH-mohñ]) *nf* An absent-minded, forgetful, slow-witted, or careless person <dope, absentminded professor, moony, pipe-dreamer, wool-gatherer, airbrain, airhead, birdbrain, blockhead, squarehead, bonehead, bubblebrain, bubblehead, buckethead, cluckhead, cementhead, clunkhead, deadhead, dumbbell, dumbcluck, dumbhead, dumbass, dumbbrain, fatbrain, fathead, flubdub, knukclebrain, knucklehead, lamebrain, lardhead, lunkhead, meathead, musclehead, noodlehead, numbskull, pointhead, scatterbrain, jerk, jerk-off, klutz, chump, creep, nerd, dork, dweeb, gweeb, geek, jackass, lummox, twerp, nerd, bozo, clod, cluck, clunk, dimwit, dingbat, dipstick, dodo, dufus, goofus, lump, lunk, nitwit, schnook, schlep, schlemiel, schmendrick, schmo,

schmuck, simp, stupe> eg *Ale gapa ze mnie. Zapomniałem prawa jazdy, panie władzo (I'm such a birdbrain. I forgot my driver's license, officer)*
See jechać na gapę

gapić się [GAH-peech shyeh] (or **gapić się jak sroka w gnat** [GAH-peech shyeh yahk SROH-kah v GNAHT]) *v* To stare or gape at someone or something <gander, take a gender, gawk, gawp, goggle, glom, glim, gun, pin, rubber, rubberneck, beam, eye, get an eyeful, give the eye, lay eyes on, set eyes on, get a load of > eg *Na co się ci wszyscy ludzie gapią? (What are all those people rubbernecking at?)*

gapiowaty [gah-pyoh-VAH-ti] *adj* Absent-minded, forgetful, slow-witted, or careless <dopey, moony, pipe-dreaming, wool-gathering, asleep on the job, not on the job, looking out the window, out to lunch, out of it> eg *Ten nowy pracownik jest bardzo gapiowaty (The new employee is pretty dopey)*

gapowicz [gah-POH-veech] *nm* Someone who travels by public transportation without paying the fare <fare dodger, stowaway> eg *Stał się ostatnio gapowiczem. Nigdy nie kupuje już biletu (He's become a fare dodger as of late. He never buys a ticket anymore)*

garbus [GAHR-boos] *nm* **1*** A hunchback <no slang equivalent> eg *Łysys garbus poprosił ją do tańca (Some bold hunchback asked her to dance)* **2** An early model of a Volkswagen, with a squat body curving down at front and rear <beetle, bug> eg *Garbus to mój ulubiony samochód (The beetle is my favorite automobile)*

gardło See przepłukać gardło

garkotłuk [gahr-KOH-twook] *nm* A person who washes dishes, esp in a restaurant <bubble dancer, pearl-diver> eg *Ile zarabia taki.garkotłuk? (How much does a pearl-diver like that earn?)*

garnuszek See być na czyimś garnuszku

garść See wziąć się do kupy

garować [gah-ROH-vahch] **1** *v* To serve a prison sentence; to be in prison <do time, serve time> eg *Garuje za gwałt (He's been doing time for rape)* **2** To wait <wait out, cool it, cool one's heels, sweat it, sweat out, be put on ice, be put on hold, hang out, hang around, stick around, sit and take it, sit tight, sit out, sit on one's ass, sit on one's butt, warm a chair, lay dead> eg *Garowałem tam na nią dwie godziny (I've been cooling my heels for her for two hours)*

gary See pobite gary, stać przy garach

gatki See gacie

gaz [gahs] **1** *nm* A gas pistol or a container with gas used for personal defense <mace, mace spray, can of mace> eg *Spryskała napastników gazem (She sprayed the assailants with a can of mace)* **2** *excl phr* (or **gaz do dechy** [gahz doh DEH-khi] or **gazu** [GAH-zoo]) (An exclamation urging someone to) Drive at full high speed or accelerate <tool it, burn rubber, burn the breeze, burn the road, step on it, step up, step on the gas, hit the gas, nail it, floor it, push it to the floor, put the pedal to the metal, , put the heel to the steel, drop the hammer down, hammer on, pour on it, pout on the coal, put on the afterburners, gun it, rev her up, open her up> eg *Zaraz nas dogonią̨c. Gaz do dechy! (They're going to get us. Step on the gas!)*
See dać sobie w gaz, dawać, na gazie

gazem See galopem

gazik [GAH-zheek] *nm* A useful and durable small military vehicle <jeep> eg *Gdzie zaparkowałeś swój gazik? (Where did you park your jeep?)*

gazować [gah-ZOH-vahch] (perf **przygazować** [pshi-gah-ZOH-vahch]) *v* **1** To drive at very high speed or to accelerate <barrel, barrel along, barrel ass, haul ass, tear, tool, burn rubber, burn the breeze, burn the road, dust, floorboard, fly, step on it, step up, step on the gas, hit the gas, nail it, floor it, push it to the floor, put the pedal to the metal, , put the heel to the steel, drop the hammer down, hammer on, pour on it, pout on the coal, put on the afterburners, gun, rev, rev up, open her up, go flat-out, go full blast, go hell-bent, go like a bat out of hell, go like a blue streak, go like blazes, go like the devil, let her rip, rip-ass, vroom, varoom, zoom> eg *Gazowała swoim Jeepem na autostradzie (She was tooling her Jeep on the highway)* **2** (or **grzać** [gzhahch]; perf **wygrzać** [VI-gzhahch] or **pogrzać** [POH-gzhahch]) *v* To drink alcohol, esp in large quantities <booze, guzzle, gargle, bend the elbow, hit the bottle, hit the sauce, knock back, lap, tank up, wet one's whistle, hang a few on, slug down, swig> eg *Ostro wczoraj gazowali (They hit the booze real hard last night); Nie lubi grzać samotnie (He hates to booze alone)*

gazu See do gazu

gazurka [gahz-ROOR-kah] *nf* Any longer piece of metal pipe, used for defense or attack <rod> eg *Zaatakował ją gazrurką (He attacked her with a rod)*

gąska See gęś

gdzie popadnie [gjeh po-PAHD-nyeh] *adv phr* Anywhere; wherever <anyplace, any old place> eg *Po prostu rzuć to gdzie popadnie (Just drop it any old place)*

gdzieś [GJEHSH] *adv* About; approximately <around, in the ballpark of, pretty near, something like, close shave, in the neighborhood of, damn near, pretty near> eg *Zarabia gdzieś z 50 000 rocznie (She earns around 50,000 a year)*

gęba [GEHM-bah] *nf* The face <kisser, puss, mug, map, phiz, mask, pan> eg *W końcu zamknął gębę (Finally he shut his yap)*
See ani pary z gęby, całą gębą, drzeć mordę, mieć niewyparzoną gębę, mocny w gębie, nie mieć co do gęby włożyć, niebo w gębie, rozdziawić gębę, zapomnieć języka w gębie

gęba na kłódkę See ani pary z gęby

gęba w kubeł See ani pary z gęby

gęś [gehnsh] (or **gąska** [GOHN-skah]) *nf* An unintelligent, naive and very conventional woman <chick, silly goose> eg *To zwykła gąska, ale za to dobrze gotuje (She's just a silly goose, but she's a good cook)*

gęsia skórka [GEHN-shyah SKOOR-kah] *nf phr* A condition in which the skin is raised up in small points because of cold or fear <goose bumps, goose flesh, goose pimples, duck bumps> eg *Nie chciałbym, żebyś się przeziębiła. Już masz gęsią skórkę (I wouldn't like you to catch cold. You're already getting goose bumps all over)*

gęsto See często gęsto

geszefciarz [geh-SHEHF-chash] *nm* A businessman, esp one involved in illegal or occasional transactions; a profiteer <big-time operator, BTO, operator, player, wheeler-dealer, tradester, cockroach, small potatoes, small-timer> eg *Jej ojciec był znanym geszefciarzem (He father was a well-known wheeler-dealer)*

geszeft [geh-SHEHFT] *nm* Business, esp if illegal or occasional <biz, deal, set-up, gesheft, monkey business> eg *Szybko wykryliśmy, że zajmuje się po prostu geszeftami (We soon discovered that he'd been doing some deals)*

gibać się [GEE-bahch shyeh] (perf **pogibać się** [poh-GEE-bahch shyeh]) *npl* To dance <rock, shake, boogie, hop, swing, jump, juke, jive, wrestle, grind> eg *Patrz, jak ta laska się umie się gibać (Look at the way that chick rocks)*

gie See gówno

gil [geel] (or **glut** [gloot]) *nm* A blob of nasal mucus <snot, booger, boogie, nose-lunger, skeet> eg *Na twoim łóżku jest gil (There's snot on your bed); Czyżbyś miała gila na ustach, czy co? (Is that a boogie on your lip, or what?)*

gimnastykować się [geem-nah-sti-KOH-vahch shyeh] *v* To think intensely about something, such as an answer; to wonder; to ponder <use one's head, rack one's brain, brainstorm, think up, noodle around, percolate, perk, head trip, skull drag, eat, bug, burn a couple of braincells> eg *Wszyscy gimnastykowali się nad sprawą (They were all noodling around the issue)*

gimnastykować się [geem-nahs-ti-KOH-vahch] *v* To think intensely; to wonder; to ponder <use one's head, rack one's brain, brainstorm, think up, noodle around, percolate, perk, head trip, skull drag, eat, bug, burn a couple of braincells> eg *Wszyscy gimnastykowali nad sprawą (They were all noodling around the issue)*

giry [GEE-ri] (or **giczoły** [gee-CHOH-wi]) *npl* A person's legs <stumps, hinders, pillars, trotters, underpinnings, pins, sticks> eg *Od tego całego łażenia bolą mnie giry (My stumps are sore from all that walking); Z takimi giczołami powninien biec dużo szybciej (With underpinnings like that, he ought to be able to win the marathon)*

gitnie [GEET-nyeh] (or **git** [GEET] or **gites** [GEE-tehs]) *adv* Extremely well; superbly <great, cool, swell, fab, rad, def, far-out, awesome, frantic, terrific, funky, gorgeous, groovy, hellacious, neat, peachy, dandy, baddest, mean, solid, super-dooper, wailing, wicked, gnarly, top-notch, ten, ace-high, A-OK, A-1, some> eg *Zobaczysz, że wszystko będzie gites (You'll see, everything is going to be great)*

gitny [GEET-ni] (or **git** [GEET] or **gites** [GEE-tehs]) *adj* Excellent; wonderful; extremely good <great, cool, swell, fab, rad, def, far-out, awesome, frantic, terrific, funky, gorgeous, groovy, hellacious, neat, peachy, dandy, baddest, mean, solid, super-dooper, wailing, wicked, gnarly, top-notch, ten, ace-high, A-OK, A-1, some> eg *Ten samochód jest na prawdę gites (This car is real cool)*

giwera [gee-VEH-rah] *nf* A pistol or rifle <blaster, gat, piece, iron, rod, heater, snubby, popper, tool, stick, boomstick, firestick, hardware, speaker, difference, persuader, convincer, equalizer, artillery, cannon, Saturday night special> eg *Zrobiła to, o co facet prosił, bo miał giwerę (She did what the guy asked because he was carrying the difference)*

glaca [GLAH-tsah] *nf* A bold spot on the head or a bold head <no slang equivalent> eg *Spójrz na glacę tego faceta. Ohyda! (Look at the bald spot on that guy. Yuck!)*

glanc See na glanc

glany [GLAH-ni] *npl* Shoes or boots, esp heavy or sturdy <stompers, wafflestompers, boondockers, clodhoppers, shitkickers> eg *Zabieraj swoje glany z mojego biurka (Get your wafflestompers out of my desk)*

gleba [GLEH-bah] *nf* The ground; the floor <deck, boards, mat, canvas> eg *Walnąłem głową o glebę i złamałem sobie nos (I hit the deck with my head and I broke my nose)*

See wyglebić się

ględzić See gadać

glina [GLEE-nah] (or **gliniarz** [GLEE-nyahsh] *nm*) *nf* A police officer <cop, copper, flatfoot, flatty, fuzz, pig, gumshoe, nabs, paddy, finest, elbow, blue, bluecoat, big John, arm, yard bull, smokey, bear, smokey bear> eg *Wynoś się, bo zawołam gliny (Get out or I call the cops)*

glizda* [GLEEZ-dah] *nf* **1** (or **gnida*** [GNEE-dah] or **gadzina** [gah-JEE-nah] *nf* or **gad** [gaht] *nm*) Someone who behaves in an unethical, immoral or dishonest way; someone one dislikes or disapproves of <asshole, fuck, fucker, fuckhead, fuckface, motherfucker, shit, shitface, shithead, shitheel, bastard, jerk, SOB, son of a bitch, son of a whore, cocksucker, prick, dick, dickhead, cuntface, schmuck, scum, scumbag, sleazebag, slimebag, dipshit, pisshead, piece of shit, pain in the ass> eg *Chodzą słuchy, że nowy szef to prawdziwa gnida (Rumor has it that your new boss is a real bastard)* **2** An earthworm or any worm-like creature <worm, inchworm, tape-worm> eg *Nie znoszę glizd (I hate worms)*

globus [GLOH-boos] *nm* The head <bean, noggin, conk, dome, gourd, skull> eg *Walnęła go prosto w globus (She hit him right on the noggin)*

glut See gil

głąb See głupek

gładko [GWAHT-koh] *adv* Very easily; effortlessly; without problems <like shit through a goose, like shit through a tin horn, easy, smooth, hands down, downhill all the way, plain sailing, running smooth> eg *W życiu wszystko szło mu gładko (Everything in his life was going like shit through a tin horn)*

głęboko See mieć coś/kogoś gdzieś

głębszy [GWEHMP-shi] *nm* A drink of liquor, esp potent <snort, finger, jigger, pull, shot, nip, gargle, guzzle, slug, hit> eg *Po paru głębszych facet widział podwójnie (After a couple of shots, the dude was seeing double)*

głośniej See dawać głośniej

głowa See bić kogoś na głowę, brać coś z sufitu, chodzić komuś po głowie, czyjaś w tym głowa, dać głowę, dać po dupie, dostać po dupie, mieć coś na głowie, mieć coś z głową, mieć mętlik w głowie, mieć olej w głowie, mieć pstro w głowie, mieć źle w głowie, nadstawiać karku, nie mieć głowy do czegoś, nie mieścić się w głowie, oczko w głowie, świtać, przewracać się komuś w głowie, puknąć się w czoło, ruszyć głową, stawać na głowie, stawiać sprawę na głowie, stracić fason, strzelić do łba, upaść na głowę, upaść na głowę, wbijać sobie coś do głowy, wpaść do głowy, wybić sobie coś z głowy, wylecieć z głowy, z głowy, zawracać komuś głowę, zawracać sobie głowę, zawracanie głowy, tak że hej

główka [GWOOF-kah] *nm* (In soccer) An act of striking the ball with the head <header, flying header, diving header> eg *Ale ładna główka! (What a nice header!)*

główkować [gwoof-KOH-vahch] *v* **1** (perf **wygłówkować** [vi-gwoof-KOH-vahch]) To think intensely about something, such as an answer; to wonder; to ponder <use one's head, rack one's brain, brainstorm, think up, noodle around, percolate, perk, head trip, skull drag, eat, bug, burn a couple of braincells> eg *Wszyscy główkowali nad sprawą (They were all noodling around the issue); Nie główkuj za bardzo, bo mózg ci się przepali (Don't rack your brain too hard. You may fry it)* **2** (perf **zagłówkować** [zah-gwoof-KOH-vahch]) *v* (In soccer) To strike the ball with the head <head> eg *Kowalski główkował dwa razy (Kowalski headed two times)*

głupek* [GWOO-pehk] (or **głupol*** [GWOO-pohl] or **głąb*** [gwohmp]) *nm* A very stupid, clumsy or ineffectual person; an idiot <airbrain, airhead, birdbrain,

blockhead, squarehead, bonehead, bubblebrain, bubblehead, buckethead, cluckhead, cementhead, clunkhead, deadhead, dumbbell, dumbcluck, dumbhead, dumbass, dumbbrain, fatbrain, fathead, flubdub, knukclebrain, knucklehead, lamebrain, lardhead, lunkhead, meathead, musclehead, noodlehead, numbskull, pointhead, scatterbrain, jerk, jerk-off, klutz, chump, creep, nerd, dork, dweeb, gweeb, geek, jackass, lummox, twerp, nerd, bozo, clod, cluck, clunk, dimwit, dingbat, dipstick, dodo, dopey, dufus, goofus, lump, lunk, nitwit, schnook, schlep, schlemiel, schmendrick, schmo, schmuck, simp, stupe> eg *Ten głupol rozbił mój samochód! (That schlemiel crashed my car!)*

głupi [GWOO-pee] **1** *adj* (or **głupawy** [gwoo-PAH-vi]) Senseless, idiotic, or clownish <loony, batty, daffy, jackass, screwloose, jerky, nerdy, kooky, sappy, crazy, crazy as a loon, dopey, ga-ga, half-baked, loopy, mental, nerts, nuts, nutty, psycho, schizo, screwy, wacky, weird, wild> eg *Nie lubię takich głupawych filmów (I don't like such loony movies); Może i jest głupawa, ale ma świetne ciało (Maybe she is dumbheaded, but she's got a great body)* **2** Unimportant, worthless, paltry or derisory <measly> eg *To go kosztowało durne dwa tysiące (It set him back measly two thousand)* **3** (Esp about a situation) Awkward, undesirable <stupid> eg *To była głupia sprawa (It was a stupid affair)*
See nie ma głupich, udawać greka, wychodzić na durnia

głupi jak but See głupszy niż ustawa przewiduje

głupi jaś [GWOO-pee YAHSH] *nm phr* An anesthetic injection which stupefies, sedates, or kills the pain <gork, knockout drop, knockout shot, knockout jab> eg *Zaserwowali mu głupiego jasia i nic nie czuł podczas operacji (They served him a knockout shot and he didn't feel anything during the operation)*

głupieć [GWOO-pyehch] (perf **zgłupieć** [ZGWOO-pyehch]) *v* To become stupid or insane <go crazy, go crazy as a loon, blow one's cork, blow one's top, blow a fuse, crack up, freak out, flip out, go ape, go bananas, go bent, go bonkers, go cracked, go dopey, go ga-ga, go half-baked, go loony, go loopy, go mental, go nerts, go nuts, go nutty, go off one's nut, go off one's rocker, go off one's base, go off the track, go off the trolley, go out one's skull, go psycho, go schizo, go screwy, go wacky, go weird, go wild, schiz out, psych out, come unglued, come unstuck, come unwrapped, come unzipped, go to pieces> eg *Można całkiem zgłupieć od tego hałasu (You can go nuts because of this noise)*

głupiego robota [gwoo-PYEH-goh roh-BOH-tah] (or **robota głupiego** [roh-BOH-tah gwoo-PYEH-goh]) *nf phr* Senseless and ineffective work that gives no satisfaction, esp time-consuming or tedious <daily grind, salt mines, nine-to-five, rat race, donkeywork, bullwork, elbow grease> eg *Dlaczego nie chcesz pracować? Bo to głupiego robota (Why don't you want to work? Because it's a donkeywork)*

głupszy niż ustawa przewiduje* [GWOOP-shi nish oo-STAH-vah psheh-vee-DOO-yeh] (or **głupi jak but*** [GWOO-pee yahk BOOT] or **głupszy od jeża*** [GWOOP-shi ohd YEH-zhah]) *adj phr* Very stupid <airbrained, airheaded, birdbrained, blockheaded, squareheaded, boneheaded, bubblebrained, bubbleheaded, bucketheaded, cluckheaded, cementheaded, clunkheaded, deadheaded, dumbclucked, dumbheaded, dumbassed, dumbbrained, fatbrained, fatheaded, flubdubbed, knukclebrained, knuckleheaded, lamebrained, lardheaded, lunkheaded, meatheaded, muscleheaded, noodleheaded, numbskulled, pointheaded, scatterbrained, nerdy, dorky, jackassed, lummoxed,

dopey, goofy> eg *Nasza nowa nauczycielka jest naprawdę głupsza od jeża (Our new teacher is real fatbrained); Dlaczego chcesz chodzić z nim? Jest głupi jak but (Why do you want to go out with him? He's scatterbrained)*

gnat [gnaht] *nm* A pistol or rifle <blaster, gat, piece, iron, rod, heater, snubby, popper, tool, stick, boomstick, firestick, hardware, speaker, difference, persuader, convincer, equalizer, artillery, cannon, Saturday night special> eg *Skądżeś wziął tego gnata? (Where did you get that boomstick?)*

gnaty [GNAH-ti] *npl* Bones, esp ribs <slats> eg *Szturchnęła go w gnaty (She poked him in the slats)*

gnić [gneech] *v* To wait <wait out, cool it, cool one's heels, sweat it, sweat out, be put on ice, be put on hold, hang out, hang around, stick around, sit and take it, sit tight, sit out, sit on one's ass, sit on one's butt, warm a chair, lay dead> eg *Gniję tu od dwóch godzin (I've been cooling my heels here for two hours)*

gnida See glizda

gniot [gnyoht] *nm* A boring or worthless book <potboiler, spyboiler, pulp> eg *Napisał tego gniota w dwa miesiące (It took him two months to write this potboiler)*

gnoić [GNOH-eech] (perf **zgnoić** [ZGNOH-eech]) *v* **1** To deliberately cause harm to someone; to ruin someone; to victimize <fuck, fuck over, fuck up, screw, screw over, screw up, shaft, sell out, sell down the river> eg *Jeśli nie będę uważał, to tych dwóch zazdrosnych skurwysynów mnie zgnoi (If I'm not careful, these two jealous pricks will fuck me)* **2** To make someone's life miserable; to torment <kick someone's ass, give someone a hard time, give someone a bad time, give someone hell, jump all over, put the heat on, put the squeeze on, put someone through the wringer, break someone's balls, bust someone's ass, lean on, twist someone's arm, hassle> eg *Jeśli nam dzisiaj nie zapłaci, zgnoimy go (If he doesn't pay us today, we'll have to lean on him)*

gnojek* [GNOH-yek] (or **gnój*** [gnooy]) *nm* A boy or a young man one dislikes or disapproves of <asshole, fuck, fucker, fuckhead, fuckface, motherfucker, shit, shitface, shithead, shitheel, bastard, jerk, SOB, son of a bitch, son of a whore, cocksucker, prick, dick, dickhead, cuntface, schmuck, scum, scumbag, sleazebag, slimebag, dipshit, pisshead, piece of shit, pain in the ass> eg *Skądżeś wytrzasnął takiego gnoja? (Where'd you find such a shithead?)*

gołodupiec See golec

goły [GOH-wi] *adj* **1** (or **goły jak święty turecki** [GOH-wi yahk SHFYEHN-ti too-REHTS-kee]) Poor or penniless <broke, dead broke, flat broke, stone broke, busted, cleaned out, cold in hand, down and out, piss-poor, poor as a church mouse, strapped, tapped out, drained, without a red cent> eg *Wszyscy wiedż, że jest goły jak święty turecki. Nawet nie ma własnego samochodu (Everybody knows that he's tapped out. He doesn't even own a car)* **2** (Of a sum) Bare; without any bonuses <net, base, plain, clean, without the frosting on the cake> eg *Dostał tylko gołą pensję (He only got his bare salary)*

goły jak święty turecki [GOH-wi yahk SHFYEHN-ti too-REHTS-kee] *adj phr* Entirely naked <bare-assed, BA, buck naked, in one's birthday suit, in the altogether, in the raw, naked as a jaybird> eg *Stał tam goły jak święty turecki, drapiąc się po brzuchu (He stood there buck naked, scratching his belly)*

godzina See młoda godzina, na czarną godzinę, po godzinach

goguś [GOH-goosh] *nm* A man, esp vain man who attaches too much importance to his physical appearance <dandy, fancypants, poser> eg *Znów chodzi z jakimś gogusiem (She's been dating some fancypants again)*

gol See strzelić gola

golas [GOH-lahs] *nm* A nude, unclad person <bare-assed, BA, buck naked, in one's birthday suit, in the altogether, in the raw> eg *Co to za golas? (Who's that bare-assed guy?)*

golec [GOH-lehts] (or **gołodupiec*** [goh-woh-DOO-pyehts]) *nm* A poor person; someone who owns nothing valuable <have-not> eg *Gołodupce szukają jakiejś szansy (The have-nots are looking for a chance)*

golnąć [GOHL-nohnch] (or **golnąć sobie** [GOHL-nohnch SOH-byeh]) *v* To have a drink of liquor, esp quick <knock back, down, slug down, swig, tank, tank up> eg *Golnij sobie trochę wódki (Why don't you swig some vodka?)*

gonić się See iść się pierdolić

gość [gohshch] (or **gostek** [GOH-stehk] or **gościu** [GOHSH-chyoo]) *nm* **1** Any man <fella, guy, dude> eg *Co to za jeden? Nie znam gościa (Who is he? I don't know that guy)* **2** A man appreciated and honored by one <article, character, item, number> eg *Tak, twój brat może być fajnym gościem, jak chce (Yes, your brother can be a cool number when he wants)*

gościówa [goh-SHCHOO-vah] *nf* **1** A woman <gal, dame, lady, missy, ma'am, dudette> eg *Z tej twojej ciotki to jest niezła gościówa! Uwielbiam jak prowadzi samochód! (That aunt of yours is a real gal. I do like the way she drives!)* **2** A woman appreciated and honored by one <article, character, item, number> eg *Ta twoja siostra, to prawdziwa gościówa (Your sister is a real article)*

gorąco See na poczekaniu

gorący See w gorącej wodzie kąpany

gorączka See dostać cholery

góra [GOO-rah] **1** *adv* Not more than; at the very most <max, tops, the mostest> eg *Na dobę emitować będziemy góra 10 minut reklam (We're going to air 10 minutes of commercials an hour, tops)* **2** *nf* Superiors or decision-makers, esp members of government or high-ranking officals <upstairs, higher-ups, brass, top> eg *Mamy rozkazy z góry (We have orders from upstairs)* **3** *nf* One's male superviser or director <boss, chief, big boy, big cheese, big enchilada, top brass, honcho, big man, man upstairs, top dog, key player, exec, numero uno> eg *Co powiedziała góra? (What did the honcho say?)*

See do góry nogami, dostać kopa w górę, iść w górę, leżeć bykiem

górka See mieć coś z górki, z górki

goryl [GOH-ril] *nm* A bodyguard <gorilla, ape, dog, lookout, bouncer, meathead, sidewinder> eg *Szkoda, że te goryle z agencji ochrony nie są grzeczniejsze (It's a shame those apes from the security agency can't be more polite)*

gorzała [goh-ZHAH-wah] (or **gorzałka** [goh-ZHAH-oo-kah]) *nf* Potent liquor such as vodka or whiskey <hard liquor, hard stuff, hooch, booze, stiff drink, poison> eg *Młodzieniec wolał gorzałę i panienki (The youth preferred hooch and chicks)*

gorzej See być gorzej komuś

gostek See gość

gotowiec [goh-TOH-vyehts] *nm* A ready composition or translation swapped during an examination and pretended to have been written during an examination

<cheat, cheat sheet, cheat note, crib sheet, crib, pony> eg *I to ma być gotowiec? (Do you call this a cheat note?)*

gotowy See silny zwarty i gotowy

gówniany* [goov-NYAH-ni] *adj* Bad, poor, worthless, or of inferior quality <shitty, crappy, lousy, awful, bush-league, cheap, cruddy, crummy, doggy, low-rent, low-ride, no-good, raggedy-ass, schlocky, stinking, tacky, trashy, two-bit, dime-a-dozen, fair to middling, garden variety, of a sort, of sorts, piddling, pissy-ass, piss-poor, run-of-the-mill, small-time> eg *To jedzenie było naprawdę gówniane (The food was real crappy)*

gówniara* [goov-NYAH-rah] *nf* A teenage girl, esp whom one despises <chick, chicklet, teen, teener, teeny-bopper, bubble-gummer, youngster, juvie, shithead, punk, snot-nose> eg *Zostaw tę smarkulę w spokoju (Leave this shithead alone)*

gówniarz* [GOOV-nyash] *nm* **1** A teenage boy, esp whom one despises <teen, teener, teeny-bopper, bubble-gummer, youngster, juvie, shithead, punk, snot-nose> eg *Byle gówniarz wie, że to koniec (Any shithead knows that it's over)* **2** A silly and irresponsible man <shithead> eg *Przestań się zachowywać jak gówniarz (Stop acting like a shithead)*

gówniarzeria* [goov-nya-ZHEHR-yah] *nf* A group of teenagers, esp whom one despises <teens, teeners, teeny-boppers, bubble-gummers, shitheads> eg *Klientela to sama gówniarzeria (The clientele is nothing but a bunch of shitheads)*

gówno See dwa razy brzydszy od gówna, wpaść

gówno kogoś obchodzić* [GOOV-noh KOH-gohsh ohp-KHOH-jeech] (or **guzik kogoś obchodzić** [GOO-zheek KOH-gohsh ohp-KHOH-jeech]) *v phr* To be indifferent to or contemptuous of; not to care at all; to ignore; to show disrespect <not give a damn, not give a fuck, not give a shit, not give a diddly-shit, not give a diddly-damn, not give a flying fuck, not give a hoot, not give a rat's ass, not give a squat, pass up, diss, skip, ig, ice, chill, freeze, cut, brush off, give the brush, give the cold shoulder, turn the cold shoulder, cold-shoulder, give the go-by, high-hat, kiss off> eg *Gówno mnie obchodzi, co myślisz (I don't give a shit what you think)*

gówno* [GOOV-noh] (or **gie** [gyeh]) **1** *nn* A worthless, unimportant, or immoral person <shit, crap, scum, slime, dirt, motherfucker, fucker> eg *On to tylko gówno (He's just a shit)* **2** *nn* Nothing at all; zero <shit, diddly shit, doodle shit, chicken shit, jack shit, shit-all, zilch, beans, damn, diddly-squat, doodly-squat, duck egg, goose egg, hoot, one red cent, one thin dime, rat's ass, zero, zippo, shit-all, fuck-all> eg *Gówno od nich dostał (He got jack shit from them)* **3** *nn* Any object or situation that is wretched, unpleasant, or bothersome <shit, crap, bitch, bummer, drag, motherfucker, fucker> eg *Zabierzcie ode mnie to gówno (Get this fucker away from me!)* **4** *nn* Feces, excrement, or a piece thereof <shit, crap, piece of shit, piece of crap> eg *Dwa razy dziś wlazł w gówno (He stepped in shit two times today)* **5** *excl* (or **gówno prawda*** [GOOV-noh PRAHV-dah]) An exclamation of defiance or disbelief <like fuck, like hell, like shit, bullshit, BS, horseshit, balls, my ass, in a pig's ass, in a pig's ear, in a pig's eye, don't shit me, are you shitting me, no shit> eg *Mówi, że zna hebrajski i arabski. Gówno! (She says she knows Hebrew and Arabic. My ass!)*

gra muzyka [GRAH moo-ZI-kah] (or **wszystko gra** [FSHIST-koh GRAH] or **szafa gra** [SHAH-fah GRAH]) *phr* Everything is in order <everything is taken care of, everything is set up> eg *Uspokój się, wszystko gra (Lighten up, everything's taken care of)*

gra nie warta świeczki [grah nyeh VAHR-tah SHFYEHCH-kee] *nf phr* A course of action that is unlikely to be rewarding or profitable; a profitless endeavor; something not worth the trouble <something for the birds, something not worth a shit, something not worth a fuck, something not worth a damn, something not worth a diddly-squat, something not worth a doodly-squat> eg *Gra nie jest warta świeczki (It's not worth a diddly-damn)*

grać [grahch] *v* To be in order; to function properly <be alright, be okay, be OK, run smooth> eg *Wszystko grało (Everything was okay)*
See kiszki komuś marsza grają

grać pod publiczkę [grahch poht poob-LEECH-keh] *v phr* To attempt to get the approval of the audience; to perform or cater to in a manner that will get the approval of the lower elements in the audience <play to the gallery, play up to> eg *To profesjonalny aktor, ale ma tendencję, żeby grać pod publiczkę (He's a competent actor, but he has a tendency to play the gallery*

grać sobie w kulki z kimś [grahch SOH-byeh f KOOL-kee s KEEMSH] (or **grać sobie w pici-polo** [grahch SOH-byeh f PEE-chee-POH-loh]) *v phr* To tease; to banter; to treat someone unseriously and frivolously; to have fun at someone's expense <poke fun at, kid, kid around, pull someone's leg, pull someone's string, fool around, jive, josh, shuck, lark, spoof, send up, fuck around with, fuck with, cut down> eg *Powiedziała mu, żeby przestał się grać z nią w kulki (She told him to stop fooling around with her)*

graba [GRAH-bah] (or **grabula** [grah-BOO-lah]) *nf* A hand <mitt, paw, duke, fiver, grabber, hook, meathook> eg *Dzieciak ma graby jak goryl (The kid's got mitts on him like a gorilla)*
See dać grabę

grajdołek [grah-ee-DOH-wehk] *nm* A small town, esp in the country; any place far from civilization <jerk town, jerkwater town, backwater, hellhole, rathole, mudhole, real hole, noplaceville, hicksville, whistle stop, dump, armpit, East Jesus, Bumfuck Egypt> eg *Dość mam życia w tym grajdołku (I have enough of living in this mudhole)*

grajek [GRAH-yehk] *nm* A musician <muso, busker, rocker, cat, band man> eg *Ile zarabia taki grajek na tydzień? (How much does such a muso make a week?)*

granda [GRAHN-dah] *nf* A scandalous fact or situation; a scandal <gas, hot potato, bad scene, bad news, can of worms, bag of worms, takedown, putdown, shit, serious shit, deep shit, deep water, drag, bind, bitch, bummer, downer, headache, double trouble, snafu, pain in the ass, pain in the neck, spot, mess, holy mess, pickle, squeeze, hard time, glitch, stinker, skeleton, skeleton in the closet, sizzler, scorcher, dynamite, Watergate, fine kettle of fish, fine how do you do, fine cup of coffee, big stink, curtains, lights out, game's over> eg *Jak mnie złapią, to będzie granda (Bad scene for me if they find me)*

grane See co jest

gras [grahs] *nm* Marijuana; cannabis <grass, pot, dope, weed, reefer, tea, hemp, Mary Jane, MJ> eg *Miała przy sobie gras, gdy ją aresztowano (She had pot on her when she was arrested); To dobry gras, koleś (This is good weed, man)*

grat [graht] *nm* Any old or used thing, esp a car or a piece of furniture <piece of junk, junk, junker, old stuff> eg *Zabieraj stąd tego grata (Get this piece of junk out of here)*

gratka [GRAHT-kah] *nf* A sudden opportunity or bargain; a sudden instance of good luck <buy, steal, deal, mazel, mazeltov, fluke, mojo, streak of luck, lucky strike, lucky hit, lucky scratch, lucky break> eg *Dostał zaproszenie z USA. Ale gratka! (He got an invitation from the USA. What a fluke!)*

grek See udawać greka

grób See być jedną nogą w grobie, przewracać się w grobie, stać nad grobem

groch z kapustą [grohkh s kah-POOS-toh] *n phr* A number of things mixed up without any sensible order <mish mash, hodge-podge, odds and ends, bits and pieces, rag-bag, mess, unholy mess, rat's nest, smorgasboard> eg *Ale groch z kapustą! (What a hodge-podge!)*

grom See jak grom z jasnego nieba, od cholery

grosz [grohsh] *nm* Money; cash <dough, bread, bank, cabbage, change, coin, folding, green, lettuce> eg *Masz trochęgrosza przy sobie? (You got some dough on you?)* See bez grosza, nie śmierdzieć groszem, złamany grosz

grosze [GROH-sheh] *npl* A small amount of money <peanuts, chicken feed, nickels and dimes, pennies, small change> eg *Płacili mu grosze (They paid him chicken feed)*

groszorób [groh-SHOH-roop] *nm* A parsimonious person; a miser <tightwad, piker, cheapskate, scrooge, pinchfist, penny-pincher, pinchpenny, nickel-nurser, nickel-squeezer> eg *Jej mąż to prawdziwy groszorób (Her husband is a real tightwad)*

groszowy [groh-SHOH-vi] *adj* Worth very little; not remunerative <cheap, nickel-and-dime> eg *Gadasz mi tu o jakimś groszowym interesie (You're telling me about some nickel-and-dime business)*

gruba kreska [GROO-bah KREHS-kah] *nf phr* Forgiveness and reconciliation, esp with reference to former communists and the communist past <burying the hatchet, letting bygones be bygones, letting sleeping dogs lie> eg *To jaskrawe grubej kreski (It is a blatant confirmation of buring the hatchet)*

gruba ryba [GROO-bah RI-bah] *nm phr* A very important, influential, or well-known person <big shot, big cheese, big enchilada, big fish, big guy, big wheel, wheel, biggie, topsider, celeb, big time operator, head honcho, BTO, VIP> eg *On musi być jakąś grubą rybą (He must be some big shot)*

grubas [GROO-bahs] *nm* An obese person <fatty, fatso, blimp, fat-ass, lard-ass, tub of lard, crisco> eg *Wszedł jakiś grubas i zamówiłł dziesięć porcji dużych frytek (Some crisco came in and ordered ten large fries)*

grube [GROO-beh] *npl* Banknotes of higher denominations <big bills> : *Daj mi dychę, mam tylko grube (Give me a tenner, all I've got is big bills)*

grube pieniądze See ciężkie pieniądze

grubo [GROO-boh] *adv* More than <cut above, way, far cry, a good bit, a fair bit, a fair sight> eg *Zapłacił grubo ponad miliard (He paid a good bit more than a million)*

gruby See walić z grubej rury

gruchot [GROO-khoht] *nm* An old and battered automobile <junker, jalopy, wreck, bucket, bucket of bolts> eg *Sprzedał tego geuchota za dwa tysiące (He sold that wreck for two thousand)*

grunt [GROONT] *nm* Something most vital, basic or essential <must, must do, bottom line, rock bottom, cold turkey, meat and potatoes, nitty-gritty, coal and ice, brass tracks> eg *Właściwy ubiór to grunt (Right apparel is a must)*

grupenseks [GROO-pehn-sehks] *nm* Group sex, esp an occasion when several males copulate with one woman; an orgy <group thing, gang bang, gang shag, train> eg *Impreza okazała się grupenseksem (The party turned out to be a group thing)*

gruszka See ni pies ni wydra

gryps [grips] *nm* A prohibited note or letter, passed around by inmates, or smuggled out of prison <kite> eg *Puszczał grypsy i w końcu wpadł (He used to fly a kite, and eventually got caught)*

grypsera [grip-SEH-rah] *nm* Cant; the secret language of the underworld, esp thieves' argot <flash, jive, lingo, double speak> eg *Rozmawiali grypserą i nic nie zrozumiałem (They were talking in flash and I couldn't understand a word)*

gryźć kogoś [grishch KOH-gohsh] *v* To be preoccupied, worried, or upset; to fret or harry oneself <eat, bug, dog, nag, stew, bleed, sweat, sweat bullets, bum out, eat one's heart out, have something at heart> eg *Spytała, co mnie gryzie (She asked what was eating me)*

gryźć się [grishch shyeh] (or **zagryzać się** [zah-GRI-zahch shyeh]) *v* To have doubts or scruples; to hesitate; be in a dilemma; to dither <fence straddle, sit on the fence, hang on the fence, run hot and cold, blow hot and cold, be between a rock and a hard place> eg *Powinna zadzwonić po policję, bo wiedziała, że to jej chłopak obrabował bank. Gryzła się (She should have called the police because she knew it was her boyfriend who robbed the bank. She was between a rock and hard place)*

gryźć ziemię [grishch ZHYEH-myeh] (or **gryźć piach** [grishch PYAHKH]) *v phr* To be dead or die <bite the dust, kiss the dust, croak, belly up, buy the farm, buy the ranch, cash in one's chips, check out, bump off, conk off, conk out, farm, give up the ghost, go home feet first, go home in a box, go west, kick in, kick off, kick the bucket, pass out, peg out, shove off, drop off, step off, pop off, push up daisies, meet one's maker, turn up one's toes, go down the tube, join the great majority, join the majority> eg *Nie wrócił, pewnie już dawno ziemię gryzie (He didn't come back. He must be pushing up daisies)*

gryz [gris] *nm* A bite of something to eat <bite> eg *Daj mi gryza, co? (Give me a bite, wil you?)*

gryzipiórek [gri-zhee-PYOO-rehk] *nm* A rank-and-file clerical worker or a low-ranking official <pencil pusher, pen driver, paper shuffler, desk jockey, white collar, pink collar, suit> eg *Chcesz być gryzipiórkiem do końca życia? (Do you want to be a paper shuffler till the end of your life?)*

gryzmoły [griz-MOH-wi] *npl* Illegible handwriting or any meaningless piece of writing <scribble, scribbling, scratching, hen tracks, chicken tracks, hen scratches, chicken scratches, hen writing, chicken writing> eg *Nie mogę rozczytać jego gryzmołów (I can't read the chicken writing of his)*

gryzmolić [griz-MKOH-leech] (perf **nagryzmolić** [nah-griz-MOH-leech]; or **gryzdać** [GRIZ-dahch] perf **nagryzdać** [nah-GRIZ-dahch]; **jak kura pazurem** [yahk KOO-rah pah-ZOO-rehm] may be added) *v* To handwrite illegibly or write anything which is meaningless <scribble, scratch> eg *Zawsze gryzmolił jak kura pazurem (He always used to scribble)*

grzać się* [GZHAHCH shyeh] (or **gzić się*** [GZHEECH shyeh]) *v* To copulate <get screwed, get fucked, get laid, screw, fuck, fork, frig, ball, bang, boink, bonk, boff, hump, poke, shag> eg *Grzali się przez całą noc (They were fucking all night long)*

grzać* [gzhahch] (perf **wygrzać*** [VI-gzhahch]) *v* To copulate with someone <fuck, screw, lay, ball, bang, boink, boff, boogie, bop, frig, hump, poke, shag> eg *Czy to prawda, że grzał tylko małolaty? (Is that true that he laid only teenagers?)*
See ani ziębić ani grzać kogoś, gazować

grzechu warty [GZHEH-khoo VAHR-ti] *adj* (Of a man) Handsome, sexually attractive <ten, drop-dead gorgeous, knock-out gorgeous, hunky, laid out> eg *Ten to jest naprawdę grzechu warty (This one is a really hunky guy)*

grzeczniś [GZHEHCH-neesh] *nm* An overly or superficially nice man; a sycophant <brown-noser, ass-kisser, ass-licker, ass-sucker, ass-wiper, back-scratcher, apple-polisher, tokus-licker, kiss-ass, yes-man> eg *Ten grzeczniś dał szefowi butelkę szampana na urodziny (That brown-noser actually gave the boss a bottle of champaigne for his birthday)*

grzyb* [gzhip] (or **stary grzyb*** [STAH-ri GZHIP]) *nm* An old man <gramps, old fart, old bugger, geezer, gaffer, old-timer, fossil> eg *Czego chciał od ciebie ten stary grzyb? (What did the geezer want from you?)*
See na diabła

grzybek [GZHI-behk] *nm* (Of an automobile) Turning upside down; capsizing <turtle, turning turtle, roofing, rolling> eg *Jazda skończyła się grzybkiem. Szczęśliwym trafem nikt nie zginął (The ride ended up in turning turtle. Luckily nobody got killed)*

grzybki [GZHIP-kee] *npl* Hallucinogenic mushrooms, used as drugs <magic mushrooms, magic shrooms, shrooms> eg *Zawsze lubiliśmy jeść grzybki na ich koncertach (We always liked to eat magic mushrooms at their concerts)*

guma [GOO-mah] *nf* **1** A rubber baton, esp police officer's <billy, billy club, nightstick, stick, hickory, rosewood, shill, bat> eg *Jeden z policjantów miał gumę (One of the policemen carried a nightstick)* **2** (or **gumka** [GOOM-kah] or **gumiak** [GOO-myahk] or **ogumienie** [oh-goo-MYEH-nyeh]) *nf* A condom <rubber, raincoat, safety, glove, scumbag, eel-skin, French-letter> eg *Znalazła gumę w kartce urodzinowej (She found a rubber in her birthday card)*
See łysa guma, złapać gumę

guzik [GOO-zheek] (or **guzik z pętelką** [GOO-zheek s pehn-TEHL-koh]) *nm* Nothing at all; zero <zilch, beans, damn, diddly-squat, doodly-squat, duck egg, goose egg, hoot, one red cent, one thin dime, rat's ass, zero, zippo, shit-all, fuck-all> eg *Co od niej dostałeś? Guzik z pentelką! (What did she get from her? Zilch!)*

guzik kogoś obchodzić See gówno kogoś obchodzić

gwałt See na gwałt

gwardia [GVAR-dyah] (or **stara gwardia** [STAH-rah GVAR-dyah]) *nf* Old people, old generation <old guard, old brigade> eg *Te nowe pomysły nigdy nie zadowolą starej gwardii (These new ideas will never please the old brigade)*

gwint See jak chuj, z gwinta

gwizdać na coś [GVEEZ-dahch nah tsohsh] *v phr* To be indifferent to or contemptuous of; not to care at all; to ignore; to show disrespect <not give a damn, not give a fuck, not give a shit, not give a diddly-shit, not give a diddly-damn, not give a flying fuck, not give a hoot, not give a rat's ass, not give a squat, pass up, diss, skip, ig, ice, chill, freeze, cut, brush off, give the brush, give the cold shoulder, turn the cold shoulder, cold-shoulder, give the go-by, high-hat, kiss off> eg *Gwiżdżę na to, co myślisz (I don't give a shit what you think)*

gwizdek See na pół gwizdka

gwizdnąć [GVEEZD-nohnch] (or **gwiznąć** [GVEEZ-nohnch]) *v* To steal; to rob <heist, boost, burgle, nurn, bag, buzz, highjack, hoist, hold up, hook, hustle, jump, kick over, knock off, knock over, lift, move, mug, nab, nick, nip, pinch, pluck, roll, rustle, snatch, snitch, stick up, swipe, take off, put the grab on, go south with> eg *Gwizdnął to z drogerii (He nicked that from a drugstore)*

gwóźdź do trumny [gvooshch doh TROOM-ni] (or **ostatni gwóźdź do trumny** [ohs-TAHT-nee gvooshch doh TROOM-ni]) *nm phr* Something bad which will bring a person's ruin one step nearer <nail in someone's coffin, last straw, last draw> eg *Ich decyzja to był ostatni gwóźdź to trumny (Their decision was a nail in his coffin)*

gzić się See **grzać się**

H

ha See tak że hej, taki że hej

haczyk [KHAH-chik] (or **hak** [khahk]) *nm* A hidden element, esp. problem or difficulty <catch, hook, snag, hitch, kicker, stinger> eg *Wszystko wygląda świetnie, ale jest w tym jeden haczyk (It all looks great, but there's a catch to it)*
See łyknąć, mieć haka na kogoś

haft [KHAHFT] *nm* Vomit <barf, puke> eg *Czy masz hafta na bucie? (Is that barf on your shoe?)*

haftować [khahf-TOH-vahch] (or **hafcić** [KHAHF-cheech] or **haftać** [KHAHF-tahch]; perf **nahaftować** [nah-khahf-TOH-vahch] or **nahafcić** [nah-KHAHF-cheech] or **nahaftać** [nah-KHAHF-tahch]) *v* To empty one's stomach; to vomit <barf, puke, blow grits, blow chunks, chuck, do a Technicolor yawn, drive the big bus, heave, pray to the porcelain god, ralph, rolf, talk to the big white phone, cry Ruth, cry Ralph, blow one's cookies, blow one's lunch, lose one's cookies, lose one's lunch, shoot one's cookies, shoot one's lunch> eg *Kto haftował w kiblu? (Who's been shooting one's cookies in the john?); Wypiła za dużo i wyszła z pokoju żeby haftować (She drank too much and left the room to blow chunks)*

haj See na haju

hajc [KHAH-eets] *nm* Money <dough, bread, bank, cabbage, change, coin, folding, green, lettuce> eg *Jeśli nie masz hajcu to do mnie nie przychodź. Za darmo nie daję (If you don't have dough, don't come to me. I don't give out for free)*

hajtać się [KHAH-ee-tahch shyeh] (or **chajtać się** [KHAH-ee-tahch shyeh]; perf **hajtnąć się** [KHAH-eet-nohnch shyeh] or **ohajtać się** [oh-KHAH-ee-tahch shyeh] or **chajtnąć się** [KHAH-eet-nohnch shyeh] or **ochajtać się** [oh-KHAH-ee-tahch shyeh]) *v* To get married; to marry <hitch, hitch up, get hitched, splice, get spliced, hook, get hooked, merge, get merged, tie the knot, walk down the aisle, take the plunge, step off the carpet> eg *Dwa tygodnie temu ochajtnąłem się (I got spliced two weeks ago)*

hak See haczyk, mieć haka na kogoś, z hakiem

haker [KHAH-kehr] (or **hacker** [KHAH-kehr] or **hakier** [KHAH-kyehr]) *nm* A very skillful, enthusiastic, and pranky computer programmer, esp who performs illegal actions such as obtaining secret information <hacker, cracker> eg *Większość hackerów to bardzo młodzi ludzie (The majority of hackers are very young people)*

harmoszka [khahr-MOHSH-kah] *nf* A harmonica <harp, mouth organ> eg *Umiesz grać na harmoszce? (Can you play a mouth organ?)*

harówa [khah-ROO-vah] (or **harówka** [khah-ROOF-kah]) *nf* A very hard work; a Herculean labor <ball-buster, bone-breaker, back-breaker, bitch, killer, grind, donkeywork, bullwork, dirty work> eg *Pisanie słowników to harówa! (Writing dictionaries is a killer!)*

harować [khah-ROH-vahch] (or **zaharowywać się** [zah-khah-roh-VI-vahch shyeh]; perf **naharować się** [nah-khah-ROH-vahch shyeh] or **zaharować się** [zah-khah-ROH-vahch shyeh]; **jak wół** [yahk VOOW] may be added) *v* To work very hard <work one's ass off, work one's fingers to the bone, work like a horse, sweat, bust one's ass off, break one's ass off, make bricks without a straw> eg *Od dwóch lat haruje jak wół (He's been working like a horse for two years)*

hasać [KHAH-sahch] (perf **pohasać** [poh-KHAH-sahch]) *v* To dance <rock, shake, boogie, hop, swing, jump, juke, jive, wrestle, grind> eg *Ta laska lubi hasać (That chick likis rocks)*

hasz [khahsh] *nm* Hashish <hash, heesh, candy> eg *Kto tu sprzedaje hasz? (Who's dealing hash around here?)*

heca [KHEH-tsah] *nf phr* An scandalous fact or situation; a scandal <gas, hot potato, bad scene, bad news, can of worms, bag of worms, takedown, putdown, shit, serious shit, deep shit, deep water, drag, bind, bitch, bummer, downer, headache, double trouble, snafu, pain in the ass, pain in the neck, spot, mess, holy mess, pickle, squeeze, hard time, glitch, stinker, skeleton, skeleton in the closet, sizzler, scorcher, dynamite, Watergate, fine kettle of fish, fine how do you do, fine cup of coffee, big stink, curtains, lights out, game's over> eg *Pies zjadł stek, który mieliśmy na obiad. Ale heca! The dog's eaten the steak we were going to have for dinner. What a gas!)*

helmut [KHEL-moot]* *nm* A male German <kraut, krauthead, sauerkraut, Fritz, Heinie, Jerry> eg *Te helmity robią całkiem dobre piwo (Those krauts make some pretty good beer)*

hera [KHEH-rah] *nf* Heroin <horse, H, hero, smack, brown sugar, doojee> eg *Lepiej trzymaj się z dala od hery (You'd better stay away from hero)*

hery [KHEH-ri] *npl* Hair <moss, wig, wool, locks> eg *Spójrz na twoje hery. Idź się ostrzyc (Take a look at your wig. Go get a haircut)*

hetera [kheh-TEH-rah] *nf* A quarrelsome, bothersome, malicious woman; a shrew <bitch, slut, cunt, broad, wench, hag, old hag, old biddy, old bag, old tart, piece of shit> eg *Dlaczego porzucił pan żonę? Bo hetera była (Why did you leave your wife? Because she was a bitch)*

historia See tak że hej, taki że hej

hit [KHEET] *nm* Anything sensational or exciting, esp news; a sensation <hit, smash-hit, bomb, bombshell, barnburner, flash, blast, eye-popper, breath-taker, heart-stopper, grabber, stand-out, stunner, gasser, sensaysh, blockbuster, sockeroo> eg *Ta informacja okazała się prawdziwym hitem (This piece of news turned out to be a real smash-hit)*

ho-ho See tak że hej, taki że hej

hołota [khoh-WOH-tah] *nf* Worthless, badly-behaved, and often poor people <riff-raff, rabble, mob, gang> eg *Czemu zaprosiła tę hołotę na imprezę? (Why did she invite all this riff-raff to the party?)*

homo-niewiadomo* [KHOH-moh nyeh-vyah-DOH-moh] *nn phr* A male homosexual or someone supposed to be one <fag, faggot, fairy, queer, fruitcake, homo, pansy, sissy, swish, daisy, limp-wrist, queen> eg *Wydaje mi się, że twój szef jest homo-niewiadomo (It seems to me that your boss is a fruitcake)*

huk See bez echa, z hukiem

hulać [KHOO-lahch] (perf **przehulać** [psheh-KHOO-lahch] or **pohulać** [poh-KHOO-lahch] or) *v* To carouse or celebrate <party, ball, have a ball, jam, paint the town red, raise hell, bar-hop, bar-crawl, go on a bender> eg *Hulali całą noc (They partied all night long)*

hulanka [khoo-LAHN-kah] *nf* A party or other usually noisy celebration <ball, bash, blast, blowout, brawl, fest, rally, shindig> eg *Podobała ci się hulanka? (Did you the ball?)*

hyś [hish] (or **hyź** [hish]) *nm* Obsession, insanity, or eccentricity <thing, kick, bag, bug, craze, freak, frenzy, weakness, bug up one's ass, bug in one's ear, bee in one's bonnet, bee, flea in one's nose, maggot, maggot in one's brain, hang-up, jones, monkey, ax to grind> eg *Zbieranie znaczków, czy to nie jest jego ostatni hyś? (Stamp collecting, isn't that his latest craze?)*

I

i po balu See po balu

icek* [EE-tsehk] *nm* A Jewish male <kike, Yid, mockie, sheeny, hooknose, eagle-beak, clipped dick, Jew boy, rabbi, Ike, Hebe, Hymie, Abe, Sammy, Goldberg> eg *Nie wiesz, czego chciał ten icek? (Don't you know what that Hymie wanted?)*

identyko [ee-dehn-TI-koh] *adj phr* Identical; the same <look-alike, dupe, clone, carbon, carbon copy, double, ditto, spitting image, dead ringer, six of one and half a dozen of the other, like two peas in a pod> eg *Jego brat był identyko jak ojciec (His brother was a dead ringer of his father)*

idiocieć [eed-YOH-chehch] (perf **zidiocieć** [zeed-YOH-chehch]) *v* To become stupid, insane, or confused <go crazy, go crazy as a loon, blow one's cork, blow one's top, blow a fuse, crack up, freak out, flip out, go ape, go bananas, go bent, go bonkers, go cracked, go dopey, go ga-ga, go half-baked, go loony, go loopy, go mental, go nerts, go nuts, go nutty, go off one's nut, go off one's rocker, go off one's base, go off the track, go off the trolley, go out one's skull, go psycho, go schizo, go screwy, go wacky, go weird, go wild, schiz out, psych out, come unglued, come unstuck, come unwrapped, come unzipped, go to pieces> eg *Można całkiem zidiocieć od tego hałasu (You can go nuts because of this noise)*

idiota See wychodzić na durnia

idiotka See słodka idiotka

igła See robić z igły widły, spod igły

ikra See z ikrą

ile wlezie [EE-leh VLEH-zhyeh] *adv phr* To an extreme degree; unrestrainedly <to the max, flat-out, all-out, all the way, like hell, like all get-out, like sin, to beat the band, like all creation, like it had gone out of style, like there was no tomorrow, like nobody's business, one's ass off, one's brains out, one's head off, the whole nine yards, nine to the dozen> eg *Pisał na komputerze ile wlezie (He typed on his computer like there was no tomorrow)*

impreza [eem-PREH-zah] (or **imprezka** [eem-PREHS-kah] or **dżampreza** [jahm-PREH-zah]) *nf* A party or other usually noisy celebration <ball, bash, blast, blowout, brawl, fest, rally, shindig> eg *Podobała ci się imprezka? (Did you like the ball?)*
See babska impreza

imprezować [eem-preh-ZOH-vahch] *v* To carouse or celebrate <party, ball, have a ball, jam, paint the town red, raise hell, bar-hop, bar-crawl, go on a bender> eg *Imprezowali całą noc (They partied all night long)*

inaczej śpiewać See cienko śpiewać

indyczyć się [een-DI-chich shyeh] (perf **naindyczyć się** [nah-een-DI-chich shyeh] or **rozindyczyć** [rohz-een-DI-chich shyeh]) *v* To be groundlessly dissatisfied or discontented; to have unfounded complaints <fuss, stink, scene, make a ceremony, beef, bleed, hassle, kvetch, bitch, beef, gripe, piss, bellyache, grouse, growl, squawk, cut a beef, make a stink, piss up a storm, raise a stink, blow up a storm, kick up a storm, eat someone's heart out, fuck around, screw around, mess around, trip> eg *Naindyczyła się, bo nie mieli tego, co chciała (She was pissing up a storm, because they didn't have what she wanted)*

inna para kaloszy [EEN-nah PAH-rah kah-LOH-shi] (or **inna broszka** [EEN-nah BROHSH-kah]; **całkiem** [TSAH-oo-kyehm] or **zupełnie** [zoo-PEH-oo-nyeh] may precede **inna**) *nf phr* Something entirely different; a separate matter <whole new ball game, whole different story, another cup of tea, different kettle of fish> eg *Jak się tam dostaniemy, to już inna para kaloszy (How we're going to get there is another cup of tea)*

inteligencik [een-teh-lee-GEHN-cheek] *nm* An intellectual <highbrow, egghead, longhair, pointhead, conehead, skull, double dome, ivory dome> eg *Wyszła za jakiegoś inteligencika (She married some egghead)*

interes [een-TEH-rehs] **1** *nm* Business <biz, deal, set-up, gesheft> eg *Szybko okazało się, że zajmuje się nielegalnymi interesami (It soon turned out that he'd been doing some illegal geshefts)* **2** The penis <cock, prick, dick, stick, joystick, dipstick, bone, meat, beef, wang, yang, dong, dummy, hammer, horn, hose, jock, joint, knob, pork, putz, rod, root, tool, flute, skin flute, love-muscle, sausage, schmuck, schlong, schvantz, cream-stick, third leg, middle leg, business, apparatus, John, Johnny, Johnson, John Thomas, Jones, pecker, peter, peepee, pisser, weenie, peenie, dingus, dingbat, thingy> eg *Fajny mam interes? (Do you like my joystick?)*
See ubić interes, złoty interes, zwijać manatki

internat [een-TEHR-naht] *nm* (Esp during the period of Martial Law in Poland) A place of intern or confinement, esp solitary <box, icebox, plant> eg *They slapped that activist in the box (Zamknęli tego działacza do internatu)*

irokez [ee-ROH-kehs] *nm* A hairstyle in which the hair on the sides is cut very short and the remaning hair is made to stand upright, popular esp among punks <punk, mohawk>: *Spójrz na jego irokeza (Check out the mohawk on that dude)*

iść [eeshch] (**rozchodzić się** [rohs-KHOH-jeech shyeh]; **jak ciepłe bułeczki** [yahk CHEHP-weh boo-WEHCH-kee] or **jak świeże bułeczki** [yahk SHFYEH-zheh boo-WEHCH-kee] or **jak woda** [yahk VOH-dah] may be added) (Of a particular merchandise) To be popular and easily sold <sell like hot cakes, go like hotcakes, sell like it's going out of style, sell like it's the best thing since sliced bread> eg *Ten gadżet jest bardzo chodliwy (This new gadget is selling like hot cakes)*

iść do łopaty [eeshch doh woh-PAH-ti] *v phr* To end up working as a menial worker, usually as a result of failing in education or losing one's career promotion <end up on the streets, end up shoveling shit, end up being a trash collector, end up in the poor house, end up a grave-digger> eg *Poszedł do łopaty jak wywalili go z kancelarii adwokackiej (He became a working stiff when they fired him from the law office)*

iść do cholery See iść w cholerę

iść do cywila [eeshch doh tsi-VEE-lah] (or **wracać do cywila** [VRAH-tsahch doh tsi-VEE-lah]) *v phr* To be discharged from the Armed Forces <get the paper, put one's papers in, end doing one's time> eg *Wrócił do cywila jakiś miesiąc temu (He ended doing his time a month ago)*

iść do diabła See iść w cholerę

iść do piachu [eeshch doh PYAH-khoo] (or **iść do Bozi** [eeshch doh BOH-zhee]) *v phr* To die <bite the dust, kiss the dust, croak, belly up, buy the farm, buy the ranch, cash in one's chips, check out, bump off, conk off, conk out, farm, give up the ghost, go home feet first, go home in a box, go west, kick in, kick off, kick the bucket, pass out, peg out, shove off, drop off, step off, pop off, push up daisies, meet one's maker, turn up one's toes, go down the tube, join the great majority, join the majority> eg *Na dłuższą metę, wszyscy pójdziemy do piachu (We'll all be pushing up daisies in the long run)*

iść do woja [eeshch doh VOH-yah] *v phr* To join the Armed Forces <follow the colors, join the colors> eg *Kiedy skończył szkołe, postanowił pójść do woja (When he left school he decided to follow the colors)*

iść jak po maśle [eeshch yahk poh MAHSH-leh] (or **iść jak z płatka** [eeshch yahk s PWAHT-kah]) *v phr* To happen or develop very easily and in the best possible way <come up roses, run smooth, go like shit through a goose, go like shit through a tin horn, easy, go smooth, go hands down, go downhill all the way, be plain sailing> eg *Nagle wszystko idzie jak z płatka (Suddenly everything's coming up roses)*

iść komuś na rękę [eeshch KOH-moosh nah REHN-keh] *v phr* To be accommodating with someone; to be willing to compromise, support, cooperate with or facilitate something for someone <play along, go along, play the game, play ball, not make waves, not rock the boat, meet someone halfway> eg *Chciałem dalej uczyć fonetyki amerykańskiej, ale dyrektor nie chciał mi pójść na rękę (I wanted to teach American phonetics, but the head of the department didn't want to play along)*

iść na łatwiznę [eeshch nah waht-FEEZ-neh] *v phr* To reduce one's efforts and esp, as a result, do things poorly and incompetently <cut corners, take the easy way, follow the line of least resistance> eg *Nie idź na łatwiznę. Zrób to porządnie (Don't cut corners. Let's do the job right)*

iść na żebry [eeshch nah ZHEH-bri] *v phr* (To be forced) To beg, esp as a result of bankruptcy or discharge <bum, hustle, sponge, cadge, chisel, tap, touch, mooch,

bite, freeload, schnor, needle, panhandle, nickel up, dime up, pass the hat, put the arm on, put the bite on, put touch on, hit the bricks> eg *Fabrykę zamknięto i wszyscy poszli na żebry (The factory was closed down and everybody hit the bricks)*

iść na całość [eeshch nah TSAH-wohshch] *v phr* To do the utmost, esp to do the sex act, as distinct from heavy petting or foreplay <go all the way, go the limit, get a homer, get a home run, hit a homer, hit a home run, get to home plate> eg *Wtedy ona zedcydowała się pójść z nim na całość (Then she decided to go all the way with him)*

iść na coś [eeshch NAH tsohsh] *v phr* To agree, accept, or believe <go for, buy, buy into, buy off, down, eat up, fall for, lap up, sign off on, swallow, take, tumble for, okay, OK, back, bless, pass on, shake on, clinch, play ball, give the green light, come across, come around> eg *Na pana miejscu poszedłbym na to (If I was you, I'd go for it)*

iść na stół See iść pod nóż

iść na zieloną trawkę [eeshch nah zhyeh-LOH-noh TRAHF-keh] (or **iść na bruk** [eeshch nah brook]) *v phr* To get dismissed or discharged from a job <hit the bricks, get fired, get laid off, get the ax, get axed, get the air, get aired, get the boot, get booted, get the sack, get sacked, get the bum's rush, get the kiss-off, get the pink slip, get one's walking papers, get one's walking ticket> eg *Jeszcze trzech profersorów poszło dziś rano na zieloną trawkę (Three more professors got the ax this morning)*

iść pod krzaczek [eeshch poht KSHAH-chehk] *v phr* To go to a secluded place to urinate, esp during a stop in a journey by car <make a pit stop, go check the plumbing, answer a call of nature, see a man about a dog, see a man about a horse> eg *Muszę iść pod krzaczek. I to szybko (I need to go check out the plumbing. Fast)*

iść pod nóż [eeshch pohd NOOSH] (or **iść na stół** [eeshch nah STOOW]) *v phr* To have a surgical operation <go under the knife, be cut> eg *Słyszałam, że idzie pod nóż w przyszłym tygodniu. Czy to prawda, że ma raka? (She goes under the knife next week, I hear. Is it true she's got cancer?*

iść się pierdolić** [eeshch shyeh pyehr-DOH-leech] (or **iść się gonić*** [eeshch shyeh GOH-neech] or **iść się jebać**** [eeshch shyeh YEH-bahch] or **iść się walić*** [eeshch shyeh VAH-leech] or **iść się leczyć** [eeshch shyeh LEH-chich]) *v phr* (Esp as an exclamation of defiance and contempt) To invite someone to perform or submit to a humiliating act <fuck you, screw you, chuck you Farley, fuck you Charley, drop dead, eat shit, eat my shorts, get lost, get fucked, get screwed, get stuffed, go fly a kite, go fuck yourself, fuck yourself, go screw yourself, screw yourself, go shit in your hat, go to hell, take a flying fuck, kiss my ass, bite my ass, piss on you, shit on you, cram it, stuff it, shove it, stick it, stick it in your ear, stick it in your ass, up your ass, up yours> eg *Powiedziała mi, że mogę się iść pierdolić! (She told me to go fuck myself)*

iść tam gdzie król chodzi piechotą [eeshch tahm gjeh krool KHOH-jee pyeh-KHOH-toh] *v phr* To go to the toilet <go to the throne room, check the plumbing, answer a call of nature, powder the face, powder one's nose, see a man about a dog, see a man about a horse, make a pit stop> eg *Poszedł tam, gdzie król chodzi piechotą (He went to see a man about the dog)*

iść w cholerę [eeshch f khoh-LEH-reh] (or **iść do cholery** [eeshch doh khoh-LEH-ri] or **iść w diabły** [eeshch v DYAHB-wi] or **iść do diabła** [eeshch doh DYAHB-wah] or **iść w pizdu**** [eeshch f PEEZ-doo] or **iść w piździec****

[eeschch peezh-JEHTS]) *v phr* (Esp in the imperative as a brusque command) To leave or depart, esp hastily <split, beat it, ankle, bag ass, blow, breeze off, burn rubber, butt out, buzz off, check out, cruise, cut and run, cut ass, cut out, drag ass, dust, ease out, fade, fade away, fade out, fuck off, get the fuck out, get the hell out , get going, get moving, get lost, get off the dime, get on one's horse, go south, haul ass, hightail, hit the bricks, hit the road, hop it, make tracks, pull out, scram, set sail, shove off, shuffle along, skate, skip out, split the scene, take off> eg *Idź w cholerę i nie denerwuj mnie! (Drag ass, stop bothering me!)*

iść w cug [eeshch f TSOOK] (or **złapać cuga** [ZWAH-pahch TSOO-gah] or **mieć cuga** [myehch TSOO-gah] or **ruszyć w cug** [ROO-shich f TSOOK] or **iść w kurs** [eeshch f KOORS] or **iść w rejs** [eeshch f REH-ees] or **iść w tango** [eeshch f TAHN-goh]) *v phr* To go on a drinking spree, esp lasting several days <go on a binge, go on a bender, go on a bust, go on a rip, go on a tear, go on a toot, go on a bat, hit the bottle, hit the booze, hit the sauce, bend the elbow> eg *Zdał egzamin i poszedł w trzydniowe tango (He passed the exam and went on a three-day binge)*

iść w długą [eeshch v DWOO-goh] (or **dać w długą** [dahch v DWOO-goh]) *v phr* To leave or depart, esp hastily <split, beat it, ankle, bag ass, blow, breeze off, burn rubber, butt out, buzz off, check out, cruise, cut and run, cut ass, cut out, drag ass, dust, ease out, fade, fade away, fade out, fuck off, get the fuck out, get the hell out , get going, get moving, get lost, get off the dime, get on one's horse, go south, haul ass, hightail, hit the bricks, hit the road, hop it, make tracks, pull out, scram, set sail, shove off, shuffle along, skate, skip out, split the scene, take off> eg *Jak tylko pojawiły się gliny, dali w długą (As soon as cops arrived, they split the scene)*

iść w diabły See iść w cholerę

iść w dół [eeshch v DOOW] *v phr* (Esp about prices or costs) To become lower; to be decreased <go down, plummet> eg *Słyszałem, że benzyna poszła w dół (I heard that the price of gas has gone down)*

iść w dyrektory [eeshch v di-rehk-TOH-ri] *v phr* To be promoted to a position of a director or top executive <become a big boss, become a big boy, become a big cheese, become a big enchilada, become a top brass, become a honcho, become a big man, become a man upstairs, become a top dog, become a key player, become a exec, become a numero uno> eg *Jego wujek poszedł w dyrektory (His uncle became a big boss)*

iść w górę [eeshch v GOO-reh] *v phr* (Esp about prices or costs) To be increased; to rise <go up, skyrocket> eg *Słyszałem, że benzyna poszła w górę (I heard that the price of gas has gone up)*

iść w kimono [eeshch f KEE-mohnoh] (or **stuknąć w kimono** [STOOK-nohnch f KEE-mohnoh] or **uderzyć w kimono** [oo-DEH-zhich f KEE-mohnoh]) *v phr* To sleep, esp to get some sleep <catch some Z's, cop some Z's, cut some Z's, bag some Z's, grab some Z's, catch a nod, cop a nod, bag a nod, grab a nod, konck a nod, collar a nod, take forty winks, bag it, snooze, conk off, caulk off, dope off, drop off, sack out, zonk out, conk out, caulk out, fall out, saw wood, rack, crash, doss, sack up, sack in, zizz, get some blanket drill, get some bunk fatigue, get some sack time, get some shuteye, hit the hay, hit the pad, hit the sack> eg *Nic nie pamiętam, bo natychmiast poszedłem w kimono (I don't remember anything, because I conked out right away)*

iść w kurs See iść w cug

iść w ministry [eeshch v mee-NEES-tri] *v phr* To be promoted to a position of a government minister <become a high man on the totem pole in the government> eg *Jej ojciec poszedł w ministry w wieku lat 40 (Her father became a high man on the totem pole in the government when he was 40)*

iść w nogi [eeshch v NOH-gee] *v phr* (Of consumed alcohol) To have an effect on someone, esp unexpectedly <go to one's head, kick in> eg *Ta wódka mi w nogi poszła (The vodka went right to my head)*

iść w odstawkę [eeshch v oht-STAHF-keh] *v phr* To lose one's position or function; to become degraded; to lose influence <get benched, get bumped, get busted, get mudslinged, get slammed> eg *Gdy nastały inne czasy, poszli w odstawkę (When new times came, they got benched)*

iść w piździec See iść w cholerę

iść w pizdu See iść w cholerę

iść w rejs See iść w cug

iść w rozsypkę [eeshch v rohs-SIP-keh] *v phr* To get broken or damaged <get smashed, get busted, get wracked> eg *Wazon poszedł w rozsypkę (The vase got smashed)*

iść w tango See iść w cug

iść z kimś do łóżka [eeshch s KEEMSH doh WOOSH-kah] (or **iść z kimś do wyra*** [eeshch s KEEMSH doh VI-rah]) *v phr* To copulate with someone <go to bed with, sleep with, do someone> eg *Czy ona naprawdę poszła z nim do łóżka, czy to tylko czcza plotka? (Did she really go to bed with him, or is it just idle goossip?)*

iść z torbami [eeshch s tohr-BAH-mee] *v phr* To go bankrupt or lose a lot of money and to get impoverished as a consequence of this <belly up, go bust, go broke, go to the cleaners, take a bath, take a beating, bust, wash out, lose out, blow, drop a bundle, go to tap out> eg *Mogli pójść z torbami, gdyby kolekcja się spaliła (They might have gone to the cleaners had the collections gotten burned)*

italianiec [ee-tah-LYAH-nyehts] *nm* An Italian <wop, dago, ginzo, greaseball, greaser, spaghetti, guinea, eytie> eg *Czego można oczekiwać od takiego italiańca? (What can you expect from a wop like that?)*

iwan* [EE-vahn] *nm* A Russian <rusky, red, Ivan, tovarich, comrade> eg *Spytaj, czy iwan chce trochę czekolady (See if Ivan wants some chocolate)*

J

ja pierdolę** [yah pyehr-DOH-leh] (or **ja cię pierdolę**** [yah chyeh pyehr-DOH-leh] or **ja pieprzę*** [yah PYEHP-sheh] or **ja cię pieprzę*** [yah chyeh PYEHP-sheh] or **ja pierniczę*** [yah pyehr-NEE-cheh] or **ja cię pierniczę*** [yah chyeh pyehr-NEE-cheh] or **ja pierdzielę*** [yah pyehr-JEH-leh] or **ja cię pierdzielę*** [yah chyeh pyehr-JEH-leh] or **ja cię kręcę** [yah chyeh KREHN-tseh] or **ja cię sunę** [yah chyeh SOO-neh]) *excl* An exclamation of surprise, shock, joy, or disappointment and irritation <shit, fuck, hell, heck, damn, damn it, goddamn it, gosh, golly, gee, jeez, holy fuck, holy cow, holy moly, holy hell, holy

mackarel, holy shit, jumping Jesus, fucking shit, fucking hell, fucking A> eg *Ja pierdolę! Spójrz na cycki tej laski! (Holy shit! Check out the jugs on that chick!)*

ja piórkuję [yah pyoor-KOO-yeh] *excl phr* (An exclamation of surprise, shock, or excitement) May I be maltreated, confounded, accursed, etc <I'll be damned, I'll be fucked, I'll be dipped in shit, I'll be hanged, I'll be jiggered, holy fuck, holy cow, holy shit, holy moly, hot damn, fuck a duck, fuck a dog, fucking a, fuck me, my ass, no shit> eg *Wygraliśmy! Ja piórkuje! (We won! I'll be damned!)*

jabłko See zbić kogoś na kwaśne jabłko

jabol [YAH-bohl] (or **jabcok** [YAHP-tsohk]) *nm* Cheap and inferior wine, esp made from apples <plonk, veeno, Mad Dog 20/20, Nighttrain, Wild Irish Rose> eg *Co powiesz na butelkę jabola? (How about a bottle of plonk?)*

jadaczka [yah-DAHCH-kah] *nf* The mouth <yap, bazoo, kisser, trap> eg *Zamknij wreszcie tę swoją jadaczkę (Shut you yap)*

jaja [YAH-yah] *npl* **1*** (or **jajca*** [YAH-ee-tsah]) *npl* The testicles <balls, sack> eg *Dostał w jaja podczas meczu (He got hit in the balls in the football game)* **2** (or **jaja jak berety** [YAH-yah yahk beh-REH-ti]) A very funny, amusing, or foolish situation <trick, laugh, laugh and a half, laugher, laughing stock, horselaugh, merry ha-ha, hoot, howl, riot, laff riot, laffer, scream, stitch, boffo, panic, knee-slapper, rib-tickler, side-splitter> eg *Zaraz na początku jakiś facet zaczął się do niej podwalać. Mówię ci, były jaja jak berety (Right at the beginning some guy started making pass at her. I'm telling you that was a laugh)* **3** (or **jaja jak berety** [YAH-yah yahk beh-REH-ti]) A scandalous fact or situation; a scandal <gas, fuss, stink, hot potato, bad scene, bad news, can of worms, bag of worms, takedown, putdown, shit, serious shit, deep shit, deep water, drag, bind, bitch, bummer, downer, headache, double trouble, snafu, pain in the ass, pain in the neck, spot, mess, holy mess, pickle, squeeze, hard time, glitch, stinker, skeleton, skeleton in the closet, sizzler, scorcher, dynamite, Watergate, fine kettle of fish, fine how do you do, fine cup of coffee, big stink, curtains, lights out, game's over> eg *Jak mnie złapią, to będą jaja (Bad scene for me if they find me)*

See bez jaj, dla jaj, robić komuś koło dupy, robić sobie jaja, z jajami, z jajem

jajcarz [YAH-ee-tsahsh] *nm* A witty, funny, and impressive person who does things for fun <artist, joker, kidder, clown, article, ham, character, item, number> eg *Popatrz tylko, co on na siebie włożył. Ale jajcarz! (Just look what he put on. What a joker!)*

jajko See kura znosząca złote jajka, obchodzić się z kimś jak z jajkiem

jajo See zrobić kogoś w konia

jak amen w pacierzu [yahk AH-mehn f pah-CHYEH-zhoo] *adv phr* Secure; very sure <sure, fer sure, sure as hell, sure as shit, sure as can be, for real, indeedy, really truly, absitively, posilutely, real, cert, def, no buts about it, wired up, cinched, taped, racked, sewed up, iced, in the bag, tied up, nailed down> eg *Wybiorą naszego kandydata jak amen w pacierzu (They will chose our candidate, no doubts about it)*

jak autobus See narąbany

jak bela See pijany jak świnia, upić się jak świnia

jak bum cyk-cyk [yahk boom tsik TSIK] (or **jak bogackiego** [yahk boh-gahts-KYEH-goh] or **jak bonie dydy** [yahk BOH-nyeh DI-di] or **jak babcię kocham** [yahk BAHP-chyeh KOH-khahm] or **jak pragnę zdrowia** [yahk

PRAHG-neh ZDROH-vyah] or **jak pragnę szczęścia** [yahk PRAHG-neh SHCHEH-shchyah]) *excl* An exclamation of extreme certainty or a promise or vow that the truth is being told <cross my heart, cross my heart and hope to die, I can swear up and down, I can swear on a stack of bibles, I can swear till I'm blue in the face, sure, fer sure, sure as hell, sure as shit, sure as can be, for real, indeedy, really truly, absitively, posilutely, real, cert, def, no buts about it> eg *Naprawdę ją przeleciał! Jak bonie dydy! (He did score her! Cross my heart)*

jak byk [yahk BIK] *adv phr* Simply; straightforwardly; evidently <in black and white, down in black and white, carved in stone, etched in stone, up front, open and shut, like it is, laid on the line, what you see is what you get, wysiwyg> eg *Tu jest napisane jak byk, że to moja własność (It says right here in black and white that it's my property)*

See zdrowy jak ryba

jak chuj** [yahk KHOO-ee] (or **jak skurwysyn**** [yahk skoor-VI-sin] or **jak cholera** [yahk khoh-LEH-rah] or **jak jasna cholera** [yahk YAHS-nah khoh-LEH-rah] or **jak diabli** [yahk DYAHB-lee] or **jak wszyscy diabli** [yahk FSHIS-tsi DYAHB-lee] or **jak jasny gwint** [yahk YAHS-ni GVEENT] or **jak nie wiem co** [yahk NYEH VYEHM tsoh]) *adv phr* Extremely; exceedingly; very <awful, god-awful, real, mighty, plenty, damn, damned, goddamn, goddamned, darn, darned, effing, flipping, forking, freaking, frigging, fucking, one's ass off, one's brains out, one's head off, to the max, like all get-out, like sin, to beat the band, like all creation, as blazes, as can be, as hell, like hell, in full swing> eg *Musisz być wściekły jak chuj (You must be mad like hell); Był pijany jak cholera (He was drunk like hell)*

jak dziki osioł See narobić się

jak groch o ścianę [yahk GROHKH oh SHCHYAH-neh] (or **jak do ściany** [yahk doh SHCHYAH-ni] or **jak do słupa** [yahk doh SWOO-pah]) *adv phr* Wasting one's time talking; talking in vain <wasting one's breath> eg *It was like wasting your breath (To było jak groch o ścianę)*

jak grom z jasnego nieba [yahk GROHM z yahs-NEH-goh NYEH-bah] *nm phr* Suddenly; unexpectedly; without warning <out of the blue, out of a clear blue sky, out of a clear blue sky, like a bolt from the blue, out in left field> eg *Wszystko zdarzyło się jak grom z jasnego nieba (Everything happened like a bolt from the blue)*

jak koń See zdrowy jak ryba

jak kura pazurem See bazgrać, gryzmolić

jak mały samochodzik See zapierdalać

jak makiem zasiał [yahk MAH-kyehm ZAH-shyah-oo] *adv phr* Silently or quitely <clammed up, closed up like a clam, buttoned up, tight-lipped, tongue-tied, unflappable, like a grave> eg *Była całkowita cisza. Jak makiem zasiał (There was complete silence. Like in a grave)*

jak mrówek [yahk MROO-vehk] (or **jak mrówków** [yahk MROOF-koof] or **jak nasrał**** [yahk NAHS-rah-oo]) *adv phr* (Of people) Plenty; many many <helluva lot, lotsa, lotta, oodles, scads, heaps, bags, barrels, loads, piles, tons, wads, jillions, zillions, enough to choke a horse, shitload, fuckload, truckload> eg *W barze było ludzi jak mrówek (There was helluva lot people in the bar); Ma pieniędzy jak nasrał (He has a fuckload of money)*

jak mur beton See mur beton

jak mysz kościelna [yahk MISH kohsh-CHYEHL-nah] *adv phr* Silent or quite <clammed up, closed up like a clam, buttoned up, tight-lipped, tongue-tied, unflappable, like a grave> eg *Siedział jak mysz kościelna. Liczył, że nikt go nie zauważy (He was like a grave. He was hoping that nobody would see him)*

jak na lekarstwo [yahk nah leh-KAHR-stfoh] *adv phr* Very few or little; almost nothing <drop in the ocean, drop in the bucket, chicken feed, smidgen, tad, wee bit, itty bit> eg *Takich klubów jest w tym mieście jak na lekarstwo (Club like that are a drop in the ocean in this town)*

jak na szpilkach [yahk nah SHPEEL-kakh] *adj phr* Eager or nervous; anxiously awaiting something <on pins and needles, champing at the bit, like a cat on hot bricks, on tenderhooks> eg *Byłem jak na szpilkach dopóki nie zadzwoniła (I was on pins and needles all evening until she finally called)*
See wiercić się jak na szpilkach

jak najęty [yahk nah-YEHN-ti] *adv phr* (Of an action) Performed to an extreme degree or unrestrainedly <to the max, flat-out, all-out, all the way, like hell, like all get-out, like sin, to beat the band, like all creation, like it had gone out of style, like there was no tomorrow, like nobody's business, one's ass off, one's brains out, one's head off, the whole nine yards, nine to the dozen> eg *Gadali jak najęci (They were chatting away nineteen to the dozen)*

jak nakręcony See gadać

jak nasrał See jak mrówek

jak nic [yahk NEETS] *adv phr* Certainly; surely <sure, fer sure, sure as hell, sure as shit, sure as can be, for real, indeedy, really truly, absitively, posilutely, real, cert, def, no buts about it, wired up, cinched, taped, racked, sewed up, iced, in the bag, tied up, nailed down> eg *On mnie jak nic wywali za drzwi (He'll bounce me, no doubts about it)*

jak nie wiem co See jak chuj

jak śliwka w gówno See wpaść

jak śliwka w kompot See wpaść

jak oparzony [yahk oh-pah-ZHOH-ni] *adv phr* (Going somewhere) immediately; very quickly <pretty damn quick, PDQ, ASAP, on the spot, on the double, double time, double clutching, like a shot, in half a mo, like now, before you know it, before you can say Jack Robinson, in a jiffy, in a flash, in half a shake, right off the bat, like a bat out of hell, like a shot out of hell, hubba-hubba, horseback, like greased lightning> eg *Gdy mnie zobaczył, wybiegł z pokoju jak oparzony (When he saw me, he ran out of the room like a bat out of hell)*

jak świnia See chlać, pijany jak świnia, upić się jak świnia

jak pączek w maśle [yahk POHN-chehk v MAHSH-leh] *adv phr* In a very good or comfortable situation, esp financially; having a pleasant or easy life <in clover, in the clover, sitting pretty> eg *Żyje jak pączek w maśle, bo jej ojciec jest bogaty (She lives in clover because her father is rich)*

jak piernik do wiatraka [yahk PYEHR-neek doh vyaht-RAH-kah] (or **jak piernik z wiatrakiem** [yahk PYEHR-neek z vyaht-RAH-kyehm] or **jak wół do karety** [yahk VOOW doh kah-REH-ti]) *v phr* (Of two things or persons) Completely unrelated <nothing to do with> eg *Te dwa obrazy mają się do siebie jak piernik do wiatraka (This painting has nothing to do with that one)*

jak pies z kotem See żyć z kimś jak pies z kotem

jak po maśle [yahk poh MAHSH-leh] (or **jak z płatka** [yahk s PWAHT-kah]) *adv phr* Very easily; effortlessly; without problems <like shit through a goose, like shit through a tin horn, easy, smooth, hands down, downhill all the way, plain sailing, running smooth> eg *W życiu wszystko szło mu jak po maśle (Everything in his life was going like shit through a tin horn); Dwa lata minęły jak z płatka (Two years have passed like a shit through a goose)*

jak pragnę szczęścia See jak bum cyk-cyk

jak pragnę zdrowia See jak bum cyk-cyk

jak ryba See zdrowy jak ryba

jak skurwysyn See jak chuj

jak smród w gaciach See ciągnąć się

jak stodoła See narąbany

jak ta lala [yahk tah LAH-lah] **1** (or **jak trza** [yahk TSHAH]) *adj phr* Fancily dressed <dolled-up, dolled-out, dressed to kill, dressed to the nines, dressed to the teeth, dressed-up, duded-up, ritzed up, swanked up, ragged out, sharp-dressed> eg *Zawsze wygląda jak ta lala (She is always dressed to kill)* **2** (or **jak złoto** [yahk ZWOH-toh]) *adj phr* Excellent; wonderful <great, cool, swell, fab, rad, def, far-out, awesome, frantic, terrific, funky, gorgeous, groovy, hellacious, neat, peachy, dandy, baddest, mean, solid, super-dooper, wailing, wicked, gnarly, top-notch, ten, ace-high, A-OK, A-1, some> eg *On to jest fachowiec jak ta lala (He's a hellacious professional)* **3** (or **jak złoto** [yahk ZWOH-toh]) *adv phr* Excellently; superbly; wonderfully <great, cool, swell, fab, rad, def, far-out, awesome, frantic, terrific, funky, gorgeous, groovy, hellacious, neat, peachy, dandy, baddest, mean, solid, super-dooper, wailing, wicked, gnarly, top-notch, ten, ace-high, A-OK, A-1, some> eg *Silnik pracuje jak ta lala (The engine's working top-notch)*
See odpierdolony

jak u Pana Boga za piecem [yahk oo PAH-nah BOH-gah zah PYEH-tsehm] *adv phr* Comfortably <comfy, cozy, homey, snug as a bug in a rug> eg *Nasz nowy dom jest cudowny. Jest przytulny i ciepły i czujesz się w nim jak w Pana Boga za piecem (Our new house is wonderful. It's nice and warm and makes you feel snug as a bug in a rug)*

jak w banku See bankowo

jak w pysk strzelił [yahk f PISK STSHEH-leew] (or **jak w mordę strzelił*** [yahk v MOHR-deh STSHEH-leew]) *adv phr* Precisely (as desired); exactly (as desired) <on the button, on the dot, on the nose, on the bean, to a tee> eg *To będzie dwa tysiące jak w mordę strzelił (It'll be two thousand on the nose)*

jak w zegarku [yahk v zeh-GAHR-koo] (or **jak w szwajcarskim zegarku** [yahk f shfah-ee-TSAHR-skeem zeh-GAHR-koo]) *adv phr* Dependably regular <as clockwork, regular as clockwork, like clockwork> eg *Przychodzi do tego sklepu codziennie jak w szwajcarskim zegarku (She comes into this store everyday, regular as clockwork)*

jak wół See narobić się, orać jak wół, zapierdalać, zasuwać

jak wszyscy diabli See jak chuj

jak z cebra See lać

jak z krzyża zdjęty [yahk s KZHI-zhah ZDYEHN-ti] *adj phr* Unusually thin and skinny <beanpole, stringbean, skin and bones, skeleton, bag of bones> eg *Twój brat wygląda jak z krzyża zdjęty. (Your brother is a real beanpole)*

jak z młodszego brata [yahk z mwoht-SHEH-goh BRAH-tah] *adj phr* (Of clothing) Too small for one <crinkled, crinkly, wrinkled, wrinkly> eg *Zawsze nosi ubrania jak z młodszego brata (He's always wearing crinkled clothes)*

jak z płatka See iść jak po maśle

jak złoto See jak ta lala

jak za zboże See płacić jak za zborze

jak ze starszego brata [yahk zeh stahr-SHEH-goh BRAH-tah] *adj phr* (Of clothing) Too big for one <hand-me-down, reach-me-down> eg *Zawsze nosi ubrania jak ze starszego brata (He's always wearing hand-me-down clothes)*

jak zmokła kura [yahk ZMOH-kwah KOO-rah] *adj phr* Drenched, soaked <soaked to the bone, drenched to the bone, like a drowned cat> eg *Śmignął jakiś samochód obok kałuży i wszyscy wyglądaliśmy jak zmokłe kury (A car drove by quickly, hit the puddle, and we all got drenched)*

jak znalazł [yahk ZNAH-lahs] *adv phr* Exactly what is needed; very adequate, suitable, or neede <handy, coming handy, hitting on all six, hitting the spot, just what the doctor ordered, on the button, on the dot, on the nose, on target, on track, that's the idea, that's the ticket, all to the mustard, nail on the head, hit in the bull's-eye> eg *Ten telefon przydał się jak znalazł (That phone number came in handy)*

jakby kij połknął [YAHK-bi KEE-ee POH-oo-knoh-oo] *adj phr* Unnaturally standoffish in a physical appearance <stiff as a bore> eg *Impreza była świetna, ale on był jakby kij połknął (The party was great but he was stiff as a bore)*

jakiś [YAH-keesh] *adv* About; approximately <around, in the ballpark of, pretty near, something like, close shave, in the neighborhood of, damn near, pretty near> eg *Chodziło o jakiś tysiąc dolarów (It was about something like a thousand dollars)*

jako tako [YAH-koh TAH-koh] *adv phr* Neither very badly nor very well; ordinarily; passably <so-so, fair to middling, vanilla, no great shakes, run of the mill, okay, OK> eg *Jak idzie praca? Jako tako (How's the work going? So-so)*

jamnik [YAHM-neek] *nm* A large portable stereo radio, cassette, or CD player <boom box, boogie box, coon box, ghetto box, ghetto blaster, nigger box> eg *Możebyś tak wyłączył tego jamnika? (I wish you'd turn that boom box off)*

jankes [ah-meh-RI-kahn] *nm* A citizen of (or a person born) in the United States of America <Yank, Yankee, Americano> eg *Słyszałeś, jankesi zaatakowali Irak (Did you hear that: The Yankees attacked Iraq)*

jaś See głupi jaś

japa [YAH-pah] *nf* The mouth <yap, bazoo, kisser, trap> eg *Trzasnąłem go w japę (I hit him on his yap)*

japoniec [yah-POH-nyehts] *nm* **1** A Japanese automobile or motorcycle <rice-burner, rice-belly, jap car, jap bike> eg *Kupił sobie japońca zamiast Mercedesa (He bought a rice-burner instead of a Mercedes)* **2*** A Japanese male <Jap, Nip, gook, slant eye> eg *Japońców wszędzie pełno (The Japs are all over)*

jarać [YAH-rahch] (perf **zajarać** [zah-YAH-rahch]) *v* **1** (perf **podjarać** [pohd-YAH-rahch] or **ujarać** [oo-YAH-rahch]) To excite someone, esp to arouse someone sexually <turn on, bring on, heat up, fire up, send, have someone's nose open> eg *Nie jara mnie ten typ kobiet (That kind of women doesn't turn me on)* **2** To smoke a cigarette <puff, drag, pull, blow, poke, toke, fume, fumigate, take a puff, take a drag, light up, torch up> eg *Muszę zajarać (I must take a drag)*

jarać się [YAH-rahch shyeh] (perf **zajarać się** [zah-YAH-rahch shyeh]) *v* **1** (perf **podjarać się** [pohd-YAH-rahch shyeh] or **ujarać się** [oo-YAH-rahch shyeh]) To get excited, esp to get aroused sexually <get turned on, be brought on, get stoked, get heated up, get fire up, be sent> eg *Podjarał się tą propozycją (He got turned on by this proposal)* **2** (perf **zjarać się** [ZYAH-rahch shyeh]) To burn; to be on fire <fry, burn down, cook down, nuke, roast, sizzle> eg *Dom obok się zjarał (The house next door got fried)*

jareccy [yah-REH-tstsi] *npl* Parents <rents, fossils, folks, old folks, old man and old lady> eg *Muszę iść spytać jareckich (I've got to go and ask the old folks)*

jarecka [yah-REH-tskah] *nf* A mother <mama, ma, mom, moms, mommy, motherkin, old lady, old woman, warden> eg *Jarecka kazała mi zostać w domu (My old lady told me to stay home)*

jarecki [yah-REH-tskee] *nm* A father <dad, daddy, pa, papa, pop, pops, guv, gaffer, padre, warden, old man> eg *Jarecki przyjechał i skończyła się wolność (My old man came home and it was the end of good times)*

jasio wędrowniczek [YAH-shyoh vehn-droh-VNEE-chehk] *nm phr* Whiskey, esp Johnnie Walker <firewater, mountain dew, shoe polish, panther piss> eg *Mój ojciec pije tylko jasia wędrowniczka (My father drinks only firewater)*

jasna cholera See cholera

jasna krew kogoś zalewa See krew kogoś zalewa

jasne [YAHS-neh] **1** *excl* Do you understand? <capeesh, kapeesh, comprende, got that> eg *Tylko jej nie zabijajcie natychmiast, jasne? (Don't kill her right away, kapeesh?)* **2** (or **jasne jak słońce** [YAHS-neh yahk SWOHŃ-tseh] *adv phr* Obvious; understandable; clearly evident <crystal clear, plain day, plain as the nose on one's face> eg *Jak to nie rozumiesz? Przecież to jest jasne jak słońce (What do you mean you don't understand? It's plain as the nose on your face)* **3** *nn* Light beer; beer in general <brew, brewski, suds, swill, froth, chill, cold one, wet one> eg *Dwie butelki jasnego, poproszę (Can I have two brews?)*

jasny See cholera, jak chuj, jak grom z jasnego nieba, pomroczność jasna

jazda [YAHZ-dah] *nf* A state of euphoria caused by drugs or alcohol <trip, high, belt, rush, jolt, riot, blast, kick, charge> eg *Po tych prochach to mam dopiero jazdę (This stuff really gives me a blast)*

jełop* [YEH-wohp] (or **jołop*** [YOH-wohp]) *nm* A very stupid, clumsy or ineffectual person; an idiot <airbrain, airhead, birdbrain, blockhead, squarehead, bonehead, bubblebrain, bubblehead, buckethead, cluckhead, cementhead, clunkhead, deadhead, dumbbell, dumbcluck, dumbhead, dumbass, dumbbrain, fatbrain, fathead, flubdub, knukclebrain, knucklehead, lamebrain, lardhead, lunkhead, meathead, musclehead, noodlehead, numbskull, pointhead, scatterbrain, jerk, jerk-off, klutz, chump, creep, nerd, dork, dweeb, gweeb, geek, jackass, lummox, twerp, nerd, bozo, clod, cluck, clunk, dimwit, dingbat, dipstick, dodo, dopey, dufus, goofus, lump, lunk, nitwit, schnook, schlep, schlemiel, schmendrick, schmo, schmuck, simp, stupe> eg *Od godziny tłumaczy tym jełopom co to oznacza (He's been explaining to these dumbheads what it means for an hour)*

jeż See głupszy niż ustawa przewiduje, obcięty na jeża, w mordę

jebać się** [YEH-bahch shyeh] *v* To copulate <get screwed, get fucked, get laid, screw, fuck, fork, frig, ball, bang, boink, bonk, boff, hump, poke, shag> eg *Jebał się z jakąś kelnerką po pracy (He used to fuck some waitress after hours)*

See iść się pierdolić

jebać w dupę See pierdolić w dupę

jebać** [YEH-bahch] (perf **wyjebać**** [vi-YEH-bahch]) *v* To copulate with someone <fuck, screw, lay, ball, bang, boink, boff, boogie, bop, frig, hump, poke, shag> eg *Nawet nie myślał, że mógłby ją wyjebać (He didn't even think he could fuck her)*

jebacz See jebak

jebadełko** [yeh-bah-DEH-oo-koh] *nn* A vibrator or any similar substitute for penis used by a woman to stimulate real copulation <dildo, fuck tool> eg *Jebadełka sprzedają za zaliczeniem pocztowym (They sell dildos by mail)*

jebak** [YEH-bahk] *nm* (or **jebaka**** [yeh-BAH-kah] or **jebacz**** [YEH-bahch]) An insatiable man who is obsessed with copulation <ass-man, cocksman, cunt-struck, cunt-happy, pussy-struck, fucking machine, hound-dog, pistol Pete> eg *Czemu przy tych dziewczynach zachowuje się tak, jakby był jakimś jebaką? (Why does he act like a hound-dog around these girls?)*

jebany** [yeh-BAH-ni] Cursed; damnable; bad <damn, damned, goddamn, goddamned, god-awful, blasted, darn, darned, effing, flipping, forking, freaking, frigging, pesky> eg *Ten jebany klucz nie pasuje (This goddamn key doesn't fit in)*

jebliwa** [jeh-BLEE-vah] *adj* (Of a woman) Readily agreeable to copulation <fuckable, hot, nympho> eg *Koło północy zrobiła się jakaś jebliwa, ale potem zasnęła (Around midnight she got sorta fuckable, and then she fell asleep)*

jebliwy** [jeh-BLEE-vi] *adj* (Of a man) Readily agreeable to copulation <fuckable, full of fuck, hot, nympho> eg *Dobra, kochasiu. Jak będziesz już jebliwy, to do mnie zadzwoń (Okay, sweetie. When you feel fuckable, call me)*

jebnąć sobie coś** [YEHB-nohnch SOH-byeh TSOHSH] *v phr* To buy something for oneself <buy oneself, get oneself, blow oneself> eg *Jebnęła sobie nowe futro (She got her a new mink coat)*

jebnięty** [yehb-NYEHN-ti] *adj* Insane, stupid or thoughtless <crazy, creazy as a loon, loony, nerts, nuts, nutso, nutsy, nutty, sick, sick in the head, sicko, wacko, wacky, psycho, shizo, screwy, off one's rocker, out of one's skull, fruity, airbrained, airheaded, birdbrained, blockheaded, squareheaded, boneheaded, bubblebrained, bubbleheaded, bucketheaded, cluckheaded, cementheaded, clunkheaded, deadheaded, dumbclucked, dumbheaded, dumbassed, dumbbrained, fatbrained, fatheaded, flubdubbed, knukclebrained, knuckleheaded, lamebrained, lardheaded, lunkheaded, meatheaded, muscleheaded, noodleheaded, numbskulled, pointheaded, scatterbrained, nerdy, dorky, jackassed, lummoxed, dopey, goofy> eg *On musi być jebnięty! Rzucić się na profesora z pyskiem? (He must be nuts! To start yelling at the professor)*

jechać do Rygi [YEH-khahch doh RI-gee] *v phr* To empty one's stomach; to vomit <barf, puke, blow grits, blow chunks, chuck, do a Technicolor yawn, drive the big bus, heave, pray to the porcelain god, ralph, rolf, talk to the big white phone, cry Ruth, cry Ralph, blow one's cookies, blow one's lunch, lose one's cookies, lose one's lunch, shoot one's cookies, shoot one's lunch> eg *Wypił całą butelkę i pojechał do Rygi (He downed the whole bottle and went to shoot his cookies)*

jechać na gapę [YEH-khahch nah GAH-peh] *v phr* To go by means of public transportation without paying for the fare <steal a ride, dodge paying one's fare> eg *Nie miał przy sobie pieniędzy, więc musiał jechać na gapę (He didn't have any money on him so he had to steal a ride)*

jeden [YEH-dehn] *nm* A drink of liquor, esp potent <snort, finger, jigger, pull, shot, nip, gargle, guzzle, slug, hit> eg *Idziemy na jednego? (Let's go out for a shot?)*
See być jedną nogą w grobie, mieć coś w małym palcu, na jednej nodze, na jedno kopyto, na jedno wychodzić, wrzucać coś do jednego worka

jednorazówka [yehd-no-rah-ZOOF-kah] *nf* Anything disposable, for a single use only <throw-away> eg *Go on, you can write on it. It's only a throw-away (Możesz po tym pisać. To tylko jednorazówka)*

jedynka [yeh-DIN-kah] *nf* A failing grade <flunk, flush, F, zip, zippo> eg *Mam trzy jedynki. Co ja teraz zrobię? (I got three flunks. What am I going to do now?)*

jędza [YEHN-dzah] *nf* A quarrelsome, bothersome, malicious woman; a shrew <bitch, slut, cunt, broad, wench, hag, old hag, old biddy, old bag, old tart, piece of shit> eg *Dlaczego porzucił pan żonę? Bo jędza była (Why did you leave your wife? Because she was a bitch)*

jedzie mi tu czołg [YEH-jeh mee too CHOH-ook] *phr* That was a stupid question; do I look like a fool <what do you take me for, tell that to the marines, tell that to the horse marines> eg *Nie mogłam przyjść, bo zachorował mi dziadek. Naprawdę? Jedzie mi tu czołg? (I couldn't make it because my granny got sick. Oh yeah? Tell that to the marines)*

jehowa [yeh-KHOH-vah] (or **jehowita** [yeh-khoh-VEE-tah] or **jehowy** [yeh-KHOH-vi]) *nm* A Jehovah witness <bible thumper, bible banger, sin hound> eg *Rozmawiałaś z tym jehową? (Did you talk to that bible thumper?)*

jeleń [YEH-lehñ] *nm* A naive and easily victimized person <patsy, sucker, easy mark, babe in the woods> eg *Zawsze się znajdzie jakiś jeleń (There will always be some sucker)*

jeść komuś z ręki [yehshch KOH-moosh z REHN-kee] *v phr* To be very willing to obey or agree with someone; to be submissive or dependent on someone <eat out of someone's hand, dance, dance to one's tune, be under someone's thumb, be under someone's spell, be in someone's pocket, be on a leash, be on a string> eg *Nowy burmistrz wkrótce będzie jadł nam z ręki (The new mayor will soon dance to our tune)*

jerychońska See trąba

jeździec See na jeźdźca

jęzor See mleć jęzorem

język See łamać sobie język, brać kogoś na języki, ciągnąć kogoś za język, język komuś kołkiem staje, mieć coś na końcu języka, mieć długi język, mieć niewyparzoną gębę, zapomnieć języka w gębie, znaleźć wspólny język

język komuś kołkiem staje [YEHN-zik KOH-moosh KOH-oo-kyehm STAH-yeh] (or **język komuś kołowacieje** [YEHN-zik KOH-moosh koh-woh-vah-CHEH-yeh]) *v phr* To be speechless because of strong feeling, surprise, confusion or fear <clam up, dummy up, button up, belt up, catch one's breath, drop dead, knock dead, drop down dead, be killed stone-dead> eg *Wiadomość była tak nieoczekiwana, że język mi kołkiem stanął (The news was so unexpected that I dropped dead)*

jołop See jełop

jubel [YOO-behl] *nm* A party or other usually noisy celebration, esp to celebrate some anniversary <ball, bash, blast, blowout, brawl, fest, rally, shindig> eg *Podobał ci się jubel? (Did you the ball?)*

jucha See psia krew

judasz [YOO-dahsh] *nm* A peephole in a door <peeper> eg *Widziałam go przez judasza (I saw him through the peeper)*

jugol* [YOO-gohl] *nm* A citizen of or someone coming from the former Yugoslavia <yugo, hunkie, hunky, bohunk, slav> eg *Czego chciał ten jugol? (What did the yugo want?)*

julek See rany

juma [YOO-mah] *nf* A theft or robbery, esp of a car <carjacking, hijacking, heist, bag job, boost, burn, crib job, five-finger discount, holdup, stickup, job, knockover, lift, pinch> eg *Juma jest tu bardzo popularna (Carjacking is very popular here)*

jumać [YOO-mahch] (perf **zajumać** [zah-YOO-mahch]) *v* To steal, esp cars <carjack, highjack, heist, boost, burgle, nurn, bag, buzz, hoist, hold up, hook, hustle, jump, kick over, knock off, knock over, lift, move, mug, nab, nick, nip, pinch, pluck, roll, rustle, snatch, snitch, stick up, swipe, take off, put the grab on, go south with> eg *W zeszłym roku zajumał Mercedesa i dwa BMW (Last year he snatched a Mercedes and two BMWs)*

jumak [YOO-mahk] (or **jumacz** [YOO-mahch]) *nm* A thief, esp a car thief <carjacker, hijacker, heist man, holdup man, stickup man, dip, cannon, tool, wire, meachanic, cutpurse, digger, file, forks, five fingers, finger, fingersmith, greasy finger, gun, knucker, picks, friskers, hooks, spitter, jostler, clipper, stickup man, lifter> eg *Policjanci właśnie aresztowali dwóch jumaków (The policemen just arrested two carjackers)*

jutro w grudniu po południu [YOO-troh v GROOD-nyoo poh poh-WOOD-nyoo] *adv phr* In the unspecified future, that is, practically never <it'll be a cold day in hell, one of these days, any day now, on the 31st of February, in a pig's eye, in a pig's ass, in a pig's ear, like hell, like fun, like shit, my ass, there's no way, someone will be damned if, someone will be fucked if, says you> eg *Oddam Ci w przyszłym tygodniu. Tak, jutro w grudniu po południu (I'll give it back next week. Yeah, like hell you will); Moją książkę dostanę jutro w rudniu po południu (It'll be a cold day in hell till I get my book back)*

K

kałach [KAH-wakh] *nm* A Kalashniokov, or any similar handheld machine gun <tommy, tommy gun, chopper, chatterbox, grease gun, typewriter, Chicago piano, remington, ack ack, automatic> eg *Był uzbrojony w kałacha (He was armed with a tommy gun)*

kabel See kablówka, kapuś

kablarz See **kapuś**

kablować See **kapować**

kablówka [kah-BLOOF-kah] (or **kabel** [KAH-behl] *nn*) *nf* A cable television <cable, cable tube, cable vid, cable telly, cable box> eg *Zainstalował sobie kablówkę w sypialni (He had cable installed in his bedroom)*

kabza See kasa, nabijać kabzę

kac [kahts] (or **kacenjamer** [kah-tsehn-YAH-mehr]) *nm* A hangover <morning after, big head> eg *Nie gadaj tak głośno, facet, mam kaca (Don't talk so loud, man, it's the morning after)*
See na kacu

kacap* [KAH-tsahp] *nm* A Russian <rusky, red, Ivan, tovarich, comrade> eg *Czego chciał ten kacap? (What did the tovarich want?)*

kaes [kah-EHS] (or **KS** [kah-EHS]) Punishment by death according to law; capital punishment <hemp, noose, necktie party, dance, chair, hot chair, hot seat, hot squat, old smokey> eg *Ta decyzja oznacza to dla niego kaes (That decision means the hemp for him)*

kafejka [kah-FEH-ee-kah] (or **kafeja** [kah-FEH-yah]) *nf* A cafe or a small and cheap restaurant <caf, coffee pot, greasy spoon, doughnut factory, dump, joint, one-arm-joint, eatery, hashery, noshery, quick and dirty> eg *Prowadzi tę kafejkę od lat (He's been running this coffe pot for years)*

kafel [KAF-fehl] *nm* Thousand, esp a thousand zloty bill <grand, G-note, thou, K> eg *Dał mi za to dwa kafle (He gave me two grand for it)*

kajtek [KAH-ee-tehk] *nm* A young child <knee biter, carpet rat, rug rat, little fella> eg *Mieszkał z żoną i dwoma kajtkami (He lived with his wife and two rug rats)*

kaktus See prędzej komuś kaktus wyrośnie

kalendarz See kopnąć w kalendarz

kalkulować [kahl-koo-LOH-vahch] (perf **wykalkulować** [vi-kahl-koo-LOH-vahch]) *v* To wonder or think intensely, and invent something <think up, fake up, cook up, dream up, cobble up, take it off the top of one's head, take it off the cuff, figure out, work out, tune in, plug in, tote up, wise up, get through one's head, get through someone's thick head, get into someone's thick head, see daylight, flash, dig, dawn on, have a brainwave, use one's head, rack one's brain, brainstorm, noodle around, percolate, perk, head trip, skull drag, eat, bug, burn a couple of braincells> eg *Cóżeś tam wykalkulował, co? (What did you think up, huh?)*

kalkulować się [kahl-koo-LOH-vahch shyeh] *v* To be profitable <pay, pay off, pay the rent, pan out> eg *Jestem pewien, że ta robota się kalkuluje (I'm sure this job pays off)*

kalosz See sędzia kalosz

kanał [KAH-nah-oo] *nm* A scandalous fact or situation; a scandal <gas, fuss, stink, hot potato, bad scene, bad news, can of worms, bag of worms, takedown, putdown, shit, serious shit, deep shit, deep water, drag, bind, bitch, bummer, downer, headache, double trouble, snafu, pain in the ass, pain in the neck, spot, mess, holy mess, pickle, squeeze, hard time, glitch, stinker, skeleton, skeleton in the closet, sizzler, scorcher, dynamite, Watergate, fine kettle of fish, fine how do you do, fine cup of coffee, big stink, curtains, lights out, game's over> eg *Prezydent nie ma żadnego alibi? Ale kanał! (The President has no alibi? What a bummer!)*
See wpuścić kogoś w maliny

kanapowy [kah-nah-POH-vi] *adj* (Of political parties) Small and insignificant <small-time, small-fry, nickel-and-dime, pissy-assed, two-bit, flea, shrimp, chirp, dinky, scratch, bush-league, farm-league> eg *Ta kanapowa partia nigdy nie wygra wyborów (This small-time party will never win the elections)*

kanar [KAH-nahr] *nm* (In public transportation) A ticket collector <chopper> eg *Kanar zażądał biletu (The chopper asked to show him his ticket)*

kant [kahnt] *nm* A swindle; a fraud; a scheme <scam, rip-off, con game, double cross, double shuffle, fast one, grift, gyp, flim-flam, hustle, number, racket, run-around, skin game, sucker game, suck-in, ride, fucking over, screwing over, hanky-panky, monkey business, song and dance, game, little game, angle> eg *Poszedł do więzienia za kanty podatkowe (He went to jail for a tax scam)*
See móc sobie w dupę wsadzić, puścić kogoś kantem

kantować [kahn-TOH-vahch] (perf **okantować** [oh-kahn-TOH-vahch]; **kiwać** [KEE-vahch] perf **okiwać** [oh-KEE-vahch] or **wykiwać** [vi-KEE-vahch]; or **kołować** [koh-WOH-vahch] perf **skołować** [skoh-WOH-vahch] or **wykołować** [vi-koh-WOH-vahch]) *v* To cheat; to swindle; to deceive; to scheme <con, rip off, shaft, roll, chisel, gyp, scam, screw, stiff, fleece, dick, do in, take in, do a number on, flim-flam, bamboozle, run a number on, take someone for a ride, take someone to the cleaners, throw someone a curve, pull a fast one, fuck over, screw over, angle, take in, snow, do a snow job, double-shuffle, fast-shuffle, flimflam, give a bun steer, give someone a line, have someone on, lead someone down the garden path, do a snow job, jerk someone's chain, pull someone's chain, pull one's leg, pull someone's string, pull the wool over someone's eyes, put someone on, snow, use smoke and mirrors> eg *Ten handlarz okantował mnie na dwie stówy (That salesman dicked me for two hundred)*

kapać [KAH-pahch] (perf **kapnąć** [KAHP-nohnch]) *v* (Of money) To flow in small amount <trickle in> eg *Ta książka zostanie wydana we wrześniu, ale pieniądze zaczną kapać dopiero w grudniu (This book will be published in September, but the money will not begin to trickle in until December)*

kapeć [KAH-pehch] *nm* A worn-out automotive tire <baldie, bald tire, shoe, skin, slick, flat, sore foot, pumpkin> eg *Masz kapcia w swoim wozie (You have one sore foot in your car)*

kapela [kah-PEH-lah] *nf* A music group <band, act, combo, outfit> eg *Jak wam się podoba ta kapela? (How do you like this band?)*

kapelusz See mieć metr pięćdziesiąt w kapeluszu

kapitalnie [kah-pee-TAHL-nyeh] (or **klawo** [KLAH-voh]) *adv* Extremely well; superbly <great, cool, swell, fab, rad, def, far-out, awesome, frantic, terrific, funky, gorgeous, groovy, hellacious, neat, peachy, dandy, baddest, mean, solid, super-dooper, wailing, wicked, gnarly, top-notch, ten, ace-high, A-OK, A-1, some> eg *Jak się dzisiaj masz? Po prostu kapitalnie. Nie mogłoby być lepiej (How are you today? I'm just great. It couldn't be better)*

kapitalny [kah-pee-TAHL-ni] (or **klawy** [KLAH-vi]) *adj* Excellent; wonderful; extremely good <great, cool, swell, fab, rad, def, far-out, awesome, frantic, terrific, funky, gorgeous, groovy, hellacious, neat, peachy, dandy, baddest, mean, solid, super-dooper, wailing, wicked, gnarly, top-notch, ten, ace-high, A-OK, A-1, some> eg *Na pewno poznasz kapitalnych ludzi (You're sure going to meet great people); To była klawa impreza. Dobrze się bawiliśmy (It was a swell party. We had fun)*

kapka [KAHP-kah] (or **kapkę** [KAHP-keh]) **1** *nf* A little bit <smidgen, tad, wee bit, itty bit> eg *I don't want the whole thing. Give me just a smidgen (Nie chcę wszystkiego. Daj mi tylko kapkę)* **2** *adv* A little; not much <bit, wee, tad, wee bit, itty bit> eg *Myślę, że ciasto jest kapkę za słodkie (I think the cake is a tad to sweet)*

kaplica [kah-PLEE-tsah] *nf* An unfavorable situation; a disaster; dead end <curtains, lights out, end of the line, bad scene, bad news, can of worms, bag of worms,

takedown, putdown, shit, serious shit, deep shit, deep water, drag, bind, bitch, bummer, downer, headache, double trouble, snafu, pain in the ass, pain in the neck, spot, mess, holy mess, pickle, squeeze, hard time, glitch, stinker> eg *Jak mnie złapią, to będzie kaplica (It's curtains for me if they find me)*

kapnąć się [KAHP-nohnch shyeh] (or **skapnąć się** [SKAHP-nohnch shyeh] or **skapować się** [skah-POH-vahch shyeh]) *v* To realize or become aware of something <figure out, work out, tune in, plug in, tote up, wise up, get through one's head, get through someone's thick head, get into someone's thick head, see daylight, flash, dig, dawn on, have a brainwave> eg *Na początku nie wiedział, że żona go zdradza. Kapnął się dopiero po roku (At the beginning he didn't know that his wife had been cheating on him. He figured that out only a year later)*

kapota [kah-POH-tah] *nf* A coat, esp old and worn-out <flogger, peacoat, greatcoat, Eisenhower> eg *Załóż kapotę i idziemy (Put your flogger and let's go)*

kapować [kah-POH-vahch] *v* **1** (perf **skapować** [skah-POH-vahch] or **pokapować** [poh-kah-POH-vahch]) To understand; to comprehend <get, get it, catch, get the drift, get the picture, get the message, get the hang of, savvy, dig, click, capeesh, read, be with it, see where one is coming from, know where one is coming from> eg *Usiłowałem mu wytłumaczyć, ale nie skapował (I tried to explain it to him but he didn't get the drift)* **2** (perf **zakapować** [zah-kah-POH-vahch]; or **kablować** [kah-BLOH-vahch] perf **zakablować** [zah-kah-BLOH-vahch]) *v* To inform the police about someone or something, esp to identify someone; to be an informer <fink, finger, snitch, squeal, beef, blab, blow, blow the whistle, canary, chirp, dime, drop a dime, go stool, leak, nark, put the finger on, rat, rat on, sell out, sing, sing out, stool, weasel> eg *Zakapowała go jako tego, który to zrobił (She fingered him as the one who did it)*

kaptować [kahp-TOH-vahch] (perf **skaptować** [skahp-TOH-vahch]) *v* To employ, hire, or recruit <head-hunt, call up, sign up, sign on, take on> eg *Udało nam się skaptować pięciu nowych pracowników (We managed to sign on five new employees)*

kapucyn See walić konia

kapuś [KAH-poosh] (or **kabel** [KAH-behl] or **kablarz** [KAHB-lahsh]) *nm* An informer, esp a police informer <fink, finger, snitch, snitcher, canary, nark, nose, pigeon, rat, singer, squeal, stool, stool pigeon, tipster, weasel, whistle-blower, whistler> eg *Zrobił się z niego kapuś. Nikt go już nie lubi (He has turned into a fink. Nobody likes him anymore)*

kapuśniak [kah-POOSH-nyahk] (or **kapuśniaczek** [kah-poosh-NYAH-chehk]) *nm* A drizzle; a light shower <spit, light drips, heavy dew, window washer, wet stuff, sky juice, cloud juice> eg *Znów pada. Nie znoszę nawet kapuśniaka (It's raining again. I hate even light drips)*

kapusta See groch z kapustą, kasa

karakan See kurdupel

kareta See jak piernik do wiatraka

kark See mieć łeb, mieć coś na głowie, na karku, nadstawiać karku, siedzieć komuś na karku, mieć ileś lat na karku

karniak [KAHR-nyahk] *nm* A drink of vodka, traditionally offered to someone who came late for the party, esp missing the first round of drinks <behind, one down> eg *A, jesteś wreszcie. Wypij karniaka! (Ah, here you are at last. You're one down!)*

karta rowerowa See żyć z kimś

kartkówka See klasówka

karwasz See kurwa

kasa [KAH-sah] (or **kabza** [KAHB-zah] or **kapusta** [kah-POO-khah]) *nf* Money <dough, bread, bank, cabbage, change, coin, folding, green, lettuce> eg *Skądżeś wziąłe tę kapustę? Obrabowałem bank (Where'd you get all that cabbage? I robbed a bank); Wynoś się, jeśli nie masz żadnej kasy (Get out of here if you don't have any dough)* See mieć forsy jak lodu, robić kokosy, wyłożyć forsę

kaseciak [kah-SEH-chyahk] *nm* A large portable stereo cassette player <boom box, boogie box, coon box, ghetto box, ghetto blaster, nigger box> eg *Możebyś tak wyłączył tego kaseciaka? (I wish you'd turn that boom box off)*

kasować [kah-SOH-vahch] (perf **zakasować** [zah-kah-SOH-vahch]) *v* To be or do better than someone else; to outdo or outsmart; to surpass <top, outgun, outfox, beat, beat one's time, burn, clobber, lick, put in the shade, skin, sweep, take the cake, come out on top, be cut above, be way far cry better> eg *Twój chłopak zakasował wszystkich. Jest taki bystry (Your boyfriend outfoxed everybody. He's so smarts)*

kasowy [kah-SOH-vi] *adj* (Esp about a film) Very remunerative or profitable <blockbuster, goldmine> eg *Jestem chyba jedyną osobą, która nie widziała tego kasowego filmu wideo I'm probably the only one who didn't see this blockbuster video)*

kasza See nie dać sobie w kaszę dmuchać

kaszka z mlekiem [KAHSH-kah z MLEH-kyehm] *nf phr* Anything easy or trivial; a trifle; a bagatelle <piece of cake, cake, cakewalk, cherry pie, duck soup, kid stuff, picnic, pushover, snap, tea party, walkaway, walkover, breeze, stroll, cinch, pipe, big deal, no big deal, no biggie, Mickey Mouse, small potatoes, small beer, fly speck, plain sailing> eg *Zwycięstwo następnym razem to będzie kaszka z mlekiem (Winning next time will be a snap)*

katabas [kah-TAH-bahs] *nm* A catechizer or theologian; a teacher of religion <preacher man, sky pilot, sky merchant, sky scout, gospel pusher, bible thumper, bible banger, sin hound> eg *Co ten katabas od ciebie chciał? (What did that sky pilot want from you?)*

katana [ka-TAH-nah] *nf* A jacket or windbreaker, esp made of jeans, typically worn by adolescents <flogger, peacoat, greatcoat, Eisenhower> eg *Załóż katanę i idziemy (Put your flogger and let's go)*

kawa See wyłożyć kawę na ławę

kawał [KAH-vah-oo] *nm* A joke <trick, rib-tickler, wisecrack, knee-slapper, gag, laugh, wheeze> eg *To był bardzao głupi kawał (That was a pretty dumb wisecrack)* See bysio, chuj, dla jaj, świński kawał

kawał byka See bysio

kawał chłopa See chłopisko

kawał chuja See chuj

kawał czasu [KAH-vah-oo CHAH-soo] *adv phr* Many years; a very long time <ages, dog's age, stretch, many a moon, month of Sundays, donkey's years, God knows how long> eg *Kawał czasu Cię nie widziałem (I haven't seen you for ages)*

kawał z brodą [KAH-vah-oo z BROH-doh] (or **kawał z myszką** [KAH-vah-oo z MISH-koh]) *nm* An old or well-known joke <joke with whiskers, old one, old wheeze, old saw, oldie, bromide, oldest joke in the world> eg *Opowiem wam kawał z brodą (Let me tell you a joke with whiskers)*

kawałek [kah-VAH-wehk] *nm* **1** A song or other short piece of music <track, cut, number, tune, track> eg *Na tej płycie są tylko cztery kawałki (There are only four numbers on this LP)* **2** A short distance <screwdriver turn away, frog's leap away, whoop, a hoop and a holler, a stone's throw, shouting distance, spitting distance> eg *Mieszkamy kawałek od stacji (We live within a stone's throw from the station)* **3** (or **kawał** [KAH-vah-oo]) *nm* Thousand, esp a thousand zloty bill <grand, G-note, thou, K> eg *Będzie to kosztowało dwa kawałki (It'll set you back two grand)*
See ciężki kawałek chleba, z hakiem

kawaler z odzysku [kah-VAH-lehr z ohd-ZIS-koo] *nm phr* A divorced man <dumpee, grass widower, ex> eg *Wszyscy wiedzą, że on jest kawalerem z odzysku (Everybody knows that he's a dumpee)*

kawalerka [kah-vah-LEHR-kah] *nf* An apartment, esp a small one <cubby, cubbyhole, crib, pad, crash pad, cave, den, joint, box, dump, heave, camp, setup, layout, flop, flophouse, shack, rack, homeplate> eg *Ma własną kawalerkę w centrum miasta (He has his own cubbyhole downtown)*

kawalerskie [kah-vah-LEHR-skyeh] *nn* An party spent the evening before the wedding by a fiancee and his colleagues <stag party, bachelor party> eg *Jak się udało twoje kawalerskie? (How was your stag party?)*

kąt [kohnt] *nm* A place to live, esp for a day or so <place, crash pad, pad, crib, digs, diggings, hangout, hideout, hive, squat, cave, den, dive, joint, flop, dump> eg *Mamy własny kąt w centrum miasta (We have a pad downtown)*
See mieszkać kątem, pierdolnąć

kiła See syf

kić [keech] *nm* A prison; a jail <slam, slammer, jug, can, bucket, cage, big cage, big house, caboose, calaboose, cannery, cooler, hole, hoosegow, icebox, lockup, mill, stir, pen, tank, college, crossbar hotel, booby hatch, pink clink, quad> eg *Jest w kiciu już od dwóch lat (He's been in the slammer for two years now)*

kibel [KEE-behl] *nm* **1** A restroom or bathroom; a toilet <john, johnny, can, crapper, potty, shitcan, shitter, shithouse, throne> eg *Gdzie tu jest kibel? (Where's the crapper in here?)* **2** A large metal container for garbage <garbage, garbage can, trash can, dumpster> eg *Gdzie moja pizza? Wyrzuciłem ją na kibel (Where's my pizza? I threw it in the garbage)*

kiblować [keeb-LOH-vahch] *v* **1** *v* To serve a prison sentence; to be in prison <do time, serve time> eg *Kibluje za gwałt (He's been doing time for rape)* **2** To wait <wait out, cool it, cool one's heels, sweat it, sweat out, be put on ice, be put on hold, hang out, hang around, stick around, sit and take it, sit tight, sit out, sit on one's ass, sit on one's butt, warm a chair, lay dead> eg *Kibluję tu od dwóch godzin (I've been cooling my heels here for two hours)* **3** To repeat a class in school or a year at the university <take over, run over, flunk the class, flunk the year> eg *Trzeba być prawdziwym idiotą, żeby kiblować (You've got to be a real idiot to flunk the year)*

kibol [KEE-bohl] *nm* An avid soccer fan <die-hard fan> eg *Pełno było tam kiboli (The place was full of die-hard soccer fans)*

kichawa See kulfon

kiciuś [KEE-chyoosh] (or **kicia** [KEE-chyah] *nf*) *nm* A cat, esp a mongrel <kitty, kitty cat, pussy, pusycat, meow meow, Garfield, Sylvester> eg *Widziałeś naszego kiciusia? (Did you see out kitty?)*

kiełbasa See nie dla psa kiełbasa

kiełbie we łbie See dostać świra, mieć świra

kiecka [KYEHTS-kah] *nf* A women's dress or skirt <outfit, rag, schmatte> eg *Kupił mi dzisiaj dwie kiecki (He bought me two rags today)*

kielich [KYEH-leekh] *nm* **1** A drink of liquor, esp potent, served in a shot glass <snort, finger, jigger, pull, shot, nip, gargle, guzzle, slug, hit> eg *Chceszs jeszcze jednego kielicha? (You want another shot?)* **2** Alcohol drinks in general, liquor <booze, stuff, juice, the bottle, the sauce> eg *Grał w karty albo szedł na kielicha (He used to play cards or go drink some stuff)*

kieliszek See zaglądać do kieliszka

kierowca See niedzielny kierowca

kieszeń See bić po kieszeni, mieć kogoś w kieszeni, mieć węża w kieszeni, trzymać się za kieszeń

kieszonkowe [kyeh-shohn-KOH-veh] *nn* Allowance <pocket money> eg *Rodzice nie dali mi kieszonkowego w zeszłym miesiącu (My parents didn't give me pocket money last month)*

kieszonkowiec [kyeh-shohn-KOH-vyehts] *nm* A professional pickpocket, esp operating in a crowd <dip, cannon, tool, wire, meachanic, cutpurse, digger, file, forks, five fingers, finger, fingersmith, greasy finger, gun, knucker, picks, friskers, hooks, spitter, jostler, clipper, stickup man, lifter> eg *Policjanci właśnie aresztowali dwóch kieszonkowców (The policemen just arresyed two dips)*

kij See chuj ci w dupę, jakby kij połknął, nie w kij dmuchał, taki że bez kija nie podchodź

kijowo [kee-YOH-voh] *adv* Extremely bad; terribly; awfully <lousy, shitty, awful> eg *Kijowo się dzisiaj czuję (I feel really lousy today)*

kijowy [kee-YOH-vi] *adj* Cursed; damnable; bad <fucking, damn, damned, goddamn, goddamned, god-awful, blasted, darn, darned, effing, flipping, forking, freaking, frigging, pesky> eg *W tym kijowym upale nie można było pracować (You couldn't work in that fukcing heat)*

kilos [KEE-lohs] *nm* A kilometer <click, klick, klik> eg *Zdarzyło się to jakieś 50 kilosów stąd (It happened some 50 clicks from here)*

kimać [KEE-mahch] (perf **przekimać się** [psheh-KEE-mahch shyeh]) *v* To sleep, esp to get some sleep <catch some Z's, cop some Z's, cut some Z's, bag some Z's, grab some Z's, catch a nod, cop a nod, bag a nod, grab a nod, konck a nod, collar a nod, take forty winks, bag it, snooze, conk off, caulk off, dope off, drop off, sack out, zonk out, conk out, caulk out, fall out, saw wood, rack, crash, doss, sack up, sack in, zizz, get some blanket drill, get some bunk fatigue, get some sack time, get some shuteye, hit the hay, hit the pad, hit the sack> eg *Muszę się przekimać, bo inaczej padnę (I've got to catch some Z's before I drop)*

kimono See iść w kimono

kino [KEE-noh] (or **komedia** [koh-MEH-dyah] *nf*) *nn* A very funny, amusing, or foolish situation <laugh, laugh and a half, laugher, laughing stock, horselaugh, merry ha-ha, hoot, howl, riot, laff riot, laffer, scream, stitch, boffo, panic, knee-slapper, rib-tickler, side-splitter> eg *Masz zamiar gotować? Ale komedia (You're going to cook? That's a laugh)*

kinol See kulfon

kip [keep] *nm* A remainder of a smoked cigarette <roach, dinch, dincher, maggot, butt, seed, skag, snipe> eg *Nie rzucaj kipów na dywan! (Don't throw your butts on the carpet!)*

kipnąć See kojfnąć

kipować [kee-POH-vahch] (perf **skipować** [skee-POH-vahch] or or **zakipować** [zah-kee-POH-vahch]) *v* To crush out a cigarette <roach, dinch> eg *Skipował papierosa i wyszedł (He dinched his cigarette and left)*

kisiel See dziesiąta woda po kisielu

kiszka See flaki się komuś przewracają, klitka

kiszki [KEESH-kah] *npl* The intestines <guts, kishkes, innards> eg *Widok był okropny. Miał kiszki na wierzchu (It was a terrible sight. His kishkes were out)*

kiszki komuś marsza grają [KEESH-kee KOH-moosh MAHR-shah GRAH-yoh] *phr* To be very hungry <be dog-hungry, have a tapeworm, have munchies, be starving, be starved, be starved to death, could eat a horse, could eat the asshole out of a bear> eg *Kiszki mi marsza grały (I was dog-hungry)*

kit [keet] *nf* **1** Anything worthless, useless, or of shoddy quality; trash <schlock, dreck, garbage, junk, lemon, crap, piece of crap, shit, piece of shit, dogshit, sleaze> eg *Kupiłem ten aparat wczoraj. To kit (I bought this camera yesterday. It's a lemon)* **2** (or **kituś-bajduś** [KEE-toosh-BAH-ee-doosh]) Nonsense; absurdities; pretentious or deceitful talk <bull, bullshit, bullshine, BS, bunk, baloney, applesauce, eyewash, hogwash, hot air, crock, crock of shit, piece of shit, pile of shit, shit, dogshit, horseshit, shit for the birds, crap, crapola, poppycock, smoke, hokum, garbage, trash, horsefeathers, smoke, all that jazz, jazz, jive, malarkey, gobbledygook, double-talk, bafflegab, blah-blah, phony-baloney, fiddle-faddle, twiddle-twaddle, mumbo-jumbo, yackety-yack> eg *Nie wciskaj mi kitu, koleś (Don't give me that baloney, man)*

See bez jaj, do dupy, kitować

kitajec* [kee-TAH-yehts] *nm* A Chinese male <Chink, Chinaman, chino, slant eyes> eg *Kitajce mają bardzo dobre jedzenie (Chinks have very good food)*

kitować [kee-TOH-vahch] (or **wciskać kit** [FCHEES-kahch KEET]) *v* To tell lies in order to deceive someone <bull, bullshit, shit, shovel the shit, string along, snow, fake it, talk through one's hat, speak with forked tongue, put someone on, pull someone's leg, pull someone's string, give someone a leg, have someone on, jack someone around, jerk someone around, kid someone around, fool someone around, jack someone's chain, spoof, cut down, mind-fuck, head-fuck, push around, upstage> eg *Mnie się zdaje, że pan kituje (I think you're shitting me)*

kiwać See kantować

kiwnąć See nie kiwnąć palcem

klamka See dom wariatów, pocałować klamkę

klamoty [klah-MOH-ti] *npl* Personal belongings, esp small and numerous articles of various kinds <stuff, crap, shit, junks, props, odds and ends, bits and pieces, thingies, gadgets, widgets, dingbats, gimmicks> eg *Zabieraj swoje klamoty z mojej szafki (Get your gadgets out of my locker)*

klapa [KLAH-pah] (or **klops** [klohps] *nm*) *nf* A failure, esp a total one <disaster, flop, bomb, blast, bust, screw-up, snafu, ruin> eg *Przedstawienie było totalną klapą (The show was a total flop)*

klapki See mieć klapki na oczach

klasa [KLAH-sah] (or **pierwsza klasa** [PYEHRF-shah KLAH-sah]) **1** *adj* Excellent; superior; superb <classy, high-class, great, cool, swell, fab, rad, def, far-out, awesome, frantic, terrific, funky, gorgeous, groovy, hellacious, neat, peachy, dandy, baddest, mean, solid, super-dooper, wailing, wicked, gnarly, top-notch, ten, ace-high, A-OK, A-1, some> eg *To prostytutka, ale klasa (She's a prostitute, but she's classy)* **2** *nf* High quality or admirable style <class> eg *On znowu pokazał klasę (He showed his class again); To jest konieta z klasą (She's a woman with class)*

klasówka [klah-SOOF-kah] (or **kartkówka** [kahrt-KOOF-kah]) *nf* An unexpected test in school <pop quiz, pop test, shotgun quiz, shotgun test, flash quiz, flash test, drop quiz, drop test> eg *Wczoraj mieliśmy dwie kartkówki z matmy (We had two pop quizzes in math yesterday)*

klata [KLAH-tah] *nf* Chest, esp man's <pecs> eg *Ten facet to ma dopiero wielką klatę! (Does this guy have big pecs!)*

klawo See kapitalnie

klawy See kapitalny

klecha* [KLEH-khah] *nm* A clergyman, esp a Roman Catholic priest <black coat, padre, sky pilot, sky merchant, sky scout, gospel pusher, bible thumper, bible banger, sin hound, rev, abbey, Holy Joe, preacher man> eg *Co ten klecha od ciebie chciał? (What did the padre want from you?)*

kleić się [KLEH-eech shyeh] (perf **przykleić się** [pshi-KLEH-eech shyeh]) *v* To mildly invite or request sexual favors <make a pass, put a move on, make a play for> eg *Zaraz po imprezie zaczęla się do niego kleić (Right after the party she started to make a pass at him)*

klepać bidę See bidować

klepka See nie mieć piątej klepki

klient [KLEE-yent] *nm* A man <fella, guy, dude> eg *Czego chciał ten klient? (What did the fella want?)*

klientka [klee-YENT-kah] *nf* A woman <gal, dame, lady, missy, ma'am, dudette> eg *Klientka mieszka w Ameryce (The gal lives in America)*

klimaty [klee-MAH-ti] *npl* What emanates from a person, object, or situation; atmosphere or feelings <vibes, vibrations, chemistry, wavelength> eg *Ona i ja czuliśmy te same klimaty od początku (She and I shared vibes right from the start); Załapałem klimaty zaraz od początku (I caught the vibes right from the start)*

klin [kleen] *nm* A drink of liquor taken as a remedy for a hangover <hair of the dog> eg *Wyglądasz strasznie. Klina ci trzeba (You look terrible. You need some hair of the dog)*
See zabić komuś klina

klitka [KLEET-kah] (or **kiszka** [KEESH-kah]) *nf* Any small room or apartment, esp narrow <cubby, cubbyhole, tight quarters, small quarters> eg *Mieszka w okropnej kiszce (He lives in a terrible cubbyhole); Popatrz na tę klitkę, w której mieszkam (Look at the tight quarters I have to live)*

klocek [KLOH-tsehk] *nm* Thousand, esp a thousand zloty bill <grand, G-note, thou, K> eg *Kosztowało go to dwa klocki (It set him back two grand)*
See dobra w te klocki, dobry w te klocki, te klocki

klop [klohp] (or **klozet** [KLOH-zeht]) *nm* A restroom or bathroom; a toilet <john, johnny, can, crapper, potty, shitcan, shitter, shithouse, throne> eg *Ta laska robiła mu laskę w klopie! (That chick gave him head in the john); Gdzie jest twój kuzyn? Rzyga w klozecie (Where's your cousin? He's puking in the shitter)*

klops See klapa

kluchy See ciepłe kluchy

kłaki [KWAH-kee] (or **kudły** [KOOD-wi]) *npl* Hair <moss, wig, wool, locks> eg *Spójrz na twoje kudły. Idź się ostrzyc (Take a look at your wig. Go get a haircut)*

kłaść na czymś/kimś lachę* [kwahshch nah chimsh/keemsh LAH-kheh] (or **kłaść na czymś/kimś lagę*** [kwahshch nah chimsh/keemsh LAH-geh] or **kłaść na czymś/kimś chuja**** [kwahshch nah chimsh/keemsh KHOO-yah]) *v phr* To be indifferent to or contemptuous of; not to care at all; to ignore; to show disrespect <not give a damn, not give a fuck, not give a shit, not give a diddly-shit, not give a diddly-damn, not give a flying fuck, not give a hoot, not give a rat's ass, not give a squat, pass up, diss, skip, ig, ice, chill, freeze, cut, brush off, give the brush, give the cold shoulder, turn the cold shoulder, cold-shoulder, give the go-by, high-hat, kiss off> eg *Kładę chuja na to, co myślisz (I don't give a shit what you think)*

kłaść uszy po sobie [KWAHSHCH OO-shi poh SOH-byeh] *v phr* To stop behaving in a superior, haughty, or self-assured manner; to moderate one's behavior <sing another tune, whistle a different tune, change one's tune, come down a peg, take down a notch, climb down, come off one's perch, get off one's high horse, eat dirt, eat humble pie, pull in one's horns, take off one's high hat> eg *Na początku zaczął się popisywać, ale potem położył uszy po sobie (At the beginning he had started to show off but later he came down a peg)*

kłapacze [kwah-PAH-cheh] (or **kły** [kwi]) *npl* The teeth <choppers, fangs, ivories, snappers> eg *Wciąż mam moje własne kłapacze (My choppers are still my own); Jego tata jest dentystą, wyrywa ludziom kły (His dad is a dentist, he pulls out people's fangs)*

kłapaczka [kwah-PAHCH-kah] (or **kopara** [koh-PAH-rah]) *nf* The mouth <yap, bazoo, kisser, trap> eg *Ma wielką kłapaczkę. I zero cycków (She has a big yap. And no tits); Chesz dostać w koparę? To ją zamknij (You want me to punch you in your yap? So shut it)*

kłębek nerwów [KWEHM-behk NEHR-voof] Someone who is nervous, anxious, or completely off-balance; a nervous wreck <basket case, nervous wreck, bundle of nerves, uptight, jumpy, jittery, shaky, shivery, nervy, edgy, antsy, clutchy, hitchy, fretty, itchy, wired, tightened-up, strung-out, on pins and needles, all hot and bothered, all shook up, worried stiff, hot and bothered, shitting razorblades, in the anxious seat, in a stew, in a sweat, in a swivet, in a tizzy, on edge> eg *Po tym spotkaniu był praktycznie kłębkiem nerwów (After that meeting he was practically a basket case)*

kłódka See ani pary z gęby

kłos See kosa

kłuć w oczy [kwooch v OH-chi] *v phr* To annoy, irritate, or make someone envious, esp by being conspicuous <turn green at the sight of> eg *Jego nowy samochód zakłuł ich w oczy (They turned green at the sight of his new car)*

kmiot [kmyoht] (or **kmiotek** [KMYOH-tehk] *nm* A slow-witted or uncultured man, esp from the country <bumpkin, hick, hillbilly, clodhopper> eg *Zupełnie nie ma gustu, jak się ubrać. Wygląda jak kmiotek (He has no taste in clothing. He looks like a country bumpkin)*

knajpa [KNAH-ee-pah] (or **knajpka** [KNAH-eep-kah]) *nf* Any bar or club, esp disrespectful <joint, dive, dump, hellhole> eg *Wynośmy się z tej knajpy (Let's get the hell out of this joint)*

knot [knoht] *nm* Something, esp a book, that is worthless or of a very low quality; a failure <potboiler, spyboiler, pulp, disaster, flop, bomb, blast, bust, screw-up, snafu, ruin> eg *Napisał tego knota w dwa miesiące (It took him two months to write this potboiler)*

kołek See język komuś kołkiem staje

kółko [KOOW-koh] *nn* A steering wheel <wheel> eg *Kto był za kókiem? (Who was behind the wheel?)*
See burdel, cztery kółka, w kółko, za kółkiem

kołnierz See nie wylewać za kołnierz

koło [KOH-woh] *nn* Thousand, esp a thousand zloty bill <grand, G-note, thou, K> eg *Dał mi za to dwa koła (He gave me two grand for it)*
See piąte koło u wozu, w kółko

kołować See kantować

kołowacieć [koh-woh-VAH-chyehch] (perf **skołowacieć** [skoh-woh-VAH-chyehch]) *v* To lose mental fitness; to become insane or eccentric <go crazy, go crazy as a loon, blow one's cork, blow one's top, blow a fuse, crack up, freak out, flip out, go ape, go bananas, go bent, go bonkers, go cracked, go dopey, go ga-ga, go half-baked, go loony, go loopy, go mental, go nerts, go nuts, go nutty, go off one's nut, go off one's rocker, go off one's base, go off the track, go off the trolley, go out one's skull, go psycho, go schizo, go screwy, go wacky, go weird, go wild, schiz out, psych out, come unglued, come unstuck, come unwrapped, come unzipped, go to pieces> eg *Całkowicie skołowaciała, gdy zdechł jej kanarek (She went to pieces when her canary died)* **2** To become bewildered, disoriented, or confused <get spaced out, get mixed up, get discombobulated, get flabbergasted, get messed up, get unscrewed, get farmisht, get balled up, get shook up, get floored, get unglued, get unzipped, get fried, get screwed-up, get fucked-up, get flummoxed, get kerflooey, get caught off base> eg *Skołowaciała, gdy to usłyszała (She got farmisht when she heard that)*
See język komuś kołkiem staje

kołowrotek [koh-woh-VROH-tehk] (or **kołomyja** [koh-woh-MI-yah] *nf* or **kotłowanina** [koht-woh-vah-NEE-nah] *nf*) *nm* A confusing situation; confusion <mess, mess-up, mix-up, fuck-up, screw-up, mess and a half, holy mess, unholy mess, all hell broke loose, ruckus, discombobulation, foofaraw, srew, sweat, swivet, tizzy, hassle, rat's nest, SNAFU> eg *Wtedy właśnie zaczęła się cała kotłowanina (Just then the whole mess started)*

kobieta See ganiać za kobietami

kobita [koh-BEET-ah] *nf* A woman <gal, dame, lady, missy, ma'am, dudette> eg *I co teraz? Co ty powiesz kobicie? (Now what? What are you gonna tell your old lady?)*

kobyła [koh-BI-wah] *nf* A thick and usually boring or worthless book <potboiler, spyboiler, pulp> eg *Napisał tę kobyłę w dwa miesiące (It took him two months to write this potboiler)*
See krowa

kobylasty [koh-bi-LAHS-ti] *adj* Big; large; sizable <gross, humongous, monstro, moby, jumbo, hefty, whopper, mother, king-size, God-size> eg *Właśnie wtedy pojawił się ten kobylasty problem (Just then that humongous problem appeared)*

kociak [KOH-chyahk] *nm* A young and attractive woman <chick, broad, gal, pussy, cunt, ass, piece of ass, piece, dish, babe, baby, dame, beauty, beaut, beauty queen, baby doll, doll, dolly, dollface, dreamboat, dream girl, eating stuff, eyeful, flavor, looker, good-looker, head-turner, traffic-stopper, honey, killer, hot number, package, knockout, oomph girl, peach, bombshell, sex bunny, sex job, sex kitten, sex pot, table grade, ten, bunny, centerfold, cheesecake, date bait, dazzler, heifer, fluff, quail, sis, skirt, tail, job, leg, tart, tomato, pussycat, cooz, twat> eg *Chciałbym poznać jakiegoś fajnego kociaka (I'd like to meet a nice pussycat)*

koczkodan* [kohch-KOH-dahn] *nm* An ugly woman <beasty, skag, skank, pig, bag, dog, cow> eg *A ten koczkodan skąd się tu znalazł? (What is this skank doing here?)*

kogut [KOH-goot] *nm* **1** A man who pursues and otherwise devotes himself to women to an unususal degree <ladies' man, lech, skirt-chaser, lady-killer, lover-boy, hound-dog, cocksman, cunt-struck, cunt-happy, pussy-struck, pistol Pete, operator, player, playboy> eg *Co za kogut z niego! Myśli tylko o kobietach (What a hound-dog he is! All he thinks is dames)* **2** The red light atop a police car, ambulance, or fire truck <cherry, bubble, Christmas tree> eg *Do wszystkich wozów. Włączyć koguty! (To all patrol cars. Hit the cherries!)*
See rany

kojfnąć [KOH-eef-nohnch] (or **kipnąć** [KEEP-nohnch]) *v* To die <bite the dust, kiss the dust, croak, belly up, buy the farm, buy the ranch, cash in one's chips, check out, bump off, conk off, conk out, farm, give up the ghost, go home feet first, go home in a box, go west, kick in, kick off, kick the bucket, pass out, peg out, shove off, drop off, step off, pop off, push up daisies, meet one's maker, turn up one's toes, go down the tube, join the great majority, join the majority> eg *Wujek kojfnął przedwczoraj (Uncle died the day before yesterday)*

koka [KOH-kah] *nf* Cocaine <coke, big-C, crack, nose candy, rich man's aspirin> eg *Nie bierzemy koki, jeśli chcesz wiedzieć (We don't do nose candy, if you want to know)*

kokosowy interes See złoty interes

kokosy [koh-KOH-si] *npl* A very profitable venture; pure profit <bonanza, gold mine, pay dirt, gravy train> eg *Nie będzie za to żadnych kokosów (You won't get any gravy out of this)*
See robić kokosy

kolano See rzucić kogoś na kolana, łysy jak kolano

koleżka See koleś

kolegować się [koh-LEHSH-kah] *v* To be friends <pal around, buddy up, be buddies, be brothers, be buddy-buddy, be palsy-walsy, hang around with, hang out with> eg *Adam i ja kolegujemy się od lat (Adam and I have palled around for years)*

kolejka [koh-LEH-ee-kah] *nf* A round of drinks <round> eg *Teraz on miał postawić kolejkę (It was his turn to buy a round)*

koleś [KOH-lehsh] (or **koleżka** [koh-LEHSH-kah]) *nm* **1** A colleague or friend <bro, brother, buddy, amigo, pal, sidekick, bosom buddy> eg *Jego koleżka ma na niego zły wpływ (His sidekick has a bad influence on him)* **2** (A term of address to) Any man, esp unknown <man, fella, feller, pal, dude, brother, buddy, buster, chief,

doc, Joe, Jack, Mac> eg *E, koleś, nie wolno tu wchodzić (Hey, buddy, you mustn't come in here)*

kolor See do wyboru do koloru

kolorowy [koh-loh-ROH-vi] *nm* A person with non-white color of skin, esp a black; a colored <nigger, niggra, bro, brother, jungle bunny, chocolate drop, darky, groid, inky-dink, blue-skin, boogie, jigaboo, zigaboo, shade, shadow, smoke, spade, spook, coon, Hershey bar> eg *Sami kolorowi w tej dzielnicy! (There are only niggers in this neighborhood)*

komar See chrapnąć sobie komara

kombinować [kohm-bee-NOH-vahch] *v* **1** To make business, esp if very clever but semi-illegal or dishonest or <wheel and deal, live by one's wits, live on one's wits> eg *Po zwolnieniu z wojska jeździł w różne strony i kombinował After his discharge from the Army, he traveled around and lived by his wits)* **2** (perf **skombinować** [skohm-bee-NOH-vahch]) To provide someone with something which is not available <fix up with> eg *Żadnych dokumentów wam nie skombinuję (I won't fix you up with any documents)* **3** (perf **wykombinować** [vi-kohm-bee-NOH-vahch]) To think intensely about something; to ponder<use one's head, rack one's brain, brainstorm, think up, noodle around, percolate, perk, head trip, skull drag, eat, bug> eg *Przyjdź do mnie, sami pokombinujemy (Come over, we'll think something up)* **4** (perf **wykombinować** [vi-kohm-bee-NOH-vahch]) To plan, plot, or devise <be up to, angle, cook up, frame up, mastermind, hatch, line up, set up, quarterback, fudge> eg *Co on kombinuje? (What is he up to?)*

komedia See kino

komin See w pół do komina

komórka [koh-MOOR-kah] *nf* (or **komórkowy** [koh-moor-KOH-vi] or **komórkowiec** [koh-moor-KOH-vyehts]) A cellular phone; a mobile phone <cell phone, cellular> eg *Ja w swoim mercu komórkowy mam (I 've got a cell phone in my Merc)*

kompakt [KOHM-pahkt] *nm* A CD player or a CD plate <CD> eg *Wydano to na taśmie czy na kompakcie? (Was it released on tape or on CD?)*

kompletne zero See zero

kompot [KOHM-poht] *nm* A home-made liquid drug made by infusing poppyseed <cut deck, phony-up> eg *Narkomani wdychali kompot (Druggies were inhaling the cut deck)*
See wpaść

komuch* [KOH-mookh] *nm* A communist <commie, comrade, red, pink, lefty, left-winger> eg *Komuchy wygrały w ostatnich wyborach (The commies won the last elections)*

komuna* [koh-MOO-nah] *nf* Communism or communist rule <commies, comrades, reds, pinks, lefties, left-wingers> eg *Komuna jest odpowiedzialna za wszystko (The reds are responsible for everything)*

kondonierka* [kohn-doh-NYEHR-kah] *nf* A small pants pocket <kick, prat kick, poke> eg *Mam coś dla Ciebie z kondonierki (I have something for you in my kick)*

koniec [KOH-nyehts] *nm* Death <end, end of the line, finish, curtains, lights out, bye-bye, kiss-off, cage, Mr. Bones> eg *Wyglądało to na koniec (It looked like curtains)*
See mieć coś na końcu języka, wiązać koniec z końcem

koniec kropka [KOH-nyehts KROHP-kah] *phr* The end; the final decision <period, that's it, that's all folks, that's all she wrote, curtains, bottom line> eg *Nie zapłacę ani centa. Koniec, kropka (I'm not about to pay not a cent. Period)*

konik [KOH-neek] *nm* **1** A person who buys tickets to be sold at higher prices; a ticket broker <scalper, digger> eg *Przed koncertem koniki sprzedawały bilety trzy razy drożej niż ich pierwotna cena (Before the concert scalpers were selling tickets three times their original price)* **2** One's hobby or extreme interest in something; an obsession <thing, kick, bag, bug, craze, freak, frenzy, weakness, bug up one's ass, bug in one's ear, bee in one's bonnet, bee, flea in one's nose, maggot, maggot in one's brain, hang-up, jones, monkey, ax to grind> eg *Zbieranie znaczków, czy to nie jest jego ostatni konik? (Stamp collecting, isn't that his latest craze?)*

konował* [koh-NOH-vah-oo] *nm* A physician or surgeon; a medical doctor <doc, bones, sawbones, bone-bender, bone-breaker, pill-pusher, pill-roller, pill-bag, pill-peddler, pill-slinger, pills, medico, croaker, butcher, Feelgood, script writer, MD> eg *Ten konował bierze za dużo (That pill pusher charges too much)*

konserwa [kohn-SEHR-vah] *nf* A person or people adversive to change; dogmatics: conservatives <hard-liner, hard-core, hard-shell, die-hard, fogy, fud> eg *Większość z nich to partyjna konserwa (Most of them are hard-liners)*

konspira [kohn-SPEE-rah] *nf* Conspiracy; secret activities <underground, top secret, undercover way, hole-and-corner way, hush-hush way> eg *Nie wiem, co to konspira (I don't know what underground means)*

konszachty [kohn-SHAHKH-ti] *npl* Powerful contacts or influenial connections, esp secret; influence <clout, drag, pull, juice, network, channels, ropes, strings, wires, suction> eg *Ma z nimi konszachty i może wszystko załatwić (He's got the pull with them and he can get everything)*

kontaktować [kohn-tahk-TOH-vahch] *v* To understand or comprehend; have orientation in something <get, get it, catch, get the drift, get the picture, get the message, get the hang of, savvy, dig, click, capeesh, read, be with it, see where one is coming from, know where one is coming from, be with it, get one's bearings> eg *On w ogóle nie kontaktuje (He doesn't get it at all)*

kontaktowy [nyeh-kohn-tahk-TOH-vi] *adj* (Of a person) Easy to communicate with or quick to understand or react <easy to talk to, casual to talk to, quick on the draw, quick on the uptake, quick on the trigger, on the ball, with it> eg *Idź spytaj mojego ojca. Jest bardzo kontaktowy (Go ask my father. He's real casual to talk to)*

kontrabanda [kohn-trah-BAHN-dah] *nf* Goods which it is illegal to bring into a country; contraband <bootleg stuff, bootleg things, swag, smuggle> eg *Miała przy sobie kontrabandę (She had some bootleg stuff on her)*

kontrolka [kohn-TROHL-kah] *nf* Any indicator light, esp in a car's dashboard <idiot light> eg *Włączyła się kontrolka (The idiot light went on)*

konus See kurdupel

koń [kohñ] *nm* **1*** The penis, esp large <cock, prick, dick, stick, joystick, dipstick, bone, meat, beef, wang, yang, dong, dummy, hammer, horn, hose, jock, joint, knob, pork, putz, rod, root, tool, flute, skin flute, love-muscle, sausage, schmuck, schlong, schvantz, cream-stick, third leg, middle leg, business, apparatus, John, Johnny, Johnson, John Thomas, Jones> eg *Złapała mnie za mojego konia (She grabbed me by my meat); Słyszałem, że wali konia co wieczór (I hear he beats his meat every evening)* **2** (or **stary koń** [STAH-ri KOHÑ]) An experienced or old man

<gramps, old fart, old bugger, geezer, gaffer, old-timer, fossil> eg *Ten stary koń dobrze wiedział, co robi (The old fart knew well what he was doing)*

See walić konia, zdrowy jak ryba, znać się jak łyse konie

kość See dać wycisk, dostać wycisk, kościotrup, przemarznąć na kość, przy kości, psia krew

kościotrup [kohsh-CHYOH-troop] (or **skóra i kości** [SKOO-rah ee KOHSH-chee] *npl phr*) *nm* An unusually thin, skinny person <beanpole, stringbean, skin and bones, skeleton, bag of bones> eg *Twój brat to prawdziwy kościotrup. (Your brother is a real beanpole)*

kop [kohp] (or **wykop** [VI-kohp]) *nm* **1** A state of euphoria or energy, esp caused by drugs or alcohol <trip, high, belt, rush, jolt, riot, blast, kick, charge> eg *Po tych prochach to mam dopiero wykop (This stuff really gives me a blast)* **2** (or **kopniak** [KOHP-nyahk]) A kick <boot> eg *Jeszcze dwa klub trzy kopniaki i jest martwy (Two or three more boots ans he's dead)*

See dać kopa, dostać kopa w górę, dostać kopa, na kopy

kopara See kłapaczka

kopcić [KOHP-cheech] (perf **nakopcić** [nah-KOHP-cheech] or perf **zakopcić** [zah-KOHP-cheech]) *v* **1** (Esp about a factory) To pollute or contaminate by emission of chimney smoke <smoke up, stink up, smog, chimney> eg *Zakład przestał w końcu kopcić (The factory finally stopped smoking up)* **2** To smoke a cigarette <puff, drag, pull, blow, poke, toke, fume, fumigate, take a puff, take a drag, light up, torch up> eg *Usiadł i zaczął kopcić (He sat down and started to puff his cigarette)*

kopę lat [KOH-peh LAHT] *adv phr* Many years; a very long time <ages, dog's age, hitch, stretch, many a moon, month of Sundays, dokey's years, God knows how long> eg *Kopę lat cię nie widziałem. Gdzieś był? (I haven't seen you for ages. Where have you been?)*

kopertówka [koh-pehr-TOOF-kah] (or **kopertówa** [koh-pehr-TOO-vah]) *nf* Money given to someone illegally or unethically; a bribe <graft, gravy, payoff, payola, smear, shmear, grease, palm grease, palm oil, boodle, kickback, envelope> eg *Minister był skorumpowany, brał kopertówy (The minister was corrupt, he was getting kickbacks)*

kopnąć w kalendarz [KOHP-nohnch f kah-LEHN-dahsh] (or **strzelić w kalendarz** [STSHEH-leech f kah-LEHN-dahsh] or **walnąć w kalendarz** [VAHL-nohnch f kah-LEHN-dahsh]) *v phr* To die <bite the dust, kiss the dust, croak, belly up, buy the farm, buy the ranch, cash in one's chips, check out, bump off, conk off, conk out, farm, give up the ghost, go home feet first, go home in a box, go west, kick in, kick off, kick the bucket, pass out, peg out, shove off, drop off, step off, pop off, push up daisies, meet one's maker, turn up one's toes, go down the tube, join the great majority, join the majority> eg *Chciałbym, żeby ten sukinsyn kopnął w kalendarz (I wish that son of a bitch kicked the bucket)*

kopnięty [kohp-NYEHN-ti] *adj* Insane, stupid, or thoughtless <crazy, creazy as a loon, loony, nerts, nuts, nutso, nutsy, nutty, sick, sick in the head, sicko, wacko, wacky, psycho, shizo, screwy, off one's rocker, out of one's skull, fruity, airbrained, airheaded, birdbrained, blockheaded, squareheaded, boneheaded, bubblebrained, bubbleheaded, bucketheaded, cluckheaded, cementheaded, clunkheaded, deadheaded, dumbclucked, dumbheaded, dumbassed,

dumbbrained, fatbrained, fatheaded, flubdubbed, knukclebrained, knuckleheaded, lamebrained, lardheaded, lunkheaded, meatheaded, muscleheaded, noodleheaded, numbskulled, pointheaded, scatterbrained, nerdy, dorky, jackassed, lummoxed, dopey, goofy> eg *On musi być kopnięty! Rzucić się na profesora z pyskiem? (He must be nuts! To start yelling at the professor)*

kopsnąć [KOHPS-nohnch] *v* To pass; to hand <hit, kick, toss, throw, drop, duke, shoot, weed, fork over> eg *Kopsnij piwo, dobra? (Toss me a beer, will you?)*

kopyta [koh-PI-tah] *npl* A person's legs <stumps, hinders, pillars, trotters, underpinnings, pins, sticks> eg *Od tego całego biegania bolą mnie kopyta (My stumps are sore from all that running)*
See na jedno kopyto, wyciągnąć nogi

korek [KOH-rehk] *nm* A traffic jam <gridlock, jam, slow and go, gawker's block, gaper's block, curiosity creep> eg *Na autostradzie jest ogromny korek (There's a big gridlock on the highway)*

korki [KOHR-kee] *npl* Private lessons; tutorials <no slang equivalent> eg *Pamiętam, że musiałem wziąć korki z matmy (I remember I had to take private lessons in math)*

koryto [ko-RI-toh] *nn* **1** Food <chow, feed, grub, scoff, eats> eg *Myśli tylko o korycie (All he thinks about is chow)* **2** A very lucrative position, esp of a high-rank government official which guarantees profit without much effort; an obvious sinecure <gravy train, gravy boat, top of the ladder, big time> eg *Ważne, żeby być przy korycie (What is important is to ride the gravy train)*

kosa [KOH-sah] *nf* **1** (or **kłos** [kwohs] *nm*) A knife considered as a weapon, esp a knife with a blade that springs out when a switch is pressed <blade, switch, switchblade, shiv, stick, ripper, steel, shank, Harlem toothpick, frog sticker> eg *Rzuć kosę, natychmiast! (Drop your blade, right now!)* **2** Drizzly weather <slush, spit> eg *Na zewnątrz była prawdziwa kosa (It was real slush outside)*

kosmiczny [kohs-MEECH-ni] *adj* (Esp about a price or sum) exorbitant; expensive <astronomical, pricey, up to here, out of sight> eg *Przed świętami ich ceny były kosmiczne (Before Christmas the prices were astronomical)*

kostucha [kohs-TOO-khah] *nf* Death personified <Grim Reaper, Mr. Grim, Mr. Bones, end, end of the line, finish, curtains, lights out, bye-bye, kiss-off, cage> eg *Kostucha go zabrała (Mr. Bones took him)*

kosz [kohsh] *nm* Basketball <hoop, cage, ball, b-ball, nigger-ball> eg *Chej ty, słuchaj, ccesz pograć w kosza? (Hey, listen, do you want to play hoop?)*
See dać kosza, dostać kosza

koszmarny [kohsh-MAHR-ni] *adj* Terrible, loathsome or disgusting <damn, damned, goddamn, goddamned, god-awful, blasted, darn, darned, effing, flipping, forking, freaking, frigging, pesky, loathsome, disgusting, gross, barfy, scuzzy, sleazy, grody, icky, yucky, gooky, grungy, ech, yech> eg *Widok był koszmarny (It was a god-awful sight)*

koszula See nosić koszulę w zębach

kot [KOHT] *nm* A draftee <boot, rookie, tenderfoot, cannon fodder, sad sack> eg *Trzeba coś zrobić z tymi kotami (We have to do something with the rookies)*
See żyć z kimś, żyć z kimś jak pies z kotem, drzeć z kimś koty, tyle co kot napłakał

kotłowanina See kołowrotek

kotek See bawić się w chowanego

Kowalski See przeciętniak

koza [KOH-zah] *nf* A young woman or teenage girl, esp one lacking wit and character <chick, silly goose> eg *Ożenił się z jakąś brzydką, nudną kozą bez żadnych zainteresowań (He married an unattractive boring chick with no interests)*
See raz kozie śmierć

kozak [KOH-zahk] *nm* A powerful, self-confident man who takes the initiative <big man on campus, big shot, big wheel> eg *To był duży kozak. Robił, co mu się tylko chciało (He was a real big shot. He could do whatever he wanted)*

kpisz czy o drogę pytasz [kpeesh chi oh DROH-geh PI-tahsh] *v phr* (An irritated answer to a question) That was a stupid question; Isn't the answer obvious? <does a bear shit in the woods, do chickens have lips, can snakes do push-ups, is the bear Catholic, is the pope Polish, is the pope Catholic, is a frog's ass waterproof, does Howdy Doody have wooden balls, does a wooden horse have a hickory dick> eg *Zapytałem Phila, czy lubi polskie laski. Kpisz, czy o drogę pytasz, odpowiedział (I asked Phil if he likes Polish chicks. Does a bear shit in the woods? He answered)*

krążek [KROHN-zhehk] *nm* A phonograph record <disc, platter, wax, vinyl, analog, LP> eg *Słyszałeś ich najnowszy krążek? (Did you hear their latest LP?)*

krążownik szos [krohn-ZHOH-vneek SHOHS] *nm phr* A large automobile, esp an American model, that uses a great deal of gasoline <gas guzzler, stretch car, hog, boat, tank, sled, Detroit Iron> eg *Nie chciałam, żebyś kupował ten krążownik szos (I didn't want you to buy this gas guzzler); Nie może pozbyć się tego krążownika szos. Nikt ich teraz nie kupuje (He can't get rid of this boat. Noone's buying them any more)*

Krakówek* [krah-KOO-vehk] *nm* Cracow (Kraków), a former capital of Poland <Cracow-shracow> eg *Bardzo lubię Kraków, więc nie nazywajcie go krakówkiem! (I like Cracow a lot, so don't call it Cracow-shracow)*

kraksa [KRAHK-sah] *nf* A violent car accident that causes traffic to stop; a crash <crack-up, pile-up, rack-up, stack-up, smash-up, crunch> eg *Dziś rano była poważna kraksa na autostradzie (There was a serious smash-up on the highway this morning)*

Krakus* [KRAH-koos] *nm* Inhabitants of Cracow (Kraków) <no slang equivalent> eg *Te Krakusy myślą, że wszystko wiedzą (These goddamn Cracow people think they know everything)*

kram [krahm] *nm* Many small articles of various kinds, esp personal belongings, located in one place <stuff, crap, shit, junks, props, odds and ends, bits and pieces, thingies, gadgets, widgets, dingbats, gimmicks> eg *Zabieraj swój kram z mojej szafki (Get your gadgets out of my locker)*

kranówa [krah-NOO-vah] (or **kranówka** [krah-NOOF-kah]) *nf* Tap water, not suitable for drinking <sewer water> eg *Nie masz chyba zamiaru pić tej kranówy, co? (You're not going to drink this sewer water, are you?)*

krasula [krah-SOO-lah] *nf* A cow <Bossie, Nellie, Elsie, moo cow, moo moo> eg *Nasza krasula zdechła nad ranem (Our Nellie died in the morning)*

kratki See za kratkami

krawężnik [krah-VEHN-zhneek] *nm* A police officer, esp a foot patrol <flatfoot, flatty, cop, copper, fuzz, pig, gumshoe, nabs, paddy, finest, elbow, blue, bluecoat, big John, arm, yard bull, smokey, bear, smokey bear> eg *Krawężnik zatrzymał się przed drzwiami (The flatty stopped at the door)*

krecha See mieć krechę u kogoś, na krechę

kręcić [KREHN-cheech] (perf **przekręcić** [psheh-KREHN-cheech]) *v* To telephone <make a call, buzz, ring, jingle, honk, horn, give someone a buzz, give someone a ring, give someone a jingle, give someone a honk, give someone a tinkle, get one on the line, get one on the horn> eg *Myślę, że powinieneś do niej przekręcić (I think you should give her a buzz)*
See ja pierdolę

kręcić lody [KREHN-cheech LOH-di] *v phr* To do a very profitable business; to make a lot of money, esp without much effort : <pull down, pick up, clean up, cash in, make a bundle, ride the gravy train> eg *Wykupił ten klub, wyremontował i teraz kręci lody (He bought this club, renovated it, and now is cashing in)*

kręcić nosem [KREHN-cheech NOH-sehm] *v phr* To show one's dissatisfaction or discontent, esp over trivialities; to have unfounded complaints <turn up one's nose, fuss, stink, scene, make a ceremony, beef, bleed, hassle, kvetch, bitch, beef, gripe, piss, bellyache, grouse, growl, squawk, cut a beef, make a stink, piss up a storm, raise a stink, blow up a storm, kick up a storm, eat someone's heart out, fuck around, screw around, mess around, trip> eg *Kręciła nosem, bo nie mieli tego, co chciała (She was pissing up a storm, because they didn't have what she wanted)*

kręcić się [KREHN-cheech shyeh] *v* (Of a venture or business) To be prosperous; to generate profit <pay, pay off, pay the rent, pan out> eg *Najważniejsze, że interes się kręci (The most important is for the business to pay off)*

kręcić się koło kogoś [KREHN-cheech shyeh KOH-woh KOH-gohsh] (or **chodzić koło kogoś** [KHOH-jeech KOH-woh KOH-gohsh]) *v phr* To follow someone in search for sexual encounter; to invite or request sexual favors <chase, cruise, tail, troll, run around, dog someone's footsteps, hunt for cunt> eg *Ostatnio kręci się koło niej jakiś blondyn (A blonde has been running around her lately)*

kręcić z kimś [KREHN-cheech s KEEMSH] *v phr* To have a steady relationship with a member of the opposite sex, esp in the teenage context <date, go steady, go together, go out, step out, have a thing going, be an item> eg *Kręci z nim już od roku (She's been going steady with him for a year)*

krempacja See bez krępacji

kreska See gruba kreska

kretyn* [KREH-tin] *nm* A stupid or thoughtless person; an idiot <airbrain, airhead, birdbrain, blockhead, squarehead, bonehead, bubblebrain, bubblehead, buckethead, cluckhead, cementhead, clunkhead, deadhead, dumbbell, dumbcluck, dumbhead, dumbass, dumbbrain, fatbrain, fathead, flubdub, knukclebrain, knucklehead, lamebrain, lardhead, lunkhead, meathead, musclehead, noodlehead, numbskull, pointhead, scatterbrain, jerk, jerk-off, klutz, chump, creep, nerd, dork, dweeb, gweeb, geek, jackass, lummox, twerp, nerd, bozo, clod, cluck, clunk, dimwit, dingbat, dipstick, dodo, dopey, dufus, goofus, lump, lunk, nitwit, schnook, schlep, schlemiel, schmendrick, schmo, schmuck, simp, stupe> eg *Wiesz co ten kretyn zrobił? Zgubił klucze (You know what that dumbass did? He lost the keys)*

kretyński [kreh-TIÑ-skee] *adj* Stupid or thoughtless <crazy, creazy as a loon, loony, nerts, nuts, nutso, nutsy, nutty, sick, sick in the head, sicko, wacko, wacky, psycho, shizo, screwy, off one's rocker, out of one's skull, fruity, airbrained, airheaded, birdbrained, blockheaded, squareheaded, boneheaded, bubblebrained, bubbleheaded, bucketheaded, cluckheaded, cementheaded, clunkheaded,

deadheaded, dumbclucked, dumbheaded, dumbassed, dumbbrained, fatbrained, fatheaded, flubdubbed, knukclebrained, knuckleheaded, lamebrained, lardheaded, lunkheaded, meatheaded, muscleheaded, noodleheaded, numbskulled, pointheaded, scatterbrained, nerdy, dorky, jackassed, lummoxed, dopey, goofy> eg *Co za kretyńska muzyka (What wacky music)*

kretyństwo [kreh-TIÑ-stfoh] *nn* Anything stupid or stupidity in general <stupid thing, silly-ass thing, stupidom, klutzdom> eg *Wlał keczup do drukarki. Co za kretyństwo! (He poured some catsoup on the printer. What a stupid thing to do!)*

krew See krew kogoś zalewa, psia krew

krew kogoś zalewa [KREHF KOH-gohsh zah-LEH-vah] (or **jasna krew kogoś zalewa** [YAHS-nah KOH-gohsh zah-LEH-vah] or **nagła krew kogoś zalewa** [NAHG-wah KOH-gohsh zah-LEH-vah]) *v phr* To be very angry or irritated <be pissed off, be peed off, be p'd off, be bent out of a shape, be pushed out of a shape, be browned off, be cheesed off, be uptight, be cranky, be edgy, be sore, be mad as a hornet, be steamed up, be ticked off, be tee'd off, be burned up, be ballistic> eg *Za każdym razem jak słyszę tego faceta, krew mnie zalewa (I get peed off everytime I listen to this guy)*

krewni i znajomi królika [KREHV-nee ee znah-YOH-mee kroo-LEE-kah] *npl phr* Everyone <everybody and his brother> eg *Na imprezie był tłum. Byli krewni i znajomi królika (The party was packed. Everybody and his brother was there)*

krewny [KREHV-ni] *adj* Indebted; owing money <in the red, into for, owe someone one,I OU, in hock> eg *Jest krewny mojemu bankowi dziesięć kawałków (He's into my bank for ten grand); Był krewny swojemu przyjacielowi pięć tysięcy (He was 5,000 in the red to his friend)*

krocie [KROH-chyeh] *npl* A large amount of money <bundle, bankroll, big bucks, megabucks, heavy bread, mint, package, hard coin> eg *Najlepsi bokserzy świata zarabiają krocie (The best boxers earn big bucks)*

krok See co rusz

król [krool] *nm* A rabbit <Bugs> eg *Muszę iść nakarmić króle (I must go feed the rabbits)* See iść tam gdzie król chodzi piechotą

król ogórków [KROOL oh-GOOR-koof] *nm phr* An owner of a large garden farm or plantation; a rich but rustic and unsophisticated businessman <big-time bumpkin, hayseed tycoon, hillbilly baron> eg *Królom ogórków ciężko jest przyzwyczaić się do życia w mieście (It's hard for these hayseeds to adjust to city life)*

królik See krewni i znajomi królika

kropelka [kroh-PEHL-kah] (or **kropla** [KROHP-lah] or **kropelka w morzu** [kroh-PEHL-kah v MOH-zhoo] or **kropla w morzu** [KROHP-lah v MOH-zhoo]) *nf* Just a little bit; not enough <drop in the ocean, drop in the bucket, chicken feed, smidgen, tad, wee bit, itty bit> eg *Dwa tysiące nie wystarczą. To kropla w morzu. Potrzebuję przynajmniej dziesięć (Two thousand is won't do. It's a drop in the ocean. I need at least ten thousand)*

kropka See koniec kropka, kubek w kubek, w kropce

kropka w kropkę See kubek w kubek

kropnąć [KROHP-nohnch] *v* To kill someone, esp ny shooting <gun, plug, blast, pop, smoke, zap, trigger, snuff, bump off, burn, blow away, erase, finish off, frag, ice, knock off, off, put away, rub, waste, wipe, take care of> eg *Kropnęli go dwa lata temu (They bumped him off two years ago)*

krowa [KROH-vah] *nf* **1*** (or **kobyła*** [koh-BI-wah]) Any large object or person <cow, monster, monstro, mungo, jumbo, moby, lunker, blimp> eg *A gdzie wstawimy tę krowę? Masz na myśli mój fortepian? (Where shall we put this monster? You mean my piano?)* **2** A 0.75-liter bottle of vodka <fifth, 20-ouncer> eg *Wykończyliśmy krowę wódki (We finished off a fifth of whiskey)* **3*** A woman, esp heavy or ugly <beasty, skag, skank, pig, bag, dog, cow> eg *Ta krowa ledwo mogła przejść przez drzwi (That cow could hardly get through the door)*

krowa dojna [KROH-vah DOH-ee-nah] (or **dojna krowa** [DOH-ee-nah KROH-vah]) *nf phr* A very profitable venture; a lucrative business <bonanza, gold mine, pay dirt, gravy train> eg *Nie sądzę, że taka pizzeria jest dojną krową (I don't consider such a pizzeria to be a gold mine)*

krwawa mańka [KRVAH-vah MAHÑ-kah] (or **krwawa mery** [KRVAH-vah MEH-ri]) *nf phr* An alcoholic cocktail "Bloody Mary" <bloody> eg *Jedną szkocką dla mnie i jedną krwawą mańkę dla mojego przyjaciela (One scotch for me and one bloody for my friend)*

kryć [krich] *v* To shield or shelter someone from something, esp responsibility or punishment; to defend and support <cover, cover up, cover someone's ass, go to bat for, stand up for, back up> eg *Wiedział, że jego szef będzie go krył (He knew his boss weould go to bat for him)*

kryminał [kri-MEE-nah-oo] **1** *nm* A prison; a jail <slam, slammer, jug, can, bucket, cage, big cage, big house, caboose, calaboose, cannery, cooler, hole, hoosegow, icebox, lockup, mill, stir, pen, tank, college, crossbar hotel, booby hatch, pink clink, quad> eg *Jest w kryminale już od dwóch lat (He's been in the slammer for two years now)* **2** *nm* Crime; criminal or illegal activity in general <caper, racket, case, dirty work, dirty job, wrongoing> eg *Gdyby to zrobił, to byłby kryminał (If he had done that, it would have meant a dirty work)* **3** A detective story or film <whodunit, shocker, chiller, thriller, cliff-hanger, grabber, spy-boiler, mystery> eg *Lubię od czasu do czasu przeczytać jakiś dobry kryminał (I like to read a good whodunit every now and then)*

krzyż See jak z krzyża zdjęty, na krzyż

krzyżówka [kshi-ZHOOF-kah] *nf* An intersection <lights, cross street, mixmaster> eg *Zatrzymaj się na następnej krzyżówce (Stop at the next lights)*

krzyżyk [KSHI-zhik] *nm* (Telling age) A period of ten years; a decade <no slang equivalent> eg *Ona jest jeszcze młoda, zaczyna dopiero drugi krzyżyk (She's still young, she's pushing twenty)*

krzyk mody [kshik MOH-di] (or **ostatni krzyk mody** [ohs-TAHT-ni kshik MOH-di]) *nm phr* Something very fashionable, trendy, and currently popular; something en vogue <the rage, the thing, go-go, hip, in-thing, latest word, latest wrinkle, craze> eg *Ostrzyż się tak jak ja. To ostatni krzyk mody (Get a haircut like mine. It's all the rage)*

krzywo See patrzeć na kogoś krzywo

krzywy See na sępa

KS See kaes

księżulek [kshehn-ZHOO-lehk] (or **księżulo** [kshehn-ZHOO-loh]) *nm* A Roman Catholic priest <black coat, padre, sky pilot, sky merchant, sky scout, gospel pusher, bible thumper, bible banger, sin hound, rev, abbey, Holy Joe, preacher man> eg *Co ten księżulo od ciebie chciał? (What did the padre want from you?)*

księżycówka [kshyehn-zhi-TSOOF-kah] *nf contempuous* Cheap, inferior, or illicit liquor, esp home-made <moonshine, moonlight, mountain dew, rotgut, swipe, tiger sweat, panther piss, coffin varnish> eg *Chciał, żebym napił się tej księżycówki (He wanted me to drink his moonshine)*

ksiuty [KSHYOO-ti] *npl* Playful sexual or amorous activity of any kind <action, dirty deed, little heavy breathing, fun and games, bouncy-bouncy, boom-boom, in-and-out, hootchie-coochie, jig-jig, roll in the hay, jelly roll, night baseball, bush patrol, hanky-panky, lovey-dovey, grab-ass, you-know-what> eg *Nie mam czasu na ksiuty (I don't have time for fun and games)*

See chodzić na dupy

ksywa [KSI-vah] (or **ksywka** [KSIF-kah]) *nf* A pseudonym <aka, handle, summer name, nickname> eg *Jaką masz ksywę? (What's your nickname?)*

kuć [kooch] (perf **wykuć** [VI-kooch]; or **obkuwać** [ohp-KOO-vahch] perf **obkuć** [OHP-kooch]; or **zakuwać** [zah-KOO-vahch] perf **zakuć** [ZAH-kooch]; or **wkuwać** [FKOO-vahch] perf **wkuć** [fkooch]; **się** [shyeh] may be added) *v* To study intensively, esp for an upcoming examination <cram, grind, dig, skull, book it, go book, hit the books, megabook, megastudy, crack the books, pound the books, bone up> eg *Zbliża się egzamin, więc lepiej zabiorę się za kucie (The exam is coming so I'd better crack the books); Przez ostatni tydzień kułem do egzaminu z matmy (For the past week I've been cramming for the math exam); Obkuwała po nocach literaturę (She was grinding literature)*

kubeł See ani pary z gęby

kubek w kubek [KOO-behk f KOO-behk] (or **kropka w kropkę** [KROHP-kah f KROHP-keh] or **toczka w toczkę** [TOHCH-kah f TOHCH-keh]) *adj phr* Identical; the same <look-alike, dupe, clone, carbon, carbon copy, double, ditto, spitting image, dead ringer, six of one and half a dozen of the other, like two peas in a pod> eg *Ich mieszkanie jest kubek w kubek jak nasze (Their apartment is a spitting image of ours); Jego brat był kropka w kropkę jak ojciec (His brother was a dead ringer of his father)*

kudły See kłaki

kujon [KOO-yohn] *nm* An overly diligent student <grind, greasy grind, wonk, tool, throat, dweeb, gweeb, grunt, cereb, bookworm, grade hound, crammer, nerd> eg *Nie jestem kujonem, po prostu jestem dobry (I'm no grind, I'm just good)*

kuku [KOO-koo] (or **kukuryku** [koo-koo-RI-koo]) *nn* A lock of hair which is sticking out in unobvious departure from one's hairstyle <cow-lick, alfalfa> eg *Gdyby nie to kukuryku, to świetnie wyglądał (He looked great but for the cow-lick)*

kuku na muniu [KOO-koo nah MOO-nyooh] *nn phr* Obsession, insanity, or eccentricity <thing, kick, bag, bug, craze, freak, frenzy, weakness, bug up one's ass, bug in one's ear, bee in one's bonnet, bee, flea in one's nose, maggot, maggot in one's brain, hang-up, jones, monkey, ax to grind> eg *Ma kuku na muniu odkąd poszedł posłuchać tego kazania (He's had a bee in his bonnet ever since he went to that sermon)*

See dostać świra, mieć świra

kukuryku See ani be ani me

kula u nogi [KOO-lah oo NOH-gee] *nf phr* A person or thing regarded as unnecessary and likely to impede <ball and chain, third wheel, excess baggage,

square peg> eg *Obawiam się, że byłem dla nich kulą u nogi (I'm afraid I was a sort of a third wheel for them)*

kulasy [KOO-lahs] *nm* A person's legs <stumps, hinders, pillars, trotters, underpinnings, pins, sticks> eg *Od tego całego biegania bolą mnie kulasy (My stumps are sore from all that running)*

kulfon [KOOL-fohn] (or **kinol** [KEE-nohl] *nm* or **kichawa** [kee-KHAH-vah] *nf*) *nm* The nose <schnozz, beak, beezer, honker, smeller, snoot> eg *Ale masz pryszcza na kinolu (That's one fine zit you got on your snoot); Z taką kichawą powinien występować w cyrku (With a schnozz like that he should be in the circus)*

kulki See grać sobie w kulki z kimś

kultura [kool-TOO-rah] (or **kulturka** [kool-TOOR-kah]) *adj* Excellent; wonderful <great, cool, swell, fab, rad, def, far-out, awesome, frantic, terrific, funky, gorgeous, groovy, hellacious, neat, peachy, dandy, baddest, mean, solid, super-dooper, wailing, wicked, gnarly, top-notch, ten, ace-high, A-OK, A-1, some> eg *Facet jest naprawdę kulturka (The guy is really cool)*

kumać [KOO-mahch] (or **kumać bazę** [KOO-mahch BAH-zeh] or **kumać blusa** [KOO-mahch BLOO-sah]; perf **skumać** [SKOO-mahch] or **wykumać** [vi-KOO-mahch]) *v* To understand; to comprehend <get, get it, catch, get the drift, get the picture, get the message, get the hang of, savvy, dig, click, capeesh, read, be with it, see where one is coming from, know where one is coming from> eg *On w ogóle nie skumał bazy (He didn't get the picture at all)*

kumać się [KOO-mahch shyeh] (perf **skumać się** [SKOO-mahch shyeh]) *v* To be friends <pal around, buddy up, be buddies, be brothers, be buddy-buddy, be palsy-walsy, hang around with, hang out with> eg *Ona skumała się z jakimś muzykiem (She has palled up with some musician)*

kumaty [koo-MAH-ti] *adj* Intelligent; clever knowledgeable <brainy, eggheaded, savvy, whiz, highbrow, long-haired, nifty, with it, cereb, nobody's fool, not born yesterday, in the know, all brains> eg *Ten facet jest bardzo kumaty (This guy is all brains)*

kumpel [KOOM-pehl] *nm* A male colleague or friend <bro, brother, buddy, amigo, pal, sidekick, bosom buddy> eg *Chciałem jechać z kumplami nad morze (I wanted to go with my pals to the seaside)*

kumpela [koom-PEH-lah] (or **kumpelka** [koom-PEHL-kah]) *nf* A female colleague or friend <gal, amiga, sister, pal, sidekick, bosom buddy> eg *Przyszły tylko dwie kumpele (Only two gals came)*

kumplować się [koom-PLOH-vahch shyeh] (or **kumplić się** [KOOM-pleech shyeh]) *v* To be friends <pal around, buddy up, be buddies, be brothers, be buddy-buddy, be palsy-walsy, hang around with, hang out with> eg *Adam i ja kumplujemy się od lat (Adam and I have palled around for years)*

kundel [KOON-dehl] *nm* A dog, esp a mongrel <doggie, mutt, pooch, pup, Fido, Pluto, Goofy, Heinz, flea bag, tail wagger, bone eater, pot hound> eg *Ile chcesz za tego kundla? (How much do you want for this mutt?)*

kupa [KOO-pah] *nf* **1** (or **kupka** [KOOP-kah]) Feces, excrement <crap, doo-doo, caca, kaka, poo, poo-poo, poop, squat> eg *Nie wdepnij w kupę (Don't step in the doo-doo)* **2** Much; many; plenty <helluva lot, lotsa, lotta, oodles, scads, heaps, bags, barrels, loads, piles, tons, wads, jillions, zillions, enough to choke a horse, shitload,

fuckload, truckload> eg *Ona ma kupę szmalu. Zastanawiam się skąd go wzięła (She has lotsa money. I wonder where did she get it from?)*

See robić kupę, trzymać się kupy, wziąć się do kupy

kupa śmiechu [KOO-pah SHMYEH-khoo] *nf phr* Something very funny, amusing or foolish; a cause of amusement, esp of derision <laugh, laugh and a half, laugher, laughing stock, horselaugh, merry ha-ha, hoot, howl, riot, laff riot, laffer, scream, stitch, boffo, panic, knee-slapper, rib-tickler, side-splitter> eg *Masz zamiar gotować? Kupa śmiechu (You're going to cook? That's a laugh)*

kuper [KOO-pehr] *nm* The buttocks, the posterior <ass, butt, bum, behind, back, back seat, seat, bottom, heinie, rear, tush, fanny, derriere, tail, bucket, tokus, keister, kazoo> eg *Wiewiórka ugryzła go w tyłek (The squirrel bit him in his behind)*

kupić [KOO-peech] *v* **1** To believe or accept <buy, buy into, buy off, down, eat up, fall for, go for, lap up, sign off on, swallow, swallow the bait, take, tumble for> eg *Nie kupuję tej twojej bajeczki. Powiedz mi prawdę (I don't buy that story. Tell me the truth)* **2** To become interested in something <buy, catch, hook, get sold into, get hooked into, get turned on> eg *Japończycy natychmiast kupili ten pomysł (The Japanase instantly bought the idea)*

kura See bazgrać, gryzmolić, jak zmokła kura, kura znosząca złote jajka

kura domowa [KOO-rah doh-MOH-vah] *nf phr* A woman whose primary interests are keeping house and raising children <housewife, hausfrau, silly goose> eg *Chciał kobietę-wampa, ożenił się z kurą domową (He wanted a vamp, he married a hausfrau)*

kura znosząca złote jajka [KOO-rah znoh-SHOHN-tsah ZWOH-teh YAH-ee-kah] (or **złota kura** [ZWOH-tah KOO-rah]) *nf phr* A very profitable venture; a lucrative business <bonanza, gold mine, pay dirt, gravy train> eg *Władze traktują to przedsięwzięcie, jak potencjalną kurę znoszącą złote jajka (The authorities treat this enterprise as a potential gold mine)*

kurczę See kurwa

kurde See kurwa

kurdupel* [koor-DOO-pehl] (or **konus*** [KOH-noos] or **karakan*** [kah-RAH-kahn]) *nm* A person of short stature <shorty, peewee, peanut, runt, squirt, shrimp, half-pint> eg *Co to za kurdupel przy drzwiach? (Who's the shrimp over by the door?);*

kurewka See kurwa

kurewski** [koo-REHF-skee] *adj* Cursed; damnable; bad <damn, damned, goddamn, goddamned, god-awful, blasted, darn, darned, effing, flipping, forking, freaking, frigging, pesky> eg *Ten kurewski klucz nie pasuje (This goddamn key doesn't fit in)*

kurewsko** [koo-REHF-skoh] *adv* **1** Extremely bad; terribly; awfully <lousy, shitty, awful> eg *Kurewsko się dzisiaj czuję (I feel really lousy today)* **2** Extremely; exceedingly; very <awful, god-awful, real, mighty, plenty, damn, damned, goddamn, goddamned, darn, darned, effing, flipping, forking, freaking, frigging, fucking, one's ass off, one's brains out, one's head off, to the max, like all get-out, like sin, to beat the band, like all creation, as blazes, as can be, as hell, like hell, in full swing> eg *Ona jest kurewsko zgrabna (She's damn shapely)*

kurewstwo** [koo-REHS-tfoh] *nn* **1** Prostitutes or prostitution in general <whoredom, hookerdom, hustlerdom> eg *Powinno się coś zrobić z tym kurewstwem (One should do something about whoredom)* 2 Anything arduous, despicable, or disagreeable <shit, bitch, fucker, motherfucker, sucker, bastard> eg *Palę tylko paczkę papierosów dziennie, bo drogie kurestwo (I only smoke a pack of cigarettes a day, because motherfuckers are expensive)*

kuroniówka See na kuroniówce

kurs See iść w cug

kurwa** [KOOR-vah] *nf* **1** (or **kurwiszon**** [koor-VEE-shohn] *nm* or **kurwiszcze**** [koor-VEESH-cheh] *nn* or **kurwena**** [koor-VEH-nah] *nf* or **kurewka**** [koo-REHF-kah] *nf* or **kurwa z matki rodem**** [KOOR-vah z MAHT-kee ROH-dehm]) *nf phr*, **lekkiego prowadzenia** [lehk-KYEH-goh proh-vah-DZEH-nyah] may be added) A prostitute <whore, hooker, hustler, slut, working girl, pro, call girl, quiff, street walker> eg *A white whore like you should earn much more (Taka biała kurwa jak ty powinna zarabiać dużo więcej)* **2** A woman, esp whom one despises <bitch, slut, cunt, broad, wench, hag, old hag, old biddy, old bag, old tart, piece of shit> eg *Co ta kurwa od ciebie chciała? (What did that cunt want from you?)* **3** (or **o kurwa**** [oh KOOR-vah] or **o żeż kurwa**** [oh zhehsh KOOR-vah] or **kurwa mać**** [KOOR-vah MAHCH] or **kurwa czyjaś mać**** [KOOR-vah CHI-yahsh MAHCH] or **do kurwy nędzy**** [doh KOOR-vi NEHN-dzi] or **u kurwy nędzy**** [oo KOOR-vi NEHN-dzi] or **kurza twarz** [KOO-zhah TFAHSH] or **kurna*** [KOOR-nah] or **kurde*** [KOOR-deh] or **kurczę** [KOOR-cheh] or **karwasz** [KAHR-vahsh] or **kurtka** [KOOR-tkah] or or **kuźwa*** [KOOZH-vah]) An exclamation of anger, irritation, disappointment, shock <shit, fuck, hell, heck, damn, damn it, goddamn it, gosh, golly, gee, jeez, holy fuck, holy cow, holy moly, holy hell, holy mackarel, holy shit, jumping Jesus, fucking shit, fucking hell> eg *Przegraliśmy ten mecz! Kurwa mać! (We lost that game! Fuck!)*

See męska dziwka, rzucać mięsem

kurwić się** [KOOR-veech shyeh] (perf **skurwić się**** [SKOOR-veech shyeh]) *v* To work as a prostitute <hustle, hook, turn tricks, peddle ass, street-walk, work the street, go whoring, whore oneself> eg *Kurwi się 7 dni w tygodniu (She street-walks seven nights a week)*

kurwiarz** [KOOR-vyahsh] *nm* A sexually voracious man, esp one who goes often to prostitutes <whore-hopper, whore-hound, whore-monger> eg *Nie był żadnym kurwiarzem, ale lubił panienki (He was no whore-hopper, but he liked call-girls)*

kurwica** [koor-VEE-tsah] *nf* A fit of extreme anger; fury; rage <fit, storm, blow-up, blow-off, flare-up, swivet, conniption fit, catfit, stew, snit, pucker, tantrum, hemorrhage, shit hemorrhage> eg *Dostał kurwicy, gdy zdał sobie sprawę z tego, że przegrali (He had a swivet when he realized they'd lost)*

See cholera kogoś bierze, dostać cholery

kurwidołek** [koor-vee-DOH-wehk] *nm* A small town, esp in the country; any place far from civilization <jerk town, jerkwater town, backwater, hellhole, rathole, mudhole, real hole, noplaceville, hicksville, whistle stop, dump, armpit, East Jesus, Bumfuck Egypt> eg *Skąd dzwonisz? Z jakiegoś kurwidołka (Where are you calling from? Bumfuck Egypt)*

kurza twarz See kurwa

kurzy móżdżek See ptasi móżdżek

kusztyczek [koosh-TI-chehk] *nm* A little drink of a potent liquor, esp vodka, served in a shot glass <snort, finger, jigger, pull, shot, nip, gargle, guzzle, slug, hit> eg *Mówi, że wypiła tylko kusztyczek (She said she only drank a finger)*

kutas** [KOO-tahs] (or **kutafon*** [koo-TAH-fohn]) *nm* A man one dislikes or disapproves of <asshole, fuck, fucker, fuckhead, fuckface, motherfucker, shit, shitface, shithead, shitheel, bastard, jerk, SOB, son of a bitch, son of a whore, cocksucker, prick, dick, dickhead, cuntface, schmuck, scum, scumbag, sleazebag, slimebag, dipshit, pisshead, piece of shit, pain in the ass> eg *Chcesz się ze mną bić, ty głupi kutasie? (You wanna pick a fight with me, you stupid prick?)*

kutwa* [KOOT-fah] *nf* A parsimonious person; a miser <tightwad, piker, cheapskate, scrooge, pinchfist, penny-pincher, pinchpenny, nickel-nurser, nickel-squeezer> eg *To kutwa, za darmo tego nie zrobi (He's a cheapskate, he won't do it for free)*

kuźwa See kurwa

kwas [kfahs] (or **kwach** [kfahkh]) *nm* LSD (lysergic acid diethylamide), a hallucinogen <acid, Lucy in the sky with diamonds, sunshine, cubes> eg *Znów jest na kwasie (She's on acid again)*

kwiatek [KFYAH-tehk] *nf* An irritating and shocking fact, event, or situation, esp one that someone wants to keep secret; a scandal <spicy info, spicy poop, skeleton, skeleton in the closet, sizzler, scorcher, dynamite, Watergate, fine kettle of fish, fine how do you do, fine cup of coffee, big stink> eg *Mogę Ci też opowiedzieć o innych kwiatkach (I can also give you some other spicy info)*
See wąchać kwiatki

kwitek See z kwitkiem

kwitnąć [KFEET-nohnch] *v* To wait <wait out, cool it, cool one's heels, sweat it, sweat out, be put on ice, be put on hold, hang out, hang around, stick around, sit and take it, sit tight, sit out, sit on one's ass, sit on one's butt, warm a chair, lay dead> eg *Kwitłem tam dwie godziny (I've been cooling my heels for her for two hours)*

L

lać [lahch] *v* **1** (perf **nalać** [NAH-lahch] or **wylać się** [VI-lahch shyeh] or **zlać się** [ZLAHCH shyeh]) To urinate <piss, leak, pee, piddle, tinkle, wee-wee, whizz> eg *Nie lej po ścianie, ty wszawy baranie (Don't leak on the wall, you lousy asshole)* **2** (or **lać jak z cebra** [lahch yahk s TSEH-brah] might be added) *v* To rain very intensely <spit, piss, piss cats and dogs, rain cats and dogs, pour cats and dogs, piss pitchforks, rain pitchforks, pour pitchforks, piss buckets, rain buckets, pour buckets, rain hammer handles, come down in buckets> eg *Nie udały nam się wakacje. Przez wszystkie dni lało jak z cebra (We didn't enjoy our vacations. It rained cats and dogs every single day* **3** (or **lać się** [LAHCH shyeh] or **lać ze śmiechu** [LAHCH zeh SHMYEH-khoo]; **sikać** [SHEE-kahch] or **szczać** [SHCHAHCH] may replace **lać**; **po nogach** [poh NOH-gakh] may precede **ze śmiechu**) *v phr* To burst with laughter <crack up, break up, split, split one's sides, die laughing, roll in the aisles, tear one apart, be in stiches, laugh fit to

burst, bust a gut laughing, pee in one's pants laughing, fall out laughing, howl, scream, horselaugh, stitch, be blue in the face, laugh till one is blue in the face> eg *Szczaliśmy ze śmiechu, gdy usłyszeliśmy tę wiadomość (We were just rolling in the aisles when we heard the news)*

lać wodę [lahch VOH-deh] *v phr* To tell lies in order to deceive someone <bull, bullshit, shit, shovel the shit, string along, snow, fake it, talk through one's hat, speak with forked tongue, put someone on, pull someone's leg, pull someone's string, give someone a leg, have someone on, jack someone around, jerk someone around, kid someone around, fool someone around, jack someone's chain, spoof, cut down, mind-fuck, head-fuck, push around, upstage> eg *Facet leje wodę, nie słyszysz? (The guy's bullshitting, can't you hear it?)*

laba [LAH-bah] *nf* A period when one does not go to school or does not work; a rest period <breather, breathing spell, downtime, time-off, fucking the dog, off> eg *Mamy jeszcze tydzień laby (We have one more week of a breather)*

lacha See kłaść na czymś/kimś lachę, laska

lachociąg* [lah-KHOH-chyohng] *nm* A person who performs fellatio <cock-sucker, dick-sucker, peter-eater, come-freak> eg *Jest strasznie brzydka, ale dobry z niej lachociąg (She's awfully ugly, but she's a good cock-sucker)*

lacz [lahch] *nm* A failing grade <flunk, flush, F, zip, zippo> eg *Dwa lacze z fizy i jeden z bioli. Ja się chyba zabiję! (Two flunks in sci and one in bio. I think I'm going to kill you!)*

See dać kopa, dostać kopa

lacze [LAH-cheh] *npl* **1** Shoes or boots, esp heavy or sturdy <stompers, wafflestompers, boondockers, clodhoppers, shitkickers> eg *Zabieraj swoje lacze z mojego biurka (Get your wafflestompers out of my desk)* **2** A person's legs <stumps, hinders, pillars, trotters, underpinnings, pins, sticks> eg *Bolą mnie trochę lacze (My stumps are sort of aching)*

lafirynda [lah-fee-RIN-dah] *nf* A promiscuous woman, esp pretensionally elegant <floozy, bimbo, slut, bitch, cunt, chippy, quiff, swinger, easy lay, easy make, alley cat, dirty-leg, roundheels, nympho, piece of ass, punchboard, town bike> eg *Gdzie żeś znalazł taką lafiryndę? (Where did you find that bimbo?)*

laga See kłaść na czymś/kimś lachę, laska

laksa* [LAKH-sah] *nf* Semen; sperm <cum, come, cream, gism, jism, jiz, love juice, scum, spunk, load, shot, wad, pearl jam> eg *Na łóżku jest trochę laksy. Wyczyść to! (There's some spunk on the bed. Clean it up!)*

lala See po balu, jak ta lala, laska, odpierdolony

lalunia See laska

laluś [LAH-loosh] *nm* A man, esp vain man who attaches too much importance to his physical appearance <dandy, fancypants, poser> eg *Zakochała się w jakimś lalusiu (She fell in love with some dandy)*

lampić się [LAHM-peech shyeh] *v* To stare or gape at someone or something <gander, take a gender, gawk, gawp, goggle, glom, glim, gun, pin, rubber, rubberneck, beam, eye, get an eyeful, give the eye, lay eyes on, set eyes on, get a load of > eg *Na co się ci wszyscy ludzie lampią? (What are all those people rubbernecking at?)*

las See święto lasu, w lesie

lasencja See laska

laska [LAHS-kah] (or **lacha** [LAH-khah]) *nf* **1** (or **lasencja** [lah-SEHN-tsyah] or **lala** [LAH-lah] (or **lola** [LOH-lah] or **lalunia** [lah-LOO-nyah]) A young and attractive woman <chick, broad, gal, pussy, cunt, ass, piece of ass, piece, dish, babe, baby, dame, beauty, beaut, beauty queen, baby doll, doll, dolly, dollface, dreamboat, dream girl, eating stuff, eyeful, flavor, looker, good-looker, head-turner, traffic-stopper, honey, killer, hot number, package, knockout, oomph girl, peach, bombshell, sex bunny, sex job, sex kitten, sex pot, table grade, ten, bunny, centerfold, cheesecake, date bait, dazzler, heifer, fluff, quail, sis, skirt, tail, job, leg, tart, tomato, pussycat, cooz, twat> eg *Co to za laska, z którą widziałem Cię wczoraj wieczór? (Who's that hot number I saw you with last night?); Muszę poderwać jakąś laskę (I must pick up some doll)* **2*** (or **laga** [LAH-gah]) *nf* The penis <cock, prick, dick, stick, joystick, dipstick, bone, meat, beef, wang, yang, dong, dummy, hammer, horn, hose, jock, joint, knob, pork, putz, rod, root, tool, flute, skin flute, love-muscle, sausage, schmuck, schlong, schvantz, cream-stick, third leg, middle leg, business, apparatus, John, Johnny, Johnson, John Thomas, Jones, pecker, peter, peepee, pisser, weenie, peenie, dingus, dingbat, thingy> eg *Robiła mi laskę (She sucked my stick)*

See obciągać, robić laskę

lata See kopę lat, mieć ileś lat na karku, mieć swoje lata

latać za kimś [LAH-tahch ZAH keemsh] (or **biegać za kimś** [BYEH-gahch ZAH keemsh] or **ganiać za kimś** [GAH-nyahch ZAH keemsh]) or **chodzić za kimś** [KHOH-jeech ZAH keemsh]) *v* To follow someone in search for sexual encounter; to invite or request sexual favors <chase, cruise, tail, troll, run around, dog someone's footsteps, hunt for cunt> eg *Lata za nim od dwóch tygodni (She's been chasing him for two weeks); Chodzi za nią jeden brunet (A brunet has been running around after her)*

latarnia See stać pod latarnią

latawica [lah-tah-VEE-tsah] *nf* A promiscuouc woman <floozy, bimbo, slut, bitch, cunt, chippy, quiff, swinger, easy lay, easy make, alley cat, dirty-leg, roundheels, nympho, piece of ass, punchboard, town bike> eg *W każdy sobotni wieczór przyprowadza do domu innego faceta. Prawdziwa z niej latawica (She comes home with a different man every Saturday night. She's a real floozy)*

leżeć [LEH-zhehch] *v* To suit one or appeal to one; to like, enjoy, or delight <fit in, suit one fine, turn on, heat up, fire up, steam up, stir up, send, give a bang, knock out, knock someone dead, knock someone' socks off, knock someone for a loop, throw someone for a loop, hit the spot, kill, murder, slay, slaughter, put someone away, tickle pink, tickle to death, tickle the piss out of someone, open one's nose> eg *Nie leży mi ta muzyka (That music doesn't bring me on)*

leżeć bykiem [LEH-zhehch BI-kyehm] (or **leżeć do góry brzuchem** [LEH-zhehch do GOO-ri BZHOO-khehm] or **leżeć na dupie*** [LEH-zhehch nah DOO-pyeh]) *v phr* To loaf or idle; to pass time lazily <bum around, hang around, hang out, goof around, fuck around, screw around, fiddle around, fiddle fart around, fart around, jack around, mess around, hack around, monkey around, knock around, kick around, fool around, horse around, piddle around, play around, rat around, schloomp around, ass around, beat around, dick around, fuck around, fuck off, screw off, goof off, jerk off, fuck the dog, rat fuck, flub the dub,

sit on one's ass, sit on one's butt, lollygag, veg out> eg *W te wakacje mam zamiar po prostu leżećdo góry brzuchem (I'm just going to goof off on this vacation)*

leżeć komuś na wątrobie [LEH-zhehch KOH-moosh nah vohn-TROH-byeh] (or **mieć na wątrobie** [myehch nah vohn-TROH-byeh]) *v phr* To be preoccupied, worried, or upset; to fret or harry oneself <eat, bug, dog, nag, stew, bleed, sweat, sweat bullets, bum out, eat one's heart out, have something at heart> eg *Spytała, co mi leży na wątrobie (She asked what was eating me); Leży mi na wątrobie, że za dwa tygodnie będę musiał zdawać egzamin (I'm bummed by the fact that I'll have to take an exam in two weeks)*

lebiega [leh-BYEH-gah] (or **lebioda** [leh-BYOH-dah]) *nf* A weak, sickly, or frail person <walking corpse, wimp> eg *Jej mąż to lebiega (Her husband is a walking corpse)*

lecieć [LEH-chyehch] *v* **1** (perf **polecieć** [poh-LEH-chyehch]) To broadcast over the radio or TV <air, get out, go on the air, telecast, televise> eg *W telewizji leciały same powtórki (They aired only reruns)* **2** To drip or trickle <come down, go down> eg *Ale mu leci po nodze! (It's dripping down his leg)* **2** (perf **przelecieć** [psheh-LEH-chyehch] or **zlecieć** [ZLEH-chyehch]) *v* (Of time) To pass <fly, fly by, run, run by> eg *Ale ten czas leci! (How time flies!); Czas szybko nam zleciał na wczorajszej imprezie. Tak dobrze się bawiliśmy (Time really flew by last night at the party. We had such a great time)*
See padać

lecieć na kogoś [LEH-chyehch] (perf **polecieć** [poh-LEH-chyehch]) *v* To be sexually or romantically interested in someone; to desire someone sexually <have the hots for, have hot pants for, have a lech for, lech after, be crazy about, be nuts about, be stuck on, be sweet on, go for, have a crush on, have a yen for> eg *Ona też na mnie leci (She's got the hots for me, too)*

lecieć sobie w chuja** [LEH-chyehch SOH-byeh f KHOO-yah] (or **lecieć sobie w głupa** [LEH-chyehch SOH-byeh v GWOO-pah]) *v phr* To tease; to banter; to treat someone unseriously and frivolously; to have fun at someone's expense <poke fun at, kid, kid around, pull someone's leg, pull someone's string, fool around, jive, josh, shuck, lark, spoof, send up, fuck around with, fuck with, cut down> eg *Powiedziała mu, żeby przestał się grać z nią w kulki (She told him to stop fucking around with her)*

lecieć w ślinę [LEH-chyehch f SHLEE-neh] *v* To kiss and possibly caress <smooch, suck face, swap spit, play kissy-kissy, play kissy-poo, play kissy-face, mash, neck, pet, smack> eg *Polecieli w ślinę szybciej niż myślicie (They swapped spit before you knew it)*

leczyć [LEH-chich] *v* To repel, anger, or irritate; to be strongly disliked <turn off, gross out, barf out, suck, scuzz one out, give one pain in the ass, make one sick, make one puke, make one barf, piss someone off, pee someone off, steam someone up, tick someone off, tee someone off, burn someone up, burn someone off, burn someone's ass, burn someone off, get someone's back up, make someone sore, make someone mad> eg *Leczy mnie ten facior (This guy grosses me out)*

leczyć się See iść się pierdolić

lejba [LEH-ee-bah] *nf* A loose-fitting woman's dress <baggy dress, pilgrim's dress> eg *Miała na sobie jakąś lejbę (She had a baggy dress on)*

lekarstwo See jak na lekarstwo

lekką ręką [LEHK-koh REHN-koh] *adv phr* Earned easily or effortlessly <without breaking one's back, without lifting one's finger> eg *Pierwsze dolary zarobił lekką ręką (He earned his first bucks without breaking his back)*

lekki See kurwa, mieć lekką rękę, panienka

lekko licząc [LEHK-koh LEE-chohnts] *adv phr* Approximately or at least <around, in the ballpark of, pretty near, something like, close shave, in the neighborhood of, damn near, pretty near, cool, clean> eg *Zarobił dziesięć baniek lekko licząc (He made a cool ten million)*

leniuchować [leh-nyoo-KHOH-vahch] *v* To loaf or idle; to pass time lazily <bum around, hang around, hang out, goof around, fuck around, screw around, fiddle around, fiddle fart around, fart around, jack around, mess around, hack around, monkey around, knock around, kick around, fool around, horse around, piddle around, play around, rat around, schloomp around, ass around, beat around, dick around, fuck around, fuck off, screw off, goof off, jerk off, fuck the dog, rat fuck, flub the dub, sit on one's ass, sit on one's butt, lollygag, veg out> eg *Przestań leniuchować i weź się do roboty (Stop fiddling around and get to work)*

leń See śmierdzący leń

lepsza połowa [LEHP-shah poh-WOH-vah] *nf phr* A wife <wifey, mama, missus, better half, old lady, little woman, ball and chain, significant other> eg *Poszedł spytać się swojej lepszej połowy (He went to ask his wifey)*

leser [LEH-sehr] *nm* A person who regulary and chronically avoids work; a shirker <goldbricker, bunk lizard, coffee cooler, feather merchant, lazybones, lazy-ass, lazy bum, bum, clock watcher, dog-fucker> eg *Powiedz temu leserowi, żeby brał się do roboty (Tell that lazybones to get to work)*

leserować [leh-seh-ROH-vahch] *v* To avoid work; to shirk duty <goldbrick, goof off, goof around, fuck around, screw around, jerk off, screw off, drag-ass, drag one's ass, drag it, dragtail, fake off, flub the dub, fuck off, fuck the dog, dog it, lollygag, sit on one's ass, soldier, skate, watch the clock> eg *On zawsze leserował (He's always been goldbricking)*

leszcz [lehshch] *nm* A man, esp rough and intimidating, a thug <hood, goon> eg *Jacyś leszcze złamali mu nos (A couple of hoods broke his nose); Ten leszcz powienien siedzieć za kratkami (That goon should be behind bars)*

lewo See dać w lewo, na lewo

lewy [LEH-vi] *adj* Illegal, unethical, or dishonest <ain't legit, ain't kosher, dirty, sleazy, crooked, crummy, foul, shady, shabby, salty, raw, heavy, hung-up, below the belt, under the counter, under the table, underhand> eg *Ma lewe dokumenty (His papers ain't kosher)*

See wstawać lewą nogą

leźć See łazić

lezba** [LEHZ-bah] (or **lezbija**** [lehz-BEE-yah]) *nf* A lesbian (either active or passive); a homosexual woman <dike, dyke, bull, bull-dyke, butch, butch-dyke, diesel, diesel-dyke, fairy lady, femme, lezbo, lez, lezzie> eg *Kobieta w skórzanej kurtce wygląda na lezbę (The woman in leather jacket looks like a butch-dyke)*

libacja [lee-BAHTS-yah] *nf* A drinking party; a carousal <bash, bender, bust, twister, wingding, winger> eg *Lubię iść na dobrą libację co jakiś czas (I like a good bender every now and then)*

liche pieniądze See psie pieniądze

licho See na diabła, cholera wie

limo *nn* [LEE-moh] An eye <peeper, blinker, lamp, ogler, peeker> eg *Dostał w limo (He was hit on his peeper)*

lipa [LEE-pah] *nf* **1** Anything worthless, useless, or of shoddy quality; trash <schlock, dreck, garbage, junk, lemon, crap, piece of crap, shit, piece of shit, dogshit, sleaze> eg *Kupiłem ten aparat wczoraj. To lipa (I bought this camera yesterday. It's a lemon)* **2** Nonsense; absurdities; pretentious or deceitful talk <bull, bullshit, bullshine, BS, bunk, baloney, applesauce, eyewash, hogwash, hot air, crock, crock of shit, piece of shit, pile of shit, shit, dogshit, horseshit, shit for the birds, crap, crapola, poppycock, smoke, hokum, garbage, trash, horsefeathers, smoke, all that jazz, jazz, jive, malarkey, gobbledygook, double-talk, bafflegab, blah-blah, phony-baloney, fiddle-faddle, twiddle-twaddle, mumbo-jumbo, yackety-yack> eg *Nie wciskaj mi lipy, koleś (Don't give me that baloney, man)*

lipny [LEEP-ni] *adj* Bad, poor, worthless, or of inferior quality <lousy, awful, bush-league, cheap, crappy, shitty, cruddy, crummy, doggy, low-rent, low-ride, no-good, raggedy-ass, schlocky, stinking, tacky, trashy, two-bit, dime-a-dozen, fair to middling, garden variety, of a sort, of sorts, piddling, pissy-ass, piss-poor, run-of-the-mill, small-time> eg *Nie można mówić, że cały ten pomysł jest lipny (You cannot say that the entire idea is lousy)*

litera See cztery litery

literatka [lee-teh-RAHT-kah] *nf* A small vodka glass <jigger, finger, shot glass, nip glass> eg *Postaw literatkę na stole (Put the jigger on the table)*

litr [leetr] (or **liter** [LEE-tehr]) *nm* A one-liter bottle of vodka <no slang equivalent> eg *Wypili litra (They drank one liter of vodka)*
See pół litra

lizać komuś dupę* [LEE-zahch KOH-moosh DOO-peh] (or **lizać kogoś po dupie*** [LEE-zahch KOH-gohsh poh DOO-pyeh] or **całować kogoś w dupę*** [tsah-WOH-vahch KOH-gohshch v DOO-peh] or **całować kogoś po dupie*** [tsah-WOH-vahch KOH-gohsh poh DOO-pyeh]) *v phr* To curry favor; to toady <brown-nose, kiss ass, lick ass, suck ass, ass-kiss, ass-lick, wipe someone's ass, apple-polish, back-scratch, bootlick, sweeten up> eg *Nie mogę na to patrzeć. Mógłby tak już przestać lizać mu dupę (I can't stand it. I wish he's stop kissing his ass)*

lizać się [LEE-zahch shyeh] (perf **polizać się** [poh-LEE-zahch shyeh] *v* To kiss and caress <smack, smooch, suck face, swap spit, play kissy-kissy, play kissy-poo, play kissy-face> eg *Lizali się prawie przez dwie godziny (They were swapping spit for nearly two hours)*

lizać* [LEE-zahch] (or **lizać patelnię**** [LEE-zahch pah-TEHL-nyeh] or **lizać cipkę**** [LEE-zahch CHEEP-keh] or **lizać rowa**** [LEE-zahch ROH-vah]; perf **wylizać*** [vi-LEE-zahch]) *v* To perform cunnilingus <lick, eat, eat pussy, cunt-lap, cunt-lick, muff dive, blow, do the face job, do it the French way, go down on, have a box lunch> eg *Chciał mnie pierw wylizać, potem przelecieć (He wanted to eat me first, then to hump me)*
See palce lizać

lizus [LEE-zoos] (or **podlizuch** [pohd-LEE-zookh])*nm* An overly or superficially nice man; a sycophant <brown-noser, ass-kisser, ass-licker, ass-sucker, ass-wiper, back-scratcher, apple-polisher, tokus-licker, kiss-ass, yes-man> eg *Zapamiętaj sobie, że nie znoszę lizusów (Remember one thing: I hate ass-kissers)*

lód See mieć forsy jak lodu, robić loda, zostawić kogoś na lodzie, kręcić lody, przełamywać lody

lodziara* [loh-JAH-rah] *nf* A woman who performs fellatio <cock-sucker, dick-sucker, peter-eater, come-freak> eg *To lodziara. Uwielbia obciągać druta (She's a come-freak. She loves to suck dick)*

lola See laska

lotek [LOH-tehk] *nm* A lottery <lotto, numbers, numbers game> eg *Stracił dużo pieniędzy grając w lotka (He lost a lot of money by playing the numbers)*

ludzie See dla ludzi, wyjść na ludzi

ludziska [loo-JEES-kah] *npl* People <folks, fellas, guys, dudes> eg *Ludziska chcieli zobaczyć ten mecz (The fellas wanted to see this game)*

ludzki [LOO-tskee] *adj* **1** (Of a person) Understanding; sympathetic; compassionate <simpatico, softhearted, softie, all heart, bleading heart, sweet as sugar, sewwt as a day> eg *Nasz nowy facet od matmy jest bardzo ludzki (Our new math prof is very softhearted)* **2** Proper; decent; good <pretty good, OK, okay> eg *Warunki są całkiem ludzkie (The conditions are pretty good)*

lufa [LOO-fah] *nf* **1** A failing grade <flunk, flush, F, zip, zippo> eg *Dlaczego jej powiedziałeś, że miałem pięć luf z matmy? (Why did you tell her that I have five flunks in math?)* **2** A drink of liquor, esp potent, served in a shot glass <snort, finger, jigger, pull, shot, nip, gargle, guzzle, slug, hit> eg *Strzelił sobie jeszcze jedną lufę (He had another shot)*

luft See do dupy

luj See niechluj

lukać [LOO-kahch] (perf **luknąć** [LOOK-nohnch]) *v* To look at; to examine or scrutinize <check out, dig, double-O, eye, eyeball, gander, take a gander, get a load of, give a look at, grab a look at, take a look at, give the once-over, give with the eye, have a look-see, make, once-over, pick up, pin, put the eye on, scope on, scope out, size up, take a reading> eg *Luknij ne tego gościa. Widziałeś kiedyś taką arogancję? (Get a load of that guy. Have you ever seen such arrogance?)*

lulać [LOO-lahch] *v* To sleep, esp to get some sleep <catch some Z's, cop some Z's, cut some Z's, bag some Z's, grab some Z's, catch a nod, cop a nod, bag a nod, grab a nod, konck a nod, collar a nod, take forty winks, bag it, snooze, conk off, caulk off, dope off, drop off, sack out, zonk out, conk out, caulk out, fall out, saw wood, rack, crash, doss, sack up, sack in, zizz, get some blanket drill, get some bunk fatigue, get some sack time, get some shuteye, hit the hay, hit the pad, hit the sack> eg *Gdzie twój brat? Poszedł lulać (Where's your brother? He went to cop some Z's)*

lulu [LOO-loo] *nn* Sleep <beddy-bye, nighty-night, snooze, catnap, forty winks, winks, shut-eye, nod, sack time, sack duty, blanket drill, bunk fatigue, Z's, zizz> eg *Pora na lulu (It's time for beddy-bye)*

lump [loomp] *nm* A vagrant, derelict or any loathsome or worthless man <bum, bo, hobo, piece of shit, hood, wino, dreg, wrongo, scum of the earth> eg *Na rogu stoi zgraja lumpów i niec nie robi (There is a bunch of bums on the corner, just doing nothing)*

lupa See brać kogoś pod lupę

lura [LOO-rah] *nf* A diluted tea, coffee, or any other liquid <dishwater, bellywash> eg *Oni to nazywają kawą? Ja to nazywam lurą (Do they call it coffee? I call it dishwater)*

lustro See pić do lustra

luz [loos] *nm* **1** Freedom; lack of any restrictions <laid-back vibes, loose feelings> eg *Wszędzie czuło się pełny luz (You could feel laid-back vibes everywhere)* **2** A period of time when one does not go to school or does not work; a rest period <breather, breathing spell, downtime, time-off, fucking the dog, off> eg *Jak będę miał trochę luzu, to przyjadę do ciebie (When I have a breather, I'll come down to see you)*
See dać sobie na luz, na luzie

luzak [LOO-zahk] *nm* A relaxed and easy-going man <laid-back guy, mellowed guy, cool guy, easy-going guy> eg *Ten Widawski to luzak. Daje zaliczenia bez większych problemów (Widawski is a cool guy. He will give you a pass without much problem)*

luzakować się [loo-zah-KOH-vahch shyeh] (perf **wyluzakować się** [vi-loo-zah-KOH-vahch shyeh] or **wyluzować się** [vi-loo-ZOH-vahch shyeh]) *v* To moderate one's behavior; to calm oneself; to relax <take it easy, hang it easy, go easy, hang loose, lay back, cool out, cool it, keep it cool, play it cool, give it a rest, don't sweat it, mellow out, lighten up, hold one's horses, keep one's shirt on> eg *Hej, wyluzakuj się. Test jest dopiero jutro (Hey, take it easy. The test's only tomorrow)*

luzara [loo-ZAH-rah] *nf* A relaxed and easy-going woman <laid-back chick, mellowed chick, cool chick, easy-going chick> eg *Ale z niej luzara! (What a cool chick she is!)*

Ł

łacha See robić komuś łachę

łachudra [wah-KHOO-drah] (or **łachmyta** [wahkh-MI-tah] *nf* or **łazęga** [wah-ZEHN-gah] *nf* or **łach** [WAHKH] *nm*) *nf* A worthless and loathsome man, esp a vagrant or derelict <bum, bo, hobo, piece of shit, hood, wino, dreg, wrongo, scum of the earth> eg *Nigdy nie ma pieniędzy. Taki z niego łachudra (He's alwaus out of money. He's such a sack of shit)*

łachy [WAH-khi] (or **łachmany** [wahkh-MAH-ni]) *nm* Clothes or clothing, esp old and worn-out <rags, schmatte, threads, drapes, duds, rags, togs, weeds, outfit> eg *Podobają mi się twoje łachy. Gdzie je kupiłaś? (I like your threads. Where did you buy them?)*
See drzeć sobie łacha z kogoś

łacina [wah-CHEE-nah] *nf* Swearwords; swearing; obscene language <French, French words, four-letter words, cuss words, dirty words, dirty talk, dirt> eg *Możebyś tak przestał używać łaciny w mojej obecności (I wish you'd stop using cuss words in my presence); Przepraszam za moją łacinę (Pardon my French)*

ładne pieniądze See ciężkie pieniądze

ładny [WAHD-ni] *adj* (Usually about a sum of money) Big <fine, whole, lump, pretty, hefty> eg *Pięć tysięcy! To ładna suma! (Five thousand! That's a pretty penny!)*

ładować [wah-DOH-vahch] (perf **władować** [vwah-DOH-vahch]; or **łoić** [WOH-eech] perf **włoić** [VWOH-eech]) *v* To beat or strike someone, esp with the fist; to punch <sock, bash, trash, clobber, bang, belt, clock, duke, dust, hammer, land one, lay one on, spank, wham, whack, bam, whip, bust, smack, poke, blast, beat the shit out of, beat the living shit out of, beat the bejejus out of, beat the

daylights out of, beat someone into the middle of next week, knock the bejejus out of, knock the daylights out of, knock someone into the middle of next week, hit someone where he lives, work over> eg *Zaraz ci włoję! (I'm going to beat the shit out of you soon!)*

ładować się [wah-DOH-vahch shyeh] (perf **władować się** [vwah-DOH-vahch shyeh]) *v* To enter or rush in rudely; to interrupt; to intrude <barge in, butt in, bust in, charge in, check in, elbow in, horn in, muscle in, crowd someone's act, get into the act, poke one's face in, poke one's nose in, stick one's face in, stick one's nose in> eg *Drzwi otworzyły się gwałtownie i dzieci władowały się do środka (The door burst open and the children barged in)*

ładować sobie w żyłę [wah-DOH-vahch SOH-byeh v ZHI-weh] (or **walić sobie w żyłę** [VAH-leech SOH-byeh v ZHI-weh] or **dać sobie w żyłę** [dahch SOH-byeh v ZHI-weh]) *v phr* To take an injection of narcotics <shoot, shoot up, bang, dope up, do up, spike up, hype, jab a vein, mainline> eg *Nie mógł się doczekać, kiedy przyjdzie do domu i będzie ładował sobie w żyłę (He couldn't wait to get home and shoot up)*

ładować w coś forsę [wah-DOH-vahch f TSOSH FOHR-seh]) *v phr* To invest money, esp in a non-profitable enterprise <sink money in, pump money into, throw money in, throw money down the drain, plunge, bankroll> eg *Mieliśmy nadzieję znaleźć kogoś, kto władowałby forsę w nasz projekt (We were hoping to find somebody to bankroll the project)*

łajba [WAH-ee-bah] *nf* A ship, boat, or yacht, esp if poorly maintained <bucket, rust bucket, tub, bathtub, can, hooker, dink, yatch, stinkpot, hole in the water, wagon, old lady> eg *Łajbę pożyczyliśmy od rybaka (We rented the bucket from some fisherman)*

łajdaczyć się [wah-ee-DAH-chich shyeh] *v* (Of a woman) To be sexually promiscuous <sleep around, screw around, fuck around, screw around the block, fuck around the block, get around, swing, bedhop> eg *Ludzie mówią, że łajdaczy się od paru miesięcy (She's been known to screw around for several months)*

łajza [WHAH-ee-zah] (or **łamaga** [wah-MAH-gah]) *nf* A bungler, esp a chronic one <screwup, goofup, goof, foozler> eg *Spójrz tylko, co ten luj zrobił! (Just look what this screwup did!)*

łamać [WAH-mahch] (or **łupać** [WOO-pahch]) *v* To ache or pain <grab, stab, kill, take someone hide and hair, hit one where one lives, have a bitch of a pain> eg *Ale mnie łamie w plecach! (I have a bitch of a pain in my back!); Łamie mnie w nogach (My legs are killing me)*

łamać się [WAH-mahch shyeh] (perf **złamać się** [ZWAH-mahch shyeh]) *v* To have doubts or scruples; to hesitate; be in a dilemma; to dither <fence straddle, sit on the fence, hang on the fence, run hot and cold, blow hot and cold, be between a rock and a hard place> eg *Powinna zadzwonić po policję, bo wiedziała, że to jej chłopak obrabował bank. Łamała się (She should have called the police because she knew it was her boyfriend who robbed the bank. She was between a rock and hard place)*

łamać sobie język [WAH-mahch SOH-byeh YEHN-zik] *v phr* To have difficulty in pronouncing a difficult or foreign word or in speaking clearly <twist one's tongue, not to get one's tongue around> eg *Anglik łamał sobie język, ale nie potrafił wymówić tych słów poprawnie (The Englishman was twisting his tongue, and couldn't pronounce this word correctly)*

łamaga See łajza

łamistrajk [wah-mee-STRAH-eek] *nm* A strikebreaker <scab, fink, rat, scissorbill, blackleg> eg *Nie potrzeba nam tu łamistrajków (We don't need no scabs)*

łapa [WAH-pah] *nf* A hand <mitt, paw, duke, fiver, grabber, hook, meathook> eg *Zabieraj swe łapy z mojego roweru! (Get your meathooks off my bike!)*
See żyć z kimś, dać komuś w łapę, dać po dupie, dostać po dupie, mieć lepkie łapy

łapać [WAH-pahch] *v* **1** (perf **złapać** [ZWAH-pahch]) To attempt to meet someone or catch something <get, grab, nail, nab, get hold of, reach out> eg *Nigdzie nie mogłem cię złapać (I couldn't get hold of you anywhere); Próbował łapać taksówkę (He tried to grab a cab)* **2** (or **łapać w lot** [WAH-pahch v LOHT]; perf **załapać** [zah-WAH-pahch]) To understand or comprehend, esp instantly <get, get it, catch, get the drift, get the picture, get the message, get the hang of, savvy, dig, click, capeesh, read, be with it, see where one is coming from, know where one is coming from> eg *Usiłowałem mu wytłumaczyć, ale nie załapał (I tried to explain it to him but he didn't get the drift); Nie łapię tego (I don't get it)* **3** (perf **złapać** [ZWAH-pahch] or (perf **załapać** [zah-WAH-pahch]) (Of disease) To start affecting someone <catch, come down with> eg *Czuję, że łapie mnie grypa (I feel like I'm coming down with the flu)*

łapać okazję [ZWAH-pahch oh-KAH-zyeh] *v phr* To get free rides, esp by standing beside a road and signaling drivers <hitchhike, hitch, hitch a lift, hitch a ride, thumb, thumb a lift, thumb a ride, bum a ride, hook a ride> eg *Złapał jakąś okazję i przybył na czas (He hitched a ride and came on time)*

łapiduch [wah-PEE-dookh] *nm* **1** A physician or surgeon; a medical doctor <doc, bones, sawbones, bone-bender, bone-breaker, pill-pusher, pill-roller, pill-bag, pill-peddler, pill-slinger, pills, medico, croaker, butcher, Feelgood, script writer, MD> eg *Ten lapiduch bierze za dużo (That pill pusher charges too much)* **2** *nm* A clergyman, esp a Roman Catholic priest <black coat, padre, sky pilot, sky merchant, sky scout, gospel pusher, bible thumper, bible banger, sin hound, rev, abbey, Holy Joe, preacher man> eg *Co ten łapiduch od ciebie chciał? (What did the padre want from you?)*

łapówka [wah-POOF-kah] (or **łapówa** [wah-POO-vah]) *nf* Money given to someone illegally or unethically; a bribe <graft, gravy, payoff, payola, smear, shmear, grease, palm grease, palm oil, boodle, kickback, envelope> eg *Wszyscy policjanci byli skorumpowani, brali łapówy od prostytutek (All the policemen were corrupt, getting kickbacks from the prostitutes)*

łapówkarz [wah-POOF-kahsh] (or **łapownik** [wah-POH-vneek]) *nm* A man who takes bribe money, esp a clerical worker or an official <someone on the take, someone on the pad, our boy, our man> eg *Nie wierzę, że burmistrz to łapownik (I don't believe that the mayor is on the take)*

łasuch [WAH-sookh] *nm* Someone who likes to eat candy <candy freak, junkfood junkie, chocoholic> eg *Mój brat to prawdziwy łasuch. Je czekoladęprzez cały czas (My brother is a real candy freak. He eats chocolate all the time)*

łatać [WAH-tahch] (perf **załatać** [zah-WAH-tahch]) *v* To make up for lost part of something <patch, patch up, clog up, fix up, doctor, pad, bump, beef up, jazz up> eg *Musieli jakoś załatać dziurę w budżecie (They had to somehow patch up the whole in the budget)*

łatwizna [waht-FEEZ-nah] *nf* Anything easy or trivial; a trifle; a bagatelle <piece of cake, cake, cakewalk, cherry pie, duck soup, kid stuff, picnic, pushover, snap, tea party, walkaway, walkover, breeze, stroll, cinch, pipe, big deal, no big deal, no biggie, Mickey Mouse, small potatoes, small beer, fly speck, plain sailing> eg *Zwycięstwo następnym razem to będzie łatwizna (Winning next time will be a snap)*
See iść na łatwiznę

ława See wyłożyć kawę na ławę

łazęga See łachudra

łazić [WAH-zheech] (or **leźć** [lehshch]; perf **poleźć** [POH-lehshch]) *v* To walk or go around, esp aimlessly <cruise, hang out, hang around, ankle, amble, leg it, hoof it, toddle, hotfoot, foot it, burn shoe leather, ride shanks mare, stomp, pound the beat, pound the pavement, gumshoe, broom, march, press the bricks, shank it, waltz> eg *Po imprezie polazła do domu (After the party she waltzed home)*

łeb [wehp] (or **łepetyna** [weh-peh-TI-nah] *nf*) *nm* The head <bean, noggin, conk, dome, gourd, skull> eg *W jego łepetynie nic nie ma, ale jest przystojny (His noggin is completely empty, but he's handsome)*
See brać się za łby, brać w łeb, mieć olej w głowie, na łebka, świtać, padać, paść komuś na mózg, przewracać się komuś w głowie, puknąć się w czoło, strzelić do łba

łeb w łeb [WEHP v WEHP] *adv phr* Simultaneously or equally <horse to horse, neck and neck> eg *Na studiach szli łeb w łeb (At the university they were neck and neck)*

łebek See łepek, po łebkach

łebski [WEHP-skee] *adj* Intelligent; clever knowledgeable <brainy, eggheaded, savvy, whiz, highbrow, long-haired, nifty, with it, cereb, nobody's fool, not born yesterday, in the know, all brains> eg *Wczoraj poznałam bardzo łebskiego faceta (Yesterday I met a very savvy guy)*

łepek [WEH-pehk] (or **łebek**) [WEH-pehk] *nm* A young man or boy <kid, punk, guy> eg *Powiedz temu łepkowi, żeby zostawił ją w spokoju (Tell the kid to leave her alone)*

łepetyna See łeb

łóżko See iść z kimś do łóżka

łóżkowy [woosh-KOH-vi] *adj* Concerning sexual activity; intimate <bedroom> eg *Było to następne łóżkowe spotkanie (It was another bedroom encounter)*

łoić See ładować

łokieć See urabiać sobie ręce

łopaciarz [woh-PAH-chahsh] *nm* An unqualified menial worker, esp one who works with a shovel; an unskilled laborer <grave-digger, wetback, blue collar, workhorse, hard hat, stiff, working stiff> eg *Łopaciarzom płacili grosze (They paid chicken feed for the blue collars)*

łopata See iść do łopaty

łupać See łamać

łyżwy [WIZH-vi] *npl* Automotive tires, esp used <shoes, skins, slicks, flats, pumpkins, used rubber> eg *Ten audik ma zjechane łyżwy! (This Audi really has used rubber)*

łykać [WI-kahch] (perf **łyknąć** [WIK-nohnch] or **nałykać się** [nah-WI-kahch shyeh]) *v* **1** To have a quick drink of alcohol <knock back, down, slug down, swig, tank, tank up> eg *Łyknął całą butelkę i zaczął bekać (He downed the whole bottle* *and started to burp)* **2** To swallow a pill of narcotics <hit, pop, drop> eg *Łyka Prozac codziennie (He pops Prozac everyday)*

łyknąć [WIK-nohnch] (or **połknąć** [POWK-nohnch]; **przynętę** [pshi-NEHN-teh] or **haczyk** [KHAH-chik] may be added) *v* To believe in some trick <swallow, swallow the bait, buy, buy into, buy off, down, eat up, fall for, go for, lap up, sign off on, take, tumble for> eg *Zaoferowano mu dobre pieniądze i połknął haczyk (He was offered good money and he swallowed the bait); Łyknęła wszystko, co jej powiedzieliśmy, głupia pinda (She bought every word we told her, dumb bitch)*

łyknąć świerzego powietrza [WIK-nohnch shfyeh-ZHEH-goh poh-VYEHT-shah] *v phr* (To go out and) To freshen up, esp to go for a walk <get a breath of fresh air, go out for a breath fresh air, change the scenery> eg *Wychodzę łyknąć świeżego powietrza (I'm going out for a breath of fresh air)*

łysa guma [WI-sah GOO-mah] (or **łysa opona** [WI-sah oh-POH-nah]) *nf phr* A worn-out automotive tire <baldie, bald tire, shoe, skin, slick, flat, sore foot, pumpkin> eg *Masz dwie łyse gumy w swoim wozie (You have two baldies in your car)*

łyskacz [WIS-kahch] (or **łycha** [WI-khah]) *nm* Whiskey <jack, firewater, mountain dew, shoe polish, panther piss> eg *Dał mi za to skrzynkę łyskacza (He gave me a box of jack)*

łyso See czuć się łyso

łysol* [WI-sohl] (or **łysa pała*** [WI-sah PAH-wah] *nf phr*) *nm* An entirely bald person <baldie, skinhead, suedehead, chrome dome, cueball, Kojak, Sinead> eg *Zrobił się łysą pałą jak miał ze dwadzieścia lat (He turned into a baldie in his twenties)*

łysy See znać się jak łyse konie

łysy jak kolano [WI-si YAHK koh-LAH-noh] *adj phr* Entirely bald <bald as an eagle, bald as an egg> eg *Jest łysy jak kolano, ale się tym nie przejmuje (He's bald as an egg but he doesn't care)*

M

ma się rozumieć [mah shyeh roh-ZOO-myehch] *phr* Obviously; apparently; understandably <sure, fer sure, sure as hell, sure as shit, sure as can be, for real, indeedy, really truly, absitively, posilutely, real, cert, def, no buts about it, barefaced, open and shut, clear as the nose on one's face, plain as the nose on one's face> eg *Zginął w lesie, ma się rozumieć (He died in the woods, no buts about it)*

mać See kurwa, psia krew

macać* [MAH-tsahch] (or **obmacywać*** [ohb-mah-TSI-vahch]; **się** [shyeh] may be added; perf **pomacać*** [poh-MAH-tsahch] or **wymacać*** [vi-MAH-tsahch]) *v phr* To touch or caress sexually; to fondle <feel, feel up, cop a feel, grope, pet, neck, play grab-ass, smooch, get physical> eg *Spoliczkowała go, gdy ją pomacał (She slapped him when he felt her); Usiłował ją wymacać, ale nie była tak pijana (He tried to feel her up, but she wasn't that drunk)*

macanka* [mah-TSAHN-kah] (or **macanko*** [mah-TSAHN-koh] *nn*) *nf* Sexual dalliance short of copulation; touching and caressing <a feel, a feel-up, grab-ass,

necking, petting, smooching> eg *Dobrze, będę spała w twoim łóżku, ale żadnej macanki (Okay, I'll sleep in your bed, but no smooching)*

machlojka [mah-KHLOH-ee-kah] *nf* A swindle; a fraud; a scheme <scam, rip-off, con game, double cross, double shuffle, fast one, grift, gyp, flim-flam, hustle, number, racket, run-around, skin game, sucker game, suck-in, ride, fucking over, screwing over, hanky-panky, monkey business, song and dance, game, little game, angle> eg *Urząd podatkowy nie znalazł żadnych śladów machlojek (The IRS found no traces of con games)*

machnąć komuś dzieciaka See zrobić komuś dzieciaka

machnąć się [MAHKH-nohnch shyeh] *v* (Of a woman) To get married; to marry <hitch, hitch up, get hitched, splice, get spliced, hook, get hooked, merge, get merged, tie the knot, walk down the aisle, take the plunge, step off the carpet> eg *Machnęła się za jakiegoś lekarza (She tied the knot with some doctor)*

Maciej See w kółko

maczać palce [MAH-chahch PAHL-tseh] *v phr* To have a part in or influence over; to be partly responsible for <take a hand in, have a hand in, be behind something> eg *Myślisz, że maczał w tym palce? (Do you think he had a hand in it?)*

Madagaskar See na Magadaskar

madziar [MAH-jahr] *nm* A Hungarian male <Hunky, Bohunk> eg *Madziary potrafią gotować całkiem niezłe jedzenie (The bohunks can really cook up some fine food)*

magiel See młyn

magisterka [mah-gee-STEHR-kah] *nf* An M.A. thesis or an M.A. degree <masters> eg *Napisałem magisterkę w dwa miesiące (I did my masters in two months)*

magnes [MAHG-nehs] *nm* Something that attract or excites people; a magnet <turn-on, pull, grab, draw, bait, hook, mousetrap> eg *Największym magnesem była oczywiście zaliczka (The advance was surely the biggest turn-on)*

magnet [MAHG-neht] *nm* A large portable stereo cassette player <boom box, boogie box, coon box, ghetto box, ghetto blaster, nigger box> eg *Możebyś tak wyłączył ten magnet? (I wish you'd turn that boom box off)*

majdan [MAH-ee-dahn] *nm* Personal belongings, esp in form of a packet <roll, bindle, biddle, load, stuff, crap, shit, junks, props, odds and ends, bits and pieces, thingies, gadgets, widgets, dingbats, gimmicks> eg *Zabieraj swój majdan i jazda stąd (Get your bindle and get out)*
See zwijać manatki

majtki See robić w gacie

mak See figa, jak makiem zasiał

makaroniarz* [mah-kah-ROH-nyahsh] (or **makaron*** [mah-KAH-rohn]) *nm* An Italian male <wop, dago, eytie, eyetalian, spaghetti, macaroni, dingbat, dino, ginzo, guinea, greaser, greaseball, spic> eg *Spytaj makaroniarza, ile za tp chce (Ask the wop how much he wants for it)*

makówka [mah-KOOF-kah] *nf* The head <bean, noggin, conk, dome, gourd, skull> eg *W jej makówce nic nie ma, ale jest zgrabna (Her noggin is completely empty, but she's stacked)*

maks See na maks

malinka [mah-LEEN-kah] *nf* A mark on the skin caused by biting or sucking during a sex act <hickey, hicky, love-bite, purple nurple> eg *Miała na sobie golf, żeby ukryć malinkę (She wore a turtleneck to cover up a hickey)*

maliny See wpuścić kogoś w maliny

maluch [MAH-lookh] *nm* A Polish Fiat 126 P, a very small automobile <no slang equivalent> eg *Wielu z nas nie może sobie pozwolić nawet na malucha (Many of us can't afford even a Fiat 126 P)*
See mały

mała See małolata

mała czarna [MAH-wah CHAHR-nah] *nf* A small cup of black coffee <black java, black ink, battery acid, caffeine fix> eg *Mała czarna zrobiłaby mi świetnie (Some black java would be real good)*
See czarnula

małe pieniądze See psie pieniądze

małe piwo [MAH-weh PEE-voh] *nn phr* Anything easy or trivial; a trifle; a bagatelle <piece of cake, cake, cakewalk, cherry pie, duck soup, kid stuff, picnic, pushover, snap, tea party, walkaway, walkover, breeze, stroll, cinch, pipe, big deal, no big deal, no biggie, Mickey Mouse, small potatoes, small beer, fly speck, plain sailing> eg *Ten egzamin to małe piwo w porównaniu z następnym (This exam is a cakewalk compared with the next one)*

mało kogoś wzruszać [MAH-woh KOH-gohsh VZROO-shahch] (or **nie wzruszać kogoś** [nyeh VZROO-shahch KOH-gohsh]) *v* To be indifferent; not to care about <make no diff, be all the same, be same old shit, be same difference, no matter how you slice it, make no never mind, be no big deal, could care less about, not care, not care a damn, not care a shit, not care a fuck, not give a damn, not give a shit, not give a fuck, be no skin off one's ass> eg *Czy chciała oddaćci pieniądze? Nie, myślę, że mało ją to wzruszało (Did she intend to give you the money back? No, I think she didn't give a damn about it)*

małolat [mah-WOH-laht] (or **młodziak** [MWOH-jahk] or **młodzian** [MWOH-jahn] or **młodzieniaszek** [mwoh-jeh-NYAH-shehk] or **młokos** *nm* [MWOH-kohs] or **mały** [MAH-wi]) *nm* A young and inexperienced man or boy; a teenager <teen, teener, teeny-bopper, bubble-gummer, youngster, juvie, son, rookie, greenhorn> eg *Nie wyglądał mi na młodzieniaszka (He did not look like a rookie to me); Osobiście nie lubię tego rodzaju muzyki, ale małolaty tak (Personally, I don't like this kind of music, but youngsters do)*

małolata [mah-woh-LAH-tah] (or **mała** [MAH-wah]) *nf* teenage girl or a young woman <chick, chicklet, teen, teener, teeny-bopper, bubble-gummer, little lady> eg *Byłam wówczas 15-letnią małolatą (I was a 15-year-old youngster then); No chodź, mała, postawię ci drinka (Come on, little girl, let me buy you a drink)*

małpa [MAH-oo-pah] (or **małpiszon** [mah-oo-PEE-shohn] *nm*) *nf* **1** A person, esp an ugly one <ape, jerk, beasty> eg *Ty wredna małpo! Zabiję cię! (You vicious ape! I'll kill you!)* **2** Someone who copies someone else's work, esp in school; an imitator <copycat, pirate, crock, stand-in, nick artist> eg *Nie bądź taki małpiszon. Wymyśl coś sam (Don't be such a copycat. Invent something of your own)*

małpka [MAH-oop-kah] *nf* A small, usually quarter-liter bottle of vodka <micky, miky> eg *Kupił tylko dwie ćwiartki (He only bought two mickies)*

mały [MAH-wi] *nm* **1** (or **maluch** [MAH-lookh]) A little drink of a potent liquor, esp vodka, served in a shot glass <snort, finger, jigger, pull, shot, nip, gargle, guzzle, slug, hit> eg *Jeszcze po jednym małym? (How about another snort?)* **2** The penis, esp small <pecker, peter, peepee, pisser, weenie, peenie, dingus, dingbat,

thingy, cock, prick, dick, stick, joystick, dipstick, bone, meat, beef, wang, yang, dong, dummy, hammer, horn, hose, jock, joint, knob, pork, putz, rod, root, tool, flute, skin flute, love-muscle, sausage, schmuck, schlong, schvantz, cream-stick, third leg, middle leg, business, apparatus, John, Johnny, Johnson, John Thomas, Jones> eg *Pokaż mi swojego małego (I want you to show me your weenie)*
See czarnula, małolat

mamisynek [mah-mee-SI-nehk] *nm* A boy or a man who allows his mother to protect him too much; any man considered weak or timid <mama's boy, mommy's boy, wimp, wuss, pussy, fraidy cat, gutless wonder, milquetoast> eg *Nie bądź taki mamisynek! Weź się w garść (Don't be such a wimp. Get hold of yourself)*

mamona [mah-MOH-nah] *nf* Money <dough, bread, bank, cabbage, change, coin, folding, green, lettuce> eg *Dba tylko o mamonę (All he cares is dough)*

mamro [MAHM-roh] *nn* A prison; a jail <slam, slammer, jug, can, bucket, cage, big cage, big house, caboose, calaboose, cannery, cooler, hole, hoosegow, icebox, lockup, mill, stir, pen, tank, college, crossbar hotel, booby hatch, pink clink, quad> eg *Jest w mamrze już od dwóch lat (He's been in the slammer for two years now)*

mamuśka [mah-MOOSH-kah] *nf* A mother or mother-in-law <mama, ma, mom, moms, mommy, motherkin, old lady, old woman, warden, battle-ax> eg *Jego mamuśka doprowadzała go do szału (His battle-ax made him furious)*

mamut See wypierdek

manatki [mah-NAHT-kee] (or **manele** [mah-NEH-leh]) *npl* Personal belongings, esp small and numerous articles of various kinds <stuff, crap, shit, junks, props, odds and ends, bits and pieces, thingies, gadgets, widgets, dingbats, gimmicks> eg *Zabieraj swoje manatki z mojej szafki (Get your gadgets out of my locker)*
See zwijać manatki

mankiet See cmoknąć w mankiet

manto See dać po dupie, dostać po dupie

mańka See krwawa mańka

mańkut [MAHÑ-koot] *nm* A left-handed eperson <left-hander, leftie, southpaw, portsider, sidewheeler> eg *Czy ten mańkut jest w waszej drużynie? (Is that leftie in your team?)*

margines [mahr-GEE-nehs] *nm* The people of the lowest standing in a society, esp criminals <dregs, dregs of society, bottom, boys uptown, wrongos, scum of the earth, F.F.V.> eg *Mordercy i handlarze narkotyków to margines (Murderers and drug dealers are the dregs of society)*

markowy [mahr-KOH-vi] *adj* Of a brand and thus, of better quality <label, make, brand-name> eg *Ona nosi tylko markowe spodnie (She only wears brand-name pants)*

marne pieniądze See psie pieniądze

marsz See kiszki komuś marsza grają, z miejsca

maruda [mah-ROO-dah] *nf* A person who is groundlessly dissatisfied or discontented; a complainer, esp a chronic malcontent <bitcher, beefer, bellyacher, griper, squawker, whiner, plainer, squealer, grouser, groucher, grumbler, moaner, sorehead, kvetch, crab, crank, gripe, grouse, grouch, forecastle lawyer, sourpuss, sourball, sourpan, picklepuss> eg *Mam już dość tej marudy (I'm sick of this sourpuss)*

marudzić [mah-ROO-jeech] (or **pomarudzić** [poh-mah-ROO-jeech]) *v* To be groundlessly dissatisfied or discontented; to have unfounded complaints <fuss, stink, scene, make a ceremony, beef, bleed, hassle, kvetch, bitch, beef, gripe,

piss, bellyache, grouse, growl, squawk, cut a beef, make a stink, piss up a storm, raise a stink, blow up a storm, kick up a storm, eat someone's heart out, fuck around, screw around, mess around, trip> eg *Przestań marudzić! (Stop kvetching!)*

marycha [mah-RI-khah] (or **maryśka** [mah-RISH-kah]) *nf* Marijuana; cannabis <grass, pot, dope, weed, reefer, tea, hemp, Mary Jane, MJ> eg *Słyszałem, że sprzedajesz marychę. Ile chcesz? (I hear you peddle grass. How much you want?)*

masło See iść jak po maśle, jak pączek w maśle, jak po maśle

masło maślane [MAHS-woh mah-SHLAH-neh] *nn phr* Words that are numerous but bring no new meaning; mere words; tautology <same old shit, babble, gobbledygok, mumbo-jumbo> eg *Enough of this mumbo-jumbo. Start talking sense (Dość już tego masła maślanego. Zacznij mówić do rzeczy)*

masa See ciemniak

maska [MAHS-kah] *nf* An automotive hood <deck lid, turtle shell, doghouse> eg *Na miłość boską, zabierz psa z maski! (For God's sake, take the dog out of the deck lid!)* See morda

masówka [mah-SOOF-kah] *nf* **1** A huge meeting or gathering, esp in a workplace <meet, get-together, huddle> eg *Nie chciał iść na tę masówkę (He didn't want to go to the get-together)* **2** A mass-produced merchandise, esp defective, unsatisfactory, or of shoddy quality <lemon, schlock, dreck, garbage, junk, crap, piece of crap, shit, piece of shit, dogshit, sleaze> eg *Ten pecet to jakaćazjatycka masówka (This PC is some Asian junk)*

maszkara* [mahsh-KAH-rah] *nf* An ugly woman <beasty, skag, skank, pig, bag, dog, cow> eg *Przyszedł na imprezę z jakąś maszkarą (He came to the party with some skag)*

Matki Boskiej Pieniężnej [MAHT-kee BOHS-kyeh-ee pyeh-NYEHN-zhneh-ee] *nm phr* A payday <eagle day, day the eagle shits, day the eagle flies, day the eagle screams, time to get paid, time to pick up the check> eg *Wszyscy w napięciu oczekiwali Matki Boskiej Pieniężnej (Everybody anxiously awaited the eagle day)*

matma [MAHT-mah] *nf* Mathematics, esp as a subject in school <math, trig, geo, algy> eg *Nigdy nie lubiłem matmy (I never liked math)*

matoł See młot

mazać się [MAH-zahch shyeh] (or **mazgaić się** [mahz-GAH-eech shyeh]) *v* To cry or weep noisily <blubber, bawl, break down, break down and cry, turn on the waterworks, cry one's eyes out, cry me a river, shed bitter tears, weep bitter tears, sing the blues, put on the weeps, let go, let it out> eg *Przestań się mazać (Stop blubbering)*

mazgaj [MAHZ-gah-ee] *nm* A person given to weeping or lamenting at the least adversity <crybaby, whiner> eg *Przestań się drzeć i nie bądź taki mazgaj! (Stop lamenting. Don't be such a cry baby!)*

mącić See mieszać

mężuś [MEHN-zhoosh] *nm* A husband <hubby, man of the house, mister, old man, worser half> eg *Co na to powiedział jej mężuś? (What did her hubby say to this?)*

mećka [MEHCH-kah] (or **mućka** [MOOCH-kah]) *nf* A cow <Bossie, Nellie, Elsie, moo cow, moo moo> eg *Nasza mećka zdechła nad ranem (Our Nellie died in the morning)*

medal See na medal

meksyk* [MEHK-sik] *nm* A male Mexican <Mex, Latino, Chicano, gringo, amigo, beaner, bean eater, chili eater, wetback, dino, greaser, oiler, spic> eg *Nie wiedziałem, dlaczego wpuszczają tu meksyki (I didn't know why they let spics in here)*

melina [meh-LEE-nah] *nf* **1** A place where alcoholic drinks are illegally sold or drunk, or any disreputable saloon <watering hole, hideaway, speakeasy, fillmill, gin dive, gin joint, gargle factory, groggery, guzzlery> eg *Spędza wiele czasu w tej melinie (He spends a lot of time at that speakeasy)* **2** A hiding place, esp for criminals; a place to escape attention or discovery <hideaway, hideout, hidey-hole, hole-up, funk hole, scatter> eg *Nie podobała mu się ich ostatnia melina. Była w centrum (He didn't like their latest hideout. It was downtown)*

melinować się [meh-lee-NOH-vahch shyeh] (perf **zamelinować się** [zah-meh-lee-NOH-vahch shyeh]) *v* To conceal oneself; to hide in some place, esp from the police <hide out, hide away, hole in, hole up, lay doggo, lay low, sit tight, tunnel> eg *Możemy zamelinować się u ciebie na dzień lub dwa? (Can we hide out in your place for a day or two?)*

melon [MEH-lohn] *nm* A million zloty <M, mil> eg *Słyszałem, że wisi ci melona (I heard she owes you a mil)*

menda* [MEHN-dah] *nf* A man one dislikes or disapproves of <asshole, fuck, fucker, fuckhead, fuckface, motherfucker, shit, shitface, shithead, shitheel, bastard, jerk, SOB, son of a bitch, son of a whore, cocksucker, prick, dick, dickhead, cuntface, schmuck, scum, scumbag, sleazebag, slimebag, dipshit, pisshead, piece of shit, pain in the ass> eg *Zabieraj pieniądze i wynocha stąd, ty mendo! (Take your money and get the hell out of here, you bastard!)*

menel [MEH-nehl] *nf* A vagrant, derelict or any loathsome or worthless man, esp drunk <bum, bo, hobo, piece of shit, hood, wino, dreg, wrongo, scum of the earth> eg *Zabierz mi tego menela sprzed oczu (Take this bum out of my sight)*

merc [MEHRTS] (or **merol** [MEH-rohl] or **meraś** [MEH-rahsh]) *nm* A Mercedes Benz <benzo, merc, MBZ> eg *Ja w swoim mercu komórkowy mam (I've got a cell phone in my MBZ)*

męska decyzja [MEHN-skah deh-TSI-zyah] *nf phr* A definite or fearless decision <ballsy decision, gutsy decision, man's gotta do what a man's gotta do> eg *Dobrze by było, gdybyś podjął męską decyzję (It would be good if you made a ballsy decision)*

męska dziwka* [MEHN-skah JEEF-kah] (or **męska kurwa**** [MEHN-skah KOOR-vah]) *nf phr* A male prostitute, not necessarily a homosexual <gigolo> eg *Powiedział, że życie męskiej dziwki nie jest takie złe, jeśli nie ma się nic przeciwko 55-letnim kobietom (He said life as a gigolo wasn't too bad if you didn't mind 55-year-old women)*

męski See po męsku

meta [MEH-tah] *nf* **1** A place where alcoholic drinks are illegally sold or drunk <watering hole, hideaway, speakeasy, fillmill, gin dive, gin joint, gargle factory, groggery, guzzlery> eg *Spędza wiele czasu w tej melinie (He spends a lot of time at that speakeasy)* **2** A place to sleep or live for a day or so, esp for young people traveling around <place to crash, crash pad, pad, crib, digs, diggings, squat, den, dive, joint, flop, dump> eg *Mamy metę w Wiedniu (We have a crash pad in Vienna)* **3** A hiding place, esp for criminals; a place to escape attention or discovery <hideaway, hideout, hidey-hole, hole-up, funk hole, scatter> eg *Nie podobała mu się ich ostatnia meta. Była w centrum (He didn't like their latest hideout. It was downtown)*

metal [MEH-tahl] (or **metalowiec** [meh-tah-LOH-vyehts]) *nm* A person who likes or plays heavy-metal music <metallurgist, metalhead, iron man, head-banger, rocker> eg *Pełno było tam metalowców (The place was full of metalheads)*

mętlik See młyn, mieć mętlik w głowie

metr See od cholery, pół litra

męty [MEHNT-ti] *nm* A person coming from the group of the lowest standing in a society, esp criminals dregs, dregs of society, bottom, boys uptown, wrongos, F.F.V.> eg *Mordercy i handlarze narkotyków to męty (Murderers and drug dealers are the dregs of society)*

miastowy [myahs-TOH-vi] *nm* - <city slicker, townee, towner> eg *Było to bardzo popularne między miastowymi (It was very popular among city slickers)*

micha [MEE-khah] *nf* Food <chow, feed, grub, scoff, eats> eg *Wszyscy wiedzą, co znaczy "micha" (Everyone knows what "grub" means)*
See morda

mieć łeb [myehch WEHP] (or **mieć głowę** [myehch GWOH-veh]; **nie od parady** [nyeh oht pah-RAH-di] or **na karku** [nah KAHR-koo] may be added) *v phr* To be clever, well-oriented or skillful at something, esp in business; to have a business acumen <have brains, have savvy, have smarts, be with it, be nobody's fool, not be born yesterday, not get off the boat, be in the know, have something on the ball, have a good head on one's shoulders, have a head on one's shoulders, have a yiddisher head, have a knack for, have what it takes, have a lot of brains upstairs> eg *Ma głowę na karku. Prawdziwa business-woman jakiej potrzebuję (She's got a good head on her shoulders. A real businesswoman, just what I need); Twój chłopak ma głowę nie od parady. Nie ma jeszcze trzydziestki, a już ma doktorat (Your boyfriend really had the brains. He's not even thirty and has already made his PhD); On ma głowę do interesów (He has a knack for business)*

mieć blade pojęcie See nie mieć zielonego pojęcia

mieć boja See mieć cykora

mieć brzucha [myehch BZHOO-khah] *v phr* To be pregnant <be knocked up, be banged up, be PG, be preggers, be puffed, be pumped, be bumped, be storked, be in the family way, have one in the oven, be infanticipating, swallow a watermelon seed, join the club> eg *Słyszałam, że ona znów ma brzucha (I hear she's in the family way again)*

mieć bzika See mieć świra

mieć ciche dni [myehch CHEE-kheh DNEE] *v phr* (Of two people) To refuse to speak to each other over a certain period of time <not be on speaking terms, not speak a word to each other> eg *Mają ciche dni od tygodnia (They haven't spoken a word to each other for a week now)*

mieć co do gęby włożyć See nie mieć co do gęby włożyć

mieć coś na głowie [myahch tsohsh nah GWOH-vyeh] (or **mieć coś na karku** [myahch tsohsh nah KAHR-koo]) *v phr* To be busily responsible for something; to be thoroughly engaged in something <have one's hands full of, have on one's hands, be on someone's mind, be tied up with, be piled up with, have something on one's back> eg *Mam na głowie masę papierkowej roboty w biurze (I'm tied up with a lot of paper work at the office)*

mieć coś na końcu języka [myehch tsohsh nah KOHÑ-tsoo yehn-ZI-kah] *v phr* Not to be quite able to remember something <have something on the tip of one's

tongue, ring a bell, disremember, disrecollect> eg *Miałem tę odpowiedź na końcu języka, ale ona była pierwsza (I had the answer on the tip of my tongue, but she was first)*

mieć coś na zbyciu [myehch TSOHSH nah ZBI-chyoo] *v phr* To have something one wants to sell; to want to dispose of stock <want to move, want to push, want to turn over, have something to get rid of> eg *Macie ten produkt na zbyciu? (Do you want to move this product?)*

mieć coś nagrane [myehch tsohsh nah-GRAH-neh] (or **mieć coś zaklepane** [myehch tsohsh zah-kleh-PAH-neh]) *v phr* To make sure in advance that something will be done; to secure; to reserve <get something wired up, get something cinched, get something taped, get something racked, get something sewed up, get something iced, get something in the bag, get something tied up, put a hold on, lay away> eg *Wybiorą naszego kandydata. Mamy to zaklepane (They will chose our candidate. We got it cinched)*

mieć coś obcykane [myehch tsohsh ohp-tsi-KAH-neh] (or **mieć coś obstukane** [myehch tsohsh ohp-stoo-KAH-neh]) *v phr* To have a thorough and ready knowledge of something; to be competent and authoritative <have something at one's fingertips, know something backwards and forwards, know something from A to Z, know something from the ground up, know all the answers, know all the tricks, know a thing or two, know one's beans, know one's stuff, know the score, know what it's all about, know what's what> eg *Lepiej spytaj mojego brata. Ma to obcykane (You'd better ask my brother. He's got the whole subject at his fingertips)*

mieć coś u kogoś [myehch oo KOH-gosh tsohsh] (or **mieć u kogoś tyły** [myehch oo KOH-gosh TI-wi]) *v phr* To be indebted; to owe someone money <be in hock, be in the red, be into for, owe someone one> eg *Mam u brata dziesięć kawałków (I'm into my brother for ten grand)*

mieć coś w małym palcu [myehch tsohsh v MAH-wim PAHL-tsoo] (or **mieć coś w jednym palcu** [myehch tsohsh v YEHD-nim PAHL-tsoo]) *v phr* To have a thorough and ready knowledge of something; to be competent and authoritative <have something at one's fingertips, know something backwards and forwards, know something from A to Z, know something from the ground up, know all the answers, know all the tricks, know a thing or two, know one's beans, know one's stuff, know the score, know what it's all about, know what's what > eg *Lepiej spytaj mojego ojca. Ma to w małym palcu (You'd better ask my father. He's got the whole subject at his fingertips)*

mieć coś z głową [myehch tsohsh z GWOH-voh] *v phr* To be or to behave as if one were insane or stupid <be off one's rocker, be off one's nut, be off one's base, be off the track, be off the trolley, be out one's skull, be out of one's mind, be crazy, be crazy as a loon, blow one's cork, blow one's top, blow a fuse, crack up, freak out, flip out, be ape, be bananas, be bent, be bonkers, be cracked, be dopey, be ga-ga, be half-baked, be loony, be loopy, be mental, be nerts, be nuts, be nutty, be psycho, be schizo, be screwy, be wacky, be weird, be wild, schiz out, psych out, come unglued, come unstuck, come unwrapped, come unzipped> eg *Co ona mówi? Ma coś z głową, czy jak? (What is she talking about? Is she out of her rocker, or what?)*

mieć coś z górki [myehch tsohsh z GOOR-kee] *v phr* To surmount the biggest difficulties or problems; to pass most of obstacles <be downhill from here on, be

downhill all the way, be plain sailing from here on> eg *Był to ciężki okres, ale minął. Teraz mamy już z górki (It was a difficult period. It's downhill from here on)*

mieć coś zaklepane See **mieć coś nagrane**

mieć coś/kogoś gdzieś [myehch tsohsh/KOH-gohsh GJEHSH] (**w dupie*** [v DOO-pyeh] or **w nosie** [v NOH-shyeh] may replece **gdzieś**; **głęboko** [gwehm-BOH-koh] may precede **w**) *v phr* To be indifferent; not to care at all; to ignore; to show disrespect <not give a damn, not give a fuck, not give a shit, not give a diddly-shit, not give a diddly-damn, not give a flying fuck, not give a hoot, not give a rat's ass, not give a squat, pass up, diss, skip, ig, ice, chill, freeze, cut, brush off, give the brush, give the cold shoulder, turn the cold shoulder, cold-shoulder, give the go-by, high-hat, kiss off> eg *Mam w dupie to, co myślisz (I don't give a shit what you think)*

mieć coś/kogoś na oku [myehch tsohsh/KOH-gohsh nah OH-koo] *v phr* **1** (or **mieć oko na coś/kogoś** [myehch OH-koh nah tsohsh/KOH-gohsh]) To observe or watch attentively; to mind or look after <keep an eye on, baby-sit> eg *Wychodzę na chcwilę. Miej oko na sklep (I must go out for a minute. Keep an eye on the store)* **2** To set one's sights on; to pick, choose, or decide <pick out, finger, lay one's finger on, put one's finger on, button down, pin down, name, tab, tag, tap, tab, slot, opt, peg> eg *No i jak? Masz coś na oku? (Well. Did you pick anything out?)*

mieć cuga See iść w cug

mieć cykora [myehch tsi-KOH-rah] (or **mieć boja** [myehch BOH-yah] or **mieć pietra** [myehch PYEHT-rah] or **mieć stracha** [myehch STRAH-khah] or **mieć pełne gacie** [myahch PEH-oo-neh GAH-chyeh]) *v phr* To be afraid; to be frightened; to be intimidated <chicken out, turn chicken, turn yellow, run scared, have cold feet, be scared stiff, be scared shitless, shit one's pants, piss one's pants, shit bullets, shit a brick, shit green, be spooked, push the panic button, wimp out> eg *Nie chciał jeje tego powiedzieć. Myślę, że miał cykora (He didn't want to tell her that. I guess he was scared stiff)*

mieć czym oddychać [myehch chim ohd-DI-khahch] *v phr* (Of a woman) To have a well developed, attractive figure, esp breasts <be built, be stacked, be constructed, be curvy, be curvaceous, be zaftig> eg *Jego nowa dziewczyna naprawdę ma czym oddychać (His new girlfriend is real stacked)*

mieć czyste ręce [myehch CHIS-teh REHN-tseh] *v phr* To be innocent; to lack guilt <be clean, have clean hands> eg *Policja go zwolniła, bo miał czyste ręce (The police let him go because he was clean)*

mieć długi język [myehch DWOO-gee YEHN-zik] *v phr* To be talkative and indiscreet; to be unable to keep a secret; to gossip <have a big mouth, bad-mouth, dish the dirt, wiggle-waggle, have diarrhea of the mouth, have verbal diarrhea, have foot in the mouth disease, put one's foot in one's mouth, spill beans, pull the cat out of the bag> eg *Lepiej z nim o tym nie rozmawiaj. Ma długi język (You'd better don't talk to him about it. He has a big mouth)*

mieć dobry spust See mieć spust

mieć fason See trzymać fason

mieć fazę [myehch FAH-zeh] (or **złapać fazę** [ZWAH-pahch FAH-zeh]) *v phr* To experience the initial euphoric effects of alcohol <get high, get buzzed, get buzzing, get happy, get kicked, get spaced, trip, fly> eg *Bardzo szybko złapała fazę (She got buzzed real quick)*

mieć fiksum-dyrdum See mieć świra

mieć fioła See mieć świra

mieć fisia See mieć świra

mieć forsy jak lodu [myehch FOHR-si yahk LOH-doo] (or **mieć kasy jak lodu** [myehch KAH-si yahk LOH-doo] or **mieć szmalu jak lodu** [myehch SHMAH-looyahk LOH-doo]) *v phr* To be very rich; to have a lot of money <have money to burn, have money to spare, be loaded, be flush, be filthy rich, be stinking rich, be dirt richy, be lousy rich, be in the bucks, be in the dough, be in the money, be rolling in it, be made of money> eg *Spójrz na niego. Możnaby pomyśleć, że ma szmalu jak lodu (Look at him. You'd think he has money to burn)*

mieć głowę See mieć łeb

mieć haka na kogoś [myehch KHAHkah nah KOHgohsh] (**haczyk** [KHAHchik] may replace **haka**, **przeciw komuś** [PSHEHchif KOHmoosh] may replace **na kogoś**) *v phr* To be in the possession of information potentially damaging to someone <have something on someone, get something on someone> eg *Myślę, że on ma coś na Ciebie (I think he has something on you)*

mieć hopla See mieć świra

mieć ileś lat na karku [myehch EE-lehsh laht nah KAHR-koo] *v phr* To reach a specific age <be on the wrong side of, have on the mileage, push, hit, get, get along, > eg *Ona ma już trzydziestkę na karku (She's on the wrong side of thirty)*

mieć kiełbie we łbie See mieć świra

mieć klapki na oczach [myehch KLAHP-kee nah OH-chyakh] *v phr* To be stubborn, bigoted, or dogmatic in one's views; to have a very limited vision on something <be a regular Archie Bunker, be head-set, be mind-set, be hard-nosed, be hard-lined, be a hard nut to crack, be locked in, have head in concrete, be stuck in concrete, be a brick wall, be stiff-necked, be stubborn as a mule> eg *Obecny dyrektor Instytutu Anglistyki ma klapki na oczach (The incumbent director of the English Institute is a regular Archie Bunker)*

mieć kogoś na boku [myehch KOH-gohsh nah BOH-koo] *v phr* To be sexually unfaithful, esp to commit adultery <cheat, two-time, chippy, get a little on the side, backdoor, have an extracurricular activity, play hanky-panky, step out on, play around, play the field> eg *Żona tego polityka miała kogoś na boku (The politician's wife has been doing some extracurricular activity)*

mieć kogoś na muszce See brać kogoś pod lupę

mieć kogoś pod lupą See brać kogoś pod lupę

mieć kogoś w kieszeni [myehch KOH-gohsh f kyeh-SHEH-nee] *v phr* To have control over someone <have someone in one's pocket, have the upper hand on, wind around one's finger, wrap around one's finger, twist around one's finger, > eg *Nie martw się o burmistrza. Będzie współpracował. Mamy go w kieszeni (Don't worry about the mayor. He'll cooperate. We have him in our pocket)*

mieć kota See mieć świra

mieć kręćka See mieć świra

mieć krechę u kogoś [myehch KREH-kheh oo KOH-gohsh] *v phr* To lose someone's trust; to fall into disfavor <be in someone's bad books, be in someone's black books, be on someone's shit list, be on someone's crap list, be in deep shit with someone, be up shit creek with someone, draw a bead on> eg *Ma krechę u profesora (He's in the bad books of the professor)*

mieć kuku na muniu See mieć świra

mieć lekką rękę [myehch LEK-koh REHN-keh] *v phr* To be wasteful; to spend money wastefully or recklessly; to squander <blow, drop, diddle away, piddle away, piss away, shell out, dish out, throw away, spend like water, pour down the drain, throw down the drain> eg *Mój wujek miał lekką rękę i szybko zbankrutował (My uncle used to spend money like water and soon went bankrupt)*

mieć lepkie łapy [myehch LEHP-kyeh WAH-pi] (or **mieć lepkie ręce** [myehch LEHP-kyeh REHN-tseh]) *v phr* To have a tendency to steal; be larcenous <have sticky fingers, have light fingers, > eg *Miał lepkie ręce i zawsze podbierał ojcu drobne (He had sticky fingers and was always taking his father's small change)*

mieć mętlik w głowie [myehch MEHNT-leek v GWOH-vyeh] (or **mieć młyn w głowie** [myehch MWIN v GWOH-vyeh]) *v phr* To be confused, disoriented, or bewildered <be dizzy, be dopey, be punchy, be spaced out, be mixed up, be discombobulated, be flabbergasted, be messed up, be unscrewed, be farmisht, be balled up, be shook up, be floored, be unglued, be unzipped, be fried, be screwed-up, be fucked-up, be flummoxed, be kerflooey, be caught off base, be in a fog, be in a haze> eg *Nie wiedziałam, co powiedzieć. Miałam mętlik w głowie (I didn't know what to say. I was mixed up)*

mieć metr pięćdziesiąt w kapeluszu [mehtr pyehn-JEH-shyohnt f kah-peh-LOO-shoo] *nm* (Of a person) To be of short stature <be shorty, be a peewee, be a peanut, be a runt, be a squirt, be a shrimp, be a half-pint> eg *Jej nowy chłopak ma metr pięćdziesiąt w kapeluszu (Her new boyfriend is a peewee)*

mieć na chleb [myehch bah KHLEHP] *v phr* To have just enough money to pay only for one's living; to maintain oneself at a minimal level <keep the wolf from the door, make cabfare, make ends meet, get by> eg *Z żoną i piątką dzieci, robił co mógł, żeby zarobić na chleb (With a wife and five children to support, he did all he could to keep the wolf from the door); Mówi, że ma dobrą pracę, ale nie ma nawet na chleb (He says he has a good job, but he doesn't even make cabfare)*

mieć na czym siedzieć [myehch nah chim SHYEH-jehch] (or **mieć na czym usiąść** [myehch nah chim OO-shyonhnshch]) *v phr* (Of a woman) To have a well developed, attractive figure, esp buttocks and hips <be built, be stacked, be constructed, be curvy, be curvaceous, be zaftig> eg *Jego nowa dziewczyna naprawdę ma na czym siedzieć (His new girlfriend is really curvy)*

mieć na wątrobie See leżeć komuś na wątrobie

mieć nasrane* [myehch nah-SRAH-neh] (or **mieć narąbane** [myehch nah-rohm-BAH-neh] or **mieć pojebane**** [myehch poh-yeh-BAH-neh] or **mieć popierdolone**** [myehch poh-pyehr-doh-LOH-neh]) *v phr* To be obsessed insane or eccentric; to act insanely <be crazy, be crazy as a loon, be ape, be bananas, be bent, be bonkers, be cracked, be dopey, be ga-ga, be half-baked, be loony, be loopy, be mental, be nerts, be nuts, be nutty, be off one's nut, be off one's rocker, be off one's base, be off the track, be off the trolley, be out one's skull, be psycho, be schizo, be screwy, be wacky, be weird, be wild, be fucked in the head, have a bug up one's ass, have a bug in one's ear, have a bee in one's bonnet, have a flea in one's nose> eg *Ten facet ma chyba nasrane. Kazał nam to wszystko przepisać (This guy must be fucked in his head. He wanted us to rewrite everything)*

mieć nie po kolei w głowie See mieć źle w głowie

mieć nierówno pod sufitem [myehch nyeh-ROOV-noh poht soo-FEE-tehm] (or **mieć nie poukładane pod sufitem** [myehch nyeh poh-ook-wah-DAH-neh poht soo-FEE-tehm]) *v phr* To be or to behave as if one were insane or stupid <be off one's rocker, be off one's nut, be off one's base, be off the track, be off the trolley, be out one's skull, be out of one's mind, be crazy, be crazy as a loon, blow one's cork, blow one's top, blow a fuse, crack up, freak out, flip out, be ape, be bananas, be bent, be bonkers, be cracked, be dopey, be ga-ga, be half-baked, be loony, be loopy, be mental, be nerts, be nuts, be nutty, be psycho, be schizo, be screwy, be wacky, be weird, be wild, schiz out, psych out, come unglued, come unstuck, come unwrapped, come unzipped> eg *Myślę, że twoja siostra ma nierówno pod sufitem (I think your sister is off her rocker)*

mieć niewyparzoną gębę [nyeh-vi-pah-ZHOH-nah GEHM-bah] (or **mieć niewyparzony język** [myehch nyeh-vi-pah-ZHOH-ni YEHN-zik] or **mieć ostry język** [myehch OHS-tri YEHN-zik]) *v phr* To speak bluntly, impudently, or obscenely <be sharp-tongued, be gutty, be lippy, be cocky, be brassy, be cheeky, be sassy, be nervy, be smart-ass, be wise-ass, back talk, back chat, talk dirty, be foul-mouthed, cuss> eg *Chcesz z nią zaczynać? Powinieneś wiedzieć, że ona ma bardzo cięty język (You want to pick a fight with her? You should know she is very cheeky)*

mieć nosa [myehch NOH-sah] (or **czuć pismo nosem** [chooch PEES-moh NOH-sehm] or **wąchać pismo nosem** [VOHN-khahch PEES-moh NOH-sehm] or **czuć przez skórę** [chooch pshehs SKOO-reh]) *v phr* To sense or suspect something; to have an intuition, esp about something wrong <smell a rat, have a sneaking suspicion, have a nose for, feel something in one's bones, feel something in one's guts, know something in one's guts, know something in one's bones, have a funny feeling, have a hunch, have vibes> eg *Jak tylko wszedłem do środka, wyczułem pismo nosem. No jasne, okradziono mnie (The minute I came in, I smelled a rat. Sure enough, I had been robbed); Pociąg się spóźnił. Miałem nosa (The train was late. I could feel it in my bones)*

mieć oko na coś/kogoś [myehch OH-koh nah tsohsh/KOH-gohsh] *v phr* To observe or watch attentively; to mind or look after <keep an eye on, baby-sit> eg *Policja ma go na oku od dwóch tygodni (The police has had an eye an him for two weeks)* See mieć coś/kogoś na oku

mieć olej w głowie [myehch OH-leh-ee v GWOH-vyeh] (or **mieć olej we łbie** [myehch OH-leh-ee VEH-wbyeh]) *v phr* To be smart, clever, or intelligent <have brains, have savvy, have smarts, be with it, be nobody's fool, not be born yesterday, not get off the boat, be in the know, have something on the ball, have a lot of brains upstairs> eg *Ten facet ma dużo oleju w głowie i nie da się nabrać (That guy has much savvy and won't be fooled)*

mieć ostry język See mieć niewyparzoną gębę

mieć świra [myehch SHFEE-rah] (**bzika** [BZHEE-kah] or **fioła** [FEE-yoh-wah] or **fisia** [FEE-shyah] or **hopla** [KHOHP-lah], **kota** [KOH-tah] or **kręćka** [KREHNCH-kah] or **pierdolca**** [pyehr-DOHL-tsah] or **zajoba*** [zah-YOH-bah] or **szmergla** [SHMEHRG-lah] or **szajbę** [SHAH-ee-beh] or **kuku na muniu** [KOO-koo nah MOO-nyooh] or **kiełbie we łbie** [KYEH-oo-byeh VEH-oo-byeh] or **fiksum-dyrdum** [FEEK-soom DIR-doom] may replace **świra**) *v phr* To be obsessed, insane or eccentric <be crazy, be crazy as a loon, be ape, be

bananas, be bent, be bonkers, be cracked, be dopey, be ga-ga, be half-baked, be loony, be loopy, be mental, be nerts, be nuts, be nutty, be off one's nut, be off one's rocker, be off one's base, be off the track, be off the trolley, be out one's skull, be psycho, be schizo, be screwy, be wacky, be weird, be wild, be fucked in the head, have a bug up one's ass, have a bug in one's ear, have a bee in one's bonnet, have a flea in one's nose> eg *Ten facet ma świra na punkcie samochodów (This guy is crazy about cars); Jego dziewczyna ma fioła na punkcie muzyki techno (His girlfriend is nuts about techno music)*

mieć pełne gacie See mieć cykora

mieć pierdolca See mieć świra

mieć pietra See mieć cykora

mieć pod czachą [myehch poht CHAH-khoh] *v phr* To be smart, clever, or intelligent <have brains, have savvy, have smarts, be with it, be nobody's fool, not be born yesterday, not get off the boat, be in the know, have something on the ball, have a lot of brains upstairs> eg *W miesiąc zarobił pięć milionów! Facet na prawdę musi mieć pod czachą! (He earned five million within a month! The guy really must have brains!)*

mieć przerwę w życiorysie [myehch PSHEHR-veh v zhi-chyoh-RI-shyeh] *nf phr* To lose consciousness as a result of heavy drinking <be knocked out, crash, pass out, conk out, zonk out> eg *Przez tę whiskey miał przerwę w życiorysie i nic nie pamięta (Thanks to this whiskey he was knocked out and does not remember anything)*

mieć przesrane* [myehch psheh-SRAH-neh] (or **mieć przerąbane** [myehch psheh-rohm-BAH-neh] or **mieć przekichane** [psheh-kee-KHAH-neh] or **mieć przechlapane** [myehch psheh-khlah-PAH-neh] or **mieć przejebane**** [myehch psheh-yeh-BAH-neh]) *v phr* To lose someone's trust or liking; to fall into disfavor <be in someone's bad books, be in someone's black books, be on someone's shit list, be on someone's crap list, be in deep shit with someone, be up shit creek with someone, draw a bead on, someone's ass is grass> eg *Po tym skandalu z pieniędzmi mam u niego przerąbane (After that scandal with the money, I'm on his shit-list); Zrób to, albo masz przechlapane (Do it or your ass is grass)*

mieć pstro w głowie [myehch PSTROH v GWOH-vyeh] (or **mieć zielono w głowie** [myehch zhyeh-LOH-noh v GWOH-vyeh] or **mieć siano w głowie** [myehch SHYAH-noh v GWOH-vyeh]) *v phr* To be silly, crazy, reckless, or frivolous, esp in the adolescent context <have a screw loose, have a loose screw, have a hole in one's head, have a few buttons missing, have one's head up one's ass, have shit for brains, not have a clue> eg *Wszyscy wiedzą, że twoja siostra ma pstro w głowie (Everybody knows that your sister has got a screw loose)*

mieć ręce i nogi [myehch REHN-tseh ee NOH-gee] *v phr* To be well-organized or well-thought-out; to be acceptable or passable <hold up, be in good shape, be OK, be okay, be kopasetic, be hunky-dory, be so-so> eg *Sądzisz, że moje wypracowanie ma ręce i nogi? (Do you think that my essay holds up?)*

mieć refleks szachisty See mieć spóźniony zapłon

mieć robaki w dupie* [myehch roh-BAH-kee v DOOP-yeh] (or **mieć robaki w tyłku** [myehch roh-BAH-kee f TIW-koo]) *v phr* To be eager or nervous to begin; to be tired of being held back <have ants in one's pants, be on pins and needles, champ at the bit, be like a cat on hot bricks> eg *Masz robaki w tyłku, czy co? (Do you have ants in your pants, or what?)*

mieć siano w głowie See mieć pstro w głowie

mieć spóźniony zapłon [myehch spoozh-NYOH-ni ZAHP-wohn] (or **mieć refleks szachisty** [myehch REHF-lehks shah-KHEES-ti]) *v phr* To think, comprehend, or react very slowly; to be slow-witted and mentally sluggish; to have slow reflexes <be slow on the draw, be slow on the uptake, be slow on the trigger, be a slow-mo, have snail speed> eg *Zawsze miał spóźniony zapłon. Nic dziwnego, że przegrał tę debatę (He's always been slow on the draw. No wonder he lost the debate)*

mieć spust [myehch SPOOST] (or **mieć dobry spust** [myehch DOH-bri SPOOST]) *v phr* **1** To be able to eat a lot; to a healthy appetite <be able to eat a horse, could eat a horse, be able to eat the asshole out of a bear, could eat the asshole out of a bear, have a tapeworm> eg *Twój brat ma dobry spust (Your brother is able to eat a horse)* **2** To be able to drink a lot <be able to drink like a fish> eg *Mój wujek to ma spust. Może wypić dziesięć piw (My uncle is able to drink like a fish. He can drink ten beers)*

mieć stracha See mieć cykora

mieć swoje lata [myehch SFOH-yeh LAH-tah] *v phr* Not to be young; to be old <not be spring chicken, be over the hill> eg *Ma swoje lata, ale wciąż gra w tenisa dwa razy w tygodniu (He is no spring chicken, but he still plays tennis twice a week); Babciu, masz już swoje lata, powinnaś odpocząć (Granny, you're a little over the hill, you should try to take it easy now)*

mieć szajbę See mieć świra

mieć szmergla See mieć świra

mieć u kogoś tyły See mieć coś u kogoś

mieć w czubie [myehch f CHOO-byeh] *v phr* To be drunk, be alcohol intoxicated <be alkied, be bagged, be blitzed, be blotto, be blown away, be bent, be boiled, be bombed, be boozed up, be blasted, be bottled, be boxed, be canned, be clobbered, be cooked, be corked, be drunk as a skunk, be edged, be embalmed, be fractured, be fried, be gassed, be ginned, be grogged, have one too many, be half under, have a load on, have an edge on, have a skinful, be high, be hooched up, be in bad shape, be in a bad way, be impaired, be illuminated, be juiced, be liquored up, be lit, be loaded, be looped, be lubricated, be lushed, be smashed, be oiled, be pickled, be plastered, be plonked, be polluted, be sauced, be shitfaced, be sloshed, be soaked, be stewed, be stiff, be stinking drunk, be swizzled, be tanked, be wiped, be zonked, be three sheets to the wind> eg *Jak można mieć w czubie po dwóch piwach? (How can anybody be bagged on two beers?)*

mieć węża w kieszeni [myehch VEHN-zhah f kyeh-SHEH-nee] *v phr* To spend money reluctantly <penny-pinch, scrimp, keep the purse strings tight> eg *Jej mąż zawsze miał węża w kieszeni, dlatego go rzuciła (Her husband kept the purse strings tight, that's why she left him)*

mieć wypite [myehch vi-PEE-teh] *v phr* To be drunk, be alcohol intoxicated <be alkied, be bagged, be blitzed, be blotto, be blown away, be bent, be boiled, be bombed, be boozed up, be blasted, be bottled, be boxed, be canned, be clobbered, be cooked, be corked, be drunk as a skunk, be edged, be embalmed, be fractured, be fried, be gassed, be ginned, be grogged, have one too many, be half under, have a load on, have an edge on, have a skinful, be high, be hooched up, be in bad shape, be in a bad way, be impaired, be illuminated, be juiced, be

liquored up, be lit, be loaded, be looped, be lubricated, be lushed, be smashed, be oiled, be pickled, be plastered, be plonked, be polluted, be sauced, be shitfaced, be sloshed, be soaked, be stewed, be stiff, be stinking drunk, be swizzled, be tanked, be wiped, be zonked, be three sheets to the wind> eg *On tego nie zrobi. Ma wypite (He can't do that. He's plastered)*

mieć źle w głowie [myehch ZHLEH v GWOH-vyeh] (or **mieć źle poukładane w głowie** [myahch ZHLEH poh-oo-kwah-DAH-neh v GWOH-vyeh] or **mieć nie po kolei w głowie** [myahch nyeh poh koh-LEH-ee v GWOH-vyeh]) *v phr* To be or to behave as if one were insane or stupid <be off one's rocker, be off one's nut, be off one's base, be off the track, be off the trolley, be out one's skull, be out of one's mind, be crazy, be crazy as a loon, blow one's cork, blow one's top, blow a fuse, crack up, freak out, flip out, be ape, be bananas, be bent, be bonkers, be cracked, be dopey, be ga-ga, be half-baked, be loony, be loopy, be mental, be nerts, be nuts, be nutty, be psycho, be schizo, be screwy, be wacky, be weird, be wild, schiz out, psych out, come unglued, come unstuck, come unwrapped, come unzipped> eg *Wszyscy wiedzą, że jego nowa dziewczyna ma nie po kolei w głowie (Everybody knows that his new girl is crazy as a loon)*

mieć z kimś na pieńku [myehch s keemsh nah PYEHŇ-koo] *v phr* To be in a state of open dislike and readiness to fight with someone <be at daggers drawn with, have a bone to pick with> eg *Mam na pieńku z dyrektorem Instytutu, bo myśli, że jestem lepszy od niego. No cóż, jestem! (I'm at daggers drawn with the director of the Institute because he thinks that I'm better. Well, I am!)*

mieć zajoba See mieć świra

mieć zdrowie do See nie mieć zdrowia do czegoś/kogoś

mieć zielono w głowie See mieć pstro w głowie

miech [myehkh] *nm* A month <moon, deano> eg *Był w więzieniu ze dwa miechy (He was in jail like two moons)*

męcho [MYEHN-khoh] *nn* Any edible animal meat or meat by-product, esp a piece <slab, chunk, side> eg *Rzuć męcho na grila (Put the slab on the grill)*

mięczak [MYEHN-chahk] *nm* A weak, timid, or effeminate male; a weakling <wimp, wuss, pussy, big baby, candy ass, milktoast, milquetoast, featherweight, gutless wonder, limp-dick, pantywaist, hard-off> eg *Czy na prawdę myślisz, że mogłabym pójść na randkę z twoim bratem? To mięczak (Do you really think I could go out on a date with your brother? He's a wimp)*

miedza See przez miedzę

między młotem a kowadłem [MYEHN-dzi MWOH-tehm ah koh-VAHD-wehm] *phr* In a very difficult situation; facing a hard decision <between a rock and a hard place, between the devil and the deep blue sea, between two fires, caught in the cross-fire, on the spot, on the hot seat, on the hornns of a dilemma> eg *Miał przed sobą dylemat. Był między młotem a kowadłem (He had a dilemma on his hands. He was clearly between a rock and a hard place)*

miejsce See z miejsca

miękkie [MYEHNK-kyeh] *npl* (or **miękka waluta** [MYEHNK-kah vah-LOO-tah]) (Esp in former communist times) Currency that is highly inflated or likely to become less valuable <soft currency, soft money> eg *Nie chciał miękkiej waluty, przyjmował tylko dolary (He didn't want soft money, he accepted only dollars)*

mieścić się w głowie See nie mieścić się w głowie

mieścina [myehsh-CHEE-nah] *nf* A small town, esp in the country; any place far from civilization <jerk town, jerkwater town, backwater, hellhole, rathole, mudhole, real hole, noplaceville, hicksville, whistle stop, dump, armpit, East Jesus, Bumfuck Egypt> eg *Skąd dzwonisz? Z jakiejś mieściny (Where are you calling from? Some mudhole)*

miernota [myehr-NOH-tah] *nf* Someone or something mediocre or of little value or significance; a mediocrity <underachiever, loser, born loser, second-rater, schlemiel, schmendrick, schmo, schnook, screwup, fuckup, hacker, muffer, scrub, dub, dool tool, turkey, lump, buterfingers, fumble-fist, goof, goof-off, goofball, eightball, foulball, klutz, also-ran, never-was, nonstarter, zero, lightweight, nobody, non, nonentity, noname, small potatoes, small timer, bush-leaguer> eg *Nowy dyrektor Instytutu postanowił promować tylko miernoty, bo sam jest miernotą (The new director of the Institute decided to promote only nonentities, because he is a nonentity himself)*

mięso See rzucać mięsem

mieszać [MYEH-shahch] (perf **namieszać** [nah-MYEH-shahch]; or **motać** [MOH-tahch] perf **namotać** [nah-MOH-tahch] or **zamotać** [zah-MOH-tahch]; or **mącić** [MOHN-cheech] perf **namącić** [nah-MOHN-cheech] or **zamącić** [zah-MOHN-cheech]) *v* To make something unclear, esp deliberately; to confuse, complicate, or lie <stir, stir up, adjy, bull, bullshit, shit, shovel the shit, string along, snow, fake it, talk through one's hat, speak with forked tongue> eg *Myślę, że facet miesza (I think the guy is bullshitting)*

mieszczuch [MYEHSH-chookh] *nm* A city dweller <towner, townee, city slicker, cliff dweller, cave dweller> eg *Nie znoszę tych mieszczuchów (I hate these townees)*

mieszkać kątem [MYEHSH-kahch KOHN-tehm] *v phr* **1** To live in someone's place <crash, crash out, nest, bunk, park, squat, perch, roost, locate, hole up, hang out, hang up one's hat> eg *Od dwóch tygodni mieszka u nich kątem (He's been crashing out at their place for two weeks)* **2** To rent a room in someone's house or apartment <rent a place> eg *Mieszka kątem we wschodniej dzielnicy (He's renting a place on the East Eside)*

mięta See czuć do kogoś miętę

migać się [MEE-gahch shyeh] *v* To avoid work; to shirk duty <goldbrick, goof off, goof around, fuck around, screw around, jerk off, screw off, drag-ass, drag one's ass, drag it, dragtail, fake off, flub the dub, fuck off, fuck the dog, dog it, lollygag, sit on one's ass, soldier, skate, watch the clock> eg *W biurze zawsze się migał (He's always been goldbricking in his office)*

migdalić się [meeg-DAH-leech shyeh] (perf **pomigdalić** [poh-meeg-DAH-leech shyeh]) *v* To touch or caress amorously; to fondle <feel, feel up, cop a feel, grope, pet, neck, play grab-ass, smooch, get physical> eg *Zaczęli migdalić się na środku pokoju (They started to play grab-ass in the middle of the room)*

migiem [MEE-gyehm] (or **w mig** [v MEEK] or **w trymiga** [f tri-mee-GAH]) *adv* Immediately; very quickly <pretty damn quick, PDQ, ASAP, on the spot, on the double, double time, double clutching, like a shot, in half a mo, like now, before you know it, before you can say Jack Robinson, in a jiffy, in a flash, in half a shake, right off the bat, like a bat out of hell, like a shot out of hell, hubba-hubba, horseback, like greased lightning> eg *Przyszedł nauczyciel i w try miga zabrali się do roboty (The teacher came in and they got to work pretty damn quick)*

mikrus [MEEK-roos] *nm* A person of short stature <shorty, peewee, peanut, runt, squirt, shrimp, half-pint> eg *Ten mikrus nawet nie wie, co mówi (The peewee doesn't know what the heck he's talking about)*

milusiński [mee-loo-SHIÑ-skee] *nm* A child <kid, pride and glory> eg *Gdzie są wasz milusiński? (Where is your pride and glory?)*

mina See barani wzrok

mineta** [mee-NEH-tah] (or **minetka**** [mee-NEHT-kah]) *nf* Cunnilingus <face job, box lunch, muff dive, cunt-eating, cunt-licking, cunt-lapping, eating-out, the French way> eg *Jakie to życie jest proste. Jedna minetka i ból głowy minął! (Life is so simple. One face job and her headache is gone!)*

miniówa [mee-NYOO-vah] *nf* A mimi-skirt <mini, mini drape, handkerchief hem> eg *Jak ci się podoba moja nowa miniówa? (How do you like my new mini?)*

minus See być na minusie

miś [meesh] *nm* **1** A fur coat <skins, dried bakers> eg *Lukniej na jej misia z norek (Check out her mink skins)* **2** (or **misiek** [MEE-shyehk] or **misio** [MEE-shyoh] or **misiu** [MEE-shyoo]) *nm* A bear <teddy, teddy bear, Yogi> eg *Jaki ładny misio! (What a nice teddy bear!)*

miód See cwaniak

misz masz [MEESH-mahsh] *nm phr* A number of things mixed up without any sensible order; a mixture or miscellany <mish mash, hodge-podge, odds and ends, bits and pieces, rag-bag, mess, unholy mess, rat's nest, smorgasboard> eg *Kto jest odpowiedzialny za ten misz masz? (Who's responsible for this mish mash?)*

mleko See kaszka z mlekiem

mleć jęzorem [mlehch jehn-ZOH-rehm] (or **mleć ozorem** [mlehch oh-ZOH-rehm]; **pytlować** [pit-LOH-vahch] or **chlapać** [KHLAH-pahch] or **trzepać** [TSHEH-pahch] may replace **mleć**) *v phr* To talk, chat, or converse, esp idly <go, gab, rap, yap, yack, yam, blab, flap, drool, patter, jaw, gum, lip, chin, chew, rattle, crack, blow, breeze, buzz, noise off, sound off, chew the fat, chew the rag, bat one's gums, beat one's gums, shoot the breeze, shoot the shit, flip one's lip, flap one's jaw, run one's mouth, talk one's ear off, talk one's ass off, wag the tongue> eg *Trzepiemy już ozorami od godziny. I'm tired (We've been batting our gums for an housr now. Jestem zmęczony)*

mleczarnie* [mleh-CHAHR-nyah] *nf* A woman's large breasts <tits, melons, knockers, bazooms, boobs, headlights, hooters, hemispheres> eg *Widziałeś mleczarnie tej laski? (Did you see the knockers on that chick?)*

młócić [MWOO-cheech] (perf **wmłócić** [VMWOO-cheech]) *v* To eat, esp voraciously <stuff oneself, pig out, scarf out, pork out> eg *Wmłócił wszystek tort (He scarfed out the whole cake)*

młoda godzina [MWOH-dah goh-JEE-nah] *adv phr* (Of the early evening) Early; an early hour; not late <night is young, night is still, early on> eg *Gdzie się tak spieszysz? Jeszcze młoda godzina (Why are you in such a rush? The night is still young)*

młody See jak z młodszego brata, czuć się jak młody bóg

młodziak See małolat

młodzian See małolat

młodzieniaszek See małolat

młokos See małolat

młot* [mwoht] (or **muł*** [moow] or **matoł*** [MAH-toh-oo]) *nm* A very stupid, clumsy or ineffectual person; an idiot <airbrain, airhead, birdbrain, blockhead, squarehead, bonehead, bubblebrain, bubblehead, buckethead, cluckhead, cementhead, clunkhead, deadhead, dumbbell, dumbcluck, dumbhead, dumbass, dumbbrain, fatbrain, fathead, flubdub, knukclebrain, knucklehead, lamebrain, lardhead, lunkhead, meathead, musclehead, noodlehead, numbskull, pointhead, scatterbrain, jerk, jerk-off, klutz, chump, creep, nerd, dork, dweeb, gweeb, geek, jackass, lummox, twerp, nerd, bozo, clod, cluck, clunk, dimwit, dingbat, dipstick, dodo, dopey, dufus, goofus, lump, lunk, nitwit, schnook, schlep, schlemiel, schmendrick, schmo, schmuck, simp, stupe> eg *Od godziny tłumaczy im, co to oznacza. Straszne młoty, nic nie rozumieją (He's been explaining to them what it means for an hour. They are real squareheads, they don't understand anything); Czy te matoły rzeczywiście uchwaliły takie głupie prawo? (Did these schlemiels really enact such a stupid law?)*

młyn [mwin] (or **magiel** [MAH-gyehl] *nm* or **mętlik** [MEHNT-leek] *nm*) *nm* A confusing situation; confusion <mess, mess-up, mix-up, fuck-up, screw-up, mess and a half, holy mess, unholy mess, all hell broke loose, ruckus, discombobulation, foofaraw, srew, sweat, swivet, tizzy, hassle, rat's nest, SNAFU> eg *Wtedy właśnie zaczął się cały magiel (Just then the whole mess started)*
See mieć mętlik w głowie

mniam-mniam [mnyahm-MNYAHM] *excl* Very tasty <yum-yum, yummy, finger-licking good> eg *O, gorące skrzydełka. Mniam-mniam! (Oh, hot wings. Yum-yum!)*

móżdżek See ptasi móżdżek

można siekierę zawiesić [MOHZH-nah shyeh-KYEH-reh zah-VYEH-sheech] (or **można siekierę powiesić** [MOHZH-nah shyeh-KYEH-reh poh-VYEH-sheech]) *phr* (Of a room) With stuffy, smoky, or stinky air; smoke-filled <chimney, smokey, stinko, whiffy, nosey, phew> eg *Nie lubiłem tego miejsca. Można tam było siekierę powiesić (I didn't like the place. It was nosey)*

móc kogoś pocałować [moots KOH-gohsh poh-tsah-WOH-vahch] (**gdzieś** [gjehsh] or **w dupę*** [v DOO-peh] or **w nos** [v nohs] or **w tyłek** [f TI-wehk] may be added) *v phr* (Used to show defiance, contempt, or refusal) To be unable to harm someone <go fuck oneself, get fucked, kiss someone's ass> eg *Pocałujcie wy mnie wszyscy w dupę! (You can kiss my ass)*

móc komuś skoczyć* [moots KOH-moosh SKOH-chich] (**naskoczyć*** [nah-SKOH-chich] or **nadmuchać*** [nah-DMOO-khahch] or **nagwizdać** [nah-GVEEZ-dahch] may replace **skoczyć**; **na chuja**** [nah KHOO-yah] may precede **skoczyć** or **naskoczyć**) *v phr* (Used to show defiance, contempt, or refusal) To be unable to harm someone <go fuck oneself, get fucked, kiss someone's ass> eg *Mogą nam naskoczyć, jesteśmy już na terytorium Polski (They can go fuck themselves. We're already on the Polish territory)*

móc sobie w dupę wsadzić* [moots SOH-byeh v DOO-peh FSAH-jeech] or **móc sobie dupę podetrzeć*** [moots SOH-byeh DOO-peh poh-DEHT-shehch] or **móc o kant dupy rozbić*** [moots oh kahnt DOO-pi ROHZ-beech] (or **moć o kant dupy potłuc*** [moots oh kahnt DOO-pi POH-twoots]) *v phr* (Someone has no benefit from something which turned out) To be bad, worthless, or useless <can stick it, can stick it up one's ass, can stick it where the sun doesn't shine, can shove it, can shove it up one's ass, can shove it where the sun doesn't

shine, can stuff it, can stuff it up one's ass, can stuff it where the sun doesn't shine, can put it in one's ear, be shitty, be crappy, be lousy, be awful, be bush-league, be cheap, be crappy, be cruddy, be doggy, be low-rent, be low-ride, be no-good, be raggedy-ass, be schlocky, be stinking, be tacky, be trashy, be two-bit, be dime-a-dozen, be fair to middling, be garden variety, be of a sort, be of sorts, be piddling, be pissy-ass, be run-of-the-mill, be small-time> eg *Ten wasz projekt można o kant dupy rozbić (You can stick this project up your ass)*

mocarz [MOH-tsahsh] *nm* A powerful, self-confident and admired man <big man on campus, big shot, big wheel> eg *Słyszałem, że twój wujek to niezły mocarz (I hear your uncle is quite a big shot)*

mocny See nie ma mocnych

mocny w gębie [MOHTS-ni f GEHM-byeh] (or **obrotny w gębie** [oh-BROHT-ni v GEHM-byeh]) *adj phr* Impudent, insolent, or brash <sharp-tongued, gutty, lippy, cocky, brassy, cheeky, sassy, nervy, smart-ass, wise-ass, foul-mouthed, cussy, bitchy> eg *Jego nowa dziewczyna jest bardzo mocna w gębie (His new girlfriend is real cheeky)*

moczymorda [moh-chi-MOHR-dah] *nm* A heavy drinker; an alcoholic <lush, bar-fly, alky, boozehound, boozer, bottle baby, dipso, elbow bender, ginhead, juicehead, loadie, sponge, soak, wino> eg *Dałem moczymordzie trochę pieniędzy (I gave some money to the wino)*

moda See krzyk mody

model [MOH-dehl] *nm* A man impressive, extravagant, or disorderly in behavior <artist, joker, clown, article, ham, character, item, number> eg *Ale z tego twojego kuzyna model. Poszedł na randkę ze swoją nauczycielką od geografii (Your cousin is a real number. He went on a date with his geography tracher!)*

modelka [moh-DEHL-kah] *nf* A woman impressive, extravagant, or disorderly in behavior <artist, joker, clown, article, ham, character, item, number> eg *Ta twoja dziewczayna, to niezła modelka (That girlfriend of yours is a real character)*

modzić [MOH-jeech] (perf **wymodzić** [vi-MOH-jeech]) *v* To think intensely, and invent something <think up, fake up, cook up, dream up, cobble up, take it off the top of one's head, take it off the cuff, figure out, work out, tune in, plug in, tote up, wise up, get through one's head, get through someone's thick head, get into someone's thick head, see daylight, flash, dig, dawn on, have a brainwave, use one's head, rack one's brain, brainstorm, noodle around, percolate, perk, head trip, skull drag, eat, bug, burn a couple of braincells> eg *Cóżeś tam wymodził, co? (What did you think up, huh?)*

mogiła [moh-GEE-wah] *nf* An unfavorable situation; a disaster; dead end <curtains, lights out, end of the line, bad scene, bad news, can of worms, bag of worms, takedown, putdown, shit, serious shit, deep shit, deep water, drag, bind, bitch, bummer, downer, headache, double trouble, snafu, pain in the ass, pain in the neck, spot, mess, holy mess, pickle, squeeze, hard time, glitch, stinker> eg *Jak mnie złapią, to będzie mogiła (It's curtains for me if they find me)*

See syf

mój [MOO-ee] *nm* One's husband <hubby, man of the house, mister, old man, worser half> eg *Mój by tak nie zrobił, bo mnie szanuje (My man wouldn't do that, because he cares for me)*

moja [MOH-yah] *nf* One's wife <wifey, mama, missus, better half, old lady, little woman, ball and chain, trouble and strife, significant other> eg *Moja mnie zdradza (My old lady has been cheating on me)*

mokra robota [MOH-krah roh-BOH-tah] (or **brudna robota** [BROOD-nah roh-BOH-tah]) *nf phr* Murder; assassination <snuff, hit, chill, offing, wasting, icing, kiss-off, knock-off, rub-out, bump-off, wipe-out> eg *Kto jest odpowiedzialny za tę mokrą robotę? (Who's responsible for that rub-out?)*

mól See zalewać robaka

monopolowy [moh-noh-poh-LOH-vi] *nm* A liquor store <corn cellar, filling station> eg *Zatrzymajmy się przy monopolowym (Let's stop off at the filling station)*

mops See nudzić się jak mops

morda na kłódkę See ani pary z gęby

morda w kubeł See ani pary z gęby

morda* [MOHR-dah] (or **micha** [MEE-khah] or **maska** [MAHS-kah]) *nf* The face <kisser, puss, mug, map, phiz, mask, pan> eg *Masz syfa na mordzie (You got a zit on your mask); Chesz dostać w michę? (You want me to punch you in your phiz?)*
See ani pary z gęby, ciemno że w mordę daj, drzeć mordę, jak w pysk strzelił, padać

mordęga [mohr-DEHN-gah] *nf* Very hard work; a Herculean labor <ball-buster, bone-breaker, back-breaker, bitch, killer, grind, donkeywork, bullwork, dirty work> eg *Ale mordęga! (What a ball-breaker it is!)*

mordownia [mohr-DOHV-nyah] *nf* A cheap and disreputable saloon <joint, dive, gin dive, gin joint, gargle factory, groggery, guzzlery, watering hole, fillmill, hideaway, speakeasy> eg *Spędza wiele czasu w tej mordowni (He spends a lot of time at that joint)*

morze See kropelka

mosiek* [MOHSHEHK] *nm* A male Jewish <kike, Yid, mockie, sheeny, hooknose, eagle-beak, clipped dick, Jew boy, rabbi, Ike, Hebe, Hymie, Abe, Sammy, Goldberg> eg *W barze siedziało dwóch mośków w jarmułkach (Two Jew boys in yarmulkas were sitting in the bar)*

most See prosto z mostu

motać See mieszać

motor [MOH-tohr] *nm* An engine <muscle, power plant, power train, pot, horses, putt putt> eg *To cacko ma super motor pod maską (This baby's got a lot of muscle under the hood)*

motyka See rzucać się z motyką na słońce

motyw [MOH-tif] *nm* An scandalous, funny, or shocking fact, event, or situation; a scandal <spicy info, spicy poop, gas, skeleton, skeleton in the closet, sizzler, scorcher, dynamite, Watergate, fine kettle of fish, fine how do you do, fine cup of coffee, big stink> eg *To, co wam powiem, to lepszy motyw (The thing I'm going to tell you is a better skeleton)*

mowa See mowa-trawa, nie ma dupy, o wilku mowa

mowa-trawa [MOH-vah TRAH-vah] **1** *nf phr* (or **drętwa mowa** [DREHN-tfah MOH-vah]) Trivial, platitudinous or deceitful talk; nonsense <small talk, bullshit, BS, applesauce, baloney, blah-blah, crap, crock of shit, eyewash, hogwash, garbage, horseshit, hot air, jive, jazz, phony-baloney, piece of shit, pile of shit, poppycock, shit, smoke, gobbledygook, double-talk, hokum, horsefeathers,

hokum, bunk> eg *Za dużo już się nasłuchałem tej mowy-trawy (I've heard enough of that baloney)* **2** *excl phr* An exclamation of incredulity or disbelief <in a pig's eye, in a pig's ass, in a pig's ear, like hell, like fun, like shit, my ass, there's no way, someone will be damned if, someone will be fucked if, says you> eg *Powiedział, że nam pomoże. Mowa trawa, akurat nam pomoże! (He said he'd help us. My ass! Like hell he would help us!)*

mózg See paść komuś na mózg, robić komuś wodę z mózgu, taki że mózg staje

mózgowiec [mooz-GOH-vyehts] *nm* A very bright and intelligent person <brain, smart apple, whiz, whiz kid, wiz, wizard> eg *Ja wiedziałem, że on jeden to potrafi. To mózgowiec! (I knew he was the only one who could do that. He's a smart apple!)*

mózgownica [mooz-gohv-NEE-tsah] *nf* The head <think-box, think-tank, bean, noggin, conk, dome, gourd, skull> eg *Chcesz dostać w mózgownicę? (You want me to punch you on the bean?)*

See ruszyć głową

mrówka [MROOF-kah] *nf* A person who crosses the border several times a day, each time taking a small amount of merchandise (esp alcohol) instead of taking it as a whole, in order to evade paying the necessary tax; a smuggler <bootlegger, legger, runner, rum runner, monkey runner> eg *Mrówki przekraczają granicę nawet dziesięćrazy dziennie (Rum runners can cross the border even ten times a day)*

See jak mrówek

mrówkowiec [mroof-KOH-vyehts] *nm* A massive, concrete apartment building with cheap apartments for working class, common in former communist times <no slang equivalent> eg *Mieszka w tym mrówkowcu (She lives in this massive apartment building)*

mruk [MROOK] *nm* A morose, melancholic, or pessimistic person <killjoy, party-pooper, wet blanket, sourpuss, sourball, drag, turn-off, grinch, crape-hanger, gloomy Gus> eg *Nie bądź taka maruda! Zabaw się trochę! (Don't be such a wet blanket! Have some fun!)*

muł See młot

mućka See mećka

mucha See taki że mucha nie siada

multum [MOOL-toom] *adv* Plenty; many many <helluva lot, lotsa, lotta, oodles, scads, heaps, bags, barrels, loads, piles, tons, wads, jillions, zillions, enough to choke a horse, shitload, fuckload, truckload> eg *W zeszłym roku zarobił multum pieniędzy (Last year he earned lotsa money)*

mur beton [moor BEH-tohn] (or **jak mur beton** [yahk moor BEH-tohn] or **na mur beton** [nah moor BEH-tohn]) *adv phr* Certainly; surely <sure, fer sure, sure as hell, sure as shit, sure as can be, for real, indeedy, really truly, absitively, posilutely, real, cert, def, no buts about it, wired up, cinched, taped, racked, sewed up, iced, in the bag, tied up, nailed down> eg *Przyjdę tam. Na mur beton (I'll be there. For sure)*

murowany [moo-roh-VAH-ni] *adj* Sure; secured <sure, fer sure, sure as hell, sure as shit, sure as can be, for real, real, cert, def, wired up, cinched, taped, racked, sewed up, iced, in the bag, tied up, nailed down> eg *Ich sukces jest murowany (Their victory is sure as shit)*

murzyn See ciemno że w mordę daj

musowo [moo-SOH-voh] *adv* Certainly; surely <sure, fer sure, sure as hell, sure as shit, sure as can be, for real, indeedy, really truly, absitively, posilutely, real, cert, def, no buts about it, wired up, cinched, taped, racked, sewed up, iced, in the bag, tied up, nailed down> eg *Widziałem już ten film. Musowo (I've already seen this movie. For sure)*

muszka See brać kogoś pod lupę

musztarda po obiedzie [moosh-TAHR-dah poh oh-BYEH-jeh] *adv phr* (It is) Too late; post factum <it is gone, it is all over, too little too late, someone missed the boat, someone blew it, kiss that one goodbye> eg *Chciał to cofnąć, ale to już była musztarda po obiedzie (He wanted to take it back, but he already missed the boat)*

musztardówka [moosh-tahr-DOOF-kah] *nf* An empty mustard jar or a glass resembling one, used for drinking alcoholic beverages <no slang equivalent> eg *Podaj mi musztardówkę (Pass me the glass)*

muzyka See gra muzyka

mydło See szwarc mydło i powidło, włazić komuś do dupy, wyjść na czymś jak Zabłocki na mydle

mydlić komuś oczy [MID-leech KOH-moosh OH-chi] *v phr* To deceive or delude someone <pull the wool over someone's eyes, beat around the bush, play games, jerk someone around, dick someone around, pussyfoot around, snow, blow smoke, play cat and mouse with, play a cat and mouse game with> eg *Usiłował zamydlić im oczy i sprzedać jakieś świństwo (He tried to pull the wool over their eyes and sell them crap)*

mysz See jak mysz kościelna

myszka See bawić się w chowanego, kawał z brodą, szara myszka, widzieć białe myszki

N

na łebka [nah WEHP-kah] (or **od łebka** [ohd WEHP-kah] or **na łeb** [nah WEH] or **na twarz** [nah TFAHSH]) *adv phr* Per person <a head> eg *Wypada po sto dolarów na łepka (It comes down to a hundred dollars a head)*

na żywo [nah ZHI-voh] *phr* (With a performance or event) Being shown as it actually happens <live> eg *Mowa prezydenta była nadana na żywo (The President's speech was broadcast live)*

na aby-aby [nah AH-bi Ah-bi] *adv phr* Carelessly and cursorily, esp because of haste; haphazardly <half-assedly, half-heartedly, helter-skelter, hit-or-miss, hit-and-miss, harum-scarum, higgedly-piggedly, ramble-scramble, arsy-varsy, with a lick and a promise, slapdash, slapbang, skewgeely, scratching the surface> eg *Zmiatał podłogę na aby aby (He was mopping the floor half-assedly)*

na bakier See być na bakier

na bani See na gazie

na bank See bankowo

na barana [nah bah-RAH-nah] *phr* (Esp about a child) Riding on someone's back or shoulders <piggyback> eg *Uwielbiał jeździćna barana (He loved riding piggyback); Weź mnie na barana! (Give me a piggyback!)*

na boku See mieć kogoś na boku, robić coś na boku

na bosaka [nah boh-SAH-kah] *adv phr* Barefoot <no slang equivalent> eg *Poszliśmy tam na bosaka (We went there barefoot)*

na bruk See iść na zieloną trawkę, posłać na zieloną trawkę

na całego [nah tsah-WEH-goh] (or **na całą parę** [nah TSAH-woh PAH-reh] or **na pełną parę** [nah PEH-oo-noh PAH-reh] or **na cały regulator** [nah TSAH-wi reh-goo-LAH-tor]) *adv phr* Truly; fully; to an extreme degree <sure, fer sure, sure as hell, sure as shit, sure as can be, for real, indeedy, really truly, absitively, posilutely, real, cert, def, no buts about it, flat-out, all-out, all the way, like hell, like all get-out, like sin, to beat the band, like all creation, to the max, as blazes, as can be, as hell, like hell, in full swing> eg *Zima jest na całego (The winter has come for real)*

na chodzie [nah KHOH-jeh] *adj phr* **1** (Of mechanical appliances) Functioning or operating <in running order, working, running, perking, ticking, clicking, humming, cooking> eg *Czy ten magnetofon jest na chodzie? (Is this tape recorder in running order?)* **2** (Esp about older people) Healthy, active, or physically fit <alive and kicking, fit as a fiddle, up to snuff, up to the mark, wrapped tight, in fine feather, in fine whack, in the pink, sound as a dollar, right as rain, full of piss and vinegar, full of beans> eg *Dziadek ma 70 lat, ale trzyma się (Grandfather is 70, but he's still fit as a fiddle)*

na cholerę [nah khoh-LEH-reh] or (**po cholerę** [poh khoh-LEH-reh] or **po jaką cholerę** [poh YAH-koh khoh-LEH-reh] *excl phr* An angry and surprised exclamation elaborating "Why?" <why the fuck, why in the fuck, why in fuck, why the hell, why in the hell, why in hell, why in fucking hell, why in the fucking hell, why in fuck's name, why in the fuck's name, why the heck, why in the heck, why in heck, why the devil, why in the devil, why in devil> eg *Po jaką cholerę marnuję czas z tymi dwoma głupkami? (Why the hell am I wasting my time with these two fools?)*

na chorobowym [nah khoh-roh-BOH-vim] *adj phr* Spending time away from a job during illness <off sick, on a sick leave> eg *Jestem na chorobowym od tygodnia (I've been on sick leave for a week)*

na chuj** [nah KHOO-ee] or **na chuja**** [nah KHOO-yah] or **po chuj**** [poh KHOO-ee] or **po chuja**** [poh KHOO-yah] or **po jakiego chuja**** [poh yah-KYEH-goh KHOO-yah] or **po kiego chuja**** [poh KYEH-goh KHOO-yah] *excl phr* An angry and surprised exclamation elaborating "Why?" <why the fuck, why in the fuck, why in fuck, why the hell, why in the hell, why in hell, why in fucking hell, why in the fucking hell, why in fuck's name, why in the fuck's name, why the heck, why in the heck, why in heck, why the devil, why in the devil, why in devil> eg *Na chuja za niego wychodziłaś? (Why the fuck did you marry him?)*

na chuja See móc komuś skoczyć

na chybił trafił [nah KHI-bee-oo TRAH-fee-oo] *adv phr* Carelessly, unplannedly, cursorily, esp because of haste; haphazardly <hit-or-miss, hit-and-miss, half-assedly, half-heartedly, slapdash, slapbang, helter-skelter, harum-scarum, higgedly-piggedly, ramble-scramble, arsy-varsy, skewgeely> eg *Nie wiedziała, który* *to był dom, więc zaczęla dzwonić do drzwi na chybił trafił (She didn't know which house it was, so he began ringing doorbells hit-or-miss)*

na cudzesa See na sępa

na cyku See na gazie

na czarną godzinę [nah CHAHR-noh goh-JEE-neh] *adv phr* For later use, esp during hard times <for a rainy day, for later, for the darkest hour> eg *Każdego dnia odkładał trochę pieniędzy na czarną godzinę (Each week she saved a little money for the darkest hour)*

na czarno See pracować na czarno

na czysto See na rękę, wyjść na czysto

na diabła [nah DYAHB-wah] (or **po diabła** [poh DYAHB-wah] or **po jakiego diabła** [poh yah-KYEH-goh DYAHB-wah] or **po kiego diabła** [poh KYEH-goh DYAHB-wah]; **czorta** [CHOHR-tah] may replace **diabła**; or **po jakiego grzyba** [poh yah-KYEH-goh GZHI-bah] or **po jakie licho** [poh YAH-kyeh LEE-khoh]) *excl phr* An angry and surprised exclamation elaborating "Why?" <why the fuck, why in the fuck, why in fuck, why the hell, why in the hell, why in hell, why in fucking hell, why in the fucking hell, why in fuck's name, why in the fuck's name, why the heck, why in the heck, why in heck, why the devil, why in the devil, why in devil> eg *Na diabła za niego wychodziłaś? (Why the heck did you marry him?)*

na dniach [nah DNYAHKH] *adv phr* In the next few days; in a short time; very soon <by and by, in a short, short short, down the line, come Sunday, coming down the pike, any day now, knocking on the front door> eg *Ciotka ma przyjechać na dniach (Aunt should be arriving any day now)*

na dokładkę [nah doh-KWAHT-keh] *adv phr* To further worsen the situation <to make it worse, to make things worse> eg *No więc rzuciła go. Na dokładkę nie zapłaciła nawet rachunków za telefon (So she dumped him. To make it worse, she didn't even pay the phone bills)*

na dupie See leżeć bykiem

na dwoje babka wróżyła [nah DVOH-yeh BAHP-kah vroo-ZHI-wah] *adv phr* Not certain; risky <chancy, iffy, dicey, rocky, touchy, up for grabs, touch and go, on a wing and a prayer, on slippery ground, on thin ice, fat chance> eg *Nie wiem, czy wybierze naszą propozycję. Na dwoje babka wróżyła (I don't know if he chhoses our proposal. It's iffy)*

na dzień dobry See na wejściu

na fali See na topie

na fleku See na gazie

na ful [nah FOOL] *adv phr* To an extreme degree; unrestrainedly <to the max, flat-out, all-out, all the way, like hell, like all get-out, like sin, to beat the band, like all creation, like it had gone out of style, like there was no tomorrow, like nobody's business, one's ass off, one's brains out, one's head off, the whole nine yards, nine to the dozen> eg *Mój wóz wyciąga stówę na ful (My car does a hundred flat-out)*

na głodniaka [nah gwohd-NYAH-kah] *adv phr* Being hungry <dog-hungry, having a tapeworm, having munchies, starving, starving to death, on empty stomach> eg *Nie pojedziemy tam chyba na głodniaka, co? (We're not going there dog-hungry, are we?)*

na garnuszku See być na czyimś garnuszku

na gazie [nah GAH-zhyeh] (or **pod gazem** [pohd GAH-zehm] or **na bani** [nah BAH-nee] or **na cyku** [nah TSI-koo] or **na fleku** [nah FLEH-koo]) *adj phr* Drunk; alcohol intoxicated <alkied, bagged, blitzed, blotto, blown away, bent, boiled, bombed, blasted, boozed, bottled, boxed, buzzed, canned, clobbered, cooked, corked, crashed, drunk as a skunk, edged, embalmed, fractured, fried, gassed, ginned, grogged, have one too many, half under, high, hooched up, in bad shape, impaired, illuminated, juiced, knocked out, liquored, lit, loaded, looped, lubricated, lushed, smashed, oiled, pickled, plastered, plonked, polluted, sauced, shitfaced, slugged, sloshed, soaked, stewed, stiff, stinking drunk, swizzled, tanked, three sheets to the wind, wiped, zonked> eg *Były na fleku, ale to nam tylko ułatwiało sprawę (They were loaded but it only helped us); Tylko mi nie mów, że facet znów jest na gazie! (Don't tell me that the guy's juiced again!)*

na glanc [nah GLAHNTS] *adv phr* Very clean or shiny <slick, spick-and-span, policed up, straightened up, spruced up, apple pie, neat as a pin, neat as a button> eg *Lubię, jak wszystko dookoła jest na glanc (I love to have everything around me spick-and-span)*

na glempa* [nah GLEHM-pah] *adv phr* With a male partner in a sex act lying over the female partner between her spread legs <in the missionary way, in the missionary position, in the missionary style, Kentucky straight> eg *Nie podobało im się robienie tego na glempa (They didn't like doing it in the missionary position)*

na gorąco See na poczekaniu

na gwałt [nah GVAH-oot] *adv phr* Immediately or badly (needed) <pretty damn quick, PDQ, ASAP, on the spot, on the double, double time, double clutching, like a shot, in half a mo, like now, before you know it, before you can say Jack Robinson, in a jiffy, in a flash, in half a shake, right off the bat, like a bat out of hell, like a shot out of hell, hubba-hubba, horseback, like greased lightning> eg *Sekretarka jest nam potrzebna. Na gwałt (We need a secretary. Pretty damn quick)*

na haju [nah KHAH-yoo] *adj phr* Intoxicated with drugs or alcohol; in a state of euphoria caused by drugs or alcohol <high, stoned, doped up, blown away, canned, cooked, corked, fried, gassed, in bad shape, impaired, illuminated, knocked out, lit, loaded, looped, pickled, polluted, shitfaced, stewed, wiped, zonked> eg *Widziałem ich na bulwarze; wszyscy byli na chaju (I saw them on the boardwalk; they were all high)*

na jednej nodze [YEH-khahch nah YEHD-neh-ee NOH-dzeh] *adv phr* **1** (Going somewhere) immediately; very quickly <pretty damn quick, PDQ, ASAP, on the spot, on the double, double time, double clutching, like a shot, in half a mo, like now, before you know it, before you can say Jack Robinson, in a jiffy, in a flash, in half a shake, right off the bat, like a bat out of hell, like a shot out of hell, hubba-hubba, horseback, like greased lightning> eg *Biegnij tam szybko, na jednej nodze! (Run over there quick, on the double!)* **2** Traveling in a tightly crowded means of public transportation <packed, jammed, jam-packed, packed like sardines, full up, up to the hilt, with not enough room to swing a cat> eg *Jechaliśmy tam na jednej nodze, taki był tłok (We were going there jam-packed, it was so crowded)*

na jedno kopyto [nah YEHD-noh koh-PI-toh] *adv phr* Identically and monotously, because done strictly according to a hakcneyed pattern; commonplace <to the same beat, lamely, flat, flat as a pancake, dull as dishwater, ho-hum, hum-drum,

dullsville, deadsville, dragsville, square, beige, blah, yawny, dragass, draggy> eg *Oni zawsze grają na jedno kopyto (They always play to the same beat)*

na jedno wychodzić [nah JEHD-noh vi-KHOH-jeech] *v phr* To make no difference <make no diff, be all the same, be same old shit, be same difference, no matter how you slice it, make no never mind, be no big deal> eg *Mamy go posłać na emeryturę czy wyrzucić? Na jedno wychodzi (Are we going to get him retired or to fire him? It's all the same)*

na jeźdźca* [nah YEHSHCH-tsah] *adv phr* With a female partner in a sex act sitting on a male partner <woman-on-top, bouncy-bouncy, horse-riding> eg *Lubi, gdy ona robi to z nim na jeźdźca (He likes her to play horse-riding)*

na języki See brać kogoś na języki

na kacu [nah KAH-tsoo] *adj phr* Suffering from a hangover <hanging, hung, with morning after, with big head> eg *Nie mieszaj piwa z whiskey. Przecież nie chcesz być jutro na kacu (Don't mix beer and whiskey. You don't want to be hanging tomorrow)*

na karku [nah KAHR-koo] *adv phr* (Esp of a busy and difficult period or event, coming) Very soon; in a short time <around the corner, in the blink of an eye, by and by, in a short, short short, down the line, come Sunday, coming down the pike, any day now, knocking on the front door> eg *Nie czekajmy z robotą, bo zima na karku (Let's not wait with the job, because winter will be here in the blink of an eye)* See mieć łeb

na końcu języka See mieć coś na końcu języka

na kość See przemarznąć na kość

na kopy [nah KOH-pi] (or **na pęczki** [nah PEHNCH-kee]) *adv phr* In surplus; in large numbers <dime a dozen, growing on trees> eg *Myśli, że dobrych posad jest na kopy (He thinks that good jobs are a dime a dozen)*

na krechę [nah KREH-kheh] *adv phr* On credit <on the cuff, on the finger, on the arm, on the bill, on the count, on tick> eg *Dostał butelkę whiskey na krechę (He got a bottle of whiskey on the cuff)*

na krzyż [NAH kshish] *adv phr* Just a few; only <is all> eg *Nasze miasteczko miało tylko trzy chałupy na krzyż (Our little town had only three houses, is all)*

na krzywy ryj See na sępa

na kuroniówce [nah koo-roh-NYOOF-tseh] *adj phr* Unemployed and getting unemployment compensation <on comp, laid off, on layoff, on the bench, on the shelf, on the beach, on the dole, on the turf, out of the rat race> eg *On nie pożyczy ci żadnych pieniędzy. Jest na kuroniówce (He won't lend you any money. He's on the lay off); Jestem na kuroniówce (I'm on comp)*

na kwaśne jabłko See zbić kogoś na kwaśne jabłko

na lekarstwo See jak na lekarstwo

na lewo [nah LEH-voh] *adv phr* Dishonestly and esp secretly or inconspicuously <under the table, underhand, on the side, on the quiet, on the QT, on the sly, in a hole-and-corner way, in holes and corners, under one's hat, under wraps, soft-pedaled, hush-hush> eg *A nie możesz to mnie zdobyć na lewo? (Can't you get it for me on the side?)*

na luzie [nah LOO-zhyeh] *adj* Relaxed; effortless; loosened up; without inhibitions <laid-back, mellow, cool, cooled out, easy-going, loose> eg *Trzeba być na luzie, żeby dobrze zdać ten egzamin (You have to be laid back to pass this exam)*

na Magadaskar [nah mah-dah-GAHS-kahr] *phr* (An exclamation used to show opposition and dislike) We do not want someone <down with, to hell with, fuck someone, screw someone, nuke someone, give someone the chair> eg *Ludzie krzyczeli: komuniści na Madagaskar! (The people shouted: Down with communists!)*

na maks [nah MAHKS] (or **na maksa** [na MAHK-sah] or **na potęgę** [nah poh-TEHN-geh]) *adv phr* To an extreme degree; unrestrainedly <to the max, flat-out, all-out, all the way, like hell, like all get-out, like sin, to beat the band, like all creation, like it had gone out of style, like there was no tomorrow, like nobody's business, one's ass off, one's brains out, one's head off, the whole nine yards, nine to the dozen> eg *Impezowaliśmy na maks (We partied to the max)*

na medal [nah MEH-dahl] (or **na piątkę** [nah PYOHNT-keh] or **na sto dwa** [na stoh-DVAH]) *adj phr* Excellently; superbly; wonderfully <great, cool, swell, fab, rad, def, far-out, awesome, frantic, terrific, funky, gorgeous, groovy, hellacious, neat, peachy, dandy, baddest, mean, solid, super-dooper, wailing, wicked, gnarly, top-notch, ten, ace-high, A-OK, A-1, some> eg *Silnik pracuje na medal (The engine's working top-notch)*; *Ten program pracuje na sto dwa (This program's working A-1)*

na minusie See być na minusie

na mur beton See mur beton

na odwal [nyeh-ZYEHM-skoh] *adv phr* Carelessly and cursorily, esp because of haste; haphazardly <half-assedly, half-heartedly, helter-skelter, hit-or-miss, hit-and-miss, harum-scarum, higgedly-piggedly, ramble-scramble, arsy-varsy, with a lick and a promise, slapdash, slapbang, skewgeely, scratching the surface> eg *Ciężko dzisiaj o dobrą sprzątaczkę. Większość sprząta na odwal (It's hard to get a good cleaning woman today. Most of them clean with a lick and a promise)*

na oko [nah OH-koh] *adv phr* About; approximately <around, in the ballpark of, pretty near, something like, close shave, in the neighborhood of, damn near, pretty near> eg *Zapłacił na oko dwa tysiące (He paid two thousand or something like that)*

na okrągło [nah oh-KROHNG-woh] *adv phr* At all times; all the time; constantly <around the clock, day and night, forever and a day> eg *Nowy sklep otwarty jest na okrągło (The new store is open around the clock)*

na świeczniku See na topie

na pałę See obcięty na jeża

na pełną parę See na całego

na pęczki See na kopy

na perłowo See zrobić kogoś na szaro

na piątkę See na medal

na pierwszy ogień [nah PYEHR-fshi OH-ghyeñ] *adv phr* Coming first; as a beginning; as a first move or suggestion <first off, for starters, for openers, from out front, from the top, from scratch> eg *Co idzie na pierwszy ogień? (What's coming for starters?)*

na pieska* [nah PYEHS-kah] *phr* With a male partner in a sex act entering the other partner from the rear <dog fashion, dog style, dog ways, doggie fashion, doggie style, doggie ways> eg *Robili to na pieska, żeby jednocześnie mogli oglądać telewizję (They did it dog style, so they could both watch television)*

na plusie See być na plusie

na pniu [nah PNYOO] *phr* (Of selling or buying) Immediately; instantly <pretty damn quick, PDQ, ASAP, on the spot, on the double, like a shot, in half a mo, like now, before you know it, before you can say Jack Robinson, in a jiffy, in a flash, right off the bat> eg *Chcieli kupić całą kolekcję na pniu (They wanted to buy the whole collection right off the bat)*

na pół gwizdka [nah poow GWEEST-kah] *adv phr* Carelessly and cursorily <half-assedly, half-heartedly, helter-skelter, hit-or-miss, hit-and-miss, harum-scarum, higgedly-piggedly, ramble-scramble, arsy-varsy, with a lick and a promise, slapdash, slapbang, skewgeely, scratching the surface> eg *Ciężko dzisiaj o dobrą sprzątaczkę. Większość sprząta na pół gwizdka (It's hard to get a good cleaning woman today. Most of them clean with a lick and a promise)*

na poczekaniu [nah poh-cheh-KAH-nyoo] (or **na gorąco** [nah goh-ROHN-tsoh]) *adv phr* At once; immediately; instantly; without any preparation <right off, right away, pretty damn quick, PDQ, ASAP, on the spot, in half a mo, like now, in a jiffy, in a flash, in half a shake, right off the bat, like a bat out of hell, like a shot out of hell, hubba-hubba, horseback, like greased lightning, before you know it, before you can say Jack Robinson> eg *Facet rozebrał się na poczekaniu (The guy stripped off before you knew it)*

na potęgę See na maks

na prawo i lewo See dawać

na prochach [nah PROH-khahkh] (or **na czymś** [nah chimsh]) *phr* Intoxicated with narcotics; drugged <high, doped, junked, tripped out, on a trip, on the stuff, on a rush, spaced out, stoned, zoned, tripping, stoning> eg *Lepiej zostaw ją w spokoju. Znów jest na prochach i zachowuje się agresywnie (You'd better leave her alone. She's doped again and she's aggressive); Czy on jest na czymś, czy jak? Czemu się tak zachowuje? (Is he high or what? Why is he acting like this?)*

na raka* [nah RAH-kah] *adv phr* With two partners engaging in a simultaneous oral sex in reciprocally inverse positions <sixty-nine> eg *Robili to zwykle na raka (They usually did it sixty-nine)*

na rauszu [nah RAH-oo-shoo] *adj phr* Experiencing the initial euphoric effects of drinking alcohol <high, buzzed, buzzing, happy, kicked> eg *Wrócili z żoną z przyjęcia na lekkim rauszu (They came back from the party a little buzzed)*

na rękę [nah REHN-keh] (or **do ręki** [doh REHN-kee] or **na czysto** [VI-eeshch nah CHIS-toh]) *adv phr* (Of an amount of money) When nothing further is to be subtracted; of a pure profit; net <cool, clean, in the clear, net, payoff, velvet, gravy, up front> eg *Zarobiliśmy 5 000 na czysto (We made a clean 5,000); Ile dostanę na rękę? (How much will I get in the clear?)*

na resorach See- bajka

na sępa [nah SEHM-pah] (or **na cudzesa** [nah tsoo-DZEH-sah] or **na krzywy ryj*** [nah KSHI-vi RI-ee]) *adv phr* (Acquired) free of charge, esp by begging; parasitically <freebie, free-o, free gratis, free lunch, freeloading, mooching, bogarting, scrounging, bumming> eg *Chciał dostać piwo na cudzesa (He wanted to get the beer free gratis)*

na spytki See brać kogoś na języki

na sto dwa See na medal

na stół See iść pod nóż

na stojaka* [nah stoh-YAH-kah] *adv phr* With both partners standing in a sex act <stand-up fuck> eg *Woli robić to na stojaka (She prefers stand-up fucks)*

na stopa See stopem

na sucho [nah SOO-khoh] (or **o suchym pysku** [oh SOO-khim PIS-koo]) *adv phr* Not drinking alcohol <on the wagon, off the booze, off the sauce, off the juice> eg *Gdzie jest wóda? Co my tak na sucho? (Where's the booze? Are we on the wagon or what?)* See ujść na sucho

na swoim [nah SFOH-eem] *adv phr* In one's house or in the familiar neighborhood <on one's own, on one's own ass, on one's own hook> eg *Od dziesięciu lat jest na swoim (He's been on his own for ten years)*

na szaro See zrobić kogoś na szaro

na szpilkach See jak na szpilkach

na tapecie *adj phr* On the agenda; to be dealt with or discussed <on the lineup, on the setup, on the spotlight, in the making, in the working> eg *Co dziś jest na tapecie? (What's on the lineup for today?)*

na topie [nah TOH-pyeh] (or **na fali** [nah FAH-lee]) *adj phr* **1** Popular, trendy, or influential <hot, hip, trendy, in, newie, latest thing, latest wrinkle, last word, in-thing, the thing, go-go, hip> eg *Czy dzwony są teraz na topie? (Are bottoms hip nowadays?)* **2** (or **na świeczniku** [nah shfyehch-NEE-koo]) In the center of attention; important or popular, esp occupying a prominent position in a social hierarchy <in the limelight, in the big league, in the major league, high profile> eg *Zawsze był na topie (He's always been in the limelight)*

na twarz See na łebka

na umór See pić na umór

na własną rękę [nah VWAHS-noh REHN-keh] *adv phr* Single-handedly; independently; unaided; at your own expense <solo, on one's own, on one's own ass, on one's own hook, on one's own sweet way, paddling one's own canoe, off one's own bat> eg *Jeśli chcesz tam iść, musisz to zrobić na własną rękę. Ja zostaję tutaj (If you want to go there, you have to go solo. I'm staying here)*

na waleta [nah vah-LEH-tah] *adv phr* Entirely naked <bare-assed, BA, buck naked, in one's birthday suit, in the altogether, in the raw, naked as a jaybird> eg *Poszliśmy tam na waleta (We went there bare-assed)*

na wejściu [nah VEH-eesh-chyoo] (or **na dzień dobry** [nah jehñ DOH-bri]) *adv phr* As a beginning; as a first move or suggestion; initial <first off, for starters, for openers, from out front, from the top, from scratch> eg *Ona mu na wejściu strzeliła w mordę (For starters, she hit him on his mug)*

na wylot See znać coś/kogoś na wylot

na zaś [na ZAHSH] *adv phr* Prematurely <just yet> eg *Nie ciesz się na zaś. Nasze zwycięstwo nie jest jeszcze pewne (Don't be happy just yet, because we can still lose)*

na zapałkę See obcięty na jeża

na zawołanie [nah zah-voh-WAH-nyeh] *adv phr* Ready to obey someone <at one's beck and call, at the snap of one's fingers> eg *He loves to have his employees at his beck and call (Lubi mieć swoich pracowników na zawołanie)*

na zbyciu See mieć coś na zbyciu

na zero See wyjść na czysto

na zicher [nah ZEE-khehr] (or **na zycher** [nah ZI-khehr]) *adv phr* Certainly; surely <sure, fer sure, sure as hell, sure as shit, sure as can be, for real, indeedy,

really truly, absitively, posilutely, real, cert, def, no buts about it, wired up, cinched, taped, racked, sewed up, iced, in the bag, tied up, nailed down> eg *Przyjdę tam. Na zicher (I'll be there. For sure)*

na zieloną trawkę See iść na zieloną trawkę

naładować akumulatory [nah-wah-DOH-vahch ah-koo-moo-lah-TOH-ri] *v phr* To regain strength, energy, or vitality <recharge someone's batteries, charge up, juice up> eg *Potrzebuję wakacji, żeby naładować akumulatory (I need a vacation to recharge my batteries)*

nałóg [NAH-wook] *nm* A heavy drinker; an alcoholic <lush, bar-fly, alky, boozehound, boozer, bottle baby, dipso, elbow bender, ginhead, juicehead, loadie, sponge, soak, wino> eg *Ten nałóg chciał trochę pieniędzy na piwo (That juicehead wanted some money for the beer)*

nałykać się Perf łykać

nażreć się See nawpierdalać się

naćpać się Perf ćpać

naćpany [nah-CHPAH-ni] *adj* Intoxicated with narcotics; drugged <high, doped, junked, tripped out, on a trip, on the stuff, on a rush, spaced out, stoned, zoned, tripping, stoning> eg *No nie, znów jest naćpany! (Oh no, he's doped again!)*

nabazgrać Perf bazgrać

nabazgrolić Perf nabazgrolić

nabić kogoś w butelkę [NAH-beech KOH-gohsh v boo-TEHL-keh] *v phr* To deceive someone, esp with smooth persuasion; to mislead <con, rip off, shaft, roll, chisel, gyp, scam, screw, stiff, fleece, dick, do in, take in, do a number on, flim-flam, bamboozle, run a number on, take someone for a ride, take someone to the cleaners, throw someone a curve, pull a fast one, fuck over, screw over, angle, take in, snow, do a snow job, double-shuffle, fast-shuffle, flimflam, give a bun steer, give someone a line, have someone on, lead someone down the garden path, do a snow job, jerk someone's chain, pull someone's chain, pull one's leg, pull someone's string, pull the wool over someone's eyes, put someone on, snow, use smoke and mirrors> eg *Ten handlarz naprawdę nabił cię w butelkę (That salesman really dicked you)*

nabierać [nah-BYEH-rahch] (perf **nabrać** [NAH-brahch]) *v* To deceive someone, esp with smooth persuasion; to mislead <con, rip off, shaft, roll, chisel, gyp, scam, screw, stiff, fleece, dick, do in, take in, do a number on, flim-flam, bamboozle, run a number on, take someone for a ride, take someone to the cleaners, throw someone a curve, pull a fast one, fuck over, screw over, angle, take in, snow, do a snow job, double-shuffle, fast-shuffle, flimflam, give a bun steer, give someone a line, have someone on, lead someone down the garden path, do a snow job, jerk someone's chain, pull someone's chain, pull one's leg, pull someone's string, pull the wool over someone's eyes, put someone on, snow, use smoke and mirrors> eg *Ten handlarz naprawdę cię nabrał (That salesman really dicked you)*

nabijać kabzę [nah-BEE-yahch KAHB-zeh] *v phr* To get rich; to make a lot of money <pull down, pick up, clean up, cash in, make a bundle, ride the gravy train> eg *Nabił kabzę na dostawach dla wojska (He made a bundle on deliveries for the army)*

nabijać się [nah-BEE-yahch shyeh] *v* To fool someone, esp by pretending; to tease; to treat someone unseriously and frivolously <put someone on, pull someone's

leg, pull someone's string, give someone a leg, have someone on, jack someone around, jerk someone around, poke fun at, kid someone around, fool someone around, jack someone's chain, spoof, cut down> eg *To nie może być prawda. Nabijasz się ze mnie (This can't be true. You're kidding me)*

nabożnisia [nah-boh-ZHNEE-shah] *nf* A overly pious woman; a devout <knee bender, Jesus freak, goody-goody, goody, tight-ass, Mother Theresa> eg *Twoja siostra to prawdziwa nabożnisia. Chodzi codziennie do kościoła (Your sister is a real knee bender. She goes to church everyday)*

nabrać się [NAH-brahch shyeh] (or **dać się nabrać** [dahch shyeh NAH-brahch] or **naciąć się** [NAH-chyohnch shyeh]) *v* To become fooled, deceived, or misled, esp with smooth persuasion <get taken in, be given a bum steer, be given a line, get conned, get ripped off, get shafted, get rolled, get chiseled, get gypped, get scammed, get screwed, get stiffed, get fleeced, get dicked, get flim-flammed, get bamboozled, be taken for a ride, be taken to the cleaners, get fucked over, get screwed over, get angled> eg *Myślałem, że to prawdziwa kamera. Dałem się nabrać (I thought it was a real camera. I got taken in)*

nabrać wody w usta [NAH-brahch VOH-di v OOS-tah] *v phr* To refrain from comment or action, and thus avoid responsibility <button one's lip, zip one's lip, button up, clam up, dummy up, wash one's hands of> eg *Minister ponownie nabrał wody w usta (The minister buttoned his lip again)*

nabujać Perf bujać

nabuzowany See narąbany

nabździć Perf bździć

nachachmęcić Perf chachmęcić

nachapać Perf chapać

nachlać się Perf chlać

nachlany See schlany

naciągać [nah-CHYOHN-gahch] (perf **naciągnąć** [nah-CHYOHNG-nohnch]) *v* **1** To induce or persuade someone, esp by flattery and endearments; to wheedle something out of someone <sweet-talk, soft-soap, twist one's arm, goose, jawbone, talk into, hook into, sponge, mooch, scrounge, milk> eg *Naciągnęli go, żeby finansował ich kampanię (They goosed him to finance their campaign); Wykorzystałaś tę okazję, żeby mnie naciągnąć (You used this opportunity to twist my arm)* **2** To cheat; swindle; deceive <con, rip off, shaft, roll, chisel, gyp, scam, screw, stiff, fleece, dick, do in, take in, do a number on, flim-flam, bamboozle, run a number on, take someone for a ride, take someone to the cleaners, throw someone a curve, pull a fast one, fuck over, screw over, angle, take in, snow, do a snow job, double-shuffle, fast-shuffle, flimflam, give a bun steer, give someone a line, have someone on, lead someone down the garden path, do a snow job, jerk someone's chain, pull someone's chain, pull one's leg, pull someone's string, pull the wool over someone's eyes, put someone on, snow, use smoke and mirrors> eg *Ten handlarz naciągnął mnie na dwie stówy (That salesman dicked me for two hundred)* **3** (or **naginać** [nah-GEE-nahch]; perf **nagiąć** [NAH-gyohnch]) To interpret something, such as a rule, flexibly and with great latitude; to operate on the fringe of law; to use semi-legal means <bend the rules, stretch the rules, stretch, stretch a point, stretch the point, bend, shade, sneak, slick, shift, phony, crook. play

dirtyeg *Naciąganiem było twierdzenie, że wszyscy zostali zaproszeni (To say that everybody was invited was stretching the point)*

naciągany [nah-chyohn-GAH-ni] *adj* False, unreliable, untrustworthy, or far-fetched <stretched, bent, shady, fishy, sneaky, shifty, fly-by-night, bogus, phony, lame, crooked, true as one can swing a cat, true as one can throw an elephant, not kosher> eg *Myślę, że ich alibi jest naciągane (I think their alibis are phony)*

nad uchem See biadolić

nadawać na tej samej fali See być na tej samej fali

nadęcie [nah-DEHN-chyeh] *adj* Conceitedness; haughtiness; self-importance or self-impression <ego-tripping, swell-headedness, big-headedness, high-nosedness, hot air> eg *Nie znoszę jego nadęcia (I hate his ego-tripping)*

nadepnąć komuś na odcisk [nah-DEHP-nohnch KOH-moosh nah OHT-cheesk] (or **nastąpić komuś na odcisk** [nah-STOHM-peech KOH-moosh nah OHT-cheesk]) *v phr* To bother, irritate, or offend someone <get under someone's skin, get on someone's nerves, push someone's button, step on someone's toes, tread on someone's toes, get down on someone, get in one's face, get on someone's back, get on someone's case, give someone the needle> eg *Nadepnął komuś na odcisk podczas ostatniej kampanii i przegrał wybory (He tread on someone's toes during the last campaign and lost the election)*

nadęty [nah-DEHN-ti] *adj* Conceited, haughty, or self-impressed <stuck-up, puffed-up, high-hat, ego-tripping, swelled-up, swell-headed, big-headed, high-nosed, blown-up, stuck on oneself, chesty, stuffy, gassy, windy, hatty, hinkty, uppity, biggety, windbag, blowhard, high on oneself, high and mighty> eg *Nowy dyrektor Instytutu to nadęty głupiec (The new director of the Institute is a stuck-up fool)*

nadmuchać See móc komuś skoczyć

nadojeść See przejeść się

nadstawiać karku [naht-STAH-vyahch KAHR-koo] (or **nadstawiać głowę** [naht-STAH-vyahch GWOH-veh] or **nadstawiać tyłek** [naht-STAH-vyahch TI-wehk]) *v phr* To put oneself at risk, esp for someone <risk one's neck, stick one's neck out, put one's ass on the line, stretch one's luck, go out on a limb, chance it, lead with one's chin> eg *Nie mam zamiaru nadstawiać za Ciebie karku (I'm not about to risk my neck for you)*

nadymać się [nah-DI-mahch shyeh] (perf **nadąć się** [NAH-dohnch shyeh] *v* To be conceited, haughty, or self-impressed <think one's shit doesn't stink, be too big for someone's shoes, ego-trip, be high on oneself, be high and mighty> eg *Młodzi biznesmeni przechwalali się i nadymali (Young businessmen were showing off and ego-tripping)*

nadziany [nah-JAH-ni] (or **dziany** [JAH-ni]) *adj* Very rich; affluent <loaded, flush, filthy rich, stinking rich, dirt richy, lousy rich, in the bucks, in the dough, in the money, rolling in it, made of money> eg *Chciałby być dziany do końca swego życia (He'd like to be stinking rich for the rest of his life)*

nafaszerować się Perf faszerować się

nagła krew kogoś zalewa See krew kogoś zalewa

naganiacz [nag-GAH-nyahch] *nm* The penis, esp large <cock, prick, dick, stick, joystick, dipstick, bone, meat, beef, wang, yang, dong, dummy, hammer, horn, hose, jock, joint, knob, pork, putz, rod, root, tool, flute, skin flute, love-muscle, sausage, schmuck, schlong, schvantz, cream-stick, third leg, middle leg, business,

apparatus, John, Johnny, Johnson, John Thomas, Jones> eg *Ociągnęła ci naganiacza? (Did she put some lipstick on your dipstick?)*

nagazowany See narąbany

nagiąć Perf naginać

naginać See naciągać

nagonka [nah-GOHN-kah] *nf* An attempt to remove from power or from membership of people whose political opinions are disapproved of or regarded as dangerous <wich-hunt> eg *Poprowadził nagonkę przeciw ludziom podejrzanym o komunizm (He led a witch-hunt against people suspected of being communists)*

nagrane See mieć coś nagrane

nagryzdać Perf gryzdać

nagryzmolić Perf gryzmolić

nagrzany [nah-GZHAH-ni] (or **napalony** [nah-pah-LOH-ni]) *adj* Sexually excited and desirous <turned-on, horny, hot, hot-assed, hot pants, hot to trot, on fire, steamed> eg *Ta dupka jest cholernie nagrzana (The chcik is so goddam hot); Byłam równie napalona, jak on (I was equally horn as he was)*

nagwizdać See móc komuś skoczyć

nahafcić See hafcić

nahaftać See haftać

nahaftować Perf haftować

naharować się Perf harować

naindyczyć się Perf indyczyć się

naiwniaczka [nah-eev-NYAHCH-kah] *nf* A naive and easily victimized woman; a dupe <sucker, patsy, easy mark, mark, fall guy, pushover, schnook, sitting duck, goat, babe in the woods> eg *Wziął mnie za jakąś naiwniaczkę, kretyn jeden (What a jerk! He took me for a sucker)*

naiwniak [nah-EEV-nyahk] (or **naiwniaczek** [nah-eev-NYAH-chehk]) *nm* A naive and easily victimized man; a dupe <sucker, patsy, easy mark, mark, fall guy, pushover, schnook, sitting duck, goat, babe in the woods> eg *Nie jestem naiwniakiem, znam moje prawa (I'm not a babe in the woods, I know my rights)*

naj [NAH-ee] *adv* Superior; superb; excellent <classy, high-class, great, cool, swell, fab, rad, def, far-out, awesome, frantic, terrific, funky, gorgeous, groovy, hellacious, neat, peachy, dandy, baddest, mean, solid, super-dooper, wailing, wicked, gnarly, top-notch, ten, ace-high, A-OK, A-1, some> eg *Wszystko w tym domu było naj (Everything in this house was top-notch)*

najebać się See napierdolić się

najebany See narąbany

najeść się strachu [NAH-yehshch shyeh STRAH-khoo] *v phr* To become afraid; to become frightened; to become intimidated <chicken out, turn chicken, turn yellow, run scared, get cold feet, get scared stiff, get scared shitless, shit one's pants, piss one's pants, shit bullets, shit a brick, shit green, get spooked, push the panic button, wimp out> eg *Film był naprawdę przerażający. Najadłem się strachu (The movie was real scary. I pissed my pants)*

najęty See jak najęty

nakopać See dać kopa

nakopcić Perf kopcić

nakręcony See skołowany

nakryć [NAH-krich] *v* To find or seize someone (esp a criminal) in the act of doing something forbidden; to catch in flagrante delicto <catch someone with the pants down, catch someone redhanded, catch someone cold, catch someone on the hop, catch someone with a smoking gun, catch someone with their hand in the cookie jar, bust, bag, claw, clip, collar, cop, flag, grab, haul in, jab, knock, pinch, nab, nail, nick, pick up, pull in, run in, sidetrack, put the collar on, put the sleeve on> eg *Wiedziałem, że policja prędzej czy później go nakryje (I knew the police would nab him sooner or later)*

nalać Perf lać

namącić Perf mącić

namiary [nah-MYAH-ri] *npl* Contact particulars such as a name, telephone number, or address <name and number, seven digits> eg *Daj mi twoje namiary (Give me the seven digits)*

namierzyć [nah-MYEH-zhich] *v* To find out where one, esp a fugitive, lives; to locate <hook, pinpoint, spot, zero in, smoke out, smell out, scope out, sniff out, hit upon, pick up on, stumble on, make a make> eg *Policja natychmiast go namierzyła (The police immediately made a make on him)*

namieszać Perf mieszać

namiot [NAH-myoht] *nm* An erect penis <hard-on, boner, bone-on, rod-on, stander, woody, stiffy> eg *Znów mam namiot w spodniach (I got a hard-on again)*

namolnie [nah-MOHL-nyeh] *adv* Obtrusively or importunately <in a pushy way> eg *Przedstawił nam projekt bardzo namolnie (He presented us his project in a very pushy way)*

namolny [nah-MOHL-ni] *adj* Aggressively obtrusive or importunate; difficult to get rid of <pushy, pain in the neck, pain in the ass> eg *Ciężko być uprzejmym wobec namolnych ludzi (It's hard to be polite to pushy people)*

namotać Perf motać

naście [NAHSH-chyeh] *adv* Of any large unspecified number over ten and below twenty <umpteen, X numer of, X amount of> eg *Napisał naście recenzji (He wrote umpteen reviews)*

napakowany [nah-pah-koh-VAH-ni] *adj* (Of a man) with well-developed muscles <built, hunky, beefy, puffed out, pumped up, built like a brick shithouse> eg *Kim jest ten napakowany dupek? (Who is that pumped up jerk?)*

napalać się [nah-PAH-lahch shyeh] (perf **napalić się** [nah-PAH-leech shyeh]) *v* To be sexually or romantically interested in someone; to desire someone sexually <have the hots for, have hot pants for, have a hard-on for, have a lech for, lech after, get turned on, get stoked, be crazy for, be nuts for, be stuck on, be sweet on, go for, have a crush on, have a yen for> eg *Nagle facet się napalił i zaproponował szybki numerek (Suddenly the guy got a hard-on for me and wanted to have a quickie); Napalił się i nie wiedział, jak nad tym zapanować (He got horny and didn't know how to handle it)*

napalony See nagrzany

naparsteczek [nah-pahr-STEH-chehk] *nm* A little drink of a potent liquor, esp vodka, served in a shot glass <snort, finger, jigger, pull, shot, nip, gargle, guzzle, slug, hit> eg *Mówi, że wypiła tylko naparsteczek (She said she only drank a finger)*

naparzać się See napierdalać się

napędzić komuś strachu [nah-PEHN-jeech KOH-moosh STRAH-khoo] *v phr* To frighten someone <spook, chill, put the chill on, scare shitless, scare stiff, scare the shit out of, scare to death, scare the bejesus out of, scare the hell out of, throw a scare into> eg *Ten wąż napędził nam wszystkim stracha (We were all spooked by that snake)*

napieprzyć Perf pieprzyć

napierdalać się** [nah-pyehr-DAH-lahch shyeh] (or **napieprzać się*** [nah-PYEHP-shahch shyeh] or **napierniczać się*** [nah-pyehr-NEE-chahch shyeh] or **napierdzielać się*** [nah-pyehr-JEH-lahch shyeh] or **nawalać się** [nah-VAH-lahch shyeh] or **naparzać się** [nah-PAH-zhahch shyeh]) *v coarse* To fight; to brawl <bang heads, bump heads, hassle, bicker, buck, romp, slug, smack, scrap, shuffle, kick up a row, put up a fight, go up against, roughhouse, take on, lock horns, set to, cross swords, pick a bone, tangle with, tangle ass with, go round and round, go toe to toe, go to it, go to the mat, have a pissing contest, have a pissing match, have a run-in, make the fur fly, put on the gloves, jump down someone's throat, duke it out> eg *Zaczęli się napierdalać (Just then they started to bump heads)*

napierdalać** [nah-pyehr-DAH-lahch] (or **napieprzać*** [nah-PYEHP-shahch] or **napierniczać*** [nah-pyehr-NEE-chahch] or **napierdzielać*** [nah-pyehr-JEH-lahch] or **nawalać** [nah-VAH-lahch]) *v* **1** To play a musical instrument very vigorously or loudly <wail, smoke, rip, strum, thrum, thump> eg *Napierdalał na swojej gitarze (He was wailing on his guitar)* **2** To ache or pain <kill, grab, stab, take someone hide and hair, hit one where one lives> eg *Ale mnie łamie w kościach! (My bones are fucking killing me!)*

napierdolić See pierdolić

napierdolić Perf pierdolić

napierdolić się** [nah-pyehr-DOH-leech shyeh] (or **napieprzyć się*** [nah-PYEHP-shich shyeh] or **napierniczyć się*** [nah-pyehr-NEE-chich shyeh] or **napierdzielić się*** [nah-pyehr-JEH-leech shyeh] or **narąbać się** [na-ROHM-bahch shyeh] or **najebać się**** [nah-YEH-bahch shyeh] or **nawalić się** [nah-VAH-leech shyeh]) *v* To get drunk <get fucked up, get alkied, get bagged, get blitzed, get blotto, get blown away, get bent, get boiled, get bombed, get boozed up, get blasted, get bottled, get boxed, get canned, get clobbered, get cooked, get corked, get drunk as a skunk, get edged, get embalmed, get fractured, get fried, get gassed, get ginned, get grogged, get high, get hooched up, get impaired, get illuminated, get juiced, get liquored up, get lit, get loaded, get looped, get lubricated, get smashed, get oiled, get pickled, get plastered, get plonked, get polluted, get sauced, get shitfaced, get sloshed, get soaked, get stewed, get stiff, get stinking drunk, get swizzled, get tanked up, get wiped, get zonked> eg *Zawsze pierwszego lubi się narąbać (He always likes to get stoned on payday); Zawsze pierwszego lubi się najebać (He always likes to get shitfaced on payday); Zawsze pierwszego lubi się narąbać (He always likes to get loaded on payday)*

napierdzielić Perf pierdzielić

napierniczyć Perf pierniczyć

napity See spity

naprany See narąbany

naprędce [nah-PREHNT-tseh] *adv* Without any preparation; impromptu <off the cuff, off the top of one's head, spur-of-the-moment> eg *Nie potrafię odpowiedzieć tak naprędce (I can't think of the answer off the top of my head)*

napyskować Perf pyskować

napyszczyć See pyszczyć

narąbać się See napierdolić się

narąbany [nah-rohm-BAH-ni] (or **nabuzowany** [nah-boo-zoh-VAH-ni] or **nagazowany** [nah-gah-zoh-VAH-ni] or **najebany**** [nah-yeh-BAH-ni] or **nawalony** [nah-vah-LOH-ni] or **naprany** [nah-PRAH-ni] or **napruty** [nah-PROO-ti] or **nagrzany** [nah-GZHAH-ni]; **jak autobus** [yahk ah-oo-TOH-boos] or **jak stodoła** [yahk stoh-DOH-wah] may be added) *adj* Drunk; alcohol intoxicated <alkied, bagged, blitzed, blotto, blown away, bent, boiled, bombed, blasted, boozed, bottled, boxed, buzzed, canned, clobbered, cooked, corked, crashed, drunk as a skunk, edged, embalmed, fractured, fried, gassed, ginned, grogged, have one too many, half under, high, hooched up, in bad shape, impaired, illuminated, juiced, knocked out, liquored, lit, loaded, looped, lubricated, lushed, smashed, oiled, pickled, plastered, plonked, polluted, sauced, shitfaced, slugged, sloshed, soaked, stewed, stiff, stinking drunk, swizzled, tanked, three sheets to the wind, wiped, zonked> eg *Do domu przyszedł nawalony jak autobus (He came home drunk as a skunk); Daj mi poprowadzić. Nie, jesteś nagazowany (Let me drive. No, you're clobbered); Był już mocno nagrzany i ledwo się trzymał na nogach (He was already loaded and he could hardly walk); Był tak nagrzany, że nie wiedział jak się nazywa (He was so clobbered he didin't even know his name)*

narobić się [nah-ROH-beech shyeh] (or **narobić się jak dziki osioł** [nah-ROH-beech shyeh yahk JEE-kee OH-shyoh-oo] or **narobić się jak wół** [nah-ROH-beech shyeh yahk VOOW] may be added) *v* To work very hard <work one's ass off, work one's fingers to the bone, work like a horse, sweat, bust one's ass off, break one's ass off, make bricks without a straw> eg *Rety, ale się wczoraj narobiłem (Man, did I work my ass off yesterday!)*

narwaniec [nahr-VAH-nyehts] *nm* A crazy or eccentric man, esp if hot-tempered or unpredictable <freak, fruitcake, goofball, cook, loon, nut, nutball, nutcase, nutter, psycho, screwball, screw-loose, sicko, wacko, weirdo, oddball> eg *Ten narwaniec rozpiął jej stanik w pięć sekund i odszedł (That freak unzipped her bra within five seconds and left)*

narwany [nahr-VAH-ni] *adj* Insane or eccentric, esp if hot-tempered or unpredictable <crazy, crazy as a loon, freaky, fruity, goofy, cooky, loony, nuts, nutty, nutty as a fruitcake, psycho, screwy, screw-loose, sicko, wacko, weirdo, schizo, wild, ape, bananas, bent, bonkers, cracked, dopey, ga-ga, half-baked, loony, loopy, mental, nerts, nuts, nutty, off one's nut, off one's rocker, off one's base, off the track, off the trolley, out one's skull, freaked-out, schizzed-out, psyched-out, flipped-out, unglued, unstuck, unwrapped, unzipped, fucked in the head, itchy, antsy, jumpy, flaky, mad, off-beat> eg *Nasz nowy facet od matmy jest naprawdę narwany (Our new math prof is real nuts)*

narzeczona See osobista narzeczona

narzeczony See osobisty narzeczony

narzygać Perf rzygać

nasiadówa [nah-shah-DOO-vah] (or **nasiadówka** [nah-shah-DOOF-kah]) *nf* A very long meeting or intense discussion, esp in a workplace <sit-in, meet, get-together, huddle, confab, clambake, rap session> eg *Poproszono mnie, żebym poprowadziła jedną nasiadówę (I was asked to lead a rap session)*

nasikać Perf sikać

nasiusiać Perf siusiać

naskoczyć See móc komuś skoczyć

nasmarkać Perf smarkać

nasmrodzić Perf smrodzić

nasrać Perf srać

nastąpić komuś na odcisk See nadepnąć komuś na odcisk

następny do golenia [nah-STEHMP-ni doh goh-LEH-nyah] *adj phr* (Of a person) Next <next off, coming up> eg *Myślę, że ty bedziesz następny (I think you may be next off)*

naszczać Perf szczać

naszprycować się Perf szprycować się

natyrać Perf **tyrać**

naważyć piwa [nah-VAH-zhich PEE-vah] *v phr* To get onself into trouble <get into shit, step into shit, get one's ass in a sling, get up shit creek without a paddle> eg *Naważył sobie piwa tą ostrą wypowiedzią (He got into deep shit by saying that remark)*

nawalać See napierdalać

nawalać [nah-VAH-lahch] (perf **nawalić** [nah-VAH-leech]) *v* (Esp about mechanical appliances) To fail or become inoperative <break down, crash, crash and burn, fry, go down, go down in flames, go south, belly up, melt down, shut down, crack up, screw up, fuck up, go blooey, go busted, go on the blink, go on the fritz, go off, go out of whack, go kerflooey> eg *Wszystko szło mi dobrze póki nie nawalił faks (Everything was doing fine until the fax crashed)*

nawalać się See napierdalać się

nawalić się See napierdolić się

nawalony See narąbany

nawet-nawet [NAH-veht NAH-veht] *adj phr* Quite good, attractive or wonderful <great, cool, swell, fab, rad, def, far-out, awesome, frantic, terrific, funky, gorgeous, groovy, hellacious, neat, peachy, dandy, baddest, mean, solid, super-dooper, wailing, wicked, gnarly, top-notch, ten, ace-high, A-OK, A-1, some, pretty good, ten, drop-dead gorgeous, knock-out gorgeous, dishy, hunky> eg *Wiesz, ten samochód jest nawet-nawet (You know, this car is cool)*

nawpierdalać się** [nahf-pyehr-DAH-lahch shyeh] (or **nawpieprzać się*** [nahf-PYEHP-shahch shyeh] or **nawpierniczać się*** [nahf-pyehr-NEE-chahch shyeh] or **nawpierdzielać się** [nahf-pyehr-JEH-lahch shyeh] or **nażreć się** [NAH-zhrehch shyeh] or **nawpychać się** [nahf-PI-khahch shyeh] or **napchać się** [NAHP-khahch shyeh] or **nawtranżalać się** [nahf-trahn-ZHAH-lahch shyeh]) *v* To overeat, eat greedily and more than needed <stuff oneself, pig out, scarf out, pork out> eg *Nawpierdalałam się czekolady (I piged out on chocolate); Nawpierdalał się ciasta i zaczął pierdzieć (He piged out on cake and started to fart)*

nędza See bida

negatyw* [neh-GAH-tif] *nm* A black person <nigger, niggra, bro, brother, jungle bunny, chocolate drop, darky, groid, inky-dink, blue-skin, boogie, jigaboo,

zigaboo, shade, shadow, smoke, spade, spook, coon, Hershey bar> eg *W tej okolicy roi się od negatywów i żółtków (This neighborhood swarms with spooks and chinks)*

nera [NEH-rah] *nf* A man's kidney <no slang equivalent> eg *Ma poważne problemy z nerami (She 's got serious problems with her kidneys)*

nerwus [NEHR-voos] *nm* Someone nervous who is easily made angry <uptight, jumpy, jittery, shaky, shivery, nervy, edgy, antsy, clutchy, hitchy, fretty, itchy, wired, tightened-up, strung-out> eg *Twój brat to prawdziwy nerwus (Your brother is really edgy)*

nerwy See kłębek nerwów, w nerwach

ni pies ni wydra [nee PYEHS nee VI-drah] (or **ni przypiął ni wypiął** [nee PSHI-pyoh-oo nee VI-pyoh-oo] or **ni przypiął ni przyłatał** [nee PSHI-pyoh-oo nee pshi-WAH-tah-oo] or **ni w pięć ni w dziesięć** [nee f PYEHNCH nee v JEH-shyehnch] or **ni w pięć ni w dziewięć** [nee f PYEHNCH nee v JEH-vyehnch] or **ni z gruszki ni z pietruszki** [nee z GROOSH-kee nee s pyeht-ROOSH-kee) *phr* Not definitely recognizable; neither of one thing nor another <neither fish nor fowl, neither fish flesh or fowl> eg *Kupiła jakiś mebel, który jest ni przypiął ni wypiął. Jest zarówno stołem, jak i krzesłem (She bought a piece of furniture which is neither fish nor fowl. It is both a table and a chair); Ten film jest ni w pięć ni w dziesięć. To jest śmieszne love story (This movie is neither fish nor fowl. It is a funny love story); Ta propozycja to ni pies ni wydra. Nie wiadomo, o co w niej chodzi (This proposal is neither fish nor fowl. I can't tell what you're proposing)*

ni w ząb See ni w ząb

niczego sobie [nee-CHEH-goh SOH-byeh] *adj phr* Quite good, attractive or wonderful <great, cool, swell, fab, rad, def, far-out, awesome, frantic, terrific, funky, gorgeous, groovy, hellacious, neat, peachy, dandy, baddest, mean, solid, super-dooper, wailing, wicked, gnarly, top-notch, ten, ace-high, A-OK, A-1, some, pretty good, ten, drop-dead gorgeous, knock-out gorgeous, dishy, hunky> eg *Myślę, że ta twoja kumpela jest niczego sobie (I think your friend is a ten)*

nie brać do ust [brahch doh OOST] *v phr* To refrain from or stop drinking alcoholic liquor <be on the wagon> eg *Od kiedy nie wziąłeś ani kropli do ust? (How long have you been on the wagon?)*

nie chodzić piechotą [nyeh KHOH-jeech pyeh-KHOH-toh] *v phr* (Of a sum of money) Not to be insignificant <ain't hay, isn't hay, ain't peanuts, isn't peanuts, ain't chopped liver, isn't chopped liver, no laughing matter, no joke> eg *Sto tysięcy piechotą nie chodzi (A hundred thousand ain't peanuts)*

nie czuć nóg [nyeh CHOOCH NOOG] *v phr* (Esp about one's legs) To be very tired; to be exhausted <dogs are barking, be dead, be dead on one's feet, be dead-tired, be dog-tired, be out of it, be out of gas, be out of juice, be all in, be all shot, be pooped, be bagged, be beat, be beat to the ground, be beat to the ankles, be bone-tired, be burned out, be bushed, be chewed, be crapped out, be done, be done in, be dragged out, be frazzled, be played out, be fucked out, be knocked out, be tuckered out, be tapped out, had it, be ready to drop, be on one's last legs> eg *Nie mogę tam iść. Nie czuję nóg (I can't go there. I'm dead on my feet)*

nie czyjaś broszka [nyeh TFOH-yah BROHSH-kah] (or **to nie czyjaś broszka** [toh nyeh TFOH-yah BROHSH-kah]) *phr* (It is) Not of someone's concern or interest <not someone's business, not someone's beeswax, not care, not care a damn, not care a shit, not care a fuck, not give a damn, not give a shit, not give a

fuck, be no skin off one's ass> eg *To nie moja broszka, czy przegrają czy nie (This is not my beeswax if they lose or not)*

nie dać się zwariować [nyeh dahch shyeh zvahr-YOH-vahch]) *v phr* Not to allow others on oneself to be deceived, confused, or mentally unbalanced <not let carried away with, let oneself get pushed around, not kid oneself, not play cat and mouse with oneself, not beat around the bush, not play games, not jerk oneself around, not dick oneself around, not pussyfoot oneself around, not snow, not blow smoke, not pull the wool over one's eyes> eg *Panowie, nie dajmy się zwariować (Gentlemen, let's not get carried away with this)*

nie dać sobie w kaszę dmuchać [nyeh dahch SOH-byeh f KAH-sheh DMOO-khahch] *v phr* Not to allow others to be manipulated or victimized; to be smart, experienced, or well-informed <let oneself get pushed around, have brains, have savvy, have smarts, be with it, be nobody's fool, not be born yesterday, not get off the boat, be in the know, have something on the ball> eg *Nie byłbym taki pewny, że nasz bluff się uda. Ten facet nie da sobie w kaszę dmuchać (I wouldn't be so sure that our bluff will work. That guy is nobody's fool)*

nie dla psa kiełbasa [nyeh dlah PSAH kyeh-oo-BAH-sah] *phr* Something or someone is not intended or fit for someone, esp because it is superior <not for someone, not someone's class, not in someone's league, not up someone's alley> eg *Mówię Ci, zostaw tę dziewczynę. Nie dla psa kiełbasa (I'm telling you, leave this girl alone. She's not in your league)*

nie do śmiechu [nyeh doh SHMYEH-khoo] *adj phr* Not funny; serious; not to be taken lightly <heavyweight, heavy number, serious jelly, serious shit, no laughing matter, no joke> eg *Ta sprawa jest nie do śmiechu (This is no laughing matter)*

nie do wyjęcia [nyeh doh vi-YEHN-chyah] (or **nie do wyjebania**** [nyeh doh vi-yeh-BAH-nyah] or **nie z tej ziemi** [nyeh s teh-ee ZHYEH-mee]) *adj phr* Excellent; wonderful; extremely good <great, cool, swell, fab, rad, def, far-out, awesome, frantic, terrific, funky, gorgeous, groovy, hellacious, neat, peachy, dandy, baddest, mean, solid, super-dooper, wailing, wicked, gnarly, top-notch, ten, ace-high, A-OK, A-1, some> eg *Ten samochód jest na prawdę nie do wyjebania (This car is real cool)*

nie do zdarcia [nyeh doh ZDAHR-chyah] *adj phr* Extremely durable, resilient, or resistant <heavy-duty, hard as nails, hardnosed, hard-assed> eg *Don't worry about him. He's hard as nails (Nie martw się o niego. Jest nie do zdarcia)*

nie kiwnąć palcem [nyeh KEEV-nohnch PAHL-tsehm] (or **nie ruszyć palcem** [nyeh ROO-shich PAHL-tsehm]; **w bucie** [v BOO-chyeh] may be added) *v phr* To do nothing to help someone <not lift one's finger, not lift one's finger to help someone> eg *Możesz sobie wyobrazić, że nawet nie kiwnął palcem? (Can you imagine that he wouldn't lift a finger?)*

nie ma dupy* [NYEH mah DOO-pi] (or **nie ma mowy** [NYEH mah MOH-vi] or **nie ma siły** [NYEH mah SHEE-wi]) *adv phr* Certainly; surely <sure, fer sure, sure as hell, sure as shit, sure as can be, for real, indeedy, really truly, absitively, posilutely, real, cert, def, no buts about it, wired up, cinched, taped, racked, sewed up, iced, in the bag, tied up, nailed down> eg *Wygra wybory? Nie ma dupy! (Will he win the elections? No buts about it!)*

nie ma głupich [nyeh mah GWOO-peekh] *phr* A phrase of disbelief or refusal telling that one will not be cheated or taken advantage of <out of the question, no

way, no way Jose, no dice, not on your life, nothing doing, no can do, you gotta be kidding, will eat one's hat, in a pig's eye, in a pig's ass, in a pig's ear, like hell, like fun, like shit, my ass, someone will be damned if, someone will be fucked if, says you> eg *Ja mam iść rozmawiać z dyrektorem? Nie ma głupich (You want me to go and speak with the principal. No way)*

nie ma mocnych [nyeh mah MOHTS-nikh] *phr* A phrase telling that noone can do anything about something; there is no remedy <nothing doing, no can do> eg *Na policjantów nie ma mocnych (Nothing doing. These cops can't be stopped)*

nie ma sprawy [nyeh mah SPRAH-vi] (or **nie ma strachu** [nyeh mah STRAH-khoo]) *phr* Forget it; Pay no more attention; Do not worry <no problem, no prob, no sweat> eg *No jasne, że naprawię pani samochód do południa. Nie ma strachu (Of course I can have your car repaired by noon. No sweat)*

nie mieć bladego pojęcia See nie mieć zielonego pojęcia

nie mieć co do gęby włożyć [nyeh myehch tsoh doh GEHM-bi VWOH-zhich] *v phr* To have no (money for) food; to be destitute <be down and out, be on the edge, be on one's ass, be on the hog, be on the rims, be down to one's last cent, be without a red cent, be without a dime to rub against another, feel the pinch, be cold in hand, be dead broke, be flat broke, be stone broke> eg *W zaszłym miesiącu nie miałem co do gęby włożyć (Last month I was down and out)*

nie mieć głowy do czegoś [nyeh myehch GWOH-vi doh CHEH-gohsh] *v phr* To be unable to think or concentrate on something in a given moment <cannot be bothered about> eg *Zostaw ojca w spokoju. Nie ma teraz głowy dla twoich pytań (Leave the father alone. He cannot be bothered about it)*

nie mieć piątej klepki [nyeh myehch PYOHN-teh-ee KLEHP-kee] (or **brakować komuś piątej klepki** [brah-KOH-vahch KOH-moosh PYOHN-teh-ee KLEHP-kee] or **nie mieć wszystkich klepek** [nyeh myehch FSHIST-keekh KLEH-pehk]) *v phr* To be silly, crazy or eccentric <have a screw loose, have a loose screw, have a hole in one's head, have a few buttons missing, have one's head up one's ass, have shit for brains, not have a clue> eg *Wszyscy wiedzą, że twojemu bratu brakuje piątej klepki (Everybody knows that your brother doesn't have a screw loose)*

nie mieć wszystkich klepek See nie mieć piątej klepki

nie mieć zdrowia do czegoś/kogoś [nyeh myehch ZDROH-vyah doh CHEH-gohsh/KOH-gohsh] *v phr* To be lacking energy, enthusiasm to do something; to be tired and unwilling to do something <be sick and tired of, be fed up with, be up to here with, have it up to here with, be sick and tired of, have no pizzazz for, have no pep for> eg *Nie mam zdrowia do tego dziecka (I'm sick and tired of this baby)*

nie mieć zielonego pojęcia [nyeh myehch zhyeh-loh-NEH-goh poh-YEHN-chah] (or **nie mieć bladego pojęcia** [nyeh myehch blah-DEH-goh poh-YEHN-chah]) *v phr* Not to know at all; to be totally ignorant or unfamiliar <not know from nothing, not know one's ass from first base, not know one's ass from a hole in the ground, not know one's ass from one's elbow, not know a rock from a hard place, not know diddly-shit, not know shit, not know shit from Shinola, not know zilch, not have a clue, not know the score, not know the time of day, not have the foggiest idea, search me> eg *Oni nie mają zielonego pojęcia o leksykografii (They know shit about lexicography)*

nie mieścić się w głowie [nyeh MYEHSH-cheech shyeh v GWOH-vyeh] *v phr* To surprise, shock, or overwhelm someone; to be inconceivable or incomprehensible <boggle one's mind, be mind-boggling, blow one's mind, be mind-blowing> eg *W głowie mi się nie mieści, jak mogła zrobić coś takiego (It boggles my mind how she could do such a thing)*

nie od parady See mieć łeb

nie śmierdzieć groszem [nyeh SHMYEHR-jehch GROH-shehm] *v phr* To have no money <be broke, be dead broke, be flat broke, be stone broke, be busted, be cleaned out, be strapped, be tapped out, be drained> eg *O ile wiem, to on nie śmierdzi groszem (As far as I know, he is flat broke)*

nie owijać w bawełnę [nyeh oh-VEE-yahch v bah-VEH-oo-neh] *v phr* To speak very directly, firmly, and plainly about something; to tell thruthfully <lay it on the line, put it on the line, talk turkey, make no bones about, not beat around the bush> eg *Była bardzo zła. Nie owijała w bawełnę i wiedzieliśmy, co miała na myśli (She was very mad. She put it on the line, and we had no doubt about what she meant)*
See owijać w bawełnę

nie pali się [nyeh PAH-lee shyeh] (or **pali się** [nyeh PAH-lee shyeh]) *excl phr* An exclamation telling someone not to be in such a hurry and to slow down <no hurry, bog down, lose steam, back off, let up, anchor it, brake, hit the brakes, ease up, hold your water, hold your horses> eg *Nie pali się. Zdążymy, mamy jeszcze dużo czasu (No hurry. We'll make it. We still have plenty of time)*

nie pisnąć ani słówka See ani pisnąć

nie popuszczać komuś [nyeh poh-POOSH-chahch KOH-moosh] (perf **nie popuścić komuś** [nyeh poh-POOSH-cheech KOH-moosh]; or **nie przepuszczać** [psheh-POOSH-chahch] perf **nie przepuścić** [psheh-POOSH-chich]) *v* Not to give in; not to forgive; to make no concessions <not let one get away with, not let it go, not let it slide, not let one off, not go easy on, not blink at, not wink at, not give an inch, give no quarter> eg *Nie popuści tym razem (He won't let it go this time)*

nie przelewać się [nyeh psheh-LEH-vahch shyeh] *v* To be poor rather than rich <be no Rockefeller> eg *Jej narzeczonemu się nie przelewa (Her fiance is no Rockefeller)*

nie przepuszczać komuś [nyeh psheh-POOSH-chahch KOH-moosh] *v phr* (Usually about men) To be indiscriminate with regard to sex partners; to readily agree to copulate with anyone <would screw anything on two legs, would screw anything with a hole in it, would screw anything that can walk, would screw anything that moves> eg *Byli tak nagrzani, że nie przepuściliby żadnej (They were so horny that they would screw anything on two legs)*

nie przymierzając [nyeh pshi-myeh-ZHAH-yohnts] *phr* (Please) Excuse the comparison <like damned, like damn, like fucking, if I do say so myself> eg *Przyszła ubrana jak, nie przymierzając, jakaś zdzira (She showed up dressed up like some goddamn slut)*

nie ruszyć palcem See nie kiwnąć palcem

nie sztuka [nyeh SHTOO-kah] (or **wielka mi sztuka** [VYEHL-kah mee SHTOO-kah] or **to nie sztuka** [toh toh nyeh SHTOO-kah]) *phr* (It is) not difficult or extraordinary at all; easy or trivial <lah-di-dah, big deal, no big deal, no biggie, piece of cake, cake, cakewalk, cherry pie, duck soup, kid stuff, picnic, pushover, snap, tea party, walkaway, walkover, breeze, stroll, cinch, pipe, Mickey

Mouse, small potatoes, small beer, fly speck> eg *Zabicie dwóch facetów to nie sztuka (Killing two guys is no big deal)*

nie tego [nyeh TEH-goh] *adj phr* Insane or eccentric <crazy, crazy as a loon, freaky, fruity, goofy, cooky, loony, nuts, nutty, nutty as a fruitcake, psycho, screwy, screw-loose, sicko, wacko, weirdo, schizo, wild, ape, bananas, bent, bonkers, cracked, dopey, ga-ga, half-baked, loony, loopy, mental, nerts, nuts, nutty, off one's nut, off one's rocker, off one's base, off the track, off the trolley, out one's skull, freaked-out, schizzed-out, psyched-out, flipped-out, unglued, unstuck, unwrapped, unzipped, fucked in the head, flaky, mad, off-beat> eg *Ten twój nowy facet jest trochę nie tego (That new boyfriend of yours is sort of fucked in the head)*

nie trawić czegoś/kogoś [nyeh TRAH-veech CHEH-gohsh/KOH-gohsh] *v phr* To hate, detest, or dislike; cannot tolerate <be gross out, be barfed out, be turned off by, have an allergy to, be allergic to, not go for, cannot stand the guts of, hate someone's guts, cannot live with, cannot put up with> eg *Obecny dyrektor Instytutu to przeciętniak, więc nie trawi ludzi ambitnych (The present director of the Institute is a mediocrity, so he can't stand the guts of ambitious people)*

nie umywać się [nyeh oo-MI-vahch shyeh] *v phr* To be far worse when compared with someone or something else; not to be fit to be compared with <pale compared with, pale by comparison with, pale in comparison with, not hold a candle to, not hold a stick to> eg *Są dobre, ale nie umywają się do zachodnich (They're good, but they can't hold a candle to Western competitors)*

nie uśmiechać się [nyeh oo-SHMYEH-khahch shyeh] *v* To dislike something and thus to be unwilling to do it <not be about to> eg *Nie uśmiechało jej się, żeby tam pojechać (She was not about to go there)*

nie w kij dmuchał [nyeh f keey DMOO-hkah-woo] *phr* (Esp about a sum of money) Not to be insignificant <ain't hay, isn't hay, ain't peanuts, isn't peanuts, ain't chopped liver, isn't chopped liver, no laughing matter, no joke> eg *Sto tysięcy to nie w kij dmuchał (A hundred thousand ain't peanuts)*

nie w sosie [nyeh f SOH-shyeh] *adj phr* Feeling unwell or annoyed; indisposed <in a bad mood, moody, out of sorts, off one's feed, green around the gills, under the weather, uptight, jumpy, jittery, shaky, shivery, nervy, edgy, antsy, clutchy, hitchy, fretty, itchy, wired, tightened-up, strung-out> eg *Widzę, że jesteś dzisiaj coś nie w sosie. Co jest? (I can see you're a little uptight today. What's up?)*

nie wylewać za kołnierz [nyeh vi-LEH-vahch zah KOH-oo-nyehsh] *v phr* To drink alcohol often and in large quantities; to enjoy drinking alcohol <like to booze, like to guzzle, like to gargle, like to bend the elbow, like to hit the bottle, like to hit the sauce, like to knock back, like to lap, like to tank up, like to wet one's whistle, like to hang a few on, like to slug down, like to swig> eg *Twój brat na pewno nie wylewa za kołnierz (Your brother sure likes to wet his whistle)*

nie wzruszać kogoś See mało kogoś wzruszać

nie z tej ziemi See nie do wyjęcia

nie ze mną te numery [nyeh ZEH mnoh teh noo-MEH-ri] (or **nie ze mną te numery Brunner** [nyeh ZEH mnoh teh noo-MEH-ri BROO-nehr] may be added) *excl* A phrase of disbelief or refusal telling that one will not be cheated or taken advantage of <out of the question, no way, no way Jose, no dice, not on your life, nothing doing, no can do, you gotta be kidding, will eat one's hat, in a pig's eye, in a pig's ass, in a pig's ear, like hell, like fun, like shit, my ass, I'll be

damned, I'll be fucked, says you> eg *Więc chcecie mi zapłacić w przyszłym miesiącu? Nie ze mną te numery (So you want to pay me next month? No way)*

niebieski See czeski, duże niebieskie oczy

niebo See jak grom z jasnego nieba, nogi po samą szyję, o niebo, w siódmym niebie

niebo w gębie [NYEH-boh v GEHM-byeh] *excl phr* Very tasty <yum-yum, yummy> eg *O, gorące skrzydełka. Niebo w gębie! ((Oh, hot wings. Yum-yum!)*

niech to [NYEHKH toh] (or **to szlag trafi** [nyehkh toh SHLAHK TRAH-fee] or **niech to jasny szlag trafi** [nyehkh toh YAHS-ni SHLAHK TRAH-fee] or **niech to diabli** [nyehkh toh DYAHB-lee] or **niech to wszyscy diabli** [nyehkh toh FSHIS-tsi DYAHB-lee] or **niech to gęś kopnie** [nyehkh toh GEHNSH KOHP-nyeh] or **niech to piorun trzaśnie** [nyehkh toh PYOH-roon TSHAHSH-nyeh] or **niech kogoś/coś kule biją** [nyehkh KOH-hosh/tsohsh KOO-leh] or **niech kogoś/coś nagła krew zaleje** [nyehkh KOH-hosh/tsohsh NAHG-wah KREHF zah-LEH-yeh]; **żeby to** [ZHEH-bi toh] may replace **niech to**; **kogoś/coś** [KOH-gohsh/tsohsh] may replace **to**) *excl* An exclamation of anger, irritation, disappointment, shock <shit, fuck, hell, heck, damn, damn it, goddamn it, gosh, golly, gee, jeez, holy fuck, holy cow, holy moly, holy hell, holy mackarel, holy shit, jumping Jesus, fucking shit, fucking hell> eg *Niech to szlag trafi! Nie wziąłem pieniędzy! (Fucking hell! I didn't take the money with me!)*

niechluj [NYEH-khloo-ee] (or **luj** [loo-ee]) *nm* A sloppy, dirty and unkempt man <dirt-bag, sleazeball, slimebag, schloomp> eg *Nie mam nic wspólnego z tym niechlujem (I have nothing to do with that dirt-bag)*

niedołęga [nyeh-doh-WEHN-gah] (or **niedorajda** [nyeh-doh-RAH-ee-dah] or **niezdara** [nyeh-ZDAH-rah] or **niezguła** [nyeh-ZGOO-wah] or **niedojda** [nyeh-DOH-ee-dah] or **niedorobiony** [nyeh-doh-roh-BYOH-ni] *nm*) *nf* An awkward, sluggish, inept, clumsy, or ineffectual person; a bungler; a fumbler <underachiever, loser, born loser, second-rater, schlemiel, schmendrick, schmo, schnook, screwup, fuckup, hacker, muffer, scrub, dub, screw-up, loser, dool tool, turkey, schmendrick, duffer, flubdub, lummox, lump, foozler, buterfingers, fumble-fist, goof, goof-off, goofball, eightball, foulball, klutz, also-ran, never-was, nonstarter, drag-ass, foot-dragger, schlepper, slowpoke, zero, lightweight, nobody, non, nonentity, noname, small potatoes, small timer, bush-leaguer> eg *Nie chcę żadnych niedołęg w moim zespole (I don't want any klutzes on my unit); Chciał to zrobić, ale taka z niego niedojda, że nie sądze, żeby to zrobił (He wanted to do it, but he's such a klutz that I don't think he will)*

niedzielny kierowca [nyeh-JEHL-ni kyeh-ROHF-tsah] *nm phr* A slow and careless driver, like one out for a leisurely Sunday drive <Sunday driver, woman driver> eg *Lepiej z nim nie jedź. To niedzielny kierowca (You'd better not go with him. He's a Sunday driver)*

niefart [NYEH-fahrt] *adj* Bad luck; misfortune <hard luck, tough luck, rotten luck, fuck luck, bad break, jinx, schlemazel, whammy, double whammy, hex> eg *Mamy przebitą oponę! Co za niefart! (We got a flat tire! What rotten luck!)*

niefartowny [nyeh-fahr-TOHV-ni] *adj* Unlucky; unfortunate <jinxed, hexed, left-handed, out of luck> eg *To była niefartowna wyprawa (It was a jinxed trip)*

niegramotny See **niekumaty**

niejadek [nyeh-YAH-dehk] *nm* A person, esp a child, that refuses to eat or eats very little <small eater, light eater> eg *Jest taki chudy, że widać, że to niejadek (He's so skinny you could tell he's a small eater)*

niekumaty [nyeh-koo-MAH-ti] (or **niegramotny** [nyeh-grah-MOHT-ni]) *adj* Slow-witted, stupid, or unintelligent <airbrained, airheaded, birdbrained, blockheaded, squareheaded, boneheaded, bubblebrained, bubbleheaded, bucketheaded, cluckheaded, cementheaded, clunkheaded, deadheaded, dumbclucked, dumbheaded, dumbassed, dumbbrained, fatbrained, fatheaded, flubdubbed, knukclebrained, knuckleheaded, lamebrained, lardheaded, lunkheaded, meatheaded, muscleheaded, noodleheaded, numbskulled, pointheaded, scatterbrained, nerdy, dorky, jackassed, lummoxed, dopey, goofy> eg *Może i jest niekumata, ale ma świetne ciało (Maybe she is dumbheaded, but she's got great body)*

nielicho See nieziemsko

nielichy [nyeh-LEE-khi] (or **niewąski** [nyeh-VOHN-skee]) *adj* Big; large; sizable <gross, humongous, monstro, moby, jumbo, hefty, whopper, mother, king-size, God-size> eg *Właśnie wtedy pojawił się nielichy problem (Just then a humongous problem appeared); Mam niewąski ból głowy (I got a mother headache)*

niemalowane See odpukać

niemiaszek* [nyeh-MYAH-shehk] *nm* A male German <kraut, krauthead, sauerkraut, Fritz, Heinie, Jerry> eg *Te niemiaszki robią całkiem dobre piwo (Those krauts make pretty good beer)*

niemiec [NYEH-myehts] *nn* The German language, esp as a subject in school <no slang equivalent> eg *Niemca uczyła nas 60-letnia panna Bernhard, kórej nie znosiłem (We were taught German by a 60-year-old Miss Berhnard, whom I hated)*

niemożebnie See nieziemsko

niemożebny [nyeh-moh-ZHEHB-ni] *adj* Unbearable; impossible; terrible; nasty <damn, damned, goddamn, goddamned, god-awful, blasted, darn, darned, effing, flipping, forking, freaking, frigging, pesky> eg *Wtedy właśnie zaczął się niemożebny hałas (Just then a darned noise started)*

niemra* [NYEHM-rah] *nf* A female German <kraut, krauthead, sauerkraut, Helga> eg *Dwie niemry wysiadły z Mercedesa (Two Helgas got out of a Mercedes)*

nieprawda See dawno i nieprawda

nierób [NYEH-roop] *nm* A person who regulary and chronically avoids work; a shirker <goldbricker, bunk lizard, coffee cooler, feather merchant, lazybones, lazy-ass, lazy bum, bum, clock watcher, dog-fucker> eg *Powiedz temu nierobowi, żeby brał się do roboty (Tell that lazybones to get to work)*

nierówno See mieć nierówno pod sufitem

niespecjalnie [nyeh-spehts-YAHL-nyeh] *adv* Not very well <not pretty well, not so good, not so hot> eg *Jak idzie praca? Niespecjalnie (How's the work going? Not so good)*

niespecjalny [nyeh-spehts-YAHL-ni] *adj* Not very good; mediocre <lousy, awful, bush-league, cheap, crappy, shitty, cruddy, doggy, low-rent, low-ride, no-good, raggedy-ass, schlocky, stinking, tacky, trashy, two-bit, dime-a-dozen, fair to middling, garden variety, of a sort, of sorts, piddling, pissy-ass, run-of-the-mill, small-time> eg *Co myślisz o ich najnowszej płycie? Myślę, że jest niespecjalna (What do you think about their latest album? I think it's no-good)*

niestrawny [nyeh-STRAHV-ni] *adj* Unacceptable or untolerable, esp because repelling or disgusting <grose, grotty, grody, gross, barfy, scuzzy, sleazy, icky, yucky, gooky, grungy, ech, yech> eg *Uważam, że ten film był całkowicie niestrawny (I think the movie was grotty to the max)*

nieudacznik [nyeh-oo-DAHCH-neek] *nm* A person who fails and reaches nothing in life <underachiever, loser, born loser, second-rater, schlemiel, schmendrick, schmo, schnook, screwup, fuckup, hacker, muffer, scrub, dub, dool tool, turkey, lump, buterfingers, fumble-fist, goof, goof-off, goofball, eightball, foulball, klutz, also-ran, never-was, nonstarter, zero, lightweight, nobody, non, nonentity, noname, small potatoes, small timer, bush-leaguer> eg *Chciał to zrobić, ale taki z niego nieudacznik, że nie sądze, żeby to zrobił (He wanted to do it, but he's such a klutz that I don't think he will)*

nieuk [NYEH-ook] *nm* An unintelligent or failing student <flunky, dropout> eg *Nie zadawaj się z tym nieukiem (Don't hang around with that flunky)*

niewąski See nielichy

niewąsko See nieziemsko

niewyżyta [nyeh-vi-ZHI-tah] *adj* (Of a woman) Sexually voracious and insatiable <good in bed, G.I.B., sex machine, fuck machine, nympho> eg *Sam nie wiem, co mam już zrobić. Ta laska jest po prostu niewyżyta i chce więcej i więcej! (I don't really know what I should do. The chick is simply a sex machine and needs more and more!)*

niewyżyty [nyeh-vi-ZHI-ti] *adj* (Of a man) Sexually voracious and insatiable <good in bed, sex machine, fuck machine, nympho> eg *Słyszałam, że jej były jest naprawdę niewyżyty (I heard her ex is really good in bed)*

niewydymka See cnotka

niewyparzony See mieć niewyparzoną gębę

niezły [WAHD-ni] *adj* **1** (Usually about a sum of money) Big <fine, whole, lump, pretty, hefty> eg *Pięć tysięcy! To ładna suma! (Five thousand! That's a pretty penny!)* **2** Quite good, attractive or wonderful <great, cool, swell, fab, rad, def, far-out, awesome, frantic, terrific, funky, gorgeous, groovy, hellacious, neat, peachy, dandy, baddest, mean, solid, super-dooper, wailing, wicked, gnarly, top-notch, ten, ace-high, A-OK, A-1, some, pretty good, dishy, hunky> eg *Ten samochód jest na prawdę niezły (This car is real cool)*

niezdara See niedołęga

niezguła See niedołęga

nieziemski [nyeh-ZYEHM-skee] *adj* Excellent; wonderful; extremely good <out of this world, great, cool, swell, fab, rad, def, far-out, awesome, frantic, terrific, funky, gorgeous, groovy, hellacious, neat, peachy, dandy, baddest, mean, solid, super-dooper, wailing, wicked, gnarly, top-notch, ten, ace-high, A-OK, A-1, some> eg *Ona jest naprawdę nieziemska! (She's truly out of this world!)*

nieziemsko [nyeh-ZYEHM-skoh] (or **nielicho** [nyeh-LEE-khoh] or **niewąsko** [nyeh-VOHN-skoh] or **niemożebnie** [nyeh-moh-ZHEHB-nyeh]) *adv* Extremely; exceedingly; very <awful, god-awful, real, mighty, plenty, damn, damned, goddamn, goddamned, darn, darned, effing, flipping, forking, freaking, frigging, fucking, one's ass off, one's brains out, one's head off, to the max, like all get-out, like sin, to beat the band, like all creation, as blazes, as can be, as hell, like hell, in full swing> eg *Byłam niewąsko przestraszona (I was darned frightened); Jestem dziś niemożebnie zmęczona (I'm damn tired today)*

niskie zawieszenie* [NEE-skyeh zah-vyeh-SHEH-nyeh] *nn phr* A woman's short legs or unshapely buttocks and hips <duck ass, piggy ass, pork chop> eg *Wcale nie przeszkadza mi jej niskie zawieszenie. Grunt to duże cycki (I don't mind her duck ass. Tits are all important)*

nisko skanalizowana* [NEES-koh skah-nah-lee-zoh-VAH-nah] *nf adj* (Of a woman) Having short legs or unshapely buttocks and hips <legless, pork-chopped, piggy assed, duck-assed> eg *Nie podoba mi się, bo jest bardzo nisko skanalizowana (I don't like her because she's very much piggy style)*

nitka See zgrać się

nóż See iść pod nóż, cios w plecy

noc See brzydki jak noc

nochal [NOH-khahl] *nm* The nose <schnozz, beak, beezer, honker, smeller, snoot> eg *Ale masz pryszcza na kulfonie Dobrze zapamiętałem jego czerwony nochal (I rememeber that red schnozz of him pretty well)*

nocka [NOHTS-kah] *nf* A night shift or a period during the night when one works <graveyard shift, lobster shift, midnight oil> eg *Nocną zmianę nazywamy tu nocką (A night-shift is called a lobster shift here)*
See zarwać nockę

nocnik See obudzić się z ręką w nocniku

noga [NOH-gah] *nf* **1** Someone who knows nothing about a given subject; an incompetent person; a dilettante <screw-up, fuck-up, loser, dool tool, turkey, schmendrick, duffer, flubdub, lummox, lump, foozler, buterfingers, fumble-fist, goof, goof-off, goofball, eightball, foulball, klutz, also-ran, never-was, nonstarter, drag-ass, foot-dragger, schlepper, slowpoke> eg *On to jest prawdziwa noga. Nic ci nie pomoże (He's a real duffer. He won't help you)* **2** Soccer <ball> eg *Zagrajmy w nogę (Let's play ball)* **3** A young and attractive woman, esp with shapely legs <chick, broad, gal, pussy, cunt, ass, piece of ass, piece, dish, babe, baby, dame, beauty, beaut, beauty queen, baby doll, doll, dolly, dollface, dreamboat, dream girl, eating stuff, eyeful, flavor, looker, good-looker, head-turner, traffic-stopper, honey, killer, hot number, package, knockout, oomph girl, peach, bombshell, sex bunny, sex job, sex kitten, sex pot, table grade, ten, bunny, centerfold, cheesecake, date bait, dazzler, heifer, fluff, quail, sis, skirt, tail, job, leg, tart, tomato, pussycat, cooz, twat> eg *Spójrz na tę nogę! (Check out that doll!)*
See być jedną nogą w grobie, chwycić Boga za nogi, dać nogę, do góry nogami, iść w nogi, kula u nogi, lać, mieć ręce i nogi, na jednej nodze, nogi po samą szyję, padać, pies z kulawą nogą, podwinęła się komuś noga, ręce opadają, traktować kogoś per noga, wstawać lewą nogą, wyciągnąć nogi, nie czuć nóg

nogi po samą szyję [NOH-gee poh SAH-moh SHI-yeh] (or **nogi do sufitu** [NOH-gee doh soo-FEE-too] or **nogi aż do nieba** [NOH-gee ahsh doh NYEH-bah]) *npl phr* Long and shapely legs (of a woman) <gams, gambs, stems> eg *Czy to ta z tymi zajebistymi nogami aż po szyję? (Is she the one with the gorgeous gams?)*

nora [NOH-rah] *nf nf* **1** Any dirty, shabby, dilapidated, or repulsive place, esp an apartment <dump, hole, hellhole, rathole, shithole, shithouse, joint, firetrap> eg *Urodził się w okropnej norze (He was born in a terrible rathole)* **2** A small town, esp in the country; any place far from civilization <jerk town, jerkwater town, backwater, hellhole, rathole, mudhole, real hole, noplaceville, hicksville, whistle stop, dump,

armpit, East Jesus, Bumfuck Egypt> eg *To miejsce to prawdziwa nora (This place is a real hole)*

normalka [nohr-MAHL-kah] *nf* A typical or normal behavior or situation <same old shit, SOS, vanilla, white bread, garden variety, everyday> eg *Wstaje, je, wychodzi do biura. Normalka (He gets up, eats, leaves for his office. Same old shit)*

nos See ciągnąć nosa, dać po dupie, dostać po dupie, kręcić nosem, mieć coś/kogoś gdzieś, mieć nosa, móc kogoś pocałować, padać, pilnować swego nosa, pod nosem, przelecieć komuś koło nosa, sprzątnąć komuś coś sprzed nosa, z palcem, zadzierać nosa

nosić kogoś na rękach [NOH-sheech KOH-gohsh nah REHN-kakh] *v phr* To treat someone with great care and tenderness, as one's favorite person; to pamper <treat with kid gloves, handle with kid gloves, treat someone as an apple of someone's eye, give someone the red carpet treatment, pet> eg *Byłam noszona na rękach (I was treated with kid gloves)*

nosić koszulę w zębach [NOH-sheech koh-SHOO-leh v ZEHM-bahkh] *v phr* To be very young; to be a mere child <be knee high to a grasshopper, rock the cradle, piss in one's pants, shit in one's pants> eg *Było to 20 lat temu, kiedy ty nosiłeś koszulę w zębach (It was 20 years ago when you were still pissing in your pants)*

nowiusieńki [noh-vyoo-SHYEHÑ-kee] *adj* New <newey, brand new, spanking new, fire new, cherry, hot off the fire, hot off the press, up to the minute> eg *Widziałeś jego nowiusieńką Mazdę? (Did you see his brand new Mazda?)*

nówka [NOOF-kah] *nf* Anything new, trendy, or popular <newie, latest thing, latest wrinkle, last word, in-thing, the thing, go-go, hip> eg *Nie chcesz tego kupić? Dlaczego? To nówka (You don't want to buy it? Why? It's a newie)*

nowobogacki [noh-voh-boh-GAH-tskee] *nm* A person having only recently become rich and often tending to tastelessly spend a lot of money to prove one's wealth; a nouveau riche <slick, new rich, new money, Johnny-come-lately> eg *Nie ma nic bardziej obrzydliwego niż nowobogaccy (There's nothing more disgusting than the new rich)*

nudny jak flaki z olejem [NOOD-ni yahk FLAH-kee z oh-LEH-yehm] *adj phr* Very dull, boring, or tedious <boring like hell, boring as hell, dull as dish-water, blah, flat, flat as a pancake, draggy, dragass, dullsville. dragsville, deadsville, dead, beige, yawny> eg *Film, który widzieliśmy, był nudny jak flaki z olejem (The movie we saw was dull as dishwater)*

nudy [NOO-di] (or **nudy na pudy** [NOO-di nah POO-di] may be added) *npl* Anything boring or boredom itself <ho-hums, hum-drum, blahs, yawn, downer, bummer, drag, drip, pain in the ass, pain in the neck, deadwood, blister, snooze act, snooze> eg *Jak wam się podobał koncert? Nudy na pudy (How did you like the concert? It was a yawn)*
See umierać z nudów

nudzić się jak mops [NOO-jeech shyeh yahk MOHPS] *v phr* To be very bored <die of boredom, be bored stiff, be bored like hell, be bored as hell, snooze, yawn> eg *Nie podobał jej się film. Nudziła się jak mops (She didn't like the movie. She was bored stiff)*

nudziara [noo-JAH-rah] *nf* A boring woman <drag, nerd, dead-ass, drip, pain in the ass> eg *Ale z ciebie nudziara! (You are nothing but a pain in the ass)*

nudziarz [NOO-jahsh] *nm* A boring man <drag, nerd, dead-ass, drip, pain in the ass> eg *O, idzie jej znajomy. Co za nudziarz! (Here comes that friend of her. What a drag!)*

numer [NOO-mehr] *nm* **1** A scandalous fact or situation; a scandal <gas, fuss, stink, hot potato, bad scene, bad news, can of worms, bag of worms, takedown, putdown, shit, serious shit, deep shit, deep water, drag, bind, bitch, bummer, downer, headache, double trouble, snafu, pain in the ass, pain in the neck, spot, mess, holy mess, pickle, squeeze, hard time, glitch, stinker, skeleton, skeleton in the closet, sizzler, scorcher, dynamite, Watergate, fine kettle of fish, fine how do you do, fine cup of coffee, big stink, curtains, lights out, game's over> eg *Jak mnie złapią, to będdzie numer (Bad scene for me if they find me)* **2** A song or other short piece of music <cut, number> eg *Na tej płycie są tylko cztery numery (There are only four numbers on this LP)*
See nie ze mną te numery, strzelić numer, wykręcić komuś numer

numerant [noo-MEH-rahnt] (or **numer** [NOO-mehr] or **numerek** [noo-MEH-rehk]) *nm* A man impressive, extravagant, or disorderly in behavior <artist, joker, clown, article, ham, character, item, number> eg *Z ciebie jest niezły numer (You're quite a number!*

numerantka [noo-meh-RAHNT-kah] (or **numer** [NOO-mehr] or **numerek** [noo-MEH-rehk]) *nf* A woman impressive, extravagant, or disorderly in behavior <artist, joker, clown, article, ham, character, item, number> eg *Numerek z ciebie panienko niewąski (You're quite a number, lady)*

numerek* [noo-MEH-rehk] (or **szybki numerek*** [SHIP-kee noo-MEH-rehk]) *nm* A sex act, esp a quick one <quickie, quick one, wham bam thank you ma'am, bunny fuck, fast fuck> eg *Ta kurewka lubi odwalać numerki, bo może w ten sposób przerobić więcej klientów (The hooker likes doing bunny fucks because she can handle more customers that way)*
See strzelić numer

numery [noo-MEH-ri] *npl* Automotive license plates <pads, plates, tags, numbers> eg *Były to zachodnie wozy na polskich numerach (They were western cars with Polish plates)*

nygus [NI-goos] *nm* A person who regulary and chronically avoids work; a shirker <goldbricker, bunk lizard, coffee cooler, feather merchant, lazybones, lazy-ass, lazy bum, bum, clock watcher, dog-fucker> eg *Powiedz temu nygusowi, żeby brał się do roboty (Tell that lazybones to get to work)*

O

o żeż kurwa See kurwa

o kurwa See kurwa

o niebo [oh NYEH-boh] *adv phr* More than <cut above, way, far cry> eg *Jest o niebo lepszy od tego, jakim był rok temu (It is a far cry better from what it was last yeat)*

o suchym pysku See na sucho

o w dupę See w mordę

o w mordę See w mordę

o w twarz See w mordę

o wilku mowa [oh VEEL-koo MOH-vah] *phr* Someone comes just when you are talking about him or her <speak of the devil, talk of the devil, look what the cat dragged in> eg *Właśnie rozmawialiśmy o twoim bracie, gdy pojawił się w drzwiach. O wilku mowa (We were just talking about your brother when he came in the door. Speak of the devil)*

obłapka* [ohb-WAHP-kah] (or **obłap*** [OHB-wahp] *nm*) *nf* Sexual dalliance, esp short of copulation; touching or caressing <a feel, a feel-up, grab-ass, necking, petting, smooching> eg *Spędziliśmy razem noc, ale nic się nie wydarzyło. Żadnej obłapki czy coś w tym stylu (We spent a night together, but nothing happened. No petting or whatever)*

obłęd [OHB-wehnt] (or **obłęd w trampkach** [OHB-wehnt TRAHMP-kakh] may be added) *nm* An extremely irritating or hilarious situation or thing <barrel of laughs, ball, blast, gas, groove, boot, charge, bang, kick, belt, buzz, charge, drive, flash, flip, jolt, riot, lift, rush, upper, wallop, whoopee, fun and games, un-fucking-believable> eg *Staliśmy cztery godziny na granicy. Obłęd! (We waited on the border for four hours. Un-fucking-believable!); Dziekan wlazł na stół zaczął śpiewać. Mówię ci, obłęd! (The dean got up on the table and started to sing. What a gas!)*

obłęd w oczach [OHB-wehnt v OH-chahkh] *nm* Great excitement bordering on insanity, esp at the sight of someone or something excellent <high, buzz, charge, rush, bang, kick, cloud nine, turn-on> eg *Miały obłęd w oczach, gdy go zobaczyły (They got a rush when they saw him)*

obłędnie [ohb-WEHND-nyeh] (or **bezbłędnie** [behz-BWEHND-nyeh]) *adv* Extremely; exceedingly; very <awful, god-awful, real, mighty, plenty, damn, damned, goddamn, goddamned, darn, darned, effing, flipping, forking, freaking, frigging, fucking, one's ass off, one's brains out, one's head off, to the max, like all get-out, like sin, to beat the band, like all creation, as blazes, as can be, as hell, like hell, in full swing> eg *Ona jest bezbłędnie zgrabna (She's darned stacked)*

obłędny [ohb-WEHND-ni] (or **bezbłędny** [behz-BWEHND-ni]) *adj* Excellent; wonderful; extremely good <great, cool, swell, fab, rad, def, far-out, awesome, frantic, terrific, funky, gorgeous, groovy, hellacious, neat, peachy, dandy, baddest, mean, solid, super-dooper, wailing, wicked, gnarly, top-notch, ten, ace-high, A-OK, A-1, some> eg *Zna judo i nikogo się nie boi. Jest bezbłędna (She knows judo and she's not afraid of anybody. She's cool)*

obłowić się [ohb-WOH-veech shyeh] *v* To earn a lot of money; to get rich <pull down, pick up, clean up, rack up, pile up, stack up, cash in, make a bundle, ride the gravy train> eg *Obłowił się na dostawach dla wojska (He made a bundle on deliveries for the army)*

obżerać się [ohb-ZHEH-rahch shyeh] (perf **obeżreć się** [oh-BEH-zhrehch shyeh]) *v* To overeat, eat greedily and more than needed <stuff oneself, pig out, scarf out, pork out> eg *Obeżarł się ciasta i zaczął rzygać (He piged out on cake and started to puke)*

obalać [oh-BAH-lahch] (perf **obalić** [oh-BAH-leech]; or **obciągać** [ohp-CHYOHN-gahch] perf **obciągnąć** [ohp-CHYOHNG-nohnch]) *v phr* To drink an entire bottle of alcohol <kill, knock back, guzzle, gargle, lap, tank up, slug down, swig> eg *W parę minut obciągnęli pół litra wódki (In a few minutes they knocked back a half-liter bottle of vodka)*

obchodzić kogoś See gówno kogoś obchodzić

obchodzić się z kimś jak z jajkiem [ohp-KHOH-jeech shyeh yahk z YAH-ee-kyehm] *v phr* To treat someone with excessive care and tenderness; to pamper <treat with kid gloves, handle with kid gloves, treat someone as an apple of someone's eye, give someone the red carpet treatment, pet> eg *On jest tutaj guru i wszyscy obchodzą się z nim jak z jajkiem (He's a guru around here and everybody treats him with kid gloves)*

obciągać** [ohp-CHYOHN-gahch] (or **ciągnąć**** [CHYOHNG-nohnch] perf **obciągnąć**** [ohp-CHYOHNG-nohnch]; **druta*** [DROO-tah] or **laskę*** [LAHS-keh] or **pałę*** [PAH-weh] or **fleta*** [FLEH-tah] may be added) To perform fellatio <suck off, blow, eat, give head, dick-lick, go down on, play the skin flute> eg *Chciała mu obciągnąć, ale poszedł spać (She wanted to suck him off, but he went to sleep)*
See obalać

obciach [OHP-chyahkh] (or **obsuwa** [ohp-SOO-vah] *nf*) *nm* A shameful or scandalous fact or situation; a shame, disgrace, or scandal <gas, come-down, put-down, take-down, dump, bummer, hot potato, bad scene, bad news, can of worms, bag of worms, takedown, putdown, shit, serious shit, deep shit, deep water, drag, bind, bitch, bummer, downer, headache, double trouble, snafu, pain in the ass, pain in the neck, spot, mess, holy mess, pickle, squeeze, hard time, glitch, stinker, skeleton, skeleton in the closet, sizzler, scorcher, dynamite, Watergate, fine kettle of fish, fine how do you do, fine cup of coffee, big stink, curtains, lights out, game's over> eg *Pies zjadł stek, który mieliśmy na obiad. Ale obciach! The dog's eaten the steak we were going to have for dinner. This is a fine kettle of fish!)*

obcięty na jeża [ohp-CHYEHN-ti nah YEH-zhah] (or **obcięty na pałę** [ohp-CHYEHN-ti nah PAH-weh] or **obcięty na zapałkę** [zah-PAH-oo-keh ohp-CHYEHN-ti nah]) *adj phr* Having very short hair <having a crew cut, having a razor cut, having a buzz cut, skinhead> eg *Nie podoba mi się ten facet obciąty na jeża (I don't like that skinhead); Kim jest ten gość ostrzyżony na pałę pod oknem (Who's that skinhead near the window)*

obcykane See mieć coś obcykane

obcyndalać się See opierdalać się

obeżreć się See obżerać się

obibok [oh-BEE-bohk] *nm* A person who regulary and chronically avoids work; a shirker <goldbricker, bunk lizard, coffee cooler, feather merchant, lazybones, lazy-ass, lazy bum, bum, clock watcher, dog-fucker> eg *Powiedz temu obibokowi, żeby brał się do roboty (Tell that lazybones to get to work)*

obiema nogami [oh-NYEH-mah noh-GAH-mee] (or **obydwoma nogami** [oh-bid-VOH-mah noh-GAH-mee]) *adv phr* Having achieved a favorable position, esp for further action <one foot in the door> eg *Ona jest obiema nogami w szoł biznesie. Jej talent daleko ją zaprowadzi (She's one foot in the door in show business. Her talent will carry her a long way)*

obijać się See opierdalać się

obkuwać See kuć

oblecieć [ohb-LEH-chyehch] *v* To be acceptable or suitable; to meet certain standards <do, wash, work, go down, cut it, make the grade, make the cut, make it, cut the mustard, pass in the dark, fill the bill, fit in, fit the bill, suit one fine, be

OK, be okay, be kopasetic, be hunky-dory, be so-so> eg *Co myślisz o tej propozycji? Obleci (What do you think about this proposal? It will make the grade)*

oblewać [ohb-LEH-vahch] *v* **1** (perf **oblać** [OHB-lahch]; or **opijać** [oh-PEE-yahch] perf **opić** [OH-peech]) (To go out and) To celebrate by drinking; to drink to a given occasion <open a bottle, paint the town red, raise hell, bar-hop, bar-crawl> eg *A więc zdałeś egzamin. Oblejmy to! (So you passed the exam. Let's open a bottle!); Zdał egzamin doktorski i poszli to opić (He passed his Ph.D. exam and they went to paint the town red)* **2** (perf **oblać** [OHB-lahch]; or **polewać** [poh-LEH-vahch] perf **polać** [POH-lahch]) To fail a student <flunk, flush, bust> eg *Ten sukinsyn znów mnie oblał (That son of a bitch flunked me again)* **3** (perf **oblać** [OHB-lahch]; or **polewać** [poh-LEH-vahch] perf **polać** [POH-lahch]) To fail an examination, course, etc <flunk, flush, bust, strike out> eg *Czy to prawda, że oblał ten egzamin? (Is that true that he flunked this exam?)*

obmacywać See macać

obrabiać komuś dupę See robić komuś koło dupy

obrotny [oh-BROHT-ni] *adj* Smart and energetic, esp in business; having business acumen <street-smart, street-wise, smart-ass, sly, cagey, foxy, sharp, smooth, cute, in the know, on the inside> eg *Jej ojciec to bardzo obrotny facet (Her father is a very street-smart guy)*

obrotny w gębie See mocny w gębie

obroty See brać kogoś do galopu

obryć Perf ryć

obrzyn [OHB-zhin] *nm* A rifle with a cut-off barrel; a sawed-off shotgun <no slang equivalent> eg *W prawym ręku trzymał obrzyn (He was holding a sawed-off gun in his right hand)*

obskakiwać [ohp-skah-KEE-vahch] (perf **obskoczyć** [ohp-SKOH-chich]) *v* **1** To quickly go from one place to another in order to take care of things, esp business <hit, cruise> eg *Trzeba obskoczyć wszystkie te miejsca i spytać, co ludzie o tym sądzą (We've got to hit all these places and ask people what they think about it)* **2** (or **skakać koło kogoś** [SKAH-kahch KOH-woh KOH-gohsh]) To treat someone with excessive care, ardor, or tenderness; to pamper <treat with kid gloves, handle with kid gloves, treat someone as an apple of someone's eye, give someone the red carpet treatment, pet> eg *On jest tutaj guru i wszyscy go obskakują (He's a guru around here and everybody treats him with kid gloves)* **3** (or **skakać koło kogoś** [SKAH-kahch KOH-woh KOH-gohsh]) To follow someone in search for sexual encounter; to invite or request sexual favors <chase, cruise, tail, troll, run around, dog someone's footsteps, hunt for cunt> eg *Ten jej były chłopak obskakuje ją gdziekolwiek ona idzie (Her ex-boyfriend is chasing her around wherever she goes)*

obstawa [ohp-STAH-vah] *nf* Bodyguards <gorillas, apes, dogs, lookouts, bouncers, meatheads, sidewinders> eg *Obstawa zatrzymała człowieka, który miał broń (The sidewinders stopped a man who was carrying a gun)*

obstukane See mieć coś obcykane

obsuwa See obciach

obudzić się z ręką w nocniku [oh-BOO-jeech shyeh z REHN-koh v nohts-NEE-koo] (or **obudzić się z palcem w nocniku** [oh-BOO-jeech shyeh z PAHL-tsehm v nohts-NEE-koo]) *v phr* To suddenly realize one is in an unfavorable position, esp because it is too late; (figuratively) to wake up <be taken aback> eg *Obudziłem się z ręką w nocniku (I was totally taken aback)*

obyczajówka [oh-bi-chah-YOOF-kah] *nf* The police unit in charge of suppressing prostitution <vice squad, pussy posse> eg *Obyczajówka aresztowała ją za prostytucję (She was arrested by the pussy posse for prostitution)*

ocena państwowa [oh-TSEH-nah pahñ-STFOH-vah] *nf phr* A grade of C <hook, pass, gentleman's C> eg *Dostał tylko ocenę państwową z tego testu (He only got a C on that test)*

ochajtać się Perf chajtać się

ochlać się Perf chlać

ochlaj [OH-khlah-ee] (or **ochlaj party** [OH-khlah-ee PAHR-ti] may be added) *nm* A drinking party; a carousal <bash, bender, bust, twister, wingding, winger> eg *Powiedz mi o tym ochlaj party (Tell me about that bender)*

ochroniarz [oh-KHROH-nyahsh] *nm* A bodyguard <gorilla, ape, dog, lookout, bouncer, meathead, sidewinder, lookout> eg *Zaczynał jako ochroniarz (He started as a gorilla)*

ochrzan See opierdol

ochujały** [oh-khoo-YAH-wi] *adj* Insane or eccentric <crazy, crazy as a loon, freaky, fruity, goofy, cooky, loony, nuts, nutty, nutty as a fruitcake, psycho, screwy, screw-loose, sicko, wacko, weirdo, schizo, wild, ape, bananas, bent, bonkers, cracked, dopey, ga-ga, half-baked, loony, loopy, mental, nerts, nuts, nutty, off one's nut, off one's rocker, off one's base, off the track, off the trolley, out one's skull, freaked-out, schizzed-out, psyched-out, flipped-out, unglued, unstuck, unwrapped, unzipped, fucked in the head, flaky, mad, off-beat> eg *Nasz nowy facet od matmy jest naprawdę ochujały (Our new math prof is real fucked in the head)*

ochujeć** [oh-KHOO-yehch] (or **ochujać**** [oh-KHOO-yahch] or **ocipieć*** [oh-CHEE-pyehch] or **oczadzieć** [oh-CHAH-jehch]) *v* **1** To lose mental fitness; to become insane or eccentric <go crazy, go crazy as a loon, blow one's cork, blow one's top, blow a fuse, crack up, freak out, flip out, go ape, go bananas, go bent, go bonkers, go cracked, go dopey, go ga-ga, go half-baked, go loony, go loopy, go mental, go nerts, go nuts, go nutty, go off one's nut, go off one's rocker, go off one's base, go off the track, go off the trolley, go out one's skull, go psycho, go schizo, go screwy, go wacky, go weird, go wild, schiz out, psych out, come unglued, come unstuck, come unwrapped, go to pieces> eg *Facet już chyba zupełnie ochujał (The guy must have gone really screwy)* **2** To become bewildered, disoriented, or confused <get spaced out, get mixed up, get discombobulated, get flabbergasted, get messed up, get unscrewed, get farmisht, get balled up, get shook up, get floored, get unglued, get unzipped, get fried, get screwed-up, get fucked-up, get flummoxed, get kerflooey, get caught off base> eg *Ochujałem zupełnie i nie wiedziałem, co zrobi/ć (I got fucked-up and had no idea what to do)*

ociupina [oh-chyoo-PEE-nah] (or **ociupinę** [oh-chyoo-PEE-neh]) **1** *nf* A little bit <smidgen, tad, wee bit, itty bit> eg *I don't want the whole thing. Give me just a smidgen (Nie chcę wszystkiego. Daj mi tylko ociupinę)* **2** *adv* A little; not much <bit, wee, tad, wee bit, itty bit> eg *Myślę, że ciasto jest ociupinę za słodkie (I think the cake is a tad too sweet)*

ocyganić [oh-tsi-GAH-neech] (or **oszwabić** [oh-SHFAH-beech]) *v* To cheat; to swindle; to deceive; to scheme <con, rip off, shaft, roll, chisel, gyp, scam, screw, stiff, fleece, dick, do in, take in, do a number on, flim-flam, bamboozle, run a number on, take someone for a ride, take someone to the cleaners, throw someone a curve, pull a fast one, fuck over, screw over, angle, take in, snow, do a snow job, double-shuffle, fast-shuffle, flimflam, give a bun steer, give someone a line, have someone on, lead someone down the garden path, do a snow job, jerk someone's chain, pull someone's chain, pull one's leg, pull someone's string, pull the wool over someone's eyes, put someone on, snow, use smoke and mirrors> eg *Ten handlarz ocyganił mnie na dwie stówy (That salesman dicked me for two hundred)*

oczadzieć See ochujeć

oczko w głowie [OHCH-koh v GWOH-vyeh] *nn phr* One's favorite person or thing <apple of someone's eye, pet, teacher's pet> eg *Jako jedyna córka była oczkiem w głowie swego ojca (As the only daughter, she was the apple of her father's eye)*

od łebka See na łebka

od biedy [ohd BYEH-di] *adv phr* Barely, hardly, or poorly (acceptable or suitable) <will do> eg *Co myślisz o tej propozycji? Od biedy może być (What do you think of this proposal? It will do)*

od cholery [oht khoh-LEH-ri] (or **od chuja**** [oht KHOO-yah] or **od groma** [ohd GROH-mah] or **od metra** [ohd MEHT-rah] or **od skurwysyna**** [oht skoor-vi-SI-nah] or **od zajebania**** [ohd zah-yeh-BAH-nyah]; **i trochę** [ee TROH-kheh] or **i ciut-ciut** [ee CHYOOT CHYOOT] may be added) *adv phr* Plenty; many <helluva lot, lotsa, lotta, oodles, scads, heaps, bags, barrels, loads, piles, tons, wads, jillions, zillions, enough to choke a horse, shitload, fuckload, truckload> eg *Było tam od cholery ludzi (The place was shithouse full of people); Zarabia od chuja pieniędzy (He earns a fuckload of money)*

od deski do deski [ohd DEHS-kee doh DEHS-kee] (or **od dechy do dechy** [ohd DEH-khi doh DEH-khi]) *adv phr* From beginning to end; thoroughly <from cover to cover, from A to Z> eg *Przeczytałem tę książkę od dechy do dechy (I read this book from cover to cover)*

od groma See od cholery

od maleńkości [ohd mah-lehñ-KOHSH-chee] *adv phr* Since childhood <since Hector was a pup, since one was knee high to a grasshopper, since one was wet behind the ears> eg *Znam go od maleńkości (I've known him since he was knee high to a grasshopper)*

od metra See od cholery

od ręki [ohd REHN-kee] (or **od zaraz** [ohd ZAH-rahs] *adv phr* At once; immediately; instantly <right off, right away, pretty damn quick, PDQ, ASAP, on the spot, in half a mo, like now, in a jiffy, in a flash, in half a shake, right off the bat, like a bat out of hell, like a shot out of hell, hubba-hubba, horseback, like greased lightning> eg *Chcę, żebyś zaczął pracę od zaraz (I want you to start work right off)*

od rzeczy See gadać od rzeczy

od skurwysyna See od cholery

od tylca* [oht TIL-tsah] *adv phr* With a male partner in a sex act entering the other partner from the rear <dog fashion, dog style, dog ways, doggie fashion, doggie

style, doggie ways> eg *Czy kiedykolwiek robiliście to od tylca? (Have you ever done it dog-ways?)*

od zajebania See od cholery

od zawsze [ohd ZAHF-sheh] *adv phr* Since always; permanently <since day one, since year one, since God was young, since Hector was a pup, since the night was day, since the sky was blue, since as long as one can remember, forever and a day> eg *Robert był fanem Motley Crue od zawsze (Robert has been a Motley Crue fan since day one)*

od zera [ohd ZEH-rah] *adv phr* (Of starting an activity) From the beginning; from nothing <from scratch, from square one, from the git-go, from the ground up, from the top, from the word go, from the drawing board> eg *Zaczynali od zera, ale teraz są bogaci (They started from scratch, but now they're rich)*

odbębniać See odfajkowywać

odbić See odbijać

odbić See odpierdolić

odbijać kogoś komuś [OHD-beech KOH-gohsh KOH-moosh] (perf **odbić** [OHD-beech]) *v phr* To take someone's girlfriend or boyfriend away <bird-dog, beat someone's time, steal> eg *Wcale nie chciałam jej odbić faceta (Honestly, I didn't want to bird-dog her); Dlaczego musiałeś odbić kobietę mnie, twojemu najlepszemu kumplowi? (Why did you have to go and bird-dog me, your best buddy?)*

odbijać się czkawką [ohd-BEE-yahch shyeh CHKAHF-koh] *v phr* To bear future repercussions <fall out, follow up, follow through, spin off, blow off, cause waves, feed back, kick back, score, open the can of worms, bottom-line, chain-react, make waves> eg *Może im się to odbić nieprzyjemną czkawką w przyszłości (It might cause waves in the future)*

odchować See chować

odchrzanić się See odpierdolić się

odcisk See nadepnąć komuś na odcisk

odczepić się See odpierdolić się

oddychać See mieć czym oddychać

odfajkowywać [oht-fah-ee-koh-VI-vahch] (perf **odfajkować** [oht-fah-ee-KOH-vahch]; or **odbębniać** [ohd-BEHMB-nyahch] perf **odbębnić** [ohd-BEHMB-neech]; or **odwalać** [ohd-VAH-lahch] perf **odwalić** [ohd-VAH-leech]) *v* To finish something very cursorily or carelessly, in order to get rid of it as soon as possible <do something half-assedly, do a half-assed job, do something half-heartedly, give something a lick and a promise> eg *Hej, nie posprzątałeś swojego pokoju! Ty to tylko odfajkowałeś (Hey, you didn't clean your room! You just gave it a lick and a promise); Sądząc po gotowym produkcie, odfajkowali to (Judging by the finished product, they did a half-assed job)*

odjazd See odlot

odjazdowo See odlotowo

odjazdowy See odlotowy

odjeżdżać See odlatywać

odjebać See odpierdolić

odjebać się See odpierdolić się

odjebany See odpierdolony

odjechać See odjeżdżać

odlatywać [ohd-lah-TI-vahch] (perf **odlecieć** [ohd-LEH-chyehch]; or **odjeżdżać** [ohd-YEHZH-jahch] perf **odjechać** [ohd-YEH-khahch]) *v* To be intoxicated with drugs or alcohol; to be in a state of euphoria caused by drugs or alcohol <be high, be stoned, be doped up, be blown away, be canned, be cooked, be corked, be fried, be gassed, be in bad shape, be impaired, be illuminated, be knocked out, be lit, be loaded, be looped, be pickled, be polluted, be shitfaced, be stewed, be wiped, be zonked> eg *Odleciała już po pięciu minutach (She got high in five minutes)* **2** To be in a state of delightful euphoria; to be thrilled <have a ball, have a blast, have a gas, have a groove, have a boot, have a charge, have a bang, have a kick, have a belt, have a buzz, have a charge, have a drive, have a flash, have a flip, have a jolt, have a riot, have a lift, have a rush, have a upper, have a wallop, have a whoopee, have fun and games> eg *Ale będzie czad! (Are we going to have a ball!)*

odlecieć na [ohd-LEH-chehch nah] *v* To lose a specific amount of money <lose out, blow, drop a bundle, go to the cleaners, take a bath, tap out, wash out, be in the red> eg *Odleciałem na dużo kasy (I blew a lot of dough)*

odlecieć Perf odlatywać

odlewać się* [ohd-LEH-vahch shyeh] (perf **odlać się*** [OHD-lahch shyeh]; or **odpryskać się*** [oht-PRIS-kahch shyeh]) *v* To urinate <piss, take a piss, leak, take a leak, whizz, take a whizz, pee, take a pee> eg *Rany, muszę się odpryskać (Gee, I need to take a leak)*

odlot [OHD-loht] (or **odjazd** [OHD-yahst]) *nm* **1** A state of euphoria caused by drugs or alcohol <trip, high, rush, jolt, riot, kick, charge> eg *Te prochy są bardzo mocne. Odlot murowany (This shit is very potent. You sure gonna get high)* **2** Any delightful and euphoric sensation; thrill <good time, barrel of laughs, ball, blast, gas, groove, boot, charge, bang, kick, belt, buzz, charge, drive, flash, flip, jolt, riot, lift, rush, upper, wallop, whoopee, fun and games> eg *Ale będzie odlot! (Are we going to have a ball!)*

odlotowo [ohd-loh-TOH-voh] (or **odjazdowo** [ohd-yah-ZDOH-voh]) *adv* Extremely well; superbly <great, cool, swell, fab, rad, def, far-out, awesome, frantic, terrific, funky, gorgeous, groovy, hellacious, neat, peachy, dandy, baddest, mean, solid, super-dooper, wailing, wicked, gnarly, top-notch, ten, ace-high, A-OK, A-1, some> eg *Skończyłem właśnie pisanie tego słownika i czuję się odlotowo (I just finished writing this dictionary and I feel great); Ubrana była naprawdę odlotowo (She was dressed really far-out)*

odlotowy [ohd-loh-TOH-vi] (or **odjazdowy** [ohd-yah-ZDOH-vi]) *adj* Excellent; wonderful; extremely good <great, cool, swell, fab, rad, def, far-out, awesome, frantic, terrific, funky, gorgeous, groovy, hellacious, neat, peachy, dandy, baddest, mean, solid, super-dooper, wailing, wicked, gnarly, top-notch, ten, ace-high, A-OK, A-1, some> eg *Ten samochód jest na prawdę odlotowy (This car is real cool)*

odpał [OHT-pah-oo] *nm* Strange, unconventional, or unpredictable behavior that goes beyond the limits of acceptability; an excess <freaky antics, weird antics, offbeat antics> eg *Dość mam tych jego odpałów (I'm sick and tired of his freaky antics)*

odpadać [oht-PAH-dahch] *v* To unacceptable, inadequate, or impossible <be out of the question, not come up to scratch, not be up to scratch, not be up to snuff, not hack it, not have it, not cut out for, will not do, will not work, will not wash, will not fly, be a no-go, not go down, not cut it, not make the grade, not make the cut, not make it, not cut the mustard, not pass in the dark, not fill the bill, not fit in,

not fit the bill, not suit one fine, not be OK, not be okay, not be kopasetic, not be hunky-dory, not be so-so> eg *Ta druga możliwość odpada (That second possibility is out of the question)*

odpalać [oht-PAH-lahch] (or **odpalać działkę** [oht-PAH-lahch JAH-oo-keh]; perf **odpalić** [oht-PAH-leech]) *v* To give someone a (portion of a larger) sum of money; to share one's profit <give someone one's cut, give someone one's bite, give someone one's whack, give someone one's piece, give someone one's slice, shoot someone one's cut, shoot someone one's bite, shoot someone one's whack, shoot someone one's piece, shoot someone one's slice> eg *Odpalił mu swoją działkę (He gave him his cut); Spytałem, czy nie odpaliłby mi działki (I asked if he could shoot me his cut)*

odpicowany See odpierdolony

odpierdolić się** [oht-pyehr-DOH-leech shyeh] (or **odpieprzyć się*** [oht-PYEHP-shich shyeh] or **odpierniczyć się*** [oht-pyehr-NEE-chich shyeh] or **odpierdzielić się*** [oht-pyehr-JEH-leech shyeh] or **odwalić się** [ohd-VAH-leech shyeh] or **odjebać się**** [ohd-YEH-bahch shyeh]) *v* **1** (or **odczepić się** [oht-CHEH-peech shyeh] or **odchrzanić się** [oht-KHZHAH-neech shyeh]) (Esp in the imperative as a brusque command) To stop bothering someone or something and leave <fuck off, fuck oneself, fuck you, get the fuck out, get the hell out, leave someone alone, give someone a break, split, beat it, ankle, bag ass, blow, breeze off, burn rubber, butt out, buzz off, check out, cruise, cut and run, cut ass, cut out, drag ass, dust, ease out, fade, fade away, fade out, get going, get moving, get lost, get off the dime, get on one's horse, go south, haul ass, hightail, hit the bricks, hit the road, hop it, make tracks, pull out, scram, set sail, shove off, shuffle along, skate, skip out, split the scene, take off> eg *Odpierdol się, bo zadzwonięna policję (Get the fuck out of here or I call the police)* **2** To dress fancily and in one's best clothes <doll up, doll out, dress up, dress out, deck up, deck out, dog up, dog out, rag up, rag out, tog up, tog out, dress to kill, dress to the nines, dress to the teeth, dress sharp, dude up, fancy up, get up, ritz up, slick up, snazz up, spiff up, swank up, put on one's best nin and tucker, put on one's glad rags, put on one's Sunday clothes, put on the dog> eg *Lubię od czasu do czasu się odpierdolić i pójść na imprezę (I like to rag out and go to a party every now and then)*

odpierdolić** [oht-pyehr-DOH-leech] (or **odpieprzyć*** [oht-PYEHP-shich] or **odpierniczyć*** [oht-pyehr-NEE-chich] or **odpierdzielić*** [oht-pyehr-JEH-leech] or **odbić** [OHD-beech] or **odwalić** [ohd-VAH-leech] or **odjebać**** [ohd-YEH-bahch]) *v* To lose mental fitness; to become insane or eccentric <get fucked up, get screwed up, get fucked in the head, get head-fucked, get mind-fucked, go crazy, go crazy as a loon, blow one's cork, blow one's top, blow a fuse, crack up, freak out, flip out, go ape, go bananas, go bent, go bonkers, go cracked, go dopey, go ga-ga, go half-baked, go loony, go loopy, go mental, go nerts, go nuts, go nutty, go off one's nut, go off one's rocker, go off one's base, go off the track, go off the trolley, go out one's skull, go psycho, go schizo, go screwy, go wacky, go weird, go wild, schiz out, psych out, come unglued, come unstuck, come unwrapped, go to pieces> eg *Był porządnym człowiekiem. Odbiło mu, gdy wygrał w totolotka (He was a decent man. He went crazy after he won on the lottery)*

odpierdolony** [oht-pyer-doh-LOH-ni] (or **odstawiony** [oht-stah-VYOH-ni] or **odpicowany** [oht-pee-tsoh-VAH-ni] or **odpierniczony*** [oht-pyer-nee-CHOH-ni] or **odjebany**** [ohd-yeh-BAH-ni] or **odsztafirowany** [oht-shtah-fee-roh-VAH-ni] or **odwalony** [ohd-vah-LOH-ni]; **jak ta lala** [yahk tah LAH-lah] may be added) *adj* Fancily dressed <dolled-up, dolled-out, dressed to kill, dressed to the nines, dressed to the teeth, dressed-up, duded-up, ritzed up, swanked up, ragged out, sharp-dressed> eg *Na piknik przyszła odstawiona jak ta lala (She showed up for the picnic dressed to the nines); Zawsze jest odpierdolona (She is always dressed to kill)*

odpryskać się See odlewać się

odpukać [oht-POO-kahch] (or **odpukać w niemalowane** [oht-POO-kahch v nyeh-mah-loh-VAH-neh]) *v* To fend off bad luck (so that something good will continue) <knock on wood> eg *Lepiej odpukaj w niemalowane! (You'd better knock on wood!); Do mojego domu jeszcze się nie włamali, odpukać (My house has not been burgled, knock on wood)*

odpuszczać [oht-POOSH-chahch] (perf **odpuścić** [oht-POOSH-cheech] *v* To give in; to forgive; to make concessions <let one get away with, let it go, let it slide, let one off, go easy on, blink at, wink at, give an inch> eg *Nie odpuści tym razem (He won't let it go this time)*

odrzucać [ohd-ZHOO-tsahch] *v* To repel and be strongly disliked <turn off, gross out, barf out, suck, scuzz one out, give one pain in the ass, make one sick, make one puke, make one barf> eg *Odrzucała mnie wtedy taka muzyka (This music grossed me out at that time)*

odsapka [oht-SAHP-kah] *nf* A short period of rest, esp in order to get stronger <breather, breathing spell, downtime, time-off> eg *Musimy mieć jakąś odsapkę (We have to take a breather)*

odskocznia [oht-SKOHCH-nyah] *nf* Something, such as an activity, done to temporarily take oneself away from one's casual activity <something on the side, get-away, step-out, stepping stone> eg *Muszę miećjakąś odskocznię, żeby dalej pracować (I've got to do something on the side to keep me going)*

odstawić See wykręcić komuś numer

odstawiony See odpierdolony

odstawka See iść w odstawkę

odsztafirowany See odpierdolony

odwalić See odpierdolić

odwalić kitę See wykitować

odwalić numer See strzelić numer

odwalić się See odpierdolić się

odwalony See odpierdolony

odwidzieć się [ohd-VEE-jehch shyeh] *v* To change one's mind, esp to stop liking or enjoying something <turn around, turn the corner, turn the tables, switch, switch over, shift gears, flip-flop, see the light, do about-face, sing another tune, whistle a different tune, change one's tune> eg *Odwidziało jej się i zmieniła pracę (She's seen the light and gotten another job)*

odwyk [OHD-vik] (or **odwykówka** [ohd-vi-KOOF-kah] *nf*) *nm* A drying-out ward or therapeutic treatment <12-step treatment, therapy> eg *Poszedł na odwyk (He went into therapy)*

ofiara [oh-FYAH-rah] (or **oferma** [oh-FEHR-mah]) *nf* A clumsy or ineffectual person lacking initiative <underachiever, loser, born loser, second-rater,

schlemiel, schmendrick, schmo, schnook, screwup, fuckup, hacker, muffer, scrub, dub, dool tool, turkey, lump, buterfingers, fumble-fist, goof, goof-off, goofball, eightball, foulball, klutz, also-ran, never-was, nonstarter, zero, lightweight, nobody, non, nonentity, noname, small potatoes, small timer, bush-leaguer> eg *Chciał to zrobić, ale taka z niego ofiara, że nie sądze, żeby to zrobił (He wanted to do it, but he's such a klutz that I don't think he will)*

oficjel [oh-FEE-tsyehl] *nm* A politician or a high-ranking official, esp a member of the government <handshaker, baby-kisser, flesh-presser, pol, suit> eg *Zjawilo się wiele oficjeli (A lot of flesh-pressers appeared)*

ogień See na pierwszy ogień

ogier [OH-gyehr] *nm* An insatiable man who is obsessed with copulation <ass-man, cocksman, cunt-struck, cunt-happy, pussy-struck, fucking machine, hound-dog, pistol Pete> eg *Czemu przy tych dziewczynach zachowuje się tak, jakby był jakimś ogierem? (Why does he act like a hound-dog around these girls?)*

ogólniak [oh-GOOL-nyahk] *nm* A high school, esp public <hi, high> eg *Chodziły do naszego ogólniaka (They attended our high)*

ogonek [oh-GOH-nehk] *nm* A number of people one behind the other; a line <no slang equivalent> eg *Ponad 20 ludzi stało w ogonku (More than 20 people were standing in a line)*

ogórek See król ogórków, sezon ogórkowy

ogromniasty [oh-grohm-NYAH-sti] *adj* Big; large; sizable <gross, humongous, monstro, moby, jumbo, hefty, whopper, mother, king-size, God-size> eg *Ale masz ogromniasty samochód! (What a humongous car you got!)*

ogumienie See guma

ohajtać się Perf hajtać się

ohyda [oh-KHI-dah] *nf* Someone or something very ugly <beast, beasty, skag, skank, pig, bag, dog, cow> eg *Skądżeś wziął taką ohydę? (Where did you get such a dog?); Co to za ohyda w Levisach? (Who's the skank in the Levi's?)*

ojczulek [oh-ee-CHOO-lehk] *nm* **1** A father <dad, daddy, pa, papa, pop, pops, guv, gaffer, padre, warden, old man> eg *Ojczulek nie dał mi ani grosza (Pops didn't give me a red cent)* **2** A Roman Catholic priest or monk <black coat, padre, sky pilot, sky merchant, sky scout, gospel pusher, bible thumper, bible banger, sin hound, rev, abbey, Holy Joe, preacher man> eg *Co ten ojczulek od ciebie chciał? (What did the padre want from you?)*

okantować Perf kantować

okazja [oh-KAH-zyah] *nf* A free ride, esp gotten by hitchhiking <hitch, lift, free ride> eg *Jak się tam dostaniesz? Spróbuję złapać jakąś okazję (How will you get there? I'll try to catch a lift)*

See łapać okazję

okienko [oh-KYEHN-koh] *nn* A period during the workday when one has free time; a recess <spare, gap, breather, breathing spell, free period, off> eg *Przyjdź o 11.30. Mam wtedy okienko (Come at 11.30. I have a breather break then); Na trzeciej godzinie mam okienko (Third class I have a spare)*

okiwać Perf kiwać

oklapnąć [oh-KLAHP-nohnch] *v* To become apathetic or tired; to lose energy or enthusiasm <be dead, be dead on one's feet, be dead-tired, be dog-tired, be out of it, be out of gas, be out of juice, be all in, be all shot, be pooped, be bagged, be

beat, be beat to the ground, be beat to the ankles, be bone-tired, be burned out, be bushed, be chewed, be crapped out, be done, be done in, be dragged out, be frazzled, be played out, be fucked out, be knocked out, be tuckered out, be tapped out, had it, be ready to drop, be on one's last legs> eg *Nie mogę już więcej pisać. Zaraz oklapnę (I can't type anymore. I'm ready to drop)*

oklepany [oh-kleh-PAH-ni] *adj* Too ordinary or banal because in too frequent use; trite <corny, cornball, corn-fed, hokum, hokey, tripe, chestnut, everyday, garden variety, dime a dozen, run of the mill, pulp, vanilla> eg *Opowiedział mi następny oklepany kawał (He told me another corny joke)*

oko See chuj ci w dupę, dawać komuś po oczach, kłuć w oczy, mieć coś/kogoś na oku, mieć klapki na oczach, mieć oko na coś/kogoś, mydlić komuś oczy, na oko, obłęd, świecić oczami, pi razy oko, postawić oczy w słup, przejrzeć na oczy, duże niebieskie oczy, przymknąć oczy, puszczać do kogoś oko

oko komuś bieleje *phr* [OH-koh KOH-moosh zbyeh-LEH-yeh] To (suddenly) become impressed, astonished, amazed <get blown away, knock one's socks off, get floored, get stuck, get stumped, get boggled, get flabbergasted> eg *Gdy pokazał jej swój nowy samochód, oko jej zbielało (After he showed her his new car, she got blown away)*

okrągło See na okrągło

okrąglak [oh-KROHNG-lahk] *nm* A rounded or oval building; a rotunda <no slang equivalent> eg *Kto mieszka w tym okrąglaku? (Who lives in this rotunda?)*

okropnie [oh-KROHP-nyeh] *adv* **1** (or **ostro** [OHS-troh]) Extremely; exceedingly; very <awful, god-awful, real, mighty, plenty, damn, damned, goddamn, goddamned, darn, darned, effing, flipping, forking, freaking, frigging, fucking, one's ass off, one's brains out, one's head off, to the max, like all get-out, like sin, to beat the band, like all creation, as blazes, as can be, as hell, like hell, in full wing> eg *Byłem okropnie głodny (I was darned hungry)* **2** Extremely bad; terribly; awfully <lousy, shitty, awful> eg *Okropnie się dzisiaj czuję (I feel really lousy today)*

okropny [oh-KROHP-ni] *adj* Cursed; damnable; bad <damn, damned, goddamn, goddamned, god-awful, blasted, darn, darned, effing, flipping, forking, freaking, frigging, pesky> eg *W tym okropnym upale nie można było pracować (You couldn't work in that goddamn heat)*

okularnica [oh-koo-lahr-NEE-tsah] *nf* A woman who wears glasses <four-eyes, professor> eg *Sam jestem okularnikiem (I'm a four-eyes myself)*

okularnik [oh-koo-LAHR-neek] *nm* A man who wears glasses <four-eyes, professor> eg *Hej, okularniku, zakład, że tego nie widzisz! (Hey, four-eyes, betcha you can't see this!)*

olej See mieć olej w głowie, nudny jak flaki z olejem

olewać [oh-LEH-vahch] (perf **olać** [OH-lahch]) *v* To be indifferent; not to care at all; to ignore; to show disrespect <not give a damn, not give a fuck, not give a shit, not give a diddly-shit, not give a diddly-damn, not give a flying fuck, not give a hoot, not give a rat's ass, not give a squat, pass up, diss, skip, ig, ice, chill, freeze, cut, brush off, give the brush, give the cold shoulder, turn the cold shoulder, cold-shoulder, give the go-by, high-hat, kiss off> eg *Olewam, co myślisz (I don't give a shit what you think); Kompletnie olała tego faceta (She completely cold-shouldered this guy)*

oparzony See jak oparzony

opchać się Perf opychać się

opchnąć Perf opychać

opędzlować [oh-pehn-DZLOH-vahch] *v* **1** To eat everything <eat up, finish off, polish off> eg *Opędzlował kurczaka w try miga (He finished off the chicken in no time at all)* **2** To steal; to rob <heist, boost, burgle, nurn, bag, buzz, highjack, hoist, hold up, hook, hustle, jump, kick over, knock off, knock over, lift, move, mug, nab, nick, nip, pinch, pluck, roll, rustle, snatch, snitch, stick up, swipe, take off, put the grab on, go south with> eg *Opędzlowali prawie sto tysięcy w gotówce (They heisted nearly a hundred thousand in cash)*

opić Perf opijać

opieprz See opierdol

opierdalać się** [oh-pyehr-DAH-lahch shyeh] (or **opieprzać się*** [oh-PYEHP-shahch shyeh] or **opierniczać się*** [oh-pyehr-NEE-chahch shyeh] or **opierdzielać się*** [oh-pyehr-JEH-lahch shyeh] or **obijać się** [oh-BEE-yahch shyeh] or **obcyndalać się** [ohp-tsin-DAH-lahch shyeh]) *v* To avoid work; to shirk duty <fuck around, fuck off, fuck the dog, goldbrick, goof off, goof around, screw around, jerk off, screw off, drag-ass, drag one's ass, drag it, dragtail, fake off, flub the dub, dog it, lollygag, sit on one's ass, soldier, skate, watch the clock> eg *Przestań się opierdalać i weź się do roboty (Stop fucking off and get to work)*

opierdalać** [oh-pyehr-DAH-lahch] (perf **opierdolić**** [oh-pyehr-DOH-leech]; or **opieprzać*** [oh-PYEHP-shahch] perf **opieprzyć*** [oh-PHYEHP-shich]; or **opierniczać*** [oh-phyehr-NEE-chahch] perf **opierniczyć*** [oh-phyehr-NEE-chich]; or **opierdzielać*** [oh-pyehr-JEH-lahch] perf **opierdzielić*** [oh-pyehr-JEH-leech]; or **opitolić** [oh-pee-TOH-leech]) *v* To reprimand, rebuke, or scold <chew, chew ass, chew out, chew out someone's ass, eat out, eat out someone's ass, bawl out, ream out, ream out someone's ass, call down, climb, climb all over, come down on, crack down on, cuss out, dress down, call on the carpet, bite someone's head off, give a piece of someone's mind, give a going over, give hell, jump on, jump all over, jump down someone's throat, land on, lay out, sound off, haul over the coals, downmouth, give someone a tongue-lashing> eg *Wiedziałam, że mój tata mnie opierniczy (I knew my dad was going to chew me out)*

opierdol** [oh-PYEHR-dohl] (or **OPR** [oh-peh-EHR] **opierdziel*** [oh-PYEHR-jehl] or or **opieprz*** [OH-pyehpsh] or **opiernicz*** [oh-PYEHR-neech] or **ochrzan** [OH-khshahn] or **ochrzantus** [oh-KHSHAHN-toos] *nm* A rebuke, reprimand, or scolding <hell, chewing, chewing out, eating out, cussing out, bawling out, going over, dressing down, reaming out, calling down, climbing, coming down, piece of someone's mind, rap on the knuckles, slap on the wrist, tongue-lashing> eg *Dostał opierdol, gdy wrócił późno do domu (He got a tongue-lashing when he got home late)*

śpiewać See cienko śpiewać

opijać See oblewać

opitolić See opierdalać

opona See łysa guma

opór See do oporu

opychać się [oh-PI-khahch] (perf **opchać się** [OHP-khahch shyeh]) *v* To overeat, eat greedily and more than needed <stuff oneself, pig out, scarf out, pork out> eg *Faceci opychali się hamburgerami i pizzą (These guys were porking out on hamburgers and pizza)*

opylać [oh-PI-lahch] (perf **opylić** [oh-PI-leech]; or **opychać** [oh-PI-khahch] perf **opchnąć** [OHPKH-nohnch]) To sell; to want dispose of a stock <move, push, turn over, pitch, drum, peddle> eg *Usiłował opylić cały ten towar (He was trying to move all this stuff)*

orżnąć* [OHR-zhnohnch] (or **oskubać** [oh-SKOO-bahch] or **oszwabić** [oh-SHFAH-beech]) *v* To cheat; to swindle; to deceive; to scheme <con, rip off, shaft, roll, chisel, gyp, scam, screw, stiff, fleece, dick, do in, take in, do a number on, flim-flam, bamboozle, run a number on, take someone for a ride, take someone to the cleaners, throw someone a curve, pull a fast one, fuck over, screw over, angle, take in, snow, do a snow job, double-shuffle, fast-shuffle, flimflam, give a bun steer, give someone a line, have someone on, lead someone down the garden path, do a snow job, jerk someone's chain, pull someone's chain, pull one's leg, pull someone's string, pull the wool over someone's eyes, put someone on, snow, use smoke and mirrors> eg *Ten handlarz orżnął mnie na dwie stówy (That salesman dicked me for two hundred)*

orać jak wół [OH-rahch yahk VOOW] *v phr* To work very hard <work one's ass off, work one's fingers to the bone, work like a horse, sweat, bust one's ass off, break one's ass off> eg *Od dwóch lat orze jak wół (He's been working like a horse for two years)*

oral* [OH-rahl] *nm* Oral sex <blow job, face job, head job, French job, deep throat> eg *Lubi wszystko a najbardziej oral (She likes everything, but blow jobs most of all)*

orgietka [ohr-GYEHT-kah] *nf* An orgy or a party which features an orgy <sex-party, fuck-party, group thing, group fuck, circle jerk, gang bang, daisy chain> eg *Urządzamy orgietkę w piątek. Przyjdziesz? (We're tossing a fuck-party on Friday. Will you come?)*

orka [OHR-kah] *nf* Very hard work; a Herculean labor <ball-buster, bone-breaker, back-breaker, bitch, killer, grind, donkeywork, bullwork, dirty work> eg *Pisanie słowników to ciężka robota, ale pisanie słowników slangu to orka! (Writing dictionaries is a hard job but writing slang dictionaries is a bitch!)*

orzeł [OH-zheh-oo] *nm* A person of extraordinary skill in specified activity; an expert <ace, whiz, whiz-kid, wiz, maven, mavin, guru> eg *Naszą szkołę reprezentował orzeł komputerowy (Our school was represented by a computer ace); Nie jesteś asem giełdowym (You're not a stock market mavin)*
See wywinąć orła

orzech See twardy orzech do zgryzienia

osa [OH-sah] *nf* A ruthless, demanding, and tenacious person, esp a teacher <toughie, stiff, ball-breaker, ball-buster, back-breaker, ass-buster, bitch, son of a bitch, badass, mean machine> eg *Słyszałem, że wasza nowa nauczycielka od matmy to prawdziwa osa (I heard your new math teacher is a real ball-breaker)*
See cięty

osiłek [oh-SHEE-wehk] *nm* A man with well-developed muscles <hunk, stud, stud-muffin, beefcake, he-man, macho, muscleman, v-man> eg *Zaczął panikować, gdy zobaczył tych osiłków (He started to chicken out when he saw these musclemen)*

osiemnastka [oh-shehm-NAHST-kah] (or **osiemnacha** [oh-shehm-NAH-khah]) *nf* **1** An eighteenth birthday party, commonly thought to mark the end of adolescence <sweet eighteen party> eg *Zaprosiła mnie na swoją osiemnastkę (I was invited to her sweet eighteen party)* **2** An eighteen-year-old girl <sweet eithteen, fresh

meat, chick, chicklet, teen, teener, teeny-bopper, bubble-gummer> eg *Słyszałem, że chodzi z jakąś osiemnachą (I heard he's been dating some 18-year-old chicklet)*

osioł [OH-shyoh-oo] *nm* A stupid, clumsy or ineffectual person; an idiot <airbrain, airhead, birdbrain, blockhead, squarehead, bonehead, bubblebrain, bubblehead, buckethead, cluckhead, cementhead, clunkhead, deadhead, dumbbell, dumbcluck, dumbhead, dumbass, dumbbrain, fatbrain, fathead, flubdub, knukclebrain, knucklehead, lamebrain, lardhead, lunkhead, meathead, musclehead, noodlehead, numbskull, pointhead, scatterbrain, jerk, jerk-off, klutz, chump, creep, nerd, dork, dweeb, gweeb, geek, jackass, lummox, twerp, nerd, bozo, clod, cluck, clunk, dimwit, dingbat, dipstick, dodo, dopey, dufus, goofus, lump, lunk, nitwit, schnook, schlep, schlemiel, schmendrick, schmo, schmuck, simp, stupe> eg *Ale osioł ze mnie. Zapomniałem prawa jazdy, panie władzo (I'm such a birdbrain. I forgot my driver's license, officer)*
See narobić się

oskubać See orżnąć

osobista narzeczona [oh-soh-BEES-tah nah-zheh-CHOH-nah] *nf phr* A fiancee <old lady, future, intended, steady, pinned, donnah, donnar, significant other> eg *Przedstawił ją jako swoją osobistą narzeczoną (He introduced her as his future)*

osobisty narzeczony [oh-soh-BEES-ti nah-zheh-CHOH-ni] *nm phr* A fiance <old man, future, intended, steady, pinned> eg *To jest jej osobisty narzeczony (This is her old man)*

ostatni See gwóźdź do trumny

ostatni dwonek [ohst-TAHT-nee DZVOH-nehk] *nm phr* The very last moment; high time <last call, eleventh hour, last mo, in the nick of time> eg *Udało mu się to zrobić na ostatni dzwonek (He managed to do it at the eleventh hour)*

ostatni krzyk mody See krzyk mody

ostro See okropnie

ostry See mieć niewyparzoną gębę

oszachrować Perf szachrować

oszołom [oh-SHOH-wohm] *nm* **1** A fanatic, esp a political or religious one; a fundamentalist <freak, crank, fan, buff, bug, freak, fiend, nut, hound, aficionado> eg *Wyczuł w tym robotę oszołomów katolickich (He sensed in it the action of Jesus freaks)* **2** A person, esp a politician, who is dogmatic, bigoted, conservative or adversive to change <hard-liner, hard-core, hard-shell, die-hard, fogy, fud, regular Archie Bunker> eg *Obecny dyrektor Instytutu Anglistyki to prawdziwy oszołom (The acting director of the English Institute is a regular Archie Bunker)*

oszwabić See ocyganić, orżnąć

otworzyć gębę See rozdziawić gębę

owca See czarna owca

owijać w bawełnę [oh-VEE-yahch v bah-VEH-oo-neh] *v phr* To avoid answering a question directly, esp because one is too careful or hesitant; to stall, hedge, or equivocate <beat around the bush, mince one's words, pussyfoot, walk on eggs> eg *Przestań owijać w bawełnę i powiedz, czego naprawdę chcesz (Stop beating around the bush and tell me what you really want)*
See nie owijać w bawełnę

ozór [OH-zoor] *nm* The tongue <stinger> eg *Masz okropnego syfa na ozorze. Lepiej idź do lekarza (You got a terrible zit on your tongue. You'd better go see a doctor)*

See mleć jęzorem

ożenek See żeniaczka

ożenić [oh-ZHEH-neech] *v* **1** To sell <move, push, turn over, pitch, drum, peddle> eg *Usiłował ożenić cały ten towar (He was trying to move all this stuff)* **2** To reconcile; to combine <meet halfway, strike a happy medium, find the middle ground, tie up with, throw in together> eg *Jak ci się udało ożenić hobby z pracą? (How did you manage to strike a happy medium between your hobby and work?)*

P

pała [PAH-wah] *nf* **1** The head <bean, noggin, conk, dome, gourd, skull> eg *Walnęła go prosto w pałę (She hit him right on the noggin)* **2*** The penis, esp large <cock, prick, dick, stick, joystick, dipstick, bone, meat, beef, wang, yang, dong, dummy, hammer, horn, hose, jock, joint, knob, pork, putz, rod, root, tool, flute, skin flute, love-muscle, sausage, schmuck, schlong, schvantz, cream-stick, third leg, middle leg, business, apparatus, John, Johnny, Johnson, John Thomas, Jones> eg *Ociągnęła ci pałę? (Did she put some lipstick on your dipstick?)* **3** A failing grade <flunk, flush, F, zip, zippo> eg *Dlaczego jej powiedziałeś, że miałem pięć pał z matmy? (Why did you tell her that I have five F's in math?)*

See łysol, obciągać, obcięty na jeża, przeginać, zakuta pała, zalać się

pałaszować [pah-wah-SHOH-vahch] *v* To eat, esp very fast <chow, scarf, scoff, pig out, scarf out, pork out> eg *Pałaszował jak wariat (He was scarfing out like a nut)*

pacan See palant

pachy See ubaw

pacierz See jak amen w pacierzu

paciorek [pah-CHYOH-rehk] *nm* A prayer, esp with the use of a rosary <no slang equivalent> eg *Codziennie mówi paciorek (She says her rosary everyday)*

paczka [PAHCH-kah] (or **paka** [PAH-kah]) *nf* A group of people who are intimate and close <folks, pack, bunch, crew, gang, clan, crowd, boys> eg *Lubiłem naszą paczkę (I really loved our gang)*

See patol

padać [PAH-dahch] (perf **paść** [pahshch]) *v* To go bankrupt or to fail <belly up, go bust, go broke, go to the cleaners, take a bath, take a beating, flop, bomb, bust, wash out> eg *Nasza firma szybko padła (Our firm soon went bust)*

padać [PAH-dahch] (perf **paść** [PAHSHCH]; **lecieć** [LEH-chehch] may replace **padać**; **na pysk** [nah PISK] or **na mordę*** [nah MOHR-deh] or **na ryj*** [nah RI-ee] or **na łeb** [nah WEHP] or **na nos** [nah NOHS] or **z nóg** [z NOOG] may be added) *v phr* To be very tired or exhausted <be dead, be dead on one's feet, be dead-tired, be dog-tired, be out of it, be out of gas, be out of juice, be all in, be all shot, be pooped, be bagged, be beat, be beat to the ground, be beat to the ankles, be bone-tired, be burned out, be bushed, be chewed, be crapped out, be done, be done in, be dragged out, be frazzled, be played out, be fucked out, be knocked out, be tuckered out, be tapped out, had it, be ready to drop, be on one's

last legs> eg *Przepraszam, ale nic już nie zrobię. Padam z nóg (I'm sorry but I'm not going to do anything, I'm all in)*

padlina [pahd-LEE-nah] *nf* Any edible but unappetizing or rotten animal meat or meat by-product <dead animal, corpse, mystery meat> eg *Widzisz, jaką padlinę mają na stole? (Can you see the corpse they have on the table?)*

padnięty [pahd-NYEHN-ti] *adj* Very tired or exhausted <dead, dead on one's feet, dead-tired, dog-tired, out of it, out of gas, out of juice, all in, all shot, pooped, bagged, beat, beat to the ground, beat to the ankles, bone-tired, burned out, bushed, chewed, crapped out, done, done in, dragged out, frazzled, played out, fucked out, knocked out, tuckered out, tapped out, had it, ready to drop, on one's last legs> eg *Ale jestem padnięta! Zaraz padnę (Am I dead-tired! I'm gonna drop in a second)*

paf See paw

pajac [PAH-yahts] *nm* A silly, witty clumsy or ineffectual person <airbrain, airhead, birdbrain, blockhead, squarehead, bonehead, bubblebrain, bubblehead, buckethead, cluckhead, cementhead, clunkhead, deadhead, dumbbell, dumbcluck, dumbhead, dumbass, dumbbrain, fatbrain, fathead, flubdub, knukclebrain, knucklehead, lamebrain, lardhead, lunkhead, meathead, musclehead, noodlehead, numbskull, pointhead, scatterbrain, jerk, jerk-off, klutz, chump, creep, nerd, dork, dweeb, gweeb, geek, jackass, lummox, twerp, nerd, bozo, clod, cluck, clunk, dimwit, dingbat, dipstick, dodo, dopey, dufus, goofus, lump, lunk, nitwit, schnook, schlep, schlemiel, schmendrick, schmo, schmuck, simp, stupe, artist, joker, kidder, clown, article, ham, character, item, number> eg *Ale pajac ze mnie. Zapomniałem prawa jazdy, panie władzo (I'm such a birdbrain. I forgot my driver's license, officer)*

paka See paczka, pierdel

pakamera [pah-kah-MAH-rah] *nf* A larder, pantry, or small warehouse; a storeroom <stash house> eg *Spał w naszej pakamerze (He used to sleep in our stash house)*

pakować [pah-KOH-vahch] (perf **wpakować** [fpah-KOH-vahch]) *v* To invest money, esp in non-profitable enterprise <sink money in, pump money into, throw money in, throw money down the drain, plunge, bankroll> eg *Mieliśmy nadzieję znaleźć kogoś, kto wpakowałby forsę w nasz projekt (We were hoping to find somebody to bankroll the project)*

pakować manatki See zwijać manatki

palant [PAH-lahnt] (or **pacan** [PAH-tsahn]) *nm* A stupid, clumsy, or naive person; an idiot <jerk, dork, geek, dumbass, dumbhead, dope, airhead, birdbrain, blockhead, dumbhead, klutz, moron> eg *Co ten porąbany palant wyrabia na dachu? (What is that loony airhead doing on the roof?); Co za palant ze mnie. Zapomniałem prawa jazdy, panie władzo (I'm such a birdbrain. I forgot my driver's license, officer); Ten twój kumpel to prawdziwy palant (That buddy of yours is a real dumbass)*

palce lizać [PAHL-tseh LEE-zahch] *adj phr* Very tasty <yum-yum, yummy, finger-licking good> eg *O, gorące skrzydełka. Mniam-mniam! (Oh, hot wings. Yum-yum!)*

palcem po wodzie pisane [PAHL-tsehm poh VOH-jeh pee-SAH-neh] (or **patykiem po wodzie pisane** [pah-TI-kyehm poh VOH-jeh pee-SAH-neh]) *phr* Not certain; risky <chancy, iffy, dicey, rocky, touchy, up for grabs, touch and go, on a wing and a prayer, on slippery ground, on thin ice, fat chance> eg *To, czy wygramy, jest patykiem po wodzie pisane (Whether we'll win is very iffy)*

palec See chodzić koło kogoś na palcach, maczać palce, mieć coś w małym palcu, nie kiwnąć palcem, obudzić się z ręką w nocniku, palcem po wodzie pisane, patrzeć przez palce, wyssać z palca, z palcem, nie pali się

palić się [PAH-leech shyeh] *v* **1** (perf **zapalić się** [zah-PAH-leech shyeh]) To desire something a lot; to display a strong willingness, readiness, or interest <be itching, be keen on, get sold into, get hooked into, get turned on, get stoked, have the hots for, have hot pants for, have a hard-on for, be crazy about, be nuts about, be stuck on, be sweet on, go for, buy, catch, hook> eg *Japończycy natychmiast zapalili się do tego pomysłu (The Japanase instantly bought the idea); Nie palił się zbytnio do przepisywania tej rozprawki (He didn't get turned on by rewriting the essay)* **2** To be in a hurry; to be late <be in hot water> eg *Był tu tylko parę minut. Paliło mu się (He was here for only few minutes. He was in hot water)*

palma [PAHL-mah] *nf* Insane self-impression or self-importance, esp as a result of one's success; egotism <ego-tripping, swell-headedness, big-headedness, high-nosedness> eg *Wiesz, jak najlepiej określić jego zachowanie jako dyrektora Instytutu? Palma (Do you know what's the best way to characterize his behavior as the director of the Institute? Ego-tripping)*

palma komuś odbiła [PAHL-mah KOH-moosh ohd-BEE-wah] (or **palma komuś uderzyła** [PAHL-mah KOH-moosh oo-deh-ZHI-wah]; **woda sodowa** [VOH-dah soh-DOH-vah] or **sodówka** [soh-DOOF-kah] may replace **palma**) *v phr* To become insanely conceited or self-impressed, esp because one has made a success <think one's shit doesn't stink, be too big for someone's shoes, ego-trip, get stuck-up, get puffed-up, get high-hat, get swelled-up, get swell-headed, get big-headed, get high-nosed, get blown-up, get stuck on oneself, get chesty, get stuffy, get gassy, get windy, get hatty, get hinkty, get uppity, get biggety, dog it, put on the dog, give oneself airs, put on airs, put on, put on the ritz> eg *Zawsze był szpanerem, ale gdzy w 1996 został dyrektorem Instytutu, to zupełnie odbiła mu palma (He had always been a blowhard, but when he became the director of the Institute in 1996, he really got big-headed)*

palnik See dać sobie w gaz

pan władza [pahn VWAH-dzah] *nm phr* A police officer <cop, copper, flatfoot, flatty, fuzz, pig, gumshoe, nabs, paddy, finest, elbow, blue, bluecoat, big John, arm, yard bull, smokey, bear, smokey bear> eg *Pan władza wlepił mi mandat (The cop gave me a ticket)*

panienka [pah-NYEHN-kah] *nf* (or **panienka lekkich obyczajów** [pah-NYEHN-kah LEHK-keekh oh-bi-CHAH-yoof]) A prostitute <hooker, hustler, pro, call girl, floozy, chippy, bimbo, quiff, slut, working girl, street walker> eg *Został przyłapany in flagranti z panienką lekkich obyczajów (He was caught red-handed, engaged with a hooker)*

panienka na telefon See dziewczynka na telefon

panikara [pah-nee-KAH-rah] *nf* A fearful, cowardly, or apprehensive woman who easily panicks <chicken, chicken heart, candy-ass, fraidy cat, scaredy cat, gutless wonder> eg *Nie bądź taka panikara. Wszystko będzie dobrze (Don't be such a fraidy cat. Everything's going to be fine)*

panikarz [pah-NEE-kahsh] *nm* A fearful, cowardly, or apprehensive man who easily panicks <chicken, chicken heart, candy-ass, fraidy cat, scaredy cat, gutless

wonder> eg *Jej chłopak, to prawdziwy panikarz. Uciekł natychmiast (Her boyfriend is a real chicken-heart. He run away right off)*

panikować [pah-nee-KOH-vahch] (perf **spanikować** [spah-nee-KOH-vahch]) *v* To panic; to be frightened, cowardly, or apprehensive <chicken out, turn chicken, turn yellow, run scared, have cold feet, be scared stiff, be scared shitless, shit one's pants, piss one's pants, shit bullets, shit a brick, shit green, be spooked, push the panic button, wimp out> eg *Spanikował przed egzaminem i wujechał z miasta (He chickened out before the exam and left the town)*

pank [pahnk]) *nm* A punk rocker <punk, punker> eg *Skini nie lubią panków (Skinheads don't like punkers)*

panna See po balu

panna z odzysku [PAHN-nah z ohd-ZIS-koo] *nf phr* A divorced woman <dumpee, grass widow, ex> eg *Wszyscy wiedzą, że ona jest panną z odzysku (Everybody knows that he's a grass widow)*

pantałyk See zbić kogoś z tropu

pantofel See pocztą pantoflową, pod pantoflem

pantoflarz [pahn-TOHF-lahsh] *nm* A man who is dominated by a woman, esp one's wife; a hen-pecked man <pussy-whipped man> eg *Mój mąż nazwałby Cię pantoflarzem (My husband would have called you a pussy-whipped man)*

państwowy See ocena państwowa

paść komuś na mózg [PAHSHCH KOH-moosh nah MOOSK] (or **rzucić się komuś na mózg** [ZHOO-cheech shyeh KOH-moosh nah MOOSK]; **rozum** [ROH-zoom] or **umysł** [OO-misw] or **łeb** [wehp] may replace **mózg**) *v phr* To lose mental fitness; to become insane or eccentric <go crazy, go crazy as a loon, blow one's cork, blow one's top, blow a fuse, crack up, freak out, flip out, go ape, go bananas, go bent, go bonkers, go cracked, go dopey, go ga-ga, go half-baked, go loony, go loopy, go mental, go nerts, go nuts, go nutty, go off one's nut, go off one's rocker, go off one's base, go off the track, go off the trolley, go out one's skull, go psycho, go schizo, go screwy, go wacky, go weird, go wild, schiz out, psych out, come unglued, come unstuck, come unwrapped, go to pieces> eg *Wygrał w totolotka i padło mu na mózg (He won the lottery and went off his rocker)*

paść Perf padać

paść trupem [pahshch TROO-pehm] *v phr* To be very shocked, surprised, or jealous, esp because of some news or at the sight of something <drop dead, knock dead, drop down dead, be killed stone-dead> eg *Jak się dowie, że zdałem egzamin lepiej od niej, to padnie trupem (When she learns that I did better on the exam, she'll drop dead)*

papier [PAH-pyehr] *nm* **1** A US dollar <buck, green, greenie, greenback, smacker, bone, clam> eg *Będzie cięto kosztowało dwieście papierów (It'll set you back two hundred bucks)* **2** (or **papierek** [pah-PYEH-rehk]) Any document, esp official <ticket, ID, doc, paper, file> eg *Kto grzebał mi w papierach? (Who messed with my docs?); Mogę zobaczyć pana papiery? (May I see your ID?)*

papierkowa robota [pah-pyehr-KOH-vah roh-BOH-tah] *nf phr* Office work, esp a less important part of it such ass keeping records or writing reports <paperwork, paper-shuffling, pen-pushing, pen-driving> eg *Miałem awersję do papierkowej roboty, więc zrezygnowałem z pracy w dyplomacji (I had an aversion to paperwork so I gave up my work in diplomacy)*

papieroch [pah-PYEH-rohkh] *nm* A cigarette <smoke, butt, cig, ciggie, fag, faggot, nail, coffin nail, stick, cancer stick, drag, bonfire, lung duster, root, cigaroot, cigareete, spark, dope, dope stick, grit, joint, pimp stick, slim, toke, weed> eg *Rety, ale mi się chce papierocha! (Man, do I need a smoke!)*

papla [PAHP-lah] *nf* A person who talks too much and cannot keep a secret <blabbermouth, babbler, blabber, bag of wind, big breeze, bigmouth, chatterbox, ear-bender, flapjaw, gabbler, gum-beater, jabberer, jawsmith, loudmouth, satchelmouth, spieler, tongue-wagger, windbag, windjammer, motormouth> eg *Twoja siostra to prawdziwa papla. Teraz wszyscy wiedzą o naszym przyjeździe (Your sister is a real chatterbox. Now everybody knows that we're coming)*

papu [PAH-poo] *nn* Food <chow, feed, grub, scoff, eats> eg *Gdzie dostanę papu? (Where can I get some chow?)*

papużki nierozłączki [pah-POOSH-kee nyeh-rohz-WOHNCH-kee] *npl phr* A pair of people, esp of the same sex, who do everything together <twosome, gruesome twosome, duo, team, bopsy twins> eg *Nazywano ich papużki-nierozłączki, bo wszędzie chodzili razem (People called them the gruesome twosome, because they used to go everywhere together)*

papuga [pah-POO-gah] (or **papuga dwudziesta druga** [pah-POO-gah dvoo-JEHS-tah DROO-gah]) *nf phr* Someone who copies someone else's work, esp in school; an imitator <copycat, pirate, crock, stand-in, nick artist> eg *Nie bądź taka papuga. Wymyśl coś sam (Don't be such a copycat. Invent something of your own)*

para See ani pary z gęby, na całego

parada See mieć łeb

parafia See z innej parafii

parapetówa [pah-rah-peh-TOO-vah] (or **parapetówka** [pah-rah-peh-TOOF-kah]) *nf* A party organized to celebrate the acquisition of a (new) apartment or a house <no slang equivalent> eg *Zrobiliśmy parapetówkę, żeby uczcić nowe mieszkanie (We threw a bash to christen our new place)*

park sztywnych [pahrk SHTIV-nikh] *nm phr* A cemetery <cold storage, bone yard, bone factory, bone orchard, marble orchard, marble town, headstone city> eg *Wyprowadził się i mieszka blisko parku sztywnych (He moved out and now lives near the marble orchard)*

parówa** [pah-ROO-vah] *nf* A man forced to perform homosexual acts, esp in prison; a passive homosexual <sugar boy, bitch, fag, faggot, fairy, queer, fruitcake, homo, pansy, sissy, swish, daisy, limp-wrist, queen> eg *Ten tu wygląda mi na parówę (This one here looks like a faggot)*

parszywy See pierdolony

party See ochlaj

partyjka [pahr-TI-ee-kah] *nf* A single round of a game, esp card game <hand> eg *Przed kościołem zagraliśmy parę partyjek pokera (We played a few hands of poker before church)*

partyjniak* [pahr-TI-ee-nyahk] *nm* (Esp in former communist times) A memeber of the Communist Party; a communist <commie, comrade, red, pink, lefty, left-winger> eg *Gdyby nie był partyjniakiem, byłby całkiem w porządku (If he wasn't a comrade, he would be quite all right)*

pas See cios poniżej pasa, za pasem

pasić See pasować

paskuda [pahs-KOO-dah] *nf* An annoying and despicable person <jerk, bitch, piece of shit, scum> eg *Ty cholero, ja się z tobą porachuję! (You piece of shit, I'll get even with you!)*

paskudnie [pahs-KOOD-nyeh] (or **potwornie** [poht-FOHR-nyeh]) *adv* **1** (or **piekielnie** [pyeh-KYEHL-nyeh]) Extremely; exceedingly; very <awful, god-awful, real, mighty, plenty, damn, damned, goddamn, goddamned, darn, darned, effing, flipping, forking, freaking, frigging, fucking, one's ass off, one's brains out, one's head off, to the max, like all get-out, like sin, to beat the band, like all creation, as blazes, as can be, as hell, like hell, in full swing> eg *Musisz być paskudnie zmęczony (You must be fucking tired);* **2** Extremely bad; terribly; awfully <lousy, shitty, awful> eg *Paskudnie mi poszło na egzaminie (I did lousy in the exam)*

paskudny See pierdolony

paskudztwo [pahs-KOOTS-tfoh] *nn* Anything annoying, disgusting, repulsive, or tasteless <shit, crap, scuzz, sleaze, drek, crud, glop, grunge, scrunge, muck, mung, goo, gook, gunk> eg *Zabierz to paskudztwo o de mnie (Take this goo out of my sight)*

pasować [pah-SOH-vahch] (or **pasić** [PAH-sheech]) *v* **1** To suit one or appeal to one; to like, enjoy, or delight <fit in, suit one fine, turn on, heat up, fire up, steam up, stir up, send, give a bang, knock out, knock someone dead, knock someone' socks off, knock someone for a loop, throw someone for a loop, hit the spot, kill, murder, slay, slaughter, put someone away, tickle pink, tickle to death, tickle the piss out of someone, open one's nose> eg *Nie pasuje mi ta muzyka (That music doesn't bring me on)* **2** To be acceptable or suitable; to meet certain standards <fit in, fit the bill, do, wash, work, do down, cut it, make the grade, make the cut, make it, cut the mustard, pass in the dark, fill the bill, suit one fine, be OK, be okay, be kopasetic, be hunky-dory, be so-so> eg *Co myślisz o tej propozycji? Pasi (What do you think about this proposal? It will make the grade)* **3** To believe, understand, or comprehend, esp something one has just said <get, get it, catch, get the drift, get the picture, get the message, get the hang of, savvy, dig, click, capeesh, read, be with it, see where one is coming from, know where one is coming from> eg *Oddał im to za darmo. Pasuje ci? (He gave it to them for free. Did you get it?)*

paszcza [PAHSH-chah] *nf* The mouth <yap, bazoo, kisser, trap> eg *Chesz dostać w paszczę? To ją zamknij (You want me to punch you in your yap? So shut it)*

paszczura See pasztet

paszoł won See won

pasztet [PAHSH-teht] *nm* **1*** (or **paszczura*** [pahsh-CHOO-rah]) An ugly woman <beasty, skag, skank, pig, bag, dog, cow> eg *Przyszedł na imprezę z jakimś pasztetem (He came to the party with some skag)* **2** An unpleasant or scandalous fact or situation; a scandal <gas, fuss, stink, hot potato, bad scene, bad news, can of worms, bag of worms, takedown, putdown, shit, serious shit, deep shit, deep water, drag, bind, bitch, bummer, downer, headache, double trouble, snafu, pain in the ass, pain in the neck, spot, mess, holy mess, pickle, squeeze, hard time, glitch, stinker, skeleton, skeleton in the closet, sizzler, scorcher, dynamite, Watergate, fine kettle of fish, fine how do you do, fine cup of coffee, big stink, curtains, lights out, game's over> eg *Prezydent nie ma żadnego alibi? Ale pasztet! (The President has no alibi? What a bummer!)*

patelnia See lizać

patelnia** [pah-TEHL-nyah] *nf* Cunnilingus <face job, box lunch, muff dive, cunt-eating, cunt-licking, cunt-lapping, eating-out, the French way> eg *Słyszałam, że twój wujek jest mistrzem patelni (I heard your uncle is a master of cunt-licking)*

patol [PAH-tohl] (or **patyk** [PAH-tik] or **paczka** [PAHCH-kah] *nf*) *nm* Thousand, esp a thousand zloty bill <grand, G-note, thou, K> eg *Dał mi za to dwa patole paczki (He gave me two grand for it)*

patrzałki [paht-SHAH-oo-kee] *npl* The eyes <peepers, blinkers, lamps, oglers, peekers> eg *Coś niedobrze z moimi patrzałkami (Something's wrong with my peepers)*

patrzeć komuś na ręce [PAHT-shehch KOH-moosh nah REHN-tseh] *v phr* To carefully observe or control someone's work or behavior; to be under observation or surveillance <breathe down someone's neck, keep an eye on, eye, eyeball, check, check out, check over, scope, scope out, figure out, track, spy, bug, spot, dig, read, case, beam, lamp, catch, case> eg *Muszę uważać, bo szef patrzy mi na ręce (I have to watch out, because the boss keeps an eye on me)*

patrzeć na kogoś krzywo [PAHT-shehch nah KOH-gohsh KSHI-voh] (or **patrzeć na kogoś wilkiem** [PAHT-shehch nah KOH-gohsh VIL-kyehm] or **patrzeć na kogoś bykiem** [PAHT-shehch nah KOH-gohsh BI-kyehm]) *v phr* To look angrily at someone; to frown at someone <look daggers at, give someone the devil eye, give someone the bad eye, give someone the dog eye, give someone a whammy> eg *Dyrektor nie lubił mnie i zawsze patrzył na mnie krzywo (The director never liked me and always gave me the evil eye)*

patrzeć przez palce [PAHT-shehch pshehs PAHL-tseh] *v phr* To pretend not to see or notice something, esp illegal <turn a blind eye to, let someone get away with, let it go, let it slide, let someone off, go easy on, blink at, wink at> eg *Skorumpowany naczelnik policji patrzył przez palce na handel narkotykami w miasteczku (The corrupt police chief turned a blind eye to the drug dealing in the town)*

patyczkować się [pah-tich-KOH-vahch shyeh] *v* To treat someone with excessive care and tenderness; to pamper <treat with kid gloves, handle with kid gloves, treat someone as an apple of someone's eye, give someone the red carpet treatment, pet> eg *Na twoim miejscu bym się z nią nie patyczkował (If I was you, I wouldn't treat her with kid gloves)*

patyk [PAH-tik] (or **patyczak** [pah-TI-chahk]) *nm* An unusually thin, skinny person <beanpole, stringbean, skin and bones, skeleton, bag of bones> eg *Twój brat to prawdziwy kościotrup. (Your brother is a real beanpole)*
See palcem po wodzie pisane, patol, wino patykiem pisane

paw See puszczać pawia

paw [pahf] (or **paf** [pahf]) *nm* Vomit <barf, puke> eg *Czy masz pawia na bucie? (Is that barf on your shoe?)*

paznokieć See tyle co kot napłakał

pazur See bazgrać, gryzmolić

pączek See jak pączek w maśle

pełną gębą See całą gębą

pełne gacie See mieć cykora

pęczek See na kopy

pedał* [PEH-dah-oo] (or **pedzio*** [PEH-joh] or **pedryl**** [PEH-dril]) *nm* A male homosexual or someone supposed to be one <fag, faggot, fairy, queer, fruitcake,

homo, pansy, sissy, swish, daisy, limp-wrist, queen> eg *Wydaje mi się, że twój szef to pedał (It seems to me that your boss is a queer)*

pedałówka See pederastka

pederastka* [peh-deh-RAHST-kah] (or **pedałówka*** [peh-dah-WOOF-kah]) *nf* A small leather hand-held pouch or purse for documents or money, popular esp among middle class men <leather, lizard, grouch bag, poke, hide, clutch> eg *W ręku trzymał pederastkę (He was holding a grouch bag in his hand)*

pęk See z cicha pęk

pękać [PEHN-kahch] (perf **pęknąć** [PEHNK-nohnch]) *v* **1** To panic; to be frightened, scared, or cowardly <chicken out, turn chicken, turn yellow, run scared, have cold feet, be scared stiff, be scared shitless, shit one's pants, piss one's pants, shit bullets, shit a brick, shit green, be spooked, push the panic button, wimp out> eg *Przestań pękać. Bierz się do roboty to zdasz ten egzamin (Stop shitting your pants. Get to work and you'll pass this exam)* **2** (Of a person) To begin to lose control of one's feelings; to begin to suffer an emotional or mental breakdown <crack up, crack, chase butterflies, blow one's cork, blow one's top, blow a fuse, crack up, freak out, flip out, go ape, go bananas, go bent, go bonkers, go cracked, go dopey, go ga-ga, go half-baked, go loony, go loopy, go mental, go nerts, go nuts, go nutty, go off one's nut, go off one's rocker, go off one's base, go off the track, go off the trolley, go out one's skull, go psycho, go schizo, go screwy, go wacky, go weird, go wild, schiz out, psych out, come unglued, come unstuck, come unwrapped, come unzipped, go to pieces> eg *Pęknął dopiero wtedy, gdy pokazali mu zdjęcie jego żony (He cracked up only when they showed him a picture of his wife)*

pękać w szwach [PEHN-kahch f shfahkh] *v phr* (or **trzeszczeć w szwach** [TSHEHSH-chehch f shfahkh]) (Of a hall or a room) To be extremely and uncomfortably full or crowded <burst at the seams, be packed, be crammed> eg *Było tak wiele ludzi, że hala pękała w szwach (There were so many people that the hall was bursting at the seams)*

pękać z zazdrości [PEHN-kahch z zah-ZDROHSH-chee] (or **skręcać z zazdrości** [SKREHN-tsahch z zah-ZDROHSH-chee]) *v phr* To become very jealous or envious <turn green, be green-eyed, eat someone's heart out, drop dead, knock dead, die over, drop down dead, be killed stone-dead> eg *Pękną z zazdrości, jak zobaczą mnie w tej sukience (They will turn green when they see me in this dress)*

pękać ze śmiechu [PEHN-kahch zeh SHMYEH-khoo] (**skręcać ze śmiechu** [SKREHN-tsahch zeh SHMYEH-khoo]) *v phr* To burst with laughter <crack up, break up, split, split one's sides, die laughing, roll in the aisles, tear one apart, be in stiches, laugh fit to burst, bust a gut laughing, pee in one's pants laughing, fall out laughing, howl, scream, horselaugh, stitch, be blue in the face, laugh till one is blue in the face> eg *Pękaliśmy ze śmiechu, gdy usłyszeliśmy tę wiadomość (We were just rolling in the aisles when we heard the news); Skręca mnie ze śmiechu, gdy oglądam tę komedię (I'm blue in the face when I watch this comedy)*

pękać ze złości [PEHN-kahch zeh ZWOHSH-chee] (**skręcać ze złości** [SKREHN-tsahch zeh ZWOHSH-chee]) *v phr* To become very angry <get pissed off, get peed off, get p'd off, get bent out of a shape, get pushed out of a shape, get browned off, get cheesed off, get uptight, get cranky, get edgy, get sore, get

mad as a hornet, get steamed up, get ticked off, get tee'd off, get burned up, go ballistic> eg *Pęknie ze złości, jak to usłyszy (He's going to go ballistic when he hears that)*

peniać [PEH-nyahch] (perf **speniać** [SPEH-nyahch]) *v* To be afraid; to be frightened; to be intimidated <chicken out, turn chicken, turn yellow, run scared, have cold feet, be scared stiff, be scared shitless, shit one's pants, piss one's pants, shit bullets, shit a brick, shit green, be spooked, push the panic button, wimp out> eg *Nie chciał wyjeżdżać. Myślę, że się peniał (He didn't want to leave. I guess he was scared stiff)*

pępek See być pępkiem świata

pępek świata [PEHMpehk SHFYAH-tah] *nm phr* (Esp ironically) Something most important; the center, esp of everyone's attention <gazed navel, center of universe, heart of the universe> eg *To miasteczko nie jest pępkiem świata (This little town is not the center of universe)*

pepik* [PEH-peek] (or **pepiczek*** [peh-PEE-chehk]) *nm* A Czech male <Czesky> eg *Pepik podał mi piwo (The Czesky passed me a beer)*

pestka [PEHST-kah] *nf* Anything easy or trivial; a trifle; a bagatelle <piece of cake, cake, cakewalk, cherry pie, duck soup, kid stuff, picnic, pushover, snap, tea party, walkaway, walkover, breeze, stroll, cinch, pipe, big deal, no big deal, no biggie, Mickey Mouse, small potatoes, small beer, fly speck, plain sailing> eg *Zwycięstwo następnym razem to pestka (Winning next time will be a snap)*
See zalany

pet [peht] *nm* **1** A cigarette <smoke, butt, cig, ciggie, fag, faggot, nail, coffin nail, stick, cancer stick, drag, bonfire, lung duster, root, cigaroot, cigareete, spark, dope, dope stick, grit, joint, pimp stick, slim, toke, weed> eg *Chcesz peta? (Do you want a smoke?)* **2** A remainder of a smoked cigarette <butt, dinch, dincher, maggot, roach, seed, skag, snipe> eg *Nie rzucaj petów na dywan! (Don't throw your butts on the carpet!)*

pętak [PEHN-tahk] *nm* A teenage boy, esp whom one despises <teen, teener, teeny-bopper, bubble-gummer, youngster, juvie, shithead, punk, snot-nose> eg *Patrz, gdzie łazisz, pętaku (Look where you're going, shithead)*

pętelka See guzik

pewniak [PEHV-nyahk] (or **pewnik** [PEHV-neek] or **pewniacha** [peh-VNYAH-khah]) *nm* **1** A certainty; something sure to happen, esp a person or team who will win easily; a sure winner <cinch, dead cinch, dead-sure thing, lead-pipe cinch, shoo-in, sure bet, safe bet, dead cert, sure shot, sure thing> eg *Te dwa konie to perniaki (These two horses are shoo-ins); Kowalski is a shoo-in (Kowalski to pewniak)* **2** A person one can count on; a trustworthy or reliable person <right guy, boy scout, pal, buddy> eg *On nas nigdy nie zwiódł. To pewniak (He never let us down. He's a real pal)*

pi razy oko [PEE RAH-zi OH-koh] (or **pi razy drzwi** [PEE RAH-zi JVEE]) *adv phr* About; approximately <around, in the ballpark of, pretty near, something like, close shave, in the neighborhood of, damn near, pretty near> eg *Dostał od nich, tak pi razy oko, pięć tysięcy (He got from them something pretty near five thousand)*

piącha [PYOHN-khah] (or **piątka** [PYOHNT-kah]) *nf* The fist <duke, five, fiver, bunch of fives> eg *Dał mi z piąchy (He hit me with his dukes)*

piątak [PYOHN-tahk] (or **piątka** [PYOHN-tkah] or **piątal** [PYOHN-tahl]) *nm* Five, esp a five zloty coin <fiver, fin, five-spot> eg *Pożycz mi piątaka, co? (Lend me a fin, will you?)*

piąte koło u wozu [PYOHN-teh KOH-woh oo VOH-zoo] *nn phr* A person or thing regarded as unnecessary and likely to impede <ball and chain, third wheel, excess baggage, square peg> eg *No cóż, spójrzmy prawdzie w oczy. Nie potrzebujemy cię. Jesteś piątym kołem u wozu (Well, let's face it. We don't need you. You are a third wheel)*

piątek czy świątek [PYOHN-tehk chi SHFYOHN-tehk] (or **w piątek czy świątek** [f PYOHN-tehk chi SHFYOHN-tehk]) *adv phr* Everyday; at all times; constantly <around the clock, day and night, forever and a day> eg *Trzeba pracować, w piątek czy świątek (You must work round the clock)*

piątka See na medal, piącha, piątak, przybić piątkę

pić do lustra [peech doh LOOS-trah] *v phr* To drink alcohol alone, esp in an attempt to forget one's troubles <drown one's sorrows, drown one's troubles> eg *Niedobrze z nim, zaczął pić do lustra (He is not well. He started to drown his sorrows)*

pić duszkiem [peech DOOSH-kyehm] *v phr* To drink down everything (in one's glass or bottle) without stopping <chug, chug-a-lug> eg *Wypił całą puszkę duszkiem (He chugged the whole can)*

pić jak szewc [peech yahk SHEHFTS] *v phr* (To be able) To drink a lot; to drink alcohol in large quantities <be able to drink like a fish, booze, guzzle, gargle, bend the elbow, hit the bottle, hit the sauce, knock back, lap, tank up, wet one's whistle, hang a few on, slug down, swig> eg *Mój wujek pije jak szewc. Może wypić dziesięć piw (My uncle is able to drink like a fish. He can drink ten beers); Jej mąż pije jak szewc (Her husband drinks like a lord)*

pić na umór [peech nah OO-moor] *v phr* To drink so much alcohol that one loses consciousness <booze, guzzle, gargle, bend the elbow, hit the bottle, hit the sauce, knock back, lap, tank up, wet one's whistle, hang a few on, slug down, swig> eg *Pili na umór przez dwa dni (They gargled for two days)*

piach See gryźć ziemię, iść do piachu

pic [peets] (or **pic na wodę** [peets nah VOH-deh] or **pic na wodę fotomontaż** [peets nah VOH-deh foh-toh-MOHN-tahsh]) *nm* A lie meant to impress or win the approval; a deceitful talk manipulating someone to think or act as one wishes <bluff, bullshit, BS, mind-fucking, head-fucking, cock-and-bull story> eg *Ona nie uwierzy w ten pic (She won't believe this bullshit)*
See dla jaj, picować

picer [PEE-tsehr] *nm* A man who has the ability to manipulate someone to think or act as one wishes, esp by lying or exaggerating <bluffer, mind-fucker, head-fucker, bullshitter, bullshit artist> eg *Twój kuzyn to prawdziwy picer. Wszystkie moje przyjaciółki mają świra na jego punkcie (Your cousin is a real head-fucker. All of my friends are crazy about him)*

pici-polo See grać sobie w kulki z kimś

picie [PEE-chyeh] *nn* Anything to drink <something to drink, something to wash one's throat with, drinkage> eg *Przynieś mi jakieś picie (Bring me something to dink)*

picować [pee-TSOH-vahch] (or **brać kogoś pod pic** [brahch KOH-gohsh pohd PEETS] or **brać kogoś pod włos** [brahch KOH-gohsh pohd VWOHS]) *v phr* (To try) To fool or deceive someone, esp by pretending; to manipulate someone to think or act as one wishes <bluff, bullshit, put someone on, pull someone's leg,

pull someone's string, give someone a leg, have someone on, jack someone around, jerk someone around, poke fun at, kid someone around, fool someone around, jack someone's chain, spoof, cut down, mind-fuck, head-fuck, push around, upstage, wind around one's finger, wrap around one's finger, twist around one's finger> eg *To nie może być prawda. Picujesz (This can't be true. You're kidding me)*

piczka See pizda

pięćdziesiątka [pyehch-jeh-SHYOHN-tkah] *nf* **1** Fifty, esp a fifty zloty bill <fifty, half a century, half a yard, fifty-spot> eg *Dali mi tylko pięćdziesiątkę (They only gave me half a century)* **2** A fifty-gram portion of alcohol, esp vodka, similar to a shot <no slang equivalent> eg *Mówi, że wypiła tylko pięćdziesiątkę (She said she only drank a finger)*

piec See jak u Pana Boga za piecem

piechota See iść tam gdzie król chodzi piechotą, nie chodzić piechotą

piekielnie See paskudnie

piekielny See pierdolony

pieklić się See pienić się

pieluchy See robić w pieluchy

pieniążki [pyeh-NYOHNSH-kee] (or **pieniądzory** [pyeh-nyehohn-DZOH-ri]) *npl* Money <dough, bread, bank, cabbage, change, coin, folding, green, lettuce> eg *Gdzie ja położyłam pieniądzory? (Where did I put my dough?)*

pieniądze See ciężkie pieniądze, psie pieniądze, siedzieć na forsie, trzymać pieniądze w skarpecie, wyłożyć forsę, za bezcen

pienić się [PYEH-neech shyeh] (perf **spienić się** [SPYEH-neech shyeh]; or **pieklić się** [PYEHK-leech shyeh] perf **wpienić się** [SPYEH-neech shyeh]) *v* To become very angry, esp so that one's mouth is filled with froth <be frothing at the mouth, foam at the mouth, get pissed off, get peed off, get p'd off, get bent out of a shape, get pushed out of a shape, get browned off, get cheesed off, get uptight, get cranky, get edgy, get sore, get mad as a hornet, get steamed up, get ticked off, get tee'd off, get burned up, go ballistic> eg *Był z tego powodu zdenerwowany? Tak, pienił się (Was he annoyed about it? Yes, he was frothing at the mouth)*

pień See mieć z kimś na pieńku, na pniu

pieścić się [PYEHSHcheech shyeh] *v* To treat someone with excessive care and tenderness; to pamper <treat with kid gloves, handle with kid gloves, treat someone as an apple of someone's eye, give someone the red carpet treatment, pet> eg *Na twoim miejscu bym się z nią nie pieścił (If I was you, I wouldn't treat her with kid gloves)*

pieprz See tam gdzie pieprz rośnie

pieprznąć See pierdolnąć

pieprznąć się See pierdolnąć się

pieprznięty See pierdolnięty

pieprzny [PYEHPSH-ni] *adj* Lewd, obscene <dirty, blue, filthy, juicy, off-color, raunchy, raw, rough, spicy, steamy, X-rated> eg *Opowiedział dwa pieprzne kawały (He cracked two raunchy jokes)*

pieprzony See pierdolony

pieprzyć See ja pierdolę, pierdolić

pieprzyć się See pierdolić się

pieprzyć w dupę See pierdolić w dupę

pierd* [PYEHRD] *nm* A release of intestinal gas, perhaps with a noise <fart, cheese, ass noise> eg *Czyj to pierd? (Whose fart was that?)*

pierdel [PYEHR-dehl] (or **pudło** [POOD-woh] or **paka** [PAH-kah]) *nm* A prison; a jail <slam, slammer, jug, can, bucket, cage, big cage, big house, caboose, calaboose, cannery, cooler, hole, hoosegow, icebox, lockup, mill, stir, pen, tank, college, crossbar hotel, booby hatch, pink clink, quad> eg *Jest w pierdlu już od dwóch lat (He's been in the slammer for two years now)*

pierdnąć Perf pierdzieć

pierdoła* [pyehr-DOH-wah] *nf* **1** An ineffectual man; a botcher <loser, schlemiel, screwup, goofup, goof, foozler> eg *Ten pierdoła nawet nie wiedział, jak zacząć (That shlemiel didn't even know how to start)* **2** (or **pierdziel*** [PYEHR-jehl] or **pryk*** [prik] *nm* or **piernik*** [PYEHR-neek] *nm*; **stary** [STAH-ri] may precede these) *nm* An old man <gramps, old fart, old bugger, geezer, gaffer, old-timer, fossil> eg *Powinni wylać tego starego pierdziela (They should lays off that old geezer); Wyszła za mąż za starego pryka (She married some old fart)*

pierdoły* [pyehr-DOH-wi] (or **pierdułki*** [pyehr-DOOW-kee] or **pierdołki*** [pyehr-DOOW-kee]) *npl* Nonsense; absurdities; pretentious, deceitful, or trivial talk <bull, bullshit, bullshine, BS, bunk, baloney, applesauce, eyewash, hogwash, hot air, crock, crock of shit, piece of shit, pile of shit, shit, dogshit, horseshit, shit for the birds, crap, crapola, poppycock, smoke, hokum, garbage, trash, horsefeathers, smoke, all that jazz, jazz, jive, malarkey, gobbledygook, double-talk, bafflegab, blah-blah, phony-baloney, fiddle-faddle, twiddle-twaddle, mumbo-jumbo, yackety-yack> eg *Mam już dość twoich intelektualnych pierdół (I'm sick and tired of your intellectual mumbo-jumbo)*

pierdolec* [pyehr-DOH-lehts] *nm* Obsession, insanity, or eccentricity <thing, kick, bag, bug, craze, freak, frenzy, weakness, bug up one's ass, bug in one's ear, bee in one's bonnet, bee, flea in one's nose, maggot, maggot in one's brain, hang-up, jones, monkey, ax to grind> eg *On ma pierdolca na punkcie Elvisa (He's got a bee in his bonnet about Elvis)*
See dostać świra, mieć świra

pierdolić komuś za uszami** [pyehr-DOH-leech zah oo-SHAH-mee] *v phr* To gossip about someone; to spread rumors about someone; to denigrate or criticize <wag some tongues, have one's name bandied about, badmouth someone, blackball someone, spitball someone, dish the dirt about someone, chew the fat about someone, cut someone up and down, cut someone into little pieces, schmooze about someone, run someone down, bring someone down, dump all over someone, dump on someone, put the shit on someone> eg *Nie rób nic głupiego, jeśli nie chcesz, żeby zaczęli pierdolić ci za uszami (Don't do anything foolish if you don't want to have your name bandied about)*

pierdolić się** [pyehr-DOH-leech shyeh] (or **pieprzyć się*** [PYEHP-schich shyeh]) *v* **1** To copulate <fuck, get fucked, get screwed, get laid, screw, fork, frig, ball, bang, boink, bonk, boff, hump, poke, shag> eg *Lubią się pierdolić w miejscach publicznych (They like to fuck in public); Gdy pieprzę się z innymi, to tak naprawdę myślę o nim (When I screw other guys, I really think about him)* **2** (or **pierniczyć się*** [pyehr-NEE-chich shyeh]) To handle someone or something too gently or slowly;

to tamper with something or someone <fuck around with, fuck with, treat with kid gloves, handle with kid gloves, play around with, play with, fool around with, fool with, mess around with, mess with, diddle around with, diddle with, fart around with, fart with, fiddle around with, fiddle with, monkey around with, monkey with, screw around with, screw with, schlep around, drag around, drag-ass> eg *Pierdolił się z tym przełącznikiem z pół godziny (He fucked around with that switch for half an hour or so)* **3** (or **pierniczyć się*** [pyehr-NEE-chich shyeh] or **pierdzielić się*** [pyehr-JEH-leech shyeh]) To get complicated or confused <get fucked up, get screwed up, get messed up, get spaced out, get mixed up, get discombobulated, get flabbergasted, get unscrewed, get farmisht, get balled up, get shook up, get floored, get unglued, get unzipped, get fried, get flummoxed, get kerflooey> eg *Wszystko zaczęło się pierdolić (Everything started to get fucked up)* **4** (or **pierniczyć się*** [pyehr-NEE-chich shyeh] or **pierdzielić się*** [pyehr-JEH-leech shyeh]) (Esp as an exclamation of defiance and contempt) To invite someone to perform or submit to a humiliating act <fuck you, screw you, chuck you Farley, fuck you Charley, drop dead, eat shit, eat my shorts, get lost, get fucked, get screwed, get stuffed, go fly a kite, go fuck yourself, fuck yourself, go screw yourself, screw yourself, go shit in your hat, go to hell, take a flying fuck, kiss my ass, bite my ass, piss on you, shit on you, cram it, stuff it, shove it, stick it, stick it in your ear, stick it in your ass, up your ass, up yours> eg *Powiedziała mi, że mogę się pierdolić! (She told me to go fuck myself); Pierdol się, jeśli tak myślisz! (Fuck you, if that's what you think)*

See iść się pierdolić

pierdolić w dupę** [pyehr-DOH-leech v DOO-peh] (**pieprzyć*** [PYEHP-shich] or **rżnąć*** [RZHNOHNCH] or **jebać**** [YEH-bahch] may replace **pierdolić**) *v phr* To do anal intercourse <ass-fuck, butt-fuck, brownhole, cornhole, bunghole, do it the Greek way, go the Hershey highway, bugger, ream> eg *Poprosił, żeby go ktoś pierdolił w dupę (He asked somebody to ass-fuck him)*

pierdolić** [pyehr-DOH-leech] *v* **1** (perf **wypierdolić**** [vi-pyehr-DOH-leech]; or **pieprzyć*** [PYEHP-schich] perf **wypieprzyć*** [vi-PYEHP-schich]) To copulate with someone <fuck, screw, lay, ball, bang, boink, boff, boogie, bop, frig, hump, poke, shag> eg *Znów mnie wszyscy będą pierdolić (I'm going to get fucked again!); Pieprzył mnie z całej siły (He banged me as hard as he could)* **2** (perf **napierdolić**** [nah-pyehr-DOH-leech]; or **pieprzyć*** [PYEHP-schich] perf **napieprzyć*** [nah-PYEHP-shich]; or **pierniczyć*** [pyehr-NEE-chich] perf **napierniczyć*** [nah-pyehr-NEE-chich]; or **pierdzielić*** [nah-pyehr-JEH-leech] perf **napierdzielić*** [nah-pyehr-JEH-leech]; **w bambus** [v BAHM-boos] may be added) To tell lies in order to deceive someone <fuck, mind-fuck, head-fuck, give someone bullshit, bull, bullshit, shit, shovel the shit, string along, snow, fake it, talk through one's hat, speak with forked tongue, put someone on, pull someone's leg, pull someone's string, give someone a leg, have someone on, jack someone around, jerk someone around, kid someone around, fool someone around, jack someone's chain, spoof, cut down, push around, upstage> eg *Nie pierdol mi o tym, że znasz się na leksykografii (Don't give me that bullshit that you know lexicography)* **3** (perf **napierdolić**** [nah-pyehr-DOH-leech]; or **pieprzyć** [PYEHP-schich] perf **napieprzyć*** [nah-PYEHP-shich] or **popieprzyć*** [poh-PYEHP-shich]; **pierniczyć*** [pyehr-NEE-chich] perf **napierniczyć*** [nah-pyehr-NEE-chich] or **popierniczyć*** [poh-pyehr-NEE-chich]; or **pierdzielić*** [pyehr-JEH-leech] perf **napierdzielić*** [nah-pyehr-JEH-leech] or **popierdzielić*** [poh-pyehr-JEH-leech]; **w bambus** [v BAHM-boos] may be added) To talk nonsense <fuck, bullshit, talk bull, talk bullshit, talk bullshine, talk BS, talk bunk, talk baloney, talk applesauce, jazz, jive, shovel the shit, blow off, blow off one's mouth> eg *Ten facet pieprzy. Nie słuchajcie go (This guy is talking bullshit. Don't listen to him)* **4** (or **pieprzyć*** [PYEHP-schich] or **pierniczyć** [pyehr-NEE-chich] or **pierdzielić*** [pyehr-JEH-leech]) To be indifferent to or contemptuous of; not to care at all; to ignore; to show disrespect <not give a damn, not give a fuck, not give a shit, not give a diddly-shit, not give a diddly-damn, not give a flying fuck, not give a hoot, not give a rat's ass, not give a squat, pass up, diss, skip, ig, ice, chill, freeze, cut, brush off, give the brush, give the cold shoulder, turn the cold shoulder, cold-shoulder, give the go-by, high-hat, kiss off> eg *Pierdolę, co myślisz (I don't give a shit what you think)*

See ja pierdolę

pierdolnąć** [pyehr-DOHL-nohnch] (or **pieprznąć*** [PYEHP-shnohnch] or **pierdyknąć*** [pyehr-DIK-nohnch]) *v* **1** To beat someone up <kick someone's ass, sock, bash, trash, clobber, bang, belt, clock, duke, dust, hammer, land one, lay one on, spank, wham, whack, bam, whip, bust, smack, poke, blast, beat the shit out of, beat the living shit out of, beat the bejejus out of, beat the daylights out of, beat someone into the middle of next week, knock the bejejus out of, knock the daylights out of, knock someone into the middle of next week, hit someone where he lives, work over> eg *Jak ci pierdolnę w mordę, to pożałujesz (I'll beat the living shit out of you and you're going to be sorry)* **2** To forcefully hit against something or collapse <hit, whack, wham, smack, bang, bump, trash, pow, fall over something> eg *Pierdolnął w drzewo (He bumped against a tree)* **3** To suddenly explode <boom, bash, bang, go off> eg *Pierdolnęła bomba (A bomb went off)* **4** To suddenly stop or give up doing something; to abandon or relinquish <walk out on, duck out on, skip out on, waltz out on, break off, give the kiss off, kiss off, leave flat, take a walk, knock it off, call it quits, drop it, bag it, can it, stow it, caulk off, come off, cut out, hang it up, lay off, take a break, drop, pull out, bail out, bow out, walk out, check out, drop out, cop out, butt out, push out, snake out, fase out, pass up, pass on, throw in the towel, throw in the sponge, toss in the sponge, toss in the towel, cry uncle, say uncle, toss it in, pack it in, cave in, buckle under, back down, fold, duck, slide, walk, leg, ditch, dump, kick off, quit cold turkey, sideline, call it a day> eg *Pierdolnął robotę i poszedł do domu (He dropped the work and went home)* **5** To fail or become inoperative; to fall into destruction <fuck up, get fucked up, screw up, get screwed up, break down, crash, crash and burn, fry, go down, go down in flames, go south, belly up, melt down, shut down, crack up, go blooey, go busted, go on the blink, go on the fritz, go off, go out of whack, go kerflooey> eg *Wszystko szło mi dobrze póki nie pieprznął faks (Everything was doing fine until the fax fucked up)* **6** To ceize to exist; to collapse or fall <fuck up, screw up, belly up, crack up, fold up, break up, break down, fall apart, go to pieces> eg *Nikt z nas nie przypuszczał, że Związek Radziecki pierdolnie tak szybko (Noone had suspected that the Soviet Union would go to pieces)* **7** To say something candidly, decidedly, or boldly; to abandon all concealment <spit it out, let it all hang out, let it out, let one's hair down, get it off one's chest, get it out of one's system, spill it,

spill one's guts, tell it like it is, open up, level, unload> eg *Pierdolnę całą prawdę (I'm going to let it all hang out)* **8** To say something blatantly improper, indiscreet, or foolish, esp carelessly; to reveal a secret or a surprise by accident <let the cat out of the bag, spill the beans, make the shit hit the fan, blab, blow> eg *To sekret. Staraj się tego nikomu nie pierdolnąć (It's a secret. Try not to blab it)* **9** (or **w cholerę** [f khoh-LEH-reh] or **w pizdu**** [f peez-DOO] or **w diabły** [v DYAH-bwi] or **w kąt** [f KOHNT] may be added; **rzucić** [ZHOO-cheech] or **zostawić** [zohs-TAH-veech] may replace **pierdolnąć**) To forcefully throw or put something <peg, toss, chuck, chunk, let fly, trun, shy> eg *Pierdolnij to na stół i chodź tu (Just fucking toss it on the table and come here)*

pierdolnąć się** [pyehr-DOHL-nohnch shyeh] (or **pieprznąć się*** [PYEHP-shnohnch shyeh] or **pierdyknąć się*** [pyehr-DIK-nohnch shyeh]) *v* **1** To make a mistake; to do something improperly <fuck up, screw up, slip, slip up, trip up, blow, flub, fluff, foozle, goof up, ball up, mess up, louse up, make a blooper, pull a blooper, drop the ball, drop a brick, put one's foot in it, stub one's toe, fall flat on one's ass, shoot oneself in the foot> eg *Pierdolnął się dopiero na ostatnim pytaniu (He fucked up on the last question)* **2** To forcefully hit against something or collapse <hit, whack, wham, smack, bang, bump, trash, pow, fall over something> eg *Pierdolnął się w kolano (He banged against his knww)* **3** To forcefully sit, lay down, or throw oneself on something <peg oneself, toss oneself, chuck oneself, chunk oneself> eg *Wrócił z pracy i zaraz pierdolnął się na łóżko (He came back home and tossed himself on the bed)*

pierdolnąć sobie coś** [pyehr-DOHL-nohnch SOH-byeh TSOHSH] (or **pieprznąć sobie coś**** [PYEHP-shnohnch SOH-byeh TSOHSH] or or **pierdyknąć sobie coś*** [pyehr-DIK-nohnch SOH-byeh TSOHSH]) *v phr* To buy something for oneself <buy oneself, get oneself, blow oneself> eg *Pierdolnąłem sobie nową kurtkę (I bought me a new jacket)*

pierdolnięty** [pyehr-dohl-NYEHN-ti] (or **pieprznięty*** [pyehpsh-NYEHN-ti]) *adj* Insane, stupid, or thoughtless <fucked in the head, fucked-up, crazy, creazy as a loon, loony, nerts, nuts, nutso, nutsy, nutty, sick, sick in the head, sicko, wacko, wacky, psycho, shizo, screwy, off one's rocker, out of one's skull, fruity, airbrained, airheaded, birdbrained, blockheaded, squareheaded, boneheaded, bubblebrained, bubbleheaded, bucketheaded, cluckheaded, cementheaded, clunkheaded, deadheaded, dumbclucked, dumbheaded, dumbassed, dumbbrained, fatbrained, fatheaded, flubdubbed, knukclebrained, knuckleheaded, lamebrained, lardheaded, lunkheaded, meatheaded, muscleheaded, noodleheaded, numbskulled, pointheaded, scatterbrained, nerdy, dorky, jackassed, lummoxed, dopey, goofy> eg *Ale ten facet jest pierdolnięty. Potrzebuje wakacji (Man, is this guy fucked-up. He needs a vacation)*

pierdolony** [pyehr-doh-LOH-ni] (or **pieprzony*** [pyehp-SHOH-ni] or **piekielny** [pyeh-KYEHL-ni] or **paskudny** [pahs-KOOD-ni] or **potworny** [poht-FOHR-ni] or **parszywy** [pahr-SHI-vi]) *adj* Cursed; damnable; bad <damn, damned, goddamn, goddamned, god-awful, blasted, darn, darned, effing, flipping, forking, freaking, frigging, pesky, gross, barfy, scuzzy, sleazy, grody, icky, yucky, gooky, grungy, ech, yech> eg *Widok był paskudny (It was a god-awful sight)*

pierdu-pierdu* [PYEHR-doo PYEHR-doo] **1** *nn phr* Trivial, platitudinous or deceitful talk; nonsense <small talk, bull, bullshit, bullshine, BS, bunk, baloney,

applesauce, eyewash, hogwash, hot air, crock, crock of shit, piece of shit, pile of shit, shit, dogshit, horseshit, shit for the birds, crap, crapola, poppycock, smoke, hokum, garbage, trash, horsefeathers, smoke, all that jazz, jazz, jive, malarkey, gobbledygook, double-talk, bafflegab, blah-blah, phony-baloney, fiddle-faddle, twiddle-twaddle, mumbo-jumbo, yackety-yack> eg *Za dużo już się nasłuchałem tego pierdu-pierdu (I've heard enough of that baloney)* **2** *excl phr* An exclamation of incredulity or disbelief <in a pig's eye, in a pig's ass, in a pig's ear, like hell, like fun, like shit, my ass, there's no way, someone will be damned if, someone will be fucked if, says you> eg *Powiedział, że nam pomoże. Pierdu-pierdu, akurat nam pomoże! (He said he'd help us. My ass! Like hell he would help us!)*

pierdyknąć See pierdolnąć

pierdyknąć się See pierdolnąć się

pierdzieć* [PYEHR-jehch] (perf **pierdnąć*** [PYEHRD-nohnch]) *v* To release intestinal gas, perhaps with a noise <fart, cut a fart, lay a fart, blow a fart, let a fart, cut the cheese, backfire, break wind, pollute the air> eg *Kto pierdnął? (Who farted?)*

pierdziel See pierdoła

pierdzielić See ja pierdolę, pierdolić

pierdzielić się See pierdolić się

pierniczyć See ja pierdolę, pierdolić

pierniczyć się See pierdolić się

piernik See co ma piernik do wiatraka, jak piernik do wiatraka, pierdoła

piersiówka [pyehr-SHYOOF-kah] *nf* A flask designed to fit into a breast pocket <breast flask> eg *Gdzie schowałeś piersiówkę? (Where did you hide your breast flask?)*

pierwszak [PYEHRF-shahk] *nm* A first-grade or first-year student <fresh, freshman, frosh, first-grader> eg *Zostaw go, to tylko pierwszak (Leave him alone, he's just a freshman)*

pierwszy See klasa, na pierwszy ogień

pies See żyć z kimś jak pies z kotem, babiarz, na pieska, ni pies ni wydra, nie dla psa kiełbasa, pod psem, zejść na psy

pies na baby See babiarz

pies z kulawą nogą [PYEHS s koo-LAH-voh NOH-goh] *nm phr* Not a single person; no one; nobody <not a soul> eg *Psa z kulawą nogą tam nie było (There was not a soul in the neighborhood)*

pięta See deptać komuś po piętach

pieter See dostać cykora, mieć cykora

piętnastka [pyehnt-NAHS-tkah] (or **piętnacha** [pyehnt-NAH-khah]) *nf* A fifteen-year-old girl, below the legal age of sexual consent <sweet fifteen, jail bait, St. Quentin quail, chick, chicklet, teen, teener, teeny-bopper, bubble-gummer> eg *Bzykanie się z tą piętnastką zaprowadzi cięza kratki (Humping this jail bait will get you behind bars)*

pietrać się [PYEHT-rahch shyeh] (perf **spietrać się** [SPYEHT-rahch shyeh]) *v* To be afraid; to be frightened; to be intimidated <chicken out, turn chicken, turn yellow, run scared, have cold feet, be scared stiff, be scared shitless, shit one's pants, piss one's pants, shit bullets, shit a brick, shit green, be spooked, push the panic button, wimp out> eg *Nie chciał wyjeżdżać. Myślę, że się pietrał (He didn't want to leave. I guess he was scared stiff)*

piętrowiec [pyehn-TROH-vyehts] (or **punktowiec** [poonk-TOH-vyehts]) *nm* A very tall modern city building <high-rise, sky-scraper, cloud-buster, cliff> eg *Mi szakamy na 20-tym piętrze piętrowca (We live on the 20th floor of a high-rise)*

piętrus [PYEHNT-roos] *nm* A bus with two levels <double-decker> eg *Zawsze lubił jeździć piętrusami (He always liked to go on double deckers)*

piguła [pee-GOO-wah] *nf* A nurse <sitter, baby-sitter, sister, nanny, mammy> eg *Możesz zawołać pigułę? (Can you call a sitter?)*

pijaczyna [pee-yah-CHI-nah] *nm* A heavy drinker; an alcoholic <lush, bar-fly, alky, boozehound, boozer, bottle baby, dipso, elbow bender, ginhead, juicehead, loadie, sponge, soak, wino> eg *Czego ten pijaczyna chciał? (What did that juicehead want?)*

pijak See po pijaku

pijany jak świnia [PYAH-ni yahk SHFEE-nyah] (**spity** [SPEE-ti] or **urżnięty** [oor-ZHNYEHN-ti] or **uchlany** [oo-KHLAH-ni] or **schlany** [SKHLAH-ni] or **zalany** [zah-LAH-ni] or **skuty** [SKOO-ti] may replace **pijany**; **w trzy dupy*** [tshi DOO-pi] or **w sztok** [PYAH-ni f shtohk] or **w trupa** [f TROO-pah] or **w butelkę** [v boo-TEHL-keh] or **jak bela** [yahk BEH-lah] may be replace **jak świnia**) *adj phr* Completely drunk <alkied, bagged, blitzed, blotto, blown away, bent, boiled, bombed, blasted, boozed, bottled, boxed, buzzed, canned, clobbered, cooked, corked, crashed, drunk as a skunk, edged, embalmed, fractured, fried, gassed, ginned, grogged, have one too many, half under, high, hooched up, in bad shape, impaired, illuminated, juiced, knocked out, liquored, lit, loaded, looped, lubricated, lushed, smashed, oiled, pickled, plastered, plonked, polluted, sauced, shitfaced, slugged, sloshed, soaked, stewed, stiff, stinking drunk, swizzled, tanked, three sheets to the wind, wiped, zonked, lit up like a Christmas tree> eg *Do domu przyszedł pijany jak świnia (He came home drunk as a skunk); Był zalany w trzy dupy (He was lit up like a Christmas tree)*

pikawa [pee-KAH-vah] *nf* The heart <ticker, pump, pumper> eg *Pikawa mu w końcu wysiadła (His ticker finally gave out)*

pilnować swego nosa [peel-NOH-vahch SFEH-goh NOH-sah] *v phr* To attend strictly to one's own affairs; not to meddle <mind one's own business, mind one's own beeswax, stick to one's knitting, keep one's nose out, butt out, keep hands off, let sleeping dogs lie> eg *Byłoby dobrze, gdyby twój brat zechciał pilnować swego nosa (It would be good if your brother would mind his own business)*

pinda See pizda

pindol* [PEEN-dohl] (or **ptaszek** [PTAH-shehk] or **ptak** [ptahk]) *nm* The penis, esp small <pecker, peter, peepee, pisser, weenie, peenie, dingus, dingbat, thingy, cock, prick, dick, stick, joystick, dipstick, bone, meat, beef, wang, yang, dong, dummy, hammer, horn, hose, jock, joint, knob, pork, putz, rod, root, tool, flute, skin flute, love-muscle, sausage, schmuck, schlong, schvantz, cream-stick, third leg, middle leg, business, apparatus, John, Johnny, Johnson, John Thomas, Jones> eg *Nie baw się ptaszkiem (Don't play with you pecker); Chciałabyś zobaczyć mojego pindolka? (Would you like to see my thingy?)*

pingwin* [PEENG-veen] *nm* A Roman Catholic nun <penguin, hood, sister> eg *Do kościoła weszły dwa pingwiny (Two hoods went into the church)*

piona [PYOH-nah] *nf* The highest grade; a perfect score <ace, A> eg *Dostałem dziś dwie piony (I got two A's today)*

pionek [PYOH-nehk] *nf* An inconsequential or insignificant person <loser, lightweight, nobody, non, nonentity, noname, small potatoes, small timer, pissant, wannabe> eg *Nie przejmuj się nim. To tylko pionek (Don't worry about him. He's just a lightweight)*

pióra [PYOO-rah] *npl* Hair <moss, wig, wool, locks> eg *Spójrz na twoje pióra. Idź się ostrzyc (Take a look at your wig. Go get a haircut)*

piórkować See ja piórkuję

piorunem [pyoh-ROO-nehm] *adv* Immediately; very quickly <pretty damn quick, PDQ, ASAP, on the spot, on the double, double time, double clutching, like a shot, in half a mo, like now, before you know it, before you can say Jack Robinson, in a jiffy, in a flash, in half a shake, right off the bat, like a bat out of hell, like a shot out of hell, hubba-hubba, horseback, like greased lightning> eg *Biegnij tam szybko, piorunem! (Run over there quick, on the double!)*

pipa See pizda

pipidówa [pee-pee-DOO-vah] *nf* A small town, esp in the country; any place far from civilization <jerk town, jerkwater town, backwater, hellhole, rathole, mudhole, real hole, noplaceville, hicksville, whistle stop, dump, armpit, East Jesus, Bumfuck Egypt> eg *Skąd dzwonisz? Z jakiejś pipidówy (Where are you calling from? Some mudhole)*

pisać See palcem po wodzie pisane

pisać się na coś [PEE-sahch shyeh NAH tsohsh] *v phr* To decide to participate in something, esp a business venture <be in, deal someone in, sign someone up> eg *Jeśli mnie pytacie, to ja się na to piszę (If you ask me, I'm in)*

pismak [PEES-mahk] *nm* A journalist or commentator, esp clumsy, dishonest, or lackey-like <news hound, news hen, scratcher, ink slinger, pencil pusher, pen driver, scribe, leg man, stringer> eg *Pod główną bramą czeka tłum pismaków (There's a crowd of news hounds at the main gate)*

pismo See mieć nosa

pisnąć See ani pisnąć

piwko [PEEF-koh] (or **pywko** [PIF-koh] or **pyfko** [PIF-koh]) *nn* Beer <brew, brewski, suds, swill, froth, chill, cold one, wet one> eg *Mogę dostać jeszcze trochę pyfka? (Could I get some more brew?*

piwo See małe piwo, naważyć piwa

piździć** [PEEZH-jeech] *v* (Of wind) To blow very intensely, often accompanied with rain <hawk, hawk like hell, blow like hell> eg *It was hawking like hell yesterday (Piździło wczoraj)*

piździawa** [peezh-JAH-vah] *nf* Windy weather <hawk stretch> eg *Mam dość tej piździawy (I have enough of this hawk stretch)*

pizda** [PEEZ-dah] (or **pipa*** [PEE-pah] or **pinda*** [PEEN-dah] or **piczka*** [PEECH-kah]) **1** *nf* A woman, esp whom one dislikes or disapproves of <bitch, slut, cunt, broad, wench, hag, old hag, old biddy, old bag, old tart, piece of shit> eg *Ta głupia pizda nie wie, czego chce (That stupid cunt doesn't know what she wants); Luknij na tę piczkę. Co za nogi! (Check out that chick. What legs!)* **2** The vulva, vagina <cunt, pussy, slit, slot, snatch, twat> eg *Ma ogoloną piczkę (She has a shaved pussy); Jej piczkę to zna połowa akademika (Half the dorm knows her cunt)*
See pierdolnąć

pizdoliz** [peez-DOH-lees] *nm* A person who performs cunnilingus <cunt-lapper, clit-licker, muff-diver> eg *Ma skłonności ku pizdolizom (She has a predilection to cunt-lappers)*

pląsać [PLOHN-sahch] (perf **popląsać** [poh-PLOHN-sahch]) *v* To dance <rock, shake, boogie, hop, swing, jump, juke, jive, wrestle, grind> eg *Ta laska lubi hasać (That chick likes to swing)*

plaża [PLAH-zhah] *nf* **1** Heat; hot weather <heat-wave, broiler, roaster, scorcher, sizzler, swelterer, sticky, steamy, sweaty> eg *Ale dzisiaj, kurwa, plaża na dworzu! (It's a fucking heat-wave outside!)* **2** Lack of something or someone; nothingness or emptiness <not a soul> eg *No i wiesz, co? Wchodzę do środka a tam plaża (Guess what. I come in and there's not a soul inside)*

plajta [PLAH-ee-tah] *nf* Bankruptcy or a total failure <belly-up, bust, foldo, disaster, flop, bomb, blast, bust, screw-up, snafu, ruin> eg *Wszystko skończyło się plajtą (Everything ended up in a bust)*

plajtować [plah-ee-TOH-vahch] (perf **splajtować** [splah-ee-TOH-vahch]) *v* To go bankrupt or to fail <belly up, go bust, go broke, go to the cleaners, take a bath, take a beating, flop, bomb, bust, wash out> eg *Nowy film splajtował (The premiere of the new movie went bust)*

plama [PLAH-mah] (or **poruta** [poh-ROO-tah] or **popelina** [poh-peh-LEE-nah]) *nf* A shameful or scandalous fact or situation; a shame, disgrace, or scandal <gas, come-down, put-down, take-down, dump, bummer, hot potato, bad scene, bad news, can of worms, bag of worms, takedown, putdown, shit, serious shit, deep shit, deep water, drag, bind, bitch, bummer, downer, headache, double trouble, snafu, pain in the ass, pain in the neck, spot, mess, holy mess, pickle, squeeze, hard time, glitch, stinker, skeleton, skeleton in the closet, sizzler, scorcher, dynamite, Watergate, fine kettle of fish, fine how do you do, fine cup of coffee, big stink, curtains, lights out, game's over> eg *Słyszałem, że ambasador nie zna angielskiego. Ale plama! (I heard the ambassador doesn't know English. What a bummer!); Jak mnie złapią, to będzie popelina (Curtains for me if they find me)*
See dać dupy

plecy [PLEH-tsi] *npl* Powerful support; influenial connections; influence <clout, drag, pull, juice, network, channels, ropes, strings, wires, suction> eg *Jemu nic nie zrobią, bo ma plecy (They won't touch him because he has much pull)*
See cios w plecy

pleść trzy po trzy [plehshch tshi POH tshi] *adv phr* To talk nonsense <bullshit, talk bull, talk bullshit, talk bullshine, talk BS, talk bunk, talk baloney, talk applesauce, jazz, jive, shovel the shit, blow off, blow off one's mouth> eg *Ten facet plecie trzy po trzy. Nie słuchajcie go (This guy is talking bullshit. Don't listen to him)*

plery [PLEH-ri] *npl* The back <traps> eg *Ale plery mu spaliło! (His traps got real sunburned)*

plota [PLOH-tah] *nf* A gossip or rumor <earful, ear dust, scuttlebutt, grapevine, clothesline, back-fence gosspip, bibful, slime, hash, gam, latrine rumor, blowup, wire, hot wire, page-oner, dirty linen, dirty wash, dirty laundry, news flash> eg *Powiem Ci najnowszą plotę (Let me fill you in on the latest dirt)*

pluć sobie w brodę [plooch SOH-byeh v BROH-deh] *v* To regret doing something <kick oneself, kick oneself in the teeth> eg *Pluł sobie w brodę, że* *sprzedał im swój stary samochód (He was kicking himself in the teeth for selling them his old car)*

plucha [PLOO-khah] *nf* Drizzly or wet weather <slush, spit> eg *Spojrzał przez okno. Plucha, powiedział (He looked through the window. Slush, he said)*

plus See być na plusie

płacić jak za zborze [PWAH-cheech yahk zah ZBOH-zheh] *v phr* To pay exorbitantly; to overpay <pay through the nose, pay an arm and a leg, pay a bundle> eg *Zapłaciliśmy za to jak za zboże (We paid an arm and a leg for this)*

płaczek [PWAH-chehk] *nm* A person given to weeping or lamenting at the least adversity <crybaby, whiner> eg *Przestań się drzeć i nie bądź taki płaczek! (Stop lamenting. Don't be such a cry baby!)*

płotka [PWOHT-kah] *nf* An inconsequential or insignificant person <loser, lightweight, nobody, non, nonentity, noname, small potatoes, small timer, pissant, wannabe> eg *Nie przejmuj się nią. To tylko płotka (Don't worry about her. She's just a lightweight)*

płyta See zmienić płytę

po łebkach [poh WEHP-kahkh] *adv phr* Carelessly and cursorily, esp because of haste; haphazardly <half-assedly, half-heartedly, helter-skelter, hit-or-miss, hit-and-miss, harum-scarum, higgedly-piggedly, ramble-scramble, arsy-varsy, with a lick and a promise, slapdash, slapbang, skewgeely, scratching the surface> eg *To miły facet, ale pracuje na odwal (He's a nice guy, but he works half-assedly)*

po balu [ee poh BAH-loo] (or **po balu panno lalu** [ee poh BAH-loo PAHN-noh LAH-loo]; **i** [ee] may precede both) *excl* (It is) over or too late <game over, it is gone, it is all over, too little too late, someone missed the boat, someone blew it, kiss that one goodbye> eg *Chciał to cofnąć, ale to już było już po balu (He wanted to take it back, but he already missed the boat)*

po bożemu* [poh boh-ZHEH-moo] *adv phr* With a male partner in a sex act lying over the female partner between her spread legs <in the missionary way, in the missionary position, in the missionary style, Kentucky straight> eg *Nie podobało im się robienie tego po bożemu (They didn't like doing it in the missionary position)*

po byku [poh BI-koo] (or **po chuju**** [poh KHOO-yoo]) *adj* **1** Excellent; wonderful; extremely good <great, cool, swell, fab, rad, def, far-out, awesome, frantic, terrific, funky, gorgeous, groovy, hellacious, neat, peachy, dandy, baddest, mean, solid, super-dooper, wailing, wicked, gnarly, top-notch, ten, ace-high, A-OK, A-1, some> eg *Naukowców mieliśmy po byku, ale sprzęt był zbyt przestarzały (We had terrific scientists, but the equipment was too old)* **2** Big; large; sizable <gross, humongous, monstro, moby, jumbo, hefty, whopper, mother, king-size, God-size> eg *Wszyscy ci zawodnicy są po byku (All these players are moby); Samochód miał po chuju. Cadillac albo Mercedes, nie pamiętam (He had a humongous car. A Cadillac or Mercedes, I can't remember now)*

po cholerę See na cholerę

po chuj See na chuj

po chuju See po byku

po czyimś trupie [poh CHI-eemsh TROO-pyeh] *adv phr* (Used to show one's determination that something will not happen) Not if someone can prevent it; never <over someone's dead body, not on your life, in a pig's eye, in a pig's ass, in

a pig's ear, someone will be damned if, someone will be fucked if> eg *Chcesz rzucić studia? Po moim trupie! (You want to quit college? Over my dead body!)*

po dawnemu See po staremu

po diabła See na diabła

po godzinach [poh goh-JEE-nahkh] *adv phr* Later than the usual times of work or business <after hours, overtime> eg *Często pracował po godzinach (He often worked after hours)*

po jaką cholerę See na cholerę

po jakie licho See na cholerę

po jakiego chuja See na chuj

po jakiego diabła See na diabła

po jakiego grzyba See na diabła

po kiego chuja See na chuj

po kiego diabła See na diabła

po męsku [poh MEHN-skoo] *adv phr* (Accepting or bearing something) Without complaint <on the chin, like a man> eg *Powinieneś to zosić po męsku (You should take it like a man)*

po pachy See ubaw

po pijaku [poh pee-YAH-koo] *adv phr* (Being) drunk; under the influence of alcohol <alkied, bagged, blitzed, blotto, blown away, bent, boiled, bombed, blasted, boozed, bottled, boxed, buzzed, canned, clobbered, cooked, corked, crashed, drunk as a skunk, edged, embalmed, fractured, fried, gassed, ginned, grogged, have one too many, half under, high, hooched up, in bad shape, impaired, illuminated, juiced, knocked out, liquored, lit, loaded, looped, lubricated, lushed, smashed, oiled, pickled, plastered, plonked, polluted, sauced, shitfaced, slugged, sloshed, soaked, stewed, stiff, stinking drunk, swizzled, tanked, three sheets to the wind, wiped, zonked> eg *Po pijaku dostawiał się do dziewczyn (Being loaded, he made a pass at the girls)*

po ptakach [poh PTAH-kakh] (or **po zawodach** [poh zah-VOH-dahkh]) *adv phr* (It is) Too late; post factum <it is gone, it is all over, too little too late, someone missed the boat, someone blew it, kiss that one goodbye> eg *Wiedział, co robić, ale było już po ptakach (He knew what to do, but he missed the boat)*

po równo [poh ROOV-noh] *adv phr* Equally for everyone or everything; equably <across the board, fifty-fifty, even-steven, half-way, the Dutch way> eg *Rada szkoły podniosła pensję wszystkim nauczycielom po równo (The school board raised the pay of all the teachers across the board); Podzielmy to po równo, co?) Let's split it fifty-fifty, okay?)*

po staremu [poh stah-REH-moo] (or **po dawnemu** [poh dahv-NEH-moo]) *adv phr* As it used to be; as it was formerly <same old shit, SOS, just like in the old days> eg *Co u Ciebie? Niewiele, wszystko po staremu (What's new with you? Not much, same old shit)*

po trupach [poh TROO-pahkh] *adv phr* By any means, legal or illegal; stubbornly and ruthlessly <by hook or by crook, no matter what> eg *Skończę tę robotę po trupach (I'll get the job done by hook or by crook)*

po uszy [poh OO-shi] *adv phr* Deeply involved; overwhelmed; surfeited; exceedingly <up to here, up to one's ass, asshole deep, up to one's eyeballs, knee

deep, head over heels> eg *Jest po uszy w długach (He's up to his eyeballs in debt); Jest w nim zakochana po sam uszy (She's head over heels in love with him)*

po zawodach See po ptakach

pół biedy [poow BYEH-di] *nf phr* A small, harmless, or unimportant predicament; nothing to be seriously worried about <nothing hot, big deal, no big deal, no biggie, Mickey Mouse, small potatoes, small beer, fly speck, piece of cake, cake, cakewalk, cherry pie, duck soup, kid stuff, picnic, pushover, snap, tea party, walkaway, walkover, breeze, stroll, cinch, pipe, plain sailing> eg *Pół biedy, jeśli dostaniesz dwóję. Gorzej, jeśli cię wyrzucą ze szkoły (It'll be no big deal if you get an F. It''ll be far worse if they expell you from school)*

pół litra [poow LEET-rah] (or **połówka** [poh-WOOF-kah] or **pół basa** [poow BAH-sah] or **pół metra** [poow MEHT-rah]) *nn phr* A half-liter bottle of vodka <no slang equivalent> eg *Wypiliśmy całe pół basa (We drank an entire half-liter vodka)*

połapać się [poh-WAH-pahch shyeh] *v* (To begin) To understand or comprehend; to get orientation in something <get, get it, catch, get the drift, get the picture, get the message, get the hang of, savvy, dig, click, capeesh, read, be with it, see where one is coming from, know where one is coming from, be with it, get one's bearings> eg *On w ogóle się w tym nie połapał (He didn't get it at all)*

półgłówek [poow-GWOO-wehk] *nm* A very stupid, clumsy or ineffectual person; an idiot <airbrain, airhead, birdbrain, blockhead, squarehead, bonehead, bubblebrain, bubblehead, buckethead, cluckhead, cementhead, clunkhead, deadhead, dumbbell, dumbcluck, dumbhead, dumbass, dumbbrain, fatbrain, fathead, flubdub, knukclebrain, knucklehead, lamebrain, lardhead, lunkhead, meathead, musclehead, noodlehead, numbskull, pointhead, scatterbrain, jerk, jerk-off, klutz, chump, creep, nerd, dork, dweeb, gweeb, geek, jackass, lummox, twerp, nerd, bozo, clod, cluck, clunk, dimwit, dingbat, dipstick, dodo, dopey, dufus, goofus, lump, lunk, nitwit, schnook, schlep, schlemiel, schmendrick, schmo, schmuck, simp, stupe> eg *Od godziny tłumaczy im, co to oznacza. Straszne półgłówki, nic nie rozumieją (He's been explaining to them what it means for an hour. They are real squareheads, they don't understand anything)*

połknąć See łyknąć

połknąć bakcyla [POH-oo-knohnch bahk-TSI-lah] *v phr* To become extremely attracted to or interested in something; to become engrossed in spmething <be really into, be heavily into, be up to here in, be all wrapped in, get sold into, get hooked, get caught, get bitten by the bug, be bitten by the bug, eat sleep and breathe something> eg *Myślę, że połknął bakcyla (I think he got bitten by the bug)*

połowa See lepsza połowa

połowica [poh-woh-VEE-tsah] *nf* A wife <wifey, mama, missus, better half, old lady, little woman, ball and chain, trouble and strife, significant other> eg *Poszedł spytać się swojej połowicy (He went to ask his wifey)*

połowinki [poh-woh-VEEN-kee] *npl* A party organized to celebrate the completion of half a period of one's university studies, usually organized in the middle of the third academic year <sophomore party> eg *Kiedy są połowinki? (When's the sophomore party?)*

połówka See pół litra

pożreć się Perf żreć się

pobawić się Perf bawić się

pobeczeć Perf beczeć

pobiadolić Perf biadolić

pobimbać Perf bimbać

pobite gary [po-BEE-teh GAH-ri] *excl* An exclamation of surrender <uncle, knock it off> eg *No dobra! Pobite gary! poddaję się! (All right! Uncle! I give in!)*

pobyczyć Perf byczyć się

pocałować See móc kogoś pocałować

pocałować klamkę [poh-tsah-WOH-vahch KLAHM-keh] *v phr* Not to find someone in their home; to knock at someone's door in vain because someone is absent <no slang equivalent> eg *Byłem u ciebie, ale pocałowałem klamkę (I came to your place, but there was noone in the house)*

pochichrać Perf chichrać

pochlać Perf chlać

pociągnąć Perf ciągnąć

pociecha [poh-CHEH-khah] *nf* A child <kid, pride and glory> eg *Uspokoił się znacznie od czasu gdy urodziła się mu pociecha (He's calmed down a lot since his pride and glory was born)*

pociupciać Perf ciupciać

pocztą pantoflową [POHCH-toh pahn-tohf-LOH-voh] *adv phr* Via an unofficial way of spreading news <on the grapevine, through the grapevine, by the grapevine> eg *Usłyszałem o twoim sukcesie pocztą pantoflową (I heard about your success through the grapevine)*

pod chmurką [poht KHMOOR-koh] *adv phr* Open-air; in the open air <under the sky, al fresco, outside> eg *Zróbmy zajęcia pod chmurką (Let's have class al fresco); Zwykle pije w knajpie pod chmurką (He normally drinks in the joint outside)*

pod gazem See na gazie

pod gruszą [pohd GROO-shoh] *adv phr* In the country <in the boondocks, in the boonies, in the sticks, in the woods, outback, up country> eg *10 % z nich spędzi wakacje pod gruszą (10 % of them will spend their vacations in the boondocks)*

pod nóż See iść pod nóż

pod nosem [pohd NOH-sehm] *adv phr* **1** In the near distance; very close; nearby <around, pretty near, screwdriver turn away, frog's leap away, whoop, within a hoop and a holler, within a stone's throw, in spitting distance, around the corner, right next door> eg *Gdzie tu jest jakaś dobra restauracja? Jest jedna, niedaleko stąd. Właściwie pod nosem (Where is any good restaurant here? There's one not far from here. Actually a screwdriver turn away from here)* **2** In a whispering or mumbling voice <under one's breath, below one's breath, beneath one's breath> eg *Liczyła coś pod nosem (She was counting under her breath)*

pod pantoflem [poht pahn-TOHF-lehm] *adj phr* (Of a man) Dominated by a woman, esp one's wife <hen-pecked, pussy-whipped, tied to one's wife apron strings, grabbed by the balls, wrapped around one's finger, twisted around one's finger> eg *On nic Ci nie powie. Jest pod pantoflem (He won't tell you anything. He's pussy-whipped)*

pod pic See picować

pod psem [poht PSEHM] *adj phr* **1** In a state of melancholy or depression; in low spirits <blue, low, down, on a downer, down in the dumps, taken down a peg, downbeat, down and out, funky, in a blue funk, in the dumps, dragged, ripped,

on a bummer, bummed out, on a down trip, having the blues, singing the blues, crying the blues, having one's ass in a sling, mopey> eg *Przez cały dzień jest pod psem. Nie wiem dlaczego (She's been on a downer the whole day. I don't know why)* **2** (Of the weather) Terrible, esp if rainy and dreary <dim, lousy, shitty, crappy> eg *Pogoda dziś pod psem (The weather's lousy today)*

pod publiczkę See grać pod publiczkę

pod siebie See robić w gacie

pod włos See picować

podłapać See złapać

podbramkowa sytuacja See sytuacja podbramkowa

podchmielony See podcięty

podchodzić [poht-KHOH-jeech] (perf **podejść** [poh-DEH-eeshch]) *v* **1** To attempt to start an action or endeavor; to approach a situation <give it a try, give it a go, give it a crack, give it a fling, have a go, have a crack, make a try, make a run at, cut and try, try one's damnedest, try on for size, have a shot at, take a shot at, take a fling at, make a stab at, tackle, bend over, go in for, go out for, go for it, take on, come at, move in on, make up to, give one a tumble, tumble> eg *Podchodzili to tego parę razy (They gave it a try several times); Podejdę to tego egzaminu w przyszłym semestrze (I'll have a go at the exam next semester)* **2** To be fully acceptable or suitable for someone <fit in, fit the bill, do, wash, work, do down, cut it, make the grade, make the cut, make it, cut the mustard, pass in the dark, fill the bill, suit one fine, be OK, be okay, be kopasetic, be hunky-dory, be so-so> eg *Podchodzi mi ta muzyka (This music fits the bill for me)*

podcięty [poht-CHEYHN-ti] (or **podchmielony** [poht-khmyeh-LOH-ni]) *adj* Drunk; alcohol intoxicated <alkied, bagged, blitzed, blotto, blown away, bent, boiled, bombed, blasted, boozed, bottled, boxed, buzzed, canned, clobbered, cooked, corked, crashed, drunk as a skunk, edged, embalmed, fractured, fried, gassed, ginned, grogged, have one too many, half under, high, hooched up, in bad shape, impaired, illuminated, juiced, knocked out, liquored, lit, loaded, looped, lubricated, lushed, smashed, oiled, pickled, plastered, plonked, polluted, sauced, shitfaced, slugged, sloshed, soaked, stewed, stiff, stinking drunk, swizzled, tanked, three sheets to the wind, wiped, zonked> eg *Myślę, że był podchmielony. Inaczej by sięd o niej nie dobierał (I think he was sauced. Otherwise he wouuldn't make a pass at her); Kierowca był nieźle podcięty (The driver was real canned)*

podejść Perf podchodzić

poderwać Perf podrywać

podetrzeć See móc sobie w dupę wsadzić

podiwanić See podpierdolić

podjarać Perf jarać

podjarać się Perf jarać się

podkładka [poht-KWAHT-kah] *nf* An official document necessary to settle down a given matter <note, paper> eg *Masz na to jakąś podkładkę? (Do you have any paper to support it?)*

podlizuch See lizus

podlizywać się [pohd-lee-ZI-vahch shyeh] (perf **podlizać się** [pohd-LEE-zahch shyeh]) *v* To curry favor; to toady <brown-nose, kiss ass, lick ass, suck ass, ass-kiss, ass-lick, wipe someone's ass, apple-polish, back-scratch, bootlick, sweeten

up> eg *Nie mogę na to patrzeć. Mógłby tak już przestać się jej podlizywać (I can't stand it. I wish he'd stop kissing her ass)*

podlotek [pohd-LOH-tehk] *nm* A teenage girl or a young woman <chick, chicklet, teen, teener, teeny-bopper, bubble-gummer, little lady> eg *Gadasz mi tu o jakichś podlotkach. Ja chcę kobiety! (You're talking about some juvies. I want a woman!)*

podminowany [pohd-mee-noh-VAH-ni] *adj* Irritated, annoyed, or nervous <cranky, uptight, jumpy, jittery, shaky, shivery, nervy, edgy, antsy, clutchy, hitchy, fretty, itchy, wired, tightened-up, strung-out> eg *Widzę, że jesteś dzisiaj wyraźnie podminowana. Co jest? (I can see you're clearly uptight today. What's up?)*

podślizgnęła się komuś noga See podwinęła się komuś noga

podpadać [pohd-PAH-dahch] (perf **podpaść** [POHT-pahshch]) *v* **1** To be suspicious or dubious <be phony, ring phony, be fishy, be funny, not be kosher> eg *Skoro mówimy o tej propozycji, to ona mi podpada (Talking about this proposal, it is somewhat fishy)* **2** To make oneself unpopular with someone; to fall into disfavor <be in someone's bad books, be in someone's black books, be on someone's shit list, be on someone's crap list, be in deep shit with someone, be up shit creek with someone, draw a bead on> eg *Podpadł u profesora (He's in the bad books of the professor)*

podpierać ścianę [poht-PYEH-rahch SHCHAH-neh] *v phr* To be peripheral and uncourted at a dance <be a wallflower> eg *Była bardzo brzydka, więc na imprezach zawsze podpierała ścianę (She was very ugly, so she was always a wallflower at the parties)*

podpierdolić** [poht-pyehr-DOH-leech] (or **podpieprzyć*** [poht-PYEHP-shich] or **podpierniczyć*** [poht-pyehr-NEE-chich] or **podpierdzielić*** [poht-pyehr-JEH-leech] or **podpiździć*** [poht-PEEZH-jeecj] or **podiwanić** [pohd-ee-VAH-neech] or **podprowadzić** [pod-proh-VAH-jeech] or **podwędzić** [pohd-VEHN-jeech]) *v* To steal; to rob <heist, boost, burgle, nurn, bag, buzz, highjack, hoist, hold up, hook, hustle, jump, kick over, knock off, knock over, lift, move, mug, nab, nick, nip, pinch, pluck, roll, rustle, snatch, snitch, stick up, swipe, take off, put the grab on, go south with> eg *Kto mi podwędził zegarek? (Who snitched my watch?)*

podpisać się pod czymś [poht-PEE-sahch shyeh poht chimsh] (or **podpisać się pod czymś obiema rękami** [poht-PEE-sahch shyeh poht chimsh oh-BYEH-mah rehn-KAH-mi]) *v phr* To support or agree with something wholeheartedly <back up, stand up for, front for, go for, sign off on, fall for, lap up, take, tumble for, okay, OK, back, bless, pass on, shake on, clinch, play ball, give the green light, come across, come around> eg *Podpisał się pod tą decyzją obiema rękami (He stood up for this proposal)*

podpity See spity

podpiździć See podpierdolić

podprowadzić See podpierdolić

podpucha [poht-POO-khah] *nf* An act or remark intended to fool someone; a more or less amiable deception or trick <put-on, leg-pull, number, spoof, con> eg *Nie widzisz, że to podpucha? (Can't you see it's a put-on?)*

podpuszczać [poht-POOSH-chahch] (perf **podpuścić** [poht-POOSH-cheech]) *v* To fool someone, esp by pretending; to tease; to treat someone unseriously and frivolously <put someone on, pull someone's leg, pull someone's string, give

someone a leg, have someone on, jack someone around, jerk someone around, poke fun at, kid someone around, fool someone around, jack someone's chain, spoof, cut down> eg *To nie może być prawda. Podpuszczasz mnie (This can't be true. You're kidding me)*

podróbka [poh-DROOP-kah] (or **podrób** [POH-droop] *nm*) *nf* Something false, fake, forged, or counterfeited <pirate label, falsie, fake, bogus, bogosity, junque, hokey> eg *Podróbki wyglądały jak autentyki (The fakes looked like the real things)*

podryw [POHD-rif] (or **podrywka** [pohd-RIF-kah] *nf*) *nm* **1** An act or attempt of becoming acquainted with someone for romantic or sexual purposes <pick-up, action> eg *Jego żona dała mu po pysku za jego niezliczone podrywki (His wife punjched his mug for his numerous pick-ups)*

podrywać [pohd-RI-vahch] (perf **poderwać** [poh-DEHR-vahch]; **zarywać** [zah-RI-vahch] or **rwać** [rvahch] perf **zarwać** [ZAHR-vahch]) *v* To become or attempt to become acquainted with someone for romantic or sexual purposes <pick up, get some action, get some ass, score> eg *Byłam dumna, że podrywa mnie starszy mężczyzna (I was proud to be picked up by an older man); Często udaje nam się zarwać jakieś małolaty (We often manage to pick up teenage girls)*

podrywacz [pohd-RI-vahch] *nm* A man who is proficient at becoming acquainted with women for romantic or sexual purposes <pick-up artist, ladies' man, heart-breaker, skirt-chaser, lady-killer, lover-boy, operator, player> eg *Uważaj na mojego brata. To prawdziwy podrywacz (Be careful with my brother. He's a real heart-breaker)*

podrywaczka [pohd-ri-VAHCH-kah] *nf* A woman who is proficient at becoming acquainted with men for romantic or sexual purposes <pick-up artist, heart-breaker, killer, vamp, operator, player, man-eater, man-trap> eg *Słyszałem, że twoja siostra to niezła podrywaczka. No man can resist her (I heard your sister is a great man-eater. Żaden facet się jej nie oprze)*

podrzucać [pohd-ZHOO-tsahch] (perf **podrzucić** [pohd-ZHOO-chich]) *v* **1** To hand something over to someone; to give <drop, slip, post, duke, shoot, pass over> eg *Rodzice podrzucali mu czasem trochę jedzenia (His parents would drop him some food from time to time)* **2** To leave at someone's place, usually for a certain period of time <drop, park, peg, nail> eg *Podrzuciliśmy dziecko teściowej i poszliśmy na tę imprezę (We dropped the baby at the mother-in-law's and went to the party)* **3** To give someone a free ride in a private vehicle <give someone a lift, give someone a ride> eg *Podrzucił mnie do domu (He gave me a lift home)*

podskakiwać [poht-skah-KEE-vahch] (perf **podskoczyć** [poht-SKOH-chich]) *v* To insolently defy, challenge, or oppose <defi, face off, face down, fly in the face, fly in the teeth, meet eyeball to eyeball, make my day, hang tough, hang in there, take one on, stick fast, stick it out, kick over traces, lip, brace, cross, put one's life on the line, stand up to, knock the chip off one's shoulder, step over the line, tangle, bump heads with, cross, square off, put down, have a bone to pick, hold no brief for, put up a fight, mess with, mess around with, fool with, fool around with, fuck with, fuck around with, screw with, screw around with, dick with, dick around with, diddle with, diddle around with, fiddle with, fiddle around with, fart with, fart around with, monkey with, monkey around with> eg *Miałem ze soba pistolet, więc żaden z nich nie podskoczył (I had a gun on me, so none of them dared to fuck with me)*

podskok See w podskokach

podstawówka [poht-stah-VOOF-kah] (or **podstawówa** [poht-stah-VOO-vah]) *nf* An elementary school, esp public <blackboard jungle, knowledge box> eg *Nie znoszę tej podstawówki (I hate this blackboard jungle)*

podtatusiały [poht-tah-too-SHYAH-wi] *adj* Aged, esp about a balding and obese man <rusty, creaky, over the hill> eg *Niektórzy faceci wydają się podtatusiali już mając trzydziestkę (Some guys seem over the hill at thirty)*

podwalać się [pohd-VAH-lahch shyeh] *v* To invite or request sexual favors <make a pass, put a move on, make a play for> eg *Pedał zaczął się do mnie podwalać, więc szybko wyszedłem z baru (The faggot started to make a pass at me, so I quickly left the bar)*

podwędzić See podpierdolić

podwinęła się komuś noga [pohd-vee-NEH-wah shyeh KOH-moosh NOH-gah] (or **podślizgnęła się komuś noga** [poh-shleezg-NEH-wah shyeh KOH-moosh NOH-gah]) *phr* To make a mistake, esp the one that is likely to ruin someone <slip, slip up, trip up, blow, flub, fluff, foozle, goof up, screw up, fuck up, ball up, mess up, louse up, make a blooper, pull a blooper, drop the ball, drop a brick, put one's foot in it, stub one's toe, fall flat on one's ass, shoot oneself in the foot> eg *Prędzej czy później podwinie mu się noga i go złapiemy (Sooner or later he's going to drop the ball)*

podwozie [pohd-VOH-zhyeh] *nn* A woman's buttocks and hips <ass, butt, bum, behind, back, back seat, seat, bottom, heinie, rear, tush, fanny, derriere, tail, bucket, tokus, keister, kazoo> eg *Jak dla mnie, to ma niezłe podwozie (As far me, she's got a nice derriere)*

pofarcić Perf farcić

pofikać Perf fikać

pogadać Perf gadać

pogibać się Perf gibać się

poględzić Perf ględzić

pogrzać Perf grzać

pohasać Perf hasać

pohulać Perf hulać

pojebany See popierdolony

pojechany See pomylony

pojechany See popierdolony

pokapować Perf kapować

pokraka* [poh-KRAH-kah] *nf* An ugly person <beasty, skag, skank, pig, bag, dog, cow> eg *Przyszedł na imprezę z jakąś pokraką (He came to the party with some skag)*

pokropek [poh-KROH-pehk] *nm* An act in which a priest consecrates with holy water, esp before lowering a coffin to the grave <hocus-pocus, mumbo-jumbo, abracadabra> eg *Ksiądz stanął nad grobem i zaczynał pokropek (The priest stood over the grave and started his mumbo-jumbo)*

pokurcz* [POH-koorch] *nm* A person of short stature <shorty, peewee, peanut, runt, squirt, shrimp, half-pint> eg *Gadasz mi tu o jakimś pokurczu (You're telling me about some peewee)*

polać Perf polewać

polaczek* [poh-LAH-chehk] *nm* A male Pole; a Pole <polack, pollack, pollock> eg *No cóż, tak to już jest między nami polaczkami (Well, that's the way we polacks are)*

polak [POH-lahk] *nm* The Polish language, esp as a subject in school <no slang equivalent> eg *Kto Cię uczył polaka w zeszłym semestrze? (Who taught you Polish last semester?)*

polecieć Perf lecieć

polewać [poh-LEH-vahch] (perf **polać** [POH-lahch]) *v* To pour alcohol into a glass <hit, give a hit> eg *Polej nam też (Hit us some, too)*
See oblewać

poleźć Perf **leźć**

polibuda [poh-lee-BOO-dah] *nf* A technical university or college <tech, poly-tech> eg *Słyszałem, że twój brat studiuje na polibudzie (I heard your brother studies at the poly-tech)*

policzek [poh-LEE-chehk] *nm* An action aimed directly and intentionally against someone else; a rebuff or insult <slap, slap in the face, knock, bringdown, put-down> eg *To był prawdziwy policzek dla jej rodziców, gdy zignorowała ich radę i zrezygnowała z pracy (It was a real slap in the face for her partents when she ignored their advice and gave up her job*

polizać się Perf lizać się

polonus* [poh-LOH-noos] *nm* A Polish emigrant <polack, pollack, pollock> eg *Wielu polonusów zdecydowało się wrócić do kraju (Many polacks decided to return to Poland)*

pomacać Perf macać

pomagier [poh-MAH-gyehr] *nm* A low-ranking male subordinate expected to help and serve to others; a helper; an assistant <help, gofer, go-for, gopher, man Friday, hired hand, sec> eg *Pojawił się wraz ze swoimi dwoma pomagierami (He showed up along with his two gofers)*

pomarudzić Perf marudzić

pomieszanie z poplątaniem [poh-myeh-SHAH-nyeh s pohp-lohn-TAH-nyehm] *nn phr* A number of things mixed up without any sensible order; a mixture or miscellany <mish mash, hodge-podge, odds and ends, bits and pieces, rag-bag, mess, unholy mess, rat's nest, smorgasboard> eg *Spójrz na jego księgi rachunkowe. Pomieszanie z poplątaniem (Have a look at his account books. It's unholy mess)*

pomigdalić się Perf migdalić się

pompka [POHMP-kah] *nf* An exercise in which someone lies face down, keeping their back straight, and pushes their body up with their arms <push-up> eg *Robi 20 pompek dziennie (He does 20 push-ups a day)*
See frajer

pompować [pohm-POH-vahch] (perf **wypompować** [vi-pohm-POH-vahch]) *v* To drink alcohol, esp quickly or in large quantities <booze, guzzle, gargle, bend the elbow, hit the bottle, hit the sauce, knock back, lap, tank up, wet one's whistle, hang a few on, slug down, swig> eg *Facet wypomopwał całą butelkę (The guy knocked back the whole bottle)*

pomroczność jasna [pohm-ROHCH-nohshch YAHS-nah] *nf phr* A mythical disease of apparent lack of memory or stupidity; amnesia <blackout, blockout, brain fade, blank, memory overload, short circuit, crash, knock-out, pass-out, conk-out, zonk-out, black-out, power outage> eg *No to jaka jest diagnoza? (So what's the diagnosis? Memory overload)*

pomyje [po-MI-yeh] *npl* **1** Defamation; slander or libel; false degrading matters <dirt, dirty linen, dirty wash, dirty laundry, mud, slime, rap, slam, smear> eg *Najlepiej było zanurzyć faceta w pomyjach (The best way was to drown the guy in mud)* **2** A diluted and unappetizing soup or any other semi-liquid food <dishwater, bellywash, pigswill> eg *Co to za pomyje? Ja mam to jeść? (What is this bellywash? Am I supposed to eat it?)*

pomyleniec [poh-mi-LEH-nyehts] (or **postrzeleniec** [poh-stsheh-LEH-nyehts] or **psychol** [PSI-khohl]) *nm* An insane or eccentric man <freak, fruitcake, goofball, cook, loon, nut, nutball, nutcase, nutter, psycho, screwball, screw-loose, sicko, wacko, weirdo, psycho, oddball> eg *Ten facet to pomyleniec. Myśli, że jest prorokiem (This guy is a freak. He thinks he's a prophet)*

pomylony [poh-mi-LOH-ni] (or **postrzelony** [poh-stsheh-LOH-ni] **pojechany** [poh-yeh-KHAH-ni] or or **psychiczny** [psi-KHEECH-ni]) *adj* Insane, stupid, or thoughtless <fucked in the head, fucked-up, crazy, creazy as a loon, loony, nerts, nuts, nutso, nutsy, nutty, sick, sick in the head, sicko, wacko, wacky, psycho, shizo, screwy, off one's rocker, out of one's skull, fruity, airbrained, airheaded, birdbrained, blockheaded, squareheaded, boneheaded, bubblebrained, bubbleheaded, bucketheaded, cluckheaded, cementheaded, clunkheaded, deadheaded, dumbclucked, dumbheaded, dumbassed, dumbbrained, fatbrained, fatheaded, flubdubbed, knukclebrained, knuckleheaded, lamebrained, lardheaded, lunkheaded, meatheaded, muscleheaded, noodleheaded, numbskulled, pointheaded, scatterbrained, nerdy, dorky, jackassed, lummoxed, dopey, goofy> eg *Ten facet jest naprawdę pomylony. Potrzebuje wakacji (This guy is really sick. He needs a vacation)*

pomyślunek [poh-mish-LOO-nehk] *nm* The ability to think quickly, reasonably, or inventively; intelligence or inventiveness <brains, savvy, smarts, it, right stuff, what is takes> eg *Ten facet to ma pomyślunek! (This guy really has the smarts)*

ponurak [poh-NOO-rahk] *nm* A morose, melancholic, or pessimistic person <killjoy, party-pooper, wet blanket, sourpuss, sourball, drag, turn-off, grinch, crape-hanger, gloomy Gus> eg *Nie bądź takim ponurakiem! Zabaw się trochę! (Don't be such a wet blanket! Have some fun!)*

pończocha See trzymać pieniądze w skarpecie

pościelówa [pohsh-cheh-LOO-vah] (or **pościelówka** [pohsh-cheh-LOOF-kah]) *nf* A very slow love song <tear-jerker, weepie, schmaltzy tune> eg *Posłuchajmy tej pościelówy (Let's listen to this tear-jerker)*

poślizg [POH-shleesk] *nm* A delay <hang-up, hold-up, slow-up, tie-up, bind, downtime, holding> eg *Przepraszam za ten poślizg. Doślę panom mansuckrypt słownika w ciągu następnych trzech tygodni (I'm sorry for the hold-up. I will send you the manuscript of the dictionary within the next three weeks)*
See z poślizgiem

pośredniak [poh-SHREHD-nyahk] *nm* An employment agency or office <flesh peddler, head hunter> eg *Tylko takie oferty mają pośredniaki (Flesh peddlers have only such offers)*

popadnie See co popadnie, gdzie popadnie

popalić See dać wycisk, dostać wycisk

popelina See plama

popierdolić** [poh-pyehr-DOH-leech] (or **popieprzyć*** [poh-PYEHP-shich] or **popierniczyć*** [poh-pyehr-NEE-chich] or **popierdzielić*** [poh-pyehr-JEH-leech]) *v* **1** To lose mental fitness; to become insane or eccentric <get fucked up, get screwed up, get fucked in the head, get head-fucked, get mind-fucked, go crazy, go crazy as a loon, blow one's cork, blow one's top, blow a fuse, crack up, freak out, flip out, go ape, go bananas, go bent, go bonkers, go cracked, go dopey, go ga-ga, go half-baked, go loony, go loopy, go mental, go nerts, go nuts, go nutty, go off one's nut, go off one's rocker, go off one's base, go off the track, go off the trolley, go out one's skull, go psycho, go schizo, go screwy, go wacky, go weird, go wild, schiz out, psych out, come unglued, come unstuck, come unwrapped, go to pieces> eg *Był porządnym człowiekiem. Popierdoliło go, gdy wygrał w totolotka (He was a decent man. He got fucked in the head after he won on the lottery)* **2** To make something unclear; to confuse, complicate, or lie <fuck up, stir, stir up, adjy, bull, bullshit, shit, shovel the shit, string along, snow, fake it, talk through one's hat, speak with forked tongue> eg *Wszystko kompletnie popierdolił (He fucked up everything)*

popierdolony** [poh-pyehr-doh-LOH-ni] (or **popieprzony*** [poh-pyehp-SHOH-ni] or **popierniczony*** [poh-pyehr-nee-CHOH-ni] or **pojechany** [poh-yeh-KHAH-ni] or **pojebany**** [poh-yeh-BAH-ni]) *adj* Insane, stupid or thoughtless <crazy, creazy as a loon, loony, nerts, nuts, nutso, nutsy, nutty, sick, sick in the head, sicko, wacko, wacky, psycho, shizo, screwy, off one's rocker, out of one's skull, fruity, airbrained, airheaded, birdbrained, blockheaded, squareheaded, boneheaded, bubblebrained, bubbleheaded, bucketheaded, cluckheaded, cementheaded, clunkheaded, deadheaded, dumbclucked, dumbheaded, dumbassed, dumbbrained, fatbrained, fatheaded, flubdubbed, knukclebrained, knuckleheaded, lamebrained, lardheaded, lunkheaded, meatheaded, muscleheaded, noodleheaded, numbskulled, pointheaded, scatterbrained, nerdy, dorky, jackassed, lummoxed, dopey, goofy> eg *On musi być popierdolony! Rzucić się na profesora z pyskiem? (He must be nuts! To start yelling at the professor)*

popijawa [poh-pee-YAH-vah] *nf* A drinking party; a carousal <bash, bender, bust, twister, wingding, winger> eg *Popijawa trwała do szóstej rano (The wingding lasted till six in the morning)*

popitka [poh-PEET-kah] (or **zapitka** [zah-PEET-kah]) *nf* A non-alcoholic drink taken after an alcoholic one; a soft drink drunk after a shot of potent alcoholic liquor <chaser, wash> eg *Chciałbym podwójną szkocką z wodą sodową na popitkę (I'd like a double scotch with a club soda chaser)*

popląsać Perf pląsać

poplątanie See pomieszanie z poplątaniem

popołudniówka [poh-poh-wood-NYOOF-kah] *nf* An evening edition of a newspaper <evening paper, evening rag, evening blat> eg *Przeczytałem o tym w jakiejś popołudniówce (I read about it in an evening paper)*

poprawka [poh-PRAHF-kah] *nf* A repeat examination <take-over, re-take, make-up exam, make-up test> eg *Po przerwie wakacyjnej będzie miała poprawkę (She will have a re-take after the vacation break)*

popuścić [poh-POOSH-cheech] *v* (Of frost) To subside; to thaw <die down> eg *Mróz popuścił (The frost has died down)*

popuszczać See nie popuszczać komuś

popychadło [poh-pi-KHAD-woh] *nn* A person without initiative who is easily victimized <patsy, doormat, easy mark, fall guy, sucker, schnook, babe in the woods> eg *Wygląda na popychadło, ale na prawdę to cwaniak (He looks like an easy mark, but he's really quite savvy)*

pornus* [POHR-noos] (or **pornos*** [POHR-nohs] *nm* or **pornol*** [POHR-nohl] *nm* or **porno** [POHR-noh] *nn*) *nm* A pornographic film <blue movie, blue flick, porn movie, porn flick, skin movie, skin flick, fuck film, flesh flick> eg *Zarobili dużo pieniędzy kręcąc pornole (They made a lot of money making skin flicks)*

portki [POHRT-kee] *npl* Pants; trousers <slacks, jeans, cords, ducks, hip huggers, kneebusters, baggies, jammies, dungarees, pegs, striders, strides, britches, knickers, drawers, longies, bags> eg *Załóż portki. Ktoś puka do drzwi (Put your slacks on. Somebody is knocking at the door)*

See robić w gacie, trząść dupą

poruchać Perf ruchać

poruta See plama

poryczeć się Perf ryczeć

porzygać się Perf rzygać

posłać na zieloną trawkę [POHS-wahch nah zhyeh-LOH-noh TRAHF-keh] (or **posłać na bruk** [POHS-wahch nah brook]) *v phr* To dismiss or discharge from a job <fire, lay off, can, ax, air, boot, sack, give the ax, give the air, give the boot, give the sack, give the bum's rush, give the kiss-off, give the pink slip, pink-slip, give one's walking papers, give one's walking ticket> eg *Posłała ich na zieloną trawkę (She's given them the kiss-off)*

posikać się Perf sikać

posiusiać się Perf siusiać

posmarować komuś łapę See dać komuś w łapę

postawić oczy w słup [poh-STAH-veech OH-chi f SWOOP] *v phr* To look hard with the eyes wide open in great surprise or shock, esp because of some news or at the sight of something <goggle, make glassy eyes, make bug eyes, drop dead, knock dead, drop down dead, be killed stone-dead> eg *Jak zobaczył tę zajebistą laskę na ulicy, to postawił oczy w słup (When he saw that gorgeous-looking chick walking down the street, he made bug eyes)*

postawić Perf stawiać

postawić się Perf stawiać się

postkomuna* [pohst-koh-MOO-nah] *nf* Postcommunists or postcommunist rule <ex-commies, ex-comrades, ex-reds, pinks> eg *Postkomuna jest odpowiedzialna za wszystko (The ex-reds are responsible for everything)*

postrzeleniec See pomyleniec

postrzelony See pomylony

posuwać się [poh-SOO-vahch shyeh] (perf **posunąć się** [poh-SOO-nohnch shyeh]) *v* To get old; to age <put mileage on, push, get along, pull pages off the calendar, get long in the tooth> eg *O rety! Ale ona się posunęła! (My! Did she put mileage on!)*

posuwać* [poh-SOO-vahch] (perf **posunąć*** [poh-SOO-nohnch]) *v* To copulate with someone <fuck, screw, lay, ball, bang, boink, boff, boogie, bop, frig, hump, poke, shag> eg *Posuwał ją przez jakąś godzinę (He humped her for an hour or so)*

poszaleć Perf szaleć

poszczać się Perf szczać

poszumieć [poh-SHOO-myehch] (perf **wyszumieć się** [vi-SHOO-myehch shyeh]) *v* To carouse or celebrate <party, ball, have a ball, jam, paint the town red, raise hell, bar-hop, bar-crawl, go on a bender> eg *Poszła tam po to, żeby się wyszumieć (She went there to have a ball)*

potłuc See móc sobie w dupę wsadzić

potłuczony See gadać od rzeczy

potańcówka [poh-tañ-TSOOF-kah] (or **potańcówa** [poh-tañ-TSOO-vah]) *nf* A dance party, esp in one's school <prom, hop, sock hop, jump, mingle, shindig, belly rub> eg *Poznaliśmy się na szkolnej potańcówce (We met at a prom)*

potęga See na maks

potwornie See paskudnie

potworny See pierdolony

powałkonić się Perf wałkonić się

powietrze See łyknąć świerzego powietrza

pozer [POH-zehr] *nm* An affected man who often fawns on women or grandstands <dandy, fancypants, poser, showboat> eg *Co to za pozer? (Who is that poser?)*

pozjadać wszystkie rozumy [pohz-YAH-dahch FSHIST-kyeh roh-ZOO-mi] *v phr* To become insanely conceited or self-impressed, esp because one has made a success <think one's shit doesn't stink, be too big for someone's shoes, ego-trip, get stuck-up, get puffed-up, get high-hat, get swelled-up, get swell-headed, get big-headed, get high-nosed, get blown-up, get stuck on oneself, get chesty, get stuffy, get gassy, get windy, get hatty, get hinkty, get uppity, get biggety, dog it, put on the dog, give oneself airs, put on airs, put on, put on the ritz> eg *Pozjadał wszystkie rozumy, gdy został dyrektorem (He got swell-headed after he became the director)*

pracoholik [prah-tsoh-KHOH-leek] (or **pracuś** [PRAH-tsoosh]) *nm* A person whose primary and obsessive interest is work; a compulsive worker <workaholic, eager-beaver, slave to the grind> eg *Napisałem ten słownik, więc jestem chyba pracoholikiem (I wrote this dictionary, so I guess I'm a workaholic)*

pracować na czarno [prah-TSOH-vahch nah CHAHR-noh] (or **robić na czarno** [ROH-beech nah CHAHR-noh]) *v phr* To work illegally <work under the table> eg *Przez ostatni miesiąć ci imigranci pracowali na czarno (For the past month the immigrants have been working under the table)*

pracuś See pracoholik

pragnąć See co dusza pragnie

prasówka [prah-SOOF-kah] *nf* An act of reading newspapers or magazines <paper-reading session> eg *Codziennie robi sobie prasówkę (Everyday he engages himself in a paper-reading session)*

prawa ręka [PRAH-vah REHN-kah] *nf phr* One's most useful and valuable helper or advisor <right hand> eg *Dzięki jej umiejętnościom została prawą rekę szefa (Thanks to her skills she became the boss's right hand)*

prawda See gówno

prawiczek* [prah-VEE-chehk] *nm* **1** A male virgin <cherry, canned goods> eg *Myślę, że on wciąż jest prawiczkiem (I think he's still a cherry)* **2** A prim and ostentatiously virtuous man; a prude <tight-ass, goody-goody, goody two-shoes, bluenose> eg *Nie bądź taka cnotka. Daj sobie na luz! (Don't be such a tight-ass. Loosen up!)*

prawiczka* [prah-VEECH-kah] *nf* **1** A female virgin <cherry, canned goods> eg *Myślę, że on wciąż jest prawiczkiem (I think he's still a cherry)* **2** A prim and ostentatiously virtuous woman; a prude <tight-ass, goody-goody, goody two-shoes, old maid, bluenose> eg *Nic z tego nie wyjdzie. To przecież prawiczka (It won't work. After all she's such a goody-goody)*

prawko [PRAHF-koh] *nf* A driver's license <license, ID, papers> eg *Mogę zobaczyć pana prawko? (May I see your license?)*

prawo See dać w prawo

prędzej komuś kaktus wyrośnie [PREHN-dzeh-ee KOH-moosh KAHK-toos vi-ROHSH-nyeh] (or **prędzej komuś kaktus na ręce wyrośnie** [PREHN-dzeh-ee KOH-moosh KAHK-toos nah REHN-tseh vi-ROHSH-nyeh]) *phr* A phrase of disbelief or refusal telling that one will not be cheated or taken advantage of <out of the question, no way, no way Jose, no dice, not on your life, nothing doing, no can do, you gotta be kidding, will eat one's hat, in a pig's eye, in a pig's ass, in a pig's ear, like hell, like fun, like shit, my ass, someone will be damned if, someone will be fucked if, says you> eg *Kaktus mi wyrośnie, jeśli pociąg przyjedzie na czas (If the train arrives on time I'll eat my hat)*

prochy [PROH-khi] *npl* Powdered drugs that are insufflated, usually cocaine or heroin <shit, stuff, nose, nose candy, snow, dusty, sugar, junk, dope> eg *Ma trochę prochów na sprzedaż (She has some nose candy for sale)*
See na prochach

prosiak [PROH-shyahk] *nm* A pig <porker, porky, cob roller, slob> eg *Kupiliśmy prosiaka (We bought a porky)*

prosto z mostu [PROHS-toh z MOHS-too] *adv phr* Sincerely; frankly; directly; holding nothing back <straight from the shoulder, from the shoulder, straight out> eg *Ona zawsze mówi prosto z mostu. Nigdy nie trzeba zgadywać, co na prawdę ma na myśli (She always speaks straight from the shoulder. You never have to guess what she really means)*

prosty jak drut [PROHS-ti yahk DROOT] *adj phr* Very simple or easy; uncomplicated <duck-soup, easy as can be, easy as hell, cherry pie, easy as pie, easy as falling off a log, snappy, cinchy, dirt-simple, simple as ABC, clear sailing, like falling off a log, like a turkey shoot, like riding a bicycle> eg *To ćwiczenie jest proste jak drut (This exercise is easy as pie)*

proszek See w proszku

prowadzić kogoś za rączkę [proh-VAH-jeech KOH-gohsh zah ROHNCH-keh] *v phr* To treat someone or steer someone's behavior with excessive care; to pamper <lead someone by the hand, treat with kid gloves, handle with kid gloves, treat someone as an apple of someone's eye, give someone the red carpet treatment, pet> eg *Nie mam zamiaru prowadzić Cię za rączkę (I'm not about to lead you by the hand)*

pryk See pierdoła

prymityw* [pri-MEE-tif] *nm* An uncultured, uncivilized person <cornball, ignoramus, clodhopper> eg *Za kogo mnie bierzesz, za jakiegoś prymitywa? (Who are you taking me for? A cornball?)*

pryszcz [prishch] *nm* Anything easy or trivial; a trifle; a bagatelle <piece of cake, cake, cakewalk, cherry pie, duck soup, kid stuff, picnic, pushover, snap, tea party, walkaway, walkover, breeze, stroll, cinch, pipe, big deal, no big deal, no biggie,

Mickey Mouse, small potatoes, small beer, fly speck, plain sailing> eg *Zabicie dwóch facetów to dla niego to pryszcz (Killing two guys is kid stuff for him)*

pryszcz na dupie See wrzód na dupie

pryszczaty* [prish-CHAH-ti] *adj* (Of a face) Pimply <crater-faced, pizza-faced> eg *Denerwuje mnie ten pryszczaty idiota (That pizza-faced idiot makes me sick)*

pryszczuch* [PRISH-chookh] *nm* Someone with a face covered with pimples <crater-face, pizza-face, pizza-puss, herpie> eg *Czego chciał ten pryszczuch? (What did that pizza-face want?)*

prywaciarz [pri-VAH-chahsh] *nm* A businessman who himeself owns and runs a company (rather than works for someone else's company); a small businessman <big-time operator, BTO, operator, player, wheeler-dealer, tradester, cockroach, small potatoes, small-timer> eg *Jej ojciec był znanym prywaciarzem (He father was a well-known wheeler-dealer)*

prywatka [pri-VAHT-kah] *nf* A private party or other celebration <ball, bash, blast, blowout, brawl, fest, rally, shindig> eg *Poznał ją na jakiejś prywatce (He met her at some blowout)*

prywatka-kopulatka* [pri-VAHT-kah koh-poo-LAHT-kah] *nf phr* A party which features mutual touching, caressing, or copulating; an orgy <circle jerk, circus love, group grope, grope-in, gang bang> eg *Zorganizujmy prywatkę-kopulatkę! (Let's organize a grope-in!)*

prząść See cienko śpiewać

przełamywać lody [psheh-wah-MI-vahch LOH-di] *v phr* To initiate social interchanges and conversation; to get something started <break the ice> eg *Byłem zdenerwowany, ale ona przełamała lody proponując drinka (I was nervous but she broke the ice by offering me a drink)*

przeżarcie [psheh-ZHAHR-cheh] *nn* An act of overeating <stuffing oneself, pigging out, scarfing out, porking out> eg *Przeżarcie nie wyszło mu na dobre. Rzygał przez cały dzień (Scarfing out didn't do him good. He was puking all day)*

przeżreć się [PSHEH-zhrehch shyeh] *v* To overeat and, esp, to feel sick <stuff oneself, pig out, scarf out, pork out> eg *Przeżarł się ciastem i musiał rzygać (He stuffed himself with the cake and had to puke)*

przebimbać Perf bimbać

przebitka [psheh-BEET-kah] *nf* A net profit (on sold merchandise or currency exchange) <net, payoff, velvet, gravy> eg *Jest z tego duża przebitka? (Is there a huge velvet out of this?)*

przechodzić komuś koło nosa See przelecieć komuś koło nosa

przechodzona* [psheh-khoh-DZOH-nah] *adj* (Of a woman) With lost virginity or sexually experienced <has been, has been around, has been around the block, has been through the mill> eg *Ona wie wiele o tych rzeczach, jest przechodzona (She knows a lot about these things, she's been around)*

przeciągać się See ciągnąć się

przeciągać strunę See przeginać

przeciek [PSHEH-chyehk] *nm* An instance of giving information to the press or other recipient secretly <leak> eg *Musiał być jakiś przeciek (There must have been some leak)*

przeciekać [psheh-CHYEH-kahch] *v* (Of information) To be given to the press or other recipient secretly <leak, fink, finger, snitch, squeal, beef, blab, blow, blow

the whistle, canary, chirp, dime, drop a dime, go stool, nark, put the finger on, rat, rat on, sell out, sing, sing out, stool, weasel> eg *Ten super tajny raport przeciekł do prasy (The top secret report was leaked to the press)*

przeciętniak [psheh-CHEHNT-nyak] (or **przeciętny zjadacz chleba** [psheh-CHYEHNT-ni ZYAH-dahch KHLEH-bah] or **przeciętny Kowalski** [psheh-CHYEHNT-ni koh-WAHL-skee]) *nm* A very average and unremarkable man<man on the street, John Doe, John Q Citizen, John Q Public, Joe Schmo, Joe Six-Pack, ordinary Joe, square John, one of the boys, every Tom Dick and Harry, ham-and-egger> eg *To typowy przeciętniak. Chciałby tylko obejrzeć jaki dobry mecz w telewizji (He's a typical Joe Six-Pack. All he wants is to watch some good game on TV); To jest dokładnie to, czego chce przeciętny Kowalski (This is just what John Doe wants)*

przedpotopowy [psheht-poh-toh-POH-vi] *adj* Old-fashioned or antiquated, esp preposterous <out, out of it, not with it, tired, passe, moth-eaten, square, corny, bent, hairy, moldy, horse-and-buggy, jurassic, dino, fossil, fuddy-duddy, jurassic> eg *Skądżeś wiął ten przedpotopowy fotel? (Where did you ge that corny armchair?)*

przedryndać Perf dryndać

przedstawienie [psheht-stah-VYEH-nyeh] *nn* A complaining and objectionable behavior; fret <fuss, stink, scene, ceremony, beef, bleed, hassle, kvetch, bitch, beef, gripe, piss, bellyache, grouse, growl, squawk> eg *Przestań robić przedstawienie i zostaw mnie w spokoju (Stop making a fuss and leave me alone)*

przegięcie [psheh-GYEHN-chyeh] *nn* A blatant exaggeration <one step too far, push, stretch, hype, ham, too-too> eg *Nie znoszę przegięć (I hate hyping things)*
See bez przegięcia

przeginać [psheh-GEE-nahch] (perf **przegiąć** [PSHEH-gyohnch]; or **przeginać pałę** [psheh-GEE-nahch PAH-weh]; or **przeciągać strunę** [psheh-CHYOH-gahch STROO-neh]) *v phr* To exaggerate <go too far, go one step too far, push, stretch, hype, ham> eg *Nie przeginaj (Don't push it)*

przegląd tygodnia [PSHEH-glohnt ti-GOHD-nyah] *nm phr* A meal composed of odds and ends, or of whatever turns up <pot luck, mystery meat, leftovers> eg *Znów zaserwowała nam przegląd tygodnia (She served us pot luck again)*

przegryźć [PSHEH-grizhch] (or **przekąsić** [psheh-KOHN-sheech] or **przetrącić** [psheh-TROHN-cheech]) *v* To eat, esp to have a light meal <have a bite, have a snack, nosh, put on the feedbag> eg *Wyskoczyli coś przegryźć (They dropped in to put something on the feedbag); Czas coś przekąsić (It's time to put something on the feedbag)*

przeholować [psheh-khoh-LOH-vahch] *v* To exaggerate <go too far, go one step too far, push, stretch, hype, ham> eg *Myślę, że przecholował (I think he went too far)*

przehulać Perf hulać

przejadać [psheh-YAH-dahch] (perf **przejeść** [PSHEH-yehshch]) *v* To spend money (saved or earned) on living or pleasure, esp on food <blow, splash, drop, shoot, throw away, piddle away, piss away> eg *Przejadł wszystkie pieniądze (He blew all his money)*

przejebać See przepierdalać

przejechać się [psheh-YEH-khahch shyeh] (or **przewieźć się** [PSHEH-vyehshch shyeh]) **1** (or **przekręcić się** [psheh-KRHN-cheech shyeh] or **przenieść się na tamten świat** [PSHEH-nyehshch shyeh nah TAHM-tehn SHFYAHT] or **przenieść się łono Abrahama** [PSHEH-nyehshch shyeh nah WOH-noh ah-brah-KHAH-mah]) *v* To die <bite the dust, kiss the dust, croak, belly up, buy the

farm, buy the ranch, cash in one's chips, check out, bump off, conk off, conk out, farm, give up the ghost, go home feet first, go home in a box, go west, kick in, kick off, kick the bucket, pass out, peg out, shove off, drop off, step off, pop off, push up daisies, meet one's maker, turn up one's toes, go down the tube, join the great majority, join the majority> eg *To niebezpieczne. Można się przewieźć (It's dangerous. You may keick the bucket); Jeśli nie przestaniesz palić, to wkrótce przeniesiesz się na tamten świat (If you don't stop smoking, you'll join the great majority before long* **2** To become cheated; to become deceived <get conned, get ripped off, get shafted, get rolled, get chiseled, get gypped, get scammed, get screwed, get stiffed, get fleeced, get dicked, get taken in, get flim-flammed, get bamboozled, be taken for a ride, be taken to the cleaners, get fucked over, get screwed over, get angled> eg *Przejechałem się z tym aparatem. Kupiłem go za więcej niż normalną cenę (I got screwed on that camera. It cost me more than its real price)*

przejeść Perf przejadać

przejeść się [PSHEH-yehshch shyeh] (or **dojeść** [DOH-yehshch] or **nadojeść** [nah-DOH-yehshch]) *v* To be bored with something, esp because of its ordinariness; to no longer feel like doing something <be fed up with, be up to here with, have it up to here with, be sick and tired of, have no pizzazz for, have no pep for> eg *Przejadły mu się te płyty (He's sick and tired of these LPs)*

przejrzeć na oczy [psheh-ee-ZHEHCH nah OH-chi] *v phr* To realize or become aware of something <figure out, work out, tune in, plug in, tote up, wise up, get through one's head, get through someone's thick head, get into someone's thick head, see daylight, flash, dig, dawn on, have a brainwave> eg *Na początku nie wiedział, że żona go zdradza. Przejrzał na oczy się dopiero po roku (At the beginning he didn't know that his wife had been cheating on him. He figured that out only a year later)*

przekąsić See przegryźć

przekimać Perf kimać

przekręcić Perf kręcić

przekręcić się See przejechać się

przekręt [PSHEH-krehnt] *nm* A swindle; a fraud; a scheme <scam, rip-off, con game, double cross, double shuffle, fast one, grift, gyp, flim-flam, hustle, number, racket, run-around, skin game, sucker game, suck-in, ride, fucking over, screwing over, hanky-panky, monkey business, song and dance, game, little game, angle> eg *Urząd podatkowy nie znalazł żadnych śladów przekrętów (The IRS found no traces of con games)*

przelecieć [psheh-LEH-chyehch] *v* To copulate with someone, esp quickly or one only time; to achieve sexual intercourse <score, fuck, screw, lay, ball, bang, boink, boff, boogie, bop, frig, hump, poke, shag> eg *W końcu ją przeleciał. Przynajmniej tak mówi (He finally scored her. At least he said that he did)*

przelecieć komuś koło nosa [psheh-LEH-chyehch KOH-moosh KOH-woh NOH-sah] (or **przechodzić komuś koło nosa** [psheh-KHOH-jeech KOH-moosh KOH-woh NOH-sah]) *v phr* To miss an opportunity <get snatched from under someone's nose, not to jump at> eg *Dyrektor Instytutu zablokował mi awans i stypendium Fulbrighta przeleciało mi koło nosa (The director of the Institute blocked my advance and the Fulbright scholarship got snatched from inder my nose)*

przelecieć Perf lecieć

przelewać się See nie przelewać się

przelotnie See w przelocie

przelotówka [psheh-loh-TOOF-kah] *nf* An arterial highway; a thru-way <rip strip, dragway, pike, bowling alley, main drag, main line> eg *Myślę, że są już teraz na przelotówce (I think they may be on the pike now)*

przemarznąć na kość [psheh-MAHRZ-nohnch nah KOHSHCH] (or **przemarznąć do szpiku kości** [psheh-MAHRZ-nohnch doh SHPEE-koo KOHSH-chee]) *v phr* To freeze <get chilled to the bone, freeze to the bone, freeze one's ass off, freeze one's balls off> eg *Czekałem na nią dwie godziny i przemarzłem na kość (I had been waiting for her for two hours and got chilled to the bone)*

przemawiać do ręki [psheh-MAH-vyahch doh REHN-kee] *v phr* To bribe someone <grease someone's palm, cross someone's palm, oil someone's palm, smear, shmear, pay off> eg *Byli skłonni przemówić mu do ręki (They were willing to grease his palm)*

przepłukać gardło [psheh-PWOO-kahch GAHRD-woh] *v phr* To have a quick drink of liquor <knock back, down, slug down, swig, tank, tank up> eg *Gdzie mógłbym przepłukać gardło? (Where could I tank something up?)*

przepadać za czymś/kimś [psheh-PAH-dahch zah chimsh/keemsh] *v phr* To like something or someone very much; to admire enormously <be crazy for, be ape for, be apeshit for, be bananas for, be bonkers for, be ga-ga for, be loony for, be mental for, be nuts for, be nutty for, be wild for, take a shine to, have a thing about, take to> eg *Ludzie za nią przepadają (People are ape for her)*

przepierdalać** [psheh-pyehr-DAH-lahch] (perf **przepierdolić**** [psheh-pyehr-DOH-leech]; or **przepieprzać*** [psheh-PYEHP-shahch] perf **przepieprzyć*** [psheh-PYEHP-shich]; or **przepierniczać*** [psheh-pyehr-NEE-chahch] perf **przepierniczyć*** [psheh-pyehr-NEE-chich]; or **przepierdzielać** [psheh-pyehr-JEH-lahch] perf **przepierdzielić*** [psheh-pyehr-JEH-leech]; or **przepuszczać** [psheh-POOSH-chahch] perf **przepuścić** [psheh-POOSH-cheech]; or **puszczać** [POOSH-chahch] perf **puścić** [POOSH-cheech]; or **przeputać** [psheh-POO-tahch]; or **przesrać*** [PSHEH-srahch]; **przejebać**** [psheh-YEH-bahch]) *v* **1** To spend money foolishly or extravagantly; to use up wastefully; to squander <blow, splash, drop, shoot, throw away, piddle away, piss away, diddle away, shell out, dish out, fork out, spend like water, pour down the drain, throw down the drain> eg *Miał fortunę, ale przejebał wszystko na torze wyścigowym (He had a fortune but he pissed it away gambling at the track); Przepierdolił całą wypłatę w dziesięć minut (He pissed away his entire wages in ten minutes); Miała fortunę, ale przepuściła wszystko w karty (She had a fortune but she blew it playing cards)* **2** To waste time doing nothing <fuck around, bum around, hang around, hang out, goof around, screw around, fiddle around, fiddle fart around, fart around, jack around, mess around, hack around, monkey around, knock around, kick around, fool around, horse around, piddle around, play around, rat around, schloomp around, ass around, beat around, dick around, fuck around, fuck off, screw off, goof off, jerk off, fuck the dog, rat fuck, flub the dub, sit on one's ass, sit on one's butt, lollygag, veg out> eg *Przepierdolił całe ferie zimowe, zamiast się przygotowaćdo testu (He fucked around during the winter break instead of preparing for the test)*

przepuszczać komuś See nie przepuszczać komuś

przerżnąć Perf rżnąć

przerabiać [psheh-RAH-byahch] (perf **przerobić** [psheh-ROH-beech]) *v* To discuss a given material in class <do, go over> eg *Czy przerabialiście tęksi/ążkę w ogólniaku (Did you do that book in your high); Na ostatnich zajęciach z literatury angielskiej przerabialiśmy sonety Szekspira (Last English class we were going over Shakespearian sonnets)*

przerwa See mieć przerwę w życiorysie

przesadyzm See bez przegięcia

przeskoczyć siebie [psheh-SKOH-chich SHYEH-byeh] *v phr* To make more than one can; to strenously attempt to get or do something; to strive <bust one's ass, bust a gut, bust one's balls, break one's ass, break one's neck, work one's ass off, do one's damnednest, give it one's all, give it one's best, go all out, go for broke, go all the way, go for it, go the extra mile, go the full yard, go the limit, go the whole nine yards, go to the wall, make a full-court press, put one's back into, hassle, sweat, dig, plug, break one's ass, bend over backward, pour it on, knock oneself out, bear down, scramble for, go after, push for, shoot for, shoot the works, spread oneself, pull oneself together, push hard> eg *On jest jednym z tych facetów, którzy przeskoczą siebie, żeby pomóc przyjacielowi (He's one of those guys who will bust their asses to help a friend)*

przespać się z kimś Perf spać z kimś

przesrać See przepierdalać

przeszastać Perf szastać

przetrącić See przegryźć

przetrzepać komuś skórę [psheh-TSHEH-pahch KOH-moosh SKOO-reh] (or **wygarbować komuś skórę** [vi-gahr-BOH-vahch KOH-moosh SKOO-reh] or **wyłoić komuś skórę** [vi-WOH-eech KOH-moosh SKOO-reh]) *v phr* To beat someone up, esp as a punishment; (figuratively) to punish someone <kick someone's ass, sock, bash, trash, clobber, bang, belt, clock, duke, dust, hammer, land one, lay one on, spank, wham, whack, bam, whip, bust, smack, poke, blast, beat the shit out of, beat the living shit out of, beat the bejejus out of, beat the daylights out of, beat someone into the middle of next week, knock the bejejus out of, knock the daylights out of, knock someone into the middle of next week, hit someone where he lives, work over> eg *Jak zaraz nieprzestaniesz, to dam ci w skórę (If you don't stop right now, I'll beat the shit out of you)*

przewieźć się See przejechać się

przewracać komuś w głowie [psheh-VRAH-tsahch KOH-moosh v GWOH-vyeh] (or **zawracać komuś w głowie** [zah-VRAH-tsahch KOH-moosh v GWOH-vyeh]; **we łbie** [veh WBYEH] may replace **w głowie**) *v phr* (For flattery or success) To distract someone; to cause someone not to be sensible <turn someone's head, fuck someone up, screw someone up, mess someone up, fuck someone's head up, screw someone's head up, mess someone's head up, head-fuck, mind-fuck> eg *Jej sukcesy przewróciły jej w głowie. Jest bardzo arogancka (Her successes fucked her head up. She's very arrogant)*

przewracać się See flaki się komuś przewracają

przewracać się komuś w głowie [psheh-VRAH-tsahch shyeh KOH-moosh v GWOH-vyeh] (or **przewracać się komuś we łbie** [psheh-VRAH-tsahch shyeh KOH-moosh veh WBYEH]) *v phr* To become insanely conceited or self-impressed, esp because one has made a success <think one's shit doesn't stink, be

too big for someone's shoes, ego-trip, get stuck-up, get puffed-up, get high-hat, get swelled-up, get swell-headed, get big-headed, get high-nosed, get blown-up, get stuck on oneself, get chesty, get stuffy, get gassy, get windy, get hatty, get hinkty, get uppity, get biggety, dog it, put on the dog, give oneself airs, put on airs, put on, put on the ritz> eg *Zawsze był szpanerem, ale gdzy w 1996 został dyrektorem Instytutu, to zupełnie przewróciło mu się w głowie (He had always been a blowhard, but when he became a director of the Institute in 1996, he really got big-headed)*

przewracać się w grobie [psheh-VRAH-tsahch shyeh v GROH-byeh] *v phr* (For a dead person) To be shocked or horrified <turn over in one's grave> eg *Gdyby Beethoven słyszał, jak ona gra jego sonaty, to przewracałby się w grobie (If Beethoven heard her play one of his sonatas, he'd turn over in his grave*

przez miedzę [pshehs MYEH-dzeh] (or **za miedzą** [zah MYEH-dzoh]) *adv phr* In the vicinity; very close; nearby <around, pretty near, screwdriver turn away, frog's leap away, whoop, within a hoop and a holler, within a stone's throw, in spitting distance, around the corner, right next door> eg *Czemuś jej nie odwiedził? Ona mieszka przecież tuż za miedzą? (Why didn't you visit her? After all she lives in spitting distance)*

przez palce See patrzeć przez palce

przezimować Perf zimować

przód See być do przodu

przy forsie [pshi FOHR-shyeh] *adj phr* Very rich; affluent <loaded, flush, filthy rich, stinking rich, dirt richy, lousy rich, in the bucks, in the dough, in the money, rolling in it, made of money> eg *Chciałbym być przy forsie do końca swego życia (I'd like to be stinking rich for the rest of my life)*

przy kości [pshi KOHSH-chee] (or **przy sobie** [pshi SOH-byeh]) *adj phr* (Of a woman) Having a well developed figure, esp sexually attractive <built, stacked, constructed, curvy, curvaceous, zaftig, big boned> eg *Ona również była przy kości (She was zaftig, too)*

przy sobie See przy kości

przyłatał See ni pies ni wydra

przybić piątkę [PSHI-beech PYOHNT-keh] *v phr* To shake hands, as a sign of agreement <slip someone five, give someone five, give someone some skin> eg *No to jak? Przybijemy piątkę? (So what do you say? Shall we slip five?)*

przydupas* [pshi-DOO-pahs] *nm* A male lover, esp one whom one pays <fuck-friend, lover-boy, boy-toy> eg *Ile zapłaciła śtwojemu przydupasowi? (How much did you pay to your lover-boy?)*

przyfarcić Perf farcić

przygazować See gazować

przygruchać [pshi-GROO-khahch] *v* To succeed in becoming acquainted with someone for romantic or sexual purposes <pick up, get some action, get some ass, score> eg *Przygruchał sobie jakąś nową panienkę, nie wiedziałeś? (He picked up a new chick, don't you know?)*

przyjemniaczek [pshi-yeh-MNYAH-chehk] *nm* An overly or superficially nice man; a sycophant <brown-noser, ass-kisser, ass-licker, ass-sucker, ass-wiper, back-scratcher, apple-polisher, tokus-licker, kiss-ass, yes-man> eg *Ten przyjemniaczek dał szefowi butelkę szampana na urodziny (That brown-noser actually gave the boss a bottle of champaigne for his birthday)*

przyjemność See średnia przyjemność

przykleić się Perf kleić się

przyklepnąć [pshi-KLEHP-nohnch] *v* To shake hands, as a sign of agreement <slip five, slap five, give someone five, give someone high-five, give someone some skin> eg *No to jak? Przyklepniesz? (So what do you say? Will you give me five?)*

przymiarka [pshi-MYAHR-kah] *nf* An attempt, esp to start an action or endeavor; an approach <try, go, crack, fling, run, shot, stab, whack, lick, header, dry run, try-on, try-out, shake-down, work-out, tackle, tumble, one's damnednest> eg *To była tylko pojedyncza przymiarka (It was only a single shot)*

przymknąć oczy [PSHIM-knohnch OH-chi] *v phr* To pretend not to see or notice something, esp illegal <turn a blind eye to, let someone get away with, let it go, let it slide, let someone off, go easy on, blink at, wink at> eg *The usher turned a blind eye to the little boy who sneaked into the theater (Bileter przymknął oczy na chłopca, który wślizgnął się do kina)*

przynętę See łyknąć

przypiął See ni pies ni wydra

przypierdalać** [pshi-pyehr-DAH-lahch] (perf **przypierdolić**** [pshi-pyehr-DOH-leech]; or **przypieprzać*** [pshi-PYEHP-shahch] perf **przypieprzyć*** [pshi-PYEHP-shich]; or **przypierniczać** [pshi-pyehr-NEE-chahch] perf **przypierniczyć*** [pshi-pyehr-NEE-chich]; or **przypierdzielać*** [pshi-pyehr-JEH-lahch] perf **przypierdzielić*** [pshi-pyehr-JEH-leech]; or **przywalać** [pshi-VAH-lahch] perf **przywalić** [pshi-VAH-leech]) *v* To beat someone up <kick someone's ass, sock, bash, trash, clobber, bang, belt, clock, duke, dust, hammer, land one, lay one on, spank, wham, whack, bam, whip, bust, smack, poke, blast, beat the shit out of, beat the living shit out of, beat the bejejus out of, beat the daylights out of, beat someone into the middle of next week, knock the bejejus out of, knock the daylights out of, knock someone into the middle of next week, hit someone where he lives, work over> eg *Zaraz mu przypierdolę! (I'm going to beat the shit out of him!)*

przypierdalać się** [pshi-pyehr-DAH-lahch shyeh] (perf **przypierdolić się**** [pshi-pyehr-DOH-leech shyeh]; or **przypieprzać się*** [pshi-PYEHP-shahch shyeh] perf **przypieprzyć się*** [pshi-PYEHP-shich shyeh]; or **przypierniczać się*** [pshi-pyehr-NEE-chahch shyeh] perf **przypierniczyć się*** [pshi-pyehr-NEE-chich shyeh]; or **przypierdzielać się*** [pshi-pyehr-JEH-lahch shyeh] perf **przypierdzielić się*** [pshi-pyehr-JEH-leech shyeh]; or **przywalać się** [pshi-VAH-lahch shyeh] perf **przywalić się** [pshi-VAH-leech shyeh]) *v* **1** To criticize someone or something, esp if not deserved; to have ungrounded complaints or remarks <pick on, trip on, nitpick, trash, bash, knock, slam, hit, clobber, blast, rake, needle, bitch, go after, stick to someone, give someone the needle, give someone the heat, give someone a hard time, give someone a bad time, give someone hell, kick someone's ass, cut in half, cut to bits, jump all over, jump on, lean on, land on, come down hard on, put down, run down, take down, throw the book at, put the heat on, put the squeeze on, put someone through the wringer, break someone's balls, bust someone's ass, twist someone's arm, hassle> eg *Czemu on się zawsze do mnie przypierdala? (Why is he always tripping on me?)* **2** To force oneself upon someone; to obtrude or intrude <push, be pushy, get on someone's back, barge in, butt in, bust in, charge in, check in, elbow in, horn in, muscle in,

crowd someone's act, get into the act, poke one's face in, poke one's nose in, stick one's face in, stick one's nose in> eg *Zrobię, co chcesz, tylko przestań się przypieprzać (I'll do what you want, just stop pushing)*

przyprawiać komuś rogi [pshi-PRAH-vyahch KOH-moosh ROH-gee] *v phr* (Esp about women) To be sexually unfaithful, esp to commit adultery <cheat, two-time, chippy, get a little on the side, backdoor, have an extracurricular activity, play hanky-panky, step out on, play around, play the field, put the horns on> eg *Żona tego polityka przyprawiałą mu rogi (The politician's wife has been involved in some backdoor activity)*

przyschnąć [PSHI-skhnohnch] *v* (Esp a scandal) To become gradually less strong until it ceases <die down, settlwe down> eg *Cała sprawa wkrótce przyschła (The whole affair soon died down)*

przystawiać się [pshi-STAH-vyahch shyeh] *v* To invite or request sexual favors <make a pass, put a move on, make a play for> eg *Pedał zaczął się do mnie przystawiać, więc szybko wyszedłem z baru (The faggot started to make a pass at me, so I quickly left the bar)*

przystojniak [pshi-STOH-ee-nyahk] (or **przystojniaczek** [pshis-toh-ee-NYAH-chehk] or **ciężki przystojniak** [CHEHNSH-kee pshi-STOH-ee-nyahk]) *nm* An attractive man <hunk, stud, stud-muffin, beefcake, he-man, macho, muscleman, v-man, ten, dreamboat> eg *Chodzi z prawdziwym przystojniakiem (She's been going out with a real beefcake)*

przyszywany [pshi-shi-VAH-ni] *adj* Someone who is not a member of a family, but is called a cousin; a very distant relative <no slang equivalent> eg *Zaprosił w gościnę przyszywanego kuzyna (He invited a distant relative to come and visit)*

przytachać się Perf tachać się

przytarabanić się Perf tarabanić się

przytargać się Perf targać się

przytaskać się Perf taskać się

przytaszczyć się Perf taszczyć się

przytekścić Perf tekścić

przytelepać się Perf telepać się

przywalać See przypierdalać

przywalać się See przypierdalać się

przyzwoitka [pshi-zvoh-EET-kah] *nf* An ostentatiously virtuous or pious woman; a prude <tight-ass, goody, goody-goody, goody two-shoes, old maid, bluenose, knee bender, Jesus freak> eg *Nie bądź taka przyzwoitka. Daj sobie na luz! (Don't be such a tight-ass. Loosen up!)*

psia krew [pshyah KREHF] (**mać** [mahch] or **jucha** [YOO-khah] or **kość** [kohshch] may replace **krew**) *excl* An exclamation of anger, irritation, disappointment, shock <shit, fuck, hell, heck, damn, damn it, goddamn it, gosh, golly, gee, jeez, holy fuck, holy cow, holy moly, holy hell, holy mackarel, holy shit, jumping Jesus, fucking shit, fucking hell> eg *Psia krew! Przegraliśmy ten mecz! Do jasnej cholery! (Holy shit! We lost that game!)*

psiak [pshayhk] *nm* A dog, esp a mongrel <doggie, mutt, pooch, pup, Fido, Pluto, Goofy, Heinz, flea bag, tail wagger, bone eater, pot hound> eg *Ile chcesz za tego psiaka? (How much do you want for this pooch?)*

psiapsiółka [pshyah-PSHYOOW-kah] *nf* A woman's female friend <gal, amiga, sister, pal, sidekick, bosom buddy> eg *Przyszły tylko dwie kumpele (Only two gals came)*

psie pieniądze [pshyeh pyeh-NYOHN-dzeh] (**małe** [MAH-weh] or **marne** [MAHR-neh] or **liche** [LEE-kheh] may replace **psie**) *npl phr* A small amount of money <peanuts, chicken feed, nickels and dimes, pennies, small change> eg *Płacili mu psie pieniądze (They paid him chicken feed)*

psikus [PSHEE-koos] *nm* A joke or prank, esp intended to fool someone <put-on, leg-pull, rib, gag, caper, spoof, hot one> eg *Kto jest odpowiedzialny za te psikusy? (Who is responsible for these put-ons?)*

pstro See mieć pstro w głowie

psu na budę [psoo nah BOO-deh] *adj phr* Bad, poor, worthless, or of inferior quality <lousy, awful, bush-league, cheap, crappy, shitty, cruddy, crummy, doggy, low-rent, low-ride, no-good, raggedy-ass, schlocky, stinking, tacky, trashy, two-bit, dime-a-dozen, fair to middling, garden variety, of a sort, of sorts, piddling, pissy-ass, piss-poor, run-of-the-mill, small-time> eg *Psu na budę ten magnetowid, który kupiłeś. Toż to lipa (The VCR that you bought is real shitty. It's a lemon)*

psuj [PSOO-ee] *nm* Someone prone to damaging everything, esp mechanical devices; a clumsy, unhandy person <butterfinges, clunker, duffer, flubdub, foozler, goof-up, fuck-up, klutz, lummox, schlep, schloomp> eg *Nie pozwolę, żeby ten psuj prowadził mój samochód (I won't let that butterfingers drive my car)*

psychiczny See pomylony

psychol See pomyleniec

ptak See pindol, po ptakach

ptasi móżdżek [PTAH-shee MOOZH-jehk] (or **kurzy móżdżek** [KOO-zhi MOOZH-jehk]) *nm phr* **1** A stupid, foolish, or ineffectual person; an idiot <shit for brains, airbrain, airhead, birdbrain, blockhead, squarehead, bonehead, bubblebrain, bubblehead, buckethead, cluckhead, cementhead, clunkhead, deadhead, dumbbell, dumbcluck, dumbhead, dumbass, dumbbrain, fatbrain, fathead, flubdub, knukclebrain, knucklehead, lamebrain, lardhead, lunkhead, meathead, musclehead, noodlehead, numbskull, pointhead, scatterbrain, jerk, jerk-off, klutz, chump, creep, nerd, dork, dweeb, gweeb, geek, jackass, lummox, twerp, nerd, bozo, clod, cluck, clunk, dimwit, dingbat, dipstick, dodo, dopey, dufus, goofus, lump, lunk, nitwit, schnook, schlep, schlemiel, schmendrick, schmo, schmuck, simp, stupe> eg *Ten twój chłopak to ptasi móżdżek (That boyfriend of yours is an airbrain)*

ptaszek See pindol

ptaszek [PTAH-shehk] *nm* A person who is a suspect, esp an ex-convict <jailbird, yardbird> eg *Szukaliśmy tego ptaszka od dwóch miesięcy (We've been looking for this jailbird for two months)*

publiczka See grać pod publiczkę

publika [poo-BLEE-kah] *nf* An audience <house> eg *Gdy zespół zaczął grać, publika zaczęła szaleć (When the band started to play, the house went wild)*

pudło [POOD-woh] *nn* **1*** (or **stare pudło*** [STAH-reh POOD-woh]) An old woman, esp overdressed <old bag, old bat, old hag, old hen, old witch> eg *Czy ja muszę słuchać tego starego pudła? (Do I have to listen to that old bag?)* **2** A television set <tv, tube, boob tube, telly, idiot box, box, vid> eg *Wyłącz to pudło. Nie mogę* *spać (Turn that box off. I can't sleep)* **3** An automobile, esp old and battered <junker, jalopy, wreck, bucket, bucket of bolts> eg *Sprzedał to pudło za dwa tysiące (He sold that wreck for two thousand)* **4** A miss <cut, pass up, bad shot> eg *Czy odpowiedzią jest „liczba pięć?"Pudło! (Is the answer "number five?" Bad shot!)*

See bez pudła, pierdel

pudy See nudy

pukawka [poo-KAHF-kah] *nf* A pistol or rifle <blaster, gat, piece, iron, rod, heater, snubby, popper, tool, stick, boomstick, firestick, hardware, speaker, difference, persuader, convincer, equalizer, artillery, cannon, Saturday night special> eg *Zrobiła to, o co facet prosił, bo miał pukawkę (She did what the guy asked because he was carrying a piece)*

puknąć się w czoło [POOK-nohnch shyeh f CHOH-woh] (or **puknąć się w łeb** [POOK-nohnch shyeh v WEHP] or **puknąć się w głowę** [POOK-nohnch shyeh v GWOH-veh]) *v* (Literally and metaphorically) To knock one's finger on one's forehead as a sign of stupidity; to come to one's senses or think something over <get a grip, get hold of oneself, wake up and smell the coffee> eg *Puknij się w czoło! O czym ty gadasz? (Wake up and smell the coffee! What are you talking about?)*

puls See trzymać rękę na pulsie

punkt See wariować na punkcie czegoś/kogoś, z miejsca

punktowiec See piętrowiec

puścić coś z dymem [POOSH-cheech tsohsh z DI-mehm] *v phr* To burn; to set something on fire <fry, burn down, cook down, nuke, roast, sizzle> eg *Jak nie oddacie pieniędzy, to puścimy z dymem cały dom (If you don't give the money back, we'll burn down the house)*

puścić kogoś kantem [POOSH-cheech KOH-gohsh KAHN-tehm] (or **puścić kogoś w trąbę** [POOSH-cheech KOH-gohsh f TROHM-beh] may replace **kantem**) *v phr* To get rid of one's romantic or sexual partner; to end up a relationship in a violent or unpleasant way <dump, break up with, ditch, bounce, put someone on hold> eg *Jest przygnębiony, bo jego dziewczyna puściła go kantem po dwóch latach (He's depressed because his girlfriend dumped him after two years); Puścił ją w trąbę i zaczął chodzić z inną (He put her on hold and started dating another woman)*

puścić kogoś z torbami [POOSH-cheech KOH-gohsh s tohr-BAH-mee] (or **puścić kogoś w skarpetkach** [POOSH-cheech KOH-gohsh f skahr-PEHT-kahkh] or **puścić kogoś w trąbę** [POOSH-cheech KOH-gohsh f TROHM-beh]) *v phr* To cheat, swindle, deceive, esp financially <con, rip off, shaft, roll, chisel, gyp, scam, screw, stiff, fleece, dick, do in, take in, do a number on, flim-flam, bamboozle, run a number on, take someone for a ride, take someone to the cleaners, throw someone a curve, pull a fast one, fuck over, screw over, angle, take in, snow, do a snow job, double-shuffle, fast-shuffle, flimflam, give a bun steer, give someone a line, have someone on, lead someone down the garden path, do a snow job, jerk someone's chain, pull someone's chain, pull one's leg, pull someone's string, pull the wool over someone's eyes, put someone on, snow, use smoke and mirrors> eg *Moja była dziewczyna puściła mnie z torbami (My ex girlfriend took me to the cleaners)*

puścić Perf puszczać

puścić się See puszczać się

puścić wiąchę [POOSH-cheech VYOHN-kheh] *v phr* To curse (someone), swear (at someone), or otherwise use foul language <cuss, talk dirty> eg *Nigdy nie puścił wiąchy (He never cussed)*

pupa [POO-pah] (or **pupka** [POOP-kah]) *nf* The buttocks, the posterior <ass, butt, bum, behind, back, back seat, seat, bottom, heinie, rear, tush, fanny, derriere, tail, bucket, tokus, keister, kazoo> eg *Jak ci się podoba moja pupa? (How do you like my bum?)*

pusty See z kwitkiem

puszczać [POOSH-chahch] (perf **puścić** [POOSH-cheech]) *v* **1** (Of washed clothes) To lose color; to dye <bleed, run> eg *Uważaj, mogą farbować (Look out, these may bleed)* **2** To broadcast over the radio or TV <air, get out, go on the air, telecast, televise> eg *Puszczali same powtórki (They aired only reruns); Puszczamy wszystko, co uznamy za ważne (We telecast whatever we find important* **3** To sell; to want dispose of a stock <move, push, turn over, pitch, drum, peddle> eg *Usiłował puścić cały ten towar (He was trying to move all this stuff)*
See przepierdalać

puszczać bąka [[POOSH-chahch BOHN-kah] *v phr* To release intestinal gas, perhaps with a noise <fart, cut a fart, lay a fart, blow a fart, let a fart, cut the cheese, backfire, break wind, pollute the air> eg *Kto puścił bąka? (Who farted?)*

puszczać do kogoś oko [POOSH-chahch doh KOH-gohsh OH-koh] (or **robić do kogoś oko** [ROH-beech doh KOH-gohsh OH-koh]) *v phr* To wink at someone seductively <make eyes at, bat one's eyes, make goo-goo eyes, give someone the eye> eg *Przestań puszczać do niej oko i weź się do roboty (Stop batting your eyes on her and get to work); Widziałam, że robił do ciebie oko (I could see he was giging you the eye)*

puszczać pawia [POOSH-chahch PAH-vyah] *v phr* To empty one's stomach; to vomit <barf, puke, blow grits, blow chunks, chuck, do a Technicolor yawn, drive the big bus, heave, pray to the porcelain god, ralph, rolf, talk to the big white phone, cry Ruth, cry Ralph, blow one's cookies, blow one's lunch, lose one's cookies, lose one's lunch, shoot one's cookies, shoot one's lunch> eg *Zaraz puści pawia (She's going to shoot her cookies)*

puszczać się [POOSH-chahch shyeh] (perf **puścić się** [POOSH-chech shyeh]) *v* (Of a woman) To be sexually promiscuous <sleep around, screw around, fuck around, screw around the block, fuck around the block, chippy around, swing, shack up, bedhop> eg *Jej matka strasznie się puszczała (Her mother screwed around like hell)*

puszczalska [poosh-CHAHL-skah] *nf* A promiscuous woman <floozy, bimbo, slut, bitch, cunt, chippy, quiff, swinger, easy lay, easy make, alley cat, dirty-leg, roundheels, nympho, piece of ass, punchboard, town bike> eg *Ma reputację puszczalskiej (She's got a reputation as an easy make)*

pycha [PI-khah] (or **pyszota** [pi-SHOH-tah]) *excl* Very tasty <yum-yum, yummy, finger-licking good> eg *O, gorące skrzydełka. Pyszota! (Oh, hot wings. Yum-yum!)*

pyfko See piwko

pysk [pisk] *nm* The face, esp ugly <mug, puss, mug, map, phiz, mask, pan> eg *Zetrzyj te gile z pyska (Wipe that goober off your mug)*
See dać pyska, drzeć mordę, jak w pysk strzelił, na sucho, padać

pyskacz [PIS-kahch] *nm* An impudent, insolent, or brash person <smart-ass, wise-ass, back talker, back chatter, sharp-tongue> eg *Nie chcę znów mieć doczynienia z tym psykaczem (I don't want to deal with that smart-ass again)*

pyskaty [pis-KAH-ti] *adj* Impudent, insolent, or brash <sharp-tongued, gutty, lippy, cocky, brassy, cheeky, sassy, nervy, smart-ass, wise-ass, foul-mouthed, cussy, bitchy> eg *Nie bądź taki pyskaty do twojej nauczycielki (Don't be so cheeky to your teacher)*

pyskować [pis-KOH-vahch] (or **pyszczyć** [PISH-chich]; perf **napyskować** [nah-pis-KOH-vahch] or **napyszczyć** [nah-PISH-chich]) *v* To offer impudent or insolent remarks <talk back, chat back, back-talk, back-chat> eg *Żadnych pyskówek! (No talking back!)*

pyskówka [pis-KOOF-kah] *nf* An impudent or impertinent remark <back-talk, back-chat, cheek, sauce, sass> eg *Masz robić to, co mówię i bez żadnych pyskówek! (Just do what I say and don't give me any sass!)*

pytać See kpisz czy o drogę pytasz

pytanie za sto złotych [pi-TAH-nyeh zah stoh ZWOH-tikh] *v phr nn phr* The most important and usually the most difficult or tricky question <sixty-four thousand dollar question, million dollar question> eg *Podczas egzaminu zadał mi pytanie za sto złotych (During the exam he asked me the sixty-four thousand dollar question*

pytlować See mleć jęzorem

pywko See piwko

pyzaty [pi-ZAH-ti] *adj* (Of a man) Having a chubby face <dipper mouth, satchel mouth> eg *Kto to jest ten pyzaty facet pod oknem (Who's the dipper mouth near the window?)*

R

radary [rah-DAH-ri] *npl* The ears, esp big <flappers, flaps, sails, cauliflowers> eg *Ten facet za dużymi radarami wydaje się mi znajomy (That guy with big flappers seems familiar to me)*

radocha [rah-DOH-khah] *nf* Something very funny, amusing or foolish; a cause of amusement <laugh, laugh and a half, laugher, laughing stock, horselaugh, merry ha-ha, hoot, howl, riot, laff riot, laffer, scream, stitch, boffo, panic, knee-slapper, rib-tickler, side-splitter> eg *Nie mielibyśmy radochy jadąc tam? (Wouldn't it be a laugh to go there?)*

rajch [RAH-eekh] *nm* Germany, not only with reference to the Third Reich <krautland, hitlerland, reich> eg *Ale se przywiózł wóz z Rajchu (Check out the car he brought from krautland)*

rajcować [rah-ee-TSOH-vahch] *v* To arouse or excite, esp sexually; to delight extremely <turn on, steam up, stir up, send, knock out, knock someone dead, knock someone' socks off, knock someone for a loop, throw someone for a loop, kill, murder, slay, slaughter, put someone away, tickle pink, tickle to death, tickle the piss out of someone> eg *Ta muzyka w ogóle mnie nie rajcuje (This music doesn't turn me on at all)*

rak See na raka

ramol* [RAH-mohl] *nm* An old man <gramps, old fart, old bugger, geezer, gaffer, old-timer, fossil> eg *Młody nie jestem stary, ale żaden zwie mnie ramol (I am not young, but I'm no old fart)*

rana See taki że do rany przyłóż

rany [RAH-ni] (**boskie** [BOH-kyeh] or **julek** [YOO-lehk] or **koguta** [koh-GOO-tah] may be added; or **rety** [REH-ti]) *excl phr* An exclamation of anger, irritation, disappointment, shock <shit, fuck, hell, heck, damn, damn it, goddamn it, gosh, golly, gee, jeez, holy fuck, holy cow, holy moly, holy hell, holy mackarel, holy shit, jumping Jesus, fucking shit, fucking hell> eg *Rany julek!! Nie wziąłem pieniędzy! (Fucking hell! I didn't take the money with me!)*

rasowy [rah-SOH-vi] *adj* True; real; genuine <born, born and bred, real McCoy, legit, kosher> eg *Mój wujek to rasowy nauczyciel (My uncle is a born and bred teacher)*

raszpla [RAHSH-plah] *nf* An old woman, esp overdressed <old bag, old bat, old hag, old hen, old witch> eg *Co powiedziała ci ta raszpla? (What did the old bag tell you?)*

rausz See na rauszu

raz dwa [rahs DVAH] *adv phr* Immediately; very quickly <pretty damn quick, PDQ, ASAP, on the spot, on the double, double time, double clutching, like a shot, in half a mo, like now, before you know it, before you can say Jack Robinson, in a jiffy, in a flash, in half a shake, right off the bat, like a bat out of hell, like a shot out of hell, hubba-hubba, horseback, like greased lightning> eg *Biegnij tam szybko, raz dwa! (Run over there quick, on the double!); Przyszedł nauczyciel i zabrali się do roboty. Raz dwa (The teacher came in and they got to work. Pretty damn quick)*

raz kozie śmierć [rahs KOH-zhyeh SHMYEHRCH] *excl phr* (Before beginning something that takes skill, luck, courage, or is very dangerous) I am ready to begin; I am now ready and willing to take the chance <here goes, here goes nothing> eg *Nigdy nie jechałem na koniu. No cóż, raz kozie śmierć! (I've never been on a horse before. Well, here goes!)*

ręce opadają [REHN-tseh oh-pah-DAH-yoh] (or **ręce i nogi opadają** [REHN-tseh ee NOH-gee oh-pah-DAH-yoh]) *phr* To be tired of someone or something (that is hopeless or miserable) and, esp, to be unable to change it <enough to make you weep, enough to make the angels weep> eg *Ręce opadają od ich głupiego zachowania (Their stupid behavior is enough to make you weep)*

rąbać [ROHM-bahch] (perf **wrąbać** [VROHM-bahch]) *v* To eat everything <To eat, esp voraciously or entirely <chow down, scarf, scoff, feed one's face, gobble up> eg *Wrąbał kurczaka w try miga (He killed the chicken in no time at all)*

rąbnąć [ROHMB-nohnhch shyeh] *v* To have a quick drink of liquor <knock back, down, slug down, swig, tank, tank up> eg *Rąbnął cztery piwa i zaczął bekać (He downed three beers and started to burp)*

rączka See złota rączka

rąsia [ROHN-shyah] *nf* A hand <mitt, paw, duke, fiver, grabber, hook, meathook> eg *Daj mi rąsię (Give me your mitt)*

rechotać [reh-KHOH-tahch] (perf **zarechotać** [zah-reh-KHOH-tahch]) *v* To burst with laughter <crack up, break up, split, split one's sides, die laughing, roll in the aisles, tear one apart, be in stiches, laugh fit to burst, bust a gut laughing, pee in one's pants laughing, fall out laughing, howl, scream, horselaugh, stitch, be blue

in the face, laugh till one is blue in the face> eg *Rechotali, gdy usłyszeli tę wiadomość (They were just rolling in the aisles when they heard the news)*

refleks See mieć spóźniony zapłon

regulator See na całego

rejs See iść w cug

ręka See dać głowę, iść komuś na rękę, jeść komuś z ręki, lekką ręką, mieć czyste ręce, mieć lekką rękę, mieć lepkie łapy, mieć ręce i nogi, na rękę, na własną rękę, nosić kogoś na rękach, obudzić się z ręką w nocniku, od ręki, patrzeć komuś na ręce, podpisać się pod czymś, prawa ręka, prędzej komuś kaktus wyrośnie, prowadzić kogoś za rączkę, przemawiać do ręki, trzymać rękę na pulsie, twarda ręka, umyć ręce, urabiać sobie ręce, wyjść z czegoś obronną ręką, z drugiej ręki, z kwitkiem, z rączki do rączki

rękaw See as w rękawie

reklamówka [reh-klah-MOOF-kah] *nf* A television or radio commercial <spot, plug, pitch, teleblurb, break, word from my sponsors> eg *Opowiem państwu więcej zaraz po reklamówce (I'll be back with you right after the break)*

repeta [reh-PEH-tah] *nf* An additional serving of food at a meal, a second helping <seconds> eg *Poprosił o repetę (He asked for seconds)*

rety See rany

różaniec See do tańca i różańca

różnica See bez różnicy

różności [roozh-NOHSH-chee] *npl* Articles of various kinds; a mixture or miscellany <combo, odds and ends, bits and pieces, mish mash, hodge-podge, rag-bag, props, thingies, smorgasboard> eg *Podobają mi się te różności (I like this mish mash)*

robak [ROH-bahk] *nm* Any insect <bug, crum, crumb, grayback> eg *Zabierz ode mnie te robaki, bo się porzygam (Take these bugs away from me or I'm going to puke)*
See mieć robaki w dupie, zalewać robaka

robić [ROH-beech] (or **robić jako ktoś** [ROH-beech YAH-koh KTOHSH] or **robić za kogoś** [ROH-beech zah KOH-gohsh] or **robić w czymś** [ROH-beech f chimsh]) *v* To work in a particular profession; to have an occupation as someone <be in, be as, do for> eg *On robi w tekstyliach (He's in the textiles); Ona tu robi jako salowa (She's here as a nurse); Ja tu robię za dyskdżokeja (I'm a DJ here)*

robić coś na boku [ROH-beech TSOHSH nah BOH-koo] *v phr* To have a part-time job, esp of an assignment nature <gig, moonlight, have a job on the side> eg *Musiał robić coś na boku, żeby mieć na wykarmienie rodziny (He had to moonlight to earn enough to feed his family)*

robić do kogoś oko See puszczać do kogoś oko

robić dzieci [ROH-beech JEH-chee] *v phr* To copulate <play doctor, play doctors and nurses, play he'n and she'n, play fun and games, do birds and bees, play in-and-out, roll in the hay, jelly roll, do you-know-what> eg *A co z tą parką? Poszli do domu robić dzieci (What about that couple? They went home to play doctors and nurses)*

robić kokosy [ROH-beech koh-KOH-si] (or **zbijać kokosy** [ZBEE-yahch koh-KOH-si] may replace **robić**; **forsę** [FOHR-seh] or **kasę** [KAH-seh] or **szmal** [SHMAHL] may replace **kokosy**) *v phr* To make a lot of money; to do a very profitable business, esp without much effort <pull down, pick up, clean up, cash in, make a bundle, ride the gravy train> eg *Zbił koksy na dostawach dla wojska (He* *made a bundle on deliveries for the army); Wykupił ten klub, wyremontował i teraz zbija koksy (He bought this club, renovated it, and now is cashing in)*

robić komuś łachę [ROH-beech KOH-moosh WAH-kheh] *v phr* To do something showing one's reluctance <do someone a favor> eg *Nie rób mi łachy. Sam to zrobię (Don't do me any favor. I'll do it myself)*

robić komuś boki [ROH-beech KOH-moosh BOH-kee] *v phr* To be sexually unfaithful, esp to commit adultery <cheat, two-time, chippy, get a little on the side, backdoor, have an extracurricular activity, play hanky-panky, step out on, play around, play the field, put the horns on> eg *Żona tego polityka robiła mu boki (The politician's wife has been involved in some backdoor activity)*

robić komuś dobrze [ROH-beech KOH-moosh DOHB-zheh] *v phr* To satisfy someone sexually, esp by performing oral sex on someone <go down on, suck off, blow, eat, lick, give head, gobble> eg *Pewnie postanowiła zrobić mu dobrze (She sure decided to do him good)*

robić komuś koło dupy* [ROH-beech KOH-moosh KOH-woh DOO-pi] (**jaj*** [YAH-EE] may replace **dupy** or **obrabiać komuś dupę*** [ohb-RAH-byahch KOH-moosh DOO-peh]) *v phr* To gossip about someone; to spread rumors about someone; to denigrate or criticize <wag some tongues, have one's name bandied about, badmouth someone, blackball someone, spitball someone, dish the dirt about someone, chew the fat about someone, cut someone up and down, cut someone into little pieces, schmooze about someone, run someone down, bring someone down, dump all over someone, dump on someone, put the shit on someone> eg *Po tym wypadku ludzie zaczęli robić jej koło dupy (After that accident people started to badmouth her)*

robić komuś wodę z mózgu [ROH-beech KOH-moosh VOH-deh z MOOZ-goo] *v phr* To deceive or confuse someone; to manipulate someone to think or act as one wishes <bluff, bullshit, put someone on, pull someone's leg, pull someone's string, give someone a leg, have someone on, jack someone around, jerk someone around, poke fun at, kid someone around, fool someone around, jack someone's chain, spoof, cut down, mind-fuck, head-fuck, push around, upstage, wind around one's finger, wrap around one's finger, twist around one's finger> eg *On jej zrobił wodę z mózgu (He mind-fucked her)*

robić kupę [ROH-beech KOO-peh] (or **rżnąć kupę*** [RZHNOHNCH KOO-peh] or **walić kupę*** [VAH-leech KOO-peh]) *v phr* To defecate <doo-doo, caca, kaka, poo, poo-poo, poop, squat, dump> eg *Musisz pamiętać, żeby robić kupę do nocnika (You must remember to doo-doo in the potty)*

robić laskę* [ROH-beech LAHS-keh] (or **stawiać laskę*** [STAH-vyahch LAHS-keh]) *v phr* To perform fellatio <suck off, blow, eat, give head, dick-lick, go down on, play the skin flute> eg *Chciała mu zrobić laskę, ale poszedł spać (She wanted to suck him off, but he went to sleep)*

robić loda* [ROH-beech LOH-dah] *v phr* To perform fellatio <suck off, blow, eat, give head, dick-lick, go down on, play the skin flute> eg *Chciała mu zrobić loda, ale poszedł spać (She wanted to suck him off, but he went to sleep)*

robić na czarno See **pracować na czarno**

robić pod siebie [ROH-beech poht SHYEH-byeh] *v phr* To defecate or urinate because of intense stress or fear; to panic; to become alarmed <shit one's pants, shit one's drawers, shit bullets, shit a brick, shit green, piss one's pants, piss one's

drawers, sweat bullets> eg *Byłem tak przerażona, że mało co nie narobiłam pod siebie (I was so terrified I nearly pissed my pants)*

robić słodkie oczy [ROH-beech SWOHT-kyeh OH-chi] *v phr* To look at someone seductively <make eyes at, make goo-goo eyes, make with bedroom eyes, make bedroom eyes at, give someone bedroom eyes, eyefuck> eg *Robiła do mnie słodkie oczy przez cały czas (She was making bedroom eyes at me all the time)*

robić siku [ROH-beech SHEE-koo] (or **robić siusiu** [ROH-beech SHYOO-shyoo]) *v phr* To urinate <piss, leak, pee, pee-pee, piddle, tinkle, wee-wee, whizz, take a piss, take a leak> eg *Ale chce mi się sikać! (Man, do I need to piss!)*

robić siusiu See **robić siku**

robić sobie dobrze [ROH-beech SOH-byeh DOHB-zheh] *v phr* To masturbate <finger, finger-fuck, play stinky-finger, play stinky-pinky, jack off, jerk off, beat off, fuck off, whack off, toss off, pull off, bang the bishop, beat one's dummy, beat the meat, pound one's meat, flog one's meat, fist-fuck, fuck one's fist, stroke, spank one's monkey, choke one's chicken, wax one's dolphin> eg *Robił sobie dobrze zawsze przed pójściem do łóżka (He always used to jerk himself before going to bed)*

robić sobie jaja [ROH-beech SOH-byeh YAH-yah] *v phr* To tease; to banter; to treat someone unseriously and frivolously; to have fun at someone's expense <poke fun at, kid, kid around, pull someone's leg, pull someone's string, fool around, jive, josh, shuck, lark, spoof, send up, cut down> eg *Powiedziała mu, żeby przestał sobie robić jaja (She told him to stop fooling around with her)*

robić w gacie [ROH-beech v GAH-chyeh] (**w majtki** [v MAH-eet-kee] or **w majtki** [v MAH-eet-kee] or **w portki** [f POHRT-kee] or **w spodnie** [f SPOHD-nyeh] or **pod siebie** [poht SHYEH-byeh] may replace **w gacie**) *v phr* **1** To defecate, esp because of intense stress or fear; to panic; to become alarmed <shit one's pants, shit one's drawers, shit bullets, shit a brick, shit green> eg *Byłem tak przerażona, że mało co nie narobiłam w gacie (I was so terrified I nearly pissed my pants)* **2** To be afraid; to be frightened; to be intimidated <chicken out, turn chicken, turn yellow, run scared, have cold feet, be scared stiff, be scared shitless, shit one's pants, piss one's pants, shit bullets, shit a brick, shit green, be spooked, push the panic button, wimp out> eg *Nie chciał wyjeżdżać. Myślę, że robił pod siebie (He didn't want to leave. I guess he was scared shitless)*

robić w pieluchy [ROH-beech f pyeh-LOO-khi] *v phr* To be very young; to be a mere child <be knee high to a grasshopper, rock the cradle, piss in one's pants, shit in one's pants> eg *Było to 20 lat temu, kiedy ty robiłeś w pieluchy (It was 20 years ago when you were still pissing in your pants)*

robić z igły widły [ROH-beech z EEG-wi VEED-wi] *v phr* To make a major issue out of a minor one; to exaggerate the importance of something <make a big deal out of something, make a mountain out of a molehill> eg *Nic się nie stało, że przybyłem pięć minut później. Przestań robić z igły widły (Arriving five minutes late was not the disaster. Stop making a mountain out of a molehill)*

robol [ROH-bohl] (or **robociarz** [roh-BOH-chahsh]) *nm* An unqualified menial worker; an unskilled laborer <grave-digger, wetback, blue collar, workhorse, hard hat, stiff, working stiff> eg *Traktowany byłem jak robol (I was treated as a workhorse)*

robota [roh-BOH-tah] *nf* **1** Work or a job, esp time-consuming or tedious <old nine-to-five, daily grind, salt mines, nine-to-five, rat race, donkeywork, bullwork, elbow grease> eg *Miałem tydzień wolnego, a teraz znów do roboty! (I had a week off,* *and now back to the salt mines!); Chciał załatwić sobie coś lepszego niż ta jego robota (He wanted to fix himself something better than his daily grind)* **2** One's place of work <salt mines> eg *Jutro rano muszę być w robocie (I have to be back in the salt mines tomorrow morning)*

See brać się, czarna robota, głupiego robota, mokra robota, papierkowa robota, wylać, wylecieć

robota głupiego See głupiego robota

rodzaj See coś w tym rodzaju

rodzinka [roh-JEEN-kah] *nf* A family <folks, kinfolks, in-laws, whole famdamnly> eg *Nie lubię jego rodzinki (I don't like his in-laws)*

rodzynek [roh-DZI-nehk] *nm* Someone who is exceptional in some way; someone who stands out <odd man out, oddball> eg *To rodzynek w naszym instytucie (He's an odd man out in our institute)*

rogacz [ROH-gahch] *nm* A man whose wife has had sex with another man since their marriage <cuckold> eg *Mój sąsiad to rogacz (My neighbor is a cuckold)*

rogi See przyprawiać komuś rogi

rok See zostać na drugi rok

rolować [roh-LOH-vahch] (perf **wyrolować** [vi-roh-LOH-vahch]) *v* To cheat; to swindle; to deceive; to scheme <con, rip off, shaft, roll, chisel, gyp, scam, screw, stiff, fleece, dick, do in, take in, do a number on, flim-flam, bamboozle, run a number on, take someone for a ride, take someone to the cleaners, throw someone a curve, pull a fast one, fuck over, screw over, angle, take in, snow, do a snow job, double-shuffle, fast-shuffle, flimflam, give a bun steer, give someone a line, have someone on, lead someone down the garden path, do a snow job, jerk someone's chain, pull someone's chain, pull one's leg, pull someone's string, pull the wool over someone's eyes, put someone on, snow, use smoke and mirrors> eg *Ten handlarz wyrolował mnie na dwie stówy (That salesman dicked me for two hundred)*

ropniak [ROHP-nyahk] *nm* A diesel automobile <smudge potter, boiler, buzz-wagon, oil burner> eg *Ten tu to ropniak (This one here is a smudge potter)*

rów See lizać

równiacha [roov-NYAH-khah] *nf* A trustworthy or pleasing person; a friend <right guy, boy scout, pal, buddy> eg *On to na prawdę równiacha (He's a real boy scout)*

równo See po równo

równy [ROOV-ni] *adj* (Of a person) Trustworthy, pleasing, friendly <right, right-on, downright, regular, cool, swell, fab, rad, def, baddest> eg *Twój kuzyn to naprawdę równy facet (Your cousin is a real cool guy)*

rozbeczeć Perf beczeć

rozbieranka [rohz-byeh-RAHN-kah] *nf* An act of undressing or a party which features such an act; a strip-tease <strip, strip-off, peel, tits and ass, T and A, tit show, flesh act, bumps and grinds> eg *Była wsławiona niezapomnianą rozbieranką podczas wykładu (She was famous for her unforgettable tit-show during the lecture)*

rozbój w biały dzień [ROHZ-boo-ee v BYAH-wi JEHÑ] *nm phr* Something very expensive or an exorbitantly high price <highway robbery, arm and a leg> eg *Dwa tysiące za coś takiego? To jest rozbój w biały dzień! (Two thousand for something like that? It's a highway robbery!)*

rozchodzić o coś See chodzić o coś

rozchodzić się [rohs-KHOH-jeech shyeh] *v* (Of money) To gradually make smaller; to gradually disappear <fade, fade away, fade out of sight, melt into the scenery, go south, do a vanishing act> eg *Gdzie pieniądze? Szybko się rozeszły (Where's the money? It quickly faded out of sight)*
See iść

rozdziawić gębę [rohz-JAH-veech GEHM-beh] (or **otworzyć gębę** [oht-FOH-zhich GEHM-beh]) *v phr* To be speechless because of strong feeling, surprise, confusion or fear <clam up, dummy up, button up, belt up, catch one's breath, drop dead, knock dead, drop down dead, be killed stone-dead> eg *Wiadomość była tak nieoczekiwana, że aż rozdziawił gębę ze zdziwienia (The news was so unexpected that he caught his breath from surprise)*

rozgryzać [rohz-GRI-zahch] (perf **rozgryźć** [ROHZ-grizhch]) *v* To understand someone or something; to find an explanation for someone or something, esp to solve a problem; to tackle <figure out, crack, work through, nail down> eg *Ciężko jest rozgryźć twoją siostrę. Nigdy nie wiadomo, o co jej chodzi (It's hard to figure out your sister. You never know what she means); Rozgryzłem wszystkie odpowiedzi (I figured all the answers out)*

rozindyczyć się Perf indyczyć się

rozjaśnić się pod sufitem [rohz-YAHSH-neech shyeh poht soo-FEE-tehm] *v phr* To (finally) understand, comprehend, or realize <figure out, work out, tune in, plug in, tote up, wise up, get through one's head, get through someone's thick head, get into someone's thick head, see daylight, flash, dig, dawn on, have a brainwave, get, get it, catch, get the drift, get the picture, get the message, get the hang of, savvy, dig, click, capeesh, read, be with it, see where one is coming from, know where one is coming from> eg *Na początku nic nie rozumiał, ale w końcu rozjaśniło mu się pod sufitem (At first he didn't understand anything, but finally he got the picture)*

rozklejać się [rohs-KLEH-yahch shyeh] (perf **rozkleić się** [rohs-KLEH-yeech shyeh]; or **rozpuszczać się** [rohs-POOSH-chahch shyeh] perf **rozpuścić się** [rohs-POOSH-cheech shyeh]) *v* To become sentimental, nostalgic, emotional; to lose one's control <get mushy, get corny, get gluey, get sappy, get schmaltzy, get sloppy, get teary, fall apart, go to pieces, come unglued, come unstuck, come unwrapped, come unzipped> eg *Tylko się nie rozklejaj z mojego powodu (Just don't get mushy on me)*

rozkręcać się [rohs-KREHN-tsahch shyeh] (perf **rozkręcić się** [rohs-KREHN-chich shyeh]) *v* (Esp about a person or the atmosphere at a party) To begin to be more lively, exciting, or stimulating <get jazzed-up, jazz oneself, jazz up oneself, gas up oneself, get gassed up, hype up oneself, get hyped up, hop up oneself, get hopped up, juice up oneself, get juiced up, jump up oneself, get jumped up, pep up oneself, get pepped up, pump up oneself, get pumped up, rev up oneself, get revved up, zazz up oneself, get zazzed up, put balls on, put hair on, be in full swing> eg *Impreza szybko się rozkręciła (The party soon was in full swing); Ludzie się rozkręcili dopiero po godzinie (People got pumped up only after an hour)*

rozlatywać się See rozpierdalać się

rozpić [ROH-speech] *v* To drink an entire bottle of alcohol <kill, knock back, guzzle, gargle, lap, tank up, slug down, swig> eg *W parę minut tozpili pół litra wódki (In a few minutes they knocked back a half-liter bottle of vodka)*

rozpierdalać** [rohs-pyehr-DAH-lahch] (perf **rozpierdolić**** [rohs-pyehr-DOH-leech]; or **rozpieprzać*** [rohs-PYEHP-shahch] perf **rozpieprzyć*** [rohs-PYEHP-shich]; or **rozpierniczać*** [rohs-pyehr-NEE-chahch] perf **rozpierniczyć*** [rohs-pyehr-NEE-chich]; or **rozpierdzielać*** [rohs-pyehr-JEH-lahch] perf **rozpierdzielić*** [rohs-pyehr-JEH-leech]; or **rozwalać** [rohz-VAH-lahch] perf **rozwalić** [rohz-VAH-leech]) *v* To destroy or wreck something <fuck up, screw up, total, waste, trash, wipe out, pile up, rack up, crack up, smash up, smack up, stack up> eg *Kto Ci powiedział, że rozwaliłem samochód ojca? (Who told you that I totaled my father's car?)*

rozpierdalać się** [rohs-pyehr-DAH-lahch shyeh] (perf **rozpierdolić się**** [rohs-pyehr-DOH-leech shyeh]; or **rozpieprzać się*** [rohs-PYEHP-shahch shyeh] perf **rozpieprzyć się*** [rohs-PYEHP-shich shyeh]; or **rozpierniczać się*** [rohs-pyehr-NEE-chahch shyeh] perf **rozpierniczyć się*** [rohs-pyehr-NEE-chich shyeh]; or **rozpierdzielać się*** [rohs-pyehr-JEH-lahch shyeh] perf **rozpierdzielić się*** [rohs-pyehr-JEH-leech shyeh]; or **rozwalać się** [rohz-VAH-lahch shyeh] perf **rozwalić się** [rohz-VAH-leech shyeh]; or **rozlatywać się** [rohz-lah-TI-vahch shyeh] perf **rozlecieć się** [rohz-LEH-chyehch shyeh]) *v* **1** To fail or become inoperative; to fall into destruction <fuck up, screw up, break down, crash, crash and burn, fry, go down, go down in flames, go south, belly up, melt down, shut down, crack up, go blooey, go busted, go on the blink, go on the fritz, go off, go out of whack, go kerflooey> eg *Wszystko szło mi dobrze póki nie rozpieprzył się faks (Everything was doing fine until the fax screwed up); Ich małżeństwo rozpierdoliło się po dwóch latach (Their marriage fucked up after two years)* **2** To forcefully hit against something or collapse <fuck up, screw up, hit, whack, wham, smack, bang, bump, trash, pow, fall over something> eg *Rozpierdolił się tym wozem (He fucked up this car)* **3** To get broken or damaged <get fucked up, get screwed up, get smashed, get busted, get wracked> eg *Wazon poszedł w rozsypkę (The vase got fucked up)*

rozprawiczać* [rohs-prah-VEE-chahch] (perf **rozprawiczyć*** [rohs-prah-VEE-chich]) *v* To terminate someone's virginity; to deflower <cherry-pop, pop someone's cherry, cop someone's cherry, take someone's cherry> eg *Była zgorzkniałe, bo ją rozprawiczył i zostawił (She was bitter because he took her cherry and left her)*

rozpuszczać się See rozklejać się

rozpylacz *nm* A handheld machine gun <tommy, tommy gun, chopper, chatterbox, grease gun, typewriter, Chicago piano, remington, ack ack, automatic> eg *Był uzbrojony w rozpylacz (He was armed with a tommy gun)*

rozryczeć się Perf ryczeć

rozsypać się Perf sypać się

rozsypka See iść w rozsypkę, w proszku

rozum See paść komuś na mózg, pozjadać wszystkie rozumy

rozumieć See ma się rozumieć, to rozumiem

rozwalać See rozpierdalać

rozwalać się See rozpierdalać się

ruchać** [ROO-khahch] (perf **poruchać**** [poh-ROO-khahch] or **wyruchać**** [vi-ROO-khahch]) *v* To copulate with someone <fuck, screw, lay, ball, bang,

boink, boff, boogie, bop, frig, hump, poke, shag> eg *Musiałem ją wyruchać, innego wyjścia nie było (I had to fuck her; there was no other way out of this)*

ruchać się** [ROO-khahch shyeh] *v* To copulate <get screwed, get fucked, get laid, screw, fuck, fork, frig, ball, bang, boink, bonk, boff, hump, poke, shag> eg *Lubią się ruchać miejscach publicznych (They like to fuck in public)*

ruda [ROO-dah] *nf* A red-headed woman <brick-top, carrot-top, carrot-head> eg *Czego chciała ta ruda? (What did the brick-top want?)*

rudera [roo-DEH-rah] *nf* An old or dilapidated house <ruin, hole, den, joint, shack, dump, cave, flophouse> eg *Nie masz zamiaru kupować tej rudery, prawda? (You're not going to buy that ruin, are you?)*

rudzielec [roo-JEH-lehts] *nm* A red-headed man <brick-top, carrot-top, carrot-head> eg *Hej, rudzielec, gdzie idziesz? (Hey, carrot-head, where are you going?)*

rupieć [ROO-pyehch] *nm* Any old or used thing <piece of junk, junk, junker, old stuff> eg *Zabieraj ode mnie te rupiecie (Get these junkers out of my sight)*

rura [ROO-rah] *nf* **1** A young and attractive woman <chick, broad, gal, pussy, cunt, ass, piece of ass, piece, dish, babe, baby, dame, beauty, beaut, beauty queen, baby doll, doll, dolly, dollface, dreamboat, dream girl, eating stuff, eyeful, flavor, looker, good-looker, head-turner, traffic-stopper, honey, killer, hot number, package, knockout, oomph girl, peach, bombshell, sex bunny, sex job, sex kitten, sex pot, table grade, ten, bunny, centerfold, cheesecake, date bait, dazzler, heifer, fluff, quail, sis, skirt, tail, job, leg, tart, tomato, pussycat, cooz, twat> eg *Jego siostra to niezła rura (His sister is some doll)* **2** (or **stara rura** [STAH-rah ROO-rah]) An old woman, esp overdressed <old bag, old bat, old hag, old hen, old witch> eg *Co powiedziała ci ta stara rura? (What did the old bag tell you?)*
See dać sobie w gaz, walić z grubej rury

rura komuś zmiękła [ROO-rah KOH-moosh ZMYEHN-kwah] *v phr* To stop behaving in a superior, haughty, or self-assured manner; to moderate one's behavior <sing another tune, whistle a different tune, change one's tune, come down a peg, take down a notch, climb down, come off one's perch, get off one's high horse, eat dirt, eat humble pie, pull in one's horns, take off one's high hat> eg *Na początku zaczął się popisywać, ale potem rura mu zmiękła (At the beginning he had started to show off but later he came down a peg)*

rusek* [ROO-sehk] (or **rusak*** [ROO-sahk] or **ruski*** [ROOS-kee]) *nm* A Russian <rusky, red, Ivan, tovarich, comrade> eg *Czego chciał ten rusek? (What did the rusky want?)*

ruski [ROOS-kee] *nm* The Russian language, esp as a subject in school <no slang equivalent> eg *Kto Cię uczył ruskiego w zeszłym semestrze? (Who taught you Russian last semester?)*

rusz See ani rusz, co rusz

ruszać [ROO-shahch] (perf **ruszyć** [ROO-shich]) *v* To arouse or excite, esp sexually; to delight extremely <turn on, bring on, steam up, stir up, send, knock out, knock someone dead, knock someone' socks off, knock someone for a loop, throw someone for a loop, kill, murder, slay, slaughter, put someone away, tickle pink, tickle to death, tickle the piss out of someone> eg *Nie rusza mnie ten typ kobiet (That kind of women doesn't turn me on)*

ruszt See wrzucić coś na ruszt

ruszyć See nie kiwnąć palcem

ruszyć głową [ROO-shich GWOH-voh] (or **ruszyć mózgownicą** [ROO-shich mooz-gohv-NEE-tsoh]) *v phr* To use one's intelligence; to start to think <use one's head, rack one's brain, brainstorm, think up, noodle around, percolate, perk, head trip, skull drag, eat, bug, burn a couple of braincells> eg *Lepiej by ci szło z matmy, gdybyś tylko ruszył głową (You could do better in math if you just used your noggin)*

ruszyć Perf ruszać

ruszyć w cug See iść w cug

rwać See podrywać

ryło See drzeć mordę, ryj

ryć [rich] (perf **obryć** [OHB-rich] or **wyryć** [VI-rich]; **się** [shyeh] may be added) *v* To study intensively, esp for an upcoming examination <cram, grind, dig, skull, book it, go book, hit the books, megabook, megastudy, crack the books, pound the books, bone up> eg *Przez ostatni tydzień ryłem do egzaminu z językoznawstwa (For the past week I've been cramming for the linguistics exam)*

ryba See czuć się jak ryba w wodzie, gruba ryba, wsio ryba, zdrowy jak ryba

rycząca czterdziestka [ri-CHOHN-tsah chtehr-JEHST-kah] (or **rycząca czterdziecha** [ri-CHOHN-tsah chtehr-JEH-khah]) *nf phr* A woman in her 40s, presumably frustrated because of her age and limited sexual popularity <Mrs. Robinson> eg *Ta rycząca czterdzioestka jest niezła w podrywaniu młodych chłopców (That Mrs. Robinson is good at picking up young boys)*

ryczeć [RI-chehch] *v* **1** (perf **rozryczeć się** [rohz-RI-chehch shyeh] or **poryczeć się** [poh-RI-chehch shyeh]) To cry or weep noisily <blubber, bawl, break down, break down and cry, turn on the waterworks, cry one's eyes out, cry me a river, shed bitter tears, weep bitter tears, sing the blues, put on the weeps, let go, let it out> eg *Rozyczała się, gdy to usłyszała (She turned on the waterworks when she heard that)* **2** (perf **poryczeć się** [poh-RI-chehch shyeh] or **ryknąć** [RIK-nohnch]) To burst with laughter <crack up, break up, split, split one's sides, die laughing, roll in the aisles, tear one apart, be in stiches, laugh fit to burst, bust a gut laughing, pee in one's pants laughing, fall out laughing, howl, scream, horselaugh, stitch, be blue in the face, laugh till one is blue in the face> eg *Ryczeliśmy ze śmiechu, gdy usłyszeliśmy tę wiadomość (We were just rolling in the aisles when we heard the news)*

Ryga See jechać do Rygi

ryj [RI-ee] (or **ryło** [RI-woh] *nn*) *nm* The face, esp ugly <mug, puss, mug, map, phiz, mask, pan> eg *Jakiś facet obili mu ryja pod domem (Some guy beat his mug near his house)*

See drzeć mordę, na sępa, padać

ryknąć Perf ryczeć

rynna See z deszczu pod rynnę

rysunki [ri-SOON-kee] *npl* Fine arts, esp as a subject in school <art, graphics, arts-crafts> eg *Chodzi na rysunki (He's taking up art)*

ryzyk-fizyk [RI-zik FEE-zik] *adv phr* Not certain; risky <chancy, iffy, dicey, rocky, touchy, up for grabs, touch and go, on a wing and a prayer, on slippery ground, on thin ice, fat chance> eg *Nie wiem, czy wybierze naszą propozycję. Ryzyk fizyk (I don't know if he chhoses our proposal. It's iffy)*

rządzić [ZHOHN-jeech] (perf **zarządzić** [zah-ZHOHN-jeech]) *v* **1** To be the best; to dominate <rule, run, run the show, be tops> eg *The Blue Jays rule! (Blue Jaysi* *rządzą!)* **2** To carouse or celebrate <party, ball, have a ball, jam, paint the town red, raise hell, bar-hop, bar-crawl, go on a bender> eg *Ale żeśmy wczoraj zarządzili na dyskotece! (Boy, did we have a ball last night in the disco!)*

rzęch [zhehnkh] *nn* An old and battered automobile <junker, jalopy, wreck, bucket, bucket of bolts> eg *Sprzedał tego rzęcha za dwa tysiące (He sold that wreck for two thousand)*

rzecz See do rzeczy, te klocki

rzępolić [zhehm-POH-leech] *v* To play a musical instrument, esp very poorly <wail, smoke, rip, strum, thrum, thump> eg *Rzępolił na swojej gitarze (He was wailing on his guitar)*

rzęsa See stawać na głowie

rzeźnik [ZHEH-zhneek] *nm* A surgeon <butcher, doc, bones, sawbones, bone-bender, bone-breaker, medico, croaker> eg *Ten rzeźnik operuje już od dwóch godzin (That butcher's been operating for two hours)*

rzucać [ZHOO-tsahch] (perf **rzucić** [ZHOO-cheech]) *v* (Esp in former communist times) To unexpectedly offer a given merchandise available to be sold ; to suddenly have in stock <have a shitload of, have a truckload of> eg *W sklepie za rogiem rzucili rajstopy (They have a shitload of pantyhose in the store around the corner)*

rzucać mięsem [ZHOO-tsahch MYEHN-sehm] (or **rzucać kurwami**** [ZHOO-tsahch koor-VAH-mee] or **rzucać chujami**** [ZHOO-tsahch khoo-YAH-mee]) *v phr* To curse (someone), swear (at someone), or otherwise use foul language <cuss, talk dirty> eg *Przestań rzucać mięsem w obecności dzieci! (Stop cussing in the presence of children)*

rzucać się [ZHOO-tsahch shyeh] *v* **1** To aggressively argue, esp if one is groundlessly dissatisfied or discontented; to have unfounded complaints <fuss, stink, scene, make a ceremony, beef, bleed, hassle, kvetch, bitch, beef, gripe, piss, bellyache, grouse, growl, squawk, cut a beef, make a stink, piss up a storm, raise a stink, blow up a storm, kick up a storm, eat someone's heart out, fuck around, screw around, mess around, trip> eg *Zaczęli się do nas rzucać (They started tripping on us)* **2** To start dealing with something, esp suddenly, energetically, or totally <set about, go about, get down to> eg *Rzucił się w końcu do roboty (He finally got down to work)*

rzucać się z motyką na słońce [ZHOO-tsahch shyeh z moh-TI-koh nah SWOHŃ-tseh] *v phr* To work very hard <work one's ass off, work one's fingers to the bone, work like a horse, sweat, bust one's ass off, break one's ass off, make bricks without a straw> eg *Pisanie słownika bez komputera to jak rzucanie się z motyką na słońce (Writing a dictionary without a computer is like making bricks without a straw)*

rzucić See pierdolnąć

rzucić kogoś na kolana [ZHOO-cheech nah koh-LAH-nah] *v phr* **1** To dazzle, charm, or enchant; to cast a spell on <throw someone to one's knees, turn on, bring on, steam up, stir up, send, knock out, knock someone dead, knock someone' socks off, knock someone for a loop, throw someone for a loop, kill, murder, slay, slaughter, put someone away, tickle pink, tickle to death, tickle the piss out of someone> eg *Ta piosenka rzuciła nas na kolana (That song really sent us)* **2** To win or defeat someone easily or totally; to beat with a great style <throw someone to one's knees, bash, trash, dish, work over, whack, whomp, whip, KO, kayo, bust, total, zap, waste, bump, kick ass, put down, smack down, shoot down,

tear down, punch out, wipe out, beat up, beat the shit out of, beat the bejejus out of, knock dead, knock out, knock the shit out of, knock the bejejus out of, blast, kill, squash, finish off, blow off, blow away> eg *Byli tak dobrzy, że mogli rzucić na kolana każdą inną drużynę (They were so good that they could kick any other team's ass)*

rzucić Perf rzucać

rzucić się czymś [ZHOO-cheech shyeh CHEEMSH] *v phr* To pass; to hand <hit, kick, toss, throw, drop, duke, shoot, weed, fork over> eg *Rzuć się śrubokrętem, co? (Toss me a screwdriver, will you?)*

rzucić się komuś na mózg See paść komuś na mózg

rzut beretem [zhoot beh-REH-tehm] *adv phr* In the vicinity; very close; nearby <around, pretty near, screwdriver turn away, frog's leap away, whoop, within a hoop and a holler, within a stone's throw, in shouting distance, in spitting distance, around the corner, right next door> eg *Mieszkam o rzut beretem od dworca (I live within a stone's throw from the railroad station)*

rzygać* [ZHI-gahch] (perf **rzygnąć*** [ZHIG-nohnch] or **narzygać*** [nah-ZHI-gahch] or **zarzygać*** [zah-ZHI-gahch] or **zrzygać się*** [ZZHI-gahch shyeh] or **zerzygać się*** [zeh-ZHI-gahch shyeh] or **porzygać się*** [poh-ZHI-gahch shyeh] or **wyrzygać się*** [vi-ZHI-gahch shyeh]) *v* To empty one's stomach; to vomit <barf, puke, blow grits, blow chunks, chuck, do a Technicolor yawn, drive the big bus, heave, pray to the porcelain god, ralph, rolf, talk to the big white phone, cry Ruth, cry Ralph, blow one's cookies, blow one's lunch, lose one's cookies, lose one's lunch, shoot one's cookies, shoot one's lunch> eg *Ktoś zerzygał się na klatce schodowej (Someone tossed his cookies on the staircase)*
See chcieć się rzygać

rzygi* [ZHI-gee] (or **rzygowiny*** [zhi-goh-VEE-ni]) *npl* Vomit <barf, puke> eg *Czy masz rzygi na bucie? (Is that barf on your shoe?)*

rżnąć* [RZHNOHNCH] *v* **1** (perf **zerżnąć*** [ZEHR-zhnohnch] or **wyrżnąć*** [VIR-zhnohnch] or **przerżnąć*** [PSHEHR-zhnohnch]) To copulate with someone <fuck, screw, lay, ball, bang, boink, boff, boogie, bop, frig, hump, poke, shag> eg *Przystojny brunet 40 lat przerżnie fachowo uległą małolatę (A handsome brunet will expertly lay a docile teenager)* **2** To play a game, such as cards <no slang equivalent> eg *W ciągu dnia jest księdzem, a w nocy rżnie w karty (He's a priest during the day; at night he messes around playing cards)*

rżnąć kupę See robić kupę

rżnąć się* [RZHNOHNCH shyeh] *v* To copulate <get screwed, get fucked, get laid, screw, fuck, fork, frig, ball, bang, boink, bonk, boff, hump, poke, shag> eg *Chcesz się rżnąć, to mnie rżnij (You want to fuck, so fuck me); Lubią się rżnąć miejscach publicznych (They like to fuck in public)*

rżnąć w dupę See pierdolić w dupę

S

sałata [sah-WAH-tah] *nf* Money <dough, bread, bank, cabbage, change, coin, folding, green, lettuce> eg *Skądżeś wziął tę sałatę? Obrabowałem bank (Where'd you get all that cabbage? I robbed a bank)*

sadło [SAHD-woh] *nn* A thickness in the waist, overweight <spare tire, love handles, heavy cream, fat city> eg *Muszę się pozbyć tego sadła (I've got to get rid of this spare tire)*
See zaleźć komuś za skórę

saks [SAHKS] *nm* A saxophone <sax> eg *Potrafisz grać na saksie? (Can you play sax?)*

saksy [SAHK-si] *npl* Seasonal work abroad, esp in Germany <no slang equivalent> eg *Pojechał na saksy w zeszłym roku (Last year he went to work in Germany)*

sala See śmiech na sali

salicyl [sah-LEE-tsil] *nm* Salicyl alcohol or any other alcohol not intended for drinking, but consumed by an addict who is in need <no slang equivalent> eg *Wypije nawet dyktę (He will even drink salicyl)*

samiec See **bal samców**

samo życie [SAH-moh ZHI-chyeh] *excl phr* That is the way things happen; such are the buffetings of fate; this is very typical or normal <such is life, that's the way the ball bounces, that's the way the cookie crumbles, that's one all over, that's how the story goes, shit happens> eg *Raz się wygrywa, raz przegrywa. Samo życie! (You win some, you lose some. That's life!)*

samochodziarz [sah-moh-KHOH-jahsh] *nm* A mechanic or an owner of a garage <grease monkey, wrench> eg *Jej ojciec jest samochodziarzem i może to naprawić (Her father is a grease monkey and he can fix it)*

samochwała [sah-moh-KHVAH-wah] *nm* A braggart; a self-aggrandizer <showoff, grandstander, showboater, hotdogger, bullshitter, bullshit artist, blowhard, pitcher, bigmouth, ego-tripper> eg *Z niej jest taka samochwała. Nie mogę jej znieść (She's such a showoff. I can't stand her!)*

samogon [sah-MOH-gohn] *nm* Cheap, inferior, or illicit liquor, esp home-made <moonshine, moonlight, mountain dew, rotgut, swipe, tiger sweat, panther piss, coffin varnish> eg *Ten samogon cię kiedyś zabije (Someday this moonshine's gonna kill you)*

sanitarka [sah-nee-TAHR-kah] *nf* An ambulance <meat wagon, butcher wagon, crash wagon, fruit wagon, band-aid wagon, blood box, bone box> eg *Sanitarka pojawiła się 15 minut później (The meat wagon showed up 15 minutes later)*

SB-ek See esbek

schaboszczak [skhah-BOHSH-chahk] *nm* A pork chop <piggy chops> eg *Nie znoszę schaboszczaków (I hate piggy chops)*

schlać się See upić się jak świnia

schlać się Perf See chlać

schlany [SKHLAH-ni] (or **uchlany** [oo-KHLAH-ni] or **nachlany** [nah-KHLAH-ni] or **zachlany** [zah-KHLAH-ni]) *adj* Drunk; alcohol intoxicated <alkied, bagged, blitzed, blotto, blown away, bent, boiled, bombed, blasted, boozed,

bottled, boxed, buzzed, canned, clobbered, cooked, corked, crashed, drunk as a skunk, edged, embalmed, fractured, fried, gassed, ginned, grogged, have one too many, half under, high, hooched up, in bad shape, impaired, illuminated, juiced, knocked out, liquored, lit, loaded, looped, lubricated, lushed, smashed, oiled, pickled, plastered, plonked, polluted, sauced, shitfaced, slugged, sloshed, soaked, stewed, stiff, stinking drunk, swizzled, tanked, three sheets to the wind, wiped, zonked> eg *Był tak nachlany, że nie wiedział jak się nazywa (He was so clobbered he didin't even know his name)*

sędzia kalosz [SEHN-jah KAH-lohsh] *nm phr* A biased and partial referee or umpire favoring one team <one-sided ref, bum ref, cold deck> eg *Wygrali, bo sędzia był kalosz (They won because of the one-sided ref)*

sekretarka See szparka sekretarka

seksbomba [sehks-BOHM-bah] (or **seksówa** [sehk-SOO-vah]) *nf* A particularly attractive woman, esp one who is sexually attractive <bombshell, chick, broad, gal, pussy, cunt, ass, piece of ass, piece, dish, babe, baby, dame, beauty, beaut, beauty queen, baby doll, doll, dolly, dollface, dreamboat, dream girl, eating stuff, eyeful, flavor, looker, good-looker, head-turner, traffic-stopper, honey, killer, hot number, package, knockout, oomph girl, peach, sex bunny, sex job, sex kitten, sex pot, table grade, ten, bunny, centerfold, cheesecake, date bait, dazzler, heifer, fluff, quail, sis, skirt, tail, job, leg, tart, tomato, pussycat, cooz, twat> eg *Nie mówiłeś mi, że twoja kuzynka to taka seksbomba (You didn't tell me that your cousin is such a sex bunny)*

sęp [SEHMP] *nm* **1** Someone who gets something without intending to repay or return; a parasite <freeloader, moocher, schnorrer, scrounger, sponger, chiseler> eg *Senatorowie to wielkie sępy (Senators are great freeloaders)* **2** A parsimonious person; a miser <tightwad, piker, cheapskate, scrooge, pinchfist, penny-pincher, pinchpenny, nickel-nurser, nickel-squeezer> eg *Nie bądź taki sęp, pożycz mi trochę pieniędzy (Don't be such a pinchfist, loan me some money)*
See na sępa

setka [SEHT-kah] **1***nf* (**seta** [SEH-tah]) A hundred-gram portion of alcohol, esp vodka <no slang equivalent> eg *Daj mi jeszcze jedną setę (Give me another shot)* **2** (or **stówa** [STOO-vah]) *nf* A speed of a 100 kilometers per hour <hundred clicks> eg *Można osiągnąć setkę w dziesięć sekund (You can reach a hundred clicks in ten seconds)* **3** (or **seta** [SEH-tah] or **stówa** [STOO-vah] or **stówka** [STOOF-kah]) *nf* Hundred, esp a hundred zloty bill <century, C, C-note, yard> eg *Podał mi stówę i powiedział, że chcę ją z powrotem w piątek (He handed me a C and said he needed it back on Friday); Pożyczyłem mu dwie stówy (I loaned him two centuries)*

sezon ogórkowy [SEH-zohn oh-goor-KOH-vi] *nm phr* The summer period during the year when most people are on vacation, many offices are closed and not much is going on; summer-time <heat time, heavy heat stretch, strawhat period, silly season, off-season> eg *Nic się nie dzieje w polityce. Sezon ogórkowy! (There's nothing going on in politics. It is the off-season!)*

sfajczyć się Perf fajczyć się

sfajdać się [SFAH-ee-dahch shyeh]) To defecate, esp in panic <crap, drop one's load, dump a load, poop, squat, take a dump, take a crap, shit bullets, shit green, shit one's pants> eg *Był tak przerażony, że się sfajdał (He was so terrified that he took a dump)*

sfiksować Perf fiksować

sflaczeć Perf flaczeć

siła See co siła, nie ma dupy

siąść Perf siadać, wysiadać

siadać [SHYAH-dahch] (perf **siąść** [SHYOHNSHCH]) *v* **1** To decline; to diminish; to deteriorate <go down, go downhill, go down the tube, go to pot, hit the skids, go to the dogs> eg *Sprzedaż nam ostatnio siadła (The sale recently has gone down)* **2** To gradually deteriorate, break down, or cease to function properly <go to hell, crack up, come apart at the seams, go to wrack and ruin, go busted, go down, go kerflooey, belly up, bust down, go off, go on the blink, go on the fritz> eg *Nie możemy grać. Wzmacniacz nam siadł (We can't play. Our amplifier has gone on the fritz*) **3** (Esp about mechanical appliances) To fail or become inoperative <break down, crash, crash and burn, fry, go down, go down in flames, go south, belly up, melt down, shut down, crack up, screw up, fuck up, go blooey, go busted, go on the blink, go on the fritz, go off, go out of whack, go kerflooey> eg *Wszystko szło mi dobrze póki nie siadł faks (Everything was doing fine until the fax crashed)*

siano See mieć pstro w głowie

siara See siki

siatka [SHAHT-kah] (or **siata** [SHAH-tah]) *nf* Volleyball <ball> eg *Zagrajmy w siatę (Let's play ball)*

siedzenie [shyeh-DZEH-nyeh] *nn* The buttocks, the posterior <ass, butt, bum, behind, back, back seat, seat, bottom, heinie, rear, tush, fanny, derriere, tail, bucket, tokus, keister, kazoo> eg *Byłem tak zły, że chciałem go kopnąć w siedzenie, gdy wychodził (I was so angry. I wanted to kick him in the seat as he left)*

siedzieć See mieć na czym siedzieć

siedzieć jak na tureckim kazaniu [SHYEH-yahk nah too-REHTS-keem kah-ZAH-nyoo] *v phr* To sit and listen to something incomprehensible or boring <sit there picking one's ass, sit there picking one's asshole> eg *Wykład był okropny. Przez godzinę siedział jak na tureckim kazaniu (The lecture was terrible. He was sitting there picking his asshole for an hour)*

siedzieć komuś na karku [SHYEH-jehch KOH-moosh nah KAHR-koo] *v phr* To carefully observe or control someone's work or behavior; to be under observation or surveillance <breathe down someone's neck, keep an eye on, eye, eyeball, check, check out, check over, scope, scope out, figure out, track, spy, bug, spot, dig, read, case, beam, lamp, catch, case> eg *Muszę uważać, bo szef siedzi mi na karku (I have to watch out, because the boss is breathing down my neck)*

siedzieć na czymś [SHYEH-jehch nah chimsh] *v phr* To have plenty of something, esp money; to be in a good financial situation <sit on, get hold of, get one's hands on, be rolling in, be sitting pretty> eg *Arabowie siedzą na ropie (The Arabs are siting on a vault of oil); On po prostu siedzi na forsie (He's simply rolling in money)*

siedzieć na drugi rok See zostać na drugi rok

siedzieć na forsie [SHYEH-jehch nah FOHR-shyeh] (or **spać na forsie** [SPAHCH nah FOHR-shyeh]; **pieniadzach** [pyeh-NYOHN-dzahkh] or **szmalu** [SHMAH-loo] may replace **forsie**) *v phr* To be very rich; to have a lot of money <have money to burn, have money to spare, be loaded, be flush, be filthy rich, be

stinking rich, be dirt richy, be lousy rich, be in the bucks, be in the dough, be in the money, be rolling in it, be made of money> eg *Spójrz na niego. Możnaby pomyśleć, że śpi na forsie (Look at him. You'd think he has money to burn)*

siedzieć w czymś [SHYEH-jehch f chimsh] *v phr* To professionally specialize in something; to be an expert in something <be in, be into, go in for, know something inside out> eg *Nie siedzę za bardzo w marketingu, ale coś o tym wiem (I'm not very much into marketing but I know a little bit about it); Siedzi w biznesie monopolowym (He's in the liquor business)*

sięgać do kieliszka See zaglądać do kieliszka

siekać [SHYEH-kahch] (perf **sieknąć** [SHYEHK-nohnch]) *v* (Of consumed alcohol) To have an effect on someone, esp unexpectedly <go to one's head, kick in> eg *Ale ta wódka mnie siekła (Did that vodka go right to my head)*

siekiera [shyeh-KYEH-rah] *nf* A very strong tea or coffee <tar, killer> eg *Co mi zrobiłeś za siekierę! (What a tar you made for me!)*
See można siekierę powiesić

sierściuch [SHEHRSH-chyookh] *nm* A man with much facial hair, esp coming from Southern Europe or the Middle East <hairy ape, bigfoot> eg *Ten sierściuch powinien się ogolić (That hairy ape needs a shave)*

sierota [shyeh-ROH-tah] *nf* A pitiful, clumsy or ineffectual person, esp a bungler <lummox, klutz, screwup, goofup, goof, foozler> eg *Patrz, coś zrobił! Ale z ciebie sierota! Look what you did! You're a real foozler!); Chciał to zrobić, ale taka z niego sierota, że nie sądze, żeby to zrobił (He wanted to do it, but he's such a klutz that I don't think he will)*

sikać* [SHEE-kahch] (perf **nasikać*** [nah-SHEE-kahch] or **wysikać się*** [vi-SHEE-kahch shyeh] or **zsikać się*** [zeh-SHEE-kahch shyeh] or **posikać się*** [poh-SHEE-kahch shyeh]; or **siusiać** [SHYOO-shyahch] perf **nasiusiać** [nah-SHYOO-shyahch]; or **wysiusiać się** [vi-SHYOO-shyahch shyeh] or **posiusiać się** [poh-SHYOO-shahch shyeh]) *v* To urinate <piss, leak, pee, pee-pee, piddle, tinkle, wee-wee, whizz, take a piss, take a leak> eg *Ale chce mi się sikać! (Man, do I need to piss!)*
See lać

siki* [SHEE-kee] (or **siuśki** [SHYOOSH-kee] or **szczochy*** [SHCHOH-khi] or **szczyny*** [SHCHCHI-ni]) *npl* **1** Urine <piss, pee-pee, wee-wee, whizz> eg *Na dywanie są siuśki. Gdzie jest ken kot? (There's piss on the carpet. Where's that cat?)* **2** A diluted tea, coffee or any other liquid <dishwater, bellywash> eg *Oni to nazywają kawą? Ja to nazywam sikami (Do they call it coffee? I call it dishwater)* **3** (or **sikacz*** [SHEE-kahch] *nm* or **siara** [SHYAH-rah] *nf*) Cheap and inferior wine <plonk, red ink, veeno, Mad Dog 20/20, Nighttrain, Wild Irish Rose> eg *Co powiesz na butelkę sikacza? (How about a bottle of plonk?)*

siksa [SHEEK-sah] (or **sziksa**) *nf* A young and unintelligent woman <chick, silly goose> eg *Ta siksa nie ma za grosz rozumu (That chick has no brains)*

siku See robić siku

silny zwarty i gotowy [SHEEL-ni ZWHAR-ti ee goh-TOH-vi] *adj phr* (Of a person) Readily agreeable, esp to copulation <fuckable, hot, nympho, signed sealed delivered, long loose and ready for use> eg *Niech wie, że jestem silny, zwarty i gotowy przez cały czas (She should know that I'm hot all the time)*

siódma woda po kisielu See dziesiąta woda po kisielu

sito [SHEE-toh] *nn* A selection or elimination, esp in a competition <competish, cut-throat competish, rat race, horse race, dog eat dog, do or die, one on one, filter> eg *Zrobili to, żeby przepuścić przez sito najlepszych kandydatów (They were filtering the best candidates)*

sitwa [SHEET-fah] *nf* Worthless, badly-behaved, and often poor people <riff-raff, rabble, mob, gang> eg *Nie lubię tej dzielnicy. Sama tu sitwa (I don't like this neighborhood. It's one big mob)*

siusiać Perf sikać

siusiak [SHYOO-shyahk] (or **siurek*** [SHYOO-rehk]) *nm* The penis, esp small <pecker, peter, peepee, pisser, weenie, peenie, dingus, dingbat, thingy, cock, prick, dick, stick, joystick, dipstick, bone, meat, beef, wang, yang, dong, dummy, hammer, horn, hose, jock, joint, knob, pork, putz, rod, root, tool, flute, skin flute, love-muscle, sausage, schmuck, schlong, schvantz, cream-stick, third leg, middle leg, business, apparatus, John, Johnny, Johnson, John Thomas, Jones> eg *Nie baw się siurkiem (Don't play with you pecker);*

siusiu See robić siku

skład See bez ładu i składu

składak [SKWAH-dahk] *nm* **1** A folding or collapsible bicycle <fold-up bike> eg *Ile chcesz za tego składaka? (How much do you want for this fold-up bike?)* **2** An automobile made from parts <chop-shop car> eg *Ja bym go nie kupował. Od razu widać, że to składak (I wouldn't buy it. You can see at a glance it's a chop-shop car)*

skąpiradło [skohm-pee-RAHD-woh] *nn* A parsimonious person; a miser <tightwad, piker, cheapskate, scrooge, pinchfist, penny-pincher, pinchpenny, nickel-nurser, nickel-squeezer> eg *Jej mąż to prawdziwe skąpiradło (Her husband is a real tightwad)*

skacowany [skah-tsoh-VAH-ni] *adj* Suffering from a hangover <hung, hanging, with morning after, with big head> eg *Wszyscy nauczyciele byli skacowani (All the teachers were hanging)*

skakać koło kogoś See obskakiwać

skanalizowana See wysoko skanalizowana, nisko skanalizowana

skapnąć się Perf kapnąć się

skapować Perf kapować

skapować się Perf kapnąć się

skaptować Perf kaptować

skarpeta See trzymać pieniądze w skarpecie, puścić kogoś z torbami

skasować [skah-SOH-vahch] *v* To destroy or wreck an automobile <total, waste, trash, wipe out, pile up, rack up, crack up, smash up, smack up, stack up> eg *Skasowała wóz zaledwie pięć minut od domu (She totaled the car not five minutes from home)*

skin [skeen] (or **skinhed** [SKEEN-heht]) *nm* A skinhead <skin> eg *Dwóch skinów zostało aresztowanych (Two skins were arrested)*

skipować Perf kipować

sklepowa [skleh-POH-vah] *nf* A female salesclerk <no slang equivalent> eg *Zawołaj sklepową (Get the clerk)*

skleroza [skleh-ROH-zah] *nf* Bad memory, forgetfulness, or absent-mindedness; sclerosis <blackout, blockout, brain fade, blank, memory overload, short circuit, crash, knock-out, pass-out, conk-out, zonk-out, black-out, power outage> eg

Chciała pojechać za granicę bez paszportu. Skleroza! (She wanted to go abroad without a passport. It was a real brain fade!)

sknera [SKNEH-rah] *nf* A parsimonious person; a miser <tightwad, piker, cheapskate, scrooge, pinchfist, penny-pincher, pinchpenny, nickel-nurser, nickel-squeezer> eg *Nie bądź taka sknera, pożycz mi trochę pieniędzy (Don't be such a pinchfist, loan me some money)*

skołować Perf kołować

skołowacieć Perf kołowacieć

skołowany [skoh-woh-VAH-ni] (or **nakręcony** [nah-krehn-TSOH-ni]; **jak ślimak w skorupie** [yahk SHLEE-mahk v skoh-ROO-pyeh] may be added)) *adj* Bewildered, disoriented, or confused <spaced out, mixed up, discombobulated, flabbergasted, messed up, unscrewed, farmisht, balled up, shook up, floored, unglued, unzipped, fried, screwed-up, fucked-up, flummoxed, kerflooey, caught off base> eg *Cały byłem skołowany i nie wiedziałem, co robić (I was all farmisht and didn't know what to do)*

skoczyć See móc komuś skoczyć

skok [skohk] *nm* A robbery <heist, boost, burn, caper, holdup, stickup, knockover, lift, pinch, ripoff, rustle, sting> eg *Kto jest odpowiedzialny za ten skok? (Who is responsible for this stickup?)*

skok w bok [SKOHK v BOHK] *nm phr* An instance of sexual infidelity, esp adultery <fling, affair, little on the side, backdoor activity, extracurricular activity, hanky-panky, cheating, two-timing, playing around> eg *Jesteś poważanym politykiem, więc od dzisiaj żadnych skoków w bok! (You're a respected politician, so from now on no cheating!)*

skombinować Perf kombinować

skonany [skoh-NAH-ni] *adj* Very tired or exhausted <dead, dead on one's feet, dead-tired, dog-tired, out of it, out of gas, out of juice, all in, all shot, pooped, bagged, beat, beat to the ground, beat to the ankles, bone-tired, burned out, bushed, chewed, crapped out, done, done in, dragged out, frazzled, played out, fucked out, knocked out, tuckered out, tapped out, had it, ready to drop, on one's last legs> eg *Ale jestem skonana! Zaraz padnę (Am I dead-tired! I'm gonna drop in a second)*

skopać See dać kopa

skóra [SKOO-rah] *nf* A leather jacket <leather> eg *Fajną masz skórę! (Nice leather you're wearing!)*
See dać po dupie, dobierać się, dostać po dupie, mieć nosa, przetrzepać komuś skórę, własna skóra, wychodzić ze skóry, zaleźć komuś za skórę, zdzierać

skóra i kości See kościotrup

skorupa See skołowany

skowronek See w siódmym niebie

skręcać [SKREHN-tsahch] (or **skręcać się** [SKREHN-tsahch shyeh]) *v* **1** To feel or experience with great intensity, esp to get excited or desirous to do something <get keen on, get sold into, get hooked into, get turned on, get stoked, have the hots for, have hot pants for, have a hard-on for, be crazy about, be nuts about, be stuck on, be sweet on, go for, buy, catch, hook> eg *Jak zobaczyłem tę nową nauczycielkę of wuefu, to natychmiast mnie skręciło mnie (When I saw that new P.T. teacher, I got turned on immediately)* **2** To repel and be strongly disliked <turn off,

gross out, barf out, suck, scuzz one out, give one pain in the ass, make one sick, make one puke, make one barf> eg *Skręca mnie już na widok tego faceta (The very sight of that guy barfs me out)*

skręcać z zazdrości See pękać z zazdrości

skręcać ze śmiechu See pękać ze śmiechu

skręcać ze złości See pękać ze złości

skręt [skrehnt] *nm* A hand-rolled cigarette, esp a marijuana cigarette <roll, joint, reefer, weed, killer, killer stick, tea stick, hemp> eg *Lubię pić piwo i palić skręty (I like to drink beer and smoke joints); Zawsze przed stosunkiem pali skręta (She always smokes a killer stick before intercourse)*

skrewić [SKREH-veech] *v* To fail spectacularly, esp by blundering; to perform very poorly and disgrace oneself <fuck up, screw up, blow, bomb, crash, flop, fold, drop the ball, lose out, strike out, fall flat on one's ass, do an el foldo, lay an egg, lose face, be shot down in flames, go down the tube, step on one's dick> eg *Aleśmy wczoraj skrewili na meczu! (Did we really blew the game yesterday!)*

skrobać* [SKROH-bahch] (perf **wyskrobać*** [vi-SKROH-bahch]) *v* To perform abortion <pull the rabbit, kill the rabbit, scrape> eg *Wyskrobał dziś dwie kobiety. Obie miały już po pięcioro dzieci (He scraped two women today. Both already had five children)*

skrobanka* [skroh-BAHN-kah] *nf* Abortion <pulling the rabbit, killing the rabbit, scaping> eg *Skrobanka jest niedopuszczalna dla katolików (Killing the rabit is intolerable for catholics)*

skuć się See upić się jak świnia

skubaniec [skoo-BAH-nyehts] (or **skurczybyk** [skoor-CHI-bik] or **skurczysyn** [skoor-CHI-sin]) *nm* A despicable or admirable person <son of a gun> eg *Jak on to zrobił? Skubaniec! (How did he do that? Son of a gun!)*

skumać Perf kumać

skumać się Perf kumać się

skurwić się Perf kurwić się

skurwysyn** [skoor-VI-sin] (or **skurwiel**** [SKOOR-vyehl] or **sukinsyn**** [soo-KEEN-sin] or **sukinkot** [soo-KEEN-koht]) *nm* A man one dislikes or disapproves of <SOB, son of a bitch, son of a whore, asshole, fuck, fucker, fuckhead, fuckface, motherfucker, shit, shitface, shithead, shitheel, bastard, jerk, cocksucker, prick, dick, dickhead, cuntface, schmuck, scum, scumbag, sleazebag, slimebag, dipshit, pisshead, piece of shit, pain in the ass> eg *Ten skurwysyn nie zapłacił mi ani grosza (That son of a bitch didn't pay me a red cent)*
See jak chuj, od cholery

skurwysyński** [skoor-vi-SIÑ-skee] *adj* Cursed; damnable; bad <damn, damned, goddamn, goddamned, god-awful, blasted, darn, darned, effing, flipping, forking, freaking, frigging, pesky> eg *Ten skurwysyński klucz nie pasuje (This goddamn key doesn't fit in)*

skuty [SKOO-ti] *adj* Completely drunk <alkied, bagged, blitzed, blotto, blown away, bent, boiled, bombed, blasted, boozed, bottled, boxed, buzzed, canned, clobbered, cooked, corked, crashed, drunk as a skunk, edged, embalmed, fractured, fried, gassed, ginned, grogged, have one too many, half under, high, hooched up, in bad shape, impaired, illuminated, juiced, knocked out, liquored, lit, loaded, looped, lubricated, lushed, smashed, oiled, pickled, plastered,

plonked, polluted, sauced, shitfaced, slugged, sloshed, soaked, stewed, stiff, stinking drunk, swizzled, tanked, three sheets to the wind, wiped, zonked, lit up like a Christmas tree> eg *Nie zrobi tego. Patrz, jest skuty (He's not going to do it. Look, he's bottled)*
See pijany jak świnia

słabeusz [swah-BEH-oosh] *nm* A soft, apathetic, sluggish or ineffectual person; a weakling <wimp, wuss, pussy, big baby, candy ass, milktoast, milquetoast, featherweight, gutless wonder, limp-dick, pantywaist, hard-off> eg *Czy na prawdę myślisz, że mogłabym pójść na randkę z twoim bratem? On to taki słabeusz (Do you really think I could go out on a date with your brother? He's a wimp)*

słabizna [swah-BEEZ-nah] *nf* Something or someone that is worthless, useless, inadequate, or too weak <schlock, dreck, garbage, junk, lemon, crap, piece of crap, shit, piece of shit, dogshit, sleaze> eg *Pierwszy model jest w porządku, ale następne to słabizna (The first model is okay, but the next ones are shlock)*

słodka idiotka [SWOHT-kah eed-YOHT-kah] *nf phr iron* A naive or stupid but highly amorous woman <bimbo, bimbette, dumb blonde, floozy> eg *Ożenił się z jakąś słodką idiotką (He married some bimbo)*

słodkości [swoht-KOHSH-chee] *npl* Candy <sweets, pogie, pogey, jawbreakers> eg *Co to za słodkości? (What are these sweets?)*

słomiana wdowa [swoh-MYAH-nah VDOH-vah] *nf phr* A divorced woman <dumpee, grass widow, ex> eg *Wszyscy wiedzą, że to słomiana wdowa (Everybody knows that he's a grass widow)*

słomiany wdowiec [swoh-MYAH-ni VDOH-vyehts] *nm phr* A divorced man <dumpee, grass widower, ex> eg *Jej brat to słowmiany wdowiec (Her brother is a dumpee)*

słońce See jasne, rzucać się z motyką na słońce

słowo See **ani pisnąć**

sługus [SWOO-goos] *nm* A man who could do everything for others in order to gain personal advantage; an overly eager or servile man <brown-noser, ass-kisser, ass-licker, ass-sucker, ass-wiper, back-scratcher, apple-polisher, tokus-licker, kiss-ass, yes-man> eg *Ten sługus dostał lepsze stanowisko niż reszta (That ass-licker got a better position than others)*

słup See jak groch o ścianę, postawić oczy w słup

słupki [SWOOP-kee] *npl* Mathematics, esp as a subject in school <math> eg *Nigdy nie lubiłem słupków (I never liked math)*

smark [SMAHRK] *nm* A blob of nasal mucus <snot, booger, boogie, nose-lunger, skeet> eg *Na twoim łóżku jest smark (There's snot on your bed)*

smarkać [SMAHR-kahch] (perf **smarknąć** [SMAHRK-nohnch] or **wysmarkać się** [vi-SMAHR-kahch shyeh] or **nasmarkać** [nah-SMAHR-kahch]) *v* Blow one's nose, esp by pinching one nostril and using no tissue <skeet shoot> eg *(Nie ma nic bardziej obrzydliwego niż zgraja smarkających facetów) There's nothing more disgusting than a bunch of fellas skeet shooting)*

smarkacz* [SMAHR-kahch] (or **smark*** [smahrk]) *nm* A teenage boy, esp whom one despises <chick, chicklet, babe, teen, teener, teeny-bopper, bubble-gummer, youngster, juvie, shithead, punk, snot-nose> eg *Kopnął smarkacza w tyłek (He kicked the punk in his ass)*

smarkula* [smahr-KOO-lah] *nf* A teenage girl, esp whom one despises <chick, chicklet, teen, teener, teeny-bopper, bubble-gummer, youngster, juvie, shithead, punk, snot-nose> eg *Zaprosił jakieś smarkule na imprezę i nie wie teraz co zrobić (He invited some shitheads to the party and now he doesn't know what to do)*

smród [smroot] (or **smrodek** [SMROH-dehk]) *nm* **1** An unpleasant, unfriendly, or scandalous atmosphere around someone or something; a scandal <gas, hot potato, bad scene, bad news, can of worms, bag of worms, takedown, putdown, shit, serious shit, deep shit, deep water, drag, bind, bitch, bummer, downer, headache, double trouble, snafu, pain in the ass, pain in the neck, spot, mess, holy mess, pickle, squeeze, hard time, glitch, stinker, skeleton, skeleton in the closet, sizzler, scorcher, dynamite, Watergate, fine kettle of fish, fine how do you do, fine cup of coffee, big stink, curtains, lights out, game's over> eg *Jak mnie złapią, to będzie smród (Bad scene for me if they find me)* **2** A release of intestinal gas, perhaps with a noise <fart, cheese, ass noise> eg *Kto puścił tego smrodka? (Who cut that fart?)* See ciągnąć się

smrodzić [SMROH-jeech] (perf **nasmrodzić** [nah-SMROH-jeech] or **zasmrodzić** [zah-SMROH-jeech]) *v* **1** To release intestinal gas, perhaps with a noise <fart, cut a fart, lay a fart, blow a fart, let a fart, cut the cheese, backfire, break wind, pollute the air> eg *Najedli się fasoli i nasmrodzili jak cholera (They ate beans and farted like hell)* **2** (Esp about a factory) To pollute or contaminate by emission of smoke <smoke up, stink up, smog, chimney> eg *Zakład przestał w końcu smrodzić (The factory finally stopped smoking up)*

smutas [SMOO-tahs] *nm* A morose, melancholic, or pessimistic person <killjoy, party-pooper, wet blanket, sourpuss, sourball, drag, turn-off, grinch, crape-hanger, gloomy Gus> eg *Nie bądź taki smutas! Zabaw się trochę! (Don't be such a wet blanket! Have some fun!)*

smykałka [smi-KAH-oo-kah] *nf* A natural tendency or special natural skill <bent, knack, hang, feel, what it takes> eg *Zawsze miała smykałkę do ikebany (She's always had a knack for ikebana)*

socjal [SOHTS-yahl] *nn* Unemployment compensation <comp> eg *Jestem na socjalu (I'm on comp); Facet żyje z socjalu (The fella's getting comp)*

sodówka See palma komuś odbiła

Sojuz [SOH-yoos] *nm* The former Soviet Union, sometimes the present-day Russia <iron curtain, Russky, reds> eg *To znany uchodźca polityczny. Właśnie uciekł z Sojuza (He's a well-known political refugee. He just escaped from behind the iron curtain)*

sól See zjeść z kimś beczkę soli

solidaruch* [soh-lee-DAH-rookh] *nm* A member of Solidarity, a Polish Trade Union <no slang equivalent> eg *Solidaruchy były bardzo niezadowolone (Solidarity members were very dissatisfied)*

sort [sohrt] *nm* A sort or kind; quality <class, make, brand, lot, batch, stock> eg *Te są lepszego sortu (These are of a better lot)*

sos See nie w sosie

spłukać się [SPWOO-kahch] *v* To lose all one's money <go broke, lose out, blow, drop a bundle, go to the cleaners, take a bath, tap out, wash out, belly up, go bust, take a beating> eg *Jestem kompletnie spłukany (I'm dead broke)*

spłukany [spwoo-KAH-ni] *adj* Completely penniless; destitute <broke, dead broke, flat broke, stone broke, busted, cleaned out, cold in hand, down and out, piss-

poor, poor as a church mouse, strapped, tapped out, drained, without a red cent> eg *Nie mogę iść z wami. Jestem spłukany (I can't go with you. I'm broke)*

spać jak zabity [spahch yahk zah-BEE-ti] (or **spać jak zarżnięty** [spahch yahk zahr-ZHNYEHN-ti]) *v phr* To sleep deeply, esp without moving <sleep like a log, sleep fast> eg *Nic nie jest w stanie mnie obudzić. Zwykle śpię jak zabity (Nothing can wake me up. I usually sleep like a log)*

spać na forsie See siedzieć na forsie

spać z kimś [SPAHCH s keemsh] (perf **przespać się** [PSHEH-spahch shyeh]) *v* To copulate with someone <sleep with, spend a night with, do someone> eg *Czy ona się z nim przespała? A co ci do tego? (Did she sleep with him? What's it to you?)*

spadać [SPAH-dahch] *v* (Esp in the imperative as a brusque command) To leave or depart, esp hastily <split, beat it, ankle, bag ass, blow, breeze off, burn rubber, butt out, buzz off, check out, cruise, cut and run, cut ass, cut out, drag ass, dust, ease out, fade, fade away, fade out, fuck off, get the fuck out, get the hell out , get going, get moving, get lost, get off the dime, get on one's horse, go south, haul ass, hightail, hit the bricks, hit the road, hop it, make tracks, pull out, scram, set sail, shove off, shuffle along, skate, skip out, split the scene, take off> eg *Spadaj, ty gnojku (Beat it, you little punk)*

spadochroniarz [spah-doh-KHROH-nyahsh] *nm* A student who repeats the grade or year <flunky, dropout> eg *W naszej klasie jest dwóch spadochroniarzy (We have two flunkies in our class)*

spanikować Perf panikować

spaślak [SPAHSH-lahk] *nm* An obese person <fatty, fatso, blimp, fat-ass, lard-ass, tub of lard, crisco> eg *Ten spaślak beka ledwo mieści się w drzwiach (That tub of lard can hardly get through the door)*

spasować [spah-SOH-vahch] *v* To give up or to give in; to resign, surrender, or abandon <drop, pull out, bail out, bow out, walk out, check out, drop out, cop out, butt out, push out, snake out, fase out, pass up, pass on, throw in the towel, throw in the sponge, toss in the sponge, toss in the towel, cry uncle, say uncle, toss it in, pack it in, cave in, buckle under, back down, fold, duck, slide, walk, leg, ditch, dump, kick off, knock off, take a walk, quit cold turkey, sideline, call it a day> eg *Zważywszy na okoliczności, będziemy musieli spasować (Under the circumstances we'll have to drop out)*

spatku [SPAHT-koo] *phr* Sleep <beddy-bye, nighty-night, snooze, catnap, forty winks, winks, shut-eye, nod, sack time, sack duty, blanket drill, bunk fatigue, Z's, zizz> eg *Pora na spatku (It's time for beddy-bye)*

spec [spehts] (or **szpec** [shpehts]) *nm* A specialist or an expert; a professional <pro, ace, whiz, whiz-kid, wiz, maven, mavin, guru> eg *Słyszałem, że twój brat to prawdziwy spec w tych sprawach (I heard your brother is a real pro in these matters)*

spęd [spehnt] *nm* A mass meeting or a rally, esp if forced <meet, get-together, huddle> eg *Nie chciał iść na ten spęd (He didn't want to go into this huddle)*

speluna [speh-LOO-nah] (or **spelunka** [speh-LOON-kah]) *nf* A cheap and disreputable saloon <joint, dive, gin dive, gin joint, gargle factory, groggery, guzzlery, watering hole, hellhole, fillmill, hideaway, speakeasy> eg *Spędza wiele czasu w tej spelunie (He spends a lot of time at that gin palace)*

speniać Perf peniać

spiąć się Perf spinać się

spić See spijać

spić się See upić się jak świnia

spienić się Perf pienić się

spierdalać** [spyehr-DAH-lahch] (perf **spierdolić**** [spyehr-DOH-leech]; or **spieprzać*** [SPYEHP-shahch] perf **spieprzyć*** [SPYEHP-shich]; or **spierniczać*** [spyehr-NEE-chahch] perf **spierniczyć*** [spyehr-NEE-chich]; or **spierdzielać** [spyehr-JEH-lahch] perf **spierdzielić*** [spyehr-JEH-leech]) *v* To leave, depart, or desert, esp hastily <fuck off, get the fuck out, split, beat it, ankle, bag ass, blow, breeze off, burn rubber, butt out, buzz off, check out, cruise, cut and run, cut ass, cut out, drag ass, dust, ease out, fade, fade away, fade out, get the hell out , get going, get moving, get lost, get off the dime, get on one's horse, go south, haul ass, hightail, hit the bricks, hit the road, hop it, make tracks, pull out, scram, set sail, shove off, shuffle along, skate, skip out, split the scene, take off> eg *Spierdalaj z mojego domu! (Get the fuck out of my house!); Spierdolił do Stanów (He pulled out to the States)*

spierdolić** [spyehr-DOH-leech] *v* To destroy or wreck something; to fail <fuck up, screw up, waste, ruin, blow, crash> eg *Spierdolił całe przedstawienie (He fucked up the entire show)*

spierdolić się** [spyehr-DOH-leech shyeh] (or **spieprzyć się**** [SPYEHP-shich shyeh] or **spierniczyć się*** [spyehr-NEE-chich shyeh] or **spierdzielić się*** [spyehr-JEH-leech shyeh]) **1** *v* To fail or become inoperative; to fall into destruction <fuck up, screw up, get fucked up, get screwed up, break down, crash, crash and burn, fry, go down, go down in flames, go south, belly up, melt down, shut down, crack up, go blooey, go busted, go on the blink, go on the fritz, go off, go out of whack, go kerflooey> eg *Wiedziałem, że silnik się spierdoli (I knew that the engine would fuck up)* **2** To fall from something <come crashing down, kiss the ground, kiss the floor, get acquainted with the pavement, take a dive> eg *Spierdolił się na ziemię (He kissed the ground)*

spietrać się Perf pietrać się

spijać [SPEE-yahch] (perf **spić** [speech]) *v* To make someone drunk <get someone alkied, get someone bagged, get someone blitzed, get someone blotto, get someone blown away, get someone bent, get someone boiled, get someone bombed, get someone boozed up, get someone blasted, get someone bottled, get someone boxed, get someone canned, get someone clobbered, get someone cooked, get someone corked, get someone drunk as a skunk, get someone edged, get someone embalmed, get someone fractured, get someone fried, get someone gassed, get someone ginned, get someone grogged, get someone high, get someone hooched up, get someone impaired, get someone illuminated, get someone juiced, get someone liquored up, get someone lit, get someone loaded, get someone looped, get someone lubricated, get someone smashed, get someone oiled, get someone pickled, get someone plastered, get someone plonked, get someone polluted, get someone sauced, get someone shitfaced, get someone sloshed, get someone soaked, get someone stewed, get someone stiff, get someone stinking drunk, get someone swizzled, get someone tanked up, get someone wiped, get someone zonked, get someone fucked up> eg *Zabrali go do miasta i spili (They took him downtown and got him zonked)*

spiknąć [SPEEK-nohnch] *v* To arrange a meeting with two or more people, esp with amorous or sexual reference; to contact <fix someone up with, set someone up with> eg *Spróbuję Cię jakoś z nią spiknąć (I'll try to fix you up with her somehow)*

spiknąć się [SPEEK-nohnch shyeh] *v* To meet or contact with one another <get together, bump into, run into, meet up, rub elbows, bunch up> eg *Spiknijmy się w przyszłym tygodniu (Let's get together next week)*

spinać się See sprężać się

spity See pijany jak świnia

spity [SPEE-ti] (or **napity** [nah-PEE-ti] or **podpity** [poht-PEE-ti] or **zapity** [zah-PEE-ti]) *adj* Drunk <alkied, bagged, blitzed, blotto, blown away, bent, boiled, bombed, blasted, boozed, bottled, boxed, buzzed, canned, clobbered, cooked, corked, crashed, drunk as a skunk, edged, embalmed, fractured, fried, gassed, ginned, grogged, have one too many, half under, high, hooched up, in bad shape, impaired, illuminated, juiced, knocked out, liquored, lit, loaded, looped, lubricated, lushed, smashed, oiled, pickled, plastered, plonked, polluted, sauced, shitfaced, slugged, sloshed, soaked, stewed, stiff, stinking drunk, swizzled, tanked, three sheets to the wind, wiped, zonked> eg *Nie lubię, gdy jesteś spity (I don't like it when you're loaded); Była już napita i chciała iść do domu (She was already sauced and she wanted to go home); O czwartej nad ranem zadzwonił sąsiad. Podpity (At four in the morning a neighbor called. He was lushed)*

splajtować Perf plajtować

spluwa [SPLOO-vah] (or **spluwaczka** [sploo-VAHCH-kah]) *nf* A pistol or rifle <blaster, gat, piece, iron, rod, heater, snubby, popper, tool, stick, boomstick, firestick, hardware, speaker, difference, persuader, convincer, equalizer, artillery, cannon, Saturday night special> eg *Nic nie mogłem zrobić. Miał spluwę (I couldn't do anything. He had a blaster)*

spod igły [spohd EEG-wi] *adj phr* New <newie, brand new, spanking new, fire new, cherry, hot off the fire, hot off the press, up to the minute> eg *To nowy model, prosto spod igły (It's a new model, spanking new)*

spódniczka [spood-NEECH-kah] *nf* A young and attractive woman <chick, broad, gal, pussy, cunt, ass, piece of ass, piece, dish, babe, baby, dame, beauty, beaut, beauty queen, baby doll, doll, dolly, dollface, dreamboat, dream girl, eating stuff, eyeful, flavor, looker, good-looker, head-turner, traffic-stopper, honey, killer, hot number, package, knockout, oomph girl, peach, bombshell, sex bunny, sex job, sex kitten, sex pot, table grade, ten, bunny, centerfold, cheesecake, date bait, dazzler, heifer, fluff, quail, sis, skirt, tail, job, leg, tart, tomato, pussycat, cooz, twat> eg *Gdzie twój brat? Ugania się za spódniczkami (Where's your brother? He's been chasing some skirts)*

spodnie See robić w gacie

spoko [SPOH-koh] (or **spokojna głowa** [spoh-KOH-ee-nah GWOH-vah]) *excl phr* An exclamation telling someone not to worry, relax, and calm oneself <take it easy, hang it easy, go easy, hang loose, lay back, cool out, cool it, keep it cool, play it cool, give it a rest, don't sweat it, mellow out, lighten up, hold one's horses, keep one's shirt on> eg *Spokojna głowa. Test jest dopiero jutro (Hey, take it easy. The test's only tomorrow)*

See dać sobie na luz

spokój See dać komuś święty spokój

spóźnialski [spoozh-NYAHL-skee] *nm* A man who is tardy to work or school, esp chronically <late-commer, Johnny-come-lately> eg *Mamy tu dwóch spóźnialskich (We've got here two late-comers)*

sprać kogoś na kwaśne jabłko See zbić kogoś na kwaśne jabłko

sprawa See nie ma sprawy, stawiać sprawę na głowie, te klocki

sprężać się [SPREHN-zhahch shyeh] (perf **sprężyć się** [SPREHN-zhich shyeh]; or **spinać się** [SPEE-nahch shyeh] perf **spiąć się** [SPYOHNCH shyeh]) *v* To concentrate all one's efforts, esp in terms of efficiency and speed; to energetically get into action; to accelerate or hurry <set about, go about, get down to, get down to business, get one's ass in gear, snap it up, snap to it, make it snappy, step on it, get the lead out, get a hump on, get a hustle on, get a move on, get one's ass, get cracking, get going, get one's finger out of one's asshole, get off one's ass, get it on, get off the dime, hop to it, hump, hustle, pour it on, pour on the coal, shake a leg, shake the lead out, gas up, goose up, hop up, jump up, pump up, rev up, buckle down> eg *Jeśli się sprężymy, to nam się uda (If we make it snappy, we can still make it); Był naprawdę leniwym studentem, ale przed egzaminem się spiął i zdał na piątkę (He was a real lazy student, but before the exam he'd buckled down and scored an A)*

sprężynowiec [sprtehn-zhi-NOH-vyehts] *nm* A knife with a blade that springs out when a switch is pressed, considered as a weapon <blade, switch, switchblade, shiv, stick, ripper, steel, shank, Harlem toothpick, frog sticker> eg *Nic nie mogłem zrobić. Miał sprężynowca (I couldn't do anything. He had a switchblade)*

spryciara [spri-CHYAH-rah] (or **spryciula** [spri-CHYOO-lah]) *nf* A smart or clever woman <smartass, wiseass, sharpie, shark, smoothie, cutie, fly> eg *Czego chciała ta spryciara? (What did this wiseass want?)*

spryciarz [SPRI-chyahsh] *nm* A smart or clever man <smartass, wiseass, sharpie, shark, smoothie, cutie, fly> eg *Ten spryciarz zażądał dwóch tysięcy. Gotówką! (That smartass wanted two thousand. In cash!)*

sprzątać [SPSHOHN-tahch] (perf **sprzątnąć** [SPSHOHNT-nohnch]) *v* To eat everything <eat up, kill> eg *Sprzątnął całego kurczaka w try miga (He killed the whole chicken in no time at all)*

sprzątnąć See sprzątać

sprzątnąć komuś coś sprzed nosa [SPSHOHNTnohnch KOHmoosh TSOHSH SPSHEHT NOHsah] (or **zdmuchnąć komuś coś sprzed nosa** [ZDMOOKHnohnch KOHmoosh TSOHSH SPSHEHT NOHsah]) *v phr* To miss an opportunity <snatch, snatch something from under someone's nose> eg *Była pierwsza i zdmuchnęła mi medal sprzed nosa (She was first and she snatched the medal from under my nose)*

spuścić wpierdol See dać wpierdol

spust See mieć spust

spuszczać [SPOOSH-chahch] (perf **spuścić** [SPOOSH-cheech]) *v* To lower the price of something <knock off, knock down, take off> eg *Kierownik sklepu spuścił z ceny płaszcza o 30 procent (The store manager knocked 30 percent off the price of the coat); Cenę spuszczono do dwóch setek (The price was knocked down to two hundred)*

spuszczać się* [SPOOSH-chach shyeh] (perf **spuścić się*** [SPOOSH-cheech shyeh]) *v* To ejaculate <come, cum, come off, blow, shoot, shoot off, shoot one's wad, cream, cream one's jeans, go off, get off, get one's rocks off, get one's nuts

off, drop one's load, explode> eg *Spuszcza się bardzo szybko, ale ma ładny uśmiech (He comes real fast, but he has a nice smile)*

spytki See brać kogoś na języki

srać* [SRAHCH] (perf **nasrać*** [NAH-srahch] or **wysrać się*** [VI-srahch shyeh] or **zesrać się*** [ZEH-srahch shyeh]) *v* To defecate, esp in panic <shit, take a shit, crap, take a crap> eg *Chce mi się srać (I feel like I need to take a shit)*

sracz* [srahch] (or **srocz*** [srohch]) *nm* A restroom or bathroom; a toilet <john, johnny, can, crapper, potty, shitcan, shitter, shithouse, throne> eg *Gdzie jest twój kuzyn? Rzyga w sraczu (Where's your cousin? He's puking in the john)*

sraczka* [SRAHCH-kah] *nf* Diarrhea; loose bowels <shits, craps, runs, trots, turistas, GIs, GI shits, gypsy tummy, quickstep, Aztec two-step, Montezuma's revenge, Basra belly, Delhi belly, Hong Kong dog, Johnny Trots, Hershey highway> eg *Nikt jeszcze nie umarł od sraczki. No, przynajmniej nie natychmiast (Nobody ever died of the turistas, right away, anyway)*

sraka* [SRAH-kah] *nf* Feces, excrement <shit, piece of shit, crock of shit, shitstick, crap, squat, dump, turd> eg *Masz srakę na bucie (You have some shit on your shoe)*

sramta-ramta* [SRAHM-tah RAHM-tah] (or **srata-tata*** [SRAH-tah TAH-tah]) **1** *nn phr* Trivial, platitudinous or deceitful talk; nonsense <talking-shmalking, small talk, bull, bullshit, bullshine, BS, bunk, baloney, applesauce, eyewash, hogwash, hot air, crock, crock of shit, piece of shit, pile of shit, shit, dogshit, horseshit, shit for the birds, crap, crapola, poppycock, smoke, hokum, garbage, trash, horsefeathers, smoke, all that jazz, jazz, jive, malarkey, gobbledygook, double-talk, bafflegab, blah-blah, phony-baloney, fiddle-faddle, twiddle-twaddle, mumbo-jumbo, yackety-yack> eg *Mam dość tego jej sramta-ramta (I'm sick of her horseshit)* **2** *excl phr* An exclamation of incredulity or disbelief <in a pig's eye, in a pig's ass, in a pig's ear, like hell, like fun, like shit, my ass, there's no way, someone will be damned if, someone will be fucked if, says you> eg *Powiedział, że nam pomoże. Sramta-ramta, akurat nam pomoże! (He said he'd help us. My ass! Like hell he would help us!)*

srata-tata See sramta-ramta

srocz See sracz

stłuczka [STWOOCH-kah] *nf* A minor car accident or a result of this <fender-bender, sideswipe, rear-ender, bump> eg *Od czasu, gdy go kupiłem, miałem tylko jedną stłuczkę (I've only had one fender-bender since I got it)*

stać* [stahch] *v* **1** (perf **stanąć*** [STAH-nohnch]) To have a penile erection <have a hard-on, have a boner, have a bone-on, have a rod-on, have a stander, have a woody, have a stiffy, have it up> eg *Znów mi stanął (I got a hard on again)* **2** To have a particular price at a given moment <go for> eg *Po ile stoi złoto? (How much is gold going for?)*

See język komuś kołkiem staje, taki że mózg staje

stać na bramce [stahch nah BRAHM-tseh] (or **być na bramce** [bich nah BRAHM-tseh]) *nf* To be employed to eject unwanted customers from a saloon or restaurant <be a bouncer, bounce> eg *Kto tutaj stoi na bramce? (Who's the bouncer here?); Stoi na bramce w klubie (He bounces at the club)*

stać nad grobem [stahch nahd GROH-behm] *v phr* To be nearly dead <be one foot in the grave, have one foot in the grave, be a goner, be on one's deathbed>

eg *Nie zostanie prezydentem. Stoi nad grobem (He won't become a president. He's one foot in the grave)*

stać pod latarnią [stahch pohd lah-TAHR-nyoh] *v phr* To work as a prostitute, esp operating on the street <hustle, hook, turn tricks, peddle ass, street-walk, work the street, go whoring, whore oneself> eg *Nie mam zamiaru iść stać pod latarnię (I'm not about to go whoring)*

stać przy garach [stahch pshi GAH-rahkh] *v phr* (Esp about women) To do the household work, esp cooking <do the chores, be a pot queen, do the chickwork, do the daily grind> eg *Nie mam zamiaru stać przy garach do końca życia (I'm not about to do the daily grind till the end of my life)*

stacyjka [stah-TSI-ee-kah] *nf* Ignition <igniter> eg *Jest taki głupi, że nawet nie wie, gdzie jest stacyjka (He's so dumb he doesn't even know where the igniter is)*

stanąć See stać

Stany [STAH-ni] *npl* United States of America <US of A, States, stateside, mainland> eg *Przyjechał do stanów jakieś dziesięćlat temu (He came to the States about ten years ago)*

stara [STAH-rah] *nf* **1** (or **staruszka** [stah-ROOSH-kah]) A mother <mama, ma, mom, moms, mommy, motherkin, old lady, old woman, warden> eg *Moja stara kazała mi zostać w domu (My old lady told me to stay home); Moja staruszka jest bardzo wredną kobietą (My old lady is a very mean woman)* **2** A wife <wifey, mama, missus, better half, old lady, little woman, ball and chain, trouble and strife, significant other> eg *Poszedł spytać się swojej starej (He went to ask his old woman)*

stara bida See bida

stara gwardia See gwardia

stara śpiewka [STAH-rah SHPYEHF-kah] *nf* Platitudinous talk <old song, same old song, old story, same old story, old tune, same old tune, familiar tune, same old shit, SOS> eg *Powiedział, że odda w przyszłym tygodniu. To jego stara śpiewka (He said he'd give it back next week. That's his old song)*

stara rura See rura

stare śmieci [STAH-reh SMYEH-chee] *npl phr* A place where one has lived for a long time <old stomping ground, old neighborhood> eg *Po tak długim okresie nieobecności wrócił na stare śmieci (After being away for such a long time, he's back in the old stomping ground)*

stare pudło See pudło

starsi See starzy

starszy See jak ze starszego brata

startować [stahr-TOH-vahch] (perf **wystartować** [vi-stahr-TOH-vahch] or **zastartować** [zah-stahr-TOH-vahch]) *v* To invite or request sexual favors <make a pass, put a move on, make a play for> eg *Startowała do niego, ale nie był zainteresowany (She mage a pass at him but he wasn't interested); Pedał startował do mnie, więc go rąbnąłem w gębę (The faggot made a pass at me, so I punched him on his mask)*

staruszek See stary

staruszka See stara

staruszkowie See starzy

stary [STAH-ri] *nm* **1** (**staruszek** [stah-ROO-shehk]) A father <dad, daddy, pa, papa, pop, pops, guv, gaffer, padre, warden, old man> eg *Stary nie dał mi ani grosza*

(The old man didn't give me a red cent) **2** A husband <hubby, man of the house, mister, old man, worser half> eg *Co na to powiedział jej stary? (What did her old man say to this?)* **3** One's male superviser or director <boss, chief, big boy, big cheese, big enchilada, top brass, honcho, big man, man upstairs, top dog, key player, exec, numero uno> eg *Co powiedział stary? (What did the big boy say?)*
See po staremu, bida, grzyb, gwardia, pierdoła, pudło, zgred

stary grzyb See grzyb

stary pierdziel See pierdoła

stary piernik See pierdoła

stary pryk See pierdoła

stary trep See trep

stary wyga [STAH-ri VI-gah] (or **stary wyjadacz** [STAH-ri vi-YAH-dahch]) *nm phr* A person experienced at doing something <old hand, old customer, pro, vet> eg *Poradzi sobie z tym. To stary wyjadacz (He'll manage it. He's an old hand)*

stary zgred See zgred

starzy [STAH-zhi] (or **staruszkowie** [stah-roosh-KOH-vyeh] or **starsi** [STAHR-shee]) *npl* Parents <rents, fossils, folks, old folks, old man and old lady> eg *Muszę iść spytać starych (I've got to go and ask the rents)*

stawać na głowie [STAH-vahch nah GWOH-vyeh] (or **stawać na rzęsach** [STAH-vahch nah ZHEHN-sahkh] or **chodzić na rzęsach** [KHOH-jeech nah ZHEHN-sahkh]) *v phr* To strive; to make one's best effort; to strenously attempt to get or do something <bust one's ass, bust a gut, bust one's balls, break one's ass, break one's neck, work one's ass off, do one's damnednest, give it one's all, give it one's best, go all out, go for broke, go all the way, go for it, go the extra mile, go the full yard, go the limit, go the whole nine yards, go to the wall, make a full-court press, put one's back into, hassle, sweat, dig, plug, break one's ass, bend over backward, pour it on, knock oneself out, bear down, scramble for, go after, push for, shoot for, shoot the works, spread oneself, pull oneself together, push hard> eg *On jest jednym z tych facetów, którzy staną na głowie, żeby pomóc przyjacielowi (He's one of those guys who will bust their asses to help a friend)*

stawiać [STAH-vyahch] (perf **postawić** [poh-STAH-veech]) *v* (To ask someone out and) *v* To pay the cost of something, esp of a drink; to treat someone to something <stand, buy, pop for, spring for, be on one, someone will get it, pick up the check, pick up the tab> eg *Nie denerwuj się. Postawię ci drinka (Don't worry. Let me buy you a drink)*

stawiać laskę See robić laskę

stawiać się [STAH-vyahch shyeh] (perf **postawić się** [poh-STAH-veech shyeh]) *v* To insolently defy, challenge, or oppose <defi, face off, face down, fly in the face, fly in the teeth, meet eyeball to eyeball, make my day, hang tough, hang in there, take one on, stick fast, stick it out, kick over traces, lip, brace, cross, put one's life on the line, stand up to, knock the chip off one's shoulder, step over the line, tangle, bump heads with, cross, square off, put down, have a bone to pick, hold no brief for, put up a fight, mess with, mess around with, fool with, fool around with, fuck with, fuck around with, screw with, screw around with, dick with, dick around with, diddle with, diddle around with, fiddle with, fiddle around with, fart with, fart around with, monkey with, monkey around with> eg

Miałem ze soba pistolet, więc żaden z nich się nie stawiał (I had a gun on me, so none of them dared to fuck with me)

stawiać sprawę na głowie [STAH-vyahch SPRAH-veh nah GWOH-vyeh] *v phr* To have things in the wrong order; to have things confused and mixed up <put the cart before the horse> eg *Zwolnij trochę i uporządkuj wszystko. Nie stawiaj sprawy na głowie! (Slow down and get organized! Don't put the cart before the horse!)*

stół See iść pod nóż

stołek [STOH-wehk] *nm* A job, position, or post, esp lucrative <seat, hot seat, top of the ladder> eg *Wszyscy zaczęli walczyć o ten wysoki stołek (Everybody started to fight to get the hot seat)*

stodoła See narąbany

stojak See na stojaka

stop [stohp] *nm* A free ride, esp gotten by hitchhiking <hitch, lift, free ride> eg *Jak się tam dostaniesz? Spróbuję złapać stopa (How will you get there? I'll try to catch a lift)*

stopem [STOH-pehm] (or **na stopa** [nah STOH-pah]) *adv* Going somewhere by hitchhiking <by hitching, by lifting, by free rideing, by thumping a lift> eg *Pojechałam na stopa do domu (I got home by hitching)*

stówa See setka

stówka See setka

strach See najeść się strachu, napędzić komuś strachu, nie ma sprawy, taki że aż strach

stracić fason [STRAH-cheech FAH-sohn] (or **stracić głowę** [STRAH-cheech GWOH-veh]) *v phr* To stop being self-assured, optimistic, or lively; to lose one's composure <lose head, lose one's cool, lose one's spirit, sing another tune, whistle a different tune, change one's tune, come down a peg, take down a notch, climb down, come off one's perch, get off one's high horse, eat dirt, eat humble pie, pull in one's horns, take off one's high hat> eg *Musiała mu powiedzieć coś okropnego, bo facet stracił fason (She must have told him something terrible, because the guy instantly lost his cool)*

straszak [STRAH-shahk] *nm* A fake gun <toy gun> eg *To nie był prawdziwy pistolet, tylko straszak (It wasn't a real gun, it was a toy gun)*

strawny [STRAHV-ni] *adj* Acceptable, passable, or tolerable <OK, okay, kopasetic, hunky-dory, so-so> eg *Na początku myślałem, że to zła książka, ale teraz wiem, że jest całkiem strawna (I thought it was a bad book at first, but now I know it's quite kopacetic)*

stroić fochy [STROH-eech FOH-khi] *v phr* To be groundlessly dissatisfied or discontented; to have unfounded complaints <fuss, stink, scene, make a ceremony, beef, bleed, hassle, kvetch, bitch, beef, gripe, piss, bellyache, grouse, growl, squawk, cut a beef, make a stink, piss up a storm, raise a stink, blow up a storm, kick up a storm, eat someone's heart out, fuck around, screw around, mess around, trip> eg *Stroiła fochy, bo nie mieli tego, co chciała (She was pissing up a storm, because they didn't have what she wanted)*

strugać wariata See udawać greka

struna See przeginać

struty [STROO-ti] *adj* In a state of melancholy or depression; in low spirits <blue, low, down, on a downer, down in the dumps, taken down a peg, downbeat, down and out, funky, in a blue funk, in the dumps, dragged, ripped, on a bummer, bummed out, on a down trip, having the blues, singing the blues, crying the

blues, having one's ass in a sling, mopey> eg *Przez cały dzień jest jak struty. Nie wiem dlaczego (He's been on a downer the whole day. I don't know why)*

stryczek [STRI-chehk] *nm* Death by hanging <hemp, noose, necktie party> eg *Oznacza to dla niego stryczek (That means the hemp for him)*

strzał w dziesiątkę [STSHAH-oo v jeh-SHYOHNT-keh] *adv phr* Exactly what is needed; very adequate, suitable, or needed <nail on the head, bull's-eye, shot on the mark, just what the doctor ordered, on the button, on the dot, on the nose, on target, on track, that's the idea, that's the ticket, all to the mustard, hitting on all six, hitting the spot> eg *Kupno tego telefonu to był strzał w dziesiątkę (Buying this phone was like hitting a nail on the head)*

strzelić [STSHEH-leech] (or **strzelić sobie** [STSHEH-leech SOH-byeh]) *v* To have a quick drink of liquor <knock back, down, slug down, swig, tank, tank up> eg *Strzelił sobie cztery piwa i zaczął bekać (He downed three beers and started to burp)*

strzelić do łba [STSHEH-leech doh WBAH] (or **strzelić do głowy** [STSHEH-leech doh GWOH-vi]) *v phr* To have a sudden idea; to come to mind briefly <cross one's mind, pass through someone's mind, dawn on, have a brainwave, spark> eg *Nagle strzeliło mu do głowy, żeby wyjechać z kraju (Suddenly it passed through his mind to leave the country)*

strzelić gola [STSHEH-leech GOH-lah] *v phr* To succeed in copulating with someone <score, make it with, make out, get in, get a homer, get a home run, hit a homer, hit a home run, get to home plate, dip one's wick, go all the way, get it on, do someone> eg *I co, strzeliłeś gola? (So what, did you make it with her?)*

strzelić numer* [STSHEH-leech NOO-mehr] (or **odwalić numer*** [ohd-VAH-leech NOO-mehr] or **zrobić numer*** [ZROH-beech NOO-mehr]; **numerek*** [NOO-meh-rehk] may replace **numer**) *v phr* To copulate with someone, esp quickly or one only time; to achieve sexual intercourse <fuck, score, screw, lay, ball, bang, boink, boff, boogie, bop, frig, hump, poke, shag> eg *Ale wczoraj strzeliłem numerek! Laska była po prostu świetna (Did I fuck last night! The chick was just great)*

strzelić sobie coś [STSHEH-leech SOH-byeh TSOHSH] *v phr* To buy something for oneself <buy oneself, get oneself, blow oneself> eg *Strzeliłem sobie nową kurtkę (I bought me a new jacket)*

strzelić w dziesiątkę [STSHEH-leech v jeh-SHYOHNT-keh] *v phr* To do exactly what is needed; to be very adequate, suitable, or needed <be handy, come handy, hit on all six, be just what the doctor ordered, be on the button, be on the nose, be on target, be on track, be the idea, be the ticket, be all to the mustard, hit the nail on the head, hit the bull's-eye> eg *Wiesz, naprawdę strzeliłeś w dziesiątkę z tym pomysłem (You know, you really hit the nail on the head with this this idea)*

strzelić w kalendarz See kopnąć w kalendarz

strzelic See stuknąć

strzemienny [stsheh-MYEHN-ni] *nm* The last drink before leaving a party <one for the road, nightcap> eg *Co powiesz na strzemiennego? (How about one for the road?)*

studenciak [stoo-DEHN-chyahk] *nm* A student of a university or college <undergrad, grad, Joe College, college boy> eg *To typowy studenciak, nie ma pieniędzy (He's a typical Joe College, he has no money)*

studniówka [stood-NYOOF-kah] *nf* A traditional party organized by a hundred days before final exams in the senior year of high school <senior prom> eg *Zaprosił mnie na studniówkę (He invited me to the senior prom)*

stuknąć [STOOK-nohnch] *v* **1** (or **strzelić** [STSHEH-leech]) To reach a specific age <push, hit, get, get along> eg *W przyszłym roku stuknie mu czterdziestka (Next year he'll be pushing forty); Ożenisz się zanim strzeli ci trzydziestka (You'll get married before you hit thirty)* **2** To hit another car <fender-bender, sideswipe, rear-ender, bump> eg *Jakiś gnojek stuknął mnie na parkingu Some punk fender-bendered me in the parking lot)*

stuknąć w kimono See iść w kimono

stuknięty [stook-NYEHN-ti] *adj* Insane, stupid, or thoughtless <fucked in the head, fucked-up, crazy, creazy as a loon, loony, nerts, nuts, nutso, nutsy, nutty, sick, sick in the head, sicko, wacko, wacky, psycho, shizo, screwy, off one's rocker, out of one's skull, fruity, airbrained, airheaded, birdbrained, blockheaded, squareheaded, boneheaded, bubblebrained, bubbleheaded, bucketheaded, cluckheaded, cementheaded, clunkheaded, deadheaded, dumbclucked, dumbheaded, dumbassed, dumbbrained, fatbrained, fatheaded, flubdubbed, knukclebrained, knuckleheaded, lamebrained, lardheaded, lunkheaded, meatheaded, muscleheaded, noodleheaded, numbskulled, pointheaded, scatterbrained, nerdy, dorky, jackassed, lummoxed, dopey, goofy> eg *Ten facet jest naprawdę stuknięty. Potrzebuje wakacji (This guy is really sick. He needs a vacation)*

stykać [STI-kahch] **1** To suit one or appeal to one; to like, enjoy, or delight <fit in, suit one fine, turn on, heat up, fire up, steam up, stir up, send, give a bang, knock out, knock someone dead, knock someone's socks off, knock someone for a loop, throw someone for a loop, hit the spot, kill, murder, slay, slaughter, put someone away, tickle pink, tickle to death, tickle the piss out of someone, open one's nose, do it for> eg *Nie styka mi ta muzyka (That music doesn't do it for me)* **2** To be acceptable or suitable; to meet certain standards <fit in, fit the bill, do, wash, work, do down, cut it, make the grade, make the cut, make it, cut the mustard, pass in the dark, fill the bill, suit one fine, be OK, be okay, be kopasetic, be hunky-dory, be so-so> eg *Co myślisz o tej propozycji? Styka (What do you think about this proposal? It will make the grade)*

sucho See na sucho, ujść na sucho, zgrać się

sufit See brać coś z sufitu, mieć nierówno pod sufitem, nogi po samą szyję, rozjaśnić się pod sufitem, z głowy

suka* [SOO-kah] (or **bura suka*** [BOO-rah SOO-kah]) *nf* A woman, esp whom one dislikes or disapproves of <bitch, slut, cunt, broad, wench, hag, old hag, old biddy, old bag, old tart, piece of shit> eg *Zabiję tę sukę (I'll kill that bitch)*

sukinkot See skurwysyn

sukinsyn See skurwysyn

sunąć See ja pierdolę

suszyć [SOO-shich] *v* **1** To suffer from an unpleasant dryness of the mouth <have cotton mouth, have dry mouth, be hanging, be hung> eg *Ale mnie suszy! (Do I have cotton mouth!)* **2** To desparately need alcohol, esp as delirium tremens <have the shakes, have the clanks, have the creeps, have the DTs, have the heebie-jeebies, have the horrors, have the jim-jams, have the jumps, have the screaming

meemies, have the blue devils> eg *O nie, znów go suszy (Oh no, he's got the DT's again)*

swój chłop [sfoo-ee KHWOHP] (or **swój człowiek** [sfoo-ee CHWOH-vyehk]) *nm phr* A trustworthy or pleasing person, a friend <right guy, boy scout, pal, buddy, one of the boys> eg *Nie będzie się przeciwstawiał. To swój chłop (He won't have any objections. He's a boy scout)*

swój człowiek See swój chłop

syf* [sif] *nm* **1** Any veneral disease, esp syphilis <bug, crud, scrud, double scrud, creeping crud, VD, clap, dose, dose of claps, drip, blue balls, syph, siph, head cold, crabs> eg *Nie używał prezerwatyw i złapał jakiegoś syfa (He didn't use any condoms so he caught clap)* **2** Dirt, filth, or mess <dustball, dust bunny, dust kitty, kitten, pussie, slut's wool, house moss, ghost turd> eg *Wszędzie syf! Nie mył łazienki co najmniej od miesiąca (It's house moss all over. He hasn't cleaned the bathroom for at least for a month)* **3** (or **syf kiła mogiła*** [sif KEE-wah moh-GEE-wah]) Anything disgusting, abhoring, repulsive <shit, crap, scuzz, sleaze, drek, crud, glop, grunge, scrunge, muck, mung, goo, gook, gunk> eg *Czy brał narkotyki? O nie, nigdy nie wziąłby tego syfu do ust (Did he do drugs? No, he wouldn't put that shit in his mouth)* **4** (or **syfek*** [SI-fehk]) *nm* A minor skin lesion or a pimple <zit, whitehead, blackhead, guber, goober, pip> eg *Nie wyciskuj swoich syfów na moim lustrze! (Don't squeeze your zits on my mirror!)*

syfiasto* [si-FYAHS-to] *adv* Extremely bad; terribly; awfully <lousy, shitty, awful> eg *Syfiasto się dzisiaj czuję (I feel really lousy today)*

syfiasty* [si-FYAHS-ti] *adj* Very bad, worthless, or of inferior quality <lousy, awful, bush-league, cheap, crappy, shitty, cruddy, crummy, doggy, low-rent, low-ride, no-good, raggedy-ass, schlocky, stinking, tacky, trashy, two-bit, dime-a-dozen, fair to middling, garden variety, of a sort, of sorts, piddling, pissy-ass, piss-poor, run-of-the-mill, small-time> eg *Jeździł jakimś syfiasttym gratem (He used to drive some schlocky jalopy)*

sylwek [SIL-vehk] *nm* A New Year's party <New Year's bash> eg *Jak się udał sylwek? (How was your New Year's bash?)*

synalek* [si-NAH-lehk] *nm* A son <junior, sprout, pride and joy> eg *Co dobrego możesz powiedzieć o jego synalku? (What good can you say about his sprout?)*

sypać się [SI-pahch shyeh] (perf **rozsypać się** [rohs-SI-pahch shyeh]) (Esp about mechanical appliances) To fail or become inoperative; to desintegrate <break down, crash, crash and burn, fry, go down, go down in flames, go south, belly up, melt down, shut down, crack up, screw up, fuck up, go blooey, go busted, go on the blink, go on the fritz, go off, go out of whack, go kerflooey> eg *Cały system rozsypał się (The entire system went bust)*

syry* [SI-ri] *npl* A person's legs <stumps, hinders, pillars, trotters, underpinnings, pins, sticks> eg *Od tego całego łażenia bolą mnie syry (My stumps are sore from all that walking)*

sytuacja podbramkowa [si-too-WAHTS-yah pohd-brahm-KOH-vah] (or **podbramkowa sytuacja** [pohd-brahm-KOH-vah si-too-WAHTS-yah]) *nf phr* A difficult situation <tight corner, tight spot, dire strait, squeeze, rut, jam> eg *Jest w sytuacji podbramkowej, bo nie może zapłacić czynszu za ten miesiąc (He's in a tight spot because he can't pay the rent this month)*

szałowo [shah-WOH-voh] *adv* Extremely well; superbly <great, cool, swell, fab, rad, def, far-out, awesome, frantic, terrific, funky, gorgeous, groovy, hellacious, neat, peachy, dandy, baddest, mean, solid, super-dooper, wailing, wicked, gnarly, top-notch, ten, ace-high, A-OK, A-1, some> eg *Zobaczysz, że wszystko będzie szałowo (You'll see, everything is going to be great)*

szałowy [shah-WOH-voh] *adj adj* Excellent; wonderful; extremely good <great, cool, swell, fab, rad, def, far-out, awesome, frantic, terrific, funky, gorgeous, groovy, hellacious, neat, peachy, dandy, baddest, mean, solid, super-dooper, wailing, wicked, gnarly, top-notch, ten, ace-high, A-OK, A-1, some> eg *Ta blondynka jest na prawdę szałowa (That blonde is real cool)*

szaber [SHAH-behr] *nm* A theft <heist, bag job, boost, burn, crib job, five-finger discount, holdup, stickup, job, knockover, lift, pinch, hijacking> eg *Siedzi za szaber (He's doing time for hijakcking)*

szabrować [shah-BROH-vahch] *v* To steal or loot <heist, boost, burgle, nurn, bag, buzz, hoist, hold up, hook, hustle, jump, kick over, knock off, knock over, lift, move, mug, nab, nick, nip, pinch, pluck, roll, rustle, snatch, snitch, stick up, swipe, take off, put the grab on, go south with, highjack> eg *Każdy, kogo przyłapiemy na szabrowaniu zostanie zastrzelony (Anyone found burgling will be shot)*

szabrownik [shah-BROHV-neek] *nm* A thief or looter <heist man, holdup man, stickup man, dip, cannon, tool, wire, meachanic, cutpurse, digger, file, forks, five fingers, finger, fingersmith, greasy finger, gun, knucker, picks, friskers, hooks, spitter, jostler, clipper, stickup man, lifter, hijacker> eg *Policja aresztowała dwóch szbrowników (The police arrested two guns)*

szachrować [shah-KHROH-vahch] (perf **oszachrować** [oh-shah-KHROH-vahch]) *v* To cheat; to swindle; to deceive; to scheme <con, rip off, shaft, roll, chisel, gyp, scam, screw, stiff, fleece, dick, do in, take in, do a number on, flim-flam, bamboozle, run a number on, take someone for a ride, take someone to the cleaners, throw someone a curve, pull a fast one, fuck over, screw over, angle, take in, snow, do a snow job, double-shuffle, fast-shuffle, flimflam, give a bun steer, give someone a line, have someone on, lead someone down the garden path, do a snow job, jerk someone's chain, pull someone's chain, pull one's leg, pull someone's string, pull the wool over someone's eyes, put someone on, snow, use smoke and mirrors> eg *Ten handlarz oszachrował mnie na dwie stówy (That salesman dicked me for two hundred)*

szafa gra See gra muzyka

szajba [SHAH-ee-bah] *nf* Obsession, insanity, or eccentricity <thing, kick, bag, bug, craze, freak, frenzy, weakness, bug up one's ass, bug in one's ear, bee in one's bonnet, bee, flea in one's nose, maggot, maggot in one's brain, hang-up, jones, monkey, ax to grind> eg *Ma szajbę na punkcie tego, że joga jest lekarstwem na wszystkie złe rzeczy tego świata (He's got a bee in his bonnet about yoga curing all the world's ills)* See dostać świra, mieć świra

szajs [SHAH-ees] (or **szmelc** [shmehlts]) *nm* Anything worthless, useless, or of shoddy quality; trash <schlock, dreck, garbage, junk, lemon, crap, piece of crap, shit, piece of shit, dogshit, sleaze> eg *Kupiłem ten aparat wczoraj. Prawdziwy szajs! (I bought this camera yesterday. It's real schlock)*

szaleć [SHAH-lehch] (perf **poszaleć** [po-SHAH-lehch] or **zaszaleć** [zah-SHAH-lehch]) *v* **1** To carouse or celebrate <party, ball, have a ball, jam, paint the town

red, raise hell, bar-hop, bar-crawl, go on a bender> eg *Szaleli całą noc (They partied all night long)* **2** To spend money foolishly or extravagantly; to use up wastefully; to squander <blow, drop, diddle away, piddle away, piss away, shell out, dish out, throw away, spend like water, pour down the drain, throw down the drain> eg *Zaszaleliśmy wczoraj w kasynie (We blew our money last night in the casino)*

szalikowiec [shah-lee-KOH-vyehts] *nm* A avid soccer fan <die-hard fan> eg *Pełno było tam szalikowców (The place was full of die-hard soccer fans)*

szamać [SHAH-mahch] *v* To eat <chow, scarf, scoff, feed one's face, grub up, put on the feedbag> eg *Zaczął szmać (He started to chow)*

szambo [SHAHM-boh] *nn* An underground container for sewage; a cesspit or cesspool <shitbox, sewer> eg *Wyrzuciliśmy to do szamba (We threw it to the sewer)*

szampon [SHAHM-pohn] *nm* Champagne or sparkling wine <bubbly, bubbles, bubble water, giggle water, sparkle water, grapes> eg *Więcej szamponu, czy może chciałabyś coś mocniejszego? (More bubble water, or do you want something stronger?)*

szara myszka [SHAH-rah MISH-kah] *nf phr* A very average and unremarkable woman <Jane, Jane Doe, Jane Q Citizen, Jane Q Public, plain Jane> eg *Prezydent jest chyba bardzo popularny wśród szarych myszek (The president seems very popular with Jane Q Citizen)*

szarak [SHAH-rahk] *nm* **1** A very average and unremarkable man <man on the street, John Doe, John Q Citizen, John Q Public, Joe Schmo, Joe Six-Pack, ordinary Joe, square John, one of the boys, every Tom Dick and Harry, ham-and-egger> eg *To szarak. Chciałby tylko obejrzeć jaki dobry mecz w telewizji (He's a Joe Six-Pack. All he wants is to watch some good game on TV)* **2** A hare <Bugs> eg *Czy to był szarak? Nic nie widziałem (Was it a hare? I haven't seen anything)*

szarówka [shah-ROOF-kah] *nf* A dawn, dusk, or any overcast and dismal day <crack of dawn, dimday, day peep, crack of dawn, early bright> eg *Była już szarówka (It was already a dimday)*

szarpidrut [shahr-PEE-droot] *nm* A guitar player, esp if not good <plunker, whanger, axman> eg *Wywalił dwóch szarpidrutów z zespołu (He fired two plunkers from the band)*

szarpnąć się [SHAHRP-nohnch shyeh] *v* To allow oneself to buy something expensive or extravagant; to squander <blow, drop, diddle away, piddle away, piss away, shell out, dish out, throw away, spend like water, pour down the drain, throw down the drain> eg *Szarpnął się na ten samochód (He dropped a lot on that car)*

szastać [SHAHS-tahch] (perf **przeszastać** [psheh-SHAHS-tahch]) *v* To spend money foolishly or extravagantly; to use up wastefully; to squander <blow, drop, diddle away, piddle away, piss away, shell out, dish out, throw away, spend like water, pour down the drain, throw down the drain> eg *Miał fortunę, ale przeszastał wszystko na torze wyścigowym (He had a fortune but he blew it gambling at the track)*

szatan [SHAH-tahn] *nm* A very strong tea or coffee <tar, killer> eg *Co mi zrobiłeś za szatana! (What a tar you made for me!)*

szatki [SHAHT-kee] *npl* Clothes or clothing; dress <threads, drapes, duds, rags, togs, weeds, outfit> eg *Podobają mi się twoje szatki. Gdzie je kupiłaś? (I like your weeds. Where did you buy them?)*

szczać* [shchahch] (perf **naszczać*** [NAH-shchahch] or **wyszczać się*** [VI-shchahch shyeh] or **zeszczać się*** [ZEH-shchahch shyeh] or **poszczać się*** [POHSH-chahch shyeh]) *v* To urinate <piss, leak, pee, pee-pee, piddle, tinkle,

wee-wee, whizz, take a piss, take a leak> eg *Ale chce mi się szczać! (Man, do I need to piss!)*
See lać

szczapa [SHCHAH-pah] (or **szkapa** [SHKAH-pah] or **szkielet** [SHKYEH-leht]) *nf* An unusually thin, skinny person <beanpole, stringbean, skin and bones, skeleton, bag of bones> eg *Twój brat to szczapa (Your brother is a skeleton)*

szczaw See **szczeniak**

szczęka komuś opada [SHCHEHN-kah KOH-moosh oh-PAH-dah] (or **szczena komuś opada** [SHCHEH-nah KOH-moosh oh-PAH-dah]) *phr* To be speechless because of shock or surprise; to be very shocked or surprised <jaw dropped down, clam up, dummy up, button up, belt up, catch one's breath, drop dead, knock dead, drop down dead, be killed stone-dead> eg *Wiadomość była tak nieoczekiwana, że szczena mi opadła ze zdziwienia (The news was so unexpected that my jaw dropped to the floor)*

szczekaczka [shcheh-KAHCH-kah] *nf* A public loudspeaker, esp hung on the wall or a post <speaker, tweeter, woofer, squawk box, hog caller, PA> eg *Wyłącz szczekaczki (Turn these speakers off)*

szczena [SHCHEH-nah] *nf* The jaw or the mouth <chops, yap, bazoo, kisser, trap> eg *Walnął go w szczenę (He knocked him on the chops)*
See szczęka komuś opada

szczeniacki [shcheh-NYAHTS-kee] *adj* Teenage; adolescent <teen, teener, teeny-bopper, bubble-gum, juvie, snot-nosed, punk, snotty> eg *Nie będę tolerował takiego szczeniackiego zachowania (I won't tolerate such snot-nosed behavior)*

szczeniactwo [shcheh-NYAHTS-tfoh] *nn* A group of teenagers or teenagers in general <teens, teeners, teeny-boppers, bubble-gummers, shitheads, punks, snot-noses> eg *Nie znoszę tego szczeniactwa (I hate these snot-noses)*

szczeniak [SHCHEH-nyak] *nm* **1** (or **szczun*** [shchoon] or **szczoch*** [shchohkh] or **szczyl*** [shchil] or **szczaw** [SHCHAHF] (or **szczawik** [SHCHAH-veek]) A teenage boy, esp whom one despises <teen, teener, teeny-bopper, bubble-gummer, youngster, juvie, shithead, punk, snot-nose> eg *Dokąd to idziesz, szczochu jeden? (Where do you think you're going, you shithead?); Sczeniak nie wiedział co zrobić (The punk didn't know what to do); Czemu pożyczyłeś nasz samochód takiemu szczawikowi? (Why did you lend our car to such a punk?)* **2** (or **szczeniaczek** [shcheh-NYAH-chehk]) *nm* A small bottle of vodka <no slang equivalent> eg *Wy to nazywacie szczniaczkiem? (Do you call this a small bottle?)* **3** (or **szczeniaczek** [shcheh-NYAH-chehk]) A little drink of a potent liquor, esp vodka, served in a shot glass <snort, finger, jigger, pull, shot, nip, gargle, guzzle, slug, hit> eg *Mówi, że wypiła tylko szczeniaczka (She said she only drank a finger)*

szczeniara [shcheh-NYAH-rah] *nf* A teenage girl, esp whom one despises <chick, chicklet, teen, teener, teeny-bopper, bubble-gummer, youngster, juvie, shithead, punk, snot-nose> eg *Nie sądzę, żeby chciała to zrobić. To jeszcze szczeniara (I don't think she'd like to do it. She's just a punk)*

szczyny* [SHCHI-ni] (or **szczochy*** [SHCHOH-khi]) *npl* Urine <piss, pee-pee, wee-wee, whizz> eg *Na dywanie są szczyny. Gdzie jest ken kot? (There's piss on the carpet. Where's that cat?)*

szczypać się [SHCHI-pahch shyeh] *v* To have doubts or scruples; to be bashful, embarrassed, or uncomfortable <fence straddle, sit on the fence, hang on the

fence, run hot and cold, blow hot and cold, be between a rock and a hard place> eg *Przestań się szczypać i powiedz, jak to się stało (Stop sitting on the fence and tell me how it happened)*

szczyt [shchit] (or **szczyty** [SHCHI-ti] *npl*) *nm* The highest degree of something <beyond the limit> eg *Paradowanie z telefonem komórkowym to obecnie szczyt snobizmu (Walking around with a cellular phone goes beyond the limit)*

szef [shehf] *nm* One's male superviser or director <boss, chief, big boy, big cheese, big enchilada, top brass, honcho, big man, man upstairs, top dog, key player, exec, numero uno> eg *Co powiedział szef? (What did the big enchilada say?)*

szefowa [sheh-FOH-vah] *nf* One's female superviser or director <boss, chief, big cheese, big enchilada, top brass, honcho, woman upstairs, top dog, key player, exec, numero uno> eg *Szefowa kazała mi to przefaksować (The woman upstairs told me to fax it)*

szefować [sheh-FOH-vahch] *v* To work as a director, leader or executive; to control; to manage <boss, be at the helm, be in the driver's seat, call the shots, crack the whip, head up, mastermind, rule the roost, wear the pants> eg *Ona szefuje dwóm firmom (She bosses two firms)*

szewc See pić jak szewc

sziksa See siksa

szkło [shkwoh] *nn* (Esp as a collective term for) A small glass for drinking vodka <shot glass, jigger, snifter> eg *Gdzie jest szkło? (Where are the shot glasses?)*

szkapa [SHKAH-pah] *nf* A horse, esp a thin, old, or neglected <hoss, hack, nag, bronco, bangtail, pony, cayuse, paint horse, old paint, dobbin, hayburner, crowbait, goat, stiff> eg *Zostaw szkapę w spokoju (Leave the hoss alone)*
See szczapa

szkielet See szczapa

szklanka [SHKLAHN-kah] (or **ślizgawica** [shleez-gah-VEE-tsah]) *nf* Glazed frost or frosty weather <sleet, icy, slippery> eg *Na drodze jest szklanka. Użytkownicy powinni zachować ostrożność (There's sleet on the road. Motorists are advised to be careful)*

szkoła See dać wycisk, dostać wycisk

szkółka [SHKOOW-kah] *nf* A school, esp a university which is small or of low standard <jail, knowledge box, blackboard jungle, brainery, diploma mill> eg *Poszedł do jakiejś pieprzonej szkółki (He went to some goddam hi)*

szkop See szwab

szkrab [shkrahp] *nm* A baby or a young child <knee biter, carpet rat, rug rat, little fella> eg *Czyj to szkrab? (Whose rug rat is that?)*

szlug [shlook] *nm* A cigarette <smoke, butt, cig, ciggie, fag, faggot, nail, coffin nail, stick, cancer stick, drag, bonfire, lung duster, root, cigaroot, cigareete, spark, dope, dope stick, grit, joint, pimp stick, slim, toke, weed> eg *Masz szluga? (Do you have a smoke?)*

szmaciarz [SHMAH-chyahsh] (or **szmaciak** [SHMAH-chyahk] or **szmatławiec** [shmaht-WAH-vyets]) *nm* A poor, loathsome and sloppy man, esp a derelict <bum, bo, hobo, piece of shit, hood, wino, dreg, wrongo, scum of the earth> eg *Nie rozmawiam ze szmaciarzami (I don't talk to bums)*

szmal [shmahl] (or **szmalec** [SHMAH-lehts]) *nm* Money <dough, bread, bank, cabbage, change, coin, folding, green, lettuce> eg *Czy on ma dużo szmalu? (Does he have a lot of dough?)*
See mieć forsy jak lodu, robić kokosy, siedzieć na forsie, wyłożyć forsę

szmalowny [shmah-LOH-vni] (or **szmalcowny** [shmahl-TSOH-vni]) *adj* Very rich; affluent <loaded, flush, filthy rich, stinking rich, dirt richy, lousy rich, in the bucks, in the dough, in the money, rolling in it, made of money> eg *Szmalowny ten twój facet. Postawił nam wszystkim obiad! (Your man is real loaded. He bought dinner for all of us!)*

szmatławiec [shmaht-WAH-vyehts] (or **szmata** [SHMAH-tah] *nf*) *nm* A tabloid, esp disreputable <rag, dirt rag, blat, bladder, scandal sheet, fish wrapper, toilet paper> eg *Gdzie to wyczytałeś? W jakimś szmatławcu (Where did you read this? In some rag)*
See szmaciarz

szmatławy [shmah-TWAH-vi] *adj* Bad, poor, worthless, or of inferior quality <lousy, awful, bush-league, cheap, crappy, shitty, cruddy, crummy, doggy, low-rent, low-ride, no-good, raggedy-ass, schlocky, stinking, tacky, trashy, two-bit, dime-a-dozen, fair to middling, garden variety, of a sort, of sorts, piddling, pissy-ass, piss-poor, run-of-the-mill, small-time> eg *Gra z jakąś szmatławą grupą (He's been playing with some cruddy band)*

szmata [SHMAH-tah] *nf* **1*** (or **szmaciara*** [shmah-CHYAH-rah] or **ściera*** [SHCHYEH-rah]) A woman, esp whom one dislikes or disapproves of <bitch, slut, cunt, broad, wench, hag, old hag, old biddy, old bag, old tart, piece of shit> eg *Słyszałem, że chodzi z jakąś szmatą (I hear he's been dating some wench)* **2*** A person one strongly dislikes, esp one who behaves in an unethical, immoral or dishonest way <asshole, fuck, fucker, fuckhead, fuckface, motherfucker, shit, shitface, shithead, shitheel, bastard, jerk, SOB, son of a bitch, son of a whore, cocksucker, prick, dick, dickhead, cuntface, schmuck, scum, scumbag, sleazebag, slimebag, dipshit, pisshead, piece of shit, pain in the ass> eg *Nie chcę mieć nic do czynienia z tą szmatą (I don't want to have anything to do with that piece of shit)* **3** Someone who is very tired or exhausted <dead, dead on one's feet, dead-tired, dog-tired, out of it, out of gas, out of juice, all in, all shot, pooped, bagged, beat, beat to the ground, beat to the ankles, bone-tired, burned out, bushed, chewed, crapped out, done, done in, dragged out, frazzled, played out, fucked out, knocked out, tuckered out, tapped out, had it, ready to drop, on one's last legs> eg *Czuję się jak szmata (I feel all in)*

szmaty [SHMAH-tah] *nf* Clothes or clothing, esp old and worn-out <rags, schmatte, threads, drapes, duds, rags, togs, weeds, outfit> eg *Co to za szmaty. Ty to nazywasz ubraniem? (What schmattes! You call these clothes?)*

szmelc See szajs

szmerek [SHMEH-rehk] *nm* The initial euphoric effects of drinking alcohol <buzz, high, kick> eg *Miał mały szmerek po winie (He got a little buzz from the wine)*

szmergiel [SHMEHR-gyehl] *nm* Obsession, insanity, or eccentricity <thing, kick, bag, bug, craze, freak, frenzy, weakness, bug up one's ass, bug in one's ear, bee in one's bonnet, bee, flea in one's nose, maggot, maggot in one's brain, hang-up, jones, monkey, ax to grind> eg *Ostatnio ma szmergla na punkcie brunetek (Brunettes are his latest craze)*

See dostać świra, mieć świra

sznaps [shnahps] *nm* A drink of liquor, esp potent, served in a shot glass <snort, finger, jigger, pull, shot, nip, gargle, guzzle, slug, hit> eg *Co powiesz na małego sznapsa? (How about a little jigger?)*

szopa [SHOH-pah] *nf* Unkempt hair on the head <mop, cow-lick, alfalfa> eg *Spójrz na jej szopę na głowie. Ohyda! (Check out the mop on her head. Yuck!)*

szopka [SHOHP-kah] *nf* A very funny, amusing, or foolish situation <laugh, laugh and a half, laugher, laughing stock, horselaugh, merry ha-ha, hoot, howl, riot, laff riot, laffer, scream, stitch, boffo, panic, knee-slapper, rib-tickler, side-splitter> eg *Ten egzamin to była prawdziwa szopka (The exam was a real laugh)*

szosa See krążownik szos

szpan [shpahn] *nm* An instance of bragging or anything attractive, stylish or unusual that makes an impression <show-off, swank, knock-out, kill-out, whizbang, humdinger, killer, killer-diller, fireworks, doozie> eg *Przywiózł masę bajerów z Ameryki (He brought a lot of humdingers from America); Rety, ale bajer! (Geez, what a knockout it is!)*

szpaner [SHPAH-nehr] *nm* A braggart; a self-aggrandizer <showoff, grandstander, showboater, hotdogger, bullshitter, bullshit artist, blowhard, pitcher, bigmouth, ego-tripper> eg *Nie lubię szpanerów takich jak twój brat (I don't like showoffs like your brother)*

szpanować [shpah-NOH-vahch] (perf **zaszpanować** [zah-shpah-NOH-vahch]) *v* To behave in an ostentatiously showy or flamboyant way in order to impress others <swank, show off, grandstand, showboat, pile it on, hotdog, bullshit, blow one's horn, blow one's trumpet, blow smoke, blow off, blow hard, signify, bigmouth, talk big> eg *Próbowała szpanować na balu dobroczynnym (She tried to grandstand at the charity ball)*

szpargały [SHPAHR-gah-oo] *nm* Indefinite or old objects, such as old papers <old stuff, old shit, old crap, junk, junker> eg *Przejrzałem moje szpargały szukając strego zdjęcia z ogólniaka (I went through my old stuff looking for my old high school photo)*

szparka [SHPAHR-kah] (or **szpara*** [SHPAH-rah]) *nf* The vulva, vagina <hole, slit, slot> eg *Wygoliłem jej szparkę (I shaved her slit)*

szparka sekretarka [SHPAHR-kah seh-kreh-TAHR-kah] *nf phr* A female secretary <sec, girl Friday, gal Friday, pink collar, gofer, go-for, gopher> eg *Poproś szparkę sekretarkę, żeby ci to skserowałą (Ask gal Friday to xerox it for you)*

szpec See spec

szpetnie [SHPEHT-nyeh] *adv* Extremely bad; terribly; awfully <lousy, shitty, awful> eg *Szpetnie się dzisiaj czuję (I feel really lousy today)*

szpetny [SHPEHT-ni] *adj* Cursed; damnable; bad; disgusting <damn, damned, goddamn, goddamned, god-awful, blasted, darn, darned, effing, flipping, forking, freaking, frigging, pesky, gross, barfy, scuzzy, sleazy, grody, icky, yucky, gooky, grungy, ech, yech> eg *Co za szpetna historia! (What a barfy story)*

szpicel [SHPEE-tsehl] *nm* An informer, esp a police informer <fink, finger, snitch, snitcher, canary, nark, nose, pigeon, rat, singer, squeal, stool, stool pigeon, tipster, weasel, whistle-blower, whistler> eg *Zrobił się z niego szpicel. Nikt go już nie lubi (He has turned into a fink. Nobody likes him anymore)*

szpiclować [shpee-TSLOH-vahch] *v* To inform the police about someone or something, esp to identify someone; to be an informer <fink, finger, snitch,

squeal, beef, blab, blow, blow the whistle, canary, chirp, dime, drop a dime, go stool, leak, nark, put the finger on, rat, rat on, sell out, sing, sing out, stool, weasel> eg *Ona zaszpicluje każdego (She'll finger anybody)*

szpilki [SHPEL-kee] (or **szpile** [SHPEE-leh]) *npl* Women's shoes with high and thin heels; stiletto heeled shoes <spike heels> eg *To ta w szpilkach (She's the one in spike heels)*
See jak na szpilkach, wiercić się jak na szpilkach

szpryca [SHPRI-tsah] *nf* **1** A hypodermic syringe and needle used to inject drugs <hype, spike, needle> eg *Zapomniała wyczyścić szprycę (She forgot to clean the hype)* **2** A dose or injection of drugs <fix, hype, needle, do-up, fix-up, hit, jab, mainline, pop, shot> eg *Muszę wziąć szprycę (I need a hype real bad)*

szprycować się [shpri-TSOH-vahch shyeh] (perf **naszprycować się** [nah-shpri-TSOH-vahch shyeh]) *v* To take an injection of narcotics <shoot, shoot up, bang, dope up, do up, spike up, hype, jab a vein, mainline> eg *Nie mógł się doczekać, kiedy przyjdzie do domu i będzie się szprycował (He couldn't wait to get home and shoot up)*

sztach [shtahkh] *nm* An inhalation of a lighted cigarette <drag, puff, pull, snort, sniff, blow, toke, fume, haul> eg *Jeszcze jeden sztach i idę (One more puff and I'm going)*

sztachać się [SHTAH-khahch shyeh] (perf **sztachnąć się** [SHTAHKH-nohnch shyeh]) *v* To inhale a lighted cigarette <drag, puff, pull, snort, sniff, blow, toke, fume, take a drag, take a puff, take a pull, take a snort, take a sniff, take a blow, take a toke, take a fume, take a haul> eg *Sztachnął się papieroskiem i uśmiechnął się (He puffed on his cigarette and smiled)*

sztama [SHTAH-mah] **1** *nf* Mutual friendship, alliance, or collaboration <deal, pact> eg *Po jakimś czasie znów była sztama (We had a deal again after some time)* **2** *excl* Shake hands with me, as a sign of agreement <slip me five, give me five, give me some skin> eg *No to jak? Sztama? (So what do you say? Will you give me five?)*

sztok See upić się jak świnia

sztuka [SHTOO-kah] *nf* An impressive, young, and attractive woman <chick, broad, gal, pussy, cunt, ass, piece of ass, piece, dish, babe, baby, dame, beauty, beaut, beauty queen, baby doll, doll, dolly, dollface, dreamboat, dream girl, eating stuff, eyeful, flavor, looker, good-looker, head-turner, traffic-stopper, honey, killer, hot number, package, knockout, oomph girl, peach, bombshell, sex bunny, sex job, sex kitten, sex pot, table grade, ten, bunny, centerfold, cheesecake, date bait, dazzler, heifer, fluff, quail, sis, skirt, tail, job, leg, tart, tomato, pussycat, cooz, twat> eg *Podoba mi się ta dziewczyna. Niezła sztuka (I like that girl. She's a real character)*
See nie sztuka

sztywniak [SHTIV-nyahk] *nm* An overly formal, unapprochable, and perhaps conceited man; someone who shows distance or lack of feeling <stiff, stiff-lip, stiff-ass, stuffed shirt, ego-tripper, windbag, blowhard, hinkty-ass, standoff, square> eg *Nigdy nie lubiłem tego sztywniaka (I never liked the stiff-ass)*

sztywny [SHTIV-ni] *adj* **1** (Of a person) Overly formal, unapprochable or conceited; showing distance or lack of feeling <stiff, stiffy, stiff-lipped, stiff-assed, stuffy, stuck-up, puffed-up, high-hat, ego-tripping, swelled-up, swell-headed, big-headed, high-nosed, blown-up, stuck on oneself, chesty, gassy, windy, hatty, hinkty, uppity, biggety, snooty, standoffish> eg *Co za sztywny facet! Próbowałam z* *nim rozmawiać przez pół godziny i nic! (What a stiff guy he is! I've been trying to start a conversation with him for half an hour and nothing happened!)* **2** Boring, monotonous, insipid, or too official and conventional <lame, flat, flat as a pancake, dull as dishwater, ho-hum, hum-drum, dullsville, deadsville, dragsville, square, beige, blah, yawny, dragass, draggy> eg *Impreza była naprawdę sztywna (The party was real lame)* **3** Not relaxed or loosened up; feeling uncomfortably alienated <cranky, uptight, jumpy, jittery, shaky, shivery, nervy, edgy, antsy, clutchy, hitchy, fretty, itchy, wired, tightened-up, strung-out> eg *Na randce był bardzo sztywny (He was real uptight on the date)* **4** Dead <stiff, stone dead, stone cold, cold, gone, dead and gone, dead as a dodo, dead as a doornail> eg *Kiedy karetka przyjechała, facet był już sztywny (When the ambulance arrived, the guy was already stone dead)* **5** Drunk <alkied, bagged, blitzed, blotto, blown away, bent, boiled, bombed, blasted, boozed, bottled, boxed, buzzed, canned, clobbered, cooked, corked, crashed, drunk as a skunk, edged, embalmed, fractured, fried, gassed, ginned, grogged, have one too many, half under, high, hooched up, in bad shape, impaired, illuminated, juiced, knocked out, liquored, lit, loaded, looped, lubricated, lushed, smashed, oiled, pickled, plastered, plonked, polluted, sauced, shitfaced, slugged, sloshed, soaked, stewed, stiff, stinking drunk, swizzled, tanked, three sheets to the wind, wiped, zonked> eg *Tylko mi nie mów, że jest sztywny. Po dwóch piwach? (Don't tell me he's blitzed. After two beers?)*

See park sztywnych

szuja* [SHOO-yah] *nf* A person one strongly dislikes, esp one who behaves in an unethical, immoral or dishonest way <asshole, fuck, fucker, fuckhead, fuckface, motherfucker, shit, shitface, shithead, shitheel, bastard, jerk, SOB, son of a bitch, son of a whore, cocksucker, prick, dick, dickhead, cuntface, schmuck, scum, scumbag, sleazebag, slimebag, dipshit, pisshead, piece of shit, pain in the ass> eg *Nie chcę mieć nic do czynienia z tą szują (I don't want to have anything to do with that piece of shit)*

szumowina* [shoo-moh-VEE-nah] *nf* A vagrant, derelict or any loathsome or worthless man, esp drunk <bum, bo, hobo, piece of shit, hood, wino, dreg, wrongo, scum of the earth> eg *Mordercy i handlarze narkotyków to margines (Murderers and drug dealers are the dregs of society)*

szurnięty [shoor-NYEHN-ti] *adj* Insane, stupid, or thoughtless <fucked in the head, fucked-up, crazy, creazy as a loon, loony, nerts, nuts, nutso, nutsy, nutty, sick, sick in the head, sicko, wacko, wacky, psycho, shizo, screwy, off one's rocker, out of one's skull, fruity, airbrained, airheaded, birdbrained, blockheaded, squareheaded, boneheaded, bubblebrained, bubbleheaded, bucketheaded, cluckheaded, cementheaded, clunkheaded, deadheaded, dumbclucked, dumbheaded, dumbassed, dumbbrained, fatbrained, fatheaded, flubdubbed, knukclebrained, knuckleheaded, lamebrained, lardheaded, lunkheaded, meatheaded, muscleheaded, noodleheaded, numbskulled, pointheaded, scatterbrained, nerdy, dorky, jackassed, lummoxed, dopey, goofy> eg *Ten facet jest naprawdę szurnięty. Potrzebuje wakacji (This guy is really sick. He needs a vacation)*

szwab* [SHFAHP] (or **szkop*** [shkohp]) *nm* A male German <kraut, krauthead, sauerkraut, Fritz, Heinie, Jerry> eg *Jakiś szwab nadjechał Beemką (Some kraut pulled up in his Beemer)*

szwajcarski See jak w zegarku

szwarc mydło i powidło [shfahrts MID-woh ee pod-VEED-woh] *npl phr* Articles of various kinds; a mixture or miscellany, esp if in disorder <mess, odds and ends, bits and pieces, mish mash, hodge-podge, rag-bag, props, thingies, combo, smorgasboard> eg *Wszystko tam było. Szwarc, mydło i powidło (Everything was there. All sorts of mish mash)*

szwendać się [SHFEHN-dahch shyeh] *v* To walk or go around, esp aimlessly <cruise, hang out, hang around, ankle, amble, leg it, hoof it, toddle, hotfoot, foot it, burn shoe leather, ride shanks mare, stomp, pound the beat, pound the pavement, gumshoe, broom, march, press the bricks, shank it, waltz> eg *Szwędał się po mieście (He used to cruise around town)*

szwindel [SHFEEN-dehl] *nm* A swindle; a fraud; a scheme <scam, rip-off, con game, double cross, double shuffle, fast one, grift, gyp, flim-flam, hustle, number, racket, run-around, skin game, sucker game, suck-in, ride, fucking over, screwing over, hanky-panky, monkey business, song and dance, game, little game, angle> eg *Urząd podatkowy nie znalazł żadnych śladów szwindli (The IRS found no traces of con games)*

szwung [SHFOONK] (or **szwunk**) *nm* Energy; initiative; verve; enthusiasm <juice, go juice, pizzazz, pep, drive, push, steam, punch, bounce, spunk, splash, get up and go, pepper-upper, piss and vinegar, snap, zap, zip, zing, pow, sock, vim> eg *Mam ostatnio szwunk, więc chyba skończę ten słownik na czas (I've been full of pizzazz recently, so I guess I will finish this dictionary on time)*

szybki Bill [SHIP-kee BEEL] *nm phr* A fast-acting or energetic man, esp reckless and without prior consideration <ball of fire, fireball, spitball, fast-burner, flash, spark plug, spring-butt, striker, live wire, piss-cutter, pisser, pistol, powerhouse, human dynamo, eager beaver, hot shot, hot number, shit on wheels, speedy Gonzales> eg *Nie jestem szybki Bill. Daj mi trochę czasu do namysłu (I'm not a fireball. Give me some time to think it over)*

szybki numerek See numerek

szycha [SHI-khah] (or **gruba szycha** [GROO-bah SHI-khah]; **szyszka** [SHISH-kah] may replace **szycha**) *nf* A very important, influential, or well-known person <big shot, big cheese, big enchilada, big fish, big guy, big wheel, wheel, biggie, topsider, celeb, big time operator, head honcho, BTO, VIP> eg *Wyszła za miejscową szychę (He married a local big shot)*

szyja See nogi po samą szyję

szykowny [shi-KOHV-ni] *adj* Elegant; fashionable; stylish; chic <sharp, dap, natty, classy, spiffy, snazzy, ritzy, plushy, swanky, nitty, fancy schmancy, jazzy, faddy, trendy, posh, swellegant> eg *Ale masz szykowną marynarkę! Gdzie ją kupiłeś? (What a ritzy jacket you got! Where did you buy it?)*

ściąga [SHCHYOHN-gah] (or **ściągaczka** [shchyohn-GAHCH-kah] or **ściągawka** [shchyohn-GAHF-kah]) *nf* A set of answers used to cheat on an examination <cheat, cheat sheet, cheat note, crib sheet, crib, pony> eg *Dobra ściąga musi być bardzo mała (A good crib must be real small)*

ściągać [SHCHYOHN-gahch] (perf **ściągnąć** [SHCHYOHNG-nohnch]) *v* **1** (Esp about money) To demand and obtain by force; to exact; to enforce <muscle, flex some muscle, arm-twist, strong-arm, put the arm on, shake, put the shake on, squeeze, put the squeeze on> eg *Musimy ściągnąć od niego wszystkie nasze pieniądze (We must arm-twist him to get all our money)* **2** To copy <cheat, crib, nick> eg *Ściągała na egzaminie i przyłapano ją (She cribbed on the exam and got caught); Usiłowałem ściągnąć niektóre odpowiedzi z jego testu (I tried to nick some answers off his test)*

ściana See podpierać ścianę, wbijać zęby w ścianę, jak groch o ścianę

ściema [SHCHYEH-mah] *nf* A shameful or scandalous fact or situation; a shame, disgrace, or scandal <gas, come-down, put-down, take-down, dump, bummer, hot potato, bad scene, bad news, can of worms, bag of worms, takedown, putdown, shit, serious shit, deep shit, deep water, drag, bind, bitch, bummer, downer, headache, double trouble, snafu, pain in the ass, pain in the neck, spot, mess, holy mess, pickle, squeeze, hard time, glitch, stinker, skeleton, skeleton in the closet, sizzler, scorcher, dynamite, Watergate, fine kettle of fish, fine how do you do, fine cup of coffee, big stink, curtains, lights out, game's over> eg *Pies zjadł stek, który mieliśmy na obiad. Ale obciach! The dog's eaten the steak we were going to have for dinner. Ain't that a bitch!)*

ściemniać [SHCHYEM-nyahch] (perf **ściemnić** [SHCHYEM-neech]) *v* To make something unclear, esp deliberately; to confuse, complicate, or lie <stir, stir up, adjy, bull, bullshit, shit, shovel the shit, string along, snow, fake it, talk through one's hat, speak with forked tongue> eg *Myślę, że facet ściemnia (I think the guy is bullshitting)*

ściera See szmata

ślamazara [shlah-mah-ZAH-rah] *nf* An ineffectual or sluggish person; a botcher <underachiever, loser, born loser, second-rater, schlemiel, schmendrick, schmo, schnook, screwup, fuckup, hacker, muffer, scrub, dub, dool tool, turkey, lump, buterfingers, fumble-fist, goof, goof-off, goofball, eightball, foulball, klutz, also-ran, never-was, nonstarter> eg *Ta ślamazara nawet nie wiedziała, jak zacząć (That shlemiel didn't even know how to start it)*

śledź [shlehch] *nm* **1** A tie <string> eg *Na twoim miejscu nie nosiłbym tego śledzia. Nie bardzo pasuje do marynarki (If I was you, I wouldn't wear this string. It doesn't go well with the jacket)* **2** (or **śledzik** [SHLEH-jeek]) A party organized on the last day of carnival <no slang equivalent> eg *Robimy śledzika. Przyjdziesz a carnical party (We're throwing a carnival party. Will you come?)* **3*** A member of Navy personnel, esp a seaman <gob, mate, shipmate, blue jacket, tar, snipe, jack, salt, old salt, sea dog, water dog swabbie> eg *Zastrzelono dwóch śledzi (Two sea dogs were shot dead)*

ślepia [SHLEH-pyah] *npl* The eyes <peepers, blinkers, lamps, oglers, peekers> eg *Podobają ci sięjeje ślepia? (Do you like her peepers?)*

ślimaczyć się [shlee-MAH-chich shyeh] *v* (Esp about time or an activity) To drag or linger; to move very slowly and, esp be delayed; to lag behind <move at a snail's pace, lag behind, drag on, drag out, drag one's feet, drag one's ass, schlep along, stretch out, crawl, toddle, tool, tail, jelly, hang around, hang up, hold up,

slow up, tie up, bind, stall, put on hold, put off, have lead in one's pants, put on the shelf> eg *Jego proces ślimaczył się przez rok (His trial dragged on for a year)*

ślimak [SHLEE-mahk] *nm* A place where a lot of roads cross over each other <spaghetti junction> eg *Przed nami ślimak, co robimy? (There's a spaghetti junction in front of us. What do we do now?)*
See skołowany

ślina See lecieć w ślinę

ślinka komuś cieknie na coś [SHLEEN-kah KOH-moosh CHYEHK-nyeh NAH tsohsh] *phr* To get aroused or excited by something <make someone's mouth water, get turned on, get stoked, get brought on, get steamed up, get stirred up, get knocked out, get knocked someone dead, be put away, be tickled pink, be tickled to death> eg *Ślinka cieknie już na samą myśl, co się stanie (Just thinking what will happen makes my mouth water)*

śliwka See wpaść

ślizgawica See szklanka

ślubna [SHLOOB-nah] *nf* A wife <wifey, mama, missus, better half, old lady, little woman, ball and chain, trouble and strife, significant other> eg *Poszedł spytać się swojej ślubnej (He went to ask his wifey)*

ślubny [SHLOOB-ni] *nm* A husband <hubby, man of the house, mister, old man, worser half> eg *Co na to powiedział jej ślubny? (What did her hubby say to this?)*

śmichy-chichy [SHMEE-khi KHEE-khi] *npl phr* Laughing or joking in general <cracking-up, breaking-up, howling, screaming, splitting, kidding, jiving, spoofing, joshing, horseplaying> eg *No dobra, dość tych śmichów chichów. Do roboty (All right, enough of this horseplaying. Let's get back to work)*

śmieć [shmyehch] *nm* A poor, loathsome, sloppy, and worthless man, esp a derelict <bum, bo, hobo, piece of shit, hood, wino, dreg, wrongo, scum of the earth> eg *Powiedział, że z takim śmieciem jak ja nie chce mieć do czynienia (He said he wants to have nothing to do with that punk)*

śmiech See lać, pękać ze śmiechu, zrywać boki, kupa śmiechu, nie do śmiechu

śmiech na sali [SHMYEHKH nah SAH-lee] *nm phr* Something very funny, amusing, preposterous, or foolish; a cause of amusement, esp of derision <laugh, laugh and a half, laugher, laughing stock, horselaugh, merry ha-ha, hoot, howl, riot, laff riot, laffer, scream, stitch, boffo, panic, knee-slapper, rib-tickler, side-splitter> eg *Ma zamiar gotować? Śmiech na sali! (Is he going to cook? That's a laugh)*

śmieci See stare śmieci

śmieciara [shmyeh-CHAH-rah] *nf* A garbage truck <dump truck, roach coach, honey wagon> eg *Przejechała go śmieciara (He was run over by a roach coach)*

śmierć See raz kozie śmierć, zapić się, do gobowej deski

śmierdzący leń [shmyehr-DZOHN-tsi LEHÑ] *nm phr* A very lazy person, esp one who chronically avoids work; a shirker <goldbricker, bunk lizard, coffee cooler, feather merchant, lazybones, lazy-ass, lazy bum, bum, clock watcher, dog-fucker> eg *Coś robił cały dzień, ty śmierdzący leniu? (What have you been doing the whole day, you lazybones?)*

śmierdzieć [SHMYEHR-jehch] To have an illegal, immoral, or scandalous quality <smell, stink, stink on ice> eg *Cała ta sprawa naprawdę śmierdzi (This whole affairs really stinks)*

śmierdzieć groszem See nie śmierdzieć groszem

śmiesznie See żeby było śmieszniej

śmiszny [SHMEESH-ni] *adj* Funny or amusing <fun, screaming, stitching, knee-slapping, rib-tickling, gut-busting, side-splitting, gas, gassy, jokey, campy, joshing, gagged-up, for grins> eg *To była na prawdę śmiszna historia (It was really a knee-slapping story)*

śpiewająco [shpyeh-vah-YOHN-tsoh] *adv* Easily and excellently <with flying colors, with bells on, with knobs on, with tits on, without mussing a hair> eg *Zdałem test z językoznawstwa śpiewająco (I passed my linguistics test with flying colors)*

śpiewka See stara śpiewka

średnia przyjemność [SHREHD-nyah pshi-YEHM-nohshch] *nf phr* Something unpleasant or unattractive <no fun, no picnic> eg *Wstawanie o szóstej rano to średnia przyjemność (Getting up at six in the morning is no fun)*

średnio na jeża [SHREHD-nhoh nah YEH-zhah] *adv phr* **1** Neither very badly nor very well; ordinarily; passably <so-so, fair to middling, vanilla, no great shakes, run of the mill, okay, OK> eg *Jak idzie praca? Średnio na jeża (How's the work going? So-so)* **2** About; approximately <around, in the ballpark of, pretty near, something like, close shave to, in the neighborhood of, damn near, pretty near> eg *Było to średnio na jeża ze dwa tysiące (It was something like two thousand)*

środowisko [shroh-doh-VEES-koh] *nn* Ecology or biology, esp as a subject in school <eco, sci> eg *Nie lubię środowiska (I don't like eco)*

świat See być jedną nogą w grobie, być pępkiem świata, pępek świata, przejechać się

światła [SHFYAHT-wah] *nf* An intersection <lights, cross street, mixmaster> eg *Zatrzymaj się na następnych światłach (Stop at the next lights)*

świeży See łyknąć świerzego powietrza

świecić oczami [SHFYEH-cheech oh-CHAH-mee] *v phr* To ashamedly endure the consequences of someone else's wrongdoings <carry the can, hold the bag, hold the sack, take the rap, take the heat, take the fall, bite the bullet, face the music, take it, put one's ass on the line> eg *Jeśli ją złapią, to ja będę za nią świecił oczami (If she gets caught, I'll take the rap for her)*

świecidełko [shfyeh-chee-DEH-oo-koh] *nn* A piece of jewelry, esp cheap and fake; a trinket <sparkler, brass, stone, rock, ice, glass, junk jewelry, gewgaw> eg *Kupił jej jakieś świecidałka (H bought her some junk jewelry)*

świeczka See gra nie warta świeczki

świecznik See na topie

świerszczyk [SHFYEHRSH-chik] *nm* A pornographic magazine <nudie, stroke book, stroke mag, stroke, rag, skin book, skin mag, skin rag, fuck book, fuck mag, porn book, porn mag, porn rag> eg *Musiałem posłużyć się świerszczykiem, żeby przełamać lody (It took a stroke book for me to break the ice)*

święto lasu [SHFYEHN-toh LAH-soo] *nn phr* A day when something exceptional happens, esp when someone is is exceptionally friendly, polite, or helpful for others <love-your-neighbor day, be-good-to-someone's-day> eg *Dlaczego ona jest dziś taka miła? Czy dziś jest święto lasu? (Why is she so nice today? Is it love-your-neighbor day?)*

świętojebliwy** [shfyehn-toh-yehb-LEE-vi] *adj* Overly pious or rekigious; devout <knee bender, Jesus freak, goody-goody, goody, tight-ass, Mother Theresa> eg

Twoja siostra jest bardzo świętojebliwa. Chodzi codziennie do kościoła (Your sister is a real knee bender. She goes to church everyday)

święty See dać komuś święty spokój, goły, goły jak święty turecki

świnia* [SHFEE-nyah] (or **wiśnia** [VEESH-nyah]) *nf* A person one strongly dislikes, esp one who behaves in an unethical, immoral or dishonest way <asshole, fuck, fucker, fuckhead, fuckface, motherfucker, shit, shitface, shithead, shitheel, bastard, jerk, SOB, son of a bitch, son of a whore, cocksucker, prick, dick, dickhead, cuntface, schmuck, scum, scumbag, sleazebag, slimebag, dipshit, pisshead, piece of shit, pain in the ass> eg *Chodzą słuchy, że nowy szef to prawdziwa świnia (Rumor has it that your new boss is a real bastard)*

See chlać, pijany jak świnia, trzeźwy jak świnia, upić się jak świnia

świniak [SHFEE-nyahk] *nm* A pig <porker, porky, cob roller, slob> eg *Kupiliśmy świniaka (We bought a porky)*

świntuch [SHFEEN-tookh] *nm* A man who pursues and otherwise devotes himself to women to an unusual degree <ladies' man, lech, skirt-chaser, lady-killer, lover-boy, hound-dog, cocksman, cunt-struck, cunt-happy, pussy-struck, pistol Pete, operator> eg *Ale z niego świntuch. Wszędzie tylko pornusy (What a lech he is. There are porn movies all over the place)*

świntuszyć [shfeen-TOO-shich] *v* To misbehave, esp tell obscene jokes <be a bad boy, be a bad girl, be a naughty boy, be a naughty girl, act up> eg *Przestań świntuszyć i zmień temat (Don't be a bad boy and change the subject)*

świński [SHFEEŃ-skee] *adj* Lewd, obscene <dirty, blue, filthy, juicy, off-color, raunchy, raw, rough, spicy, steamy, X-rated> eg *Opowiedział dwa świńskie kawały (He told two raunchy jokes)*

świński blondyn [SHFEEŃ-skee BLOHN-din] *nm phr* A blond man with light complexion, esp of Scandinavian looks <no slang equivalent> eg *Kto to jest ten świski blondyn? (Who is that blond guy over there)*

świński kawał [SHFEEŃ-skee KAH-vah-oo] *nm* An obscene joke <dirty joke, filthy joke, raunchy joke> eg *On zawsze lubił opowiadać świńskie kawały w towarzystwie konbiet (He always liked to tell dirty jokes in the company of women)*

świński* [SHFEEŃ-skee] *adj* Unethical, immoral, or dishonest; nasty <bad-assed, nasty-assed, bitchy, barfy, mean, creepy, crumb, bent, crooked> eg *Jego nowa dziewczyna ma bardzo świński charakter. Na jego miejscu bym z nią zerwał, i to szybko (His new girlfriend has a real bitchy character. If I was him, I would break up with her fast)*

świństwa [SHFEEŃ-stfah] *n pl* Sexual perversity, esp in the form of pornography <dirt, filth, porn, nudie, sleaze> eg *Oglądali te świństwa na okrągło (They would watch this filth day and night)*

świństwo [SHFEEŃ-stfoh] *nn* **1** A wicked, mean, or malicious act <dirty trick, rotten trick, dirty pool, dirty work, shady business, jiggery-pokery, skull-duggery> eg *Zrobiła mu świństwo (She played a dirty trick on him)* **2** Anything disgusting, abhoring, repulsive <shit, crap, scuzz, sleaze, drek, crud, glop, grunge, scrunge, muck, mung, goo, gook, gunk> eg *Czy brał narkotyki? O nie, nigdy nie wziąłby tego świństwa do ust (Did he do drugs? No, he wouldn't put this shit in his mouth)*

świr [shfeer] *nm* **1** (or **świrus** [SHFEE-roos]) An insane or eccentric man <freak, fruitcake, goofball, cook, loon, nut, nutball, nutcase, nutter, psycho, screwball,

screw-loose, sicko, wacko, weirdo, psycho, oddball> eg *Ten facet to świr. Myśli, że jest prorokiem (This guy is a freak. He thinks he's a prophet)* **2** Obsession, insanity, or eccentricity <thing, kick, bag, bug, craze, freak, frenzy, weakness, bug up one's ass, bug in one's ear, bee in one's bonnet, bee, flea in one's nose, maggot, maggot in one's brain, hang-up, jones, monkey, ax to grind> eg *Zbieranie znaczków, czy to nie jest jego ostatni świr? (Stamp collecting, isn't that his latest craze?)*

świrować [shfee-ROH-vahch] (perf **ześwirować** [zeh-shfee-ROH-vahch]) *v* **1** To lose mental fitness; to become insane or eccentric <go crazy, go crazy as a loon, blow one's cork, blow one's top, blow a fuse, crack up, freak out, flip out, go ape, go bananas, go bent, go bonkers, go cracked, go dopey, go ga-ga, go half-baked, go loony, go loopy, go mental, go nerts, go nuts, go nutty, go off one's nut, go off one's rocker, go off one's base, go off the track, go off the trolley, go out one's skull, go psycho, go schizo, go screwy, go wacky, go weird, go wild, schiz out, psych out, come unglued, come unstuck, come unwrapped, go to pieces> eg *Całkowicie ześwirowała, gdy zdechł jej kanarek (She went to pieces when her canary died)* **2** To become bewildered, disoriented, or confused <get spaced out, get mixed up, get discombobulated, get flabbergasted, get messed up, get unscrewed, get farmisht, get balled up, get shook up, get floored, get unglued, get unzipped, get fried, get screwed-up, get fucked-up, get flummoxed, get kerflooey, get caught off base> eg *Ześwirowała, gdy to usłyszała (She got farmisht when she heard that)*

świstek [SHFEES-tehk] *nm* A sheet of paper, esp a document <paper> eg *Pokazała mi jakiś świstek (She showed me some paper)*

świtać [SHFEE-tahch] (perf **zaświtać** [zah-SHFEE-tahch]; **w głowie** [v GWOH-vyeh] or **we łbie** [veh WBYEH] may be added) *v* To have a sudden idea; to come to mind briefly <cross one's mind, pass through someone's mind, dawn on, have a brainwave, spark> eg *Powiem ci, co mi właśnie zaświtało w głowie (Let me tell you what just crossed my mind)*

T

tablice [tah-BLEE-tseh] *npl* Automotive license plates <pads, plates, tags, numbers> eg *Były to zachodnie wozy na polskich tablicach (They were western cars with Polish plates)*

tabun [TAH-boon] *nm* A tight crush of people; a crowd of people <jam, mob, horde, everybody and his brother> eg *Widziałeś ten tabun na zewnątrz? (Did you see that mob outside?)*

tachać się See telepać się

tak że hej [tahk zheh KHEH-ee] ((**ha** [khah] or **ho-ho** [khoh-KHOH] or **historia** [khee-STOH-tyah] or **głowa mała** [GWOH-vah MAH-wah] or **chuj** [KHOO-ee] may replace **hej**) *adv phr* Extremely; exceedingly; very <awful, god-awful, real, mighty, plenty, damn, damned, goddamn, goddamned, darn, darned, effing, flipping, forking, freaking, frigging, fucking, one's ass off, one's brains out, one's head off, to the max, like all get-out, like sin, to beat the band, like all creation, as

blazes, as can be, as hell, like hell, in full swing> eg *Był pijany, że hej (He was drunk like hell)*

taki że aż strach [TAH-kee ZHEH ahsh STRAHKH] *adj phr* Frightening; terrifying; eerie <scary, creepy, hairy, shivery, furry> eg *Ten stary dom był taki, że aż strach (This old house was real creepy)*

taki że bez kija nie podchodź [TAH-kee ZHEH behs KEE-yah nyeh POHT-khohch] *adj phr* (Of a person) Dangerous-looking, aggressive, or belligerent <defi, ornery, feisty, bitchy, cussed, scrappy, snorky, flip, salty, spiky, mean, bad-assed, nasty-assed, gutty, lippy, cocky, brassy, cheeky, sassy, nervy, smart-ass, wise-ass, foul-mouthed> eg *Ona jest taka, że bez kija nie podchodź (She's real sassy)*

taki że do rany przyłóż [TAH-kee zheh doh RAH-ni PSHI-woosh] *adj phr* (Of a person) Gentle; obliging; understanding <sweet as sugar, sweet as a day, simpatico, softhearted, softie, all heart, bleading heart> eg *Nasz nowy facet od matmy jest taki, że do rany przyłóż (Our new math prof is very softhearted)*

taki że hej [TAH-kee zheh KHEH-ee] (**ha** [khah] or **ho-ho** [khoh-KHOH] or **historia** [khee-STOH-tyah] or **głowa mała** [GWOH-vah MAH-wah] or **chuj** [KHOO-ee] may replace **hej**) *adj phr* Excellent; wonderful; extremely good <great, cool, swell, fab, rad, def, far-out, awesome, frantic, terrific, funky, gorgeous, groovy, hellacious, neat, peachy, dandy, baddest, mean, solid, super-dooper, wailing, wicked, gnarly, top-notch, ten, ace-high, A-OK, A-1, some> eg *Ona ma takiego ojca, że hej! Na pewno ci pomoże (She has a swell dad. He'll sure help you)*

taki że mózg staje [moosk STAH-yeh] *adj phr* [TAH-kee zheh moosk STAH-yeh]) Amazing; unusual; extraordinary; inconceivable <mind-boggle, mind-blowing> eg *Ich nowoczesne pojazdy są takie, że mózg staje (Their high-tech vehicles are mind-boggling)*

taki że mucha nie siada [MOO-khah nyeh SHYAH-dah] (or **że mucha nie siada** [zheh MOO-khah nyeh SHYAH-dah]) *adj phr* Excellent; beyond reproach <great, cool, swell, fab, rad, def, far-out, awesome, frantic, terrific, funky, gorgeous, groovy, hellacious, neat, peachy, dandy, baddest, mean, solid, super-dooper, wailing, wicked, gnarly, top-notch, ten, ace-high, A-OK, A-1, some> eg *Mówię ci, ten samochód jest bardzo dobry. Mucha nie siada (I'm telling you, this car is very good. Real cool)*

taki chuj See chuj

taki sobie [TAH-kee SOH-byeh] (or **taki tam** [TAH-kee tahm]) *adj phr* Not very good; mediocre <lousy, awful, bush-league, cheap, crappy, shitty, cruddy, doggy, low-rent, low-ride, no-good, raggedy-ass, schlocky, stinking, tacky, trashy, two-bit, dime-a-dozen, fair to middling, garden variety, of a sort, of sorts, piddling, pissy-ass, run-of-the-mill, small-time> eg *Co myślisz o ich najnowszej płycie? Myślę, że jest taka sobie (What do you think about their latest album? I think it's no-good)*

takiego chuja See chuj

taksa See taryfa

taksiarz [TAHK-shahsh] *nm* A taxicab driver <hack, hacker, hackie, cabbie> eg *Taksiarz nie miał drobnych (The hack didn't have any change)*

tam gdzie pieprz rośnie [tahm gjeh PYEHPSH ROSH-nyeh] (or **tam gdzie diabeł mówi dobranoc** [tahm gjeh DYAH-beh-oo MOO-vee doh-BRAH-nohts]) *nn phr* A small town, esp in the country; any place far from civilization

<jerk town, jerkwater town, backwater, hellhole, rathole, mudhole, real hole, noplaceville, hicksville, whistle stop, dump, armpit, East Jesus, Bumfuck Egypt> eg *Pojechał tam, gdzie pieprza rośnie (He went to some Bumfuck Egypt)*

tam i nazad [tahm ee NAH-zahd] (or **tam i siam** [tahm ee SHYAHM] or **w tę i nazad** [f teh ee NAH-zaht]) *adv* Back and forth; backwards and forwards; from one side to the other <to and fro, there and back> eg *Przez cały dzień łazi tam i nazad (He's been going to and fro all day)*

tango See iść w cug

tani jak barszcz [TAH-nee yahk BAHRSHCH] *adj phr* Very cheap; inexpensive <dirt cheap, cheap as dirt, dog cheap, steal> eg *Ten rower był tani jak barszcz (This bike was cheap as dirt)*

taniec See do tańca i różańca

taniocha [tah-NYOH-khah] *nf* Something very cheap; something inexpensive <cheapie, el cheapo, bargain, steal> eg *Pięć stów za coś takiego? To taniocha! (Five hundred for a thing like that? It's a steal!)*

tankować [tahn-KOH-vahch] (perf **zatankować** [zah-tahn-KOH-vahch]) *v* To drink alcohol, esp in large quantities <tank up, booze, guzzle, gargle, bend the elbow, hit the bottle, hit the sauce, knock back, lap, tank up, wet one's whistle, hang a few on, slug down, swig> eg *Twój brat to dopiero lubi zatankować (Your brother sure likes to wet his whistle)*

tańczyć koło kogoś [TAHÑ-chich KOH-woh KOH-gohsh] *v phr* To treat someone with excessive care, ardor, or tenderness; to pamper <treat with kid gloves, handle with kid gloves, treat someone as an apple of someone's eye, give someone the red carpet treatment, pet> eg *On jest tutaj guru i wszyscy koło niego tańczą (He's a guru around here and everybody treats him with kid gloves)*

tapeta See brać na warsztat, na tapecie

tarabanić się See telepać się

targać się See telepać się

taryfa [tah-RI-fah] (or **taksa** [TAHK-sah]) *nf* A taxicab <cab, hack> eg *Zadzwoń po taryfę, dobra? (Call a cab, will you?);Gdzie mogę tu złapać taksę? (Where can I get a cab here?)*

taryfiarz [tah-RI-fyahsh] *nm* A taxicab driver <hack, hacker, hackie, cabbie> eg *Taryfiarz nie miał drobnych (The hack didn't have any change)*

tasiemcowy [tah-syehm-TSOH-vi] *adj* (Esp about about a line) Very long <mile long, spun out, strung out, dragged out, stretched> eg *Kolejka była tasiemcowe (The line was a mile long)*

tasiemiec [tah-SHYEH-myehts] *nm* A television daily dramatic series showing the painful or passionate amours and disasters of ordinary people, consisting of many episodes <soap opera, tapeworm series> eg *Nie przepada za Brazylijskimi tasiemcami (She's not very much into Brazilian soap operas)*

taskać się See telepać się

taszczyć się See telepać się

tauzen [TAH-oo-zehn] (or **tysiak** [TI-shyahk]) *nm* Thousand, esp a thousand zloty bill <grand, G-note, thou, K> eg *Dał mi za to dwa tauzeny (He gave me two grand for it)*

te klocki [teh KLOHTS-kee] (or **te sprawy** [teh SPRAH-vi] or **te rzeczy** [teh ZHEH-chi]) *npl phr* Copulation in general <you-know-what, it> eg *Jeśli nie możesz* *być dobry, to bądź chociaż dobry w te klocki (If you can't be good, be good at it); Myślę, że ona lubi te klocki (I think she likes you-know-what)*

tekścić [TEHKSH-cheech] (perf **przytekścić** [pshi-TEHKSH-cheech]) *v* To say something funny, shocking, impressive, or important, esp very accurately and cogently <say a line, say a one-liner, say a mouthful, say an earful, make a spiel, make a pitch> eg *Ale przytekściła! (She sure said a mouthful!)*

tekściarz [TEHKSH-chahsh] *nm* An eloquent man prone to playing verbal tricks <wordsmith, spieler, pitcher, artist, joker, kidder, clown, article, ham, character, item, number> eg *Z tego twojego kuzyna to prawdziwy tekściarz. Ale jej powiedział! (Your cousin is a real joker. Did he give her an earful!)*

tekst [tehkst] *nm* Any statement, esp funny, impressive, or important, and very accurate and cogent <line, one-liner, mouthful, earful, spiel, pitch> eg *Słyszałeś ten tekst? (Did you hear that mouthful?)*

telefon See dziewczynka na telefon

telepać się [teh-LEH-pahch shyeh] (perf **przytelepać się** [pshi-teh-LEH-pahch shyeh]; or **tachać się** TAH-khahch shyeh] perf **przytachać się** pshi-TAH-khahch shyeh]; or **tarabanić się** tah-rah-BAH-neech shyeh] perf **przytarabanić się** pshi-tah-rah-BAH-neech shyeh]; or **targać się** TAHR-gahch shyeh] perf **przytargać się** pshi-TAHR-gahch shyeh]; or **taskać się** TAHS-kahch shyeh] perf **przytaskać się** pshi-TAHS-kahch shyeh];or **taszczyć się** TAHSH-chich shyeh] perf **przytaszczyć się** pshi-TAHSH-chich shyeh]) *v* To move or carry something with difficulty <schlep, drag, hump, cart, hump, tote, lug> eg *Mam się telepać z tym plecakiem całą drogę z powrotem do ciebie? (Am I supposed to lug this backpack all the way back to your place?)*

telewizor See w telewizorze

tępak See tłumok

tępy* [TEHM-pi] *adj* Stupid or unintelligent <airbrained, airheaded, birdbrained, blockheaded, squareheaded, boneheaded, bubblebrained, bubbleheaded, bucketheaded, cluckheaded, cementheaded, clunkheaded, deadheaded, dumbclucked, dumbheaded, dumbassed, dumbbrained, fatbrained, fatheaded, flubdubbed, knukclebrained, knuckleheaded, lamebrained, lardheaded, lunkheaded, meatheaded, muscleheaded, noodleheaded, numbskulled, pointheaded, scatterbrained, nerdy, dorky, jackassed, lummoxed, dopey, goofy> eg *Co za tępa laska! Nie rozumie ani słowa (What a airheaded chick! She doesn't understand a word)*

tip top [teep TOHP] *adj phr* Excellent; wonderful; extremely good <classy, high-class, great, cool, swell, fab, rad, def, far-out, awesome, frantic, terrific, funky, gorgeous, groovy, hellacious, neat, peachy, dandy, baddest, mean, solid, super-dooper, wailing, wicked, gnarly, top-notch, ten, ace-high, A-OK, A-1, some> eg *Wyposażenie było tip top (The equipment was was top-notch)*

tłok See ujść

tłumok* [TWOO-mohk] (or **tłuk*** [TWOOK] or **tępak*** [TEHM-pahk] or **tuman*** [TOO-mahn] or **trep*** [trehp]) *nm* A very stupid, clumsy or ineffectual person; an idiot <airbrain, airhead, birdbrain, blockhead, squarehead, bonehead, bubblebrain, bubblehead, buckethead, cluckhead, cementhead, clunkhead, deadhead, dumbbell, dumbcluck, dumbhead, dumbass, dumbbrain, fatbrain, fathead, flubdub, knukclebrain, knucklehead, lamebrain, lardhead, lunkhead,

meathead, musclehead, noodlehead, numbskull, pointhead, scatterbrain, jerk, jerk-off, klutz, chump, creep, nerd, dork, dweeb, gweeb, geek, jackass, lummox, twerp, nerd, bozo, clod, cluck, clunk, dimwit, dingbat, dipstick, dodo, dopey, dufus, goofus, lump, lunk, nitwit, schnook, schlep, schlemiel, schmendrick, schmo, schmuck, simp, stupe> eg *Od godziny tłumaczy im, co to oznacza. Straszne tłumoki, nic nie rozumieją (He's been explaining to them what it means for an hour. They are real squareheads, they don't understand anything)*

tłuścioch [TWOOSH-chyohkh] *nm* An obese person <fatty, fatso, blimp, fat-ass, lard-ass, tub of lard, crisco> eg *Ten tłuścioch beka ledwo mieści się w drzwiach (That tub of lard can hardly get through the door)*

to nie czyjaś broszka See nie czyjaś broszka

to nie sztuka See nie sztuka

to rozumiem [toh roh-ZOO-myehm] (or **to ja rozumiem** [toh yah roh-ZOO-myehm]) *phr* Now you are saying the right things or doing what you should be doing <now you're talking, now you're cooking> eg *Gdy skończył grać, nauczyciel powiedział „To rozumien!"(As he finished playing, the teacher said, "Now you're cooking!")*

toczka w toczkę See kubek w kubek

top See na topie, tip top

torba See iść z torbami, puścić kogoś z torbami

totalnie [toh-TAHL-nyeh] *adv* Extremely; exceedingly; very <awful, god-awful, real, mighty, plenty, damn, damned, goddamn, goddamned, darn, darned, effing, flipping, forking, freaking, frigging, fucking, one's ass off, one's brains out, one's head off, to the max, like all get-out, like sin, to beat the band, like all creation, as blazes, as can be, as hell, like hell, in full swing> eg *Byliśmy totalnie zmęczeni (We were darn tired)*

totalny [toh-TAHL-ni] *adj* Big; large; sizable; extreme <gross, humongous, monstro, moby, jumbo, hefty, whopper, mother, king-size, God-size, awful, god-awful, real, damn, damned, goddamn, goddamned, blasted, darn, darned, effing, flipping, forking, freaking, frigging, pesky> eg *Jego pokój to bybł totalny bałagan (His room was a god-awful mess)*

totek [TOH-tehk] *nm* A lottery <lotto, numbers, numbers game> eg *Stracił dużo pieniędzy grając w lotka (He lost a lot of money by playing the numbers)*

towar [TOH-vahr] *nm* A young and attractive woman <chick, broad, gal, pussy, cunt, ass, piece of ass, piece, dish, babe, baby, dame, beauty, beaut, beauty queen, baby doll, doll, dolly, dollface, dreamboat, dream girl, eating stuff, eyeful, flavor, looker, good-looker, head-turner, traffic-stopper, honey, killer, hot number, package, knockout, oomph girl, peach, bombshell, sex bunny, sex job, sex kitten, sex pot, table grade, ten, bunny, centerfold, cheesecake, date bait, dazzler, heifer, fluff, quail, sis, skirt, tail, job, leg, tart, tomato, pussycat, cooz, twat> eg *Powiedz mi więcej o tym towarze (Tell me more about that babe)*

towarzycho [toh-vah-ZHI-khoh] *nn* A group of people who are intimate and close; a company <scene, folks, pack, bunch, crew, gang, clan, crowd, boys> eg *Całe towarzycho w końcu dortarła tu wczoraj (The whole crew finally got here yesterday); Zaczęła szlajać się z ćpunami. To nie było towarzycho dla mnie (She started to hang out with druggies. It wasn't my scene)*

trąba* [TROHM-bah] (or **trąba jerychońska*** [TROHM-bah yeh-ri-KHOHÑ-skah] may be added) *nf* A pitiful, clumsy or ineffectual person, esp a bungler <lummox, klutz, screwup, goofup, goof, foozler> eg *Jak mogłeś zrobić cośtakiego? Ale z Ciebie trąba! (How could you do that? What a klutzz you are!)*
See puścić kogoś kantem, puścić kogoś z torbami

traktor See trep

traktować kogoś per noga [trahk-TOH-vahch KOH-gohsh pehr NOH-gah] *v phr* To deal with in a humiliating, haughty, or oppressive manner <treat someone like a doormat, treat someone like shit> eg *Dyrektor traktuje mnie per noga, bo jestem lepszy od niego (The director has been treating me like shit because I'm better than he is)*

trampki See obłęd

trasa See być w trasie

trawa [TRAH-vah] (or **trawka** [TRAHF-kah]) *nf* Marijuana; cannabis <grass, pot, dope, weed, reefer, tea, hemp, Mary Jane, MJ> eg *Miała przy sobie trawkę, gdy ją aresztowano (She had pot on her when she was arrested)*
See mowa-trawa, iść na zieloną trawkę, posłać na zieloną trawkę

trep [trehp] **1** *nm* (or **traktor** [TRAHK-tohr]) A shoe or boot, esp an old one <stomper, wafflestomper, boondocker, clodhopper, shitkicker> eg *Zabieraj trepy z mojego biurka (Get your wafflestompers off my desk)* **2*** (or **stary trep*** [STAH-ri trehp]) *nm* An old man <gramps, old fart, old bugger, geezer, gaffer, old-timer, fossil> eg *Czego chciał od ciebie ten stary trep? (What did the geezer want from you?)*
See tłumok

trójczyna [troo-ee-CHI-nah] *nf phr* A grade of C <hook, pass, gentleman's C> eg *Dostał tylko ocenę państwową z tego testu (He only got a C on that test)*

trop See zbić kogoś z tropu

trumna See gwóźdź do trumny

trup See paść trupem, pijany jak świnia, po czyimś trupie, po trupach, upić się jak świnia

trupiarnia [troo-PYAHR-nyah] *nf* A mortuary or morgue <icebox, cooler, freezer, slab, ward X> eg *Ciało zabrano do trupiarni (The body was taken to the ice box)*

truposz [TROO-pohsh] *nm* A dead body; a corpse <stiff, dead meat, goner, dead duck, dead pigeon, crowbait, worm-food> eg *Zeszłej nocy wyciągnęli z rzeki następnego truposza (They pulled another stiff out of the river last night)*

truteń [TROO-tehñ] *nm* A person who regulary and chronically avoids work; a shirker <goldbricker, bunk lizard, coffee cooler, feather merchant, lazybones, lazy-ass, lazy bum, bum, clock watcher, dog-fucker> eg *Twój brat to prawdziwy truteń. Nawet nie zabrał sięjeszcze do roboty (Your brother is a real goldbricker. He hasn't even started working)*

tryper* [TRI-pehr] (or **trynio*** [TRI-nyoh]) *nm* Gonorrhea, or any other veneral disease <bug, crud, scrud, double scrud, creeping crud, VD, clap, dose, dose of claps, drip, blue balls, syph, siph, head cold, crabs> eg *Nie używał prezerwatyw i złapał trynia (He didn't use any condoms so he caught VD)*

trząść dupą* [TSHOHNSCHCH DOO-poh] (or **trząść portkami** [TSHOHNSCHCH pohrt-KAH-mee]) *v phr* To be afraid; to be frightened; to be intimidated <chicken out, turn chicken, turn yellow, run scared, have cold feet, be scared stiff, be scared shitless, shit one's pants, piss one's pants, shit bullets,

shit a brick, shit green, be spooked, push the panic button, wimp out> eg *Było widać, że przez cały czas trząsł dupą (You could tell he was pissing his pants all the time)*

trzasnąć [TSHAHS-nohnch] *v* To have a quick drink of liquor <knock back, down, slug down, swig, tank, tank up> eg *Trzasnął cztery piwa i zaczął bekać (He downed three beers and started to burp)*

trzepać See mleć jęzorem

trzepać konia See walić konia

trzepnięty [tshehp-NYEHN-ti] *adj* Insane, stupid, or thoughtless <fucked in the head, fucked-up, crazy, creazy as a loon, loony, nerts, nuts, nutso, nutsy, nutty, sick, sick in the head, sicko, wacko, wacky, psycho, shizo, screwy, off one's rocker, out of one's skull, fruity, airbrained, airheaded, birdbrained, blockheaded, squareheaded, boneheaded, bubblebrained, bubbleheaded, bucketheaded, cluckheaded, cementheaded, clunkheaded, deadheaded, dumbclucked, dumbheaded, dumbassed, dumbbrained, fatbrained, fatheaded, flubdubbed, knukclebrained, knuckleheaded, lamebrained, lardheaded, lunkheaded, meatheaded, muscleheaded, noodleheaded, numbskulled, pointheaded, scatterbrained, nerdy, dorky, jackassed, lummoxed, dopey, goofy> eg *Ten facet jest naprawdę trzepnięty. Potrzebuje wakacji (This guy is really sick. He needs a vacation)*

trzeszczeć w szwach See pękać w szwach

trzeźwy jak świnia* [TSHEH-zhvi yahk SHFEE-nyah] *adj phr* Completely sober <cold sober, stone cold sober, sober as a judge, on the wagon, dry> eg *Twierdził, że był trzeźwy jak świnia (He claimed he was sober as a judge)*

trzy razy brzydszy od gówna See dwa razy brzydszy od gówna

trzymać fason [TSHI-mahch FAH-sohn] (o **mieć fason** [myehch FAH-sohn]) *v phr* To be self-assured, optimistic, or lively; to keep one's composure <keep cool, not lose head, pull through, make it through, keep up one's spirit, pull oneself together, hold oneself together, keep it together> eg *Mimo tego, że wujek zmarł, ciotka trzyma fason (Despite the fact that uncle died, auntie has been making it through)*

trzymać pieniądze w skarpecie [TSHI-mahch pyeh-NYOHN-dzeh f skahr-PEH-cheh] (or **trzymać pieniądze w pończosze** [TSHI-mahch pyeh-NYOHN-dzeh f pohñ-CHOH-sheh]) *v phr* To keep or hide one's savings home rather than in a bank <squirrel away, sock away, stash, stache, rathole> eg *Myślę, że trzyma te pieniądze w skarpecie (I think he socked the money away)*

trzymać rękę na pulsie [TSHI-mahch REHN-keh nah POOL-shyeh] *v phr* To carefully listen or pay attention hoping to get advance warning of something; to control <have one's ear to the ground, keep one's ear to the ground, play by ear> eg *Będę trzymał rękę na pulsie i dam ci znać, czego się dowiedziałem (I'll keep my ear to the ground and let you know what I find out)*

trzymać się [TSHI-mahch shyeh] *v* **1** (Esp about older people) To be healthy, active, or physically fit <be alive and kicking, be fit as a fiddle, be up to snuff, be up to the mark, be hale and hearty, be wrapped tight, be in fine feather, be in fine whack, be in the pink, be sound as a dollar, be right as rain, be full of piss and vinegar, be full of beans> eg *Dziadek ma 70 lat, ale trzyma się (Grandfather is 70, but he's still fit as a fiddle)* **2** (To try) To remain mentally unaffected or balanced; to keep one's composure; to control oneself <keep cool, not lose head, make it through, keep up one's spirit, pull oneself together, keep it together> eg *Mimo* *tego, że wujek zmarł, ciotka trzyma się (Despite the fact that uncle died, auntie has been making it through)*

trzymać się kupy [TSHI-mahch shyeh KOO-pi] *v phr* To make sense; to be plausible and reasonable <figure, add up, hang together, hold together, hold up, hold water, stack up, wash, work, do, go down> eg *To, że opuściła miasto po prostu nie trzyma się kupy (It just doesn't figure that she would leave town)*

trzymać się za kieszeń [TSHI-mahch shyeh zah KYEH-shehñ] *v phr* To spend money reluctantly <penny-pinch, scrimp> eg *Jej mąż trzymał się bez przewry za kieszeń (Her husband penny-pinched all the time)*

trzymać z kimś [TSHI-mahch s KEEMSH] *v* To be friends with someone <pal around, buddy up, be buddies, be brothers, be buddy-buddy, be palsy-walsy, hang around with, hang out with> eg *Zawsze trzymał z komunistami (He always palled with the communists)*

trzynastka [tshi-NAHST-kah] *nf* An additional salary paid once a year around Christmas <Christmas bonus, Christmas frosting on the cake> eg *W tym roku liczyłem na całkiem niezłą trzynastkę, ale nic nie dostałem (This year I was hoping for a nice juicy Christmas bonus, but I got nothing)*

tuman See tłumok

twarda ręka [TFAHR-dah REHN-kah] *nf phr* Severe governing; tight control <rod of iron, iron fist, iron hand> eg *Prezydent rządził twardą ręką (The President ruled with an iron hand)*

twarde [TFAHR-deh] (or **twarda waluta** [TFAHR-dah vah-LOO-tah]) *npl* (Esp in former communist times) Currency that is strong in the market and backed by considerable economic power <hard currency, hard money> eg *Nie chciał miękkiej waluty, przyjmował tylko twarde (He didn't want soft money, he was only interested in hard money)*

twardy [TFAHR-di] *adj* **1** Uncompromising, tenacious, or persistent <hard-line, hard-core, locked, bound, bound and determined, set, tough, stiff, stiff-necked, stubborn as a mule, mulish> eg **2** Ruthless, hard, and demanding <tough, rough, stiff, ball-breaking, ball-busting, back-breaking, ass-busting, bitchy, badass, cussed, feisty> eg *Słyszałem, że wasz nowy nauczyciel od matmy jest twardy (I heard your new math teacher is real tough)*

twardy orzech do zgryzienia [TFAHR-di OH-zhehkh doh zgri-ZHYEH-nyah] *nm phr* A difficult person or thing to deal with <hard nut to crack, tough nut to crack> eg *Twój kuzyn to twardzy orzech do zgryzienia. Nie mogę go rozgryźć (Your cousin is a hard nut to crack. I can't figure him out)*

twarz See na łebka

tył See być do tyłu, mieć coś u kogoś

tyłek [TI-wehk] *nm* The buttocks, the posterior <ass, butt, bum, behind, back, back seat, seat, bottom, heinie, rear, tush, fanny, derriere, tail, bucket, tokus, keister, kazoo> eg *Mam cię kopnąć w tyłek? No to lepiej bierz siędo roboty (You want me to kick you in the ass? So you'd better get moving)*
See mieć robaki w dupie, móc kogoś pocałować, nadstawiać karku

tyci [TI-chee] *adj* Very small; tiny <teeny, teeny-weeny, teensy, teensy-weensy, bitty, bitsy, itsy-bitsy, wee, short, yea high, yea big, pint-sized, half-pint, knee high> eg *Dostał tylko tyci kawałek (All he got was a teeny-weeny piece)*

tydzień See przegląd tygodnia

tyle co kot napłakał [TI-leh tsoh KOHT nah-PWAH-kah-oo] (or **tyle co brudu pod paznokciem** [TI-leh tsoh BROO-doo poht pah-ZNOHK-chyhem] or **tyle co brudu za paznokciem** [TI-leh tsoh BROO-doo poht pah-ZNOHK-chyhem]) *adv phr* Very little; almost nothing <drop in the ocean, drop in the bucket, chicken feed, smidgen, tad, wee bit, itty bit> eg *Pieniędzy dostaliśmy tyle, co kot napłakał (The money we got was a drop in the ocean); Czy on ma pieniądze? Tyle, co brudu za paznokciem (Does he have any money? A smidgen)*

tylec See od tylca

typ [tip] (or **typek** [TI-pehk]) *nm* A man one dislikes or disapproves of <asshole, fuck, fucker, fuckhead, fuckface, motherfucker, shit, shitface, shithead, shitheel, bastard, jerk, SOB, son of a bitch, son of a whore, cocksucker, prick, dick, dickhead, cuntface, schmuck, scum, scumbag, sleazebag, slimebag, dipshit, pisshead, piece of shit, pain in the ass> eg *Jak mogła się przespać z takim typem? (How could she go to bed with such a dickhead?)*

tyrać [TI-rahch] (or **tyrać jak wół** [TI-rahch yahk VOOW] perf **natyrać** [nah-TI-rahch]) *v* To work very hard <work one's ass off, work one's fingers to the bone, work like a horse, sweat, bust one's ass off, break one's ass off, make bricks without a straw> eg *Od dwóch lat tyra jak wół (He's been working like a horse for two years)*

tyrać [TI-rahch] (or **tyrać jak wół** [TI-rahch yahk VOOW]) *v* To work very hard <work one's ass off, work one's fingers to the bone, work like a horse, sweat, bust one's ass off, break one's ass off> eg *Od dwóch lat tyra jak wół (He's been working like a horse for two years)*

tysiak See tauzen

U

u chuja See chuj

u diabła See do diabła

u kurwy nędzy See kurwa

ubaw [OO-bahf] (or **ubaw po pachy** [OO-bahf poh PAH-khi] or **ubaw po same pachy** [OO-bahf poh SAH-meh PAH-khi]) *nm* Something very funny, amusing or foolish; a cause of amusement, esp of derision <laugh, laugh and a half, laugher, laughing stock, horselaugh, merry ha-ha, hoot, howl, riot, laff riot, laffer, scream, stitch, boffo, panic, knee-slapper, rib-tickler, side-splitter> eg *Masz zamiar gotować? Ale ubaw! (You're going to cook? That's a laugh); Nie mielibyśmy ubawu jadąc tam? (Wouldn't it be a hoot to go there?)*

ubecja* [oo-BEHTS-yah] *nf* (Esp in former communist times) Secret Police <the eye, undercovers, plainclothes, spooks, peepers, dicks, ops> eg *Ubecja go dorwała (The plainclothes caught him)*

ubek* [OO-behk] (or **ubol*** [OO-bohl]) *nm* (In former communist times) A member of Secret Police <the eye, undercover, plainclothes, spook, peeper, dick, op> eg *Zabito wczoraj dwóch ubeków (Two spooks were killed yesterday)*

ubić interes [OO-beech een-TEH-rehs] *v phr* To make or conclude an arrangement, esp to reach an agreement on price for something <strike a bargain, make a deal, cut a deal, crack a deal> eg *Targowaliśmy się przez jakiś czas, ale w końcu ubiliśmy interes (We argued for a long time, but finally struck a bargain)*

ubogi See dla ubogich

ubzdryngolić się See urżnąć się

ubzdryngolony See urżnięty

ubzdurać sobie [oo-BZDOO-rahch SOH-byeh] *v* To persuade oneself; to confirm oneself in the conviction <get something into one's head, put oneself across, turn one's head around, twist one's arm> eg *Ubzdurała sobie, że zostanie lekarzem (She got it into her head that she would become a doctor)*

uchlać się See upić się jak świnia

uchlać się Perf See chlać

uchlany See pijany jak świnia, schlany

ucho See biadolić, cwaniak, dać po dupie, dostać po dupie, kłaść uszy po sobie, pierdolić komuś za uszami, po uszy

uciąć See dać głowę

uciułać Perf ciułać

udawać greka [oo-DAH-vahch GREH-kah] (or **udawać głupiego** [oo-DAH-vahch gwoo-PYEH-goh] or **udawać wariata** [oo-DAH-vahch vahr-YAH-tah] or **strugać wariata** [STROO-gahch vahr-YAH-tah]) *v phr* To pretend one does not understand or did not pay any attention <play dumb, play possum> eg *Tylko nie udawaj Greka! Dobrze wiem, że wiesz, o co chodzi (Just don't play possum! I know well you know what's going on)*

uderzać po kieszeni See bić po kieszeni

uderzyć w gaz See dać sobie w gaz

uderzyć w kimono See iść w kimono

uganiać się za kobietami See ganiać za kobietami

ugryźć [OO-grizhch] *v* To start finding an explanation for someone or something, esp to solve a problem; to tackle <figure out, crack, work through, nail down> eg *Nie wiem, jamk to ugryźć (I don't know how to figure this out)*

ujaić See upierdalać

ujarać Perf jarać

ujebać See upierdalać

ujść [OO-eeshch] (or **ujść w tłoku** [OO-eeshch f TWOH-koo]) *v* To be barely acceptable or suitable; to barely meet certain standards <do, wash, work, do down, cut it, make the grade, make the cut, make it, cut the mustard, pass in the dark, fill the bill, fit in, fit the bill, suit one fine, be OK, be okay, be kopasetic, be hunky-dory, be so-so> eg *Co myślisz o tej propozycji? Ujdzie w tłoku (What do you think about this proposal? It will pass in the dark)*

ujść na sucho [OO-eeshch nah SOO-khoh] (or **upiec się** [OO-pyehts shyeh]) *v* To go unpunished; to be acquitted of a crime <go scot-free, get off scot-free, be saved by the bell> eg *Ściągała na klasówce, została przyłapana, ale uszło jej to na sucho)*

układy [oo-KWAH-di] *npl* Powerful contacts; influenial connections; influence <clout, drag, pull, juice, network, channels, ropes, strings, wires, suction> eg *Ma układy i może wszystko załatwić (He's got the pull and he can get everything)*

ul [OOL] *nm* **1** A prison; a jail <slam, slammer, jug, can, bucket, cage, big cage, big house, caboose, calaboose, cannery, cooler, hole, hoosegow, icebox, lockup, mill, stir, pen, tank, college, crossbar hotel, booby hatch, pink clink, quad> eg *Jest w ulu już od dwóch lat (He's been in the slammer for two years now)* **2** A restroom or bathroom; a toilet <john, johnny, can, crapper, potty, shitcan, shitter, shithouse, throne> eg *Gdzie jest twój kuzyn? Rzyga w ulu (Where's your cousin? He's puking in the john)*

ululany See urżnięty

umarlak [oo-MAHR-lahk] (or **umrzyk** [OOM-zhik]) *nm* A dead body; a corpse <stiff, dead meat, goner, dead duck, dead pigeon, crowbait, worm-food> eg *Zeszłej nocy wyciągnęli z rzeki następnego umrzyka (They pulled another stiff out of the river last night)*

umierać z nudów [oo-MYEH-rahch z NOO-doof] *v phr* To be very bored <die of boredom, be bored stiff, snooze, yawn> eg *Nie podobał jej się film. Umierała z nudów (She didn't like the movie. She was bored stiff)*

umoczyć [oo-MOH-chich] *v* To lose a lot of money <go broke, lose out, blow, drop a bundle, go to the cleaners, take a bath, tap out, wash out, belly up, go bust, take a beating> eg *Myślę, że umoczą na tym interesie (I think they're going to drop a bundle on that deal)*

umrzyk See umarlak

umyć ręce [OO-mich REHN-tseh] (or **umyć ręce od czegoś** [OO-mich REHN-tseh oht CHEH-gohsh]) *v phr* To withdraw from or refuse to be responsible for <wash one's hands of, button one's lip, zip one's lip, button up, clam up, dummy up> eg *Szkoła umyła ręce od zachowania uczniów podczas przerwy wiosennej (The school washed its hands of the students' behavior during spring recess*

umysł See paść komuś na mózg

umysłowy [oo-mi-SWOH-vi] *nm* An educated employee who works mentally rather than physically, esp a clerical worker <pencil pusher, pen driver, paper shuffler, desk jockey, white collar, pink collar, suit> eg *Pomyśł nie podobał się to umysłowym (The white collars didn't like the idea)*

umywać się See nie umywać się

uniwerek [oo-nee-VEH-rehk] *nm* A college or university <u, knowledge box, brainery, campus> eg *Naszy uniwerek jest spoko (Our brainery is okay); Studiuje na uniwerku (She studies at the u)*

uścisnąć grabę See dać grabę

uśmiechać się See nie uśmiechać się

upaść na głowę [OO-pahshch nah GWOH-veh] *v phr* To be or to behave as if one were insane or stupid <be off one's rocker, be off one's nut, be off one's base, be off the track, be off the trolley, be out one's skull, be out of one's mind, be crazy, be crazy as a loon, blow one's cork, blow one's top, blow a fuse, crack up, freak out, flip out, be ape, be bananas, be bent, be bonkers, be cracked, be dopey, be ga-ga, be half-baked, be loony, be loopy, be mental, be nerts, be nuts, be nutty, be psycho, be schizo, be screwy, be wacky, be weird, be wild, schiz out, psych out, come unglued, come unstuck, come unwrapped, come unzipped, get fucked up, get screwed up, get fucked in the head, get head-fucked, get mind-fucked> eg *Co on gada? Upadł na głowę, czy jak? (What is he talking about? Is he out of her rocker, or what?)*

upić się jak świnia* [OO-peech shyeh yahk SHFEE-nyah] (**spić** [speech] or **urżnąć** [OOR-zhnohnch] or **uchlać** [OO-khlahch] or **schlać** [skhlahch] or **zalać** [ZAH-lahch] or **skuć się** [skooch] may replace **upić**; **w trzy dupy*** [tshi DOO-pi] or **w sztok** [PYAH-ni f shtohk] or **w trupa** [f TROO-pah] or **w butelkę** [v boo-TEHL-keh] or **jak bela** [yahk BEH-lah] may be replace **jak świnia**) *v phr* To get drunk <get alkied, get bagged, get blitzed, get blotto, get blown away, get bent, get boiled, get bombed, get boozed up, get blasted, get bottled, get boxed, get canned, get clobbered, get cooked, get corked, get drunk as a skunk, get edged, get embalmed, get fractured, get fried, get gassed, get ginned, get grogged, get high, get hooched up, get impaired, get illuminated, get juiced, get liquored up, get lit, get loaded, get looped, get lubricated, get smashed, get oiled, get pickled, get plastered, get plonked, get polluted, get sauced, get shitfaced, get sloshed, get soaked, get stewed, get stiff, get stinking drunk, get swizzled, get tanked up, get wiped, get zonked, get fucked up> eg *Wczoraj znów się spił (He got canned yesterday again)*

upiec się See ujść na sucho

upierdalać** [oo-pyehr-DAH-lahch] (perf **upierdolić**** [oo-pyehr-DOH-leech]; or **upieprzać*** [oo-PYEHP-shahch] perf **upieprzyć*** [oo-pyehr-DOH-leech]; or **upierniczać*** [oo-pyehr-NEE-chahch] perf **upierniczyć*** [oo-pyehr-NEE-chich]; or **upierdzielać*** [oo-pyehr-JEH-lahch] perf **upierdzielić*** [oo-pyehr-JEH-leech]; or **ujebać**** [oo-YEH-bahch] or **ujaić*** [oo-YAH-yeech] or **utrącić** [oo-TROHN-cheech] or **usadzić** [oo-SAH-jeech] or **urządzić** [oo-ZHOHN-jeech]) *v* To deliberately cause harm to someone; to ruin someone; to victimize <fuck, fuck over, fuck up, screw, screw over, screw up, shaft, sell out, sell down the river> eg *Uważaj, on chce cię upierdolić (Watch it, he wants to fuck you over); Jeśli nie będę uważał, to tych dwóch zazdrosnych skurwysynów mnie upierdoli (If I'm not careful, these two jealous pricks will fuck me)*

upierdliwy* [oo-pyehr-DLEE-vi] *adj* Aggressively obtrusive, importunate, or overly meticulous; difficult to get rid of <pushy, pain in the neck, pain in the ass> eg *To dobry szef, ale potrafi być czasem bardzo upierdliwy (He's a good boss, but he can be very pushy sometimes)*

upierdolić się** [oo-pyehr-DOH-leech shyeh] (or **upieprzyć się*** [oo-pyehr-DOH-leech shyeh] or **upierniczyć się*** [oo-pyehr-NEE-chich shyeh] or **upierdzielić się*** [oo-pyehr-JEH-leech shyeh]) *v* **1** To get drunk <get fucked up, get alkied, get bagged, get blitzed, get blotto, get blown away, get bent, get boiled, get bombed, get boozed up, get blasted, get bottled, get boxed, get canned, get clobbered, get cooked, get corked, get drunk as a skunk, get edged, get embalmed, get fractured, get fried, get gassed, get ginned, get grogged, get high, get hooched up, get impaired, get illuminated, get juiced, get liquored up, get lit, get loaded, get looped, get lubricated, get smashed, get oiled, get pickled, get plastered, get plonked, get polluted, get sauced, get shitfaced, get sloshed, get soaked, get stewed, get stiff, get stinking drunk, get swizzled, get tanked up, get wiped, get zonked> eg *Wczoraj znów się upierdolił się (He got canned yesterday again)* **2** To get dirty or blotted, esp with any grease or lubricant <mess up, muss up, sleaze up, muck up, crud up, crum up, mung up, pigpen, get something all over> eg *Upierdoliłem się jakąś mazią (I messed up myself with some gook)*

urżnąć się [OO-rzhnohnch shyeh] (or **ubzdryngolić się** [oo-bzdrin-GOH-leech shyeh]) *v* To get drunk <get alkied, get bagged, get blitzed, get blotto, get blown away, get bent, get boiled, get bombed, get boozed up, get blasted, get bottled, get boxed, get canned, get clobbered, get cooked, get corked, get drunk as a skunk, get edged, get embalmed, get fractured, get fried, get gassed, get ginned, get grogged, get high, get hooched up, get impaired, get illuminated, get juiced, get liquored up, get lit, get loaded, get looped, get lubricated, get smashed, get oiled, get pickled, get plastered, get plonked, get polluted, get sauced, get shitfaced, get sloshed, get soaked, get stewed, get stiff, get stinking drunk, get swizzled, get tanked up, get wiped, get zonked, get fucked up> eg *Zawsze w sobotę lubi się ubzdryngolić (He always likes to get shitfaced on Saturday)*
See upić się jak świnia

urżnięty [oo-RZHNYEHN-ti] (or **ubzdryngolony** [oo-bzdrin-goh-LOH-ni] or **ululany** [oo-loo-LAH-ni]) *adj* Drunk; alcohol intoxicated <alkied, bagged, blitzed, blotto, blown away, bent, boiled, bombed, blasted, boozed, bottled, boxed, buzzed, canned, clobbered, cooked, corked, crashed, drunk as a skunk, edged, embalmed, fractured, fried, gassed, ginned, grogged, have one too many, half under, high, hooched up, in bad shape, impaired, illuminated, juiced, knocked out, liquored, lit, loaded, looped, lubricated, lushed, smashed, oiled, pickled, plastered, plonked, polluted, sauced, shitfaced, slugged, sloshed, soaked, stewed, stiff, stinking drunk, swizzled, tanked, three sheets to the wind, wiped, zonked> eg *Facet znów jest ubzdryngolony (The guy is juiced again)*
See pijany jak świnia

urabiać sobie ręce [oo-RAH-byahch SOH-byeh REHN-tseh] (or **urabiać sobie ręce po łokcie** [oo-RAH-byahch SOH-byeh REHN-tseh poh WOHK-chyeh]) *v phr* To work very hard <work one's ass off, work one's fingers to the bone, work like a horse, sweat, bust one's ass off, break one's ass off> eg *Urobiłem sobie ręce wczoraj (I worked my ass off yesterday)*

urządzić See upierdalać

urzędas [oo-ZHEHN-dahs] *nm* A rank-and-file clerical worker or a low-ranking official <pencil pusher, pen driver, paper shuffler, desk jockey, white collar, pink collar, suit> eg *Chcesz być urzędasem do końca życia? (Do you want to be a paper shuffler till the end of your life?)*

urzędolić [oo-zhehn-DOHleech] *v* To work as a rank-and-file clerical worker or a low-ranking official <push a pen, drive a pen, shuffle papers, office> eg *Czemu miałbym chcieć urzędolić do końca życia? (Why should I want to push a pen for the rest of my life?); Gdzie urzędolisz? (Where do you office?)*

usadzić See upierdalać

usiąść See mieć na czym siedzieć

usrany See do gobowej deski

usta See nabrać wody w usta, nie brać do ust

ustawić się [oos-TAH-veech shyeh] *v* To settle down professionally or financially <get located, come to one's own, strike out on one's own, take the plunge, be sitting pretty> eg *Masz już 28 lat. Pora już się ustawić (You're already 28. It's about time for you to take the plunge)*

ustawiony [oo-stah-VYOH-ni] *adj* Comfortably settled down professionally, financially, or personally; in a good position <located, sitting pretty> eg *Jego rodzina jest bogata. Jest ustawiony (His family is well off. He's sitting pretty)*

ustrojstwo [oo-STROH-ee-stfoh] *nn* Any apparatus, appliance or device; any object <thingy, thingamajig, thingum, thingdad, gismo, giz, gadget, widget, dingbat, dingus, grabber, gimmick, whatchamacallit, whatzis, goofus, jigamaree, gigmaree, doodad, doodle, doofunny, doohickey, doojigger, jigger, stuff, bitch, fucker, baby, idiot box> eg *Jak to ustrojstwo działa? (How does this gismo work?)*

uszatek [oo-SHAH-tehk] *npl* Someone with large ears <dumbo, cauliflower> eg *Rety, patrz na tego uszatka! (Wow, look at that dumbo!)*

uszy* [OO-shee] *npl* A woman's breasts, esp large <tits, melons, knockers, bazooms, boobs, headlights, hooters, lungs, hemispheres> eg *Szukam dziewczyny o dużych uszach (I'm looking for a girl with big lungs)*

utrącić See upierdalać

utrwalacz [oo-TRFAH-lahch] *nm* Beer drunk after potent alcohol <beer chaser> eg *Daj mi setkę whiskey i utrwalacz (Give me a shot of whiskey and a beer chaser)*

uziemić [ooZHEHmeech] *v* To prevent a child from going out as a punishment <ground> eg *Jako karę zostałem uziemiony na tydzień (As a punishment I got grounded for a week)*

W

w błoto See wyrzucić w błoto

w biały dzień [v BYAH-wi JEHÑ] *adv phr* Publicly visible in the daytime <in broad daylight> eg *Złodziej ukradł ten samochód w biały dzień (The thief stole the car in broad daylight)*

w biegu [v BYEH-goo] *adv phr* In motion; moving from one place to another; going somewhere <on the run, on the move, on the wing> eg *Zjedzmy pizzę w biegu (Let's have pizza on the run)*

w butelkę See pijany jak świnia, upić się jak świnia

w cholerę See iść w cholerę, pierdolnąć

w chowanego See bawić się w chowanego

w czepku urodzony [f CHEHP-koo oo-roh-DZOH-ni] *adj phr* Born with many advantages <born with a silver spoon in one's mouth> eg *Ona jest w czepku urodzona (She was born with a silver spoon in her mouth)*

w długą See iść w długą

w dechę [v DEH-kheh] **1** *adj phr* (or **wdechowy** [vdeh-KHOH-vi]) Excellent; wonderful <great, cool, swell, fab, rad, def, far-out, awesome, frantic, terrific, funky, gorgeous, groovy, hellacious, neat, peachy, dandy, baddest, mean, solid, super-dooper, wailing, wicked, gnarly, top-notch, ten, ace-high, A-OK, A-1, some> eg *Ten samochód jest na prawdę w dechę (This car is real cool)* **2** *adv phr* (or **wdechowo** [vdeh-KHOH-voh]) *adv* Excellently; superbly; wonderfully <great, cool, swell, fab, rad, def, far-out, awesome, frantic, terrific, funky, gorgeous, groovy, hellacious, neat, peachy, dandy, baddest, mean, solid, super-dooper,

wailing, wicked, gnarly, top-notch, ten, ace-high, A-OK, A-1, some> eg *Jak się dzisiaj masz? Po prostu w dechę. Nie mogłoby być lepiej (How are you today? I'm just great. It couldn't be better)*

w diabły See iść w cholerę, pierdolnąć

w dupę See móc kogoś pocałować, w mordę, włazić komuś do dupy

w dupie See mieć coś/kogoś gdzieś

w gorącej wodzie kąpany [v goh-ROHN-tseh-ee VOH-jeh kohm-PAH-ni] *adj phr* Impatient, impetuous, or quick-tempered; eagerly desirous <in hot water, itchy, itching, antsy, flaky, spitball, bursting, busting, gung ho, hopped-up, hot-eyed, hot to trot, hurting, hyper, ranged, red-hot, wild, wired, steamed-up, boiling, off the hip, up and down> eg *Nie czekał, natychmiast do niej zadzwonił. Był na prawdę w gorącej wodzie kąpany (He didn't wait, but called her right away. He was really gung ho)*

w kąt See pierdolnąć

w kółko [f KOOW-koh] (or **w koło** [f KOH-woh]; **Macieju** [mah-CHYEH-yoo] or **Wojtek** [VOH-ee-tehk] may be added) *adv phr* Non stop; continuously; all the time <<around the clock, day and night, forever and a day, over and over, again and again> eg *Ona gada tak w kółko (She's been saying this around the clock)*

w kropce [f KROHP-tseh] *adv phr* In a very difficult situation; facing a hard decision <on the spot, on the hot seat, between a rock and a hard place, between the devil and the deep blue sea, between two fires, caught in the cross-fire, on the hornns of a dilemma> eg *Przez jakiś czas byłam w kropce i nie wiedziałam, co robić (I was really in the hot seat for a while and didn't know what to do)*

w lesie [v LEH-shyeh] (or **daleko w lesie** [dah-LEH-koh v LEH-shyeh]) *adv phr* Only at the beginning; lagging behind; delayed <hung-up, held-up, slowed-up, tied-up, binded, sidelined, sidetracked, passed-up, shelved, on hold> eg *Jak ci idzie robota? Wciąż jestem w lesie (How are you getting on with your work? I'm still tied-up)*

w locie [v LOH-chyeh] *adv phr* In motion; moving from one place to another; going somewhere <on the run, on the move, on the wing> eg *Jej mąż jest obwoźnym sprzedawcą. Zawsze jest w locie (Her husband is a traveling salesman. He's always on the wing)*

w lot See łapać, chwycić

w mig See migiem

w mordę* [v MOHR-deh] (or **w mordę jeża*** [v MOHR-deh YEH-zhah] or **w dupę*** [v DOO-peh] or **w dupę jeża*** [v DOO-peh YEH-zhah] or **w twarz** [f TFAHSH]; **o** [oh] may precede **w**) *excl phr* An exclamation of anger, irritation, disappointment, shock <shit, fuck, hell, heck, damn, damn it, goddamn it, gosh, golly, gee, jeez, holy fuck, holy cow, holy moly, holy hell, holy mackarel, holy shit, jumping Jesus, fucking shit, fucking hell> eg *O w mordę! Nie wziąłem pieniędzy! (Fucking hell! I didn't take the money with me!)*

w nerwach [v NEHR-vahkh] (or **cały w nerwach** [TSAH-wi v NEHR-vahkh]) *adj phr* Apprehensive, worried, or nervous <worried stiff, jittery, jumpy, shaky, shivery, quivery, fraidy, scaredy, frozen, panicky, spooked, yellow, cold-feeted, scared spitless, cranky, uptight, nervy, edgy, antsy, clutchy, hitchy, fretty, itchy, wired, tightened-up, strung-outin a dither, in a doodah, in a flutter, in a lather, in a sweat, in a cold sweat, in a tizzy> eg *Minęła północ. Byłam cała w nerwach i* *postanowiłam zadzwonić na policję (It was after midnight. I was all shaky and I decided to call the police)*

w nosie See mieć coś/kogoś gdzieś

w obroty See brać kogoś do galopu

w pestkę See zalany

w piździec See iść w cholerę

w pizdu See iść w cholerę, pierdolnąć

w pół do komina [f POOW doh koh-MEE-nah] *phr* A rude response to someone's asking the time <time to get a watch, half-past the monkey's ass quarter to its balls> eg *Która godzina? W pół do komina (What time is it? Time to get a watch)*

w podskokach [f poht-SKOH-kahkh] *adv phr* Immediately; very quickly <pretty damn quick, PDQ, ASAP, on the spot, on the double, double time, double clutching, like a shot, in half a mo, like now, before you know it, before you can say Jack Robinson, in a jiffy, in a flash, in half a shake, right off the bat, like a bat out of hell, like a shot out of hell, hubba-hubba, horseback, like greased lightning> eg *Przyszedł nauczyciel i zabrali się do roboty. W podskokach (The teacher came in and they got to work. Pretty damn quick)*

w porywach [f poh-RI-vahkh] *adv phr* Maximally; the most; to a highest degree <max, tops, the mostest> eg *Kolejka czasami liczyła w porywach do stu osób (The line was sometimes consisted of a hundred people, tops)*

w porządeczku [f poh-zhohn-DEHCH-koo] (or **w porząsiu** [f poh-ZHOHN-shyoo]) *adv phr* All right; agreeable; fine <OK, okay, okey-dokey, okie-dokie, A-OK, right, righto, right on> eg *A gdybym przyjechał po ciebie o piątej? W porząsiu (Suppose I pick you up at five? Okey-dokey)*

w proszku [f PROHSH-koo] (or **w rozsypce** [v rohs-SIP-tseh]) *adj phr* Broken or fragmented; damaged; in pieces <into smithereens, to smithereens> eg *Waza była w rozsypce (The vase was shot to smithereens)*

w przelocie [f psheh-LOH-chyeh] (or **przelotnie** [psheh-LOHT-nyeh]) *adv phr* Temporarily; briefly; from time to time <every now and then, every now and again, every so often, on and off> eg *Widywali się tylko w przelocie, bo byli tak zajęci (They were seeing each other on and off)*

w siódmym niebie [f SHYOOD-mim NYEH-byeh] (or **w skowronkach** [f skoh-VROHN-kakh]) *adj phr* Extremely happy <in seventh heaven, on a cloud, on cloud nine, on cloud seven, chirpy, corky, perky, up, upbeat, flying high, floating on air, sunny side up, wowed, pleased as punch, happy as a clam, tickled, tickled pink, high as a kite, gassed> eg *Był w siódmym niebie, gdy jego żona urodziła mu chłopczyka (He was on cloud nine after his wife had a baby boy); Miał wkrótce przyjść. Cała byłam w skowronkach (He would come real soon. I was happy as a clam)*

w sosie See nie w sosie

w sztok See pijany jak świnia, upić się jak świnia

w tłoku See ujść

w tę i we w tę [fteh ee VEH fteh] *adv phr* Back and forth; backwards and forwards; from one side to the other <to and fro, there and back> eg *Przez cały dzień łazi w tę i we w tę (He's been walking around to-and-fro all day)*

w telewizorze [f teh-leh-vee-ZOH-zheh] *nm phr* Broadcast by television <on tv, on the tube, on the telly, on the box> eg *Widziałem to w telewizorze (I saw it on tv)*

w trasie See być w trasie

w trupa See pijany jak świnia, upić się jak świnia

w trymiga See migiem

w trzy dupy See pijany jak świnia, upić się jak świnia

w twarz See w mordę

w zawiasach [v zah-VYAH-sahkh] *adj phr* (Of a sentence) Suspended <no slang equivalent> eg *Dostał sześć miesięcy i dwa lata w zawiasach (He was given a six-month jail sentence suspended for two years)*

w życiu [v ZHI-chyoo] *adv phr* (Used to show one's determination that something will not happen) Never <over someone's dead body, not on your life, in a pig's eye, in a pig's ass, in a pig's ear, someone will be damned if, someone will be fucked if> eg *Chcesz rzucić studia? W życiu! (You want to quit college? Over my dead body!)*

wał* [VAH-oo] *nm* A stupid or foolish man, an idiot <jerk, dork, geek, dumbass, dumbhead, dope, airhead, birdbrain, blockhead, dumbhead, klutz> eg *Co ten wał wyrabia na dachu? (What is that airhead doing on the roof?)*

wałkonić się [vah-oo-KOH-neech shyeh] (perf **powałkonić się** [poh-vah-oo-KOH-neech shyeh]) *v* To loaf or idle; to pass time lazily <bum around, hang around, hang out, goof around, fuck around, screw around, fiddle around, fiddle fart around, fart around, jack around, mess around, hack around, monkey around, knock around, kick around, fool around, horse around, piddle around, play around, rat around, schloomp around, ass around, beat around, dick around, fuck around, fuck off, screw off, goof off, jerk off, fuck the dog, rat fuck, flub the dub, sit on one's ass, sit on one's butt, lollygag, veg out> eg *W te wakacje mam zamiar po prostu się powałkonić (I'm just going to goof off on this vacation)*

wałkoń [VAH-oo-kohñ] *nm* A very lazy person, esp one who chronically avoids work; a shirker <goldbricker, bunk lizard, coffee cooler, feather merchant, lazybones, lazy-ass, lazy bum, bum, clock watcher, dog-fucker> eg *Twój brat to prawdziwy wałkoń. Nawet nie zabrał sięjeszcze do roboty (Your brother is a real goldbricker. He hasn't even started working)*

wałówka [vah-WOOF-kah] (or **wałówa** [vah-WOO-vah]) *nf* Food brought with someone somewhere, esp intended as a gift or given to a sick person <care package> eg *Matka przywiozła ze sobą wałówkę, jak zwykle (Mother brought care package with her, as always)*

ważniak [VAHZH-nyak] *nm* **1** A man who is very important or thinks that he is very important <big shot, high roller, wheeler-dealer> eg *To dobra szansa spotkania ważniaków (It's a good opportunity to meet some big shots)* **2** A conceited, self-important, or or self-impressed person <ego-tripper, high-hatter, swelled-head, big-head, high-nose, stuffed shirt> eg *Nowy dyrektor Instytutu Anglistyki to ważniak (The new director of the English Institute is an ego-tripper)*

wafel [VAH-fehl] *nm* A small round mat placed under a glass or bottle <coaster, beer plate> eg *Masz, weź podstawkę (Here, take a coaster)*

wagarować [vah-gah-ROH-vahch] *v* To stay away from school without an excuse; to be truant <play hooky, hooky, juke, go awol, skip class, cut class, ditch class, blow off class> eg *Chodźmy jutro na wagary, co? (Let's skip classes tomorrow, huh?)*

wagarowicz [vah-gah-ROH-veech] *nm* A student who stays away from school without an excuse <skipper, awol> eg *Dziś znów mamy dwóch wagarowiczów (Today we've got two skippers again)*

wagary [vah-GAH-ri] *npl* An instance of staying away from school without an excuse; being truant <awol, hooky, no-show, cut> eg *Znów poszedł na wagary (He's gone awol again)*

wajcha [VAH-ee-khah] (or **wichajster** [vee-KHAH-ees-tehr] *nm*) *nf* Any lever, shift, or crank <stick> eg *Złap za żółtą wajchę i pociągnij (Grab the yellow stick and pull)*

waksy [VAHK-si] *npl* (A period of) Vacation, esp in school or university <vacs, liberty> eg *Kiedy macie waksy? (When do you have vacs?)*

walić konia** [VAH-leech KOH-nyah] (or **bić konia**** [BEECH KOH-nyah] or **trzepać konia**** [TSHEH-pahch KOH-nyah]; **kapucyna**** [kah-poo-TSI-nah] may replace **konia**) *v phr* (Of a man) To masturbate <jack off, jerk off, beat off, fuck off, whack off, toss off, pull off, bang the bishop, beat one's dummy, beat the meat, pound one's meat, flog one's meat, fist-fuck, fuck one's fist, stroke, spank one's monkey, choke one's chicken, wax one's dolphin> eg *Widziałem, jak walił konia w toalecie (I saw him jerking off in the bathroom)*

walić kupę See robić kupę

walić się See iść się pierdolić

walić się* [VAH-leech shyeh] *v* To copulate <get screwed, get fucked, get laid, screw, fuck, fork, frig, ball, bang, boink, bonk, boff, hump, poke, shag> eg *Lubią się walić miejscach publicznych (They like to fuck in public)*

walić sobie w żyłę See ładować sobie w żyłę

walić z grubej rury [VAH-leech z GROO-beh-ee ROO-ri] *v phr* To exaggerate praise; to flatter of cajole <soft-soap, sweet-talk, grease, schmear, honey up, butter up, dish out the applesauce, lay it on thick, pour it on thick, spread it on thick, pile it on thick, put it on thick> eg *Mój brat zawsze wali z grubej rury. I dobrze na tym wychodzi (My brother always spreads it on thick. And it works well for him)*

walić* [VAH-leech] (perf **walnąć*** [VAHL-nohnch]) *v* To copulate with someone <fuck, screw, lay, ball, bang, boink, boff, boogie, bop, frig, hump, poke, shag> eg *Walił ją od tyłu, tak jak chciała (He was screwing her from the back, the way he liked it)*

walnąć [VAHL-nohnch] *v* To have a quick drink of liquor <knock back, down, slug down, swig, tank, tank up> eg *Walnął cztery piwa i zaczął bekać (He downed three beers and started to burp)*

walnąć o glebę See wyglebić się

walnąć w kalendarz See **kopnąć w kalendarz**

walory [vah-LOH-ri] *nm pl* A woman's breasts, esp large <tits, melons, knockers, bazooms, boobs, headlights, hooters, hemispheres> eg *Jego siostra to ma dopiero ma walory! (His sister really has some melons!)*

waluciarz [vah-LOO-chyahsh] *nm* A money changer, esp illegal <no slang equivalent> eg *Jego brat jest cinkciarzem (His brother is a money changer)*

waluta See miękkie, twarde

wapniak* [VAHP-nyak] (or **wapno*** [VAHP-noh]) *nm* An old man, esp a parent <gramps, old fart, old bugger, geezer, gaffer, old-timer, fossil> eg *Rzuć wapno na druty (Put the old fart on the line)*

wariackie papiery [vah-RYAHTS-kyeh pah-PYEH-ri] (or **żółte papiery** [ZHOOW-teh pah-PYEH-ri]) *npl phr* An official document issued by a psychiatrist stating someone's mental sickness; mental instability in general

<section eight, nutter's ID> eg *Uniknął wojska, bo ma żółte papiery (He managed to evade the draft because of section eight)*

wariat See udawać greka

wariatkowo See dom wariatów

wariować na punkcie czegoś/kogoś [vahr-YOH-vahch nah POONK-chyeh CHEH-gohsh/KOH-gohsh] (or **wariować za czymś/kimś** [vahr-YOH-vahch zah chimsh/keemsh]) *v phr* To like someone very much; to admire enormously <be crazy for, be ape for, be apeshit for, be bananas for, be bonkers for, be ga-ga for, be loony for, be mental for, be nuts for, be nutty for, be wild for, take a shine to, have a thing about, take to> eg *Ludzie za nią wariują (People are ga-ga for her)*

Warszawka* [vahr-SHAHF-kah] **1** *nf* Warsaw (Warszawa), the capital of Poland <Warsaw-schmarsaw> eg *Jest tu kto z warszawki? (Is there anyone from Warsaw-schmarsaw)* **2** Inhabitants of Warsaw <no slang equivalent> eg *Warszawka się tu zjeżdża co rok (These goddamn Warsaw people come here every year)*

warsztat See brać na warsztat

wart See chuja wart, grzechu warty

wazelina [vah-zeh-LEE-nah] (or **wazeliniarstwo** [vah-zeh-lee-NYAHR-stfoh]) *nf* Currying favor or flattery in general <brown-nosing, ass-kissing, ass-licking, ass-wiping, apple-polishing, back-scratching, sweet-talking, bootlicking, smoke, stroke, hogwash, goo, hokum, soft soap, soap, eyewash, hogwash, shot in the arm, shot in the ass> eg *Nie znoszę wazeliny (I hate ass-kissing)*

See włazić komuś do dupy

wazeliniarz [vah-zeh-LEE-nyahsh] *nm* An overly or superficially nice man; a sycophant <brown-noser, ass-kisser, ass-licker, ass-sucker, ass-wiper, back-scratcher, apple-polisher, tokus-licker, kiss-ass, yes-man> eg *Wygląda na to, że wszyscy w biurze z wyjątkiem mnie to wazeliniarze (It looks like everybody in the office is an apple polisher but me)*

wąż See mieć węża w kieszeni

wąchać kwiatki [VOHN-khahch KFYAHT-kee] (or **wąchać kwiatki od spodu** [VOHN-khahch KFYAHT-keeoht SPOH-doo]) *v phr* To be dead or die <bite the dust, kiss the dust, croak, belly up, buy the farm, buy the ranch, cash in one's chips, check out, bump off, conk off, conk out, farm, give up the ghost, go home feet first, go home in a box, go west, kick in, kick off, kick the bucket, pass out, peg out, shove off, drop off, step off, pop off, push up daisies, meet one's maker, turn up one's toes, go down the tube, join the great majority, join the majority> eg *Chcesz skończyć wąchając kwiatki? (Do you want to end up pushing up daisies?)*

wąchać pismo nosem See mieć nosa

wąchy [VOHN-khee] *npl* Mustache <lip fuzz, peach fuzz, pez, stash, stache> eg *Nie lubię jego wąchów (I don't like his lip fuzz)*

wątroba See leżeć komuś na wątrobie

wbijać sobie coś do głowy [VBEE-yahch SOH-byeh tsohsh doh GWOH-vi] **1** *v phr* To persuade oneself; to confirm oneself in the conviction <get something into one's head, put oneself across, turn one's head around, twist one's arm> eg *Wbiła sobie do głowy, że zostanie lekarzem (She got it into her head that she would become a doctor)* **2** *v phr* To study, esp with difficulty; to try to master something <cram, grind, dig, skull, book it, go book, hit the books, megabook, megastudy, crack the books, pound the books, bone up> eg *Przez dwa tygodnie usiłowałem wbić sobie to do* *głowy, ale rezultat jest mizerny (I've been hitting the books for two weeks, but the results are miserable)*

wbijać zęby w ścianę [VBEE-yahch ZEHM-bi f SHCHAH-neh] *v phr* To save on food in order to make ends meet <scrimp and scrape, scrimp and save, tighten the belt> eg *Przez ostatni rok wbili zęby w ścianę, żeby móc kupić sobie nowy samochód (For the past year they've been scrimping and scraping in order to afford a new car)*

wchodzić coś [FKHOH-jeech f TSOSH] *v* To (decide to) participate in a business venture <be in, deal someone in, sign someone up> eg *Jeśli mnie pytacie, to ja wchodzę (If you ask me, I'm in)*

wchodzić komuś do dupy See włazić komuś do dupy

wciąć Perf wcinać

wcinać [FCHEE-nahch] (perf **wciąć** [fchyonch]) *v* To eat, esp voraciously <stuff oneself, pig out, scarf out, pork out> eg *Chłopcy wcinali hamburgery wszystek tort (The boys were pigging out on hamburgers)*

wciry See dać wycisk, dostać wycisk

wciskać kit See kitować

wciskać w siebie See wpychać w siebie

wdechowo See w dechę

wdechowy See w dechę

wdowa See słomiana wdowa

wdowiec See słomiany wdowiec

wejścia [VEH-eesh-chyeh] (or **wtyki** [FTI-kee]) *nm pl* Powerful contacts; influenial connections; influence <clout, drag, pull, juice, network, channels, ropes, strings, wires, suction> eg *Nie miał żadnych dojść (He didn't have any pull); Ma wtyki i może wszystko załatwić (He's got the pull and he can get everything)*

wejście See na wejściu

wejściówka [veh-eesh-CHYOOF-kah] *nf* An admission ticket or invitation <pass, chit, paper, bid> eg *Mogę zobaczyć pańską wejściówkę? (Can I see your pass?)*

wezwać kogoś na dywanik [VEH-zvahch KOH-gohsh nah di-VAH-neek] (or **brać kogoś na dywanik** [brahch KOH-gohsh nah di-VAH-neek]) *v phr* To (call someone to his office and) reprimand <call someone on the carpet> eg *Jeszcze jeden taki błąd i szef wezwie cię na dywanik (One more error like that and the boss will call you on the carpet)*

wiącha See puścić wiąchę

wiącha [VYOHN-khah] *nf* **1** (or **wiecheć** [VYEH-khehch] *nm*) A bouquet of flowers <no slang equivalent> eg *Przyniósł jej wiąchę kwiatów (He brought her a bouquet of flowers)* **2** (or **wiązanka** [vyohn-ZAHN-kah] A hail of abuse; a sentence of sweardwords or curses <French words, four-letter words, cuss words, dirty words, dirty talks, dirt> eg *Dostał manadat, bo puścił wiąchę do policjanta (He got a ticket because he used cuss words in front of a policeman)*

wiązać koniec z końcem [VYOHN-zahch KOH-nyehts s KOHÑ-tsehm] (or **wiązać koniec z końcem ledwo** [LEHD-voh VYOHN-zahch KOH-nyehts s KOHÑ-tsehm] or **z trudem wiązać koniec z końcem** [s TROO-dehm VYOHN-zahch KOH-nyehts s KOHÑ-tsehm]) *v phr* To (hardly) manage to live on a small amount of money <make ends meet, make both ends meet, scratch a living> eg *Ciężko w tych czasach wiązać koniec z końcem (It's hard these days to make ends meet)*

wiązanka See wiącha

wiać See zwiewać

wiara [VYAH-rah] *nf* A group of people <folks, pack, bunch, crew, gang, clan, crowd, boys> eg *Poszedłem do kina z całą wiarą (I went to the movies with the whole gang)*

wiatr See wystawić kogoś do wiatru

wiatrak See co ma piernik do wiatraka, jak piernik do wiatraka

wic [veets] (or **wist** [veest]) *nm* A joke <trick, rib-tickler, wisecrack, knee-slapper, gag, laugh, wheeze> eg *Chciałem im opowiedzieć jakiegoś wica (I wanted to tell them a knee-slapper)*

wichajster See wajcha

widły See robić z igły widły

widziały gały co brały [vee-JAH-wi GAH-wi TSOH BRAH-wi] *excl phr* You knew whom you would marry and now it is too late to regret your decision <you wanted it you got it, what you see is what you get> eg *Nie trzeba było się żenić. Widziały gały co brały (You shouldn't have gotten married. You wanted it, you got it)*

widzieć białe myszki [VEE-jehch BYAH-weh MISH-kee] *v phr* To see hallucinatory creatures during the delirium tremens <see pink elephants, see pink spiders> eg *Mówił, że widział białe myszki (He said he saw pink elephants)*

widzieć się komuś [VEE-jehch shyeh KOH-moosh] *v* To like someone or something <dig, go for> eg *Ja ci się widzi ta dupcia? (How do you dig that chick?); Nie widzimi się jedzenie wieprzowiny (I don't dig pork)*

widzimisię [vee-jee-MI-shyeh] *nn* One's own caprice, whim, or opinion; discretion <call, judge and jury, fool notion> eg *Wylał ją z powodu swojego widzimisię (It was only his call to flunk her)*

wiedźma [VYEHJ-mah] *nf* A woman, esp shrewish, whom one dislikes or disapproves of <bitch, slut, cunt, broad, wench, hag, old hag, old biddy, old bag, old tart, piece of shit> eg *Otworzyła nam jakaś wiedźma (Some wench opened the door for us)*

wiedzieć o co biega [VYEH-jehch oh tsoh BYEH-gah] *v phr* To be cognizant, well-oriented, or well-informed <get, get it, catch, get the drift, get the picture, get the message, get the hang of, savvy, dig, click, capeesh, read, be with it, see where one is coming from, know where one is coming from, be with it, get one's bearings> eg *On w ogóle nie wie, o co biega (He doesn't get it at all)*

wiedzieć z czym to się je [VYEH-jehch s chim toh shyeh YEH] *v phr* To know the facts, esp about life and its difficulties; to experience something <do, live through, know the score, know where it's at, know what's what, been there oneself, been there done that> eg *Już raz przedtem byłeś żonaty, więc powienieneś wiedzieć, z czym to się je (You'd been married once before so you should know the score)*

wielka mi sztuka See nie sztuka

wieś See dziura

wieśniacki [vyehsh-NYAHTS-kee] *adj* Conventional; oldfahioned; neither modern nor fashinable <square, corny, clonish, drippy, drizzly, droid, fuddy-duddy, squaresville, uncool, unhep> eg *Co za wieśniack ciuch! (What a corny outfit!)*

wieśniak [VYEHSH-nyahk] *nm* A conventional man, esp dressed in an old-fashioned way; a man who is not fashinable, modern, or au courant <square, squarehead, clone, cornball, cube, drip, drizzle, droid, flat tire, fuddy-duddy, zoid, Jeff, Ken> eg *Nie rozmawiam z tym wieśniakiem (I don't talk to this squarehead)*

wieśniara [vyehsh-NYAH-rah] *nf* A conventional woman, esp dressed in an old-fashioned way; a woman who is not fashinable, modern, or au courant <square, squarehead, clone, cornball, cube, drip, drizzle, droid, flat tire, fuddy-duddy, zoid, Zelda> eg *Zaręczył sięz jakąś wieśniarą (He married some suarehead)*

wieprz [vyehpsh] *nm* An obese person <fatty, fatso, blimp, fat-ass, lard-ass, tub of lard, crisco> eg *Ten wieprz beka ledwo mieści się w drzwiach (That tub of lard can hardly get through the door)*

wiercić się jak na szpilkach [VYEHR-cheech shyeh yahk nah SHPEEL-kakh] *v phr* To be eager or nervous to begin; to be tired of being held back <be on pins and needles, champ at the bit, be like a cat on hot bricks> eg *Za karę został po szkole dwie godziny. Wiercił się jak na szpilkach (w As a punishment he was kept after school for two hours. He was champing at the bit to go out)*

wiesieć na włosku [VI-shyehch nah VWOHS-koo] *v phr* To hang in the balance <hang by a skin of one's teeth, hang by a thread, hang by a hair> eg *Życie tego starego człowieka wisiało na włosku (The old man's life hung by a thread)*

wietnamiec* [vyeht-NAH-myehts] *nm* A male Vietnamese <dink, gook, slope, slant-eye, zip> eg *Te wietnamce, to potrafią gotować! (These gooks sure can cook!)*

wilk See o wilku mowa, patrzeć na kogoś krzywo

winkiel See za winklem

wino patykiem pisane [VEE-noh pah-TI-kyehm pee-SAH-neh] (or **wino marki wino** [MAHR-kee VEE-noh]) *nn phr* Cheap and inferior wine <plonk, red ink, veeno, Mad Dog 20/20, Nighttrain, Wild Irish Rose> eg *Przyniósł ze sobą jakieś wino marki wino (He brought some plonk with him)*

wiochmen See wsiun

wiśnia See świnia

wiosłować [vyohs-WOH-vahch] *v* To eat a soup, esp very fast <slurp down, drink down> eg *Wiosłował jakby był koniec świata (He slurped down his soup like there was no tomorrow)*

wisieć komuś See zwisać komuś

wisieć komuś coś [VI-shyehch KOH-moosh tsohsh] *v* To be indebted; to owe someone money <be in hock, be in the red, be into for, owe someone one> eg *Wiszę twojemu bratu dziesięć kawałków (I'm into your brother for ten grand)*

wist See wic

wkurwiać** [FKOOR-vyahch] (perf **wkurwić**** [FKOOR-veech]; or **wkurzać*** [FKOO-zhahch] perf **wkurzyć*** [FKOO-zhich]; or **wnerwiać** [VNEHR-vyahch] perf **wnerwić** [VNEHR-veech]) *v* To annoy, irritate, or anger someone <piss someone off, pee someone off, steam someone up, tick someone off, tee someone off, burn someone up, burn someone off, burn someone's ass, burn someone off, get someone's back up, make someone sore, make someone mad, turn off, gross out, barf out, suck, scuzz one out, give one pain in the ass, make one sick, make one puke, make one barf, make someone's blood boil, bring to the boil> eg *Ten facet mnie wkurwia (This guy pisses me off)*

wkurwiać się** [FKOOR-vyahch shyeh] (perf **wkurwić się**** [FKOOR-veech shyeh]; or **wkurzać się*** [FKOO-zhahch shyeh] perf **wkurzyć się*** [FKOO-zhich shyeh]; or **wnerwiać się** [VNEHR-vyahch shyeh] perf **wnerwić się** [VNEHR-veech shyeh]; or **wściekać się** [FSHCHEH-kahch shyeh] perf **wściec się** [FSHCHYEHTS shyeh]) *v* To be annoyed, irritated, or angry <be

pissed off, be peed off, be p'd off, be bent out of a shape, be pushed out of a shape, be browned off, be cheesed off, be uptight, be cranky, be edgy, be sore, be mad as a hornet, be steamed up, be ticked off, be tee'd off, be burned up, be ballistic, fly off the handle, flip one's lid, hit the ceiling, see red > eg *Za każdym razem jak słyszę tego faceta, to się wściekam (I get peed off everytime I listen to this guy)*

wkurwiony** [fkoor-VYOH-ni] (or **wkurzony*** [fkoo-ZHOH-ni] or **wnerwiony** [vnehr-VYOH-ni] or **wściekły-zapiekły** [FSHCHYEHK-wi zah-PYEHK-wi]) *adj* Annoyed, irritated, or angry <pissed off, peed off, p'd off, bent out of a shape, pushed out of a shape, browned off, cheesed off, uptight, cranky, edgy, sore, mad as a hornet, steamed up, ticked off, tee'd off, burned up, ballistic> eg *Chyba była bardzo wkurwiona (Sje must have been real pissed off)*

wkuwać See kuć

wleźć See ile wlezie

władować Perf ładować

władować się Perf ładować się

władza See pan władza

własna skóra [VWAHS-nah SKOO-rah] (or **własna dupa*** [VWAHS-nah DOO-pah]) *nf phr* The whole self; the person <one's ass, one's butt, one's neck> eg *Kłamał w sądzie, żeby uratować własną skórę (He lied in the court to save his neck); Zabieraj stąd swoją dupę! (Get your ass out of here!)*

włazić komuś do dupy* [VWAH-zheech KOH-moosh doh DOO-pi] (or **wskakiwać komuś do dupy*** [fskah-KEE-vahch KOH-moosh doh DOO-pi] or **wchodzić komuś do dupy*** [FKHOH-jeech KOH-moosh doh DOO-pi]; **w dupę*** [v DOO-peh] may replace **do dupy**; **bez mydła** [behz MID-wah] or **bez wazeliny** [behz vah-zeh-LEE-ni] may be added) *v phr* To curry favor; to toady <brown-nose, kiss ass, lick ass, suck ass, ass-kiss, ass-lick, wipe someone's ass, apple-polish, back-scratch, bootlick, sweeten up> eg *Nie mogę na to patrzeć. Mógłby tak już przestać włazić mu do dupy (I can't stand it. I wish he's stop kissing his ass)*

włożyć See nie mieć co do gęby włożyć

włoić Perf łoić

włos See brać kogoś pod włos, picować, wiesieć na włosku

wmłócić Perf młócić

wół See harować, jak piernik do wiatraka, narobić się, orać jak wół, tyrać, zapierdalać, zasuwać

wołowy See dupa

wściekły-zapiekły See wkurwiony

wściekle [FSHCHYEHK-leh] *adv* Extremely; exceedingly; very <awful, god-awful, real, mighty, plenty, damn, damned, goddamn, goddamned, darn, darned, effing, flipping, forking, freaking, frigging, fucking, one's ass off, one's brains out, one's head off, to the max, like all get-out, like sin, to beat the band, like all creation, as blazes, as can be, as hell, like hell, in full swing> eg *Myślę, że ona jest wściekle piękna (I think she's goddamned beautiful)*

woda See cicha woda, czuć się jak ryba w wodzie, dużo wody w Wiśle upłynie, dziesiąta woda po kisielu, iść, lać wodę, nabrać wody w usta, palcem po wodzie pisane, palma komuś odbiła, pic, robić komuś wodę z mózgu, w gorącej wodzie kąpany

wóda [VOO-dah] (or **wódzia** [VOO-jah]) *nf* Vodka or any other potent alcohol <hard liquor, hard stuff, hooch, booze, stiff drink, poison> eg *Po kolacji zaproponował nam wódę (After supper he suggested that we drink hard stuff)*

wodotrysk [voh-DOH-trisk] *nm* Insane self-impression or self-importance, esp as a result of one's success; egotism <ego-tripping, swell-headedness, big-headedness, high-nosedness, hot air> eg *Wiesz, jak najlepiej określić jego zachowanie jako dyrektora Instytutu? Wodotrysk (Do you know what's the best way to characterize his behavior as the director of the Institute? Ego-tripping)*

wojaczka [voh-YAHCH-kah] *nf* War in general <action, battle, line of duty> eg *Ten żołnierz zginął podczas wojaczki (That soldier died in action)*

wojak [VOH-yahk] *nm* A soldier <G.I., G.I. Joe, Joe, Joe Blow, dogface, doughfoot, doughboy, trooper> eg *Był z niego dobry wojak (He was a good G.I. Joe)*

wojo See iść do woja

wojo [VOH-yoh] *nn* Armed Forces <Uncle Sam, green machine, khaki tit> eg *Wojo go wzięło (Uncle Sam's got him)*

Wojtek See w kółko

won** [vohn] (or **wynocha** [vi-NOH-khah] or **paszoł won**** [PAH-show VOHN]) *excl* A brusque exclamation telling someone to leave or depart <split, beat it, ankle, bag ass, blow, breeze off, burn rubber, butt out, buzz off, check out, cruise, cut and run, cut ass, cut out, drag ass, dust, ease out, fade, fade away, fade out, fuck off, get the fuck out, get the hell out , get going, get moving, get lost, get off the dime, get on one's horse, go south, haul ass, hightail, hit the bricks, hit the road, hop it, make tracks, pull out, scram, set sail, shove off, shuffle along, skate, skip out, split the scene, take off> eg *Won stąd, ty świnio! (Get the fuck out of here, you pig!)*

worek See wrzucać coś do jednego worka

wóz See piąte koło u wozu

wóz [voos] (**wózek** [VOO-zehk]) *nm* An automobile <wheels, set of wheels, crate, ride, cage, trans, transportation, four wheeler, boat, buggy> eg *Gdzie zaparkowałeś swój wóz? (Where did you park your wheels?)*

wóz albo przewóz [voos AHL-boh PSHEH-voos] *phr* (A demand to) Do one thing or another, but stop dithering; take action <shit or get off the pot, piss or get off the pot, fish or cut off bait, neck or nothing> eg *Nie można dalej zwlekać. Wóz albo przewóz (We can't wait any longer. Fish or cut bait)*

wpadka [FPAHT-kah] *nf* **1** Unwanted pregnancy, possibly due to failure in contraception <knock-up, PG> eg *Ma depresję z powodu tej wpadki (She's depressed because of this knock-up)* **2** A careless but blatant mistake, esp the one that is likely to ruin someone <slip, slip-up, flub, fluff, foozle, goof-up, screw-up, fuck-up, ball-up, mess-up, louse-up, blooper> eg *Była to kolejna wpadka (It was another slip-up)*

wpakować See pakować

wpaść [fpahshch] *v* **1** To get pregnant unexpectedly or unwantedly, possibly due to failure in contraception <get knocked up, get banged up, get PG, get preggers, get puffed, get pumped, get bumped, get storked> eg *Wpadła zanim skończyła ogólniak (She got knocked up before she finished high school)* **2** (or **wpaść jak śliwka w kompot** [fpahshch yahk SHLEEF-kah f KOHM-poht] or **wpaść jak śliwka w gówno*** [fpahshch yahk SHLEEF-kah v GOOV-noh]) To make a careless but blatant mistake, esp the one that is likely to ruin someone; to accidentally get onself into trouble <slip, slip up, trip up, blow, flub, fluff, foozle, goof up, screw up, fuck up, ball up, mess up, louse up, make a blooper, pull a blooper, drop the ball, drop a brick, put one's foot in it, stub one's toe, fall flat on one's ass, shoot oneself in the foot, get into shit, step into shit, get one's ass in a sling, get up shit creek without a paddle> eg *Prędzej czy później wpadnie i go złapią (He'll slip up sooner or later and will get caught)*

wpaść do głowy [fpahshch doh GWOH-vi] *v phr* To have a sudden idea; to come to mind briefly <cross one's mind, pass through someone's mind, dawn on, have a brainwave, spark> eg *Powiem ci, co mi właśnie wpadło do głowy (Let me tell you what just crossed my mind)*

wpienić się Perf pienić się

wpieprz See dać wpierdol, dostać wpierdol

wpierdalać się** [fpyehr-DAH-lahch shyeh] (perf **wpierdolić się**** [fpyehr-DOH-leech shyeh]; or **wpieprzać się*** [FPYEHP-shahch shyeh] perf **wpieprzyć się*** [FPYEHP-shich shyeh]; or **wpierniczać się*** [fpyehr-NEE-chahch shyeh] perf **wpierniczyć się*** [fpyehr-NEE-chich shyeh]; or **wpierdzielać się*** [fpyehr-JEH-lahch shyeh] perf **wpierdzielić się*** [fpyehr-JEH-leech shyeh]) *v* **1** To interfere, interrupt, or intrude, esp rudely; to pry into someone's affairs <fuck around with, fuck with, barge in, butt in, bust in, charge in, check in, elbow in, horn in, muscle in, crowd someone's act, get into the act, poke one's face in, poke one's nose in, stick one's face in, stick one's nose in> eg *Zaraz po ich ślubie teściowa zaczęła wpierdalać się w ich życie (Right after their wedding the mother-in-law started to butt into their life)* **2** To get onself into trouble <get fucked, get into shit, step into shit, get one's ass in a sling, get up shit creek without a paddle> eg *Ale się wpierdolił przy tym interesie (Did he really step into shit on that deal!)* **3** To forcefully step into something, collapse, or hit against something <hit, whack, wham, smack, bang, bump, trash, pow, fall over something> *Wpierdolił się w drzewo (He bumped against a tree)*

wpierdalać** [fpyehr-DAH-lahch] perf **wpierdolić**** [fpyehr-DOH-leech]; or **wpieprzać*** [FPHEHP-shahch] perf **wpieprzyć*** [FPYEHP-shich]; **wpierniczać*** [fpyehr-NEE-chahch] perf **wpierniczyć*** [fpyehr-NEE-chihch]; or **wpierdzielać*** [fpyehr-JEH-lahch] perf **wpierdzielić*** [fpyehr-JEH-lahch]; or **wsuwać** [FSOO-vahch] perf **wsunąć** [VSOO-nohnch]; or **wtranżalać** [ftrahn-ZHAH-lahch] perf **wtranżolić** [ftrahn-ZHOH-leech]) *v* **1** To eat, esp very fast <chow, scarf, scoff, pig out, scarf out, pork out> eg *Widzisz panów wpieprzających jajka na twardo? (Can you see these guys scarfing out on hard-boiled eggs?); Wtranżolił całego indyka (He scarfed the whole turkey)* **2** To beat someone up <kick someone's ass, sock, bash, trash, clobber, bang, belt, clock, duke, dust, hammer, land one, lay one on, spank, wham, whack, bam, whip, bust, smack, poke, blast, beat the shit out of, beat the living shit out of, beat the bejejus out of, beat the daylights out of, beat someone into the middle of next week, knock the bejejus out of, knock the daylights out of, knock someone into the middle of next week, hit someone where he lives, work over> eg *Zaraz mu wpierdolę! (I'm going to beat the shit out of him!)*

wpierdol See dać wpierdol, dostać wpierdol

wpuścić kogoś w maliny [FPOOSH-cheech KOH-gohsh v mah-LEE-ni] (or **wpuścić kogoś w kanał** [FPOOSH-cheech KOH-gohsh v KAH-nah-oo]) *v phr*

To cheat; to swindle; to deceive; to make a fool out of someone <con, rip off, shaft, roll, chisel, gyp, scam, screw, stiff, fleece, dick, do in, take in, do a number on, flim-flam, bamboozle, run a number on, take someone for a ride, take someone to the cleaners, throw someone a curve, pull a fast one, fuck over, screw over, angle, take in, snow, do a snow job, double-shuffle, fast-shuffle, flimflam, give a bun steer, give someone a line, have someone on, lead someone down the garden path, do a snow job, jerk someone's chain, pull someone's chain, pull one's leg, pull someone's string, pull the wool over someone's eyes, put someone on, snow, use smoke and mirrors> eg *Prawnicy wpuścili go w maliny (The lawyers led him down to the garden path)*

wpychać w siebie [FPI-khahch f SHYEH-byeh] (or **wciskać w siebie** [FCHEES-kahch f SHYEH-byeh]) *v* To overeat, eat greedily and more than needed <stuff oneself, pig out, scarf out, pork out> eg *Wciska w siebie czekoladę i hamburgery (He porks out on chocolate and hamburgers)*

wrąbać Perf rąbać

wracać do cywila See iść do cywila

wredny [VREHD-ni] *adj* Vicious, malicious, or mean <meanie, bad-assed, nasty-assed, bitchy, dirty, lousy, cussed> eg *Co za wredna laska. Cokolwiek robię, to mówi, że źle (What a bitchy chick. Whatever I do, she says I do wrong)*

wrzód na dupie* [vzhoot nah DOO-pyeh] (or **pryszcz na dupie*** [prishch nah DOO-pyeh]) *nm phr* An irritating obstacle, hindrance, or something out of place <pain in the ass, setback, wart on someone's ass, needle in someone's eye> eg *Ten facet to wrzód na dupie. Nie pasuje do naszego zespołu (This guy is a wart on my ass. He doesn't fit in our company)*

wrzucać coś do jednego worka [VZHOO-tsahch doh yehd-NEH-goh VOHR-kah] *v phr* To fail do discern differences and treat as the same or equal; to wrongly generalize <rank something in the same pot, put something in the same pot> eg *Wrzucił Japończyków i Chińczyków do jednego worka (He's put the Japanese and the Chinese to the same pot)*

wrzucić coś na ruszt [VZHOO-cheech tsohsh nah ROOSHT] *v phr* To eat, esp to have a light meal <chow, scarf, scoff, feed one's face, grub up, put on the feedbag, grab a bite> eg *Czas wrzucić coś na ruszt (It's time to put something on the feedbag)*

wsadzić See móc sobie w dupę wsadzić

wsiąknąć [FSHYOHNK-nohnch] (or **wyparować** [vi-pah-ROH-vahch]) *v* To disappear without a trace <fade, fade away, fade out of sight, melt into the scenery, go south, do a vanishing act> eg *Wsiąknął gdzieś dwa lata temu (He faded out of sight two years ago)*

wsio ryba [fshyoh RI-bah] (or **wsio rybka** [fshyoh RIP-kah] or **wsio rawno** [fshyoh rahv-NOH]) *adv phr* (Something makes) No difference; (Something is) insignificant <no diff, all the same, same old shit, same difference, no matter how you slice it, makes no never mind, makes no difference, anything goes> eg *Czy go wyrzucą, czy sam odejdzie, to wsio ryba (They fire him or he quits, it's the same difference)*

wsiun* [fshyoon] (or **wsiok*** [fshyook] or **wsiowy*** [FSHYOH-vi] or **wiochmen*** [VYOHKH-mehn]) *nm* A rural man, a rustic <hick, hayseed, apple-knocker, hillbilly, shitkicker> eg *Nieważne, że to wsiun. Ma masę pieniędzy (It doesn't matter that he's a shitkicker. He's got a lot of money!); Chodzi z jakimś wiochmenem (She's been dating some hick)*

wskakiwać komuś do dupy See włazić komuś do dupy

wstawać lewą nogą [FSTAH-vahch LEH-voh NOH-goh] *v phr* To get up in the morning in a bad mood; to have a bad mood <get up on the wrong side of the bed, get out of the wrong side of the bed> eg *Co z tobą jest? Wstałeś dziś lewą nogą? (What's wrong woth you? Did you get up on the wrong side of the bed today?)*

wstawić się [FSTAH-veech shyeh] *v* To get drunk <get alkied, get bagged, get blitzed, get blotto, get blown away, get bent, get boiled, get bombed, get boozed up, get blasted, get bottled, get boxed, get canned, get clobbered, get cooked, get corked, get drunk as a skunk, get edged, get embalmed, get fractured, get fried, get gassed, get ginned, get grogged, get high, get hooched up, get impaired, get illuminated, get juiced, get liquored up, get lit, get loaded, get looped, get lubricated, get smashed, get oiled, get pickled, get plastered, get plonked, get polluted, get sauced, get shitfaced, get sloshed, get soaked, get stewed, get stiff, get stinking drunk, get swizzled, get tanked up, get wiped, get zonked, get fucked up> eg *Zawsze w sobotę lubi się wstawić (He always likes to get shitfaced on Saturday)*

wstawiony [fstah-VYOH-ni] *adj* Drunk; alcohol intoxicated <alkied, bagged, blitzed, blotto, blown away, bent, boiled, bombed, blasted, boozed, bottled, boxed, buzzed, canned, clobbered, cooked, corked, crashed, drunk as a skunk, edged, embalmed, fractured, fried, gassed, ginned, grogged, have one too many, half under, high, hooched up, in bad shape, impaired, illuminated, juiced, knocked out, liquored, lit, loaded, looped, lubricated, lushed, smashed, oiled, pickled, plastered, plonked, polluted, sauced, shitfaced, slugged, sloshed, soaked, stewed, stiff, stinking drunk, swizzled, tanked, three sheets to the wind, wiped, zonked> eg *Tylko mi nie mów, że znów jest wstawionay (Don't tell me he's blitzed again)*

wsuwać See wpierdalać

wszarz* [fshahsh] *nm* A despicable, loathsome and sloppy man, esp a derelict <louse, bum, bo, hobo, piece of shit, hood, wino, dreg, wrongo, scum of the earth> eg *Wszarz nie chciał dać nam spokoju (The bum didn't want to leave us alone)*

wszystko gra See gra muzyka

wtenczas [FTEHN-chahs] **1** *adv* Then; at that time <back then, in those days> eg *Wtenczas byliśmy bardzo biedni (We were very poor in those days)*

wtranżalać See wpierdalać

wtrząchnąć [FTZHOHNKH-nohnch] *v* To eat, esp everything <chow, scarf, scoff, pig out, scarf out, pork out> eg *Wtrząchnął całego indyka (He scarfed the whole turkey)*

wtyki See wejścia

wucet [VOO-tseht] *nm* A restroom or bathroom; a toilet <john, johnny, can, crapper, potty, shitcan, shitter, shithouse, throne> eg *Gdzie jest twój kuzyn? Jest w wucecie (Where's your cousin? He's in the john)*

wuef [voo-EHF] *nm* Physical education, a subject in school <PT, PE, phy ed, phys ed, gym> eg *Myślę, że urwę się z wuefu (I think I'm going to cut PE)*

wyłazić ze skóry See wychodzić ze skóry

wyłożyć forsę [vi-WOH-zhich FOHR-seh] (or **pieniądze** [pyeh-NYOHN-dzeh] or **kasę** [KAH-seh] or **szmal** [shmahl] may replace **forsę**) *v phr* To invest money, esp to start an enterprise <bankroll, go in for> eg *Japończycy wyłożyli forsę na ten projekt (The Japanese bankrolled the project)*

wyłożyć kawę na ławę [vi-WOH-zhich KAH-veh nah WAH-veh] *v phr* To speak very directly, firmly, and plainly about something; to tell thruthfully <lay it on the line, put it on the line, get down to the nitty-gritty, get down to the facts> eg *Dobra, wyłożę ci kawęna ławę. Musisz ciężej pracować, jeśli chcesz zdać (Okay, I'm going to lay it on the line for you. You must work harder if you want to pass)*

wyłoić komuś skórę See przetrzepać komuś skórę

wyżerka [vi-ZHEHR-kah] *nf* An act of eating up delicious food or delicious food itself <spread, great grub, great chow> eg *Na imprezie była świetna wyżerka (There was an awesome spread at the party)*

wyżreć Perf żreć

wyżyłować się [vi-zhi-WOH-vahch shyeh] *v* To spend all one's money; to spend a sum of money that is inadequate to one's budget <go broke, lose out, blow, drop a bundle, go to the cleaners, take a bath, tap out, wash out, belly up, go bust, take a beating> eg *Wyżyłował się na tym mieszkaniu (He dropped a bundle on that apartment)*

See wykańczać się

wybić sobie coś z głowy [VI-beech SOH-byeh tsosh z GWOH-vi] *v phr* To stop thinking about (doing) something; to persuade oneself (often as a result of exterior influence) not to do something <get something out of one's head, forget about it> eg *Chcesz tam lecieć samolotem? Wybij to sobie z głowy, to zbyt kosztowne (Do you want to fly there? Get it out of your head, it's too expensive)*

wybór See do wyboru do koloru

wybrzydzać [vi-BZHI-dzahch] (or **wydziwiać** [vi-JEE-vyahch]) *v* To be groundlessly dissatisfied or discontented; to have unfounded complaints <fuss, stink, scene, make a ceremony, beef, bleed, hassle, kvetch, bitch, beef, gripe, piss, bellyache, grouse, growl, squawk, cut a beef, make a stink, piss up a storm, raise a stink, blow up a storm, kick up a storm, eat someone's heart out, fuck around, screw around, mess around, trip> eg *Wybrzydzała, bo nie mieli tego, co chciała (She was pissing up a storm, because they didn't have what she wanted)*

wybudować się Perf budować się

wybulić See bulić

wybyczyć Perf byczyć się

wybzykać Perf bzykać

wychlać Perf chlać

wychlapać Perf chlapać

wychodek [vi-KHOH-dehk] *nm* A restroom or bathroom; a toilet <john, johnny, can, crapper, potty, shitcan, shitter, shithouse, throne> eg *Gdzie jest twój kuzyn? Poszedł do wychodka (Where's your cousin? He went to the john)*

wychodzić na durnia [vi-KHOH-jeech nah DOOR-nyah] (or **wychodzić na głupiego** [vi-KHOH-jeech nah gwohh-PYEH-goh] or **wychodzić na idiotę** [vi-KHOH-jeech nah ee-DYOH-teh]) *v phr* To make a fool of oneself <make a laughing stock out of oneself> eg *Wyszła na durnia tą ostatnią uwagą (She made a laughing stock of herself by that last remark)*

wychodzić ze skóry [vi-SKOH-chich zeh SKOO-ri] (or **wyłazić ze skóry** [vi-WAH-zheech zeh SKOO-ri] or **wyskoczyć ze skóry** [vis-KOH-chich zeh SKOO-ri]) *v phr* **1** To strive; to make one's best effort; to strenously attempt to get or do something <bust one's ass, bust a gut, bust one's balls, break one's ass,

break one's neck, work one's ass off, do one's damnednest, give it one's all, give it one's best, go all out, go for broke, go all the way, go for it, go the extra mile, go the full yard, go the limit, go the whole nine yards, go to the wall, make a full-court press, put one's back into, hassle, sweat, dig, plug, break one's ass, bend over backward, pour it on, knock oneself out, bear down, scramble for, go after, push for, shoot for, shoot the works, spread oneself, pull oneself together, push hard> eg *On jest jednym z tych facetów, którzy wyjdą ze skóry, żeby pomóc przyjacielowi (He's one of those guys who will bust their asses to help a friend)* **2** (or **wychodzić z siebie** [vi-KHOH-jeech s SHYEH-byeh]) To be very angry or irritated and to lose control; to be emotionally uncontrolled because of anger or irritation <be beside oneself, be pissed off, be peed off, be p'd off, be bent out of a shape, be pushed out of a shape, be browned off, be cranky, be uptight, be jumpy, be edgy, be sore, be mad as a hornet, be steamed up, be ticked off, be tee'd off, be burned up, be ballistic> eg *Był tak wściekły, że prawie wyskoczył ze skóry (He was so furious that he was almost beside himself)*

wychylić [vi-KHI-leech] *v* To have a quick drink of liquor <knock back, down, slug down, swig, tank, tank up> eg *Wychylił cztery piwa i zaczął bekać (He downed three beers and started to burp)*

wyciąć See wykręcić komuś numer

wyciągać [vi-CHYOHN-gahch] (perf **wyciągnąć** [vi-CHYOHNG-nohnch]) *v* **1** To earn a specific amount of money, esp as a salary <make, knock down, pull down, pull in, rack in, pick up, clean up, rack up, pile up, stack up, cash in> eg *Ile wyciągasz na miesiąć? (How much do you make a month?)* **2** (Of an automobile) To reach a given maximum speed <do, turn, hit, climb> eg *Ten wóz wyciąga około stówy na godzinę (This car will hit around a hundred per hour); Wyciąga górę setę (She does a hundred max)*

wyciągnąć nogi [vi-CHYOHNG-nohnch NOH-gee] (or **wyciągnąć kopyta*** [vi-CHYOHNG-nohnch koh-PI-tah] or **wyjść nogami do przodu** [VI-eeshch noh-GAH-mee doh PSHOH-doo]) *v phr* To die <bite the dust, kiss the dust, croak, belly up, buy the farm, buy the ranch, cash in one's chips, check out, bump off, conk off, conk out, farm, give up the ghost, go home feet first, go home in a box, go west, kick in, kick off, kick the bucket, pass out, peg out, shove off, drop off, step off, pop off, push up daisies, meet one's maker, turn up one's toes, go down the tube, join the great majority, join the majority> eg *Który pierwszy wyciągnął kopyta? (Who was the first to kick the bucket?); Nie rób tego, chyba, że chcesz wyjść nogami do przodu (Don't do it, unless you want to turn up your toes)*

wyciągnąć Perf ciągnąć

wycisk See dać wycisk, dostać wycisk

wyciupciać Perf ciupciać

wycwanić się [vi-TSFAH-neech shyeh]) *v* To become shrewdly aware; to apprehend reality; to smarten <wise up, smarten up, get smart, get wise, get with it, pull up one's socks, tie one's shoes> eg *Oszukanie go może być trudniejsze, bo się wycwanił (Fooling him may be more difficult because he wised up)*

wydębić [vi-DEHM-beech] *v* **1** To wheedle something out of someone; to get without intending to repay or return; to beg <freeload, sponge, mooch, scrounge, bum, chisel, dog it, hit up, put the lug on, put the touch on, touch up, stick for> eg *Koleś, mogę wydębić od ciebie papierosa? (Can I chisel a cigarette from you, pal?)*

wydobrzeć See wylizać się
wydoić Perf doić
wydra See ni pies ni wydra
wydupczyć Perf dupczyć
wydymać Perf dymać
wydziwiać See wybrzydzać
wygłówkować Perf główkować
wyga See stary wyga
wygadany [vi-gah-DAH-ni] (or **wyszczekany** [vi-shcheh-KAH-ni]) *adj* Able to express or defend ideas readily and effectively; eloquently brash <sharp-tongued, gutty, lippy, cocky, brassy, cheeky, sassy, nervy, smart-ass, wise-ass, foul-mouthed, cussy, bitchy> eg *Twoja siostrzyczka jest naprawdę wyszczekana. Ale im nagadała! (Your little sister is real sassy. Did she give them an earful!)*
wygarbować komuś skórę See **przetrzepać komuś skórę**
wygibasy [vi-gee-BAH-si] *npl* Movements done when dancing; dancing itself <rocking, shaking, booging, hopping, swinging, jumping, juking, jiving, grinding> eg *Enough of this booging (Wystarczy tych wygibasów)*
wyglebić się [vi-GLEH-beech shyeh] (or **walnąć o glebę** [VAHL-nohnch oh GLEH-beh] or **zaliczyć glebę** [zah-LEE-chich GLEH-beh]) *v* To fall from something <come crashing down, kiss the ground, kiss the floor, get acquainted with the pavement, take a dive> eg *Kozioł zaliczył glebę (The goat kissed the ground)*
wygodnicki [vi-goh-DNEE-tskee] *adj* Overly concerned with own comfort; accustomed to comfort or laziness <Mr. Lazy-ass, Mr. Lazybones, Mr. Lazy-bum, Mr. Comfort, Prince Comfort> eg *Czego chce ten wygodnicki? (What does Mr. Lzaybones want?)*
wygrzać Perf grzać
wygwizdów [vi-GVEEZ-doof] (or **wygwizdowo** [vi-gvee-ZDOH-voh] *nn*) *nm* A small town, esp in the country; any place far from civilization <jerk town, jerkwater town, backwater, hellhole, rathole, mudhole, real hole, noplaceville, hicksville, whistle stop, dump, armpit, East Jesus, Bumfuck Egypt> eg *Skąd dzwonisz? Z jakiegoś wygwizdowa (Where are you calling from? Some mudhole)*
wyjadacz See stary wyga
wyjebać See jebać
wyjść na czymś jak Zabłocki na mydle [VI-eeshch nah chimsh yahk zah-BWOHYS-kee nah MID-leh] *v phr* To lose a lot of money <go broke, lose out, blow, drop a bundle, go to the cleaners, take a bath, tap out, wash out, belly up, go bust, take a beating> eg *Myślę, że wyjdą na tym interesie jak Zabłocki na mydle (I think they're going to drop a bundle on that deal)*
wyjść na czysto [VI-eeshch nah CHIS-toh] (or **wyjść na zero** [VI-eeshch nah nah ZEH-roh]) *v phr* To make a zero net profit; to earn exactly as much as one invested <break even> eg *Okazało się, że to przedsięwzięcie nie było tak intratne, jak oczekiwaliśmy. Wyszliśmy jedynie na czysto (It turned out that the business venture wasn't as luctrative as we expected. We only managed to break even)*
wyjść na ludzi [VI-eeshch nah LOO-jee] *v phr* To steer one's life in such a way that one becomes a valuable individual; to achieve something in life <make a man> eg *Jest jeszcze szansa, że wyjdziesz na ludzi (There's still hope you can still make a man of yourself)*

wyjść na minus See być na minusie

wyjść na plus See być na plusie

wyjść na swoje See być na plusie

wyjść nogami do przodu See wyciągnąć nogi

wyjść z czegoś [VI-eeshch s CHEH-gohsh] *v phr* Not to have something on one's possession <be out of, not have on one> eg *Masz drobne? Wyszłam z drobnych (Do you have any change? I'm out of any change)*

wyjść z czegoś obronną ręką [VI-eeshch s CHEH-gohsh ohb-ROHN-noh REHN-koh] *v phr* To go unpunished; to be acquitted of a crime <go scot-free, get off scot-free, be saved by the bell> eg *Ściągała na klasówce, została przyłapana, ale wyszła z tego obronną ręką)*

wykalkulować Perf **kalkulować**

wykańczać się [vi-KAHÑ-chahch shyeh] (perf **wykończyć się** [vi-KOÑ-chich shyeh]; or **wyżyłować się** [vi-shi-WOH-vahch shyeh] or **wypompować się** [vi-pohm-POH-vahch shyeh]) *v phr* To be very tired or exhausted <be dead, be dead on one's feet, be dead-tired, be dog-tired, be out of it, be out of gas, be out of juice, be all in, be all shot, be pooped, be bagged, be beat, be beat to the ground, be beat to the ankles, be bone-tired, be burned out, be bushed, be chewed, be crapped out, be done, be done in, be dragged out, be frazzled, be played out, be fucked out, be knocked out, be tuckered out, be tapped out, had it, be ready to drop, be on one's last legs> eg *Nie pracuj tak ciężko, bo się zaraz wykończysz (Don't work so hard, because you'll be out of gas soon)*

wykapany [vi-kah-PAH-ni] *adj* (Esp about persons) Exactly similar; identical; the same <spitting image of, chip off the old block, double, look-alike, dead ringer> eg *Z jego zachowania można było wywnioskować, że to wykapany ojciec (From his behavior you could see that he was the spitting image of his father)*

wykidajło [vi-kee-DAH-ee-woh] *nm* A person employed to eject unwanted customers from a saloon or restaurant <bouncer> eg *Jej brat miał czarny pas w karate i został wykidajłem w jakimś nocnym klubie (Her brother had a black belt in karate and became a bouncer in some night club)*

wykitować [vi-kee-TOH-vahch] (or **odwalić kitę** [ohd-VAH-leech KEE-teh]) *v* To die <bite the dust, kiss the dust, croak, belly up, buy the farm, buy the ranch, cash in one's chips, check out, bump off, conk off, conk out, farm, give up the ghost, go home feet first, go home in a box, go west, kick in, kick off, kick the bucket, pass out, peg out, shove off, drop off, step off, pop off, push up daisies, meet one's maker, turn up one's toes, go down the tube, join the great majority, join the majority> eg *Jest zbyt młody, żeby wykitować (He's too young to kick the bucket)*

wykiwać Perf kiwać

wykołować Perf kołować

wykolejeniec [vi-koh-leh-YEH-nyehts] *nm* An outcast, esp a criminal; a bad person <badass, bad guy, bad egg, baddie, wrong number, wrongo, piece of shit, dreg, scum of the earth, hood, hoodlum, hooligan, goon, con, ex-con, crook, mugger, dropper, finger, racketeer, jailbird, yardbird, mobster, gangster> eg *Do tego baru przychodzą sami wykolejeńcy (This bar is frequented only by bad guys)*

wykombinować Perf kombinować

wykoncypować [vi-kohn-tsi-POH-vahch] *v* To devise, invent, or realize something <use one's head, rack one's brain, brainstorm, think up, noodle around, percolate,

perk, head trip, skull drag, eat, bug, burn a couple of braincells, figure out, work out, tune in, plug in, tote up, wise up, get through one's head, get through someone's thick head, get into someone's thick head, see daylight, flash, dig, dawn on, have a brainwave> eg *Cóżeś tam wykoncypował, co? (What did you think up, huh?)*

wykończony [vi-KOHÑ-choh-ni] (or **wypluty** [vi-PLOO-ti] or **wypompowany** [vi-pohm-poh-VAH-ni] or **wyprany** [vi-PRAH-ni] or **wypruty** [vi-PROO-ti]) *adj* Very tired or exhausted <dead, dead on one's feet, dead-tired, dog-tired, out of it, out of gas, out of juice, all in, all shot, pooped, bagged, beat, beat to the ground, beat to the ankles, bone-tired, burned out, bushed, chewed, crapped out, done, done in, dragged out, frazzled, played out, fucked out, knocked out, tuckered out, tapped out, had it, ready to drop, on one's last legs> eg *Ale jestem wykończony! Zaraz padnę (Am I dead-tired! I'm gonna drop in a second)*

wykończyć się Perf wykańczać się

wykop See kop

wykorkować [vi-kohr-KOH-vahch] *v* To die <bite the dust, kiss the dust, croak, belly up, buy the farm, buy the ranch, cash in one's chips, check out, bump off, conk off, conk out, farm, give up the ghost, go home feet first, go home in a box, go west, kick in, kick off, kick the bucket, pass out, peg out, shove off, drop off, step off, pop off, push up daisies, meet one's maker, turn up one's toes, go down the tube, join the great majority, join the majority> eg *Który pierwszy wykorkował? (Who was the first to kick the bucket?)*

wykręcić komuś numer [vi-KREHN-cheech KOH-moosh NOO-mehr] (**odstawić** [oht-STAH-veech] or **wyciąć** [VI-chyohnch] or **wywinąć** [vi-VEE-nohnch] or **zrobić** [ZROH-beech] may replace **wykręcić**) *v phr* To cheat; to swindle; to deceive; to make a fool out of someone <con, rip off, shaft, roll, chisel, gyp, scam, screw, stiff, fleece, dick, do in, take in, do a number on, flim-flam, bamboozle, run a number on, take someone for a ride, take someone to the cleaners, throw someone a curve, pull a fast one, fuck over, screw over, angle, take in, snow, do a snow job, double-shuffle, fast-shuffle, flimflam, give a bun steer, give someone a line, have someone on, lead someone down the garden path, do a snow job, jerk someone's chain, pull someone's chain, pull one's leg, pull someone's string, pull the wool over someone's eyes, put someone on, snow, use smoke and mirrors> eg *Moja była dziewczyna wykręciła mi niezły numer (My ex girlfriend really took me for a ride)*

wykuć Perf kuć

wykumać Perf kumać

wylać [VI-lahch] *v* **1** To expell or relegate a student from school or university <flunk out, flush out, bust out, bounce out, kick out, bilge out, boot out> eg *Pił dużo, więc go wylali ze szkoły (He was a heavy-drinking student so they flunked him out from school)* **2** (or **wylać z roboty** [VI-lahch z roh-BOH-ti]) *v* To dismiss or discharge from a job, esp forcefully <fire, lay off, can, ax, air, boot, sack, give the ax, give the air, give the boot, give the sack, give the bum's rush, give the kiss-off, give the pink slip, pink-slip, give one's walking papers, give one's walking ticket> eg *Wylała ich obydwu (She's given them both the kiss-off)*

wylać dziecko z kąpielą [VI-lahch JEHTS-koh s kohm-PYEH-loh] *v phr* To lose the most important part of something when getting rid of the bad or unwanted part <throw the baby out with the bathwater> eg *Musimy uważać, żeby nie wylać dziecka z kąpielą. Naszym zadaniem jest kontrola techniki, a nie odwracanie się od niej (We must be careful not to throw the baby out with the bathwater. Our task is to control technology, not to turn away from it)*

wylać Perf lać

wylecieć [vi-LEH-chehch] **1** To be expelled or relegated from school or university <get flunked out, get flushed out, get busted out, get bounced out, get kicked out, get bilged out, get booted out> eg *Pił dużo, więc go wyleciał (He was a heavy-drinking student so he got flunked out)* **2** (or **wylecieć z roboty** [vi-LEH-chehch z roh-BOH-ti]) *v* To get dismissed or discharged from a job, esp forcefully <get fired, get laid off, get the ax, get axed, get the air, get aired, get the boot, get booted, get the sack, get sacked, get the bum's rush, get the kiss-off, get the pink slip, get one's walking papers, get one's walking ticket> eg *Jeszcze trzech profersorów wyleciało dziś rano (Three more professors got the ax this morning)*

wylecieć z głowy [vi-LEH·chyech z GWOH-vi] *v phr* (For something which was to be remembered) To be forgotten; to forget <slip one's mind, clean forget, draw a blank, blow up, go up> eg *Po drodze do domu miałem wstąpić do spożywczego, ale wyleciało mi z głowy (I meant to go to the grocery store on the way home, but it slipped my mind)*

wylewać za kołnierz See nie wylewać za kołnierz

wylizać Perf lizać

wylizać się [vi-LEE-zahch shyeh] (or **wydobrzeć** [vi-DOHB-zhehch]) *v* To live in spite of illness or wounds; to regain health <pull through, pull around, get well, come around> eg *Ma wiele ran, ale się wyliże (She has many wounds, but she'll pull through)*

wylotówka [vi-loh-TOOF-kah] *nf* An exit route <no slang equivalent> eg *Weźcie następną wylotówkę (Take the next exit route)*

wyluzakować się Perf luzakować się

wyluzować się Perf luzować się

wymacać Perf macać

wymiękać [vi-MYEHN-kahch] (perf **wymięknąć** [vi-MYEHNK-nohnch]) *v* To be afraid; to be frightened; to be intimidated <chicken out, turn chicken, turn yellow, run scared, have cold feet, be scared stiff, be scared shitless, shit one's pants, piss one's pants, shit bullets, shit a brick, shit green, be spooked, push the panic button, wimp out> eg *Facet wymiękł już na sam widok (The guy chickened out right at the very sight)*

wymoczek [vi-MOH-chehk] *nm* A young, inexperienced, sickly or frail man <walking corpse, wimp> eg *Jej mąż to wygląda jak jakiś wymoczek (Her husband looks like some kind of a walking corpse)*

wymodzić Perf modzić

wynocha See won

wyśrubowany [vi-shroo-boh-VAH-ni] *adj* (Esp about a price or sum) Exorbitant; expensive <pricey, up to here, out of sight> eg *Nigdy nie robi zakupów w tym sklepie, bo uważa, że ceny są tam zbyt wyśrubowane (She never shops in this store because she finds the prices too pricey)*

wyświechtany [vi-shfyehkh-TAH-ni] *adj* **1** Shabby and threadbare <worn-out, done-in, beat-up, ratty, tacky, frowzy, used-up, in a bad way> eg *Te spodnie są zbyt* *wyświechtane, nie założe ich (These pants are too beat-up, I won't put them on)* **2** (Of a phrase or word) Used too often; hackneyed <corny, hokey, tripe, square> eg *Używał wyświechtanych słów (He used corny words)*

wypad See zrobić wypad

wypalić [vi-PAH-leech] *v* **1** To come into effect; to succeed <work out, come out, pan out, not fall through, not fall down, not fall flat, not drop through, not tumble down, not fuck up, not get fucked up, not screw up, not get screwed up, not get crimped, not get cramped, not get stymied> eg *Wypalił wam plan? (Did your plan work out?)* **2** To say something blatantly improper, indiscreet, or foolish, esp carelessly; to reveal a secret or a surprise by accident <let the cat out of the bag, spill the beans, make the shit hit the fan, blab, blow> eg *Rety, ale wypalił! (Boy, did he blab it!)*

wyparować See wsiąknąć

wypiął See ni pies ni wydra

wypiąć się Perf wypinać się

wypieprzyć Perf pieprzyć

wypierdalać** [vi-pyehr-DAH-lahch] (perf **wypierdolić**** [vi-pyehr-DOH-leech]; or **wypieprzać*** [vi-PYEHP-shahch] perf **wypieprzyć*** [vi-PYEHP-shich] or **wypierniczać*** [vi-pyehr-NEE-chahch] perf **wypierniczyć*** [vi-pyehr-NEE-chich]; or **wypierdzielać*** [vi-pyehr-JEH-lahch] perf **wypierdzielić*** [vi-pyehr-JEH-leech]) *v* **1** To leave, depart, or desert, esp hastily <fuck off, get the fuck out, split, beat it, ankle, bag ass, blow, breeze off, burn rubber, butt out, buzz off, check out, cruise, cut and run, cut ass, cut out, drag ass, dust, ease out, fade, fade away, fade out, get the hell out , get going, get moving, get lost, get off the dime, get on one's horse, go south, haul ass, hightail, hit the bricks, hit the road, hop it, make tracks, pull out, scram, set sail, shove off, shuffle along, skate, skip out, split the scene, take off> eg *Wypierdalaj z mojego domu! (Get the fuck out of my house!)* **2** To eject by force <bounce, boot out, bum-rush, give the bum's rush, chuck, kick out, put the skids to, turn out, throw on the ass> eg *Przyszedł właściciel i nas wypieprzył (The owner came up and bounced us)* **3** To discard; to get rid of oneself of <chuck, ax, bag, boot, can, deep-six, ditch, dump, eighty-six, junk, kiss goodbye, put the skids to, shitcan, toss overboard, unload> eg *Powinienem wypieprzyć ten telewizor już dawno temu (I should have deep-six this old T.V. set long ago)*

wypierdek* [vi-PYEHR-dehk] (or **wypierdek mamuta*** [vi-PYEHR-dehk mah-MOO-tah]) *nm* A man one dislikes or disapproves of <asshole, fuck, fucker, fuckhead, fuckface, motherfucker, shit, shitface, shithead, shitheel, bastard, jerk, SOB, son of a bitch, son of a whore, cocksucker, prick, dick, dickhead, cuntface, schmuck, scum, scumbag, sleazebag, slimebag, dipshit, pisshead, piece of shit, pain in the ass> eg *Powiedz temu wypierdkowi, żeby zjeżdżał stąd (Tell that jerk to beat it)*

wypierdolić Perf pierdolić

wypierdolić się** [vi-pyehr-DOH-leech shyeh] (or **wypieprzyć się*** [vi-PYEHP-shich shyeh] or **wypierniczyć się*** [vi-pyehr-NEE-chich shyeh] or **wypierdzielić się*** [vi-pyehr-JEH-leech shyeh]) *v* To tip over and fall; to collapse <hit, whack, wham, smack, bang, bump, trash, pow, fall over something> eg *Wpierdolił się na skórce od banana (He fell over a fucking banana peel)*

wypinać dupę See wypinać się

wypinać się [vi-PEE-nahch shyeh] (or **wypinać dupę*** [vi-PEE-nahch DOO-peh] perf **wypiąć się** [VI-pyohnch shyeh]) *v phr* To be indifferent; not to care at all; to ignore; to show disrespect <not give a damn, not give a fuck, not give a shit, not give a diddly-shit, not give a diddly-damn, not give a flying fuck, not give a hoot, not give a rat's ass, not give a squat, pass up, diss, skip, ig, ice, chill, freeze, cut, brush off, give the brush, give the cold shoulder, turn the cold shoulder, cold-shoulder, give the go-by, high-hat, kiss off> eg *Kompletnie wypięła dupę na tego faceta (She completely cold-shouldered this guy)*

wypindrzony [vi-peend-ZHOH-nah] *adj* Fancily dressed <dolled-up, dolled-out, dressed to kill, dressed to the nines, dressed to the teeth, dressed-up, duded-up, ritzed up, swanked up, ragged out, sharp-dressed> eg *Kim jest ten wypindrzony facet? (Who's that sharp-dressed man?)*

wypisz wymaluj [VI-peesh vi-MAH-loo-ee] *adj* (Esp about persons) Exactly similar; identical; the same <spitting image of, chip off the old block, double, look-alike, dead ringer> eg *Nosi białe skarpetki i czerwony krawat. Wypisz wymaluj jego ojciec (He wears white socks and red tie. He's a spitting image of his father)*

wypluty See wykończony

wypociny [vi-poh-CHEE-ni] *npl* An unimaginative, meaningless, or mediocre piece of written work, esp an essay <scribble, scribbling, scratching, comp, stuff, wipe-ass, ass-wipe> eg *Jak byś ocenił te wypociny? (How would you grade this scribble?)*

wypompować się See wykańczać się

wypompowany See wykończony

wyprany See wykończony

wypruty See wykończony

wypruwać sobie flaki [vi-PROO-vahch SOH-byeh FLAH-kee] (or **wypruwać z siebie flaki** [vi-PROO-vahch s SHYEH-byeh FLAH-kee]; **żyły** [ZHI-wi] may replace **flaki**) *v phr* To work very hard <work one's ass off, work one's fingers to the bone, work like a horse, sweat, bust one's ass off, break one's ass off, make bricks without a straw> eg *Wyrpuwał z siebie flaki przez pięć lat, żeby kimś zostać (He worked his ass off for five years to become somebody)*

wypuszczać *v* [vi-POOSH-chahch] (perf **wypuścić** [vi-POOSH-cheech]) To show a new product for sale on the market; to release <bring out> eg *Niedawno firma wypuściła dwa nowe modele (The company has brought out two new models recently)*

wyrżnąć Perf rżnąć

wyrabiać się [vi-RAH-beech shyeh] (perf **wyrobić się** [vi-ROH-beech shyeh]) *v* **1** To be able or to manage to do something, esp on time; to succeed <make it, make out, get on, get along, come on, come along, handle, cut the mustard> eg *Nie wyrobił się na wirażu i rozbił się (He didn't make it on the curve and crashed); Możemy się nie wyrobić na czas (We may not cut the mustard)* **2** To gain experience or skill <make the grade, come into one's own> eg *Wyrobił się jako bokser (As a boxer, he really came into his own)*

wyrko [VIR-koh] (or **wyro** [VI-roh]) *nn* A bed <hay, pad, sack, flop, rack, snooze bin, fleabag, fart sack, whank-pit, workbench> eg *Nie zmieniałem pościeli w moim wyrku przez miesiąc. Może dwa (I haven't changed the sheets in my whank-pit for a month. Or is it two?)*

wyro See iść z kimś do łóżka, wyrko

wyrobić się Perf wyrabiać się

wyrodek* [vi-ROH-dehk] *nm* Someone who is thought by his family to have brought shame to the family; the worst member in the family <black sheep, black sheep of the family, rotten apple> eg *Moja siostra to wyrodek w naszej rodzinie. Zawsze ma problemy z policją (My sister is the black sheep in our family. She's always in trouble with the police)*

wyrolować Perf rolować

wyruchać Perf ruchać

wyryć Perf ryć

wyrzucić w błoto [vi-ZHOO-cheech v BWOH-toh] (or **wywalać w błoto** [vi-VAH-lahch v BWOH-toh]) *v phr* To spend money foolishly <throw away, pour down the drain, throw down the drain> eg *Został wyrzucony ponieważ wyrzucał pieniądze w błoto (He was expelled because he had been throwing money down the drain)*

wyrzygać się Perf rzygać

wysępić [vi-SEHM-peech]) *v* To wheedle something out of someone; to get without intending to repay or return; to beg <freeload, sponge, mooch, scrounge, bum, chisel, dog it, hit up, put the lug on, put the touch on, touch up, stick for> eg *Wysępiał papierosy od kolegów (He would bum cigarettes from his colleagues)*

wysiadać [vi-SHYAH-dahch] (perf **siąść** [VI-shyonshch]) *v* (Esp about mechanical appliances) To fail or become inoperative <break down, crash, crash and burn, fry, go down, go down in flames, go south, belly up, melt down, shut down, crack up, screw up, fuck up, go blooey, go busted, go on the blink, go on the fritz, go off, go out of whack, go kerflooey> eg *Wszystko szło mi dobrze póki nie wysiadł faks (Everything was doing fine until the fax crashed)*

wysikać się Perf sikać

wysiusiać się Perf siusiać

wyskoczyć z ciuchów [vi-SKOH-chich s CHYOO-khoof] *v phr* To undress; to get naked <strip, strip off, peel> eg *Szybko wyskoczyła z ciuszków, gdy pokazał jej swój interes (She quickly stripped off when he showed her his joystick)*

wyskoczyć ze skóry See wychodzić ze skóry

wyskok [VIS-kohk] *v phr* Strange, unconventional, or unpredictable behavior that goes beyond the limits of acceptability; an excess <freaky antics, weird antics, offbeat antics> eg *Dość mam tych jego wyskoków (I'm sick and tired of his offbeat antics)*

wyskrobać [vi-SKROH-bahch] *v* To find and acquire money needed for something, esp with difficulty <scrape up, scrape together> eg *Wyskrobała trochę pieniędzy, ale to nie wystarczyło (She managed to scrape up some money but it wasn't enough)*

wyskrobać Perf skrobać

wysmarkać się Perf smarkać

wysokie zawieszenie [vi-SOH-khyeh zah-vyeh-SHEH-nyeh] *nn phr* A woman's long legs or shapely buttocks and hips <legs up to her ass> eg *Miała wysokie zawieszenie (She had legs up to her ass)*

wysoko skanalizowana [vi-SOH-koh skah-nah-lee-zoh-VAH-nah] *nf adj* (Of a woman) Having long legs or shapely buttocks and hips <leggy> eg *Moja dziewczyna jest wysoko skanalizowana. Poza tym jest bardzo inteligentna (My girlfried is leggy. Aside from that, she's pretty intelligent)*

wysrać się Perf srać

wyssać z palca [VIS-sahch s PAHL-tsah] *adj phr* To devise or invent, esp impromptu, something not based on facts; to hastily fabricate <think up, fake up, cook up, dream up, cobble up, take it off the top of one's head, take it off the cuff, take it spur-of-the-moment> eg *Całą tę historię wyssał z palca (He cooked up the all story)*

wystartować Perf startować

wystawić kogoś do wiatru [vi-STAH-veech KOH-gohsh doh VYAHT-roo] *v phr* To cheat; to swindle; to deceive; to make a fool out of someone <con, rip off, shaft, roll, chisel, gyp, scam, screw, stiff, fleece, dick, do in, take in, do a number on, flim-flam, bamboozle, run a number on, take someone for a ride, take someone to the cleaners, throw someone a curve, pull a fast one, fuck over, screw over, angle, take in, snow, do a snow job, double-shuffle, fast-shuffle, flimflam, give a bun steer, give someone a line, have someone on, lead someone down the garden path, do a snow job, jerk someone's chain, pull someone's chain, pull one's leg, pull someone's string, pull the wool over someone's eyes, put someone on, snow, use smoke and mirrors> eg *Prawnicy wystawili go do wiatru (The lawyers led him down to the garden path)*

wystrychnąć kogoś na dudka [vis-TRIKH-nohnch KOH-gohsh nah DOOT-kah] *v phr* To cheat; to swindle; to deceive; to make a fool out of someone <con, rip off, shaft, roll, chisel, gyp, scam, screw, stiff, fleece, dick, do in, take in, do a number on, flim-flam, bamboozle, run a number on, take someone for a ride, take someone to the cleaners, throw someone a curve, pull a fast one, fuck over, screw over, angle, take in, snow, do a snow job, double-shuffle, fast-shuffle, flimflam, give a bun steer, give someone a line, have someone on, lead someone down the garden path, do a snow job, jerk someone's chain, pull someone's chain, pull one's leg, pull someone's string, pull the wool over someone's eyes, put someone on, snow, use smoke and mirrors> eg *Prawnicy wystrychnęli go na dutka (The lawyers led him down to the garden path)*

wystrzałowo [vist-shah-WOH-voh] *adv* Extremely well; superbly <great, cool, swell, fab, rad, def, far-out, awesome, frantic, terrific, funky, gorgeous, groovy, hellacious, neat, peachy, dandy, baddest, mean, solid, super-dooper, wailing, wicked, gnarly, top-notch, ten, ace-high, A-OK, A-1, some> eg *Zobaczysz, że będzie wystrzałowo (You'll see,it'll be great)*

wystrzałowy [vist-shah-WOH-vi] *adj* Excellent; wonderful; extremely good <great, cool, swell, fab, rad, def, far-out, awesome, frantic, terrific, funky, gorgeous, groovy, hellacious, neat, peachy, dandy, baddest, mean, solid, super-dooper, wailing, wicked, gnarly, top-notch, ten, ace-high, A-OK, A-1, some> eg *Ale wystrzałowy samochód! Skąd go masz? (What a gorgeous car! Where did you get it from?)*

wyszczać się Perf szczać

wyszczekany See wygadany

wyszumieć się See poszumieć

wytrąbić [vi-TROHM-beech]) *v* To drink an entire bottle of alcohol, esp quickly <kill, knock back, guzzle, gargle, lap, tank up, slug down, swig> eg *W parę minut wytrąbił pół litra wódki (In a few minutes he knocked back a half-liter bottle of vodka)*

wywłoka* [viv-WOH-kah] *nf* A woman, esp esp ugly and promiscuous, whom one dislikes or disapproves of <ho', skag, skank, pig, bag, beasty, bitch, slut, cunt,

broad, wench, hag, old hag, old biddy, old bag, old tart, piece of shit> eg *Co tu robi ta wywłoka? (What is that skag doing here?)*

wywalać w błoto See wyrzucić w błoto

wywinąć See wykręcić komuś numer

wywinąć orła [vi-VEE-nohnch OHR-wah] *v phr* To die <bite the dust, kiss the dust, croak, belly up, buy the farm, buy the ranch, cash in one's chips, check out, bump off, conk off, conk out, farm, give up the ghost, go home feet first, go home in a box, go west, kick in, kick off, kick the bucket, pass out, peg out, shove off, drop off, step off, pop off, push up daisies, meet one's maker, turn up one's toes, go down the tube, join the great majority, join the majority> eg *Wypił dużo wódki, dostał krwotoku i wywinął orła (He drank a lot of vodka, started to bleed, and croaked)*

wzdychać do kogoś [VZDI-khahch doh KOH-gohsh] *v* To desire or love someone, esp secretly; hanker after someone <have a yen for, have eyes for, have big eyes for, itch for, go for, fall for, die over, have it bad for, have a mash for> eg *Wzdycha do niej od zeszłego lata (He's been having a mash for her since last summer)*

wziąć Perf brać

wziąć się do kupy [vzhyohnch shyeh doh KOO-pi] (or **wziąć się w garść** [vzhyohnch shyeh v gahrshch]; **pozbierać** [poh-ZBYEH-rahch] or **zebrać** [ZEH-brahch] may replace **wziąć**) *v phr* (To try) To remain mentally unaffected or balanced; to keep one's composure; to get in control of oneself <pull oneself together, keep cool, not lose head, make it through, keep up one's spirit, get a grip on oneself, get hold of oneself, take hold of oneself, keep it together> eg *Trudno mu jest wziąć się w garść po śmierci dziadka (It is hard for him to pull himself together after his grandfather's death)*

wziąć się Perf brać się

wziąć sobie na luz See dać sobie na luz

wziąć sobie na wstrzymanie See dać sobie na wstrzymanie

wzrok See barani wzrok

Z

z [Z] (or **ze** [ZEH]) *adv* About; approximately <around, in the ballpark of, pretty near, something like, close shave, in the neighborhood of, damn near, pretty near> eg *To będzie ze dwa kilometry (It'll be something like two kilometers)*

z brzuchem [z BZHOO-khehm] *adj phr* Pregnant <knocked up, banged up, PG, preggers, puffed, pumped, bumped, storked, in the family way, have one in the oven, infanticipating, swallowed a watermelon seed, in the club> eg *Słyszałeś nowość? Lula jest z brzuchem (Did you hear the big news? Lula's in the club)*

z byka spaść [z BI-kah spahshch] *v phr* To be or to behave as if one were insane or stupid; to lose one's senses <be off one's rocker, be off one's nut, be off one's base, be off the track, be off the trolley, be out one's skull, be out of one's mind, be crazy, be crazy as a loon, blow one's cork, blow one's top, blow a fuse, crack up, freak out, flip out, be ape, be bananas, be bent, be bonkers, be cracked, be dopey, be ga-ga, be half-baked, be loony, be loopy, be mental, be nerts, be nuts, be

nutty, be psycho, be schizo, be screwy, be wacky, be weird, be wild, schiz out, psych out, come unglued, come unstuck, come unwrapped, come unzipped> eg *Co ona mówi? Z byka spadła, czy jak? (What is she talking about? Is she out of her rocker, or what?)*

z cebra See lać

z cicha pęk [s chee-khah PEHNK] *nm phr* Suddenly; unexpectedly; without warning <out of the blue, out of a clear blue sky, out of a clear blue sky, like a bolt from the blue, out from left field> eg *Wypowiedział te słowa nagle z cicha pęk (He said those words out of a clear blue sky)*

z czym to się je See wiedzieć z czym to się je

z deszczu pod rynnę [z DEHSH-choo pohd RIN-neh] *adv phr* From a bad situation to a worse situation <from bad to worse, out of the frying pan into the fire> eg *Byłem w długach. A potem wpadłem z deszczu pod rynnę, bo straciłem pracę (I was deeply in debt. Then I really went out of the frying pan into the fire when I lost my job)*

z doskoku [z dohs-KOH-koo] *adv phr* Temporarily; sporadically; from time to time <every now and then, every now and again, every so often, on and off> eg *Widywali się z doskoku, bo byli tak zajęci (They were seeing each other on and off)*

z drugiej ręki [z DROO-gyeh-ee REHN-kee] *adj phr* Owned or used by someone else before; not new <second hand, hand-me-down, reach-me-down> eg *Kupił jakiś wóz z drugiej ręki (He bought some second-hand car)*

z fasonem [s fah-SOH-nehm] *adj phr* (Esp about someone's dress) With unrestrained and self-assured elegance; stylish <with class, classy, spiffy, snazzy, ritzy, plushy, swanky, nitty, fancy schmancy, natty, jazzy, faddy, trendy, sharp, posh, swellegant> eg *Nasz profesor to byl człowiek z fasonem (Our professor was a man with class)*

z fleka See dać kopa, dostać kopa

z głowy [z GWOH-vi] *adv phr* **1** (or **z sufitu** [s soo-FEE-too]) Without any preparation; impromptu <off the cuff, off the top of one's head, spur-of-the-moment> eg *Nie potrafię odpowiedzieć tak z głowy (I can't think of the answer off the top of my head); Jej pytania były z sufitu, ale były nardzo dobre (Her questions were from the cuff, but were very good)* **2** Having finished (doing) something; no longer bothering one <done with, all over, all set, be through, wrapped up, finished up, wound up, washed up, buttoned up, mopped up, cleaned up, tied up, closed up, packed up> eg *Zdałam ostatni egzamin i całą sesję miałam z głowy (I passed the last exam and the whole session was all over)*

z górki [z GOOR-kee] *adv phr* **1** In the last phase; in the final stage <downhill from here on, plain sailing from here on> eg *Był to ciężki okres, ale minął. Teraz jest już z górki (It was a difficult period. It's downhill from here on)* **2** Easily; effortlessly; without problems <like shit through a goose, like shit through a tin horn, easy, smooth, hands down, downhill all the way, plain sailing> eg *W życiu wszystko szło mu z górki (Everything in life was downhill all the way for him); Wszystko pójdzie z górki (It's all plain sailing now)*

See mieć coś z górki

z grubsza [z GROOP-shah] *adv phr* Roughly; approximately <around, in the ballpark of, pretty near, something like, close shave, in the neighborhood of, damn near, pretty near> eg *Zapłacił z grubsza dwa tysiące (He paid something like two thousand)*

z gwinta [z GVEEN-tah] *adv phr* Drunk straight from the bottle <swig, pull> eg *He took a swig of beer (Wypił piwo z gwinta)*

z hakiem [s KHAH-kyehm] (or **z kawałkiem** [s kah-WAH-oo-kyehm]) *adv phr* Over; more than <cut above, and change, plus change> eg *Zapłacił 2 000 z hakiem (He paid a cut above 2,000)*

z hukiem [s KHOO-kyehm] *adv phr* Grandly; conspicuously; with repercussions <with a bang, with a splash, with a fallout, with a follow-up, with a follow-through, with a spin-off, with a feedback, with a kickback, with making waves> eg *Przyjazd prezydenta odebrano w mediach z hukeim (The President's arrival was met with a bang in the media)*

z ikrą [z EEK-roh] *adj phr* (Esp about a man) Courageous, daring, or fearless <gutsy, gutty, gritty, ballsy, spunky, nervy, hairy, brassy, cocky, cheeky, sassy, crusty, bodacious, braver than Dick Tracy, game, dead game, stand-up> eg *Dlaczego głosowałeś na niego? Bo to facet z ikrą (Why did you vote for him? Because he's a gutsy guy)*

z innej parafii [z EEN-neh-ee pah-RAHF-yee] (or **z innej beczki** [z EEN-neh-ee BEHCH-kee]) *adj phr* Entirely different, esp if unusual <dif, diff, whale different, offbeat, far cry, whole new ball game, whole different story, another cup of tea, different kettle of fish> eg *Zadał pytanie zupełnie z innej parafii, którego nikt nie zrozumiał (He asked a whale different question that no one understood)*

z jajami* [z yah-YAH-mee] *adj phr* (Esp about a man) Courageous, daring, or fearless <with balls, ballsy, gutsy, gutty, gritty, spunky, nervy, hairy, brassy, cocky, cheeky, sassy, crusty, bodacious, breaver than Dick Tracy, game, dead game, stand-up> eg *Nasz szef to facet z jajami (Our boss is a ballsy guy)*

z jajem [z YAH-yehm] *adj phr* Impressive and hilarious or amusing <great, cool, swell, fab, rad, def, far-out, awesome, frantic, terrific, funky, gorgeous, groovy, hellacious, neat, peachy, dandy, baddest, mean, solid, super-dooper, wailing, wicked, gnarly, top-notch, ten, ace-high, A-OK, A-1, some, jokey, gassy, screaming, gut-busting, side-splitting, knee-slapping, rib-tickling> eg *To był wykład z jajem (It was a gut-busting lecture)*

z jakiej paki [z YAH-kyeh-ee PAH-kee] *phr* A questioning or angry exclamation elaborating "Why?" or "For what reason?" <says who, sez who, name one good reason why, why the fuck, why in the fuck, why in fuck, why the hell, why in the hell, why in hell, why in fucking hell, why in the fucking hell, why in fuck's name, why in the fuck's name, why the heck, why in the heck, why in heck, why the devil, why in the devil, why in devil> eg *Ja jestem tutaj szefem. Taak? Z jakiej paki? (I'm the boss here. Oh yeah? Name one good reason why)*

z kawałkiem See z hakiem

z kopa See dać kopa, dostać kopa

z kwitkiem [s KFEET-kyehm] (or **z pustymi rękami** [s poos-TI-mee rehn-KAH-mee]) *adv phr* (Departing) With nothing <empty-handed> eg *Przyszli mając nadzieję na coś do jedzenia, ale odeszli z kwitkiem (They came hoping for some food, but they went away empty-handed)*

z lacza See dać kopa, dostać kopa

z miejsca [z MYEH-ees-tsah] (or **z mety** [z MEH-ti] or **z marszu** [z MAHR-shoo] or **z punktu** [z POONK-too]) *adv phr* Immediately, quickly, or without any preparation <pretty damn quick, PDQ, ASAP, on the spot, on the double, double

time, double clutching, like a shot, in half a mo, like now, before you know it, before you can say Jack Robinson, in a jiffy, in a flash, in half a shake, right off the bat, like a bat out of hell, like a shot out of hell, hubba-hubba, horseback, like greased lightning, off the cuff, off the top of one's head, spur-of-the-moment> eg *Nie potrafię odpowiedzieć tak z miejsca (I can't think of the answer off the top of my head)*

z miodem w uszach See cwaniak

z odzysku See kawaler z odzysku, panna z odzysku

z płatka See iść jak po maśle

z palcem [s PAHL-tsehm] *adv phr* (**z palcem w dupie*** [s PAHL-tsehm v DOO-pyeh] or **z palcem w nosie** [s PAHL-tsehm v NOH-shyeh]) *adv phr* Certainly, surely, easily, or without problems <sure, fer sure, sure as hell, sure as shit, sure as can be, for real, indeedy, really truly, absitively, posilutely, real, cert, def, no buts about it, wired up, cinched, taped, racked, sewed up, iced, in the bag, tied up, nailed down, like shit through a goose, like shit through a tin horn, easy, smooth, hands down, downhill all the way, plain sailing, running smooth> eg *Wygra wybory? Z palcem w dupie! (Will he win the elections? No buts about it!)*

z poślizgiem [s poh-SHLEZ-gyehm] *adv phr* With a delay; delayed <hung-up, held-up, slowed-up, tied-up, bound, downtimed> eg *Doślę panom mansuckrypt słownika z małym poślizgiem (I will send you the manuscript of the dictionary with a little hold-up)*

z punktu See z miejsca

z pustymi rękami See z kwitkiem

z rączki do rączki [z ROHNCH-kee doh ROHNCH-kee] *adv phr* (Esp about sums of money) Quickly being handed over from one person to another; in quick circulation <from hand to hand> eg *Pieniądze przechodziły z rączki do rączki (The money was going from hand to hand)*

z sufitu See z głowy

z zaskoku [z zahs-KOH-koo] *nm phr* Suddenly; unexpectedly; surprisingly <out of the blue, out of a clear blue sky, out of a clear blue sky, like a bolt from the blue, out in left field> eg *Wszystko zdarzyło się z zaskoku (Everything happened like a bolt from the blue)*

za bezcen [zah BEHS-tsehn] (**za psie pieniądze** [zah PSHEH pyeh-NYOHN-dzeh]) *adv phr* (Sold, bought, or acquired) Very cheaply <for peanuts, for chicken feed, for nickels and dimes, for pennies, for small change> eg *Kupiłem to za bezcen (I bought it for peanuts)*

za Boga See za cholerę

za Chiny Ludowe See za cholerę

za chińskiego Boga See za cholerę

za cholerę [zah khoh-LEH-reh] (or **za chuj**** [zah KHOO-ee] or **za chuja**** [zah KHOO-yah] or **za Chiny Ludowe** [zah KHEE-ni loo-DOH-veh] or **za chińskiego Boga** [zah kheeñ-SKYEH-goh BOH-gah] or **za Boga** [zah BOH-gah]) *adv phr* A phrase of refusal or disbelief telling that one will never do something or something will never happen; never; not for anything <over someone's dead body, in a pig's eye, in a pig's ass, in a pig's ear, someone will be damned if, someone will be fucked if, not for the world, not for anything in the world, not for love or money, no way, no way Jose, no dice, not on your life, nothing doing, no can do> eg *On tego nie zrobi. Za cholerę! (He won't do it! No way!)*

za chuj See za cholerę

za frajer [zah FRAH-yehr] (or **za friko** [zah FREE-koh] or **za frico** [zah FREE-koh]) *adv phr* (Sold, bought, or acquired) Very cheaply or free of charge <freebie, free-o, free gratis, free lunch> eg *Możecie tu parkować za frajer (You can park here for free)*

za kółkiem [zah KOOW-kyehm] *adv phr* Driving an automobile <behind the wheel, wheeling> eg *Kto siedział za kókiem? (Who was behind the wheel?)*

za kratkami [zah kraht-KAH-mee] *adv phr* In prison <behind bars> eg

za miedzą See przez miedzę

za pasem [zah PAH-sehm] *adv phr* Very soon; in a short time <by and by, in a short, short short, down the line, come Sunday, coming down the pike, knocking on the front door> eg *Nie czekajmy z robotą, bo zima za pasem (Let's not wait with the job, because winter is down the line)*

za pięć dwunasta [zah pyehch dvoo-NAHS-tah] *nm phr* The very last moment; high time <last call, eleventh hour, last mo, in the nick of time> eg *Udało mu się to zrobić na za pięć dwunasta (He managed to do it at the eleventh hour)*

za psie pieniądze See za bezcen

za winklem [zah VEENK-lehm] *nm* Around the corner <no slang equivalent> eg *Najbliższy bar jest zaraz za winklem (The nearest bar is just around the corner)*

załapać [zah-WAH-pahch] *v* To understand or comprehend; to get orientation in something <get, get it, catch, get the drift, get the picture, get the message, get the hang of, savvy, dig, click, capeesh, read, be with it, see where one is coming from, know where one is coming from, be with it, get one's bearings> eg *On w ogóle tego nie załapał (He didn't get it at all)*
See złapać, łapać

załatać Perf łatać

załoga [zah-WOH-gah] *nf* A group of people who are intimate and close; a company <folks, pack, bunch, crew, gang, clan, crowd, boys> eg *Cała towarzycho w końcu dortarła tu wczoraj (The whole crew finally got here yesterday)*

Zabłocki See wyjść na czymś jak Zabłocki na mydle

zabalować Perf balować

zabawiać się [zah-BAH-vyahch shyeh] (perf **zabawić się** [zah-BAH-veech shyeh]) *v* To caress sexually or to copulate <play with someone, feel up, cop a feel, grope, pet, neck, play grab-ass, smooch, get physical> eg *Zabawiali się przez cały wieczór (They were playing grab-ass the whole evening)*
See bawić się

zabić komuś klina [ZAH-beech KOH-moosh KLEE-nah] *v phr* To ask someone embarassing or difficult questions and, as a result of this, to force them to intense thinking <put someone on the spot, catch someone off balance, throw someone off balance, get someone off someone's heels, put someone on the spot, catch someone off guard> eg *To mi pani zabiła klina tym pytaniem! (Your question surely put me on the spot!)*

zabierać See brać kogoś

zabijać czas [zah-BEE-yahch chahs] *v phr* To spend or waste time <kill time, while away the time, while the time> eg *Czytał książkę tylko po to, żeby zabić czas (He was reading a book just to kill time)*

zabity See dziura, spać jak zabity

zabrylować Perf brylować

zabrzęczeć Perf brzęczeć

zabujać się Perf bujać się

zabulić See bulić

zabździć Perf bździć

zachciewajka [zah-khcheh-VAY-kah] *nf* **1** (**zachcianka** [zakh-CHYAHN-kah]) One's whim or caprice; a sudden desire, esp a fantastic or eccentric one <call, judge and jury, fool notion> eg *Miała zachciankę, żeby odwiedzić wszystkich jej krewnych (She had a fool notion to visit all her relatives)* **2** A minor skin lesion, a pimple <zit, guber, goober, hickey, pip> eg *Masz zachciewajkę na nosie! (You got a zit ony nose!)*

zachlany See schlany

zachomikować Perf chomikować

zachrzantus See zapierdol

zadać się Perf zadawać się

zadawać się [KOO-mahch shyeh] (perf **zadać się** [SKOO-mahch shyeh]) *v* To be friends <pal around, buddy up, be buddies, be brothers, be buddy-buddy, be palsy-walsy, hang around with, hang out with> eg *Zadaje się z jakimś muzykiem (She has palled up with some musician)*

zadekować się Perf dekować się

zadrinkować Perf zadrinkować

zadrynkować Perf zadrynkować

zadrzeć Perf zadzierać

zadupie* [zah-DOO-pyeh] (or **zapchajdziura** [zahh-khah-ee-JOO-rah]) *nn* A small town, esp in the country; any place far from civilization <jerk town, jerkwater town, backwater, hellhole, rathole, mudhole, real hole, noplaceville, hicksville, whistle stop, dump, armpit, East Jesus, Bumfuck Egypt> eg *Skąd dzwonisz? Z jakiegoś zadupia (Where are you calling from? Some mudhole)*

zadyma [zah-DI-mah] *nf* A noisy and violent street demonstration, esp with the use of police; a riot <demo, walkout, march, rally> eg *Z marszu zrobiła się zadyma (A rally broke out during the march)*

zadzierać [zahJEHrahch] (perf **zadrzeć** [ZAHDzhehch]) *v* To defy or challenge; to provoke <defi, face off, face down, fly in the face, fly in the teeth, meet eyeball to eyeball, make my day, hang tough, hang in there, take one on, stick fast, stick it out, kick over traces, lip, brace, cross, put one's life on the line, stand up to, knock the chip off one's shoulder, step over the line, tangle, bump heads with, cross, square off, put down, have a bone to pick, hold no brief for, put up a fight, mess with, mess around with, fool with, fool around with, fuck with, fuck around with, screw with, screw around with, dick with, dick around with, diddle with, diddle around with, fiddle with, fiddle around with, fart with, fart around with, monkey with, monkey around with> eg *Nie zadzieraj ze mną, chyba że życie ci niemiłe (Don't mess with me unless you're tired of living)*

zadzierać nosa [zahJEHrahch NOHsah] *v phr* To act superior; to be conceited and snobbish <think one's shit doesn't stink, be too big for someone's shoes, ego-trip, get stuck-up, get puffed-up, get high-hat, get swelled-up, get swell-headed, get big-headed, get high-nosed, get blown-up, get stuck on oneself, get chesty, get stuffy, get gassy, get windy, get hatty, get hinkty, get uppity, get biggety, dog it,

put on the dog, give oneself airs, put on airs, put on, put on the ritz> eg *Nie zadzieraj nosa. Baw się razem z nami (Stop putting on airs. Come and play with us)*

zadziorny [zah-JOHR-ni] *adj* Defiantly quarrelsome or aggressive; belligerent <defi, ornery, feisty, bitchy, cussed, scrappy, snorky, flip, salty, spiky, mean, bad-assed, nasty-assed, gutty, lippy, cocky, brassy, cheeky, sassy, nervy, smart-ass, wise-ass, foul-mouthed> eg *Nie bądź taki zadziorny, dobra? (Don't be so cheeky, will you?)*

zafajdany See zasrany

zagłówkować Perf główkować

zaganiacz [zah-GAH-nyahch] *nm* The penis, esp large <cock, prick, dick, stick, joystick, dipstick, bone, meat, beef, wang, yang, dong, dummy, hammer, horn, hose, jock, joint, knob, pork, putz, rod, root, tool, flute, skin flute, love-muscle, sausage, schmuck, schlong, schvantz, cream-stick, third leg, middle leg, business, apparatus, John, Johnny, Johnson, John Thomas, Jones> eg *Złapała mnie za zaganiacza (She grabbed me by my meat)*

zaganiany See zalatany

zaglądać do kieliszka [zah-GLOHN-dahch doh kyeh-LEESH-kah] (or **sięgać do kieliszka** [SHYEHN-gahch doh kyeh-LEESH-kah]) *v phr* To drink alcohol often and in large quantities; to enjoy drinking alcohol <like to booze, like to guzzle, like to gargle, like to bend the elbow, like to hit the bottle, like to hit the sauce, like to knock back, like to lap, like to tank up, like to wet one's whistle, like to hang a few on, like to slug down, like to swig> eg *Zaglądał często do kieliszka (He often liked to wet one's whistle)*

zagoniony See zalatany

zagraniczniak [zah-grah-NEECH-nyahk] *nm* A foreigner <furriner, outsider, stranger, jaboney, jiboney> eg *Coraz więcej zagraniczniaków przyjeżdża to naszego miasta (More and more furriners come to see our city)*

zagranie [zah-GRAH-nyeh] *nn* Strange, unconventional, or unpredictable behavior that goes beyond the limits of acceptability <freaky antics, weird antics, offbeat antics> eg *Dość mam tych jego zagrań (I'm sick and tired of his freaky antics)*

zagrycha [zah-GRI-khah] *nf* A light snack eaten after drinking alcoholic <bite, snack, nosh, something to chew on, something to munch on> eg *Daj mi jakąś zagrychę (Give me something to chew on)*

zagwozdka [zah-GVOHST-kah] *nf* A complicated or difficult thing to deal with, esp a problem <hard nut to crack, tough nut to crack> eg *Mam zagwozdkę. Nie wiem, co z tym zrobić (I have a hard nut to crack. I don't know what to do with it)*

zahaczyć [zah-KHAH-chich] *v* **1** To ask about; to want to know <hit, hit upon, touch upon, go over, work over> eg *Dziennikarz zahaczył o ich najnowszą płytę (The journalist touched upon about their latest album)* **2** To mention, allude, or hint <bring up, drag up, spring, spring one's duke, tip one's duke, tip one's hand> eg *Prezydent zahaczył o kwestię bezrobocia (The President brought up the issue of unemployment)* **3** To stop on one's way at a given place <hit, pull over, stop over, cover> eg *Zahaczmy jeszcze o monpolowy (Let's stop over at a liquor store)*

zaharować się Perf harować

zaharowywać się See harować

zahukany [zah-khoo-KAH-ni] *adj* Meek, submissive, or shy, esp because of a despotic treatment; cowed or intimidated <buffaloed, bulldozed, pushed around, whipped around, bowled down, on a string, on a leash, chickened out, spooked,

chilled, yellow, scared stiff, scared shitless, fraidy, scaredy, frozen, panicky, spooked, yellow, cold-feeted> eg *To dobra dziewczyna, ale jest totalnie zahukana przez despotycznego ojca (She's a nice girl, but she's totally whipped around by her despotic father)*

zajarać Perf jarać

zajarać się Perf jarać się

zajebiście* [zah-yeh-BISH-chyeh] *adv* **1** Extremely well; superbly <awful, god-awful, real, mighty, plenty, damn, damned, goddamn, goddamned, darn, darned, effing, flipping, forking, freaking, frigging, fucking, one's ass off, one's brains out, one's head off, to the max, like all get-out, like sin, to beat the band, like all creation, as blazes, as can be, as hell, like hell> eg *Skończyłem właśnie pisanie tego słownika i czuję się zajebiście (I just finished writing this dictionary and I feel great)* **2** Extremely; exceedingly; very <awful, god-awful, real, mighty, plenty, damn, damned, goddamn, goddamned, darn, darned, effing, flipping, forking, freaking, frigging, fucking, one's ass off, one's brains out, one's head off, to the max, like all get-out, like sin, to beat the band, like all creation, as blazes, as can be, as hell, like hell, in full swing> eg *Ona jest zajebiście zgrabna (She's fucking shapely)*

zajebisty* [zah-yeh-BIS-ti] *adj* Excellent; wonderful; extremely good <great, cool, swell, fab, rad, def, far-out, awesome, frantic, terrific, funky, gorgeous, groovy, hellacious, neat, peachy, dandy, baddest, mean, solid, super-dooper, wailing, wicked, gnarly, top-notch, ten, ace-high, A-OK, A-1, some> eg *Ten samochód jest na prawdę zajebisty (This car is real cool)*

zajob* [ZAH-yohp] *nm* Obsession, insanity, or eccentricity <thing, kick, bag, bug, craze, freak, frenzy, weakness, bug up one's ass, bug in one's ear, bee in one's bonnet, bee, flea in one's nose, maggot, maggot in one's brain, hang-up, jones, monkey, ax to grind> eg *Judo to jego ostatni zajob (Judo is his latest craze)*
See dostać świra, mieć świra

zajumać Perf jumać

zakała [zah-KAH-wah] *nf* Someone who is thought by his family to have brought shame to the family; the worst member in the family <black sheep, black sheep of the family, rotten apple> eg *Moja siostra jest zakałą rodziny naszej rodziny. Zawsze ma problemy z policją (My sister is the black sheep in our family. She's always in trouble with the police)*

zakablować Perf kablować

zakapior [zah-KAH-pyor] *nm* A despicable, loathsome and sloppy man, esp a derelict <bum, bo, hobo, piece of shit, hood, wino, dreg, wrongo, scum of the earth> eg *Zatrzymaliśmy się przy monopolowym i przyczepił się do nas jakiś zakapior (We stopped at the liquor store and some hood started giving us a hard time)*

zakapować Perf kapować

zakasować Perf kasować

zakichany See zasrany

zakipować Perf kipować

zaklepać [zah-KLEH-pahch] *v* To make sure in advance that something will be done; to secure; to reserve <put a hold on, lay away, get something wired up, get something cinched, get something taped, get something racked, get something sewed up, get something iced, get something in the bag, get something tied up> eg *Jego wybór jest zaklepany (His election is in the bag)*

zaklepane See mieć coś nagrane

zakonserwowany [zah-kohn-sehr-voh-VAH-ni] *adj* (Esp about older people) Healthy, active, or physically fit <alive and kicking, fit as a fiddle, up to snuff, up to the mark, wrapped tight, in fine feather, in fine whack, in the pink, sound as a dollar, right as rain, full of piss and vinegar, full of beans> eg *Dziadek ma 70 lat, ale trzyma się (Grandfather is 70, but he's still fit as a fiddle)*

zakopcić Perf kopcić

zakrapiany [zah-krah-PYAH-ni] *adj* (Of a party) Featuring alcohol consumption <booze, boozy> eg *Mieliśmy polować na kaczki, a wyszła z tego zakrapiana impreza (We were supposed to go duck hunting, but it turned out to be a booze party)*

zakuć Perf zakuwać

zakuta pała* [zah-KOO-tah PAH-wah] *nf phr* A very stupid, clumsy or ineffectual person; an idiot <airbrain, airhead, birdbrain, blockhead, squarehead, bonehead, bubblebrain, bubblehead, buckethead, cluckhead, cementhead, clunkhead, deadhead, dumbbell, dumbcluck, dumbhead, dumbass, dumbbrain, fatbrain, fathead, flubdub, knukclebrain, knucklehead, lamebrain, lardhead, lunkhead, meathead, musclehead, noodlehead, numbskull, pointhead, scatterbrain, jerk, jerk-off, klutz, chump, creep, nerd, dork, dweeb, gweeb, geek, jackass, lummox, twerp, nerd, bozo, clod, cluck, clunk, dimwit, dingbat, dipstick, dodo, dopey, dufus, goofus, lump, lunk, nitwit, schnook, schlep, schlemiel, schmendrick, schmo, schmuck, simp, stupe> eg *Twój brat to zakuta pała. Nic nie zrozumiał (Your brother is a musclehead. He didn't understand anything)*

zakuty łeb See baran

zakuwać See kuć

zalać komuś sadła za skórę See zaleźć komuś za skórę

zalać się See **upić się jak świnia**

zalać się [ZAH-lahch shyeh] (or **zalać pałę** [ZAH-lahch PAH-weh]) *v phr* To get drunk <get alkied, get bagged, get blitzed, get blotto, get blown away, get bent, get boiled, get bombed, get boozed up, get blasted, get bottled, get boxed, get canned, get clobbered, get cooked, get corked, get drunk as a skunk, get edged, get embalmed, get fractured, get fried, get gassed, get ginned, get grogged, get high, get hooched up, get impaired, get illuminated, get juiced, get liquored up, get lit, get loaded, get looped, get lubricated, get smashed, get oiled, get pickled, get plastered, get plonked, get polluted, get sauced, get shitfaced, get sloshed, get soaked, get stewed, get stiff, get stinking drunk, get swizzled, get tanked up, get wiped, get zonked, get fucked up> eg *Zawsze w sobotę lubi zalać pałę (He always likes to get shitfaced on Saturday)*

zalany [zah-LAH-ni] (or **zalany w pestkę** [f PEHST-keh zah-LAH-ni]) *adj* Drunk; alcohol intoxicated <alkied, bagged, blitzed, blotto, blown away, bent, boiled, bombed, blasted, boozed, bottled, boxed, buzzed, canned, clobbered, cooked, corked, crashed, drunk as a skunk, edged, embalmed, fractured, fried, gassed, ginned, grogged, have one too many, half under, high, hooched up, in bad shape, impaired, illuminated, juiced, knocked out, liquored, lit, loaded, looped, lubricated, lushed, smashed, oiled, pickled, plastered, plonked, polluted, sauced, shitfaced, slugged, sloshed, soaked, stewed, stiff, stinking drunk, swizzled, tanked, three sheets to the wind, wiped, zonked> eg *Nie może prowadzić. Jest zalany w pestkę (He can't drive. He's bottled)*

See pijany jak świnia

zalatany [zah-lah-TAH-ni] (or **zaganiany** [zah-gah-NYAH-ni] or **zagoniony** [zah-goh-NYOH-ni]) *adj* Busy, in constant move <busy as a bee, busy as a beaver, on the hop, on the jump, on the move> eg *On jest dziś bardzo zalatany (He's really on the jump today)*

zalewać See krew kogoś zalewa

zalewać robaka [zah-LEH-vahch roh-BAH-kah] (or **zapijać robaka** [zah-PEE-yahch roh-BAH-kah]; **mola** [MOH-lah] may replace **robaka**) *v phr* To drink alcohol in an attempt to forget one's troubles <drown one's sorrows, drown one's troubles, find the cure in a bottle> eg *Gdy zmarła jego siostra, zalał robaka (When his sister died, he drowned his sorrows)*

zaleźć komuś za skórę [ZAH-lehshch KOH-moosh zah SKOO-reh] (or **zalać komuś sadła za skórę** [ZAH-lahch KOH-moosh SAH-Dwah zah SKOO-reh]) *v phr* To bother, irritate, or offend someone <get under someone's skin, get on someone's nerves, push someone's button, step on someone's toes, tread on someone's toes, get down on someone, get in one's face, get on someone's back, get on someone's case, give someone the needle> eg *Zalazł komuś za skórę podczas ostatniej kampanii i przegrał wybory (He tread on someone's toes during the last campaign and lost the election)*

zaliczać [zah-LEE-chahch] (perf **zaliczyć** [zah-LEE-chich]) *v* **1*** To succeed in copulating with someone <score, make it with, make out, get in, get a homer, get a home run, hit a homer, hit a home run, get to home plate, dip one's wick, go all the way, get it on> eg *I heard he scored with most of the girls in our class (Słyszałem, że zaliczył większość dziewczyn z naszej klasy); Zaliczyła wszystkich trzech (She made it with all three)* **2** To visit many places, esp by traveling <hit, do, fall by, swing by, play> eg *Wczoraj zaliczyliśmy dwa muzea (We did two museums yesterday)* **3** To experience something <do, live through, know the score, know where it's at, know what's what, been there oneself, been there done that> eg *Zaliczył dwa małżeństwa (He lived through two marriages)*

zaliczyć glebę See wyglebić się

zamącić Perf mącić

zamelinować się Perf melinować się

zamiatać [zah-MYAH-tahch] *v* To eat a meal, esp very fast <chow, scarf, scoff, pig out, scarf out, pork out> eg *Zamiatał jakby był koniec świata (He scarfed out like there was no tomorrow)*

zamknąć się [ZAHMK-nohnch shyeh] *v* To stop talking <shut up, put a sock in it, button your lip, zip your lip, bag your head, keep your mouth shut, don't let out a peep, shut your yap, can it, cork it, button it, bottle it, clam up> eg *Zamknij się do cholery! (Shut the fuck up!)*

zamotać Perf motać

zamurować [zah-moo-ROH-vahch] (or **zatkać** [ZAHTK-nohnch]) *v* To shock, surprise, overwhelm, and esp make someone speechless <floor, rock, shake someone up, give someone a turn, flabbergast, put someone away, spring something on, knock someone over, blow away, blow one's mind, clam up, dummy up, button up, belt up, catch one's breath, drop dead, knock dead, drop down dead, be killed stone-dead> eg *Ta wiadomość mnie zamurowała. Nie* *wiedziałem, co powiedzieć (The news knocked me dead. I didn't know what to say); Zatkało mnie, gdy usłyszałam tę wiadomość (I caught my breath when I heard that news)*

zaś See na zaś

zaobrączkować się [zah-ohb-rohnch-KOH-vahch] *v* To get married; to marry <hitch, hitch up, get hitched, splice, get spliced, hook, get hooked, merge, get merged, tie the knot, walk down the aisle, take the plunge, step off the carpet> eg *Zaobrączkowali się dwa tygodnie temu (They got spliced two weeks ago)*

zaobrączkowana [zah-ohb-rohnch-koh-VAH-nah] *adj* (Of a woman) Married <hitched, hooked, tied, spliced, merged, wearing a hat> eg *Nie wiem, czy jest zaobrączkowana (I don't know if she's hitched)*

zaobrączkowany [zah-ohb-rohnch-koh-VAH-ni] *adj* (Of a man) Married <hitched, hooked, tied, spliced, merged, wearing a hat> eg *Jest zaobrączkowany od dwóch miesięcy (He's been hitched for two months)*

zaśpiewać [zah-SHPYEH-vahch] *v* To charge a price that is much too high <come out with a price of> eg *Zaśpiewał 4,000 za ten samochód (He came out with a price of 4,000 for that car)*

zaświtać Perf świtać

zapłon See mieć spóźniony zapłon

zapałka See obcięty na jeża

zapalać [zah-PAH-lahch] (perf **zapalić** [zah-PAH-leech]; **zapuszczać** [zah-POOSH-chahch] perf **zapuścić** [zah-POOSH-cheech]) *v* To start an engine <crank up, start up, turn over, kick over> eg *Silnik był tak bardzo zimny, że nie mogłem go zapalić (My car engine was so cold that it wouldn't turn over)*

zapalić się Perf palić się

zapchajdziura See zadupie

zapić się [ZAH-peech shyeh] (or **zapić się na śmierć** [ZAH-peech shyeh nah SHMYEHRCH]) *v* To get drunk to the point when one can die; to die because of overdrinking <drink oneself to death, O.D. on drinking> eg *Zapił się na śmierć (He drunk himself to death)*

zapieprz See zapierdol

zapierdalać** [zah-pyehr-DAH-lahch] (perf **zapierdolić**** [zah-pyehr-DOH-leech]; or **zapieprzać*** [zah-PYEHP-shahch] perf **zapieprzyć*** [zah-pyehr-DOH-leech]; or **zapierniczać*** [zah-pyehr-NEE-chahch] perf **zapierniczyć*** [zah-pyehr-NEE-chich]; or **zapierdzielać*** [zah-pyehr-JEH-lahch] perf **zapierdzielić*** [zah-pyehr-JEH-leech])) *v* **1** To kill or beat someone up <fuck, fuck over, fuck up, screw, screw over, screw up> eg *Wstawaj, kurwa, bo cię zapierdolę! (Get up or I'll fuck you up)* **2** (**jak wół** [yahk VOOW] or **jak mały samochodzik** [yahk MAH-wi sah-moh-KHOH-jeek] may be added) To work very hard <work one's ass off, work one's fingers to the bone, work like a horse, sweat, bust one's ass off, break one's ass off, make bricks without a straw> eg *Zapierdalał całe życie (All his life he's been working like a horse)* **3** To steal; to rob <heist, boost, burgle, nurn, bag, buzz, highjack, hoist, hold up, hook, hustle, jump, kick over, knock off, knock over, lift, move, mug, nab, nick, nip, pinch, pluck, roll, rustle, snatch, snitch, stick up, swipe, take off, put the grab on, go south with> eg *Ktoś zapierdolił mu zegarek (Somebody snitched his watch)* **3** To go or drive very fast <barrel, barrel along, barrel ass, haul ass, tear, tool, burn rubber, burn the breeze, burn the road, dust, floorboard, fly, step on it, step up, step on

the gas, hit the gas, nail it, floor it, push it to the floor, put the pedal to the metal, put the heel to the steel, drop the hammer down, hammer on, pour on it, pour on the coal, put on the afterburners, gun, rev, rev up, open her up, go flat-out, go full blast, go hell-bent, go like a bat out of hell, go like a blue streak, go like blazes, go like the devil, let her rip, rip-ass, vroom, varoom, zoom> eg *Zapierdalał swoim Porsche na autostradzie (He flew down the highway in his Porsche)*

zapierdol** [zah-PYEHR-dohl] (or **zapieprz*** [ZAH-pyehpsh] or **zapierdziel**** [zah-PYEHR-jehl] or **zapierdas*** [zah-PYEHR-dahs] or **zachrzantus** [zah-KHZHAHN-toos]) *nm* A very hard work; a Herculean labor <ball-buster, bone-breaker, back-breaker, bitch, killer, grind, donkeywork, bullwork, dirty work> eg *Gdy wrócę do domu, znów czeka mnie zapierdol (When I'm back home, it's bullwork again); Rety! Mieliśmy z tym wszystkim zachrzantus! (Boy! Was that a real ball-buster!)*

zapijać robaka See zalewać robaka

zapitka See popitka

zapity See spity

zapomnieć języka w gębie [zah-POHM-nyehch yehn-ZI-kah v GEHM-byeh] *v phr* To be speechless because of strong feeling, surprise, confusion or fear <clam up, dummy up, button up, belt up, catch one's breath, drop dead, knock dead, drop down dead, be killed stone-dead> eg *Wiadomość była tak nieoczekiwana, że zapomniałem języka w gębie (The news was so unexpected that I caught my breath from shock)*

zaprawić się [zah-PRAH-veech shyeh]) (or **doprawić się** [doh-PRAH-veech shyeh]) *v phr* To get drunk <get alkied, get bagged, get blitzed, get blotto, get blown away, get bent, get boiled, get bombed, get boozed up, get blasted, get bottled, get boxed, get canned, get clobbered, get cooked, get corked, get drunk as a skunk, get edged, get embalmed, get fractured, get fried, get gassed, get ginned, get grogged, get high, get hooched up, get impaired, get illuminated, get juiced, get liquored up, get lit, get loaded, get looped, get lubricated, get smashed, get oiled, get pickled, get plastered, get plonked, get polluted, get sauced, get shitfaced, get sloshed, get soaked, get stewed, get stiff, get stinking drunk, get swizzled, get tanked up, get wiped, get zonked, get fucked up> eg *Zaprawił się wódką (He got boiled on vodka)*

zaprawiony [zah-prah-VYOH-ni] (or **zaprószony** [zah-proo-SHOH-ni] or **zawiany** [zah-VYAH-ni]) *adj* Drunk; alcohol intoxicated <alkied, bagged, blitzed, blotto, blown away, bent, boiled, bombed, blasted, boozed, bottled, boxed, buzzed, canned, clobbered, cooked, corked, crashed, drunk as a skunk, edged, embalmed, fractured, fried, gassed, ginned, grogged, have one too many, half under, high, hooched up, in bad shape, impaired, illuminated, juiced, knocked out, liquored, lit, loaded, looped, lubricated, lushed, smashed, oiled, pickled, plastered, plonked, polluted, sauced, shitfaced, slugged, sloshed, soaked, stewed, stiff, stinking drunk, swizzled, tanked, three sheets to the wind, wiped, zonked> eg *Nie może prowadzić. Jest nieźle zaprawiony (He can't drive. He's really bottled); Tylko mi nie mów, że znów jest zawiany (Don't tell me he's blitzed again)*

zapuszczać See zapalać

zarżnięty See spać jak zabity

zarżnięty See zdechły

zarabiać na chleb [zah-RAH-byahch nah KHLEHP] *v phr* To earn enough to support oneself and one's family <bring home the bacon, bring home the groceries, earn bread and butter, keep the wolf from the door> eg *Mam rodzinę, muszę zarabiać na chleb (I have family, I must bring home the bacon)*

zarabiać na dupie* [zah-RAH-byahch nah DOO-pyeh] *v phr* To work as a prostitute <hustle, hook, turn tricks, peddle ass, street-walk, work the street, go whoring, whore oneself> eg *Od jak dawna zarabiasz na dupie? (How long have you been turning tricks?)*

zaraz [ZAH-rahs] *adv* In the near distance; very close; nearby <around, pretty near, screwdriver turn away, frog's leap away, whoop, within a hoop and a holler, within a stone's throw, in spitting distance, around the corner, right next door> eg *Mieszkam zaraz koło dworca (I live within a stone's throw from the railroad station)*

zarechotać Perf rechotać

zarwać See rwać

zarwać nockę [ZAHR-vahch NOHTS-keh] *v phr* To work or study during the night <burn the midnight oil, pull an all-nighter> eg *Wyglądasz na zmęczonego. Zarywałeś ostatnio nockę? (You look tired. Have you been burning the midnight oil recently?*

zarywać See podrywać

zarządzić Perf rządzić

zarzygać Perf rzygać

zaskok See z zaskoku

zaskórniaki [zah-SKOOR-nyahk] *nm pl* Petty savings for special purposes, esp hidden from one's spouse <pinched money, pinched dough, mad money> eg *Ma trochę zaskórniaków, więc może zapłacić (She's got some pinched money, so she can pay)*

zasmarkany* [zah-smahr-KAH-ni] *adj* Teenage and immature, esp if foolish or irresponsible <teen, teener, teeny-bopper, bubble-gum, juvie, shitheaded, punk, snot-nosed> eg *Nie mam niewspólnego z tym zasmarkanym idiotą (I have nothing to do with this snot-nosed idiot)*

zasmrodzić Perf smrodzić

zasraniec* [zahs-RAH-nyehts] (or **zasmarkaniec*** [zah-smahr-KAH-nyets]) *nm* A teenage boy, esp whom one despises <teen, teener, teeny-bopper, bubble-gummer, youngster, juvie, shithead, punk, snot-nose> eg *Nie będzie mi taki zasraniec mówił, co mam robić (This snot-nose will not tell me what to do)*

zasrany* [zahs-RAH-ni] (or **zafajdany** [zah-fah-ee-DAH-ni] or **zakichany** [zah-kee-KHAH-ni] *adj* Cursed; damnable; bad <damn, damned, goddamn, goddamned, god-awful, blasted, darn, darned, effing, flipping, forking, freaking, frigging, pesky> eg *W tym zakichanym upale nie można było pracować (You couldn't work in that goddamn heat)*

zastartować Perf startować

zastrzyk [ZAHST-shik] *nm* Something that gives someone energy or enables further action, esp money <boos, shot in the arm, shot in the ass, kick in the arm, kick in the ass, pick-me-up> eg *Dzięki za czek. To był prawdziwy zastrzyk (Thank you for the check. It was a real shot in the arm)*

zasuwać [zah-SOO-vahch] (or **zasuwać jak wół** [zah-SOO-vahch yahk VOOW]) *v* To work very hard <work one's ass off, work one's fingers to the bone, work like a

horse, sweat, bust one's ass off, break one's ass off> eg *Od dwóch lat zasuwa jak wół (He's been working like a horse for two years)*

zaszaleć Perf szaleć

zaszpanować Perf szpanować

zatankować Perf tankować

zatkać See zamurować

zatrzęsienie [zaht-shehn-SHYEH-nyeh] *nn* Plenty; many many <helluva lot, lotsa, lotta, oodles, scads, heaps, bags, barrels, loads, piles, tons, wads, jillions, zillions, enough to choke a horse, shitload, fuckload, truckload> eg *W pubie było zatrzęsnienie ludzi (There was helluva lot people in the pub)*

zawiany See zaprawiony

zawieszenie See niskie zawieszenie, wysokie zawieszenie

zawodnik [zah-VOHD-neek] *nm* A man impressive, extravagant, or disorderly in behavior <artist, joker, clown, article, ham, character, item, number> eg *Z tego twojego kuzyna to prawdziwy zawodnik; poszedł na egzamin końcowy w szortach! (Your cousin is a real joker: He went to his final exam wearing shorts!)*

zawody See po ptakach

zawracać komuś głowę [zah-VRAH-tsahch KOH-moosh GWOH-weh] (or **zawracać komuś dupę*** [zah-VRAH-tsahch KOH-moosh DOO-peh]) *v phr* To bother, annoy, or harry someone, especially by taking someone's time <eat, bug, dog, nag, drag, nudge, bitch, bellyache, stew, bleed, sweat, sweat bullets, bum out, eat one's heart out, have something at heart> eg *Nie zawracaj mi głowy tymi bzdurami (Stop nagging me about it)*

zawracać sobie głowę [zah-VRAH-tsahch SOH-byeh GWOH-veh] (or **zawracać sobie dupę*** [zah-VRAH-tsahch SOH-byeh DOO-peh]) *v phr* To bother or harry oneself <eat, bug, dog, nag, drag, nudge, bitch, bellyache, stew, bleed, sweat, sweat bullets, bum out, eat one's heart out, have something at heart> eg *Nie zawracaj sobie głowy (Don't sweat it)*

zawracanie głowy [zah-vrah-TSAH-nyeh GWOH-vi] (or **zawracanie dupy*** [zah-vrah-TSAH-nyeh DOO-pi]) *nn phr* Anything trivial, unimportant, but often bothersome <big deal, no big deal, no biggie, Mickey Mouse, small potatoes, small beer, fly speck, piece of cake, cake, cakewalk, cherry pie, duck soup, kid stuff, picnic, pushover, snap, tea party, walkaway, walkover, breeze, stroll, cinch, pipe, plain sailing> eg *Chcesz tylko pieniędzy? Zawracanie głowy. Myślałem, że chodzi ci o coś innego (Is money all you want? It's no big deal. I thought you wanted something else)*

zazdrość See pękać z zazdrości

ząb See ani w ząb, coś na ząb, nosić koszulę w zębach, wbijać zęby w ścianę

zbłaźnić się [ZBWAH-zhneech shyeh] *v* To make a fool of oneself <make a laughing stock out of oneself, make an ass of oneself, make a jerk of oneself> eg *Zbłaźniła się tą ostatnią uwagą (She made a laughing stock of herself by that last remark)*

zbajerować Perf bajerować

zbaranieć [zbah-RAH-nyehch] (or **zdębieć** [ZDEHM-byehch]) *v* To become bewildered, disoriented, or confused <get spaced out, get mixed up, get discombobulated, get flabbergasted, get messed up, get unscrewed, get farmisht, get balled up, get shook up, get floored, get unglued, get unzipped, get fried, get screwed-up, get fucked-up, get flummoxed, get kerflooey, get caught off base> eg

Zbaraniała, gdy to usłyszała (She got farmisht when she heard that); Zdębiałam, gdy usłyszałam tę wiadomość (I caught my breath when I heard that news)

zbić kogoś na kwaśne jabłko [zbeech KOH-gohsh nah KFAHSH-neh YAHP-koh] (or **sprać kogoś na kwaśne jabłko** [sprahch KOH-gohsh nah KFAHSH-neh YAHP-koh]) *v phr* To beat someone up, esp as a punishment <kick someone's ass, sock, bash, trash, clobber, bang, belt, clock, duke, dust, hammer, land one, lay one on, spank, wham, whack, bam, whip, bust, smack, poke, blast, beat the shit out of, beat the living shit out of, beat the bejejus out of, beat the daylights out of, beat someone into the middle of next week, knock the bejejus out of, knock the daylights out of, knock someone into the middle of next week, hit someone where he lives, work over> eg *Jak zaraz nieprzestaniesz, to cię zbiję na kwaśne jabłko (If you don't stop right now, I'll beat the shit out of you)*

zbić kogoś z tropu [zbeech s TROH-poo] (or **zbić kogoś z pantałyku** [zbeech s pahn-tah-WI-koo]) *v phr* To surprise someone immensely; to catch a person unprepared, esp by asking embarassing or difficult questions <put someone on the spot, catch someone off balance, throw someone off balance, get someone off someone's heels, put someone on the spot, catch someone off guard> eg *Nie wiedziałem, co powiedzieć. Zbiła mnie z tropu (I didn't know what to say. She caught me off balance)*

zbijać bąki [ZBEE-yahch BOHN-kee] *v phr* To loaf or idle; to pass time lazily <bum around, hang around, hang out, goof around, fuck around, screw around, fiddle around, fiddle fart around, fart around, jack around, mess around, hack around, monkey around, knock around, kick around, fool around, horse around, piddle around, play around, rat around, schloomp around, ass around, beat around, dick around, fuck around, fuck off, screw off, goof off, jerk off, fuck the dog, rat fuck, flub the dub, sit on one's ass, sit on one's butt, lollygag, veg out> eg *W te wakacje mam zamiar po prostu zbijać bąki (I'm just going to goof off on this vacation)*

zbijać kokosy See robić kokosy

zbluzgać Perf bluzgać

zbok [zbohk] *nm* A pervert <freak, geek, perv, pervo, twister, kink, kinko, panty thief> eg *Każdy wie, co znaczy słowo „zbok" (Everybody knows what "freak" means)*

zborze See płacić jak za zborze

zbzikować Perf bzikować

zdębieć See zbaranieć

zdechły [ZDEHKH-wi] (or **zdechlak** [ZDEHKH-lahk] or **zjebany**** [zyeh-BAH-ni] or **zmachany** [zmah-KHAH-ni] or **zarżnięty** [zahr-ZHNYEHN-ti]) *adj* Very tired or exhausted <dead, dead on one's feet, dead-tired, dog-tired, out of it, out of gas, out of juice, all in, all shot, pooped, bagged, beat, beat to the ground, beat to the ankles, bone-tired, burned out, bushed, chewed, crapped out, done, done in, dragged out, frazzled, played out, fucked out, knocked out, tuckered out, tapped out, had it, ready to drop, on one's last legs> eg *Ale jestem dzisiaj zdechły! Zaraz padnę (Am I dead-tired today! I'm gonna drop in a second)*

zdechnąć Perf zdychać

zdeczko See deczko

zderzaki [zdeh-ZHAH-kee] *npl* A woman's breasts, esp large <tits, melons, knockers, bazooms, boobs, headlights, hooters, hemispheres> eg *Z takimi zderzakami, powinna grać w filmach (With boobs like that, she ought to be in the movies)*

zdmuchnąć komuś coś sprzed nosa See sprzątnąć komuś coś sprzed nosa

zdołować Perf dołować

zdrowaśka [zdroh-VAHSH-kah] *nm* A prayer to Holy Mary <Hail Mary> eg *Codziennie mówi zdrowaśkę (She says Hail Mary everyday)*

zdrowie See jak bum cyk-cyk, nie mieć zdrowia do czegoś/kogoś

zdrowo [ZDROH-voh] *adv* Extremely; exceedingly; very <awful, god-awful, real, mighty, plenty, damn, damned, goddamn, goddamned, darn, darned, effing, flipping, forking, freaking, frigging, fucking, one's ass off, one's brains out, one's head off, to the max, like all get-out, like sin, to beat the band, like all creation, as blazes, as can be, as hell, like hell, in full swing> eg *Był zdrowo pijany (He was drunk like hell)*

zdrowy [ZDROH-vi] *adj* Big; large; sizable <gross, humongous, monstro, moby, jumbo, hefty, whopper, mother, king-size, God-size> eg *Zjadł zdrowy kawał tortu (He ate a humongous piece of cake)*

zdrowy jak ryba [ZDROH-vi yahk KOHŃ] (or **zdrowy jak byk** [ZDROH-vi yahk BIK] or **zdrowy jak koń** [ZDROH-vi yahk KOHñ]) *adj phr* Very healthy <alive and kicking, fit as a fiddle, up to snuff, up to the mark, wrapped tight, in fine feather, in fine whack, in the pink, sound as a dollar, right as rain, full of piss and vinegar, full of beans> eg *Dziadek ma 70 lat, ale jest zdrów jak ryba (Grandfather is 70, but he's still fit as a fiddle)*

zdurnieć Perf durnieć

zdychać [ZDI-khahch] (perf **zdechnąć** [ZDEHKH-nohnch]) *v* **1** To lose strength or energy; to be become very tired or exhausted <be dead, be dead on one's feet, be dead-tired, be dog-tired, be out of it, be out of gas, be out of juice, be all in, be all shot, be pooped, be bagged, be beat, be beat to the ground, be beat to the ankles, be bone-tired, be burned out, be bushed, be chewed, be crapped out, be done, be done in, be dragged out, be frazzled, be played out, be fucked out, be knocked out, be tuckered out, be tapped out, had it, be ready to drop, be on one's last legs> eg *Właśnie skończyłem i zdycham (I just finished and I'm all in)* **2*** To die or be dying <bite the dust, kiss the dust, croak, belly up, buy the farm, buy the ranch, cash in one's chips, check out, bump off, conk off, conk out, farm, give up the ghost, go home feet first, go home in a box, go west, kick in, kick off, kick the bucket, pass out, peg out, shove off, drop off, step off, pop off, push up daisies, meet one's maker, turn up one's toes, go down the tube, join the great majority, join the majority> eg *Chciałbym, żeby ten sukinsyn zdechł. Zasługuje na to (I wish that son of a bitch kicked the bucket. He deserves it)*

zdziadziały See zramolały

zdziebko See deczko

zdzierać [ZJEH-rahch] (or **zdzierać skórę z kogoś** [ZJEH-rahch SKOO-reh s KOH-gohsh]; perf **zedrzeć** [ZEHD-zhehch]) *v* To charge someone too much; to deceive financially; to swindle <con, rip off, shaft, roll, chisel, gyp, scam, screw, stiff, fleece, dick, do in, take in, do a number on, flim-flam, bamboozle, run a number on, take someone for a ride, take someone to the cleaners, throw someone a curve, pull a fast one, fuck over, screw over, angle, take in, snow, do a snow job, double-shuffle, fast-shuffle, flimflam, give a bun steer, give someone a line, have someone on, lead someone down the garden path, do a snow job, jerk someone's chain, pull someone's chain, pull one's leg, pull someone's string, pull

the wool over someone's eyes, put someone on, snow, use smoke and mirrors> eg *Nie wiem, kto bardziej z nas zdziera, kościół czy rząd (I don't know who rips us off more, the church or the government); Tamten handlarz zdarł ze mnie dwie stówy (That salesman dicked me for two centuries); Zdarłem z niego parę dolarów (I conned him out of a couple of dollars)*

zdzierstwo [ZJEHR-stfoh] *nn* An act of overcharging; a swindle <rip-off, con game, gyp, jip, scam> eg *To było prawdziwe zdzierstwo (It was a real rip-off)*

zdzira* [ZJEE-rah] *nf* A woman, esp esp ugly and promiscuous, whom one dislikes or disapproves of <ho', skag, skank, pig, bag, beasty, bitch, slut, cunt, broad, wench, hag, old hag, old biddy, old bag, old tart, piece of shit> eg *Co tu robi ta zdzira? (What is that skag doing here?)*

zeżreć Perf żreć

zebrać See wziąć się do kupy

zedrzeć Perf zdzierać

zegarek See jak w zegarku

zejść na psy [ZEH-eeshch nah PSI] *v phr* To deteriorate; to go to riun <go to the dogs, go to the devil, go to pot, go to seed, run to seed> eg *Po śmierci właściciela interes zszedł na psy (After the owner died the business went to the dogs)*

ześwirować Perf świrować

zerżnąć Perf rżnąć, zrzynać

zero [ZEH-roh] *nn* **1** (or **kompletne zero** [kohm-PLEHT-neh ZEH-roh]) An inconsequential or insignificant person <loser, lightweight, nobody, non, nonentity, noname, small potatoes, small timer, chromosome> eg *Jak mogła wyjść za takie zero? (How could she marry such a loser?)* **2** [ZEH-roh] *nn* (Of an amount of money) Nothing at all; zero <zilch, beans, damn, diddly-squat, doodly-squat, duck egg, goose egg, hoot, one red cent, one thin dime, rat's ass, zero, zippo, shit-all, fuck-all> eg *Nie dali mu zero (They gave him zilch)*

See od zera, wyjść na czysto

zerzygać się Perf rzygać

zesrać się Perf srać

zeszczać się Perf szczać

zet [zeht] (or **złocisz** [ZWOH-cheesh]) *nm* A zloty, Polish currency <no slang equivalent> eg *Dał mi za to dziesięć zetów (He gave me ten zloty for it)*

zetpete [zeht-peh-TEH] *nn* A hand or technical works, a subject in school <workshop> eg *Dziś na zetpete uczymy się, jak piłować (Today in workshop we're learning how to saw)*

zgłupieć See głupieć

zgarniać [ZGAHR-nyahch] *v* To earn a specific amount of money, esp as a salary <make, knock down, pull down, pull in, rack in, pick up, clean up, rack up, pile up, stack up, cash in> eg *Wiesz, ile on zgarnia na miesiąc? (Do you know how much he pulls down a month?)*

zgnoić See gnoić

zgrać się [ZGRAHCH shyeh] (or **zgrać się do suchej nitki** [ZGRAHCH shyeh doh SOO-kheh-ee NEET-kee]) *v* To lose all one's money on gambling <blow on gambling, drop on gambling> eg *Zgrał się do suchej nitki i postanowił popełnićsamobójstwo (He blew all his money on gambling and decided to commit suicide)*

zgraja [ZGRAH-yah] *nf* A group of people <folks, pack, bunch, crew, gang, clan, crowd, boys> eg *Instytut Anglistyki to zgraja wariatów (The English Department is a pack of nuts)*

zgred* [zgreht] (or **stary zgred*** [STAH-ri ZGREHT]) *nm* An old man, esp if unpleasant <gramps, old fart, old bugger, geezer, gaffer, old-timer, fossil> eg *Wyszła za mąż za starego zgreda (She marries some old fart)*

zgrywa [ZGRI-vah] *nf* A joke intended to fool or deceive someone; a more or less amiable trick <put-on, leg-pull, number, spoof, con> eg *Nie widzisz, że to zgrywa? (Can't you see it's a put-on?)*
See dla jaj

zgrywać się [ZGRI-vahch shyeh] *v* To behave in an unconvential or unusual way, esp in order to fool someone; to pretend <fake, fake out, jive, jazz, put someone on, pull someone's leg, pull someone's string, give someone a leg, have someone on, jack someone around, jerk someone around, poke fun at, kid someone around, fool someone around, jack someone's chain, spoof, cut down> eg *Przestań się zgrywać (Stop jacking me around)*

zgrywus [ZGRI-voos] *nm* A man prone to playing tricks <artist, joker, kidder, clown, article, ham, character, item, number> eg *Z tego twojego kuzyna to prawdziwy zgrywus; poszedł na egzamin końcowy w szortach! (Your cousin is a real joker: He went to his final exam wearing shorts!)*

zidiocieć Perf idiocieć

ziębić See ani ziębić ani grzać kogoś

zieleniak [zheh-LEH-nyahk] *nm* A grocery store <corner store, deli> eg *Skocz do zieleniaka i kup trochę jabłek (Go down to the corner store and buy some apples)*

zielone [zheyh-LOH-neh] *npl* US dollars <bucks, greenies, greens, greenback> eg *Będzie cię to kosztowało dwieście zielonych (It'll set you back two hundred greenbacks)*

zielony [zheh-LOH-ni] *adj* Inexperienced or incompetent <green, greeny, green-ass, greenhorn, rookie, virgin, wet behind the ears> eg *On nic o tym nie wie, jest zielony (He doesn't know anything about it, he's greeny)*
See iść na zieloną trawkę, mieć pstro w głowie, nie mieć zielonego pojęcia, posłać na zieloną trawkę

zielsko [ZHEHL-skoh] *nn* Any weed-like plant <weed> eg *Co to za zielsko? (What kind of weed is that?)*

ziemia See gryźć ziemię, nie do wyjęcia

zimnica [zheem-NEE-tsah] *nf* Chill; cold weather <cold tit, colder than a witch's tit, colder than a frozen fish's asshole, freezing one's tits off, freezing one's balls off, one-dog night, coolth, freezer> eg *Wczoraj była zimnica (Yesterday it was colder than a witch's tit)*

zimno że dupę urywa* [ZHEEM-noh zheh DOO-peh oo-RI-vah] *adv phr* Chill; cold weather <cold tit, colder than a witch's tit, colder than a frozen fish's asshole, freezing one's tits off, freezing one's balls off, one-dog night, coolth, freezer> eg *Zimno, że dupę urywa! (It's colder than a witch's tit!)*

zimować [zhee-MOH-vahch] (perf **przezimować** [psheh-zhee-MOH-vahch]) *v* To repeat a class in school or a year at the university <take over, run over, flunk the class, flunk the year> eg *Trzeba być prawdziwym idiotą, żeby zimować (You've got to be a real idiot to flunk the year)*

zjarać się Perf jarać się

zjebany See zdechły

zjeść z kimś beczkę soli [zyehshch s keemsh BEHCH-keh SOH-lee] *v phr* To know and understand someone very well, esp because of shared past hardships <be like blood brothers, been through, read someone, read someone like a book, know someone like a book, know someone like the back of one's hand, know someone like the palm of one's hand, know what makes someone tick, have someone's number> eg *Zjadłem z nim beczkę soli. Byliśmy razem w wojsku (I know him like a book. We were in the Army together)*

zlać Perf lać

zlatywać się [zlah-TI-vahch shyeh] (perf **zlecieć się** [ZLEH-chyehch shyeh]; or **złazić się** [ZWAH-zhich shyeh] perf **zleźć się** [ZLEHZHCH shyeh]) *v* (Of people) To suddenly arrive or gather in large numbers; to crowd or congregate <flock, flock in, drop in, pop in, drag in, fall in, blow in, breeze in, flood in, sky in, barge in, roll in, spring in, bust in, pull in, check in, hit, make the scene> eg *Sąsiedzi zlecieli się, żeby zobaczyć jej nowy samochód (Neighbors flocked in to see her new car)*

zlecieć Perf lecieć

zlewka [ZLEHF-kah] *nf* A liquid meal composed of odds and ends, or of whatever turns up <pot luck, leftovers> eg *Znów zaserwowała nam jakąś zlewkę (She served us some pot luck again)*

zleźć się Perf złazić się

złamać się Perf łamać się

złamany grosz [zwah-MAH-ni GROHSH] *nm phr* (Of an amount of money) Nothing at all; zero <zilch, beans, damn, diddly-squat, doodly-squat, duck egg, goose egg, hoot, one red cent, one thin dime, rat's ass, zero, zippo, shit-all, fuck-all> eg *Nie dali mi złamanego grosza (They gave me zilch)*

złamas [ZWAH-mahs] *nm* A man one dislikes or disapproves of <asshole, fuck, fucker, fuckhead, fuckface, motherfucker, shit, shitface, shithead, shitheel, bastard, jerk, SOB, son of a bitch, son of a whore, cocksucker, prick, dick, dickhead, cuntface, schmuck, scum, scumbag, sleazebag, slimebag, dipshit, pisshead, piece of shit, pain in the ass> eg *Wiesz, co mi zrobił ten złamas? (Do you know what the prick did to me?)*

złapać [WAH-pahch] (or **załapać** [zah-WAH-pahch] or **podłapać** [pohd-WAH-pahch]) *v* To contract a disease, esp veneral <catch, grab, come down with> eg *Chodzili do burdeli często, ale żaden z nas nie złapał syfa (They would visit brothels often, but nobody caught a syph)*

złapać cuga See iść w cug

złapać fazę See mieć fazę

złapać gumę [ZWAH-pahch GOO-meh] *v phr* To catch a flat tire <catch a flat> eg *Właśnie wtedy złapaliśmy gumę (Just then we caught a flat)*

złapać Perf łapać

złazić się See zlatywać się

złocisz See zet

złodziejka [zwoh-JEH-ee-kah] *nf* An electric extension <no slang equivalent> eg *Możesz mi podać złodziejkę? (Can you pass me the extension?)*

złość See pękać ze złości

złota rączka [ZWOH-tah ROHNCH-kah] *nf phr* A person who is skillful or knowledgeable in many areas <jack of all trades, crackerjack, know it all> eg *Spytaj mojego tatę. To złota rączka (Ask my dad. He's a jack of all trades)*

złoto See jak ta lala

złoty See kura znosząca złote jajka

złoty interes [ZWOH-ti een-TEH-rehs] (or **kokosowy interes** [koh-koh-SOH-vi een-TEH-rehs]) *nm phr* A very profitable venture <bonanza, gold mine, pay dirt, gravy train> eg *Obawiam się, że to nie będzie kokosowy interes (It won't be a bonanza, I'm afraid)*

zmachać się [ZMAH-khahch shyeh] *v* To be very tired or exhausted, esp because of hard work <be dead, be dead on one's feet, be dead-tired, be dog-tired, be out of it, be out of gas, be out of juice, be all in, be all shot, be pooped, be bagged, be beat, be beat to the ground, be beat to the ankles, be bone-tired, be burned out, be bushed, be chewed, be crapped out, be done, be done in, be dragged out, be frazzled, be played out, be fucked out, be knocked out, be tuckered out, be tapped out, had it, be ready to drop, be on one's last legs> eg *Nie pracuj tak ciężko, bo się zaraz zmachasz (Don't work so hard, because you'll be out of gas soon)*

zmachany See zdechły

zmajstrować komuś dzieciaka See zrobić komuś dzieciaka

zmienić płytę [ZMYEH-neech PWI-teh] *v* To shift the topic of conversation <change the channel, change the tune> eg *Zmień płytę, bo jesteś nudny (Change the channel, because you're boring)*

zmyłka [ZMI-oo-kah] *nf* A fact or remark which is intended to mislead, esp to draw people's attention away from the main point <red herring, put-on, frame-up, set-up, fake> eg *To oskarżenie było tylko zmyłką, aby zdyskredytować jego pozycję (The charge was just a red herring designed to discredit his standing)*
See dla zmyłki

znać coś/kogoś na wylot [znahch tsohsh/KOH-gohsh nah VI-loht] *v phr* To understand something or someone very well <been through, read someone, read someone like a book, know someone like a book, know someone like the back of one's hand, know someone like the palm of one's hand, know what makes someone tick, have someone's number, live in someone's pockets> eg *Moja dziewczyna zna mnie na wylot (My girlfriend can read me like a book)*

znać się jak łyse konie [znahch shyeh yahk WI-seh KOH-nyeh] *v phr* To know and understand each other very well <been through, read someone, read someone like a book, know someone like a book, know someone like the back of one's hand, know someone like the palm of one's hand, know what makes someone tick, have someone's number, live in someone's pockets> eg *Znamy się jak łyse konie. Byliśmy razem na studiach (We know each other like a book. We went to college together)*

znać ten ból [znahch tehn BOOL] *v phr* To understand and relate to someone's position, esp because of similar past experience <know what someone means, know where someone is coming from, know where it's at, been there oneself, have the same vibes, know the feeling> eg *Znam ten ból. Sam to widziałem (I know where you're coming from. I saw it myself)*

znajda [ZNAH-ee-dah] *nf* A child of unknown parents <bastard> eg *Nie chcemy tu żadnych znajd (We don't want any bastards here)*

znajomek [znah-YOH-mehk] *nm* An acquaintance <bro, brother, buddy, amigo, pal, sidekick> eg *To tylko jeden z moich znajomków (He's just one of my amigos)*

znajomy See krewni i znajomi królika

znaleźć wspólny język [ZNAH-lehshch FSPOOL-ni YEHN-zik] *nm phr* To become perfectly understood of felt by someone; to make oneself understood; to start to communicate <get across, get one's point across, interface, relate, touch base, be on the same wavelength, be on someone's wavelength, have the same vibes, be tuned in, find a common ground> eg *Nie znaleźliśmy wspólnego języka, więc zerwaliśmy ze sobą (We didn't find a common ground, so we broke up)* **2** To reach an agreement; to compromise <okay, OK, shake hands, shake on, sign on, clinch, cut, go along with, play ball, come across, come around, trade off, meet halfway, strike a happy medium, make a deal, fit in> eg *Nie martw się, w końcu znajdą wspólny język (Don't worry, they'll eventually meet halfway)*

zołza [ZOW-zah] (or **zrzęda** [ZZHEHN-dah]) *nf* A woman whom one dislikes or disapproves of, esp a woman who is groundlessly dissatisfied or discontented <bitch, slut, cunt, broad, wench, hag, old hag, old biddy, old bag, old tart, piece of shit, bitcher, beefer, bellyacher, griper, squawker, whiner, plainer, squealer, grouser, groucher, grumbler, moaner, sorehead, kvetch, crab, crank, gripe, grouse, grouch, forecastle lawyer, sourpuss, sourball, sourpan, picklepuss> eg *Słyszałem, że jego życie to piekło. Ożenił się z taką zołzą (I hear his life is real hell. He married such a beefer)*

zostać na drugi rok [ZOH-stahch nah DROO-gee rohk] (or **siedzieć na drugi rok** [SHYEH-jehch nah DROO-gee rohk]) *v phr* To repeat a class in school or a year at the university <take over, run over, flunk the class, flunk the year> eg *Trzeba być prawdziwym idiotą, żeby zostać drugi rok (You've got to be a real idiot to flunk the year)*

zostawić See pierdolnąć

zostawić kogoś na lodzie [zoh-STAH-veech KOH-gohsh nah LOH-jeh] *v phr* To cheat, swindle, deceive, esp financially <con, rip off, shaft, roll, chisel, gyp, scam, screw, stiff, fleece, dick, do in, take in, do a number on, flim-flam, bamboozle, run a number on, take someone for a ride, take someone to the cleaners, throw someone a curve, pull a fast one, fuck over, screw over, angle, take in, snow, do a snow job, double-shuffle, fast-shuffle, flimflam, give a bun steer, give someone a line, have someone on, lead someone down the garden path, do a snow job, jerk someone's chain, pull someone's chain, pull one's leg, pull someone's string, pull the wool over someone's eyes, put someone on, snow, use smoke and mirrors> eg *Moja była dziewczyna zostawiła mnie na lodzie (My ex girlfriend took me to the cleaners)*

zramolały* [zrah-moh-LAH-wi] (or **zdziadziały*** [zjah-JAH-wi]) *adj* Aged, esp about a balding and obese man <rusty, creaky, over the hill> eg *Spójrz na tego zramolałego idiotę. Przystawia się do studentki (Look at that rusty idiot. He's making a pass at some student); Niektórzy faceci wydają się zdziadziali już mając trzydziestkę (Some guys seem over the hill at thirty)*

zrobić See wykręcić komuś numer

zrobić kogoś na szaro [ZROH-beech KOH-gohsh nah SHAH-roh] (or **zrobić kogoś na perłowo** [ZROH-beech KOH-gohsh nah pehr-WOH-voh] or **zrobić kogoś bez mydła** [ZROH-beech KOH-gohsh behz MID-wah]) *v phr* To cheat, swindle, deceive, esp financially <con, rip off, shaft, roll, chisel, gyp, scam, screw, stiff, fleece, dick, do in, take in, do a number on, flim-flam, bamboozle, run a number on, take someone for a ride, take someone to the cleaners, throw someone a curve, pull a fast one, fuck over, screw over, angle, take in, snow, do a snow job, double-shuffle, fast-shuffle, flimflam, give a bun steer, give someone a line, have someone on, lead someone down the garden path, do a snow job, jerk someone's chain, pull someone's chain, pull one's leg, pull someone's string, pull the wool over someone's eyes, put someone on, snow, use smoke and mirrors> eg *Moja była dziewczyna zrobiła mnie na szaro (My ex girlfriend took me to the cleaners)*

zrobić kogoś w konia [ZROH-beech KOH-gohsh f KOH-nyah] (**balona** [bah-LOH-nah] or **bambuko** [bahm-BOO-koh] or **bambusa** [bahm-BOO-sah] or **chuja**** [KHOO-yah] or **w jajo** [YAH-yoh] may replace **konia**) *v phr* To cheat; to swindle; to deceive; to make a fool out of someone <con, rip off, shaft, roll, chisel, gyp, scam, screw, stiff, fleece, dick, do in, take in, do a number on, flim-flam, bamboozle, run a number on, take someone for a ride, take someone to the cleaners, throw someone a curve, pull a fast one, fuck over, screw over, angle, take in, snow, do a snow job, double-shuffle, fast-shuffle, flimflam, give a bun steer, give someone a line, have someone on, lead someone down the garden path, do a snow job, jerk someone's chain, pull someone's chain, pull one's leg, pull someone's string, pull the wool over someone's eyes, put someone on, snow, use smoke and mirrors> eg *Może próbować zrobić się w balona. Uważaj na niego (He may try to take you in. Keep an eye on him)*

zrobić komuś dzieciaka [ZROH-beech KOH-moosh jeh-CHAH-kah] (or **machnąć komuś dzieciaka** [MAHKH-nohnch KOH-moosh jeh-CHAH-kah] or **zmajstrować komuś dzieciaka** [zmah-ee-STROH-vahch KOH-moosh jeh-CHAH-kah]; **dziecko** [JEHTS-koh] or **brzucha** [BZHOO-khah] may replace **dzieciaka**) *v phr* To make pregnant <knock up, bang up, bump, stork> eg *Musiała kogoś obwinić za to, że zrobił jej dzieciaka (She had to blame someone for bumping her); Kto zmajstrował jej dziecko? (Who knocked her up?)*

zrobić numer See strzelić numer

zrobić wypad [ZROH-beech VI-pahd] *v phr* To visit a given place, esp to go downtown or go on a short pleasure trip <hit, do, fall by, swing by> eg *Postanowiliśmy zrobić wypad do miasta (We decided to hit the town); Let's do Europe this summer, shall we?(Zróbmy wypad do Europy tego lata, co?)*

zrobić z kogoś człowieka [ZROH-beech s KOH-gohsh chwoh-VYEH-kah] *v phr* To steer someone's life in such a way that they become a valuable individual <make a man out of someone> eg *Proszę się nie martwić. Zrobimy z niego człowieka (Don't worry. We'll make a man out of him)*

zrobiona [zroh-BYOH-nah] *adj* (Of a woman) Made-up and fancily dressed <made-up to kill, dolled-up, dolled-out, dressed to kill, dressed to the nines, dressed to the teeth, dressed-up, duded-up, ritzed up, swanked up, ragged out, sharp-dressed> eg *Luknij na tę lalę. Ale jest zrobiona! (Check out that doll. Is she made up to kill!)*

zrywać boki [ZRI-vahch BOH-kee] (or **zrywać boki ze śmiechu** [ZRI-vahch BOH-kee zeh SHMYEH-khoo]) *v phr* To burst with laughter <crack up, break up, split, split one's sides, die laughing, roll in the aisles, tear one apart, be in stiches, laugh fit to burst, bust a gut laughing, pee in one's pants laughing, fall out

laughing, howl, scream, horselaugh, stitch, be blue in the face, laugh till one is blue in the face> eg *Mało co nie pękli ze śmiechu, gdy powiedziałem im, dlaczego się spóźniłem (They nearly split their sides when I told them my reason for being late)*

zrzęda See zołza

zrzucać się [ZZHOO-tsahch shyeh] *v* To contribute, esp a share of some expense <kick in, chip in, pitch in, fork up, fork over, fork out, feed the kitty, pass the hat> eg *Wszyscy zrzuciliśmy się po parę dolców na prezent dla niego (We all pitched in a couple bucks to get him a present)*

zrzutka [ZZHOOT-kah] *nm* A collection of money among a group of people; a contributed fund <kick-in, chip-in, pitch-in, kitty, pool> eg *Zróbmy zrzutkę, co? (Let's make a pitch-in, huh?)*

zrzygać się Perf rzygać

zrzynać [ZZHI-nahch] (perf **zerżnąć** [ZEHRZH-nohnch]; or **zwalać** [ZVAH-lahch] perf **zwalić** [ZVAH-leech]) *v* To copy <cheat, crib, nick> eg *Zrzynała na egzaminie i przyłapano ją (She nicked on the exam and got caught)*

zsikać się Perf sikać

zupełnie See inna para kaloszy

zwalać See zrzynać

zwalić Perf zwalać

zwalić się** [ZVAH-leech shyeh] *v phr* To ejaculate semen <come, come off, blow off, drop one's load, get it off, get one's nuts off, get one's rocks off, go off, shoot, shoot one's load, shoot one's wad, spunk> eg *Zrelaksuj się, zanim się spuścisz (Relax before you come)*

zwariować See nie dać się zwariować

zwarty See silny zwarty i gotowy

zwędzić See zwinąć

zwierzak [ZVYEH-zhahk] *nm* Any animal <critter, dog, mutt> eg *dę nakarmić wierzaki? (I'm going to feed the critters)*

zwierzę See dzień dobroci dla zwierząt

zwiewać [ZVYEH-vahch] (or **wiać** [vyahch] perf **zwiać** [zvyahch]) *v* To leave or depart, esp hastily <split, beat it, ankle, bag ass, blow, breeze off, burn rubber, butt out, buzz off, check out, cruise, cut and run, cut ass, cut out, drag ass, dust, ease out, fade, fade away, fade out, fuck off, get the fuck out, get the hell out , get going, get moving, get lost, get off the dime, get on one's horse, go south, haul ass, hightail, hit the bricks, hit the road, hop it, make tracks, pull out, scram, set sail, shove off, shuffle along, skate, skip out, split the scene, take off> eg *Gliny już tu są. Zwiewamy! (The cops are already here. Let's split!)*

zwijać manatki [ZVEE-yahch mah-NAHT-kee] (or **pakować manatki** [pah-KOH-vahch mah-NAHT-kee]; **manele** [mah-NEH-leh] or **żagle** [ZHAH-gleh] or **interes** [een-TEH-rehs] or **majdan** [MAH-ee-dahn] may replace **manatki**) *npl* To leave one's job or home <pull up stakes, pack up> eg *Mam zamiar zwinąć manatki i przenieść się do Ameryki lub Australii (I'm going to pull up stakes and move to America or Australia)*

zwinąć [ZWEE-nohnch] *v* **1** (or **zwędzić** [ZVEHN-jeech]) To steal; to rob <heist, boost, burgle, nurn, bag, buzz, highjack, hoist, hold up, hook, hustle, jump, kick over, knock off, knock over, lift, move, mug, nab, nick, nip, pinch, pluck, roll, rustle, snatch, snitch, stick up, swipe, take off, put the grab on, go south with> eg

Zwędził to z drogerii (He nicked that from a drugstore) **2** To catch a criminal; to arrest <bust, bag, claw, clip, collar, cop, flag, grab, haul in, jab, knock, pinch, nab, nail, nick, pick up, pull in, run in, sidetrack, put the collar on, put the sleeve on> eg *Wiedziałem, że policja prędzej czy później go zwinie (I knew the police would nab him sooner or later)*

zwisać komuś [ZVEE-sahch KOH-moosh] (or **wisieć komuś** [VI-shyehch KOH-moosh]) *v phr* To be indifferent; not to care at all; to ignore <not give a damn, not give a fuck, not give a shit, not give a diddly-shit, not give a diddly-damn, not give a flying fuck, not give a hoot, not give a rat's ass, not give a squat, pass up, diss, skip, ig, ice, chill, freeze, cut, brush off, give the brush, give the cold shoulder, turn the cold shoulder, cold-shoulder, give the go-by, high-hat, kiss off> eg *Zwisa mi, co myślisz (I don't give a shit what you think)*

Ż

żabojad* [zhah-BOH-yaht] *nm* A French person <frog, froggy, frog-eater, Frenchy> eg *Cały problem z żabojadami polega na tym, że ich język jest taki dziwny (The problem with the frogs is that their language is so strange)*

żaden *adj* [ZHAH-dehn] Not very good; miserable <saddest excuse for, lousy, awful, bush-league, cheap, crappy, shitty, cruddy, crummy, doggy, low-rent, low-ride, no-good, raggedy-ass, schlocky, stinking, tacky, trashy, two-bit, dime-a-dozen, fair to middling, garden variety, of a sort, of sorts, piddling, pissy-ass, piss-poor, run-of-the-mill, small-time> eg *Spójrz na samochód, który kupiłem. Stary, to żaden samochód! (Check out the car I just bought. Man, that's the saddest excuse for a car I ever saw!)*

żagle See zwijać manatki

żarłok [ZHAR-wohk] *nm* A glutton <pig, hog, bellygod, greedyguts, foodie, chow hound, slob> eg *Mój brat to żarłok. Nigdy nie ma dość (My brother is a pig. He never has enough)*

żarcie [ZHAHR-chyeh] (or **żarło** [ZHAHR-woh]) *nn* Food <chow, feed, grub, scoff, eats> eg *Chodźmy na żarcie (Let's go get some grub)*

że aż strach See taki że aż strach

że bez kija nie podchodź See taki że bez kija nie podchodź

że do rany przyłóż See taki że do rany przyłóż

że hej See tak że hej, taki że hej

że mózg staje See taki że mózg staje

że mucha nie siada See taki że mucha nie siada

żebry See iść na żebry

żeby było śmieszniej *phr* To further worsen the situation, esp in to a tragicomic or sarcastic effect <to make it funnier, to make it worse, to make things worse> eg *No więc rzuciła go. Żeby było śmieszniej, nie zapłaciła nawet rachunków za telefon (So she dumped him. To make it worse, she didn't even pay the phone bills)*

żeby to See niech to

żelastwo [zheh-LAHS-tfoh] *nn* An object or objects made from iron, esp old and useless; hardware <iron wreck, iron junk, iron scraps, iron heaps> eg *W piwnicy trzymał żelastwo, które obrastało kurzem (He had iron junk lying in the basement, collecting dust)*

żeniaczka [zheh-NYAHCH-kah] (or **ożenek** [oh-ZHEH-nehk] *nm*) *nf* An instance of getting married; marriage <bells, wedding bells, getting hitched, getting spliced, getting hooked, getting merged> eg *Ona myśli tylko o żeniaczce (All she cares about is wedding bells)*

żłób [zhwoop] *nm* A very lucrative position, esp of a high-rank government official which guarantees profit without much effort; an obvious sinecure <gravy train, gravy boat, top of the ladder> eg *Ważne, żeby być przy żłobie (What is important is to ride the gravy train)*

żłobek [ZHWOH-behk] *nm* A jail cell where drunks are kept <drunk tank, drunk pound> eg *Te parę godzin w żłobku naprawdę spowodowało, że zacząłem myśleć o alkoholu (A couple of hours in the drunk tank really made me think about alcohol)*

żołądkować się [zhoh-wohnt-KOH-vahch shyeh] *v* To be very angry or irritated <be pissed off, be peed off, be p'd off, be bent out of a shape, be pushed out of a shape, be browned off, be cranky, be edgy, be sore, be mad as a hornet, be steamed up, be ticked off, be tee'd off, be burned up, be ballistic> eg *Nie wiem, o co się tak żołądkował (I don't know what made him so ballistic)*

żółte papiery See wariackie papiery

żółtek [ZHOOW-tehk] *nm* An Asian; an Oriental <gook, dink, slope, slant eye, gooney, rice grinder> eg *Nikt nie chciał iść na wojnę z żółtkami (Nobody wanted to go to war against the gooks)*

żółtodziób [zhoow-TOH-joop] *nm* An inexperienced person; a newcomer; a novice <greenhorn, rookie, rook, boot, tenderfoot, new kid on the block, Johnny-come-lately, wetnose, snotnose, yardbird> eg *On ci nic nie pomoże. To żółtodziób (He won't help you much. He's a greenhorn)*

żonka [ZHOHN-kah] *nf* A wife <wifey, mama, missus, better half, old lady, little woman, ball and chain, significant other, significant other> eg *Poszedł spytać się swojej żonki (He went to ask his wifey)*

żonkoś [ZHOHN-kohsh] *nm* A recently married man who is (still) in love with his wife; a newly-wed husband <hubby> eg *Co powie na to jej żonkoś? (What will her hubby say to that?)*

żreć [zhrehch] (perf **zeżreć** [ZEH-zhrehch] or **wyżreć** [VI-zhrehch]) *v* To eat, esp voraciously or entirely <chow down, scarf, scoff, feed one's face, gobble up> eg *Ten dzieciak zeżarł całą czekoladę (This kid scoffed the whole chocolate)*

żreć się [zhrehch shyeh] (perf **pożreć się** [POH-zhrehch shyeh]) *v* To quarrel or argue; to actively disagree; to fight <hassle, bump heads, take on, lock horns, set to, scrap, cross swords, pick a bone, tangle with, tangle ass with, go up against, put up a fight, bicker, go round and round, go toe to toe, go to it, go to the mat, have a pissing contest, have a pissing match, have a run-in, kick up a row, make the fur fly, put on the gloves, lead a cat-and-dog life, have a cat-and-dog life, fight like cat and dog, jump down someone's throat, be at loggerheads with> eg *Żrą się obecnie z właścicielami (They are currently bumping heads with the owners)*

żur [zhoor] *nm* A heavy drinker, an alcoholic <lush, bar-fly, alky, boozehound, boozer, bottle baby, dipso, elbow bender, ginhead, juicehead, loadie, sponge,

soak, wino> eg *Ten żur chciał trochę pieniędzy na piwo (That boozer wanted some money for beer)*

żyła [ZHI-wah] *nf* **1** A ruthless, demanding, and tenacious person <toughie, stiff, ball-breaker, ball-buster, back-breaker, ass-buster, bitch, son of a bitch, badass, mean machine> eg *Słyszałem, że wasz nowy nauczyciel od matmy to prawdziwy żyła (I heard your new math teacher is a real ball-breaker)* **2** A parsimonious person; a miser <tightwad, piker, cheapskate, scrooge, pinchfist, penny-pincher, pinchpenny, nickel-nurser, nickel-squeezer> eg *Jej mąż to prawdziwa żyła. Nic jej nie kupił (Her husband is a real tightwad. He bought her nothing)*
See ładować sobie w żyłę, wypruwać sobie flaki

żyła złota [ZHI-wah ZWOH-tah] *nf phr* A very profitable venture; a lucrative business <bonanza, gold mine, pay dirt, gravy train, cash cow> eg *Wydaje się, że to przedsięwzięcie to jest żyła złota (This enterprise seems to be a gold mine)*

żyłka [ZHIW-kah] *nf* A natural tendency or special natural skill <bent, knack, hang, feel, what it takes> eg *On nie ma żyłki do sztuki (He doesn't have a knack for art)*

żyć na czyimś garnuszku See być na czyimś garnuszku

żyć z kimś [ZHICH s KEMSH] (or **żyć z kimś na kocią łapę** [ZHICH s KEMSH nah KOH-chyoh WAH-peh] or **żyć z kimś na kartę rowerową** [ZHICH s KEMSH nah KAHR-teh roh-veh-ROH-voh]) *v phr* To live together without marriage <shack up, play house> eg *Żył na kocią łapę z czterdziestoletnią wdową (He shacked up with a 40-year-old widow)*

żyć z kimś jak pies z kotem [ZHICH s KEEMSH yahk PYEHS s KOH-tehm] (or **drzeć z kimś koty** [dzhehch s keemsh KOH-ti]) *v phr* To constantly quarrel with someone with whom one lives or works <lead a cat-and-dog life, have a cat-and-dog life, fight like cat and dog, hassle, bump heads, lock horns, cross swords, pick a bone, tangle with, put up a fight, jump down someone's throat, be at loggerheads with> eg *We wczesnych latach małżeństwa żyli ze sobą jak pies z kotem (In the early years of their marriage they had led a cat-and-dog life)*

życie See samo życie, w życiu

życiorys See mieć przerwę w życiorysie

żydek* [ZHI-dehk] or **żydziak*** [ZHI-jahk] or **żydzior*** [ZHI-johr]) *nm* A Jewish male <kike, Yid, mockie, sheeny, hooknose, eagle-beak, clipped dick, Jew boy, rabbi, Ike, Hebe, Hymie, Abe, Sammy, Goldberg> eg *Nie lubię ludzi, którzy nazywają Żydów "żydziorami" (I don't like people who call Jews "kikes")*

żydowica* [zhi-doh-VEE-tsah] *nf* A Jew female <Jew girl, Jewish American Princess, JAP> eg *Możebyś tak przestała używać określenia"żydowica"? (I wish you'd stop using the expression "Jew girl")*

żygolak [zhi-GOH-lahk] *nm* A male prostitute, not necessarily a homosexual <gigolo> eg *Powiedział, że życie żygolaka nie jest takie złe, jeśli nie ma się nic przeciwko 55-letnim kobietom (He said life as a gigolo wasn't too bad if you didn't mind 55-year-old women)*

żyjątko [zhi-YOHN-tkoh] *nn* A petty animal <critter, little critter> eg *Czy te żyjątka są niebezpieczne? (Are these critters safe?)*

żytniówka [zhit-NYOOF-kah] (or **żyto** [ZHI-toh] *nn*) *nf* Vodka produced from rye <rye> eg *Daj mi trochę żyta i sok jabłkowy na popitkę (Give me some rye and apple juice as a chaser)*

Bibliography

Anusiewicz, J. & J. Skawiński. 1996. *Słownik polszczyzny potocznej*. Warszawa: PWN
Czarnecka, K. & H. Zgółkowa. 1991. *Słownik gwary uczniowskiej*. Poznań: SAWW
Grochowski, M. 1995. *Słownik polskich przekleństw i wulgaryzmów*. Warszawa: PWN
Kaczmarek, L. & T. Skubalanka & S. Grabias. 1994. *Słownik gwary studenckiej*. Lublin: UMCS
Kania, S. 1985. *Słownik argotyzmów*. Warszawa: Wiedza Powszechna
Stępniak, K. 1993. *Słownik Tajemnych gwar przestępczych*. Londyn: Puls Publications
Tuftanka, U. 1993. Zakazane wyrazy. *Słownik sprośności i wulgaryzmów*. Warszawa: Wydawnictwo O
Widawski, M. 1992. *Słownik slangu i potocznej angielszczyzny*. Gdańsk: Slang Books
----------, M. 1994. *The Fucktionary*. Gdańsk-Elbląg: Comprendo

Allen, I. 1993. *The City in Slang*. New York: OUP
Anderson, D. 1975. *The Book of Slang*. Middle Village, NY: Jonathan David Publishers
Andersson, L. & P. Trudgill. 1992. *Bad Language*. London: Penguin Books
Ash, R. & B. Highton. 1991. *Private Parts*. Kraków: Bull Publishing House
Ayto, J. & J. Simpson. 1992. *The Oxford Dictionary of Modern Slang*. Oxford: OUP
Beale, P. 1990. *A Dictionary of Catch Phrases*. London: Routledge and Kegan Paul
----------, P. 1991. *A Concise Dictionary of Slang and Unconventional English*. London: Routledge and Kegan Paul
Blowdryer, J. 1985. *Modern English: A Trendy Slang Dictionary*. San Francisco: Last Gasp Press
Cassidy, F. 1991. *Dictionary of American Regional English*. Cambridge, Mass.: Belknap Press and Harvard University Press
Chapman, R. 1986. *New Dictionary of American Slang*. New York: Harper and Row Publishers
----------, R. 1989. *Thesaurus of American Slang*. New York: Harper and Row Publishers
De Sola, R. 1982. *Crime Dictionary*. New York: Facts on File
Dickson, P. 1990. *Slang! The Topic-by-Topic Dictionary of Contemporary American Lingoes*. New York: Pocket Books
----------, P. 1994. *War Slang*. New York: Pocket Books
Eble, C. 1989. *College Slang 101*. Georgetown, CT: Lane Press
----------, C. 1996. *Slang and Sociability*. Chapel Hill: University of North Carolina Press
Elting, J. & D. Cragg. 1984. *A Dictionary of Soldier Talk*. New York: Charles Scribner's Sons
Flexner, S. 1976. *I Hear America Talking*. New York: Van Norstrand Reinhold
----------, S. 1982. *Listening to America*. New York: Simon and Schuster
Green, J. 1984. *The Dictionary of Contemporary Slang*. London: Pan Books
----------, J. 1986. *The Slang Thesaurus*. London: Pan Books
----------, J. 1993. *Slang Down the Ages*. London: Kyle Cathie Limited
Hailey, F. 1982. *Soldier Talk*. Braintree, Mass.: Irving and Co. Publishing
Holder, R. 1987. *A Dictionary of American and British Euphemisms*. Bath: Bath University Press
Hughes, G. 1991. *Swearing*. Oxford: Basil Blackwell
Kogos, F. 1967. *A Dictionary of Yiddish Slang and Idioms*. Secaucus, NJ: Citadel Press
Lambodian, W. 1979. *Doublespeak Dictionary*. Los Angeles: Pinnacle Books

Lewin, E. & A. Lewin. 1988. *The Random House Thesaurus of Slang.* New York: Random House
Lighter, J. 1994. *Random House Historical Dictionary of American Slang.* New York: Random House
Major, C. 1994. *Juba to Jive: A Dictionary of African-American Slang.* New York: Penguin Books
Makkai, A. 1987. *A Dictionary of American Idioms.* Hauppauge, NY: Barron's Educational Series
McDonald. 1989. *A Dictionary of Obscenity, Taboo, and Euphemism.* London: Sphere Books
Mills, J. 1993. *Sexwords.* London: Penguin Books
Munro, P. 1984. *UCLA Slang.* Los Angeles: UCLA Press
Neaman, J. & C. Silver. 1991. *Kind Words: A Thesaurus of Euphemisms.* New York: Aron Books
Palmatier, R. & H. Ray. 1995. *Dictionary of Sports Idioms.* Lincolnwood, IL: NTC Publishing Group
Paros, L. 1988. *The Erotic Tongue.* London: Arlington Books
Partridge, 1984. *A Dictionary of Slang and Unconventional English.* 8th ed. P. Beale. New York: Macmillan
Pearl, A. 1980. *Dictionary of Popular Slang.* Middle Village, NY: Jonathan David
Pythian, B. 1989. *A Conscise Dictionary of English Slang.* Dunton Green, Sevenoaks: Hodder and Stoughton
Rawson, H. 1981. *A Dictionary of Euphemisms and Other Doubletalk.* New York: Crown Publishers
Raymond, E. 1991. *The New Hacker's Dictionary.* Cambridge, Mass.: MIT
Rees, N. 1991. *Bloomsboory Dictionary of Popular Phrases.* London: Bloomsbury Publishing
Richter, A. 1991. *A Dictionary of Sexual Slang.* New York: John Wiley and Sons
Rogers, J. 1989. *The Dictionary of Cliches.* New York: Ballantine Books
Rosten, L. 1958. *The Joys of Yiddish.* New York: McGraw-Hill
Safire, W. 1978. *Safire's Political Dictionary.* New York: Random House
Sheidlower, J. 1995. *The F-word.* New York: Random House
Spears, R. 1982. *Slang and Euphemism.* New York: Signet Books
----------, R. 1986. *The Slang and Jargon of Drugs and Drink.* Metuchen, NJ: Scarecrow Press
----------, R. 1986. *NTC's American Idioms Dictionary.* Lincolnwood, IL: NTC Publishing Group
----------, R. 1990. *Forbidden American English.* Lincolnwood, IL: NTC Publishing Group
----------, R. 1992. *Common American Phrases in Everyday Contexts.* Lincolnwood, IL: NTC Publishing Group
----------, R. 1986. *Contemporary American Slang.* Lincolnwood, IL: NTC Publishing Group
----------, R. 1992. *NTC's Dictionary of American Slang and Colloquial Expressions.* Lincolnwood, IL: NTC Publishing Group
----------, R. 1996. *NTC's Dictionary of American Slang and Colloquial Expressions.* Lincolnwood, IL: NTC Publishing Group
Steele, G. 1983. *The Hacker's Dictionary.* New York: Harper and Row Publishers
Summers, D. 1992. *Longman Dictionary of English Language and Culture.* Burnt Hill, Harlow: Longman
Thorne, T. 1990. *Bloomsbury Dictionary of Slang.* London: Bloomsbury Publishing
Watts, K. 1994. *The 21st Century Dictionary of Slang.* New York: Dell Publishing
Wentworth, H. & S. Flexner. 1975. *Dictionary of American Slang.* New York: Thomas Y. Crowell

English Index

A

B

D

E

F

G

H

I

L

M

N

O

P

Q

R

T

Related Titles from Hippocrene . .

Dictionaries

POLISH-ENGLISH UNABRIDGED DICTIONARY
3,800 pp • 250,000 entries, 3-vols • 0-7818-0441-8 • $200.00hc • (526)

POLISH HANDY EXTRA DICTIONARY
125 pp • 4 x 6 • 0-7818-0504-X • $11.95pb • (607)

HIGHLANDER POLISH-ENGLISH/ENGLISH-HIGHLANDER POLISH DICTIONARY
111pp • 4 x 6 • 2,000 entries • 0- 7818-0303-9 • $9.95pb • (297)

POLISH-ENGLISH/ENGLISH-POLISH CONCISE DICTIONARY, with complete phonetics
408pp • 3 5/8 x 7 • 8,000 entries • 0-7818-0133-8 • $9.95pb • (268)

POLISH-ENGLISH/ENGLISH-POLISH COMPACT DICTIONARY
240pp • 4 x 6 • 9,000 entries • 0-7818-0496-5 • $8.95pb • (609)

POLISH-ENGLISH/ENGLISH-POLISH PRACTICAL DICTIONARY
708 pp • 5 ½ x 8 ½ • 32,000 entries • 0-7818-0085-4 • $119.95pb • (450)

POLISH-ENGLISH/ENGLISH-POLISH STANDARD DICTIONARY, revised edition with business terms
780pp • 5 ½ x 8 ½ • 32,000 entries • 0-7 818-0282-2 • $19.95pb • (298)

POLISH PHRASEBOOK AND DICTIONARY
252pp • 5 ½ X 8 ½ • 0-7818-0134-6 • $9.95pb • (192)
2 Cassettes, Vol I: 0-7818-0340-3 • $12.95 • (492)
2 Cassettes, Vol II: 0-7818-0384-5 • $12.95 • (486)

Tutorial

AMERICAN PHRASEBOOK FOR POLES, 2nd Edition
153pp • 5 ½ x 8 ½ • 0-7818-0554-6 • $8.95pb • (644)

ENGLISH CONVERSATIONS FOR POLES
250pp • 5 ½ x 8 ½ • 0-87052-873-4 • $9.95pb • (225)

ENGLISH FOR POLES SELF-TAUGHT
496pp • 6 x 8⅜ • 455 lessons • 3,600 dictionary entries • 0-7818-0273-3 • $19.95pb • (317)

BEGINNER'S POLISH
200pp • 5 ½ x 8 ½ • 0-7818-0299-7 • $9.95pb • (82)
Casettes: 0-7818-0330-6 • $12.95 • (56)

MASTERING POLISH
288pp • 5 ½ x 8 ½ • 0-7818-0015-3 • $14.95pb • (381)
Cassettes: 0-7818-0016-1 • $12.95 • (389)

GRADED READER OF CLASSIC POLISH LITERATURE
130pp • 5 ½ x 8 ½ • 0-7818-0326-8 • $9.95 • (80)

Proverbs

A TREASURY OF POLISH APHORISMS, A Bilingual Edition
140pp 5 ½ x 8 ½ • 20 illus • 0-7818-0549-X • $12.95 • (647)

DICTIONARY OF 1,000 POLISH PROVERBS
131pp • 5 ½ x 8 ½ • 0-7818-0482-5 • $11.95pb • (628)

History

THADDEUS KOSCIUSZKO: The Purest Son of Liberty
350pp • 0-7818-0576-7 • $29.95hc • (704)

THE LAST KING FO POLAND
560pp • 48pp illus • 0-7818-0603-8 • $35.00hc • (676)

FORGOTTEN HOLOCAUST:
The Poles under German Occupation 1939-1945, Revised Edition
300pp • 6 x 9 • illus • 0-7818-0528-7 • $22.50hc • (639)

JEWS IN POLAND: A Documentary History
402 pp • 0-7818-0604-6 • $19.95pb • (677)

Literature

TREASURY OF CLASSIC POLISH LOVE SHORT STORIES IN POLISH AND ENGLISH
128 pp • 5 x 7 • 0-7818-0297-0 • $11.95 • (185)
Cassettes: 0-7818-0361-6 • $12.95 • (576)

POLISH FABLES, Bilingual Edition
250pp • 6 x 9 • 0-7818-0548-1 • $19.95hc • (646)

GLASS MOUNTAIN, 26 Ancient Polish Folktales and Fables
160pp • 6 x 9 • illus • 0-7818-0552-X • $14.95hc • (645)

QUO VADIS?
589pp • 6 x 9 • 0-7818-0550-3 • $19.95pb • (648)

Travel

PODHALE: A Companion Guide to the Polish Highlands
276pp • 6 x 9 36 illus • 0-7818-0552-8 • $19.95hc • (652)

POLAND'S JEWISH HERITAGE INSIDER'S GUIDE
208pp 5 ½ x 8 ½ • 36 illus • 0- 7818-0522-8 • $19.95hc • (652)

POLAND COMPANION GUIDE, Revised Edition
220pp 5 ½ x 8 ½ • 0-7818-0077-3 • $14.95pb • (380)

POLAND INSIDER'S GUIDE
233pp • 5 ½ x 8 ½ • 0-87052-880-7 • $9.95pb • (29)

Cookbooks

POLISH HERITAGE COOKERY, illustrated edition
915 pp • 16pp color photos • over 2,200 recipes • 6 x 9 • 0-7818-0558-9 • $39.95 • (658)

OLD POLISH TRADITIONS IN THE KITCHEN AND AT THE TABLE
304pp • 5 x 8 ½ • 0-7818-0488-4 • $11.95pb • (546)

THE BEST OF POLISH COOKING, revised edition
219pp • 5 ½ x 8 ½ • 0-7818-0123-3 • $8.95pb • (391)

Calendar

A Polish Heritage Publication
POLISH HERITAGE ART CALENDAR, 1998
A Celebration of Wilno/Vilnius
24pp • 12 X 12 • 13 color illus • 0-7818-0551-1 • $10.95 • (640)